"Lars Kierspel has taken charting to a whole new level. This book provides an incredible number of charts—often quite detailed—on virtually every dimension of Paul imaginable. There are the usual charts that we have come to expect regarding dates and places, but Kierspel has provided a whole new level of information in various other charts on theology, comparisons of Paul to others, and a variety of contextual matters. Students and scholars will also find at the end of the book detailed comments and a very useful bibliography. I can't imagine students not finding this a very helpful resource."

—Stanley E. Porter,
President and Dean, Professor of New Testament,
McMaster Divinity College

"Lars Kierspel has brought together a wealth of information on Paul's life, mission, and thought. His work can be a useful tool for those who are trying to sort out both the biblical data and current questions."

—Mark Seifrid,
The Mildred and Ernest Hogan Professor of New Testament Interpretation,
Southern Baptist Theological Seminary

"A very useful resource text for a course on Paul. This is a single resource for the data I have commonly distributed to students. It seems just about every handout I ever passed out, plus many I had not considered, have been gathered and thoughtfully organized by Lars Kierspel. The chart format makes it easy for me to direct students to specific material. Each chart is laid out in a way accessible even to undergraduate students in an intro course; yet, other charts have the types of technical information helpful to graduate students. This is the type of book students like to keep. After the 100+ charts, Kierspel provides for each chart a nuanced and thoughtful explanation with extensive bibliographic support, not merely a list of sources but the major players and their views (with citations). Like all Pauline research, one will dispute this or that conclusion; nonetheless, Kierspel presents the common, evangelical thought. Besides expected charts on virtues or vices in Paul, readers might particularly enjoy his charts on 'Faith of Jesus Christ': What does it mean?, The 'Already' and 'Not Yet,' The Imperative in Paul's Letters, Women in Ministry, and The 'New Perspective' on Paul. This will be a required secondary text in my next course on Paul!"

—E. Randolph Richards,
Professor of Biblical Studies,
Palm Beach Atlantic University

"This useful contribution by Lars Kierspel provides us with a treasure trove of information on Paul's world, life and ministry, churches, letters, and thought. All of this is condensed into a format of some 111 charts, each covering a different topic related to Paul and his epistles. The charts are arranged into four categories, covering Paul's background and context, his life and ministry, his letters, and finally his theological concepts. Though not completely exhaustive in scope, Kierspel covers the main issues in each category, such as the religious and political context of Paul's world and the setting of each Pauline letter, with brief introductions ('snapshots') of its contents. Current scholarly debates about such things as authorship and interpretation of problem passages are treated thoroughly and in a balanced presentation, with ample bibliographical notes for further investigation. Especially valuable are his treatments of topics of particular current interest and scholarly debate, such as the role of women in Paul's churches, the meaning of his phrase 'faith (of) Christ,' and the 'new perspective' on Paul, to mention but a few. Whether student, pastor, or teacher, anyone working in Paul will find this a valuable reference tool."

—John Polhill
Senior Professor of New Testament,
The Southern Baptist Theological Seminary

"Extremely helpful in the classroom!"

—Terry L. Wilder,
Professor and Wesley Harrison Chair of New Testament,
Southwestern Baptist Theological Seminary

KREGEL
CHARTS OF THE
BIBLE

Charts on the Life, Letters, and Theology of Paul

Lars Kierspel

Charts on the Life, Letters, and Theology of Paul

© 2012 by Lars Kierspel

Published by Kregel Publications, a division of Kregel, Inc., P.O. Box 2607, Grand Rapids, MI 49501.

The Greek font GraecaU and the Hebrew font NewJerusalemCU are both available from www.linguistsoftware.com/lgku.htm, +1-425-775-1130.

Library of Congress Cataloging-in-Publication Data
Kierspel, Lars, 1972-
Charts on the life, letters, and theology of Paul / Lars Kierspel.
    p. cm
    Includes bibliographical references.
  1. Paul, the Apostle, Saint—Charts, diagrams, etc. 2. Bible. N.T. Epistles of Paul—Criticism, interpretation, etc.—Charts, diagrams, etc. 3. Bible. N.T. Epistles of Paul—Theology—Charts, diagrams, etc.—I. Title.
    BS2506.3.K54 2012
    225.9'2—dc23
                                              2012036694

ISBN 978-0-8254-2936-1

Printed in the United States of America
12 13 14 15 16 / 5 4 3 2 1

Contents

C. PAUL'S LETTERS

D. PAUL'S THEOLOGICAL CONCEPTS

Preface

Paul made ample use of lists on a variety of subjects such as sins (e.g., Rom. 1:29–31), sufferings (e.g., 2 Cor. 11:23–27), salvation (e.g., Rom. 8:28–30), and spiritual gifts (e.g., 1 Cor. 12:8–10, 28–30). Maybe that is why preparing these charts often helped me discover the apostle on his own turf. The different angles reflected here constantly highlighted new aspects and offered unexpected insights. Given the nature of the apostle's life and letters, this book is not for the lazy reader. While the charts ease access to information, they demand every ounce of intellectual and creative energy to avoid consuming them as biographical and theological fragments. Needless to say, Paul's life is richer than these charts are able to reflect; and studies of Paul ask and answer more questions than I was able to review, understand, and display. My limits in book space, time, and abilities forced me to make selections.

The comments offer a variety of helps, from mere references to secondary sources to the analysis of single observations and brief syntheses of subjects. The little space provided for them at the back of the book never allowed for sufficient discussion of any single aspect. The reader will do well to keep these limits in mind and use the charts and the comments in conjunction with well informed discussions, some of them referenced in the bibliography. The Greek terms in the charts and references to German literature in the comments may enhance the value of the book for some readers but should not hinder its use otherwise. My best hope is that these charts not only inform but also inspire the reader to analysis and discovery beyond the pages of this book.

Special thanks are extended to the proofreaders of the manuscript, my wife Laura, my colleagues Ron Clutter and Jeff Forrey, and Jim Weaver from Kregel Publications, all of whom saved me from embarassing mistakes and oversights. Any remaining errors are my responsibility. All translations of Paul's letters were taken from the *New American Standard Version* unless noted otherwise.

Abbreviations

1 Apol.	Justin Martyr, *Apologia I* (*First Apology*)
1 Clem.	*1 Clement*
1 En.	*1 Enoch*
1 Macc.	1 Maccabees
1QS	Community Rule (Dead Sea Scrolls)
2 Bar.	2 Baruch
2 Macc.	2 Maccabees
3 Bar.	3 Baruch (Greek Apocalypse)
3 Macc.	3 Maccabees
4 Macc.	4 Maccabees
Abr.	Philo, *De Abrahamo* (*On the Life of Abraham*)
A.J.	Josephus, *Antiquitates judaicae* (*Jewish Antiquities*)
ANF	Anti-Nicene Fathers
Ann.	Tacitus, *Annals*
Apoc. El.	*Apocalypse of Elijah*
As. Mos.	*Assumption of Moses*
Bapt.	Tertullian, *De Baptismo* (*Baptism*)
Bar.	Baruch
Barn.	*Barnabas*
BDAG	*A Greek-English Lexicon of the New Testament*, 3rd ed. (2000)
B.J.	Josephus, *Bellum judaicum* (*Jewish War*)
C. Ap.	Josephus, *Contra Apionem* (*Against Apion*)
CD	Cairo Geniza copy of the *Damascus Document* (Dead Sea Scrolls)
Cels.	Origen, *Contra Celsum* (*Against Celsus*)
Civ.	Augustine, *De Civitate Dei* (*The City of God*)
Contempl.	Philo, *De vita contemplative* (*On the Contemplative Life*)
Did.	*Didache*
Ebr.	Philo, *De ebrietate* (*On Drunkenness*)
Ep.	Seneca, *Epistolae morales*
Eth. Nic.	Aristotle, *Ethica Nichomachea* [*Nichomachean Ethics*]
Geogr.	Strabo, *Geographica*
Hist. Eccl.	Eusebius, *Historia ecclesiastica*
Hypoth.	Philo, *Hypothetica*
Ign. *Magn.*	Ignatius, *To the Magnesians*
Ign. *Pol.*	Ignatius, *To Polycarp*
Inst.	Lactantius, *Divinarum institutionum* [*The Divine Institutes*]
Jubil.	*Jubilees*
L.A.B.	*Pseudo-Philo* (OT Pseudepigraphon)
L.A.E.	*Life of Adam and Eve* (OT Pseudepigraphon)

Legat.	Philo, *Legatio Ad Gaium* (*On the Embassy to Gaius*)
Mort.	Lactantius, *De morte persecutorum* [*The Deaths of the Persecutors*]
Nat. Hist.	Pliny the Elder, *Naturalis Historia*
NPNF	*Nicene and Post-Nicene Fathers*
Pol.	Aristotle, *Politica* [*Politics*]
Pol. Phil.	Polycarp, *To the Philippians*
Pss. Sol.	*Psalms of Solomon*
Scorp.	Tertullian, *Scorpiace* [*Antidote for the Scorpion's Sting*]
Sir.	Sirach/Ecclesiasticus
Spec.	Philo, *De specialibus legibus* (*On the Special Laws*)
Strom.	Clement of Alexandria, *Stromata*
T. Benj.	*Testament of Benjamin*
T. Dan	*Testament of Dan*
T. Jos.	*Testament of Joseph*
T. Levi	*Testament of Levi*
T. Reu.	*Testament of Reuben*
T. Sol.	*Testament of Solomon*
T. Zeb.	*Testament of Zebulon*
t.*Sukkah*	Tosefta, tractate *Sukkah*
Tg. Ps.-J.	*Targum Pseudo-Jonathan*
Tg. Pss.	*Targum Psalms*
Tract. ep. Jo.	Augustine, *In epistulam Johannis ad Parthos tractatus*
Wis.	Wisdom of Solomon
y.*Gitt*	Palestinian (Yerushalmi) Talmud, tractate *Gittin*

BIBLE VERSIONS AND TRANSLATIONS

ASV	American Standard Version
ESV	English Standard Version
HCSB	Holman Christian Standard Bible
JB	Jerusalem Bible
KJV	King James Version
NAB	New American Bible
NAS	New American Standard Bible
NET	New English Translation
NIV	New International Version
NJB	New Jerusalem Bible
NKJ	New King James Version
NLT	New Living Translation
NRS	New Revised Standard Version
RSV	Revised Standard Version

Part A

PAUL'S BACKGROUND & CONTEXT

Roman Emperors before and during Paul's Life

CHART 1

Name	Events and Ideas of Direct or Indirect Significance for Paul's Life and Ministry
Julius Caesar (100-44 BC)	• He rebuilt Corinth as a Roman colony • He built an aqueduct in Antioch (Syria) to supply the city with water • He was deified posthumously in 42 BC, a decision initiated by his successor Augustus to legitimate his rule with the title *divi filius* ('son of the god') • Caesar, and later Augustus, made Judaism a legal religion ('religio licita'), declaring the Jews of Alexandria, for example, citizens of the city (*A.J.* 14.188)
Augustus (27 BC – AD 14)	• He was the adopted son of Julius Caesar (therefore "*Caesar* Augustus") • Herod the Great established games in Jerusalem, held every five years, in honor of Augustus • Tarsus was home to Athenodorus, a Stoic teacher and close companion of Augustus • An edict by Augustus in 12 BC guaranteed that Jews could send money to Jerusalem (see 2 Cor. 8–9; Rom. 15:25–31) • In 7 BC, six thousand Pharisees refused to give an oath of loyalty to Herod and Augustus (*A.J.* 17.42) • In AD 6, Augustus annexed Judea and made it a Roman province until AD 41 when King Herod Agrippa I was appointed as king • Emperors since Augustus were often called "lord" and "savior" (see Rom. 1:4; 4:24; 16:2; Phil. 2:11; 3:20) • Augustus said: "I made the sea peaceful and freed it of pirates" (*Res Gestae* 25)—a happy condition for a traveler such as Paul
Tiberius (AD 14-37)	• He married Augustus' daughter and was adopted by the emperor • Named in the honor of Tiberius, Herod Antipas built Tiberias as the capitol of Galilee in AD 20 • Pilate erected a building in honor of Tiberius in Caesare Maritima • Jesus was crucified (Luke 3:1) • Tiberius indulged in excessive homoerotic pleasures (Suetonius, *Tiberius* 43–44) • Tiberius banished all Jews from Rome (*A.J.* 18.83)
Gaius Caligula (AD 37-41)	• He gave Aretas jurisdiction over Damascus (2 Cor. 11:32) • Paul converted during the reign of Caligula (Acts 9) • He ordered the erection of his statue in Jerusalem's temple but died before it could be done
Claudius (AD 41-54)	• Caligula was his nephew; Claudius' daughter Octavia was Nero's first wife • Paul and Barnabas delivered a collection for believers in Judea who suffered from a famine during Claudius' reign (Acts 11:28–30) • In Thessalonica, Paul was accused of acting against the decrees of Caesar (Claudius) by "saying that there is another king, Jesus" (Acts 17:7) • Though otherwise known for his "tolerant edicts" for the Jews (see *A.J.* 19.281–311; 20:11–14), Claudius expelled Jews from Rome in 49 AD "on account of Chrestus" (Suetonius, *Claudius* 25.4; see Acts 18:2); Christians were still very much associated with Judaism. The expulsion brought Aquila and Priscilla to Corinth where they met Paul (Acts 18:2; 1 Cor. 16:19; Rom. 16:3) • Paul's confrontation with Peter (Gal. 2:11–21) happened during his reign
Nero (AD 54-68)	• Paul made his appeal to this emperor (Acts 26:32) • Paul wrote of a Christian's duty to civil obedience (Rom. 13:4) during the early years of Nero's reign which stood under the influence of his mother Agrippina, of Seneca and the praetorian prefect Burrus. That changed in AD 59, after he had killed his mother, Burrus had died, and Seneca had retired. • Seneca called the republic Nero's "body" of which the emperor was "the head" (Seneca, *De Clem.* 1.5.1, 2.2.1; see 1 Cor. 11:3; 12:12–27; Eph. 1:22; 4:15; 5:23; Col. 1:18; 2:10, 19) • After the great fire in AD 64, Nero persecuted Christians and Paul was killed. The emperor's exclusive focus on Christians shows the break between them and Judaism • Is the "Narcissus" of Rom. 16:11 the freedman of Tiberius who was powerful under Claudius and executed by Nero in AD 54?

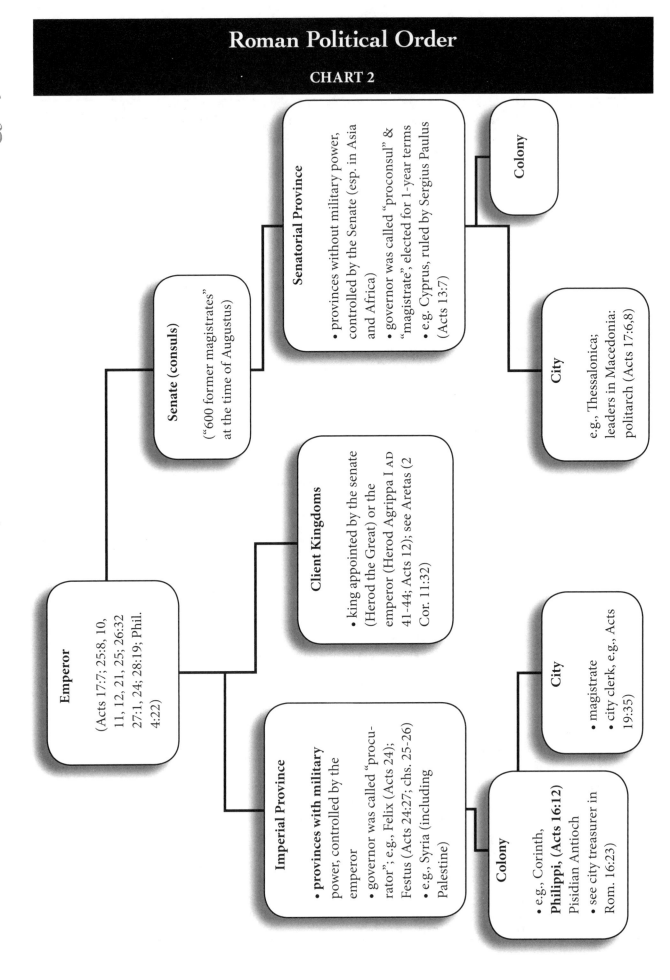

Roman Political Order

CHART 2

Emperor

(Acts 17:7; 25:8, 10, 11, 12, 21, 25; 26:32 27:1, 24; 28:19; Phil. 4:22)

Senate (consuls)

("600 former magistrates" at the time of Augustus)

Senatorial Province

• provinces without military power, controlled by the Senate (esp. in Asia and Africa)
• governor was called "proconsul" & "magistrate", elected for 1-year terms
• e.g. Cyprus, ruled by Sergius Paulus (Acts 13:7)

Colony

City

e.g., Thessalonica; leaders in Macedonia: politarch (Acts 17:6,8)

Client Kingdoms

• king appointed by the senate (Herod the Great) or the emperor (Herod Agrippa I AD 41-44; Acts 12); see Aretas (2 Cor. 11:32)

Imperial Province

• **provinces with military power, controlled by the emperor**
• governor was called "procurator"; e.g., Felix (Acts 24); Festus (Acts 24:27; chs. 25–26)
• e.g., Syria (including Palestine)

City

• magistrate
• city clerk, e.g., Acts 19:35

Colony

• e.g., Corinth, **Philippi, (Acts 16:12)** Pisidian Antioch
• see city treasurer in Rom. 16:23)

Roman Social Order

CHART 3

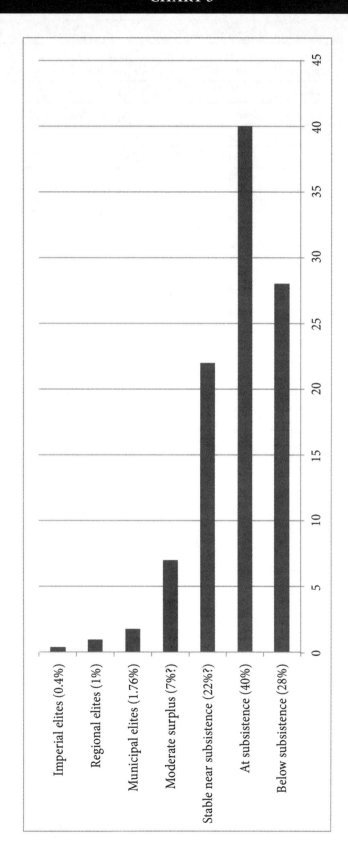

Roman Military Structure

CHART 4

Name		Strength	Commander
(1) PRAETORIAN GUARD	This imperial bodyguard consisted of handpicked Italian soldiers who often intervened in Rome's politics and received double the pay of legionaries		
9 cohorts total with 500 soldiers each		4,500–6,000	
(2) LEGION	The major Roman military force that required wealth and citizenship for enlistment		
25 legions total		120,000	
1 legion (10 cohorts; e.g., Mk 5:9)		4,800	Legate
1 cohort (6 centuries)		480	Military Tribune
1 century (10 contubernia)		80	Centurion
1 contubernium		8	
(3) AUXILIARIES	Non-Roman forces (cavalry & infantry) which received full citizenship after honorable service (since the emperor Claudius)		
1 alae (cavalry)		500	
1 turmae (squadron)		20–30	
1 cohort (infantry) (σπεῖρα; e.g., Acts 10:1; 21:31; 27:1)		500	Commander (χιλίαρχος, e.g., Acts 21:31, 37)
1 century		80	Centurion (ἑκατοντάρχης, e.g., Acts 10:1)
1 equestrian cohort (cavalry & infantry)		1,000	
(4) NAVY	The Roman navy was subordinated to the legions and recruited from the lower ranks of society, with citizenship as a reward upon discharge		

Greco-Roman Religions, Cults, and Philosophies

CHART 5

Greco-Roman Gods and Goddesses

The Major 12 Olympian gods and goddesses

1. Jupiter (Latin)	Zeus (Greek)	Father of the gods	Acts 14:12-13 (Lystra)
2. Juno	Hera	Women	
3. Neptune	Poseidon	Sea	
4. Pluto	Hades	God of the underworld	
5. Apollo	Apollo	Youth, music, prophecy	
6. Diana	Artemis	Woods, moon, women	Acts 19:24-25 (Ephesus)
7. Vulcan	Hephaestus	Fire, smiths	
8. Minerva	Athena	Crafts, war	
9. Mars	Ares	War	
10. Venus	Aphrodite	Love	
11. Mercury	Hermes	Messenger of the gods	Acts 14:12 (Lystra)
12. Vesta	Hestia	Hearth, household activities	

Minor Deities

Ceres	Demeter	Fertility, grain	
Bacchus	Dionysus	Wine, debauchery	
Fortuna	Tyche	Farming, good luck	
Castor/Pollux	Castor/Pollux	Sailors (twin gods)	Acts 28:11 (Alexandrian ship)
Dike		Justice	Acts 28:1–6 (Malta)

Deified Heroes and "unknown gods"

Aesculapius	Asklepios	Healing	
"unknown god"			Acts 17:23 (Athens)

Imperial Cult (e.g., Acts 12:20-23)

Augustus (27 BC – AD 14)	Herod the Great built temples for the goddess Roma and the emperor Augustus in *Casarea* Philippi, *Caesarea* Maritima and in *Sebaste* (Greek name which is "Augustus" in Latin). Augustus claimed to have inaugurated the "age of peace" and erected the famous *Ara Pacis* ('altar of peace') in Rome (see 1 Thess. 5:2). Philo said that Augustus received honors worldwide "equal to those of the Olympian gods" (*Legat.* 149–150).
Tiberius (AD 14–37)	In AD 19, Herod Antipas built the city Tiberias as the capitol of Galilee in honor of Augustus' successor. Pontius Pilate added a "Tiberium" in Caesarea Maritima. Although Tiberius rejected similar building projects in Spain (*Ann.* 4.37–37), temples dedicated to him with priest and cult are known from eleven cities in Asia Minor, and at least some of them go back to his lifetime.
Gaius Caligula (AD 37–41)	He deified himself and demanded the worship of his statue in Jerusalem's temple (*A.J.* 18.257–309; 19.4; *Legat.* 201, 354–357).
Claudius (AD 41–54)	Just as Tiberius, Claudius rejected desires to erect statues and temples in his honor. In 49 AD, he expelled Jews from Rome (Acts 18:2) because of a "Chrestus" (Suetonius, *Claud.* 25.4). This expulsion brought the Jewish couple Aquila and Priscilla to Corinth, where they met Paul and became fellow workers in Ephesus (Acts 18:26; 2 Tim. 4:19) and Rome (Rom. 16:3).

Nero (AD 54-68)	In 55 AD, the Senate in Rome set up a statue of Nero in the temple of Mars Ultor (Tacitus *Ann.* 13.8.1)—the first time since Caesar that an emperor had been directly associated with a god in Rome. In 65 AD, he rejected a proposed temple to "the divine Nero," citing the tradition that only dead emperors were divine. But he did erect in his place a hundred-foot bronze statue of himself as the sun with a star-shaped crown.
Mystery Cults	
Cult of Eleusis	The god of the underworld stole Demeter's daughter. She threatened with famine until Zeus ruled that the daughter was to spend 2/3 of the year with her mother. The rites were celebrated annually in Eleusis (near Athens) at a sanctuary and included fasting, songs with jokes and mockery and a special drink.
Cult of Dionysus	The contents of the myths surrounding the god of wine, Dionysus, change from the time of Euripides' drama *Bacchae* (405 BC) to the first century. In the imperial period with the senate's restrictive policies, the Dionysian rites included preparatory fasting and sexual abstinence followed by a bath of purification, striking with rods, processions, dancing, music, meals and drinking parties. The cult spread widely since it was not connected to a special place or priest.
Cult of Isis	In the final version of the myth in Plutarch, Osiris died by drowning in a sea. Isis, his consort, found him and brought him back to Egypt. Seth, the antagonist, cut Osiris into fourteen pieces and scattered them. Isis found them and buried them in different graves. This Egyptian mystery cult spread far into the Greco-Roman Mediterranean world.
Cult of Mithra	The god Mithra killed a bull whose shedding of blood became the source of salvation. Among the rites that accompany seven different grades of initiation were the use of bread and a cup of water with words spoken over them, reminding of the Lord's Supper. Women were excluded from the cult which recruited primarily among civil servants and soldiers. It dates as early as the first century BC and reaches its height in the third century AD, with hundreds of *mithraea* (temples of the cult) found all over the Roman empire.
Popular Beliefs	
Miracles of healing	While Hippocrates became the classical symbol for healing through empirical observation, Asclepius was considered the god who heals through miraculous intervention in combination with therapeutic treatments such as sleep, baths, consecrated (and therefore) health-giving food, etc. Temples (*Asklepieion*) were dedicated.
Miracles of healing	to him in cities like Epidaurus, Athens, Corinth, Rome, and most importantly Pergamum. The power of miraculous healing was also ascribed to other gods (Hercules; Isis) and heroes such as Greek classical philosophers (Pythagoras; Empedocles), rulers (King Pyrrhus of Epirus; Augustus; Vespasian), the physician Asclepiades and the itinerant philosopher Apollonius of Tyana.
Fortune-telling	Fortune-tellers (or *diviners, soothsayers*) interpreted auspicious signs as divine revelation about the present and the future. Practically everything in life could be interpreted as a hint from a divine power, ranging from trivialities (stumbling, sneezing) to earthquakes and the eclipse of the sun. Divination as an art specialized on particular signs such as dreams, the flight of birds (augurs), casting lots, the internal organs of a sacrificed animal (healthy or changed in some way), the way chicken eat their food (greedy or reluctant), the rising of incense clouds, the turning of a spindle, etc.
Magic	Magic in antiquity was based on the belief that certain materials (amulettes, hair, fat, feathers, animals, etc.), words (magical formulas), and rites could be used (a) to protect oneself from gods, demons, spirits or human enemies, to use these powers (b) for altering one's fate or cure illnesses or (c) even to harm an enemy. It compares best today with witchcraft, sorcery, and the occult.
Astrology	As one particular form of fortune-telling, ancient astrology was not only preoccupied with the science of the stars (astronomy), but also with the interpretation of a person's character and destiny from the position of the stars, either in the hour of his birth (*horoscope*) or of the moment in which an important decision had to be made. All emperors from Tiberius to Hadrian (except Trajan) made frequent use of astrology in their politics.

Philosophies	
Epicureanism	Based on the Greek philosopher Epicurus (341–271 BC), Epicureanism emphasizes natural causes (vs. magical worldview) and free will (vs. fatalism) in order to free people from fears and promote tranquility of the mind. The practice of asceticism (training in a life based on philosophy) and therapy (healing and help through conversation and confession) were characteristics of the Epicurean school. Already during his lifetime, Epicurus was regarded a "savior" and his image was venerated. Slaves and women were allowed among the students. Among those that kept Epicurus' philosophy alive in following centuries were Lucretius (c. 96–55 BC) and, in part, Seneca (4 BC – AD 65).
Stoicism	The founder Zeno (360–260 BC) emphasized God's presence in everything material (pantheism). The focus in the first century AD was on ethics that prized individual virtue as supreme and health, wealth, beauty, even life or death as "indifferent" (*adiaphora*). Seneca (4 BC – AD 65) and Epictetus (c. AD 55–135) were the most famous Stoics in Paul's lifetime.
Middle Platonism (80 BC – AD 220)	Following Plato's ancient Greek philosophy, Middle Platonism (see Plutarch AD 50–120) thought of God as being served by intermediary beings who attend sacrifices and mystery celebrations. People use philosophy for ascent toward deity so that the soul can be liberated from reincarnation and attachment to a body.

Paul's Greco-Roman Background

CHART 6

Paul's Life

Tarsus	Paul's place of birth and city of his early years; capital of Cilicia, "no insignificant city" (Acts 21:39): Strabo, a Greek geographer († AD 24), said: "The people at Tarsus have devoted themselves so eagerly, not only to philosophy, but also to the whole round of education in general, that they have surpassed Athens, Alexandria, or any other place" (*Geogr.* 14.5.13).
Greek Language	Paul's primary language was Greek; all of Paul's letters were written in Greek
Greek Bible	Paul quoted the Old Testament mostly from the Septuagint, the Greek translation
Greco-Roman Education	Paul was able to argue from Greek grammar (Gal. 3:16, singular vs. plural), use the Greek letter form current in his days, and employ techniques of Greco-Roman composition and rhetoric in his letters. Hundreds of parallels to pagan writings can be found, and Paul cited explicitly three, possibly four, pagan authors: • Menander (ca. 344–392 BC): "Bad company corrupts good morals" (1 Cor. 15:33) • Aratus (ca. 315–240 BC): "For we also are His children" (Acts 17:28) • Epimenides (6th or 7th c. BC): "Cretans are always liars, evil beasts, lazy gluttons" (Titus 1:12) • Maybe also Bion the sophist: "the love of money is a root of all sorts of evil" (1 Tim. 6:10)
Roman Citizenship	Paul was a Roman citizen by birth (see Acts 16:37-39; 22:25-29; 23:27; 25:10-12)

Paul's Teaching

Patron-Client	patriarchal father-children hierarchy with regard to God and Christians: e.g., 1 Cor. 8:6; 10:26; 11:3; 15:24–28
Shame / Honor	Paul can use shame/blame within its typical pagan understanding (e.g., 1 Cor. 11:4–6; 15:34; 2 Thess. 3:14). But the message of the crucified Christ turns conventional notions of honor upside down (Rom. 1:16–17; 1 Cor. 1:23; 4:5; 2 Cor. 10:12; 12:9).
Vices and Virtues	1 Cor. 5:9–11; 6:9–10; 2 Cor. 6:6–8; 12:20; Gal. 5:19–23; Eph. 4:25–32; 5:3–5; Phil. 4:8–9; Col. 3:5, 8, 12; 1 Tim. 1:9–10; 4:12; 6:11; 2 Tim. 2:22; 3:2–5
Metaphors	
Family	• "adoption" (υἱοθεσία, Rom. 8:15, 23; 9:4; Gal. 4:5; Eph. 1:5) • "reconciliation" (καταλλαγή, e.g., Rom. 5:11), used in Greek marital records
Religion	• pagan temple (1 Cor. 6:19–20) • libation (Phil. 2:17; 2 Tim. 4:6)
Slavery	See 1 Cor 7:21-23
Sports	• race, prize, run, wreath, box (1 Cor. 9:24–27) • "striving" (συναθλέω, Phil. 1:27)
Commerce	• "down payment" (ἀρραβών, 2 Cor. 1:22) • "certificate of debt" (χειρόγραφον, Col. 2:14)

Military	• triumphal procession (2 Cor. 2:14–16) • soldier (Eph. 6:11-17; 1 Thess. 5:8; 1 Tim. 6:12) • "triumph" (Col. 2:15)
Education	• "tutor" / "guardian" / "custodian" (παιδαγωγός, Gal. 3:24)
Legal system	• "judgment seat" (βῆμα, 2 Cor. 5:10; Rom. 14:10) • "decree" (δόγμα, Col. 2:14; see Luke 2:1; Acts 17:7)
Politics	• "citizenship" (συμπολίτης Eph 2:19; πολιτεύομ. Acts 23:1; Phil. 1:27; πολίτευμα Phil. 3:20) • "coming" (παρουσία, e.g. 1 Cor. 15:23; 1 Thess. 2:19; 4:15) • "meeting" (ἀπάντησις, 1 Thess. 4:17)
Philosophy	• "virtue" (ἀρετή, Phil. 4:8) • "content" (αὐτάρκης, Phil. 4:11; also 2 Cor. 9:8; 1 Tim. 6:6) • "self-control" (ἐγκράτεια, Gal. 5:23) • "conscience" (συνείδησις, e.g., Rom. 2:15; 9:1; 13:5; 1 Cor. 8:7, 10, 12; 10:25, 27–29)

First-Century Judaisms: Different Groups

CHART 7

First-Century Judaisms	Important Concepts
ESSENES	According to Josephus, the Essenes were a group of around four thousand people (*A.J.* 18.18–22; also *Contempl.* 1.1) who lived in various cities in Palestine and dressed in white clothes (*B.J.* 2.123–124). Essenes believed that "fate governs all things" (*A.J.* 13.172). They devalued marriage and riches and shared their possessions (*B.J.* 2.120–122).
HELLENISTS	Jews who spoke Greek and embraced at least parts of the Greek culture, in contrast to "the Hebrews" (Acts 6:1). In the NT, only Luke mentions "Hellenists" (Ἑλληνιστής): in Jerusalem (Acts 6:1; 9:29) and Antioch (ESV Acts 11:20; NAS translates "Greeks").
PHARISEES	Josephus described the beliefs of Pharisees, including resurrection of the dead, eternal judgment (*A.J.* 18.13–14), and oral "regulations by the fathers" (*A.J.* 13.297). While only six thousand people counted themselves among them (*A.J.* 18.13-22), they had the "multitude on their side" (*A.J.* 13.298). Paul called himself a "Pharisee" (Acts 23:6; Phil. 3:5) and labeled it the "strictest sect of our religion" (Acts 26:5). Though not without discussion, the *Psalms of Solomon* (1st century BC) are frequently regarded as an expression of Pharisaic beliefs.
• Conservative School of Shammai	This Pharisaic school understood, for example, the legitimate reason for divorce mentioned in Deut. 24:1 ("indecent thing") as a reference to unlawful sexual behavior.
• Liberal school of Hillel	Hillel's school, on the other hand, gave "indecent thing" a much broader meaning, including childlessness, cultic offenses, and even "if she spoiled his dish" (*y.Git* 9, 1).
PHILO	Philo (25 BC – AD 50) was an educated Jew in Alexandria who, according to Josephus, was "not unskillful in philosophy" (*A.J.* 18:259). The more than forty writings of Philo include works of theology, biblical commentary, and philosophy. With special reverence for Plato (e.g., *Fug* 1.63), Philo used the help of ancient Greek philosphers to explain the Jewish faith to Greek outsiders.
SADDUCEES	According to Josephus, Sadducees believed that there is no resurrection ("souls die with their bodies"; also Matt. 22:23; Acts 23:8), there is no fate (*A.J.* 13.173), there is no obligation to obey oral traditions of the forefathers, but only the written word of Moses instead (*A.J.* 13.297; see Acts 23:8). Their influence was limited to the rich (*A.J.* 13.298).
SICARII	Josephus tells us this about the Sicarii (*B.J.* 2:254–256): "When the country was purged of these, there sprang up another type of robbers in Jerusalem, which were called Sicarii, who slew men in the daytime, and in the midst of the city: this they did chiefly at the festivals, when they mingled themselves among the multitude, and concealed daggers under their garments, with which they stabbed those who were their enemies; and when any fell down dead, the murderers became a part of those who had indignation against them; by which means they appeared persons of such reputation, that they could by no means be discovered."
ZEALOTS	Josephus called this the "fourth sect of Jewish philosophy" (*A.J.* 18.23) whose founder, Judas the Galilean, rebuked his countrymen "if they submitted to paying taxes to Romans and tolerated human masters after serving God" (*B.J.* 2.118).
THERAPEUTAE	Mostly Egyptian Jews whom Philo described in *De Vita Contemplativa* with admiration as "philosophers." They donated their wealth to the poor, lived simply in the rural areas, especially outside Alexandria, and were devoted to solitude, "studying in that place the laws and the sacred oracles of God enunciated by the holy prophets, and hymns, and psalms" (1:25) through allegorical interpretation (1:28).
CHRIST-BELIEVING JEWS	Before the conversion of Cornelius, the first Christian Gentile (Acts 10), the early church consisted nearly exclusively of Jews who maintained their loyalty to the Torah (Acts 21:21) and to the temple (Luke 24:53; Acts 2:46). Among them were synagogue leaders (Acts 18:8, 17), Pharisees (Acts 15:5; 23:6), Hellenists, and Hebrews (Acts 6:1).

First-Century Judaisms: Common Characteristics

CHART 8

Monotheism

DEUTERONOMY 6:4–5: "[4] Hear, O Israel! The LORD is our God, the LORD is one! [5] You shall love the LORD your God with all your heart and with all your soul and with all your might."

JUDITH 8:18–20 (RSV): "[18] For never in our generation, nor in these present days, has there been any tribe or family or people or city of ours which worshiped gods made with hands, as was done in days gone by—[19] and that was why our fathers were handed over to the sword, and to be plundered, and so they suffered a great catastrophe before our enemies. [20] But we know no other god but him, and therefore we hope that he will not disdain us or any of our nation."

PHILO, *Ebr.* 1:45: "Therefore he would never have ventured to compare the true and faithful God to those falsely named gods, if he had really known him; but ignorance of the one God has caused him to entertain a belief of many as gods, who have in reality no existence at all."

1 CORINTHIANS 8:5–6: "[5] For even if there are so-called gods whether in heaven or on earth, as indeed there are many gods and many lords, [6] yet for us there is but one God, the Father, from whom are all things, and we exist for Him; and one Lord, Jesus Christ, by whom are all things, and we exist through Him."

TACITUS (56–120 CE), *Histories* 5.5.2–5: "Those who come over to their religion … have this lesson first instilled into them, to despise all gods, to disown their country, and set at nought parents, children, and brethren."

Election of Israel

DEUTERONOMY 7:6–8: "[6] For you are a holy people to the LORD your God; the LORD your God has chosen you to be a people for His own possession out of all the peoples who are on the face of the earth. [7] The LORD did not set His love on you nor choose you because you were more in number than any of the peoples, for you were the fewest of all peoples, [8] but because the LORD loved you and kept the oath which He swore to your forefathers, the LORD brought you out by a mighty hand and redeemed you from the house of slavery, …"

PHILO, *Abr.* 1:98: "In this manner the chastity of the woman [Sarah] was preserved, and God condescended to display the excellence and piety of her husband [Abraham], giving him the noblest reward, namely, his marriage free from all injury, and even from all insult, so as no longer to be in danger of being violated; a marriage which however was not intended to produce any limited number of sons and daughters, but an entire nation – the most God-loving of all nations – and one which appears to me to have received the offices of priesthood and prophecy on behalf of the whole human race."

ROMANS 9:3–5: "[3] For I could wish that I myself were accursed, separated from Christ for the sake of my brethren, my kinsmen according to the flesh, [4] who are Israelites, to whom belongs the adoption as sons, and the glory and the covenants and the giving of the Law and the temple service and the promises, [5] whose are the fathers, and from whom is the Christ according to the flesh, who is over all, God blessed forever. Amen."

ROMANS 11:2, 5, 28–29: "[2] God has not rejected His people whom He foreknew. … [5] In the same way then, there has also come to be at the present time a remnant according to God's gracious choice. … [28] From the standpoint of the gospel they are enemies for your sake, but from the standpoint of God's choice they are beloved for the sake of the fathers; [29] for the gifts and the calling of God are irrevocable."

JOSEPHUS, *A.J.* 3.313 (about golden calf incident, Exodus 32): "and that on this account, though he [God] would not indeed kill them all, nor utterly exterminate their nation, which he had honoured more than any other part of mankind, yet he would not permit them to take possession of the land of Canaan, nor enjoy its happiness."

4 EZRA 5:23: "O sovereign Lord, from every forest of the earth and from all its trees you have chosen one vine, and from all the lands of the world you have chosen for yourself one region, and from all the flowers of the world you have chosen for yourself one lily, and from all the depths of the sea you have filled for yourself one river, and from all the cities that have been built you have consecrated Zion for yourself, and from all the birds that have been created you have named for yourself one dove, and from all the flocks that have been fashioned you have provided for yourself one sheep, and from all the multitude of people you have gotten for yourself one people; and to this people, whom you have loved, you have given the Law which is approved by all."

Circumcision

GENESIS 17:10, 14: "[10] This is My covenant, which you shall keep, between Me and you and your descendants after you: every male among you shall be circumcised. ... [14] But an uncircumcised male who is not circumcised in the flesh of his foreskin, that person shall be cut off from his people; he has broken My covenant."

1 MACCABEES 1:14–15, 60–61 (NRS): "[14] So they [lawless men from Israel] built a gymnasium in Jerusalem, according to Gentile custom, [15] and removed the marks of circumcision, and abandoned the holy covenant. They joined with the Gentiles and sold themselves to do evil. ... [60] In accordance with the decree, they put to death the women who had their children circumcised, [61] and their families and those who circumcised them; ..."

JUBILEES 15:26: "And every one that is born, the flesh of whose foreskin is not circumcised on the eighth day, belongs not to the children of the covenant which the Lord made with Abraham, but to the children of destruction; nor is there, moreover, any sign on him that he is the Lord's, but (he is destined) to be destroyed and slain from the earth, and to be rooted out of the earth, for he has broken the covenant of the Lord our God."

PHILO, *Spec* 1:2–7: "[2] The ordinance of circumcision of the parts of generation is ridiculed, though it is an act which is practiced to no slight degree among other nations also, and most especially by the Egyptians, who appear to me to be the most populous of all nations, and the most abounding in all kinds of wisdom. ... [4] First of all, that it is a preventive of a painful disease, ... [5] Secondly, it secures the cleanliness of the whole body ... [6] Thirdly, there is the resemblance of the part that is circumcised to the heart; ... [7] The fourth, and most important, ... those nations which practice circumcision are the most prolific and the most populous."

PSEUDO-PHILO 9:13: "Now that child was born in the covenant of God and the covenant of the flesh." (About Moses as a baby in Egypt. The idea here is that Moses was born circumcised)

ACTS 11:2–3: "[2] And when Peter came up to Jerusalem, those who were circumcised took issue with him, [3] saying, 'You went to uncircumcised men and ate with them.'"

ACTS 15:1, 5: "[1] Some men came down from Judea to Antioch and were teaching the brothers: 'Unless you are circumcised according to the custom of Moses, you cannot be saved.'. . .[5] But some of the sect of the Pharisees stood up, saying, 'It is necessary to circumcise them and to direct them to observe the Law of Moses.'"

GALATIANS 6:12–13: "[12] Those who desire to make a good showing in the flesh try to compel you to be circumcised, simply so they will not be persecuted for the cross of Christ. [13] For those who are circumcised do not even keep the Law themselves, but they desire to have you circumcised so that they may boast in your flesh."

TACITUS (56–120 CE), *Histories* 5.5.2–5: "Circumcision was adopted by them as a mark of difference from other men. Those who come over to their religion adopt the practice, and have this lesson first instilled into them, to despise all gods, to disown their country, and set at nought parents, children, and brethren. Still they provide for the increase of their numbers. It is a crime among them to kill any newly-born infant."

Separation from Gentiles

JUBILEES 22:16: "Separate yourself from the Gentiles, and do not eat with them, and do not perform deeds like theirs. And do not become associates of theirs. Because their deeds are defiled, and all of their ways are contaminated and despicable, and abominable."

WISDOM OF SOLOMON 11:9: "For when they (Israel) were tried, though they were being disciplined in mercy, they learned how the ungodly (Gentiles) were tormented when judged in wrath. [10] For thou didst test them (Israel) as a father does in warning, but thou didst examine the ungodly (Gentiles) as a stern king does in condemnation."

LETTER OF ARISTEAS 139, 142: "In his wisdom the legislator ... surrounded us with unbroken palisades and iron walls to prevent our mixing with any of the other peoples in any matter. ... so to prevent our being perverted by contact with others or by mixing with bad influences, he hedged us in on all sides with strict observances connected with meat and drink and touch and hearing and sight, after the manner of the Law."

GALATIANS 2:11–12, 14–16: "[11] But when Cephas came to Antioch, I opposed him to his face, because he stood condemned. [12] For prior to the coming of certain men from James, he used to eat with the Gentiles; but when they came, he began to withdraw and hold himself aloof, fearing the party of the circumcision. ... [14] But when I saw that they were not straightforward about the truth of the gospel, I said to Cephas in the presence of all, 'If you, being a Jew, live like the Gentiles and not like the Jews, how is it that you compel the Gentiles to live like Jews? [15] We are Jews by nature and not sinners from among the Gentiles; [16] nevertheless knowing that a man is not justified by the works of the Law but through faith in Christ Jesus, even we have believed in Christ Jesus, so that we may be justified by faith in Christ and not by the works of the Law; since by the works of the Law no flesh will be justified.'"

TACITUS, *Hist.* 5.5.2–5: "The most degraded out of other races, scorning their national beliefs, brought to them their contributions and presents. This augmented the wealth of the Jews, as also did the fact, that among themselves they are inflexibly honest and ever ready to shew compassion, though they regard the rest of mankind with all the hatred of enemies. They sit apart at meals, they sleep apart, and though, as a nation, they are singularly prone to lust, they abstain from intercourse with foreign women; among themselves nothing is unlawful."

Paul's Jewish Background

CHART 9

Paul's Life	
"From the tribe of Benjamin"	Phil. 3:5; Rom. 11:1; the 'loyal south' of King David, center of post-exilic community and including Jerusalem and the temple
"A Hebrew"	Phil. 3:5; pure ancestry, in contrast to Greek-speaking Hellenists (2 Cor. 11:22)
Parents	Paul's parents were Jews ("of Hebrews" Phil. 3:5) and Pharisees (Acts 23:6). Jerome reported that Paul's parents came from Gischala in Galilee.
"Pharisee"	Phil 3:5-6; Acts 23:6; 26:5; also 22:3; he held to the oral Law (Gal. 1:14)
Hebrew language	Paul spoke in "Hebrew dialect" (Ἑβραΐδι διαλέκτῳ, Acts 21:40; 22:2), the same one in which the resurrected Jesus talked to him (Acts 26:14). (Tarsus is close to Syria, which produced Aramaic literature). Even in his Greek letters, Paul used Hebrew ("amen," "Sabbath," and "Satan") and Aramaic ("Abba," "Maranatha") words.
Jewish education	Education under Gamaliel (Acts 22:3), grandson or son of the famous Hillel
Practice of Judaism	• Routine visits to synagogues (Acts 13:5, 14; 14:1; 17:1, 10, …) • Paul circumcised Timothy (Acts 16:3) • Paul took a Nazirite vow (Acts 18:18; 21:24; see Num. 6:2–21)
Agony over Jewish unbelief	Rom 9:1-5
Paul's Teaching	

Use of Jewish literature and traditions
  a) Old Testament
  b) Intertestamental traditions
  c) Other Jewish traditions
	• 136 OT quotations and over 450 allusions (see chart 45)
	• The Law was given by angels (Gal. 3:19): LXX Deut 33:2; *Tg. Ps.-J.* Deut. 33:2; *Jubil.* 1:27–29
	• "Jannes and Jambres" (2 Tim. 3:8): *Tg. Ps.-J.* on Ex 7:11. *T. Sol.* 25:4
	• "first Adam" (1 Cor. 15:45–47): *Tg. Pss.* 49:2; 69:32; *3 Bar.* 9:7
	• "and he *gave* gifts to men" (Eph. 4:8): *Tg. Pss.* 68:18 (MT/LXX "took")
	• The moveable well (1 Cor. 10:4): *t.Sukkah* 3.11
	• "Belial" (2 Cor. 6:15): *Sib. Or.* 2.165; *T. Reu.* 4:7

Jewish *Concepts*	• Adam's sin as the fall of humanity (Rom. 5:12): 4 Ezra 3:21–22; *L.A.E.* 44:2 • Universal sin (Rom. 3:10–18): Ps. 14:1-3; 51:5; Eccl. 7:20; 4 Ezra 8:35 • Davidic Messiah (Rom. 1:3): Ps. 110:1; Jer. 23:5; Amos 9:11; *Pss. Sol.* 17:23–51 • Positive view of the Law (e.g., Rom. 13:9): Ex. 20:13–17; 2 Bar. 51:7; *L.A.B.* 9:8 • Negative view of idols (Acts 19:26; 1 Cor. 8:4): Ex. 20:3–4; Isa. 40:18–20; Wis. 11:15–16 • New covenant (1 Cor. 11:25; 2 Cor. 3:6): Jer. 31:31–34; Eze. 36:24–27; CD A 6.18–19 • Justification by faith (Rom. 4:1–5; Gal. 3:6-9): Gen. 15:6; Hab. 2:4; maybe 1QS 11:2–3 • God's grace (Rom. 5:15–21): Gen. 6:8; Ex. 33:12–34:9; Isa. 60:10; Wis. 3:9; 1QH 12.37 • God's love (Rom. 5:8): Ex. 34:6; Ps. 86:15; Joel 2:13; Jonah 4:2; Wis. 11:26 • Apocalypticism (Rom. 11:25–27; 1 Thess. 4:16–17): Isa. 27:13; 59:20–21; 1 Enoch; 4 Ezra
Jewish *Terms*	• "sanctify" (ἁγιάζω, e.g., Rom 15:16): Ex 28:41; Sir 33:12; 45:4; Zeph 1:7 • circumcision (Phil 3:3; Col 2:11): Gen 17:10-14; Ex 4:24-26; Lev 12:1-3 • Jesus as "mercy seat" (ἱλαστήριον, Rom 3:25): see Exod 25:17-22 • "Maranatha" (1 Cor 16:22), Aramaic for "Our Lord, come!" • "Abba" ('father') for God (Rom 8:15; Gal 4:6; see Mark 14:36) • "devil" (διάβολος, Eph 4:27): see 1 Chr 21:1; Job 1:6 • "Amen" (15xPaul, e.g., Rom 1:25): see 1 Chr 16:36; Neh 8:6 • "son of" expressions (e.g., Eph 2:2; 1 Thess 5:5): see Gen 29:1; Matt 23:15 • "walk" as a term for lifestyle (see Prov 8:20): e.g., Rom 6:4; Gal 6:16

Part B

PAUL'S LIFE & MINISTRY

Chronology of Paul's Life

CHART 10

Event	Date	Age	Reference
Birth in Tarsus	ca. 5		
Move to Jerusalem	ca. 10	ca. 5	
Studies under Rabbi Gamaliel	ca. 15–20	ca. 10–15	
Death of Jesus	30	25	
Conversion of Paul	33	28	Acts 9
Paul in Arabia		Gal 1:17	
Jerusalem I (Cephas, James)	35	30	Acts 9:26; Gal 1:18
Paul in Cilicia	ca. 36–42	ca. 31–37	Acts 9:30; Gal 1:21
Paul in Antioch	ca. 42	ca. 37	Acts 11:25–26
Jerusalem II: Collection		Acts 11:30; 12:25? Gal 2?	
First missionary journey	ca. 45–47	ca. 40–42	Acts 13:1–14:28
(Seleucia, Cyprus, Perga, Antioch, Iconium, Lystra, Derbe, Antioch)			
Jerusalem III (Apostolic council)	48	43	Acts 15:1–35; Gal 2?
Incident in Antioch with Peter	48	43	Gal 2:11-21
Second missionary journey	48 (late summer)–51/52		Acts 15:36–18:22
(Syria, Cilicia, Derbe, Lystra, Troas, Philippi, Thessalonica, Berea, Athens, Corinth, Syria)			
1.5 years in Corinth	50/51	45–46	Acts 18:1–17
Jerusalem IV		Acts 18:21–22	
Antioch	51/52	46–47	Acts 18:22–23
Third missionary journey	52–55/56	47–50/51	Acts 18:23–21:16
(Galatia, Phrygia, Ephesus, Macedonia, Troas, Miletus, Syria)			
3 years in Ephesus	52–54/55	47–49/50	Acts 19:1–41
Macedonia & Greece	55	50	Acts 20:1–2
Last stay in Corinth	56 (early in the year)		Acts 20:3
Jerusalem V	56 (early summer)		Acts 21:17
Imprisonment in Caesarea	56–58	51–53	Acts 23:33
Change of office, Felix/Festus	58	53	Acts 24:27
Arrival in Rome	59	54	Acts 28
Death of Paul	64		

Parallels between Acts and the Pauline Corpus

CHART 11

		Paul in Acts	Paul in His Letters
Biographical Parallels			
1.	Paul persecuted Christians before his conversion	8:1; 9:4–5; 22:4; 26:11	1 Cor. 15:19; Gal. 1:13, 23; Phil. 3:6
2.	Conversion	Chs. 9 / 22 / 26	1 Cor. 9:1; 15:8; Gal. 1:13–17; etc.
3.	Paul escapes in a "basket"	9:25 (σπυρίς)	2 Cor. 11:33 (σαργάνη)
4.	Paul preached in Jerusalem	9:28	Rom. 15:19
5.	Jewish opposition in Judea	9:29–30	1 Thess. 2:14–15
6.	Jewish push to force circumcision on Gentiles	15:1–5	Rom. 2:24–29; Gal. 5:1–12; Phil. 3:2
7.	Wish not to be a burden to churches	20:33–34	1 Cor. 9; 2 Cor. 11:7–11; 1 Thess. 2
8.	Paul worked with his hands	18:3 (tentmaker)	1 Thess. 4:1; 1 Cor. 4:12
9.	Famine relief efforts	11:27–30	Rom. 15:25–27; 1 Cor. 16:1–3
10.	Paul and the pillars in Jerusalem	15:1–21	Gal. 2:1–10
11.	Paul is willing to die for Jesus Christ	20:24; 21:13	Rom. 14:8; Phil. 1:20–21
Verbal Parallels			
12.	A zealous Pharisee (ζηλωτὴς ὑπάρχων)	22:3; also 9:1–2; 26:4–5	Gal. 1:14; also 2 Cor. 11:22; Phil. 3:5
13.	Let down through a wall (χαλᾶν διὰ τοῦ τείχους)	9:25	2 Cor. 11:33
14.	Paul wanted to "destroy" (πορθέω) churches	9:21	Gal. 1:13
15.	Paul suffered (see 2 Cor 11:23–28) persecution (διωγμός, διώκω) affliction (θλῖψις) beatings (πληγαί) imprisonment (φυλακή, δέσμιος, …) in chains (ἄλυσις)	13:50 14:22; 20:23 16:23; 21:32 τύπτω 16:23; 21:33; 23:18; 28:16 21:33; 28:20	1 Cor. 4:12; Gal. 5:11; 2 Tim. 3:11, etc. Rom. 5:3; 2 Cor. 1:4; Phil. 4:14; etc. 2 Cor. 6:5; 11:23 2 Cor. 6:5; 11:23; Eph. 3:1; Phil. 1:7, 13; Col. 4:3; Philem. 1:1, 13 Eph. 6:20; 2 Tim. 1:16
16.	How he lived when being with his converts	20:17–18	1 Thess. 2:1–2; 5:10–11; Phil. 4:15
17.	"Serving the Lord"	20:19	Rom. 12:11
18.	"Jews and Greeks"	20:21	Rom. 1:16; 1 Cor. 1:22; Gal. 3:28
19.	"The gospel of the grace of God"	20:24	Rom. 15:16; 1 Thess. 2:2, 8–9
20.	Being innocent of his converts' blood	20:26	1 Thess. 2:10
21.	"Admonish" (νουθετέω)	20:31	Rom. 15:14; 1 Cor. 4:14; …
22.	"Working hard" (κοπιάω)	20:34–35	1 Cor. 4:12; 1 Thess. 5:12

Theological Parallels		
CHRISTOLOGY		
23. Jesus is the Son of David	13:22–23	Rom. 1:3; 2 Tim. 2:8
24. Jesus was rejected in Judea	13:27–28	1 Thess. 2:14–15
25. Jesus died on the cross	13:29	1 Cor. 1:17–18; Phil. 2:8; Col. 1:20
26. God raised Jesus from the dead	13:30, 37	Rom. 10:9; 1 Cor. 6:14; 1 Thess. 1:10
27. Jesus "appeared" (ὤφθη) to his disciples	13:31	1 Cor. 15:5–8
28. His death and resurrection fulfill Scripture	13:27, 32–35	Rom. 1:2; 3:21; 16:26; 1 Cor. 15:3–4
29. God will judge through Jesus	17:31	Rom. 2:16; 1 Cor. 4:4–5
SOTERIOLOGY		
30. No freedom through the Law of Moses	13:39	Rom. 3:20–21; 4:15; Gal. 4:19–5:4
31. Believe and you will be saved	16:31	Rom. 10:9
32. Forgiveness of sins	13:38; 26:18	Eph. 1:7; Col. 1:14
33. Eternal life	13:46, 48	Rom. 5:21; Rom. 6:22–23

Differences between Acts and the Pauline Corpus

CHART 12

		Paul in Acts	Paul in His Letters
		Information in Acts but Not in Paul's Letters	
1.	From Tarsus	9:11; 21:39; 22:3	Not mentioned
2.	Roman Citizenship	mentioned in 16:37–39; 22:25–29 (v. 28 by birth!); 23:27; 25:10–12	Not mentioned
3.	Jewish "Saul"	Used for Paul: 7:58, . . . 13:9, etc.	Not mentioned
4.	Education	in Jerusalem under Gamaliel (22:3)	Not mentioned
5.	Miracles	Luke mentions many miracles of Paul	Only general references (see chart 26)
6.	God-fearers	13:16, 26, 50; 16:14; 17:4, 17; 18:7	Not mentioned
7.	Synagogue	13:5, 14; 14:1; 17:1, 10, 17; 18:4, 19, etc.	Not mentioned
8.	Names	Stephen (8:1; 22:20), Ananias (9:10), etc.	Not mentioned
9.	Shipwrecks	One shipwreck on his voyage to Rome (27:41–44) not mentioned in Paul	Three shipwrecks (2 Cor. 11:25) which happened before the one in Acts 27
		Information in Paul's Letters but Not in Acts	
10.	Paul's Letters	Not mentioned	e.g., 2 Cor. 10:10
11.	Places	Not mentioned	Arabia (Gal. 1:17), Colossae (Col. 1:2), Crete (Titus 1:5), Hierapolis (Col. 4:12), Laodicea (Col. 4:12), Spain (Rom. 15:24)
12.	Non-Jewish Elements	Not mentioned	uncircumcised Titus (Gal. 2:3); "apostle of Gentiles" (Rom. 11:13)
13.	Union with Christ	Not mentioned	See Rom. 6:1–11; 2 Cor. 5:17; Eph. 3:17
14.	Soteriology	Only 20:28 refers to expiatory benefits	See Rom. 3:25; Gal. 3:13; etc.
15.	Vs. the Law	Only in 13:38–39	Rom. 3:20; 4:13; 5:13, 20; Gal. 3:10–12
16.	Justification by Faith	Only in 10:34 and 13:38–39 and here similar to Paul in content, not in form	Rom. 3:26, 28, 30; 5:1; Gal. 2:16; 3:8, 24
17.	"Apostle"	Only used twice for Paul (14:4, 14) and applied to Barnabas in the same context	Used over thirty times by Paul for himself
18.	Sickness	Not mentioned	Paul (Gal. 4:13; 2 Cor. 12:7), Epaphroditus (Phil. 2:25–27), Timothy (1 Tim. 5:23), Trophimus (2 Tim. 4:20)

		Discrepancies Between Acts and Paul's Letters	
19.	Paul and the Apostles	Luke subordinates Paul under apostles in Jerusalem (9:27–28; 15:1–35; 16:4)	Paul emphasizes independence from the apostles in Jerusalem (Gal. 2:1-10)
20.	After Paul's Conversion	Paul spent some days with disciples in Damascus (9:19)	Paul "did not immediately consult with flesh and blood" (Gal. 1:16)
21.	In Damascus	"Jews" plotted against Paul (Acts 9:23–24)	Ethnarch under king Aretas ordered to arrest Paul (2 Cor. 11:32)
22.	Paul's Visits to Jerusalem	Four to five visits: 9:26–30; 11:30 & 12:25; 15:1–30; 18:22 (implied in ἀναβάς, κατέβη); 21:17; 22:17–21	Only two visits: Gal. 1:18–24 ("three years later"); 2:1–10 ("after an interval of fourteen years")
23.	Second Visit to Jerusalem	Paul comes to relieve famine in Judea (11:27–30); first visit 9:26–30	Paul comes to discuss mission to the Gentiles (Gal. 2:1–10); first visit 1:18–24
24.	Faith and Works	No sharp distinction: 26:20, see *inclusio* with Luke 3:8	Sharp distinction: Rom. 3:20–21; 2 Cor. 3:6; Gal. 3:6–14; Eph. 2:8–9, 15
25.	Attitude to Mosaic Law	Mostly positive (16:3; 18:18; 20:6,16; 21:17–27; 23:6–9), but also 13:38–39	Mostly critical (Rom. 3:20; 7:5; Gal. 3:10–12), but also Rom. 3:31; 7:14; etc.
26.	Break with Judea & Jews	Pragmatics: because of Jewish hostility and opposition, see 13:46; 18:6; 28:28	For theological reasons: faith in Christ is antithetical to the law
27.	Spelling	Silas; Priscilla	Silvanus; Prisca

Parallels between Jesus in Luke, and Paul in Acts

CHART 13

	Parallel	Jesus in Luke	Paul in Acts	
1.	True Israelite	2:21–24, 41–42	16:3–4; 18:8; 22:3; 23:6; etc.	
2.	God's "chosen" instrument	9:35 (ὁ ἐκλελεγμένος)	9:15 (σκεῦος ἐκλογῆς)	
3.	Divinely sent	4:18 (ἀπέσταλκέν με), 43; etc.	22:21; 26:17 (ἀποστέλλω σε)	
4.	"light … to the Gentiles"	2:32 (φῶς εἰς ἀποκάλ. ἐθνῶν)	13:47 (εἰς φῶς ἐθνῶν, Isa 49:6)	
5.	In the synagogue from the beginning	4:15	9:20; 13:5	
6.	Visit the synagogue as a "custom" (εἰωθὸς)	4:16	17:2	
7.	First detailed visit in a synagogue:	4:16–30 (Nazareth)	13:14–52 (Pis. Antioch / Thess.)	
	a) Synagogue situation	4:16–17	13:14–16a;	17:1–2
	b) Scriptural fulfillment	4:18–21	13:16b–41;	17:2b–3
	c) Initial acceptance	4:22	13:42–43;	17:4
	d) Eventual rejection	4:23–28	13:44–49;	17:5
	e) Lethal attack	4:29–30	13:50–52;	17:5b–9
8.	Gospel summary	24:44–47	26:22–23	
9.	Both "explain" (διανοίγω) the Scriptures	24:32	17:2–3	
10.	a) Scriptures	4:21; 24:27	17:2	
11.	b) Moses, Psalms, Prophets	18:31; 22:37; 24:44	13:33; 13:27, 40; 26:22	
12.	c) Isaiah 6:9–10	8:10	28:25–28	
13.	Divine necessity (δεῖ) in life and ministry	2:49; 4:43; 13:33; 19:5; 17:25; etc.	9:6, 16; 19:21; 23:11; 27:24	
14.	esp. suffering (δεῖ … παθεῖν)	9:22; 17:3, 25; 24:7, 26	9:16 (see 14:22)	
15.	Both make known the "word of His grace"	4:22 λόγοι τῆς χάριτος	14:3 λόγος τῆς χάριτος; 20:32	
16.	Resurrection: "all live to Him"	20:38 πάντες γὰρ αὐτῷ ζῶσιν	17:28 Ἐν αὐτῷ γὰρ ζῶμεν	
17.	Opposition against Sadducees who deny resurrection of the dead	20:27	23:8	
18.	Exorcism (ἐξέρχομαι)	4:33–37; 8:26–39; 11:20	16:16–18	
19.	Curing a fever (πυρετός)	4:38–39	28:7–9	
20.	Raising someone from the dead after stating that the person is not really dead	8:49–56	20:9–12	
21.	Both attract the "crowd" (ὄχλος)	5:1, 19; 8:19; 9:12	11:26; 14:14; 17:8; 19:26, etc.	
22.	Wealthy female benefactors	8:2–3	16:11–15; 17:4, 12	

23.	Response of people with wrath (θυμός)	4:28 (in Nazareth)	19:28 (in Ephesus)
24.	Last intentional trip to Jerusalem	9:51–52	19:21–22
25.	Farewell address	Chs. 22–23 ("My blood," 22:20)	20:18–35 ("His own blood," 20:28)
26.	"not a hair of your head will perish"	21:18	27:34
27.	Plotting against them (ἐνεδρεύω)	11:54	23:21
28.	Accused of opposing Caesar	23:2	17:7
29.	Chief priests and leaders try to kill them	19:47 ἀρχιερεῖς καὶ … οἱ πρῶτοι	25:2–3 ἀρχιερεῖς καὶ οἱ πρῶτοι
30.	Prophesied delivery into Gentile hands	18:31–33	21:20–11
31.	Arrested by the Jews	22:54	23:27; 24:6; 28:17
32.	Trial in four parts	Sanhedrin, Pilate, Herod, Pilate	Sanhedrin, Felix, Festus, Herod
33.	Trials before the high priest	Chs. 22–23; (Annas in 3:2)	23:2; 24:1 (Ananias)
34.	Trial before a Roman governor	23:1–5, 17–25 (Pilate)	24:1–27 (Felix), 25:1–12 (Festus)
35.	Trial before the Herods	23:7–11 (Antipas)	25:13–26:32 (Agrippa II)
36.	Roman authorities find no guilt	23:4, 15, 22	23:29; 25:25; 26:31; 28:18
37.	Both are delivered by Romans to captors	23:25 παρέδωκεν	27:1 παρεδίδουν
38.	Each is followed by a great crowd	23:27 ἠκολ. … πλῆθος τοῦ λαοῦ	21:36 ἠκολ. …πλῆθος τοῦ λαοῦ
39.	Multitude cries: "Away with him!"	23:18 ἀνέκραγον … Αἶρε τοῦτον	21:36 κράζοντες, Αἶρε αὐτόν

Parallels in Acts between Peter and Paul

CHART 14

	Parallel	Peter	Paul
1.	Signs and wonders (τέρατα καὶ σημεῖα)	2:43; 4:30; 5:12	14:3; 15:12
2.	Healing of a lame man	in Jerusalem (3:1–10)	in Lystra (14:8–10)
3.	Healing without touching	through his shadow (5:15)	with his handkerchiefs (19:12)
4.	Healing of sick people	paralytic Aeneas (9:28)	Publius' sick father (28:7–9)
5.	Raising from the dead	Tabitha (9:36–42)	Eutychus (20:9–12)
6.	Miraculous escape from prison	5:19; 12:5–11	16:25–26
7.	Cursing a magician	Simon (8:9, 20–23)	Elymas (13:6–10)
8.	Visions (ὅραμα) to expand the Gospel	10:17, 19	9:15; 16:9–10; also 18:9
9.	Trance (ἔκστασις)	10:10	22:17
10.	Comparison with rebels	5:36–37 (Theudas)	21:38 (the Egyptian)
11.	Apotheosis	in Caesarea (10:25–26)	in Lystra (14:8–20); Philippi (16:25–34); Malta (28:1–6)
12.	Defense before Sanhedrin	4:1–22; 5:17–42	21:26–23:10
13.	Silver and/or gold (ἀργύριον καὶ χρυσίον)	3:6	20:33
14.	Filled with the Spirit (πλησθεὶς πνεύματος ἁγίου)	4:8	13:9
15.	Fear falls upon all (φόβος μέγας ἐπὶ πάντας)	5:5, 11	19:17
16.	Jews filled with jealousy (ἐπλήσθησαν ζήλου)	5:17	13:45
17.	Gamaliel / Gallio divert anger against apostles	5:34–39 (Gamaliel)	18:14–17 (Gallio)
18.	Laying on of hands	8:17–18	19:6
19.	Speaking in tongues	10:46	19:6
20.	Converts with Latin names	Cornelius	Sergius Paulus
21.	Caesarea and centurions	10:1 (Cornelius)	27:1 (Julius)
22.	Stories told three times, involving a voice from heaven at midday	10:9–16, 28; 10:5–10	9:1–9; 22:6–7; 26:12–13
23.	Visions in the above stories	10:3 (Cornelius)	9:10 (Ananias)
24.	Falling at feet	10:25 (Cornelius)	16:29 (Philippian jailer)
25.	Earthquakes "shake" (σαλεύω), following prayer	4:31	16:26

Autobiographical Information

CHART 15

	Autobiographical Statement	Reference
1.	Jewish origin and identity	2 Cor. 11:22; Gal. 1:13–14; 2:15; Phil. 3:5–6; Rom. 9:3; 11:1
2.	Relatives	συγγενεῖς in Rom. 16:7, 11, 21 (see Acts 23:16)
3.	Persecutor of the church	1 Cor. 15:9; Gal. 1:13, 23; Phil. 3:6; 1 Tim. 1:13
4.	Manual laborer	1 Cor. 4:12; 9:6; 2 Cor. 6:5; 11:23, 27; 1 Thess. 2:9; 2 Thess. 3:8 (see Acts 18:3; 20:34–35)
5.	Notes on missionary activity	1 Cor. 2:1–5; 3:1–10; 1 Thess. 1:2–8; 3:1–5
6.	(Travel) plans	1 Cor. 16:5–9; Rom. 15:22–32; Gal. 1:17–2:12; Phil. 2:19–24
7.	Calling and apostleship	Rom. 15:15–16; 1 Cor. 1:17; 9:1; 15:3–10; Gal. 1:11–17; Eph. 3:8; Phil. 3:4–11; 1 Tim. 1:12–16
8.	Apostolic lifestyle	1 Cor. 9; 2 Cor. 11:7–9; Phil. 3:12–14; 4:11–18
9.	Signs and wonders	Rom. 15:19; 1 Cor. 2:4; 2 Cor. 12:12; Gal. 3:5; 1 Thess. 1:5 (?)
10.	Sickness	Gal. 4:13; 6:17; 2 Cor. 12:7
11.	Accepting financial support	1 Cor. 9:3–12; 2 Cor. 11:8; Phil. 4:10–20
12.	Refusing financial support	1 Thess. 2:9–12; 1 Cor. 9:8–18; 2 Cor. 2:17; 11:7–11
13.	Collection for Jerusalem	1 Cor. 16:1–4; 2 Cor. 8:1–9:15; Gal. 2:9–10; Rom. 15:14–32
14.	Sufferings, persecution, imprisonment	Rom. 16:7; 1 Cor. 4:7–12; 15:32; 2 Cor. 1:8–10; 4:7–12; 6:4–10; 11:23–29; Eph. 3:1; 4:1; Col. 4:10; 1 Thess. 2:2; Philem. 1:9, 23
15.	Special revelations	1 Cor. 11:23; 2 Cor. 12:1–10; Gal. 1:15–16; 2:2
16.	References to his own letters	2 Cor. 2:1–4; 7:8–9; Col. 4:16
17.	Generic "I"	Rom. 7:7–25; 1 Cor. 13:1–3, 11

Comparison of Three Accounts of Paul's Conversion in Acts

CHART 16

		ACTS 9:1–19	ACTS 22:3–16	ACTS 26:4–18
1.	Persecution of Christians	7:58–8:3	22:3–5	26:4–5, 9–11
2.	On the road to Damascus	9:3	22:6	26:12
3.	Time of the christophany	—	noontime (22:6)	midday (26:13)
4.	Light from heaven	"³ suddenly a **light from heaven** flashed around him"	"⁶ a very bright **light** suddenly flashed **from heaven** all around me"	"¹³ a **light from heaven**, brighter than the sun, shining all around me"
5.	Falling to the ground	"⁴ he **fell to the ground**"	"⁷ I **fell to the ground**"	"¹⁴ we had all **fallen to the ground**"
6.	Jesus' voice	"⁴ **heard a voice** saying to him, 'Saul, Saul, why are you persecuting Me?'"	"⁷ and **heard a voice** saying to me, 'Saul, Saul, why are you persecuting me?'"	"¹⁴ I **heard a voice** saying to me in the Hebrew dialect, 'Saul, Saul, why are you persecuting me?' It is hard for you to kick against the goads.'"
7.	Paul's question	"⁵ Who are You, Lord?"	"⁸ Who are You, Lord?"	"¹⁵ Who are You, Lord?"
8.	Jesus' answer	"⁵ **I am Jesus whom you are persecuting.** ⁶ but get up and enter the city, and it will be told you what you must do."	"⁸ **I am Jesus the Nazarene, whom you are persecuting.**"	"¹⁵ **I am Jesus whom you are persecuting.** ¹⁶ But get up and stand on your feet; for this purpose I have appeared to you, to appoint you a minister and a witness not only to the things which you have seen, but also to the things in which I will appear to you; ¹⁷ delivering you from the Jewish people and from the Gentiles, to whom I am sending you, ¹⁸ to open their eyes so that they may turn from darkness to light and from the dominion of Satan to God, in order that they may receive forgiveness of sins and an inheritance among those who have been sanctified by faith in Me."
9.	Paul's company	"⁷ hearing the voice, but seeing no one"	"⁹ saw the light, …, but did not understand the voice …"	—
10.	Paul's question	—	"⁹ What shall I do, Lord?"	—
11.	Jesus' answer	—	"¹⁰ Get up and go on into Damascus, and there you will be told of all that has been appointed for you to do."	—

		ACTS 9:1–19	ACTS 22:3–16	ACTS 26:4–18
12.	Paul's blindness	**Paul was blind three days, did not eat or drink, and was led into Damascus (v. 8–9)**	**Paul was blind and led into Damascus (v. 11)**	—
13.	Jesus appears to Ananias	"¹⁰ Now there was a disciple at Damascus named **Ananias**; and the Lord said to him in a vision, 'Ananias.' And he said, 'Here I am, Lord.' ¹¹ And the Lord said to him, 'Get up and go to the street called Straight, and inquire at the house of Judas for a man from Tarsus named Saul, for he is praying, ¹² and he has seen in a vision a man named Ananias come in and lay his hands on him, so that he might regain his sight.' ¹³ But Ananias answered, 'Lord, I have heard from many about this man, how much harm he did to Your saints at Jerusalem; ¹⁴ and here he has authority from the chief priests to bind all who call on Your name.' ¹⁵ But the Lord said to him, "Go, for he is a chosen instrument of Mine, to bear My name before the Gentiles and kings and the sons of Israel; ¹⁶ for I will show him how much he must suffer for My name's sake."	"¹² A certain **Ananias**, a man who was devout by the standard of the Law, and well spoken of by all the Jews who lived there, …"	—
14.	Ananias meets Paul	"¹⁷ **Brother Saul**, the Lord Jesus, who appeared to you on the road by which you were coming, has sent me so that you may regain your sight and be filled with the Holy Spirit.' And immediately there fell from his eyes something like scales, and he regained his sight and he **got up and was baptized;** ¹⁹ and he took food and was strengthened."	"¹³ … '**Brother Saul**, receive your sight!' And at that very time I looked up at him. ¹⁴ And he said, "The God of our fathers has appointed you to know His will and to see the Righteous One and to hear an utterance from His mouth. ¹⁵ For you will be a witness for Him to all men of what you have seen and heard. ¹⁶ Now why do you delay? **Get up and be baptized,** and wash away your sins, calling on His name.'"	—

Saul—Paul: Did the Apostle Change His Name?

CHART 17

	A) NO, PAUL ALWAYS HAD TWO NAMES	
(1)	"Saul" was his Jewish name (*supernomen*) and "Paul" his Gentile name (*cognomen*). It was not atypical for Jews in the diaspora to have two names that were phonetically similar.	Deissmann, Zahn, Harrer, F. F. Bruce, Murphy O'Connor, Schnelle
	B) YES, PAUL CHANGED HIS NAME	
(2)	The change of names happened in Acts 9 to indicate Paul's conversion from a persecutor to God's advocate.	Epiphanius; Gregory Nazianzen
(2b)	"Saul" and "Paul" are Greek names, meaning to "shake" (*saleuo*) and "to cease" (*pauomai*). The change of names thus indicates that the apostle once "assaulted" the church ('Saul') but has now ceased to do so ('Paul').	Euthalius the Deacon; mentioned but rejected by Chrysostom, *On the Changing of Names* 2
(3a)	The change of names happened in Acts 13. Since Paul converted/"conquered" the proconsul Sergius Paulus (13:7), he now chooses his name, analogous to Scipio who adopted the cognomen Africanus after defeating Hannibal in Africa ("triumphalist" view).	Origen, Jerome, *Commentary on Philemon*; *Catalogues of Virtuous Men* 5.
(3b)	The name change in Acts 13:9 shows that Paul was adopted by the proconsul Sergius Paulus or at least used the politician's name with his permission.	Dessau, Harrer, S. Mitchell, Fadinger, Pearson, Barnett
(4)	Paul was conquered by the Holy Spirit who renames Saul in order to place him under His authority, just as Nebuchadnezzar renames Hananiah, Azariah, and Mishahel and calls them Shadrach, Meshach, and Abednego. The *life*-change happened in Acts 9, but the *name*-change is delayed until Acts 13 so that diaspora Jews who knew Saul the persecutor only by name (Gal. 1:21–23) would recognize that this same Saul now believes the Gospel ("defeatist" view).	Chrysostom, *On the Changing of Names* 3
(5)	The change of name illustrates Paul's transformation. "Saul" reminds of David's opponent "Saul son of Kish," mentioned in the NT only in Acts 13:21. "Paul" means "little one" in Latin and indicates thus the change of heart. Augustine: "When he was Saul, he was proud, exalted; when he was Paul, he was lowly and little" (*Tract. ep. Jo.* 8)	Augustine, *On the Spirit and the Letter* 7.12, McDonough

Paul's Missionary Journeys

CHART 18

		FIRST JOURNEY	SECOND JOURNEY	THIRD JOURNEY	FOURTH JOURNEY
1.	Acts	13:1–14:28	15:36–18:22	18:23–21:16	21:17–28:16
2.	Date	AD 47–48	AD 50–52	AD 52–57	AD 57–60
3.	Cities and regions	Antioch (Syria), Seleucia, Cyprus, Perga, Pisidian Antioch (Galatia), Iconium, Lystra, Derbe, Antioch (Galatia)	Antioch (Syria), Syria, Cilicia, Derbe, Lystra, Troas, Philippi, Thessalonica, Berea, Athens, Corinth, Caesarea, Antioch	Antioch (Syria), Galatia, Phrygia, Ephesus, Macedonia, Troas, Miletus, Syria	Jerusalem, Caesarea, Sidon, Crete, Clauda, Malta, Syracuse, Rhegium, Puteoli, Rome
4.	Major visits	A "long time" in Antioch (Syria) (14:28)	Eighteen months in Corinth (18:11)	Three years in Ephesus (19:10; 20:31)	Two years in Caesarea (24:27) Two years in Rome (28:30)
5.	Divine leading	13:2, 4	16:6, 7, 9–10; 18:9	19:21–22; 21:4, 10–11	23:1
6.	Visits to synagogues	13:5, 14; 14:1	(16:13, 16) 17:1, 10, 17; 18:4, 19	19:8	Temple (21:17, 26)
7.	Jewish rejection	(9:22–25) 13:48–51; 14:19	17:5–9, 13–14; 18:5–6, 12–16	20:3, 19	(21:11) 21:27–32, 36; 22:30; 23:1–5, 12–31; 24:1–9; 25:2–3, 7–8, 24
8.	"turn to Gentiles"	13:46 (see 22:17–21)	18:6		28:28
9.	Prominent Co-worker	*Barnabas* (13:2, 7, 42–43, 46, 50; 14:12, 14, 20; see 15:37–40; Gal. 2:1, 9, 13), a Levite and Jewish Christian from Cyprus (4:36)	*Silas* (15:40; 16:19, 25, 29; 17:4, 10; 1 Thess. 1:1; 2 Thess. 1:1 2 Cor. 1:19), a Jewish Christian leader (15:22) and prophet (15:32) from Jerusalem, maybe also a Roman citizen (16:37)	*Timothy* (19:22; 20:4; 1 Cor. 4:17; etc.), an uncircumcised believer from Lystra with a Jewish mother and a Greek father (16:1–3); Paul gets to know Apollos (18:24–19:1)	*Luke* (see 'we' sections: 16:10–17; 20:5–15; 21:1–18; 27:1–28:16)
10.	Big Speeches	13:16–47 (to Jews in Antioch)	17:22–31 (to Gentiles in Athens)	20:18–35 (to Christians in Ephesus)	22:1, 3–21 (to Jews in Jerusalem); 24:10b–21 (to Felix); 26:2–23 (to King Agrippa)
11.	Internal Problems	Jewish believers in Jerusalem, some of them Pharisees, demand that Gentile Christians should be circumcised and keep the law of Moses (15:1, 5).	Paul separated from John Mark, Barnabas' cousin (Col. 4:10), because he deserted Paul in Pamphylia (15:37–40).	Jewish Christians in Jerusalem were concerned that Paul taught Jews in the diaspora "to forsake Moses, telling them not to circumcise their children nor to walk according to the customs" (21:21).	

	FIRST JOURNEY	SECOND JOURNEY	THIRD JOURNEY	FOURTH JOURNEY
12. **Major Opposition**	Jews stoned Paul in Lystra (14:19–20).	After healing a fortune-telling slave girl in Philippi, city authorities ordered a public beating and prison for Paul and Silas without a trial (16:22–24, 37).	In Ephesus, Paul's preaching of monotheism disturbed business with figurines of the goddess Artemis and led to a huge riot against Christians (19:23–41).	In Jerusalem, Paul barely escaped Roman flogging (22:24–29) and repeated Jewish plots to kill him (23:12–24; 25:3) and traveled as a prisoner to stand trial before authorities in Caesarea and Rome.
13. **Respectable converts**	Sergius Paul, proconsul of Cyprus (Acts 13:7–12).	"leading women" of Thessalonica (17:4) and Berea (17:12); Dionysius the Areopagite (17:34); Crispus, the leader of the synagogue in Corinth (18:8).		Publius, a "leading" man from the island of Malta (28:7); "leading" Jews in Rome (28:17, 24).
14. **Prominent supporters**	Manaen from the church in Antioch, "who had been brought up with Herod the tetrarch" (13:1).	Gallio, proconsul of Achaia, rejected Jewish accusations against Paul in Corinth (18:12–16).	Asiarchs (19:31); the town clerk (ὁ γραμματεύς) of Ephesus rejected accusations against Paul (19:35–41).	Pharisees in Jerusalem: "We find nothing wrong with this man" (23:9). The Roman commander Claudius Lysias (23:29), Felix (24:22–23) and Festus rejected Jewish accusations (25:18–19, 24–27) as did King Agrippa (26:30–32).
15. **Later fruits from earlier efforts**		Timothy from Lystra (16:1); Gaius from Derbe (20:4)	Secundus (20:4) and Aristarchus (19:29; 27:2) from Thessalonica	Trophimus from Ephesus (21:29)

Paul's Coworkers

CHART 19

30 Male Coworkers	Achaicus (1 Cor. 16:15–18); Andronicus (Rom. 16:7); Apollos (1 Cor. 16:12); Aquila (Rom. 16:3–5); Archippus (Col. 4:17); Aristarchus (Col. 4:10); Barnabas (Acts 14:4); Clement (Phil. 4:2–3); Demas (Philem. 1:24); Epaphras (Col. 1:7); Epaphroditus (Phil. 2:25); Erastus (Acts 19:22); Fortunatus (1 Cor. 16:15–18); Gaius of Derbe (Acts 20:4); Justus (Col. 4:10–11); Luke (Philem. 1:24); Mark (2 Tim. 4:11); Onesimus (Col. 4:9); Philemon (Philem. 1:7); Quartus (Rom. 16:23); Secundus (Acts 20:4); Sopater (Acts 20:4); Sosthenes (1 Cor. 1:1); Silas (Acts 15:22); Stephanas (1 Cor. 16:15–18); Timothy (Acts 16:1); Titus (2 Cor. 2:13); Trophimus (Acts 20:4); Tychicus (Eph. 6:21); Urbanus (Rom. 16:9)
11 Female Coworkers	Apphia (Philem. 1:2); Euodia (Phil. 4:2-3); Junia? (Rom. 16:7); Mary (Rom. 16:6); Nympha (Col. 4:15); Persis (Rom. 16:12); Phoebe (Rom. 16:1); Prisca (Rom. 16:3–5); Syntyche (Phil. 4:2-3); Tryphaena & Tryphosa (Rom. 16:12)
Those who housed Paul in their homes	Ananias (Damascus, Acts 9:10–18; 22:12–13); Judas (Damascus, Acts 9:11); an unnamed jailer (Philippi, Acts 16:33–34); Lydia (Philippi, Acts 16:40); Jason (Thessalonica; Acts 17:7); Aquila and Priscilla (Corinth, Acts 18:3); Titus Justus (Corinth, Acts 18:7); Mnason (Jerusalem, Acts 21:16); Gaius (Corinth, Rom. 16:23); Peter (Jerusalem, Gal. 1:18)
Additional "support staff"	Rufus' mother: motherly care (Rom. 16:13) Tertius: secretarial service (Rom. 16:22) Macedonian Christians: material support (2 Cor. 11:9; Phil. 4:10–20) Carpus: storage of Paul's belongings (2 Tim. 4:13)

All Cities Visited by Paul

CHART 20

PALESTINE, SYRIA AND ARABIA		ACTS	PAULINE CORPUS
1.	Jerusalem	Acts 8:1; 9:26; 22:3; 13:27; 21:11–23:22; 26:4, 10	Gal. 1:18; 2:1
2.	Caesarea Maritima	Acts 18:22; 21:8; 23:23; 25:6	
3.	Damascus	Acts 9:8, 19-25; 2 Cor 11:31–33	Gal. 1:17
4.	Arabia		Gal. 1:17
5.	Antioch	Acts 11:26; 13:1; 14:26; 15:22, 30; 18:22	Gal. 2:11
6.	Seleukia	Acts 13:4	
7.	Tyre	Acts 21:3–4	
8.	Sidon	Acts 27:3	
9.	Ptolemais	Acts 21:7	
CYPRUS AND SOUTHERN ASIA MINOR			
10.	Tarsus	Acts 9:11; 21:39; 22:3; 9:30; 11:25	
11.	Cyprus	Acts 13:4	
12.	Attalia	Acts 14:25	
13.	Perga	Acts 13:13–14; 14:25	
14.	Pisidian Antioch	Acts 13:14–52; 14:21	2 Tim. 3:11
15.	Iconium	Acts 13:51–14:6; 14:21	2 Tim. 3:11
16.	Lystra	Acts 14:20–21; 16:1	2 Tim. 3:11
17.	Derbe	Acts 14:6–20; 16:1	
18.	Myra	Acts 27:5	
WESTERN ASIA MINOR			
19.	Ephesus	Acts 18:19; 19:1–20:1;	1 Cor. 15:32; 16:8; 1 Tim. 1:3, 18
20.	Troas	Acts 16:8–11; 20:5–6	2 Cor. 2:12; 2 Tim. 4:13
21.	Assos	Acts 20:13–14	
22.	Mitylene	Acts 20:14	
23.	Chios	Acts 20:15	
24.	Samos	Acts 20:15	
25.	Miletus	Acts 20:15, 17	2 Tim. 4:20
26.	Cos	Acts 21:1	
27.	Rhodes	Acts 21:1	
28.	Patara	Acts 21:1	
GREECE AND MACEDONIA			
29.	Samothrace	Acts 16:11	
30.	Neapolis	Acts 16:11	
31.	Philippi	Acts 16:12–40; 20:6	Phil. 1:3–5, 30; 2:22, 28; 1 Thess. 2:2
32.	Amphipolis	Acts 17:1	
33.	Apollonia	Acts 17:1	

34.	Thessalonica	Acts 17:1–9	Phil. 4:16
35.	Berea	Acts 17:10–14	
36.	Athens	Acts 17:15–18:1	1 Thess. 3:1
37.	Corinth	Acts 18:1–18	1 Cor. 1:6, 14, 16; 3:5; 4:15; etc.
38.	Cenchreae	Acts 18:18	Rom. 16:1
39.	Crete	Acts 27:7, 12–13, 21	Titus 1:5
ROME AND THE WEST			
40.	Syracuse	Acts 28:12	
41.	Rhegium	Acts 28:13	
42.	Puteoli	Acts 28:13	
43.	Rome	Acts 19:21; 23:11; 28:14–31	2 Tim. 1:17

Major Cities in Paul's Ministry

CHART 21

ANTIOCH (Syria)	With about 300,000 people of mixed origin and ethnicity, Antioch was not only the "metropolis" of Syria but, after Rome and Alexandria, "the third city in the habitable earth what was under the Roman empire" (*B.J.* 3.29). Although Paul mentioned this city only once (Gal. 2:11), its significance for his ministry cannot be overestimated. It emerged, beside Jerusalem, as the second center of early Christianity and consisted of Gentiles for the most part (Acts 11:19). The church in Antioch sent the apostle out to his first and second missionary journeys (Acts 13:1; 16:1) and it is to this city where he returned and rested both times (Acts 14:26–28; 18:22). Jews from Judea went to Antioch to circumcise Gentile Christians, which led to the first and famous Christian council in Jerusalem (Acts 15:1-35).
CAESAREA MARITIMA	Caesarea Maritima housed the official residence of the Roman governor (*praetorium*) and headquarters for the Roman troops in Palestine. Its harbor provided a connection to the Western world. Josephus called Caesarea "a very great (μεγίστην) city of Judea, and for the greatest part inhabited by Greeks" (Ἑλλήνων; *B.J.* 3.409). Paul was rescued from Jerusalem to Caesarea (about seventy miles apart) after a Jewish plot to kill him was uncovered (Acts 23:12–35). The apostle remained imprisoned in Caesarea for over two years (Acts 24:27) before he was sent to Rome for his trial.
CORINTH	Corinth was a port city with two harbors, Lechaion on the west (Adriatic) and Cenchrea on the east (Aegean). An isthmus of 2½ miles at narrowest point connected both seas. With a population of ca. 100,000 people, Corinth was, in contrast to Athens, the most important commercial and cultural center in Southern Greece. The seat of the Roman government of Achaia resided here from 27 BC on. It hosted the Isthmian Games—second only to the Olympics. Cynic philosophy was at home here (see Diogenes, 5th century BC), as well as shrines and temples to many gods (see 1 Cor. 8:5), e.g., Apollo, Aphrodite, including a "synagogue to the Hebrews" (inscription; Acts 18). Paul spent eighteen months in Corinth on his second missionary journey (Acts 18:11).
EPHESUS	With probably 100,000 to 150,000 people, Ephesus was superseded in size only by Rome, Alexandria and Antioch (Syria). Ephesus was the "metropolis of Asia" (πρωτευούσῃ τῆς Ἀσίας, *A.J.* 14.224). Its location as a port city guaranteed commerce and wealth. The Ephesians worshiped multiple gods and goddesses (e.g., Aphrodite, Apollo, Asclepius, Pluto, Poseidon, Zeus). But they took special pride in being called "twice neokoros" on coins, meaning that they were the guardians of the goddess Artemis and of the emperor cult. Paul spent close to three years in Ephesus (Acts 19:10; 20:31) on the third missionary journey.
JERUSALEM	Jerusalem, the capitol of Palestine, was not only "by far the most famous city of the East" (Pliny the Elder [AD 23/24-79], *Nat. Hist.* 5.15.70), but was perceived already in late biblical traditions as the "center of the earth" (see Ezek. 5:5 [Rom. 15:19]; also *Jubil.* 8:12; *1 En.* 26.1). This certainly proved true for the life and destiny of Jesus (Luke 9:51-52) and Paul (Acts 19:21-22; 22:3) and for the origin and mission of the early Church ("Jerusalem" occurs 61 times in Acts). Estimates about the city's population range from at least 60,000 to 120,000. Paul mentions "Jerusalem" in Rom. 15:19, 25–26, 31; 1 Cor. 16:3; Gal. 1:17–18; 2:1; 4:25–26.
PHILIPPI	With a population between 5,000 and 15,000 people, Philippi was smaller than Thessalonica or Amphipolis. And yet, Luke calls it a "leading" (πρώτη[ς], Acts 16:12) city and Roman colony in Macedonia, a northern province of Greece. The social elites of the city consisted entirely of retired veterans from the Roman military, which gave Philippi the most Roman character among any city east of Rome. Latin was the language of the leaders. Roman architecture characterized the city. Roman gods such as Jupiter, Neptune, and Mercury were honored by the residents. Paul founded the first church in Europe here.

ROME	Rome was the capitol of the Roman empire and had a population of ca. 700,000—1 million people. Among them were a high number of Jews, around 50,000, who repeatedly experienced anti-Semitism to the point of expulsion from the city (so under emperors Tiberius [*A.J.* 18.81-84] and Claudius [Acts 18:2]). Tacitus (c. AD 56-120) writes: "Rome, where all things hideous and shameful from every part of the world find their centre and become popular" (*Ann.*, 15.44). Roman pilgrims to Jerusalem during Pentecost in the early 30s of the first century might have been the first Christians in the capitol (Acts 2:10). Decades later, Paul lived at least two years in Rome as a prisoner awaiting trial (Acts 28:30). His presence there was not merely a matter of legal circumstances but of divine necessity (Acts 19:21; 23:11).
THESSALONICA	Thessalonica was a harbor city and metropolis of Macedonia (which is a province of Greece). Estimates about its population vary from 20,000 to 100,000 people. The chief deity of the city was called "Cabirus" who was worshipped together with other gods such as Zeus, Asclepius, Aphrodite, Demeter, etc. Located along the Via Egnatia, the strategic location of both Philippi and Thessalonica helped spread the Gospel westward toward Rome.

All Women Mentioned by and around Paul

CHART 22

	A) WOMEN IN ACTS		
1.	Bernice	Sister of Herod Agrippa II	Acts 25:13, 23; 26:30
2.	Damaris	From Athens; she believed in response to Paul's preaching	Acts 17:34
3.	Drusilla	Daughter of Agrippa I and sister of Agrippa II	Acts 24:24
4.	Lydia	A seller of purple fabrics and a worshiper of God from Thyatira who worked in Philippi where she met Paul	Acts 16:14, 40
5.	Slave girl	In Philippi; Paul exorcises her demons	Acts 16:16-18
6.	Prominent women	In Thessalonica and Berea; they believe Paul's gospel	Acts 17:4, 12
7.	Prophetesses	Virgin daughters of Philip the evangelist, they prophesied	Acts 21:8–9
	B) WOMEN IN PAUL'S LETTERS		
8.	Apphia	"the sister" who is addressed in Paul's letter to Philemon	Philem. 1:2
9.	Chloe	Members of her house told Paul about the Corinthian church	1 Cor. 1:11
10.	Claudia	A believer	2 Tim. 4:21
11.	Euodia	She has "struggled" with Paul (συνήθλησάν) in the Gospel	Phil. 4:2–3
12.	Eve	She was created after Adam and deceived by the serpent	2 Cor. 11:3; 1 Tim. 2:13
13.	Hagar	An Egyptian "slave-girl" (NRS Gen 16:1) who became the concubine of the patriarch Abraham	Gal. 4:24–25
14.	Junia?	Paul's fellow-prisoner, "outstanding among the apostles"	Rom. 16:7
15.	Julia	A believer in Rome	Rom. 16:15
16.	Mary	She worked very hard for the Christians in Rome	Rom. 16:6
17.	Nympha	She was a leader of a house church in Laodicea	Col. 4:15
18.	Persis	The "beloved, who has worked hard in the Lord"	Rom. 16:12
19.	Phoebe	She was a deacon (dia,konoj) and patron (prosta,tij) in Cenchrea	Rom. 16:1
20.	Sarah	Wife of the patriarch Abraham	Rom. 4:19; 9:9
21.	Syntyche	She "struggled" with Paul (sunh,qlhsa,n) in the Gospel	Phil. 4:2–3
22.	Tryphaena	A "worker in the Lord"	Rom. 16:12
23.	Tryphosa	A "worker in the Lord"	Rom. 16:12
24.	Rufus' mother		Rom. 16:13
25.	Nereus' sister		Rom. 16:15
	C) WOMEN IN ACTS AND PAUL'S LETTERS		
26.	Priscilla (Acts) Prisca (Letters)	She risked her life for Paul	Acts 18:2, 18, 26; Rom. 16:3; 1 Cor. 16:19; 2 Tim. 4:19

All Men Mentioned by and around Paul

CHART 23

A) MEN IN ACTS

1.	Agabus	A Christian prophet who prophesied to Paul twice	Acts 11:28; 21:10
2.	Ananias	A Christian in Damascus whom Jesus sent to Paul	Acts 9:10–18
3.	Ananias	High priest, ca. AD 48	Acts 23:2; 24:1
4.	Bar Jesus	Also "Elymas;" a Jewish sorcerer on Cyprus who was an attendant of the proconsul Sergius Paulus	Acts 13:6-12
5.	Demetrius	A silversmith in Ephesus who opposed Paul	Acts 19:23
6.	Dionysius	A member of the Areopagus in Athens who believes after Paul evangelizes there	Acts 17:34
7.	Eutychus	Young man in Troas who fell out of a window	Acts 20:7–12
8.	Felix	Procurator of Judea from AD 52–60	Acts 23:24–24:27
9.	Festus	Procurator of Judea, ca. AD 59–62	Acts 24:27–26:32
10.	Gaius	From Macedonia; Paul's "travel companion"	Acts 19:29
11.	Gaius	From Derbe (?); he accompanied Paul	Acts 20:4
12.	Gallio	Roman proconsul of Achaia who refused to judge Paul in Corinth	Acts 18:12–17
13.	Gamaliel	Member of the Sanhedrin, teacher of Paul	Acts 5:34; 22:3
14.	Herod Agr. I	He persecuted the early church in Jerusalem	Acts 12:1–23
15.	Herod Agr. II	The king who listened to Paul's defense	Acts 25:13–26:32
16.	Judas	Also called "Barsabbas"; he brought the letter of the Jerusalem council to the church in Antioch	Acts 15:22, 27, 32
17.	Manaen	A Christian at Antioch who had been brought up with Herod Antipas	Acts 13:1
18.	Philip	Evangelist from Caesarea, one of the Seven	Acts 21:8; 6:5
19.	Sceva	A Jewish chief priest from whose seven sons exorcized in the name of Jesus	Acts 19:13–16
20.	Secundus	From Thessalonica, travelling with Paul	Acts 20:4
21.	Simon	Called "Niger"; a leader of the church in Antioch	Acts 13:1
22.	Sopater	"of Berea, the son of Pyrrhus", travels with Paul	Acts 20:4
23.	Tertullus	Ananias the high priest's lawyer who accused Paul	Acts 24:1–2
24.	Titius Justus	A "godfearer" in Corinth; Paul goes to his house after the Jews resisted and blasphemed him	Acts 18:6

NAMELESS INDIVIDUALS

25.	Jailer	Jailer in Philippi who became a Christian	Acts 16:19–34
26.	Philosophers	Epicurean and Stoic philosophers argue with Paul	Acts 17:18
27.	Elders	Of the church in Ephesus	Acts 20:17

B) MEN IN PAUL'S LETTERS

28.	Achaicus	He supplied what the Corinthians lacked	1 Cor. 16:17–18
29.	Adam	The first man created by God	Rom. 5:14; 1 Cor. 15:22, 45; 1 Tim. 2:13–14
30.	Ampliatus	Paul's "beloved in the Lord"	Rom. 16:8

31.	Andronicus	A Jew who converted before Paul, was imprisoned and is "outstanding among the apostles"	Rom. 16:7
32.	Apelles	"the approved (δόκιμον) in Christ"	Rom. 16:10
33.	Archippus		Col. 4:17; Philem. 1:2
34.	Aristobulus	Paul asks to greet those of Aristobulus' house	Rom. 16:10
35.	Artemas	Coworker of Paul	Titus 3:12
36.	Asyncritus		Rom. 16:14
37.	Carpus		2 Tim. 4:13
38.	Clement	Fellow-worker of Paul	Phil. 4:2–3
39.	Crescens		2 Tim. 4:10
40.	Demas	A "fellow worker" who later "loved this present world" and deserted Paul	Philem. 1:24; Col. 4:11; 2 Tim. 4:10
41.	Epaphras	From Colossae, possibly the founder of the church	Col. 1:7; 4:12; Philem. 1:23
42.	Epaphroditus	From Philippi; "my brother and fellow worker and fellow soldier, who is also your messenger and minister to my need"	Phil. 2:25; 4:18
43.	Epaenetus	The first convert in province of Asia	Rom. 16:5
44.	Eubulus	He sents greetings through Paul to Timothy	2 Tim. 4:21
45.	Fortunatus		1 Cor. 16:15–18
46.	Gaius	from Achaia (Corinth), baptized by Paul; he is a "host" (ξένος) of the apostle	1 Cor. 1:14; Rom. 16:23
47.	Hermas		Rom. 16:14
48.	Hermes		Rom. 16:14
49.	Hermogenes	He turned away from Paul	2 Tim. 1:15
50.	Herodion	Paul's "kinsman" (συγγενῆ)	Rom. 16:11
51.	Hymenaeus	"whom I have handed over to Satan, so that [he] will be taught not to blaspheme"; he believed that the resurrection had already happened	1 Tim. 1:20; 2 Tim. 2:17–18
52.	Justus	Jesus called "Justus," a Jewish fellow-worker	Col. 4:10–11
53	Linus	He sents greetings to Timothy through Paul	2 Tim. 4:21
54.	Luke	"the beloved physician" (ὁ ἰατρὸς ὁ ἀγαπητὸς)	Col. 4:11, 14; 2 Tim. 4:11; Philem. 1:24; "we" passages in Acts: 16:11, etc.
55.	Narcissus	Christians meet in his house	Rom. 16:11
56.	Nereus		Rom. 16:15
57.	Olympas		Rom. 16:15
58.	Onesimus	A slave from Colossae who worked with Paul	Col. 4:9; Philem. 1:10
59.	Onesiphorus		2 Tim. 1:16; 4:19
60.	Patrobas		Rom. 16:14
61.	Philemon		Philem. 1:1
62.	Philetus	He said that "the resurrection has already taken place" and thus upset the faith of some	2 Tim. 2:17–18
63.	Philologus		Rom. 16:15
64.	Phlegon		Rom. 16:14
65.	Phygelus	He turned away from Paul	2 Tim. 1:15
66.	Pudens	He sents greetings to Timothy through Paul	2 Tim. 4:21

67.	Quartus	"the brother"	Rom. 16:23
68.	Rufus	"a choice-man (τὸν ἐκλεκτὸν) in the Lord"	Rom. 16:13
69.	Sosipater	One of Paul's "kinsmen" (συγγενεῖς)	Rom. 16:21
70.	Stachys	"my beloved"	Rom. 16:9
71.	Stephanas		1 Cor. 1:16; 16:15, 17
72.	Tertius	Paul's amanuensis for writing *Romans*	Rom. 16:22
73.	Titus	A "Greek" (Gal. 2:3); Paul calls him "my brother" (2 Cor. 2:13), "my partner and fellow worker" (2 Cor. 8:23), and "my true child in a common faith" (Titus 1:4)	2 Cor. 2:13; 7:6, 13–14; 8:6, 16, 23; 12:18; Gal. 2:1, 3; 2 Tim. 4:10; Titus 1:4
74.	Urbanus	"our fellow-worker in Christ"	Rom. 16:9
75.	Zenas	"the lawyer" (τὸν νομικὸν)	Titus 3:13
C) MEN IN ACTS AND PAUL'S LETTERS			
76.	Alexander	The coppersmith "whom I have handed over to Satan, so that [he] will be taught not to blaspheme"	1 Tim. 1:20; 2 Tim. 4:14 (maybe Acts 19:33)
77.	Apollos	A Jew native from Alexandria, coworker of Paul	Acts 18:24; 19:1; 1 Cor. 1:12; 3:4–5, 22; 4:6; 16:12; Titus 3:13
78.	Aquila	A Jewish believer, native of Pontus, who risked his life for Paul (Rom. 16:4)	Acts 18:2, 18, 26; Rom. 16:3; 1 Cor. 16:19; 2 Tim. 4:19
79.	Aristarchus	From Thessalonica, Paul's "fellow-prisoner" (συναιχμάλωτος, Col. 4:10) and one of the few Jewish fellow-workers	Acts 19:29; 20:4; 27:2; Col. 4:10; Philem. 1:24
80.	Barnabas	A Levite who became a Christian before Paul; he connected Paul with the apostles in Jerusalem and later joined him on the first missionary journey	Acts 4:36; 9:27; 1 Cor. 9:6; Gal. 2:1, 9, 13; Col. 4:10
81.	Crispus	Synagogue leader from Corinth, baptized by Paul	Acts 18:8; 1 Cor. 1:14
82.	Erastus	The "city-treasurer" (ὁ οἰκονόμος τῆς πόλεως) who "ministered" (διακονούντων) to Paul	Rom. 16:23; Acts 19:22; 2 Tim. 4:20
83.	Jason	From Thessalonica, one of Paul's "kinsmen" (συγγενεῖς)	Acts 17:5–9; Rom. 16:21
84.	Lucius	One of Paul's "kinsmen" (συγγενεῖς)	Rom. 16:21 (also Acts 13:1?)
85.	Mark	Barnabas' cousin, also called "John," and one of the few Jewish fellow-workers of Paul	Acts 12:12, 25; 15:37–39; Col. 4:10; 2 Tim. 4:11; Philem. 1:24
86.	Peter	Called "Cephas" in 1 Cor. 1:12; 3:22; 9:5; 15:5; Gal. 1:18; 2:9, 11, 14	Acts 15:7; Gal. 2:7–8
87.	Silas (Acts) Silvanus (Paul)	A Roman citizen and Jewish Christian prophet who joined Paul on his second missionary journey	Acts 15:22–40; 16:19–29; 17:4–15; 18:5; 2 Cor. 1:19; 1 Thess. 1:1; 2 Thess. 1:1; (also 1 Peter 5:12)
88.	Sosthenes	Synagogue leader in Corinth who was beaten	Acts 18:17; 1 Cor. 1:1
89.	Timothy	His mother was Jewish, his father was Greek; Paul calls him "my beloved and faithful child in the Lord" (1 Cor. 4:17) and his "fellow worker" (Rom. 16:21); Timothy served, among others, in Berea, Corinth, and Ephesus	Acts 16:1; 17:14–15; 18:5; 19:22; 20:4; Rom. 16:21; 1 Cor. 4:17; 16:10; 2 Cor. 1:1, 19; Phil. 1:1; 2:19; Col. 1:1; 1 Thess. 1:1; 3:2, 6; 2 Thess. 1:1; 1 Tim. 1:2, 18; 6:20; 2 Tim. 1:2; Philem. 1:1
90.	Trophimus	A Christian from Ephesus who traveled with Paul	Acts 20:4; 21:29; 2 Tim. 4:20
91.	Tychicus	"the beloved brother and faithful minister in the Lord"	Acts 20:4; Eph. 6:21; Col. 4:7; 2 Tim. 4:12; Titus 3:12

Speeches of Paul in Acts

CHART 24

MISSIONARY SPEECHES	SPOKEN TO	742 WORDS
1. at Antioch of Pisidia (13:16b–41, 46–47)	Jews	471
2. at Lystra, together with Barnabas (14:15–17)	Gentiles	68
3. at Philippi to the jailor, together with Silas (16:31)	Gentile	12
4. at the Areopagus (17:22–31)	Gentiles	191
APOLOGETIC SPEECHES		**1493 WORDS**
5. to the Corinthians (18:6b-d)	Jews	16
6. to disciples in Caesarea (21:13b-c)	Christians	26
7. to the Jews in Jerusalem (22:1, 3–21)	Jews	322
8. before the Sanhedrin (23:1b, 3, 5, 6b)	Jews	63
9. before Felix (24:10b–21)	Gentile	198
10. before Festus (25:8b, 10b–11)	Gentile	62
11. before King Agrippa (26:2–23, 25–27, 29)	Jew	497
12. during the sea voyage to Rome (27:10b, 21b-26, 31b, 33b–34)	276 people (v.37)	154
13. to the Roman Jewish leaders (28:17c–20, 25b–28)	Jews	155
FAREWELL SPEECH		**320 WORDS**
14. to the Ephesian elders (20:18–35)	Christians	320
TOTAL WORDS		**2555**

Contextualization in Paul's Missionary Speeches

CHART 25

CATEGORIES	ACTS 13:13–52	ACTS 14:8–20	ACTS 17:16–34
Geographic location	Pisidian Antioch	Lystra, small remote mountain village	Athens, large coastal city
Locality	Diaspora synagogue	Public forum	Areopagus council
Audience	Diaspora Jews and God-fearing Gentiles	Indigenous Lycaonians	"Epicurean [practical atheists] and Stoic [natural revelation] philosophers" (v.18)
Social-cultural Setting	Ancient diaspora Jews	Isolated rural Gentiles who speak a local dialect (v.11) and are loyal to ancient religious customs and beliefs (v.12–13)	Developed civilization, open to new ideas (v.19–21)
Symbolical Value	Encounter with Judaism	Encounter with Paganism	Encounter with Hellenism
Address	"Men of Israel, and you who fear God" (v.16, 26)	"Men, why are you doing these things?" (v.15)	"Men of Athens" (v.22)
Occasion for the Sermon	Visit in the synagogue	Healing of a lame person	Discussion in the marketplace
Point of Contact	History of Israel (v.17–22), "promise" to the fathers (v. 23, 32, 33)	God gave you rain, food and gladness (v.17)	Inscription to an "unknown God"; "ignorance" (v.23, 30); Stoic concept of people being made to seek God (v.27)
Quotations	Ps 2:7; Isa 55:3; Ps 16:10; Hab 1:5; Isa 49:6 (33–35)	Implicit: Ex 20:11 // Ps 146:6 "who made the heaven and the earth" (v.15)	"For we also are His children" (by Aratus, one "of your own poets," v.28), showing natural connection between God and human beings
Point of Contrast	Jews in Jerusalem and their rulers rejected Jesus (v.27–29); Law of Moses could not free the Jews (v.39); their own prophets warn against unbelief (v.41)	Paul and Barnabas reject their idolatrous deification (v.15)	Paul preaches "strange deities" (Ξένων δαιμονίων, v.18); Athenians worship in "ignorance" (v.23); God does not dwell in human temples (v.25); against idolatry (v.29)
Description of God	"God of this people Israel" (v.17)	"a living God" (v.15)	"The God who made the world and all things in it" (v. 24)
God's Dealings with People in the Past	God's positive history of Israel (v.17–22)	"In the generations gone by He permitted all the nations to go their own ways" (v.16)	God made every nation and placed them geographically (v.26-27); God overlooked previous "ignorance" (v.30)
Call to Conversion	"forgiveness of sins is proclaimed to you … everyone who believes is freed from all things" (v.38–39)	"turn from these vain things to a living God" (v.15)	"that all people everywhere should repent" (v.30)

Paul's Miracles

CHART 26

	MIRACLE	TEXT
1.	Jesus appears to Saul, a light and voice from heaven	Acts 9:3–4
2.	Saul's sight restored	Acts 9:17–18
3.	Paul blinds Elymas, the magician, on Cyprus	Acts 13:8–11
4.	Paul cures a lame man in Lystra	Acts 14:8–10
5.	Paul casts out a demon from a girl in Philippi	Acts 16:16–18
6.	Paul exits a prison in Philippi through an earthquake	Acts 16:26
7.	Paul performs miracles in Ephesus with handkerchiefs	Acts 19:11–12
8.	Paul raises Eutychus in Troas	Acts 20:9–10
9.	Paul remains unharmed despite a viper's bite on Malta	Acts 28:3–5
10.	Paul heals Publius's father on Malta from fever	Acts 28:7–9
11.	General references to "signs and wonders" performed by Paul	Acts 14:3; 15:12; 28:9 Rom. 15:19; 1 Cor. 2:4; 2 Cor. 12:12; Gal. 3:5; 1 Thess. 1:5 (?)

MIRACLES IN THE *ACTS OF PAUL* (2nd century AD)

1.	Paul raises the boy of Anchares and Phila in Antioch	Acts of Paul 2
2.	Paul raises Hermocrates and Dion, two men in Myra	Acts of Paul 4
3.	Paul blinds Hermippus and restores his sight again	Acts of Paul 4
4.	Paul prays and the temple of Apollo in Sidon collapses	Acts of Paul 5
5.	Paul exorcises demons in Tyre	Acts of Paul 6
6.	Paul miraculously escapes the fight with beasts in Ephesus	Acts of Paul 7
7.	Paul raises Frontina	Acts of Paul 8
8.	Paul raises Patroclus, the cupbearer of emperor Nero	Acts of Paul 11
9.	The deceased Paul appears Nero in a dream	Acts of Paul 11

Paul's Prayers

CHART 27

	Romans
1:7–10	[7] Grace to you and peace from God our Father and the Lord Jesus Christ. [8] First, I thank my God through Jesus Christ for you all, because your faith is being proclaimed throughout the whole world. [9] For God, whom I serve in my spirit in the preaching of the gospel of His Son, is my witness as to how unceasingly I make mention of you, [10] always in my prayers making request, if perhaps now at last by the will of God I may succeed in coming to you.
10:1	Brethren, my heart's desire and my prayer to God for them is for their salvation.
15:5–6	[5] Now may the God who gives perseverance and encouragement grant you to be of the same mind with one another according to Christ Jesus; [6] that with one accord you may with one voice glorify the God and Father of our Lord Jesus Christ.
15:13	Now may the God of hope fill you with all joy and peace in believing, that you may abound in hope by the power of the Holy Spirit.
15:33	Now the God of peace be with you all. Amen.
16:20	The grace of our Lord Jesus be with you.
16:25–27	[25] Now to Him who is able to establish you according to my gospel and the preaching of Jesus Christ, according to the revelation of the mystery which has been kept secret for long ages past, [26] but now is manifested, and by the Scriptures of the prophets, according to the commandment of the eternal God, has been made known to all the nations, leading to obedience of faith; [27] to the only wise God, through Jesus Christ, be the glory forever. Amen.

	1 Corinthians
1:3–9	[3] Grace to you and peace from God our Father and the Lord Jesus Christ. [4] I thank my God always concerning you, for the grace of God which was given you in Christ Jesus, [5] that in everything you were enriched in Him, in all speech and all knowledge, [6] even as the testimony concerning Christ was confirmed in you, [7] so that you are not lacking in any gift, awaiting eagerly the revelation of our Lord Jesus Christ, [8] who shall also confirm you to the end, blameless in the day of our Lord Jesus Christ. [9] God is faithful, through whom you were called into fellowship with His Son, Jesus Christ our Lord.
1:14	I thank God that I baptized none of you except Crispus and Gaius, …
16:22	Maranatha.
16:23	The grace of the Lord Jesus be with you.

	2 Corinthians
1:2-4	[2] Grace to you and peace from God our Father and the Lord Jesus Christ. [3] Blessed be the God and Father of our Lord Jesus Christ, the Father of mercies and God of all comfort; [4] who comforts us in all our affliction so that we may be able to comfort those who are in any affliction with the comfort with which we ourselves are comforted by God.
9:15	Thanks be to God for His indescribable gift!
12:8	Concerning this [thorn in the flesh] I implored the Lord three times that it might leave me.
13:7–10	[7] Now we pray to God that you do no wrong; not that we ourselves may appear approved, but that you may do what is right, even though we should appear unapproved. [8] For we can do nothing against the truth, but only for the truth. [9] For we rejoice when we ourselves are weak but you are strong; this we also pray for, that you be made complete. [10] For this reason I am writing these things while absent, in order that when present I may not use severity, in accordance with the authority which the Lord gave me, for building up and not for tearing down.
13:14	The grace of the Lord Jesus Christ, and the love of God, and the fellowship of the Holy Spirit, be with you all.

Galatians	
1:3–5	[3] Grace to you and peace from God our Father, and the Lord Jesus Christ, [4] who gave Himself for our sins, that He might deliver us out of this present evil age, according to the will of our God and Father, [5] to whom be the glory forevermore. Amen.
6:16	And those who will walk by this rule, peace and mercy be upon them, and upon the Israel of God.
6:18	The grace of our Lord Jesus Christ be with your spirit, brethren. Amen.

Ephesians	
1:2–4	Grace to you and peace from God our Father and the Lord Jesus Christ. [3] Blessed be the God and Father of our Lord Jesus Christ, who has blessed us with every spiritual blessing in the heavenly places in Christ, [4] just as He chose us in Him before the foundation of the world, that we should be holy and blameless before Him.
1:15–23	[15] For this reason I too, having heard of the faith in the Lord Jesus which exists among you, and your love for all the saints, [16] do not cease giving thanks for you, while making mention of you in my prayers; [17] that the God of our Lord Jesus Christ, the Father of glory, may give to you a spirit of wisdom and of revelation in the knowledge of Him. [18] I pray that the eyes of your heart may be enlightened, so that you may know what is the hope of His calling, what are the riches of the glory of His inheritance in the saints, [19] and what is the surpassing greatness of His power toward us who believe. These are in accordance with the working of the strength of His might [20] which He brought about in Christ, when He raised Him from the dead, and seated Him at His right hand in the heavenly places, [21] far above all rule and authority and power and dominion, and every name that is named, not only in this age, but also in the one to come. [22] And He put all things in subjection under His feet, and gave Him as head over all things to the church, [23] which is His body, the fulness of Him who fills all in all.
3:14–21	[14] For this reason, I bow my knees before the Father, [15] from whom every family in heaven and on earth derives its name, [16] that He would grant you, according to the riches of His glory, to be strengthened with power through His Spirit in the inner man; [17] so that Christ may dwell in your hearts through faith; and that you, being rooted and grounded in love, [18] may be able to comprehend with all the saints what is the breadth and length and height and depth, [19] and to know the love of Christ which surpasses knowledge, that you may be filled up to all the fulness of God. [20] Now to Him who is able to do exceeding abundantly beyond all that we ask or think, according to the power that works within us, [21] to Him be the glory in the church and in Christ Jesus to all generations forever and ever. Amen.
6:23–24	[23] Peace be to the brethren, and love with faith, from God the Father and the Lord Jesus Christ. [24] Grace be with all those who love our Lord Jesus Christ with a love incorruptible.

Philippians	
1:2–5	[2] Grace to you and peace from God our Father and the Lord Jesus Christ. [3] I thank my God in all my remembrance of you, [4] always offering prayer with joy in my every prayer for you all, [5] in view of your participation in the gospel from the first day until now.
1:9–11	[9] And this I pray, that your love may abound still more and more in real knowledge and all discernment, [10] so that you may approve the things that are excellent, in order to be sincere and blameless until the day of Christ; [11] having been filled with the fruit of righteousness which comes through Jesus Christ, to the glory and praise of God.
4:20	Now to our God and Father be the glory forever and ever. Amen.
4:23	The grace of the Lord Jesus Christ be with your spirit.

Colossians	
1:2–4	[2] Grace to you and peace from God our Father. [3] We give thanks to God, the Father of our Lord Jesus Christ, praying always for you, [4] since we heard of your faith in Christ Jesus and the love which you have for all the saints;

1:9–12	[9] For this reason also, since the day we heard of it, we have not ceased to pray for you and to ask that you may be filled with the knowledge of His will in all spiritual wisdom and understanding, [10] so that you may walk in a manner worthy of the Lord, to please Him in all respects, bearing fruit in every good work and increasing in the knowledge of God; [11] strengthened with all power, according to His glorious might, for the attaining of all steadfastness and patience; joyously [12] giving thanks to the Father, who has qualified us to share in the inheritance of the saints in Light.
4:3–4	[3] praying at the same time for us as well, that God may open up to us a door for the word, so that we may speak forth the mystery of Christ, for which I have also been imprisoned; [4] in order that I may make it clear in the way I ought to speak.
4:12	Epaphras, who is one of your number, a bondslave of Jesus Christ, sends you his greetings, always laboring earnestly for you in his prayers, that you may stand perfect and fully assured in all the will of God.
4:18	Grace be with you.
	1 Thessalonians
1:1–5	[1] Grace to you and peace. [2] We give thanks to God always for all of you, making mention of you in our prayers; [3] constantly bearing in mind your work of faith and labor of love and steadfastness of hope in our Lord Jesus Christ in the presence of our God and Father, [4] knowing, brethren beloved by God, His choice of you; [5] for our gospel did not come to you in word only, but also in power and in the Holy Spirit and with full conviction; just as you know what kind of men we proved to be among you for your sake.
2:13	For this reason we also constantly thank God that when you received the word of God which you heard from us, you accepted it not as the word of men, but for what it really is, the word of God, which also performs its work in you who believe.
3:10–13	[10] as we night and day keep praying most earnestly that we may see your face, and may complete what is lacking in your faith? [11] Now may our God and Father Himself and Jesus our Lord direct our way to you; [12] and may the Lord cause you to increase and abound in love for one another, and for all men, just as we also do for you; [13] so that He may establish your hearts unblamable in holiness before our God and Father at the coming of our Lord Jesus with all His saints.
5:23	Now may the God of peace Himself sanctify you entirely; and may your spirit and soul and body be preserved complete, without blame at the coming of our Lord Jesus Christ.
5:28	The grace of our Lord Jesus Christ be with you.
	2 Thessalonians
1:2–4	[2] Grace to you and peace from God the Father and the Lord Jesus Christ. [3] We ought always to give thanks to God for you, brethren, as is only fitting, because your faith is greatly enlarged, and the love of each one of you toward one another grows ever greater; [4] therefore, we ourselves speak proudly of you among the churches of God for your perseverance and faith in the midst of all your persecutions and afflictions which you endure.
1:11–12	[11] To this end also we pray for you always that our God may count you worthy of your calling, and fulfill every desire for goodness and the work of faith with power; [12] in order that the name of our Lord Jesus may be glorified in you, and you in Him, according to the grace of our God and the Lord Jesus Christ.
2:13–14	[13] But we should always give thanks to God for you, brethren beloved by the Lord, because God has chosen you from the beginning for salvation through sanctification by the Spirit and faith in the truth. [14] And it was for this He called you through our gospel, that you may gain the glory of our Lord Jesus Christ.
2:16–17	[16] Now may our Lord Jesus Christ Himself and God our Father, who has loved us and given us eternal comfort and good hope by grace, [17] comfort and strengthen your hearts in every good work and word.
3:1–2	[1] Finally, brethren, pray for us that the word of the Lord may spread rapidly and be glorified, just as it did also with you; [2] and that we may be delivered from perverse and evil men; for not all have faith.
3:5	And may the Lord direct your hearts into the love of God and into the steadfastness of Christ.

3:16	Now may the Lord of peace Himself continually grant you peace in every circumstance. The Lord be with you all!
3:18	The grace of our Lord Jesus Christ be with you all.
1 Timothy	
1:2	Grace, mercy and peace from God the Father and Christ Jesus our Lord.
1:12	I thank Christ Jesus our Lord, who has strengthened me, because He considered me faithful, putting me into service;
1:17	Now to the King eternal, immortal, invisible, the only God, be honor and glory forever and ever. Amen.
6:16	To Him be honor and eternal dominion! Amen.
6:21	Grace be with you [plural: ὑμῶν].
2 Timothy	
1:2–3	[2] Grace, mercy and peace from God the Father and Christ Jesus our Lord. [3] I thank God, whom I serve with a clear conscience the way my forefathers did, as I constantly remember you in my prayers night and day, …
1:16–18	[16] The Lord grant mercy to the house of Onesiphorus for he often refreshed me, and was not ashamed of my chains; [17] but when he was in Rome, he eagerly searched for me, and found me— [18] the Lord grant to him to find mercy from the Lord on that day—and you know very well what services he rendered at Ephesus.
4:14–16	[14] Alexander the coppersmith did me much harm; the Lord will repay him according to his deeds. [15] Be on guard against him yourself, for he vigorously opposed our teaching. [16] At my first defense no one supported me, but all deserted me; may it not be counted against them.
4:18	The Lord will rescue me from every evil deed, and will bring me safely to His heavenly kingdom; to Him be the glory forever and ever. Amen.
4:22	The Lord be with your spirit [singular, πνεύματός σου]. Grace be with you [plural: ὑμῶν].
Titus	
1:4	Grace and peace from God the Father and Christ Jesus our Savior.
3:15	Grace be with you all [plural: ὑμῶν].
Philemon	
1:3–6	[3] Grace to you and peace from God our Father and the Lord Jesus Christ. [4] I thank my God always, making mention of you in my prayers, [5] because I hear of your love, and of the faith which you have toward the Lord Jesus, and toward all the saints; [6] and I pray that the fellowship of your faith may become effective through the knowledge of every good thing which is in you for Christ's sake.
1:25	The grace of the Lord Jesus Christ be with your spirit [plural: πνεύματος ὑμῶν].

Names, Titles, and Metaphors for Paul and His Ministry

CHART 28

NAMES

Paul (Παῦλος)	157 times used of the apostle Paul (1x for a proconsul in Cyprus, Acts 13:7): Acts 13: 9, 13, 16, 43, 45, 46, 50; 14:9, 11, 12, 14, 19; 15:2 [2x], 12, 22, 25, 35, 36, 38, 40; 16:3, 9, 14, 17, 18, 19, 25, 28, 29, 36, 37; 17:2, 4, 10, 13, 14, 15, 16, 22, 33; 18:5, 9, 12, 14, 18; 19:1, 4, 6, 11, 13, 15, 21, 26, 29, 30; 20:1, 7, 9, 10, 16, 37; 21:4, 11, 13, 18, 26, 29, 30, 32, 37, 39, 40; 22:25, 28, 30; 23:1, 3, 5, 6, 10, 12, 14, 16 [2x], 17, 18, 20, 24, 31, 33; 24:1, 10, 24, 26, 27; etc.; Rom. 1:1; 1 Cor. 1:1, 12, 13; 3:4, 5, 22; 16:21; 2 Cor. 1:1; 10:1; Gal. 1:1; 5:2; Eph. 1:1; 3:1; Phil. 1:1; Col. 1:1, 23; 4:18; 1 Thess. 1:1; 2:18; 2 Thess. 1:1; 3:17; 1 Tim. 1:1; 2 Tim. 1:1; Titus 1:1; Philem. 1:1, 9, 19; 2 Peter 3:15
Saul (Σαῦλος, Greek form)	15xNT: Acts 7:58; 8:1, 3; 9:1, 8, 11, 22, 24; 11:25, 30; 12:25; 13:1,2, 7, 9
(Σαούλ, Hebrew form)	9xNT: Acts 9:4, 17; 22:7, 13; 26:14 (once for Saul, king of Israel: Acts 13:21)

TITLES AND METAPHORS

Abortion (ἔκτρωμα)	1 Cor. 15:8
Apostle (ἀπόστολος)	Rom. 1:1; 1 Cor. 4:9; 9:1, 2, 5; 15:9; 1 Tim. 2:7; 2 Tim 1:11
Apostle of (Jesus) Christ	1 Cor. 1:1; 2 Cor. 1:1; Eph. 1:1; Col. 1:1; 1 Thess. 2:6; 1 Tim. 1:1; 2 Tim. 1:1; Titus 1:1
Apostle through Jesus Christ	Gal. 1:1
Apostle of/to the Gentiles	Rom. 11:13; Gal. 2:8
The least of the apostles	1 Cor. 15:9
Architect (ἀρχιτέκτων)	1 Cor. 3:10
Athlete	1 Cor. 9:24–27; Phil 2:16
Chosen instrument	Acts 9:15 (σκεῦος ἐκλογῆς; see 22:14)
Father (πατήρ)	1 Cor. 4:15, 17; 2 Cor. 11:2 (see 6:13; 12:14); Phil. 2:22; 1 Thess. 2:11
my (beloved) child(ren)	1 Cor. 4:14, 17; Gal. 4:19; see also 2 Cor. 6:13; 12:14; Phil. 2:22; 1 Thess. 2:7, 11; 1 Tim. 1:2, 18; 2 Tim. 2:1; Titus 1:4; Philem. 1:10
mother/nurse (τροφός)	1 Thess. 2:7; see also 1 Cor. 3:2; Gal. 4:19; Philem. 1:10 (ἐγέννησα)
Fellow-worker (συνεργός)	2 Cor. 1:24 (f. of your joy); see also Rom. 16:3, 9, 21; 2 Cor. 8:23; Phil. 2:25; 4:3
God's fellow worker	1 Cor. 3:9 (for Timothy in 1 Thess. 3:2)
Light of the Gentiles	Acts 13:47 (quoting Isa. 49:6)
Matchmaker	2 Cor. 11:1–4
Preacher (κῆρυξ)	1 Tim. 2:7; 2 Tim. 1:11; see the verb "to preach" (κηρύσσω) in 1 Cor. 1:23; 9:27; 15:11, 12; 2 Cor. 1:19; 4:5; 11:4; Gal. 2:2; 5:11; Col. 1:23; 1 Thess. 2:9; Acts 9:20; 15:35; 19:13; 20:25; 28:31
Priest (ἱερουργέω)	Rom. 15:16; see 1:9 (λατρεύω); 1 Cor. 9:13
minister (λειτουργός)	Rom. 15:16 ("to the Gentiles"); see also 2 Cor. 9:12; Phil. 2:17
drink offering	Phil. 2:17; 2 Tim. 4:6 (see 2 Cor. 2:14–16 "fragrance of Christ")
Prisoner (δέσμιος)	Eph. 3:1 (of Christ); 4:1 (of the Lord); 2 Tim. 1:8 (his pr.); Philem. 1:1, 9 (of Christ Jesus)

Servant (διάκονος)	1 Cor. 3:5; 2 Cor. 3:6 (s. of the new covenant); 6:4 (s. of God); 11:23 (s. of Christ); Eph. 3:7; Col. 1:23, 25
Servant (ὑπηρέτης) of Christ	1 Cor. 4:1; Acts 26:16
TITLES AND METAPHORS	
Slave (δοῦλος)	2 Cor. 4:5; Col. 1:7; 4:7; Acts 16:17; see 1 Cor. 9:19, 27
Slave of Christ	Rom. 1:1; Gal. 1:10; Phil. 1:1 (see 1 Cor. 7:22; Eph. 6:6; Col. 4:12)
Slave of God	Titus 1:1 (see Acts 16:17; James 1:1; 1 Peter 2:16; Rev. 7:3; 15:3)
Slave of the Corinthians	2 Cor. 4:5
Soldier ([συ]στρατιώτης)	Phil. 2:25 (see also Philem. 1:2; 1 Cor. 9:7; 2 Cor. 10:3–5; 2 Tim. 2:3–4)
Paul defeated	2 Cor. 2:14
Paul's weapons	2 Cor. 6:7; 10:1–6; see Eph. 6:13–17
Steward (οἰκονόμος)	1 Cor. 4:1 (s. of the mysteries of God)
Teacher (διδάσκαλος)	1 Tim. 2:7 (t. of the Gentiles); 2 Tim. 1:11; 3:10; see the verb "to teach" (διδάσκω) in Acts 11:26; 15:35; 18:11; 20:20; 21:21, 28; 28:31; 1 Cor. 4:17; Col. 1:28; 2 Thess. 2:15; see the two nouns for "teaching": a) διδαχή in Acts 13:12; 17:19; Titus 1:9; and b) διδασκαλία in 1 Tim. 4:6; 2 Tim. 3:10; Titus 2:10
Witness (μάρτυς)	Acts 22:15; 26:16; see the verb "to witness" (μαρτύρομαι) in Acts 26:22 and "to testify" (διαμαρτύρομαι) in Acts 18:5; 20:21, 24; 28:23

Tracking Paul's Opponents

CHART 29

ROMANS	
3:8	… (as we are **slanderously reported** and as some claim that we say), "Let us do evil that good may come "?
5:3	And not only this, but we also exult in **our tribulations**, knowing that tribulation brings about perseverance
8:17–18	[17] and if children, heirs also, heirs of God and fellow heirs with Christ, if indeed we **suffer** with Him in order that we may also be glorified with Him. [18] For I consider that the **sufferings of this present time** are not worthy to be compared with the glory that is to be revealed to us.
8:35–37	[35] Who will separate us from the love of Christ? Will **tribulation**, or **distress**, or **persecution**, or **famine**, or **nakedness**, or **peril**, or **sword**? [36] Just as it is written, "**For Thy sake we are being put to death all day long; We were considered as sheep to be slaughtered**" [Ps 44:22]. [37] But in all these things we overwhelmingly conquer through Him who loved us.
12:14,17	[14] Bless **those who persecute you**; bless and curse not. … [17] Never pay back **evil** for evil to anyone. …
15:30–31	[30] Now I urge you, brethren, by our Lord Jesus Christ and by the love of the Spirit, to strive together with me in your prayers to God for me, [31] that **I may be rescued from those who are disobedient in Judea**, and **that my service for Jerusalem may prove acceptable to the saints**;
16:3–4	[3] Greet Prisca and Aquila, my fellow workers in Christ Jesus, [4] **who for my life risked their own necks**,
16:17–18, 20	[17] Now I urge you, brethren, keep your eye on **those who cause dissensions and hindrances** contrary to the teaching which you learned, and turn away from them. [18] For such men are **slaves**, not of our Lord Christ but **of their own appetites**; and **by their smooth and flattering speech they deceive the hearts of the unsuspecting**. … [20] The God of peace will soon crush **Satan** under your feet. The grace of our Lord Jesus be with you.
1 CORINTHIANS	
1:12	Now I mean this, that each one of you is saying, "I am of Paul," and "I of Apollos," and "I of Cephas," and "I of Christ."
4:3	But to me it is a very small thing that I should be examined by you, or by any **human court**; in fact, I do not even examine myself.
4:9–13	[9] For, I think, God has exhibited us apostles last of all, as men condemned to death; because we have become a spectacle to the world, both to angels and to men. [10] We are fools for Christ's sake, but you are prudent in Christ; we are weak, but you are strong; you are distinguished, but we are **without honor**. [11] To this present hour we are both **hungry** and **thirsty**, and are **poorly clothed**, and are **roughly treated**, and are **homeless**; [12] and we toil, working with our own hands; when we are **reviled**, we bless; when we are **persecuted**, we endure; [13] when we are **slandered**, we try to conciliate; we have become as the **scum of the world**, the dregs of all things, even until now.
5:11	But actually, I wrote to you not to associate with any **so-called brother** if he should be an immoral person, or covetous, or an idolater, or a reviler, or a drunkard, or a swindler—not even to eat with such a one.
9:3–4	My defense to those who examine me is this: [4] Do we not have a right to eat and drink?
15:15	Moreover we are even **found to be false witnesses of God**, because we witnessed against God that He raised Christ, whom He did not raise, if in fact the dead are not raised.
15:32	If from human motives **I fought with wild beasts at Ephesus**, what does it profit me? If the dead are not raised, let us eat and drink, for tomorrow we die.
16:8–9	[8] But I will remain in Ephesus until Pentecost; [9] for a wide door for effective service has opened to me, **and there are many adversaries**.

	2 CORINTHIANS
1:8–10	[8] For we do not want you to be unaware, brethren, of **our affliction which came to us in Asia**, that we were **burdened excessively, beyond our strength, so that we despaired even of life**; [9] indeed, we had the **sentence of death** within ourselves so that we would not trust in ourselves, but in God who raises the dead; [10] who delivered us from **so great a peril of death**, and will deliver us, He on whom we have set our hope.
4:7–12	[7] But we have this treasure in earthen vessels, so that the surpassing greatness of the power will be of God and not from ourselves; [8] we are **afflicted in every way**, but not **crushed**; perplexed, but not despairing; [9] **persecuted**, but not forsaken; **struck down**, but not destroyed; [10] always carrying about in the body the dying of Jesus, that the life of Jesus also may be manifested in our body. [11] For we who live are **constantly being delivered over to death** for Jesus' sake, that the life of Jesus also may be manifested in our mortal flesh. [12] So death works in us, but life in you.
6:4–10	[4] … but in everything commending ourselves as servants of God, in much endurance, in **afflictions**, in **hardships**, in **distresses**, [5] in **beatings**, in **imprisonments**, in **tumults**, in **labors**, in **sleeplessness**, in **hunger**, [6] in purity, in knowledge, in patience, in kindness, in the Holy Spirit, in genuine love, [7] in the word of truth, in the power of God; by the weapons of righteousness for the right hand and the left, [8] by glory and **dishonor**, by **evil report** and good report; **regarded as deceivers** and yet true; [9] **as unknown** yet well-known, **as dying** yet behold, we live; **as punished** yet not put to death, [10] **as sorrowful** yet always rejoicing, **as poor** yet making many rich, **as having nothing** yet possessing all things.
11:12–15, 19–20	[12] But what I am doing, I will continue to do, that I may cut off opportunity from those who desire an opportunity to be regarded just as we are in the matter about which they are boasting. [13] For such men are **false apostles, deceitful workers, disguising themselves as apostles of Christ**. No wonder, for even **Satan** disguises himself as an angel of light. [15] Therefore it is not surprising if **his servants** also disguise themselves as servants of righteousness, whose end will be according to their deeds. … [19] For you, being so wise, tolerate the foolish gladly. [20] For you tolerate it if anyone **enslaves you, anyone devours you, anyone takes advantage of you, anyone exalts himself, anyone hits you in the face**.
11:23–27	[23] Are they servants of Christ?—I speak as if insane—I more so; in far more labors, in far more **imprisonments, beaten** times without number, often in danger of death. [24] **Five times I received from the Jews thirty-nine lashes**. [25] **Three times I was beaten with rods, once I was stoned**, three times I was shipwrecked, a night and a day I have spent in the deep. [26] I have been on frequent journeys, in dangers from **rivers**, dangers from **robbers**, dangers from my **countrymen**, dangers from the **Gentiles**, dangers in the **city**, dangers in the **wilderness**, dangers on the **sea**, dangers among **false brethren**; [27] I have been in labor and hardship, through **many sleepless nights**, in **hunger** and **thirst, often without food**, in **cold** and **exposure**.
12:9–11	[9] And He has said to me, "My grace is sufficient for you, for power is perfected in weakness." Most gladly, therefore, I will rather boast about my weaknesses, that the power of Christ may dwell in me. [10] Therefore I am well content with weaknesses, with **insults**, with **distresses**, with **persecutions**, with **difficulties**, for Christ's sake; for when I am weak, then I am strong. [11] I have become foolish; you yourselves compelled me. Actually I should have been commended by you, for in no respect was I inferior to **the most eminent apostles**, even though I am a nobody.
	GALATIANS
1:6–7	[6] I am amazed that you are so quickly deserting Him who called you by the grace of Christ, for a **different gospel**; [7] which is really not another; only there are **some who are disturbing you**, and want to distort the gospel of Christ.
2:1–4	[1] Then after an interval of fourteen years I went up again to Jerusalem with Barnabas, taking Titus along also. [3] But not even Titus who was with me, though he was a Greek, was **compelled to be circumcised**. [4] But it was because of the **false brethren** who had sneaked in to spy out our liberty which we have in Christ Jesus, in order to bring us into bondage.
3:1, 4	You foolish Galatians, who has **bewitched** you, before whose eyes Jesus Christ was publicly portrayed as crucified?' … [4] Did you **suffer** so many things in vain—if indeed it was in vain?
4:16–17	[16] So have I become your enemy by telling you the truth? [17] They eagerly seek you, not commendably, but they wish to **shut you out**, in order that you will seek them.

5:7–12	[7] You were running well; who hindered you from obeying the truth? [8] **This persuasion** did not come from Him who calls you. [9] A little leaven leavens the whole lump of dough. [10] I have confidence in you in the Lord, that you will adopt no other view; but **the one who is disturbing you** shall bear his judgment, whoever he is. [11] But I, brethren, if I still preach **circumcision**, why am I still **persecuted**? Then the stumbling block of the cross has been abolished. [12] Would that those who are troubling you would even **mutilate themselves**.
6:12	Those who desire to make a good showing in the flesh try to **compel you to be circumcised**, simply that they may not be persecuted for the cross of Christ.
EPHESIANS	
2:11	Therefore remember, that formerly you, the Gentiles in the flesh, **who are called "Uncircumcision" by the so-called "Circumcision,"** which is performed in the flesh by human hands—
3:1	For this reason I, Paul, the prisoner of Christ Jesus for the sake of you Gentiles— … (also 4:1)
3:13	Therefore I ask you not to lose heart at **my tribulations** on your behalf, for they are your glory.
4:1	Therefore I, **the prisoner of the Lord**, implore you to walk in a manner worthy of the calling with which you have been called,…
4:14	As a result, we are no longer to be children, tossed here and there by waves and carried about by every **wind of doctrine**, by the **trickery of men**, by **craftiness in deceitful scheming;** …
4:17–19	[17] So this I say, and affirm together with the Lord, that you walk no longer just as the **Gentiles also walk, in the futility of their mind**, [18] being darkened in their understanding, excluded from the life of God, because of the ignorance that is in them, because of the hardness of their heart; [19] and they, having become callous, have given themselves over to sensuality, for the practice of every kind of impurity with greediness.
5:5–6	[5] For this you know with certainty, that no immoral or impure person or covetous man, who is an idolater, has an inheritance in the kingdom of Christ and God. [6] **Let no one deceive you with empty words**, for because of these things the wrath of God comes upon the sons of disobedience.
6:11–12	[11] Put on the full armor of God, that you will be able to stand firm against the **schemes of the devil**. [12] **For our struggle** is not against flesh and blood, but against **the rulers, against the powers, against the world forces of this darkness, against the spiritual forces of wickedness in the heavenly places**.
6:19–20	[19] and pray on my behalf, that utterance may be given to me in the opening of my mouth, to make known with boldness the mystery of the gospel, [20] for which **I am an ambassador in chains**; that in proclaiming it I may speak boldly, as I ought to speak.
PHILIPPIANS	
1:12–17	[12] Now I want you to know, brethren, that my circumstances have turned out for the greater progress of the gospel, [13] so that my **imprisonment** in the cause of Christ has become well known throughout the whole praetorian guard and to everyone else, [14] and that most of the brethren, trusting in the Lord because of my imprisonment, have far more courage to speak the word of God without fear. [15] **Some, to be sure, are preaching Christ even from envy and strife**, but some also from good will; [16] the latter do it out of love, knowing that I am appointed for the defense of the gospel; [17] the former **proclaim Christ out of selfish ambition**, rather than from pure motives, **thinking to cause me distress in my imprisonment**.
1:28–30	[28] in no way alarmed by your **opponents**—which is a sign of destruction for them, but of salvation for you, and that too, from God. [29] For to you it has been granted for Christ's sake, not only to believe in Him, but also to **suffer for His sake**, [30] experiencing the **same conflict** which you saw in me, and now hear to be in me.
2:15	so that you will prove yourselves to be blameless and innocent, children of God above reproach in the midst of a **crooked and perverse generation**, among whom you appear as lights in the world,
2:21	For they all seek after their own interests, not those of Christ Jesus.
3:2–3	[2] **Beware of the dogs, beware of the evil workers, beware of the false circumcision;** [3] for we are the true circumcision, who worship in the Spirit of God and glory in Christ Jesus and put no confidence in the flesh,…

3:18–19	[18] For many walk, of whom I often told you, and now tell you even weeping, that they are **enemies of the cross of Christ**, [19] whose end is destruction, whose god is their appetite, and whose glory is in their shame, who set their minds on earthly things.
	COLOSSIANS
2:8	See to it that no one takes you captive through philosophy and **empty deception**, according to the tradition of men, according to the elementary principles of the world, rather than according to Christ.
2:11	and in Him you were also **circumcised** with a circumcision made without hands, in the removal of the body of the flesh by the circumcision of Christ;
2:16–23	[16] Therefore **no one is to act as your judge** in regard to food or drink or in respect to a **festival** or a **new moon or a Sabbath day**— [17] things which are a mere shadow of what is to come; but the substance belongs to Christ. [18] Let no one keep defrauding you of your prize by delighting in **self-abasement** and the **worship of the angels**, taking his stand on **visions** he has seen, inflated without cause by his fleshly mind, [19] and not holding fast to the head, from whom the entire body, being supplied and held together by the joints and ligaments, grows with a growth which is from God. [20] If you have died with Christ to the elementary principles of the world, why, as if you were living in the world, do you submit yourself to decrees, such as, [21] "**Do not handle, do not taste, do not touch!**" [22] (which all refer to things destined to perish with the using)—in accordance with the commandments and teachings of men? [23] These are matters which have, to be sure, the appearance of wisdom in **self-made religion and self-abasement and severe treatment of the body**, but are of no value against fleshly indulgence.
4:3, 10, 18	[3] praying at the same time for us as well, that God will open up to us a door for the word, so that we may speak forth the mystery of Christ, for which I have also been **imprisoned**; … [10] Aristarchus, my **fellow prisoner**, sends you his greetings; … [18] … Remember my **imprisonment**. Grace be with you.
	1 THESSALONIANS
1:6	You also became imitators of us and of the Lord, having received the word in **much tribulation** with the joy of the Holy Spirit,
2:2	but after **we had already suffered and been mistreated in Philippi**, as you know, we had the boldness in our God to speak to you the gospel of God amid **much opposition**.
2:14–16	[14] For you, brethren, became imitators of the churches of God in Christ Jesus that are in Judea, for **you also endured the same sufferings at the hands of your own countrymen**, even as they did from the Jews, [15] who both killed the Lord Jesus and the prophets, and drove us out. They are not pleasing to God, but hostile to all men, [16] **hindering us from speaking to the Gentiles** that they may be saved; with the result that they always fill up the measure of their sins. But wrath has come upon them to the utmost.
3:4	For indeed when we were with you, we kept telling you in advance that we were going to **suffer affliction**; and so it came to pass, as you know. …
3:7	… brethren, in all our distress and affliction we were comforted about you through your faith;
	2 THESSALONIANS
1:4–5	[4] therefore, we ourselves speak proudly of you among the churches of God for your perseverance and faith in the midst of all **your persecutions and afflictions** which you endure. [5] This is a plain indication of God's righteous judgment so that you will be considered worthy of the kingdom of God, for which indeed **you are suffering**.
2:1–4	[1] Now we request you, brethren, with regard to the coming of our Lord Jesus Christ, and our gathering together to Him, [2] that you not be quickly shaken from your composure or be disturbed either by a spirit or a message or a letter as if from us, to the effect that the day of the Lord has come. [3] **Let no one in any way deceive you**, for it will not come unless the apostasy comes first, and the man of lawlessness is revealed, the son of destruction, [4] who opposes and exalts himself above every so-called god or object of worship, so that he takes his seat in the temple of God, …
3:2	and that we will be **rescued from perverse and evil men**; for not all have faith.

1 TIMOTHY	
1:3–7	[3] As I urged you upon my departure for Macedonia, remain on at Ephesus so that you may instruct certain men not to teach **strange doctrines**, [4] nor to pay attention to **myths** and endless **genealogies**, which give rise to mere speculation rather than furthering the administration of God which is by faith. [5] But the goal of our instruction is love from a pure heart and a good conscience and a sincere faith. [6] For some men, **straying** from these things, **have turned aside** to fruitless discussion, [7] wanting to be teachers of the Law, even though they do not understand either what they are saying or the matters about which they make confident assertions.
1:19–20	[19] keeping faith and a good conscience, which some have rejected and **suffered shipwreck in regard to their faith** [20] Among these are **Hymenaeus** and **Alexander**, whom I have delivered over to Satan, so that they will be taught not to blaspheme.
4:1–3, 7	[1] But the Spirit explicitly says that in later times some will fall away from the faith, paying attention to **deceitful spirits and doctrines of demons**, [2] by means of the **hypocrisy of liars** seared in their own conscience as with a branding iron, [3] men who **forbid marriage and advocate abstaining from foods**, which God has created to be gratefully shared in by those who believe and know the truth. … [7] But have nothing to do with **worldly fables** fit only for old women.
5:14–15	[14] Therefore, I want younger widows to get married, bear children, keep house, and give the enemy no occasion for reproach; [15] for some have already **turned aside to follow Satan.**
6:3–4, 10	[3] If anyone advocates a different doctrine, and does not agree with sound words, those of our Lord Jesus Christ, and with the doctrine conforming to godliness, [4] he is conceited and understands nothing; but he has a morbid interest in **controversial questions and disputes about words**, out of which arise envy, strife, abusive language, evil suspicions, and constant friction between men of depraved mind and deprived of the truth, **who suppose that godliness is a means of gain.** … [10] For the **love of money** is a root of all sorts of evil, and some by longing for it have **wandered away from the faith**, and pierced themselves with many griefs.
6:20–21	[20] O Timothy, guard what has been entrusted to you, avoiding worldly and empty chatter and the opposing arguments of **what is falsely called "knowledge"**— [21] which some have professed and thus **gone astray from the faith.**
2 TIMOTHY	
1:15	You are aware of the fact that all who are in Asia turned away from me, among whom are **Phygelus** and **Hermogenes**.
2:14–18, 23	[14] Remind them of these things, and solemnly charge them in the presence of God not to **wrangle about words**, which is useless and leads to the ruin of the hearers. [15] Be diligent to present yourself approved to God as a workman who does not need to be ashamed, accurately handling the word of truth. [16] But avoid **worldly and empty chatter**, for it will lead to further ungodliness, [17] and **their talk will spread like gangrene**. Among them are **Hymenaeus** and **Philetus**, [18] men who have gone astray from the truth saying that **the resurrection has already taken place**, and they upset the faith of some. … [23] But refuse **foolish and ignorant speculations**, knowing that they produce quarrels.
3:1–9, 10–13	[1] But realize this, that in the last days difficult times will come. [2] For **men will be lovers of self, lovers of money**, boastful, arrogant, revilers, disobedient to parents, ungrateful, unholy, [3] unloving, irreconcilable, malicious gossips, without self-control, brutal, haters of good, [4] treacherous, reckless, conceited, lovers of pleasure rather than lovers of God; [5] holding to a form of godliness, although they have denied its power; and avoid such men as these. [6] For among them are those who **enter into households and captivate weak women** weighed down with sins, led on by various impulses, [7] always learning and never able to come to the knowledge of the truth. [8] And just as Jannes and Jambres opposed Moses, so **these men also oppose the truth**, men of depraved mind, rejected as regards the faith. [9] But they will not make further progress; for their folly will be obvious to all, just as Jannes's and Jambres's folly was also. [10] Now you followed my teaching, conduct, purpose, faith, patience, love, perseverance, [11] **persecutions**, **and sufferings**, such as happened to me at Antioch, at Iconium and at Lystra; what **persecutions** I endured, and out of them all the Lord rescued me! [12] Indeed, **all who desire to live godly in Christ Jesus will be persecuted.** [13] But **evil men** and **impostors** will proceed from bad to worse, deceiving and being deceived.

4:3–4, 10, 14	[3] For the time will come when they will not endure sound doctrine; but wanting to have their ears tickled, they will accumulate for themselves teachers in accordance to their own desires; [4] and will turn away their ears from the truth, and will turn aside to **myths**. … [10] for **Demas**, having loved this present world, has deserted me and gone to Thessalonica; Crescens has gone to Galatia, Titus to Dalmatia. . . . [14] **Alexander** the coppersmith did me much harm; the Lord will repay him according to his deeds.

TITUS	
1:10–16	[10] For there are many **rebellious men, empty talkers** and **deceivers**, especially **those of the circumcision**, [11] who must be silenced because they are upsetting whole families, teaching things they should not *teach*, for the sake of sordid gain. [12] One of themselves, a prophet of their own, said, "Cretans are always liars, evil beasts, lazy gluttons." [13] This testimony is true. For this cause reprove them severely that they may be sound in the faith, [14] not paying attention to **Jewish myths** and **commandments of men** who turn away from the truth. [15] To the pure, all things are pure; but to those who are **defiled** and **unbelieving**, nothing is pure, but both their mind and their conscience are defiled. [16] They profess to know God, but **by their deeds they deny Him, being detestable and disobedient, and worthless for any good deed**.
3:9–11	[9] But avoid **foolish controversies** and **genealogies** and **strife and disputes about the Law**; for they are unprofitable and worthless. [10] Reject a **factious man** after a first and second warning, [11] knowing that such a man is perverted and is sinning, being self-condemned.

PHILEMON	
1:1	Paul, a **prisoner of Christ Jesus**, and Timothy our brother, to Philemon …
1:10	I appeal to you for my child Onesimus, whom I have begotten in **my imprisonment**,
1:13	whom I wished to keep with me, so that on your behalf he might minister to me in **my imprisonment** for the gospel;
1:23	Epaphras, my **fellow prisoner** in Christ Jesus, greets you.

Accusations against, and Misunderstandings of, Paul

CHART 30

	TEXTS	ACCUSATIONS AND MISUNDERSTANDINGS
1.	Acts 16:20–21	In **Philippi**, Paul exorcised a fortunetelling slave-girl. "But when her masters saw that their hope of profit was gone" (16:19), they accused Paul and Silas before the chief magistrates of practicing Jewish magic that disrupted Roman economy.
2.	Acts 17:6–7	In **Thessalonica**, "jealous" Jews (17:5) accused Paul before city authorities of leading a sedition by placing Jesus against Caesar.
3.	Acts 17:32	In **Athens**, people "sneered" at Paul's teaching on resurrection.
4.	Acts 18:12–16	In Corinth, Jews accused Paul before Gallio, the proconsul of Achaia, of persuading "men to worship God contrary to the law."
5.	Acts 19:23–41	In **Ephesus**, Paul converted people from idolatry. The silversmith Demetrius and other craftsmen of idolatrous figurines accused Paul of being "robbers of temples" and "blasphemers of our goddess [Artemis]" (19:37, also 27).
6.	Acts 21:21, 28–29	In **Jerusalem**, *Jews* accused Paul of "teaching all the Jews who are among the Gentiles to forsake Moses, telling them not to circumcise their children nor to walk according to the customs." Some days later, Jews from Asia accused Paul in Jerusalem of preaching "against our people and the Law and this place; and besides he has even brought Greeks into the temple and has defiled this holy place."
7.	Acts 21:38	The *Roman* commander mistook Paul for an Egyptian terrorist.
8.	Acts 24:5–6	In **Caesarea Maritima**, the attorney Tertullus, hired by the Jews, accused Paul before the governor Felix of stirring "up dissension among all the Jews throughout the world," that Paul was "a ringleader of the sect of the Nazarenes" who "even tried to desecrate the temple." (see 25:8, 18-19, 25; 26:6-7)
9.	Rom. 3:1	Paul betrayed God's people: "Then what advantage has the Jew [over the Gentile]?"
10.	Rom. 3:3	God is unfaithful to his promise because Jews are unfaithful to him.
11.	Rom. 3:8; 6:1	Paul subverts law and order: "Let us do evil that good may come[.]"
12.	1 Cor. 5:9–11	Paul advocates complete withdrawal from unbelievers (previous letter; see 2 Cor 6:14).
13.	2 Cor. 1:15–17	Paul's changing travel plans indicate an unstable character.
14.	2 Cor. 2:17	Paul changes the word of God and lies (also 4:1-2; see 1:12).
15.	2 Cor. 6:8	Paul and Timothy are regarded as deceivers (ὡς πλάνοι).
16.	2 Cor. 10:10	"For they say, 'His letters are weighty and strong, but his personal presence is unimpressive, and his speech contemptible'" (also 10:1).
17.	Gal. 1:1, 10, 16	Paul is a people-pleaser (see also 2:2, 6; 2 Cor. 1:12; 2:17; 4:1-2).
18.	Gal. 2:15–21	Christ promotes sin since justification is by faith and not by law.
18.	Gal. 5:11	Paul still preaches circumcision
20.	1 Thess. 2:1-16	Out of greed Paul flatters people so that they give him their money
21.	2 Thess. 2:2	The day of the Lord has already come (see 1 Thess. 4:15-17).

Paul's Sufferings

CHART 31

SUFFERINGS		REFERENCE
1.	without honor	ἄτιμοι	1 Cor. 4:10; 2 Cor. 6:8
2.	hungry and thirsty	πεινάω, νηστεία, διψάω	1 Cor. 4:11; 2 Cor. 6:5; 11:27
3.	poorly clothed	γυμνιτεύω	1 Cor. 4:11; 2 Cor. 11:27
4.	roughly treated	κολαφίζω	1 Cor. 4:11
5.	homeless	ἀστατέω	1 Cor. 4: 11
6.	toil with own hands	κοπιῶμεν … τ. ἰδ. χερσίν	1 Cor. 4:12; 2 Cor. 11:23, 27
7.	reviled, slandered	λοιδορούμενοι, δυσφημούμενοι, βλασφημοῦμαι	1 Cor. 4:12–13; 2 Cor 6:8; see Rom. 3:8; 1 Cor. 10:30; Acts 16:20–21; 17:6–7; 18:13; 24:5–6; 25:2, 7–8, 15, 24;
8.	persecuted	διωκόμενοι, διωγμός	1 Cor. 4:12; 2 Cor. 4:8; see Acts 13:50; Rom. 8:35; 2 Cor. 12:10; Gal. 5:11; 1 Thess. 2:15; 2 Tim. 3:11–12
9.	scum and dirt of the world	περικαθάρματα, περίψημα	1 Cor. 4:13
10.	perplexed	ἀπορούμενοι	2 Cor. 4:8
11.	struck down	καταβαλλόμενοι	2 Cor. 4:9
12.	delivered over to death	εἰς θάνατον παραδιδόμεθα	2 Cor. 4:11; 11:23
13.	afflictions, sufferings	θλῖψις, θλίβομαι, παθήματα, πάσχω	2 Cor. 1:6; 4:8; 6:4; 7:5; Eph. 3:13; 1 Thess. 3:4, 7; 2 Tim. 1:12
14.	hardships, distresses	ἀνάγκαι, στενοχωρίαι	2 Cor. 6:4; 12:10; 1 Thess. 3:7
15.	beatings	πληγαί	2 Cor. 6:5; 11:23; see Acts 21:32
16.	many imprisonments	φυλακαῖ, δεσμός, δέσμιος	2 Cor. 6:5; 11:23; Phil. 1:13; Philem. 1:1; • Philippi (Acts 16:19–40) • Ephesus? (AD 50–22; Rom. 16:3, 7; 1 Cor. 15:30–32; 2 Cor. 11:23) • Caesarea (AD 58–60; Acts 24–26) • Rome (AD 60–62; Acts 28)
17.	tumults	ἀκαταστασίαι	2 Cor. 6:5
18.	sleeplessness	ἀγρυπνίαι	2 Cor. 6:5; 11:27 ("often")
19.	viewed as deceiver	ὡς πλάνοι	2 Cor. 6:8
20.	unknown	ὡς ἀγνοούμενοι	2 Cor. 6:9
21.	dying	ὡς ἀποθνήσκοντες	2 Cor. 6:9
22.	punished	ὡς παιδευόμενοι	2 Cor. 6:9
23.	sorrowful	ὡς λυπούμενοι	2 Cor. 6:10; see 2:1, 4; Rom. 9:2
24.	poor	ὡς πτωχοὶ … μηδὲν ἔχοντες	2 Cor. 6:10
25.	five times 39 lashes	πεντάκις τεσσερ. παρὰ μίαν	2 Cor. 11:24
26.	three times beaten with rods	τρὶς ἐραβδίσθην	2 Cor. 11:25; e.g., Acts 16:22–23
27.	once I was stoned	ἅπαξ ἐλιθάσθην	2 Cor. 11:25; see Acts 14:19

SUFFERINGS		REFERENCE
28.	three times I was shipwrecked	τρὶς ἐναυάγησα	2 Cor. 11:25; see Acts 27:39–44
29.	a night and a day in the deep	νυχθήμερον ἐν τῷ βυθῷ	2 Cor. 11:25
30.	frequent journeys	ὁδοιπορίαις πολλάκις	2 Cor. 11:26
31.	dangers from rivers	κινδύνοις ποταμῶν	2 Cor. 11:26
32.	… robbers	κινδύνοις λῃστῶν	2 Cor. 11:26
33.	… from my countrymen	κινδύνοις ἐκ γένους	2 Cor. 11:26; see Acts 13:50; 14:2, 5, 19; 17:5; 20:3, 19; 21:11; 23:12, 20–21; 25:3; 26:21
34.	… from the Gentiles	κινδύνοις ἐξ ἐθνῶν	2 Cor. 11:26; see Acts 14:5, 19; 16:16–24; 19:23–20:1
35.	… in the city	κινδύνοις ἐν πόλει	2 Cor. 11:26; e.g., 1 Thess. 2:2
36.	… in the wilderness	κινδύνοις ἐν ἐρημίᾳ	2 Cor. 11:26
37.	… on the sea	κινδύνοις ἐν θαλάσσῃ	2 Cor. 11:26; see Acts 27:7–44
38.	… among false brethren	κινδύνοις ἐν ψευδαδέλφοις	2 Cor. 11:26; see 11:13; Gal. 2:4
39.	insults, mistreat	ὕβρις, ὑβρίζω	2 Cor. 12:10; 1 Thess. 2:2; see Acts 14:5

Why Did Luke Finish Acts without Reporting Paul's End?

CHART 32

	HISTORICAL EXPLANATIONS	PROPONENTS
1.	Luke did not know anything about Paul's martyrdom, either because Paul was still alive when Luke finished Acts or because Luke did not know about Paul's death.	Canon Muratori; Harnack; Walasky
2.	Acts is written as a legal defense in Paul's trial for Roman officials, which means that he could not have known yet about Paul's death.	Munck; Wikenhauser
3.	Luke did not mention Paul's end because he was embarrassed about the failure of Christians to support him in his trial and execution (see *1 Clem.* 5:5–7; 2 Tim. 4:16)	Cullmann; Barrett; Walasky
4.	Luke did not report Paul's end because his readers knew about it already.	Hanson
	THEOLOGICAL EXPLANATIONS	
5.	With Paul's arrival in Rome, Luke accomplished his purpose as expressed in Acts 1:8, namely to show that the early church was commissioned to preach the Gospel "to the remotest part of the earth."	J. A. Bengel
6.	Luke finished with Paul's final and failed attempt to convert Jews, followed by the apostle's turn to the Gentiles (Acts 28:25–28) because Luke regarded this as the hermeneutical key for Luke (see Acts 13:46–47; 18:6), and as the theological key to Paul's mission among the Gentiles.	Conzelmann
7.	Luke did not report Paul's death because he could not create a parallel to Jesus' resurrection.	Jülicher, Fascher
8.	Luke did not report Paul's martyrdom because he did not want to prepare readers from such fate but spare them from it.	Haenchen
9.	Luke's pro-Roman apologetics did not permit to report the embarrassing negative result of Paul's trial in Rome.	Roloff, Holloway
	LITERARY-RHETORICAL EXPLANATIONS	
10.	Luke planned a third volume but did not finish it.	Th. Zahn; W. Ramsay; Van Bruggen
11.	The Pastoral Epistles are the third volume with which Luke concluded the story of Paul begun in Acts.	J. D. Quinn; S. G. Wilson
12.	The abrupt end of the Gospel of Mark served Luke as a model. The absence of Paul's martyrdom sends the reader back to Jesus' end.	W. F. Brosend II
13.	The "rhetoric of silence" is a literary convention of Luke's time and requires the reader himself to reconstruct Paul's end. Literary clues lead the reader to conclude that Paul the accused became the judge and the model preacher who fulfilled the plan of Acts 1:8.	Daniel Marguerat

Traditions of Paul's Missionary Journey to Spain

CHART 33

Romans 15:22–24, 28	[22] "For this reason I have often been prevented from coming to you; [23] but now, with no further place for me in these regions, and since I have had for many years a longing to come to you [24] whenever I go to **Spain**—for I hope to see you in passing, . . . [28] Therefore, when I have finished this, and have put my seal on this fruit of theirs, I will go on by way of you to **Spain**."
I Clement (AD 93/97)	"Owing to envy, Paul also obtained the reward of patient endurance, after being seven times thrown into captivity, compelled to flee, and stoned. After preaching both in the east and west, he gained the illustrious reputation due to his faith, having taught righteousness to the whole world, and come **to the extreme limit of the west**, and suffered martyrdom under the prefects." [chapter 5; *ANF* I.6]
Muratorian Canon (2nd century)	"For the 'most excellent Theophilus' Luke summarises the several things that in his own presence have come to pass, as also by the omission of the passion of Peter he makes quite clear, and equally by (the omission) of the journey of Paul, who from the city (of Rome) proceeded to Spain." [lines 35-39; Schneemelcher I.35]
The Acts of Peter (3rd century)	"While Paul was spending some time in Rome and strengthening many in the faith, it happened that a woman by name Candida, the wife of Quartus, a prison officer, heard Paul speak and paid attention to his words and believed. And when she had instructed her husband also and he believed, Quartus gave leave to Paul to leave the city (and go) where he wished. But Paul said to him, 'If it is God's will, He himself will reveal it to me.' And when he had fasted for three days and asked of the Lord what was right for him, Paul then saw a vision, the Lord saying to him, 'Paul, arise and be a physician to those who are in **Spain**.'"[Schneemelcher II.287]
Hippolytus (AD 170–236)	13. "And Paul entered into the apostleship a year after the assumption of Christ; and beginning at Jerusalem, he advanced as far as Illyricum, and Italy, **and Spain**, preaching the Gospel for five-and-thirty years. And in the time of Nero he was beheaded at Rome, and was buried there." ["Hyppolytus on the twelve apostles," ANF 5:255]
The Acts of Xanthippe, Polyxena, and Rebekka (3rd century)	VII. "But Xanthippe was always keeping watch through the doors into the streets of the city, and the blessed Paul, the preacher and teacher and illuminator of the world, left Rome and came even into Spain by the fore-knowledge of God. And coming up to the gates of the city he stood and prayed, and crossing himself entered the city." [*ANF* 10:206]
Jerome (AD 345–419)	"4. ... If I choose to say, 'the apostle Paul before he went to Spain was put in fetters at Rome,' . . . must Paul on being released at once go to **Spain** . . .?" ["Against Helvidius", *NPNF* II.6.335]
John Chrysostom (AD 347–407)	"And it is a plain proof of this, that the word shall surely be preached everywhere in the world, so much shall ye be above the things that alarm you. For, that they may not say, how then shall we live? He said more, Ye shall both live and preach everywhere. Therefore He added moreover, 'And this gospel shall be preached in the whole world for a witness to all nations, and then shall the end come' [Rom 10:18], of the downfall of Jerusalem. "For in proof that He meant this, and that before the taking of Jerusalem the gospel was preached, hear what Paul saith, "Their sound went into all the earth [Col 1:23];' and again, 'The gospel which was preached to every creature which is under Heaven [Col 1:6].' And seest thou him running from Jerusalem unto **Spain**? And if one took so large a portion, consider what the rest also wrought. For writing to others also, Paul again saith concerning the gospel, that 'it is bringing forth fruit, and growing up in every creature which is under Heaven [Col 1:23].'" ["Homilies on Matthew: Homily 75," *NPNF* I.10.452]
John Chrysostom (AD 347–407)	"2. . . . For as yet he was not arrested. Two years then he passed bound, in Rome; then he was set free; then, **having gone into Spain**, he saw Jews also in like manner; and then he returned to Rome, where also he was slain by Nero. The Epistle to Timothy then was later than this Epistle [Hebrews]. For there he says, 'For I am now ready to be offered'" [2 Tim 4:6]. ["Homilies on the Epistle to the Hebrews," *NPNF* I.14.364]

Traditions of Paul's Martyrdom

CHART 34

I Clement 5:5–8 (AD 93/97)	"Because of jealousy and strife Paul showed the way to the prize for patient endurance. After he had been seven times in chains, had been driven into exile, had been stoned, and had preached in the east and in the west, he won the genuine glory for his faith, having taught righteousness to the whole world and having reached the farthest limits of the west. Finally, when he had given his testimony before the rulers, he thus departed from the world and went to the holy place, having become an outstanding example of patient endurance."
The Acts of Paul 11.5 (2nd cent. AD)	"Then Paul stood with his face to the east and lifted up his hands unto heaven and prayed at length, and after communing in prayer in Hebrew with the fathers he stretched out his neck without speaking further. And when the executioner (speculator) struck off his head, milk spurted upon the soldier's clothing. And when they saw it, the soldiers and all who stood by were amazed, and glorified God who had given Paul such glory: and they went off and reported to Caesar what had happened."
Clement of Alexandria (died after AD 215), *Strom.* VII 106,3	"For the teaching of our Lord at His advent, beginning with Augustus and Tiberius, was completed in the middle of the times of Tiberius. And that of the apostles, embracing the ministry of Paul, ends with Nero."
Tertullian (ca. AD 150-220), in Eusebius, *Hist. Eccl.* 2.25.4	"Look at your records: there you will find that Nero was the first to persecute this belief when, having overcome the whole East, he was especially cruel in Rome against all. We boast that such a man was the author of our chastisement; for he who knows him can understand that nothing would have been condemned by Nero had it not been great and good."
Tertullian (ca. AD 160–220), *Scorp.* 15,3	"And if a heretic wants a faith backed by public record, let the archives of the empire speak, as would the stones of Jerusalem. We read the lives of the Caesars. In Rome Nero was the first to stain with blood the rising faith. Peter was girded about by another, when he was made fast to the cross. Paul obtained a birth suited to Roman citizenship, when in that city he was given re-birth by an ennobling martyrdom."
Lactantius (ca. AD 240–320), *Inst.*, IV 21	"For at His departure He had endowed them with power and strength, by which the system of their new announcement might be founded and confirmed. But He also opened to them all things which were about to happen, which Peter and Paul preached at Rome; and this preaching being written for the sake of remembrance, became permanent, in which they both declared other wonderful things, and also said that it was about to come to pass, that after a short time God would send against them a king who would subdue the Jews, and level their cities to the ground, and besiege the people themselves, worn out with hunger and thirst. Then it should come to pass that they should feed on the bodies of their own children, and consume one another. Lastly, that they should be taken captive, and come into the hands of their enemies, and should see their wives most cruelly harassed before their eyes, their virgins ravished and polluted, their sons torn in pieces, their little ones dashed to the ground; and lastly, everything laid waste with fire and sword, the captives banished for ever from their own lands, because they had exulted over the well-beloved and most approved Son of God. And so, after their decease, when Nero had put them to death, Vespasian destroyed the name and nation of the Jews, and did all things which they had foretold as about to come to pass."

Part C

PAUL'S LETTERS

Manuscripts (Papyri and Uncials) of Paul's Letters

CHART 35

DATE	PAPYRI	CONTENT
Ca. 200	P 32	Titus 1:11–15; 2:3–8
	P 46	Rom. 5:17–6:3, 5–14; 8:15–25, 27–35; 8:37–9:32; 10:1–11:22,24–33; 11:35–15:9; 15:11–33; 16:1–23, 25–27; 1 Cor.; 2 Cor.; Eph.; Gal.; Phil.; Col.; 1 Thess. 1:1; 1:9–2:3; 5:5–9, 23–28 [Pastoral Epistles are missing]
3rd cent.	P 15	1 Cor. 7:18–32; 7:32–8:4
	P 27	Rom. 8:12–22, 24–27; 8:33–9:3; 9:5–9
	P 30	1 Thess. 4:12–13, 16–17; 5:3, 8–10, 12–18; 2 Thess. 1:1–2
	P 40	Rom. 1:24–27; 1:31–2:3; 3:21–4:8; 6:4–5, 16; 9:16–17, 27
	P 49	Eph. 4:16–29; 4:32–5:13
	P 65	1 Thess. 1:2–3; 2:1, 6–13
	P 87	Philem. 1:13–15, 24–25
	P 113	Rom. 2:12–13, 29
	P 118	Rom. 15:26–27, 32–33; 16:1, 4–7, 11–12
3rd / 4th cent.	P 16	Phil. 3:10–17; 4:2–8
	P 92	Eph. 1:11–13, 19–21; 2 Thess. 1:4–5, 11–12
4th cent.	P 10	Rom. 1:1–7
4th / 5th cent.	P 117	2 Cor. 7:6–8, 9–11
Ca. 400	P 51	Gal. 1:2–10, 13, 16–20
	P 99	Rom. 1:1; 2 Cor. 1:3–6, 6–17, 20–24; 2:1–9; 2:9–5:3; 5:13–6:3; 6:3–8:13; 8:14–22; 9:2–11:8; 11:9–23; 11:26–13:11; Gal. 1:4–11; 1:18–6:15; 1:14–2:4; 2:4–3:19; 3:19–4:9; Eph. 1:4–2:21; 1:22?; 3:8–6:24
5th / 6th cent.	P 94	Rom. 6:10–13, 19–22
6th cent.	P 11	1 Cor. 1:17–22; 2:9–12, 14; 3:1–3, 5–6; 4:3–5; 5:7–8; 6:5–9, 11–18; 7:3–6, 10–14
	P 14	1 Cor. 1:25–27; 2:6–8; 3:8–10:20
Ca. 600	P 26	Rom. 1:1–9, 9–16
7th cent.	P 31	Rom. 12:3–8
	P 34	1 Cor. 16:4–7, 10; 2 Cor. 5:18–19, 19–21; 10:13–14; 11:2, 4, 6–7
7th cent.?	P 68	1 Cor. 4:12–17; 4:19–5:3
Ca. 700	P 61	Rom. 16:23–27; 1 Cor. 1:1–2, 4–6; 5:1–3, 5–6, 9–13; Phil. 3:5–9, 12–16; Col. 1:3–7, 9–13; 4:15; 1 Thess. 1:2–3; Titus 3:1–5, 8–11, 14–15; Philem. 1:4–7

DATE	UNCIALS	CONTENT
4th cent.	ℵ 01	Codex Sinaiticus: contains all Pauline letters
5th cent.	A 02	Codex Alexandrianus: 2 Cor. 4:13–12:6 is missing
4th cent.	B 03	Codex Vaticanus: 1–2 Tim., Titus, Philem. are missing
4th cent.	C 04	Codex Ephraemi: portions of every letter except 2 Thess.
6th cent.	Dᴾ 06	Codex Claromontanus: contains all Pauline letters

Secretaries, Cowriters, and Carriers

CHART 36

Secretaries *(amanuensis)*	Rom. 16:22 "I, Tertius, who write this letter, greet you in the Lord." 1 Cor. 16:21 "The greeting is in my own hand— Paul." Gal. 6:11 "See with what large letters I am writing to you with my own hand." Col. 4:18 "I, Paul, write this greeting with my own hand." 2 Thess. 3:17 "I, Paul, write this greeting with my own hand, and this is a distinguishing mark in every letter; this is the way I write."	
Cowriters	Romans 1 Corinthians 2 Corinthians Galatians Ephesians Philippians Colossians 1 Thessalonians 2 Thessalonians 1 Timothy 2 Timothy Titus Philemon	— "Paul, … apostle … and Sosthenes our brother" (1:1) "Paul , an apostle … and Timothy our brother" (1:1) "Paul, an apostle … and all the brethren who are with me" (1:1–2) — "Paul and Timothy, bond-servants of Christ Jesus" (1:1) "Paul, an apostle … and Timothy our brother" (1:1) "Paul and Silvanus and Timothy" (1:1; see 2 Cor 1:19 for all three) "Paul and Silvanus and Timothy" (1:1) — — — "Paul, a prisoner of Christ … and Timothy, the brother" (1:1)
Carriers	Romans 1 Corinthians 2 Corinthians Galatians Ephesians Philippians Colossians 1 Thessalonians 2 Thessalonians 1 Timothy 2 Timothy Titus Philemon	Timothy (Rom. 16:21)? Tertius (Rom. 16:22)? Timothy (1 Cor. 16:10) Titus (and Timothy?) (2 Cor. 8:6, 16–18) — Tychicus (Eph. 6:21) Epaphroditus (Phil. 2:25–30) Tychicus (Col. 4:7–9) — — Tychicus (2 Tim. 4:12)? Luke (2 Tim. 4:11)? Tychicus (2 Tim. 4:12)? Luke (2 Tim. 4:11)? Artemas & Tychicus (Titus 3:12) or Zenas & Apollos (3:13)? Tychicus and Onesimus (Col. 4:7–9)?

Various Groupings of Paul's Letters

CHART 37

Undisputed/Authentic Letters	(1)	Romans
	(2)	1 Corinthians
	(3)	2 Corinthians
	(4)	Galatians
	(5)	Philippians
	(6)	1 Thessalonians
	(7)	Philemon
Disputed/Deutero-Pauline Letters	(1)	Colossians
	(2)	Ephesians
	(3)	2 Thessalonians
Pseudepigraphic Letters	(1)	1 Timothy
	(2)	2 Timothy
	(3)	Titus
Prison Letters/ Captivity Letters	(1)	Ephesians (see 3:1; 4:1; 6:20)
	(2)	Philippians (see 1:7, 13–14, 17)
	(3)	Colossians (see 4:3, 10, 18; also 1:24)
	(4)	Philemon (see 1:1, 9–10, 13, 23)
Pastoral Letters	(1)	1 Timothy
	(2)	2 Timothy
	(3)	Titus
Major Letters	(1)	Romans
	(2)	1 Corinthians
	(3)	2 Corinthians
	(4)	Galatians

How Many Letters Did Paul Write?

CHART 38

No. of Letters	Rom.	1Cor	2Cor	Gal	Eph	Phil	Col	1Th	2Th	1Tim	2Tim	Tit	Phlm	Proponents
0	—	—	—	—	—	—	—	—	—	—	—	—	—	Dutch Radicals (1878-1957)
4	X	X	X	X	—	—	—	—	—	—	—	—	—	F. C. Baur, Tübinger School
5	X	X	X	X	—	—	—	—	—	—	—	—	X	Morton & McLeman (1966)
6	X	X	X	X	—	X	—	—	X	—	—	—	—	Ledger (1995)
7	X	X	X	X	—	X	—	X	—	—	—	—	X	Roetzel (1998), Schnelle (2005)
8a	X	X	X	X	—	X	—	X	—	—	X	—	X	Murphy O'Connor (1996)
8b	X	X	X	X	—	X	—	X	X	—	—	—	X	Mealand (1995)
9	X	X	X	X	—	X	X	X	X	—	—	—	X	Ross (1925), Kümmel (1964)
10	X	X	X	X	X	X	X	X	X	—	—	—	X	I. Marshall, Witherington
12	X	X	X	X	X	X	X	X	X	X	X	—	X	Kenny (1986)
13	X	X	X	X	X	X	X	X	X	X	X	X	X	Polhill (1999), L.T. Johnson (2002), Reicke (2001)
14	X	X	X	X	X	X	X	X	X	X	X	X	X	Including the letter to the Hebrews: Farrar (1891); Reymond (2003)

X means the scholar considers the letter to be written by Paul
— means the scholar does not think that Paul wrote this letter

Other Literature Ascribed to Paul

CHART 39

	WRITING	DATE	CONTENT
1.	Letter allegedly from Paul	1st century	Unknown (see 2 Thess. 2:2)
2.	Acts of Paul	2nd century	Only partially complete account about "one great journey by the apostle" (Schneemelcher II:232) from Damascus to Rome that ends with his martyrdom under Nero
3.	3 Corinthians	2nd century	Paul's response to a letter from the Corinthians
4.	Martyrdom of Paul	2nd century	Originally part of the Acts of Paul, this document about Paul's martyrdom under Nero was separated and transmitted independently
5.	Prayer of Paul	after the mid-2nd century	Part of a leaf of Codex I of the Nag Hammadi literature
6.	Apocalypse of Paul II	2nd-3rd century	Christian Gnostic work (same name but different from Apocalypse of Paul) that describes Paul's journey into the tenth heaven
7.	Epistle of Paul and Seneca	3rd-4th century	Fourteen Latin letters of correspondence between Paul and Seneca, a stoic philosopher, six of them ascribed to Paul. The letters date from the 3rd or 4th century and are known already by Augustine and Jerome, though not necessarily approved as authentic
8.	Epistle to the Laodiceans	?	A short Latin collection of phrases from Pauline letters, mostly Philippians
9.	Apocalypse of Paul	4th-5th century	Apocryphal work that elaborates on the "rapture" of Paul as mentioned in 2 Corinthians 12:2–4

Paul's Letters: Total Numbers of Words and Vocabulary

CHART 40

	LETTER	WORDS	STICHOI	VOCABULARY	PAGES
Nine letters to churches	Romans	7,111	920	1,068	16
	1 Corinthians	6,829	870	967	16
	2 Corinthians	4,477	590	792	10
	Galatians	2,230	293	526	5
	Ephesians	2,422	312	529	6
	Philippians	1,629	208	448	4
	Colossians	1,582	208	431	4
	1 Thessalonians	1,481	193	366	4
	2 Thessalonians	823	106	250	2
Four letters to individuals	1 Timothy	1,591	230	541	4
	2 Timothy	1,238	172	458	3
	Titus	659	97	303	2
	Philemon	335	38	141	1
Total	13	32,303	4,237	2,648	

Various Arrangements of Paul's Letters

CHART 41

Marcion	P46	Muratorian Canon	01, A, B, C, Athanasius	D, Augustine, Gelasius	The Sahidic Canon	Ephraem's Com. on Paul (Armen.)
2nd cent.	2nd cent.	2-3rd cent.	4th cent.	5th cent.	6th cent.	12th cent.
Gal.	Rom.	Corinthians	Rom.	Rom.	Rom.	Rom.
1 Cor.	Heb.	Eph.	1 Cor.	1 Cor.	1 Cor.	1 Cor.
2 Cor.	1 Cor.	Phil.	2 Cor.	2 Cor.	1 Cor.	1 Cor.
Rom.	2 Cor.	Col.	Gal.	Gal.	Heb.	3 Cor.
1 Thess.	Eph.	Gal.	Eph.	Eph.	Gal.	Gal.
2 Thess.	Gal.	"Thessalonians"	Phil.	Col.	Eph.	Eph.
Laodiceans	Phil.	Rom.	Col.	Phil.	Phil.	Phil.
Col.	Col.	"Again to Corinth."	1 Thess.	1 Thess.	Col.	Col.
Phil.	1 Thess.	"Again to Thess."	2 Thess.	2 Thess.	1 Thess.	1 Thess.
Philem.		Titus	Heb.	1 Tim.	2 Thess.	2 Thess.
		"Two to Timothy"	1 Tim.	2 Tim.	1 Tim.	Heb.
			2 Tim.	Titus	2 Tim.	1 Tim.
			Titus	Philem.	Titus	2 Tim.
			Philem.	Heb.	Philem.	Titus

Formal Structural Components of Paul's Letters

CHART 42

			Rom.	1Cor	2Cor	Gal	Eph	Phil	Col	1Thes	2Thes	1Tim	2Tim	Tit	Phlm
Salutation	Prescript	Superscriptio (sender)	1:1-6	1:1	1:1a	1:1-2a	1:1a	1:1a	1:1	1:1a	1:1a	1:1	1:1	1:1-3	1a
		Adscriptio (recipient)	1:7a	1:2	1:1b	1:2b	1:1b	1:1b	1:2a	1:1b	1:1b	1:2a	1:2a	1:4a	1b-2
		Salutatio (Greetings)	1:7b	1:3	1:2	1:3-5	1:2	1:2	1:2b	1:1c	1:2	1:2b	1:2b	1:4b	3
		Thanks	1:8-15	1:4-9			1:15-23	1:3-8	1:3-8	1:2-10	1:3-10		1:3-5		4-7
	Preface	Prayer						1:9-11	1:9-14		1:11-12				
		Praise ("Blessed")			1:3-11		1:3-14								
	Personal notes	Travelogue/'apostolic parousia'	15:14-29	16:1-9 (4:14-21)	12:14-13:10	4:11-20		(2:19-24)		(2:17-3:13)	(8:16-24; 9:1-5)		4:9-20	3:12	21-22
Subscription		Request for prayer	15:30-33				6:19-20		4:3	5:25	3:1-2			3:15	
		Greetings to/commendation	16:3-15	16:10-18			6:21-22	4:21	4:7-9	5:12-13			4:14-20	3:13-14	
		Kiss	16:16a	16:20b	13:12					5:26					
		Greetings fRom.	16:16b-24	16:19-20a	13:13			4:22	4:10-15				4:21	3:15	23-24
		Signature "own hand"		16:21		6:11			4:18		3:17				19
		Blessings		16:23	13:11, 14	6:16, 18	6:23-24	4:23	4:18	5:23-24, 28	3:16, 18	6:21	4:22	3:15	25
		Doxology	16:25-27					4:20					4:18		

Hapax Legomena in Paul's Letters

CHART 43

	Words	Hapax	%
Rom.	7,094	115	1.62
1 Cor.	6,807	84	1.23
2 Cor.	4,448	67	1.50
Gal.	2,220	31	1.39
Eph.	2,425	35	1.44
Phil.	1,624	40	2.46
Col.	1,577	37	2.34
1 Thess.	1,472	18	1.22
2 Thess.	824	8	0.97
1 Tim.	1,586	66	4.16
2 Tim.	1,235	60	4.85
Titus	663	32	4.82
Philem.	328	8	2.43
Total	32,303	601	1.86

	Vocab	Hapax	%
Rom.	1,068	115	10.76
1 Cor.	967	84	8.68
2 Cor.	792	67	8.45
Gal.	526	31	5.89
Eph.	529	35	6.61
Phil.	448	40	8.92
Col.	431	37	8.58
1 Thess.	366	18	4.91
2 Thess.	250	8	3.2
1 Tim.	541	66	12.19
2 Tim.	458	60	13.10
Titus	303	32	10.56
Philem.	141	8	5.67
Total	2,648	601	22.69

ROMANS							
		Ῥεβέκκα	9:10	Τρυφῶσα	16:12	πυκτεύω	9:26
συμπαρακαλέομαι	1:12	πλάσμα	9:20	Περσίς	16:12	δουλαγωγέω	9:27
Θειότης	1:20	Ὡσηέ	9:25	Ἀσύγκριτος	16:14	καταστρώννυμι	10:5
Καθοράω	1:20	ὑπόλειμμα	9:27	Φλέγων	16:14	ἐπιθυμητής	10:6
Ματαιόομαι	1:21	συντέμνω	9:28	Πατροβᾶς	16:14	παίζω	10:7
Σεβάζομαι	1:25	ἀποτολμάω	10:20	Ἑρμᾶς	16:14	εἰκοσιτρεῖς	10:8
ἐκκαίομαι	1:27	ἐκπετάννυμι	10:21	Φιλόλογος	16:15	ὀλοθρευτής	10:10
ὄρεξις	1:27	ὑπολείπομαι	11:3	Ἰουλία	16:15	τυπικῶς	10:11
κακοήθεια	1:29	χρηματισμός	11:4	Νηρεύς	16:15	μάκελλον	10:25
ψιθυριστής	1:29	ἑπτακισχίλιοι	11:4	Ὀλυμπᾶς	16:15	ἱερόθυτος	10:28
κατάλαλος	1:30	Βάαλ	11:4	χρηστολογία	16:18	κόμη	11:15
θεοστυγής	1:30	λεῖμμα	11:5	ἀφικνέομαι	16:19	φιλόνεικος	11:16
ἐφευρετής	1:30	κατάνυξις	11:8	Σωσίπατρος	16:21	ἀναξίως	11:27
ἀσύνθετος	1:31	θήρα	11:9	Τέρτιος	16:22	ὄσφρησις	12:17
ἀνελεήμων	1:31	νῶτος	11:10	Κούαρτος	16:23	ἀσχήμων	12:23
εὐσχημοσύνη	12:23	συγκάμπτω	11:10	**1 CORINTHIANS**			
ἀμετανόητος	2:5	πρόσλημψις	11:15	Χλόη	1:11	ἀντίλημψις	12:28
δικαιοκρισία	2:5	πιότης	11:17	συζητητής	1:20	κυβέρνησις	12:28
γραπτός	2:15	ἀποτομία	11:22	ἀγενής	1:28	ἠχέω	13:1
ἐπονομάζομαι	2:17	καλλιέλαιος	11:24	πειθός	2:4	κύμβαλον	13:1
ἱεροσυλέω	2:22	ἀνεξεραύνητος	11:33	ἀπόδειξις	2:4	χρηστεύομαι	13:4
ψεῦσμα	3:7	σύμβουλος	11:34	γεώργιον	3:9	περπερεύομαι	13:4
προέχομαι	3:9	προδίδωμι	11:35	ἀρχιτέκτων	3:10	αἴνιγμα	13:12
προαιτιάομαι	3:9	ὑπερφρονέω	12:3	καλάμη	3:12	παραμυθία	14:3
ἀχρειόομαι	3:12	ἀναλογία	12:6	δράσσομαι	3:19	ἄψυχος	14:7
λάρυγξ	3:13	ἱλαρότης	12:8	ἐπιθανάτιος	4:9	αὐλός	14:7
δολιόω	3:13	ἀποστυγέω	12:9	γυμνιτεύω	4:11	εὔσημος	14:9
ἀσπίς	3:13	φιλόστοργος	12:10	ἀστατέω	4:11	νηπιάζω	14:20
ἀρά	3:14	προηγέομαι	12:10	δυσφημέω	4:13	ἑτερόγλωσσος	14:21
σύντριμμα	3:16	ἄνθραξ	12:20	περικάθαρμα	4:13	διερμηνευτής	14:28
ὑπόδικος	3:19	ἀσθένημα	15:1	περίψημα	4:13	ὡσπερεί	15:8
πάρεσις	3:25	τολμηρότερον	15:15	ἑορτάζω	5:8	ἔκτρωμα	15:8
προγίνομαι	3:25	ἐπαναμιμνήσκω	15:15	ἐξαίρω	5:13	τάγμα	15:23
προπάτωρ	4:1	ἱερουργέω	15:16	ἀνάξιος	6:2	νή	15:31
ἐπικαλύπτω	4:7	Ἰλλυρικόν	15:19	σύμφωνον	7:5	θηριομαχέω	15:32
ἑκατονταετής	4:19	ἐπιποθία	15:23	συγγνώμη	7:6	ὁμιλία	15:33
ἐλλογέω	5:13	συναγωνίζομαι	15:30	ἐπισπάομαι	7:18	ἦθος	15:33
σύμφυτος	6:5	συναναπαύομαι	15:32	ἀπελεύθερος	7:22	ἐκνήφω	15:34
ἤτοι	6:16	Φοίβη	16:1	λύσις	7:27	πτηνόν	15:39
ὕπανδρος	7:2	προστάτις	16:2	βρόχος	7:35	ἄτομος	15:52
παλαιότης	7:6	Ἐπαίνετος	16:5	ἀπερισπάστως	7:35	ῥιπή	15:52
σύμφημι	7:16	Ἀνδρόνικος	16:7	εὐπάρεδρον	7:35	ἀμετακίνητος	15:58
συνήδομαι	7:22	Ἰουνία	16:7	ὑπέρακμος	7:36	πάροδος	16:7
ἀντιστρατεύομαι	7:23	Ἀμπλιᾶτος	16:8	εἰδωλεῖον	8:10	ἀνδρίζομαι	16:13
συνδοξάζομαι	8:17	Οὐρβανός	16:9	κημόω	9:9	Φορτουνᾶτος	16:17
συστενάζω	8:22	Στάχυς	16:9	ἐγκοπή	9:12	Ἀχαϊκός	16:17
συνωδίνω	8:22	Ἀπελλῆς	16:10	παρεδρεύω	9:13	Μαρανα	16:22
ὑπερεντυγχάνω	8:26	Ἀριστόβουλος	16:10	συμμερίζομαι	9:13	θα	16:22
ἀλάλητος	8:26	Ἡρωδίων	16:11	ἄκων	9:17		
ὑπερνικάω	8:37	Νάρκισσος	16:11	ἀδάπανος	9:18		
νομοθεσία	9:4	Τρύφαινα	16:12	ἀδήλως	9:26		

2 CORINTHIANS							
2 CORINTHIANS		βυθός	11:25	προελπίζω	1:12	συμμιμητής	3:17
ἀπόκριμα	1:9	δίψος	11:27	μέγεθος	1:19	πολίτευμα	3:20
συνυπουργέω	1:11	Δαμασκός	11:32	ἄθεος	2:12	ἐπιπόθητος	4:1
ἐλαφρία	1:17	ἐθνάρχης	11:32	μεσότοιχον	2:14	Εὐοδία	4:2
ἐπιτιμία	2:6	Ἀρέτας	11:32	συμπολίτης	2:19	Συντύχη	4:2
καπηλεύω	2:17	σαργάνη	11:33	συνοικοδομοῦμαι	2:22	σύζυγος	4:3
συστατικός	3:1	ἄρρητος	12:4	σύσσωμος	3:6	Κλήμης	4:3
ἱκανότης	3:5	σκόλοψ	12:7	πολυποίκιλος	3:10	προσφιλής	4:8
ἐντυπόω	3:7	ἐπισκηνόω	12:9	ἐξισχύω	3:18	εὔφημος	4:8
κατοπτρίζομαι	3:18	ἑσσόομαι	12:13	αἰχμαλωτεύω	4:8	μεγάλως	4:10
ἀπολέγομαι	4:2	ἐκδαπανάω	12:15	κατώτερος	4:9	ἀναθάλλω	4:10
δολόω	4:2	καταβαρέω	12:16	καταρτισμός	4:12	ἀκαιρέομαι	4:10
αὐγάζω	4:4	πανοῦργος	12:16	κλυδωνίζομαι	4:14	αὐτάρκης	4:11
παραυτίκα	4:17	συναποστέλλω	12:18	κυβεία	4:14	μυέομαι	4:12
ἐπακούω	6:2	ψιθυρισμός	12:20	ἀπαλγέω	4:19	Φιλιππήσιος	4:15
προσκοπή	6:3	φυσίωσις	12:20	ἀνανεόομαι	4:23	λῆμψις	4:15
δυσφημία	6:8	κατάρτισις	13:9	ἐπιδύω	4:26	**COLOSSIANS**	
εὐφημία	6:8	**GALATIANS**		παροργισμός	4:26	Κολοσσαί	1:2
ἑτεροζυγέω	6:14	συνηλικιώτης	1:14	αἰσχρότης	5:4	προακούω	1:5
μετοχή	6:14	πατρικός	1:14	μωρολογία	5:4	ἀρεσκεία	1:10
συμφώνησις	6:15	ἱστορέω	1:18	εὐτραπελία	5:4	ὁρατός	1:16
Βελιάρ	6:15	παρείσακτος	2:4	κρυφῇ	5:12	πρωτεύω	1:18
συγκατάθεσις	6:16	κατασκοπέω	2:4	ἐπιφαύσκω	5:14	εἰρηνοποιέω	1:20
ἐμπεριπατέω	6:16	εἴκω	2:5	ἄσοφος	5:15	μετακινέω	1:23
εἰσδέχομαι	6:17	συνυποκρίνομαι	2:13	ῥυτίς	5:27	ἀνταναπληρόω	1:24
μολυσμός	7:1	ὀρθοποδέω	2:14	μακροχρόνιος	6:3	πιθανολογία	2:4
ἀγανάκτησις	7:11	ἐθνικῶς	2:14	εὔνοια	6:7	στερέωμα	2:5
πτωχεύω	8:9	Ἰουδαϊκῶς	2:14	πάλη	6:12	συλαγωγέω	2:8
ἐλαττονέω	8:15	ἰουδαΐζω	2:14	κοσμοκράτωρ	6:12	φιλοσοφία	2:8
ἁδρότης	8:20	baskai,nw	3:1	ἑτοιμασία	6:15	θεότης	2:9
ἀπαρασκεύαστος	9:4	Γαλάτης	3:1	θυρεός	6:16	σωματικῶς	2:9
προκαταρτίζω	9:5	προευαγγελίζομαι	3:8	βέλος	6:16	ἀπέκδυσις	2:11
προαιρέομαι	9:7	ἐπιδιατάσσομαι	3:15	προσκαρτέρησις	6:18	χειρόγραφον	2:14
ἱλαρός	9:7	προκυρόω	3:17	ἄνοιξις	6:19	προσηλόω	2:14
δότης	9:7	τετρακοσιοικαιτριάκοντα	3:17	**PHILIPPIANS**		νεομηνία	2:16
πένης	9:9	προθεσμία	4:2	αἴσθησις	1:9	καταβραβεύω	2:18
ἀνεκδιήγητος	9:15	ἐκπτύω	4:14	ἁγνῶς	1:17	ἐμβατεύω	2:18
ὀχύρωμα	10:4	μορφόω	4:19	πτύρομαι	1:28	δογματίζομαι	2:20
ἐκφοβέω	10:9	ἀλληγορέω	4:24	παραμύθιον	2:1	ἀπόχρησις	2:22
ἐγκρίνω	10:12	συστοιχέω	4:25	σύμψυχος	2:2	ἐθελοθρησκία	2:23
ὑπερεκτείνω	10:14	πεισμονή	5:8	κενοδοξία \	2:3	ἀφειδία	2:23
ὑπερέκεινα	10:16	δάκνω	5:15	ἁρπαγμός	2:6	πλησμονή	2:23
ἁρμόζω	11:2	κενόδοξος	5:26	ὑπερυψόω	2:9	αἰσχρολογία	3:8
Συλάω	11:8	προκαλέομαι	5:26	καταχθόνιος	2:10	Σκύθης	3:11
ἀβαρής	11:9	φθονέω	5:26	ὀκταήμερος	3:5	μομφή	3:13
ψευδαπόστολος	11:13	φρεναπατάω	6:3	σκύβαλον	3:8	βραβεύω	3:15
δόλιος	11:13	μυκτηρίζω	6:7	συμμορφίζομαι	3:10	εὐχάριστος	3:15
παραφρονέω	11:23	εὐπροσωπέω	6:12	ἐξανάστασις	3:11	ἀθυμέω	3:21
ὑπερβαλλόντως	11:23	στίγμα	6:17	ἐπεκτείνομαι	3:13	ἀνταπόδοσις	3:24
πεντάκις	11:24	**EPHESIANS**		σκοπός	3:14	ἀνεψιός	4:10
νυχθήμερον	11:25	κληρόω	1:11	ἑτέρως	3:15	παρηγορία	4:11

Word	Ref	Word	Ref	Word	Ref	Word	Ref
Ἱεράπολις	4:13	αὐθεντέω	2:12	**2 TIMOTHY**		φαιλόνης	4:13
Νύμφα	4:15	τεκνογονία	2:15	μάμμη	1:5	Κάρπος	4:13
Λαοδικεύς	4:16	νεόφυτος	3:6	Λωΐς	1:5	μεμβράνα	4:13
1 THESSALONIANS		δίλογος	3:8	Εὐνίκη	1:5	χαλκεύς	4:14
ἐξηχέομαι	1:8	βαθμός	3:13	ἀναζωπυρέω	1:6	Εὔβουλος	4:21
ἀναμένω	1:10	ἑδραίωμα	3:15	δειλία	1:7	Λίνος	4:21
προπάσχω	2:2	ὁμολογουμένως	3:16	Φύγελος	1:15	Κλαυδία	4:21
κολακεία	2:5	ῥητῶς	4:1	Ἑρμογένης	1:15	**TITUS**	
τροφός	2:7	ψευδολόγος	4:2	ἀναψύχω	1:16	ἀψευδής	1:2
ὁμείρομαι	2:8	καυστηριάζομαι	4:2	βέλτιον	1:18	ἐπιδιορθόω	1:5
ὁσίως	2:10	μετάλημψις	4:3	στρατολογέω	2:4	ὀργίλος	1:7
ἀμέμπτως	2:10	ἀπόβλητος	4:4	λογομαχέω	2:14	φιλάγαθος	1:8
συμφυλέτης	2:14	ἐντρέφω	4:6	χρήσιμος	2:14	ἐγκρατής	1:8
ἐκδιώκω	2:15	γραώδης	4:7	ἀνεπαίσχυντος	2:15	ματαιολόγος	1:10
ἀπορφανίζω	2:17	γυμνασία	4:8	ὀρθοτομέω	2:15	φρεναπάτης	1:10
σαίνομαι	3:3	ἐπιπλήσσω	5:1	γάγγραινα	2:17	ἐπιστομίζω	1:11
ὑπερβαίνω	4:6	ἔκγονον	5:4	Φίλητος	2:17	Ἰουδαϊκός	1:14
θεοδίδακτος	4:9	ἀμοιβή	5:4	νεωτερικός	2:22	βδελυκτός	1:16
περιλείπομαι	4:15	μονόομαι	5:5	ἀπαίδευτος	2:23	πρεσβύτης	2:2
κέλευσμα	4:16	καταλέγω	5:9	ἤπιος	2:24	κατάστημα	2:3
περικεφαλαία	5:8	τεκνοτροφέω	5:10	ἀνεξίκακος	2:24	ἱεροπρεπής	2:3
ἄτακτος	5:14	ξενοδοχέω	5:10	ἀντιδιατίθεμαι	2:25	καλοδιδάσκαλος	2:3
ὀλιγόψυχος	5:14	καταστρηνιάω	5:11	ἀνανήφω	2:26	σωφρονίζω	2:4
ὁλοτελής	5:23	φλύαρος	5:13	φίλαυτος	3:2	φίλανδρος	2:4
ἐνορκίζω	5:27	τεκνογονέω	5:14	ἄσπονδος	3:3	φιλότεκνος	2:4
2 THESSALONIANS		οἰκοδεσποτέω	5:14	ἀκρατής	3:3	οἰκουργός	2:5
ὑπεραυξάνω	1:3	πρόκριμα	5:21	ἀνήμερος	3:3	ἀφθορία	2:7
ἐγκαυχάομαι	1:4	πρόσκλισις	5:21	ἀφιλάγαθος	3:3	ἀκατάγνωστος	2:8
ἔνδειγμα	1:5	ὑδροποτέω	5:23	φιλήδονος	3:4	σωτήριος	2:11
τίνω	1:9	στόμαχος	5:23	φιλόθεος	3:4	σωφρόνως	2:12
ἀτακτέω	3:7	ἄλλως	5:25	ἀποτρέπω	3:5	περιούσιος	2:14
περιεργάζομαι	3:11	νοσέω	6:4	ἐνδύνω	3:6	περιφρονέω	2:15
καλοποιέω	3:13	λογομαχία	6:4	γυναικάριον	3:6	στυγητός	3:3
σημειόομαι	3:14	ὑπόνοια	6:4	μηδέποτε	3:7	φροντίζω	3:8
1 TIMOTHY		διαπαρατριβή	6:5	Ἰάννης	3:8	αἱρετικός	3:10
ἀπέραντος	1:4	διατροφή	6:8	Ἰαμβρῆς	3:8	ἐκστρέφομαι	3:11
ἐκζήτησις	1:4	σκέπασμα	6:8	καταφθείρω	3:8	αὐτοκατάκριτος	3:11
ματαιολογία	1:6	βλαβερός	6:9	ἔκδηλος	3:9	Ἀρτεμᾶς	3:12
πατρολῴας	1:9	φιλαργυρία	6:10	ἀγωγή	3:10	Νικόπολις	3:12
μητρολῴας	1:9	περιπείρω	6:10	γόης	3:13	Ζηνᾶς	3:13
ἀνδροφόνος	1:9	πραϋπάθεια	6:11	πιστόω	3:14	**PHILEMON**	
ἀνδραποδιστής	1:10	ἀπρόσιτος	6:16	θεόπνευστος	3:16	Φιλήμων	1:1
ἐπίορκος	1:10	ὑψηλοφρονέω	6:17	ἐλεγμός	3:16	Ἀπφία	1:2
διώκτης	1:13	ἀδηλότης	6:17	ἐπανόρθωσις	3:16	ἄχρηστος	1:11
ὑπερπλεονάζω	1:14	ἀγαθοεργέω	6:18	ἄρτιος	3:17	ἑκούσιος	1:14
ἤρεμος	2:2	εὐμετάδοτος	6:18	ἀκαίρως	4:2	ἐλλογέω	1:18
ἀντίλυτρον	2:6	κοινωνικός	6:18	ἐπισωρεύω	4:3	ἀποτίνω	1:19
καταστολή	2:9	ἀποθησαυρίζω	6:19	κνήθω	4:3	προσοφείλω	1:19
αἰδώς	2:9	ἀντίθεσις	6:20	ἀνάλυσις	4:6	ὀνίναμαι	1:20
πλέγμα	2:9	ψευδώνυμος	6:20	Κρήσκης	4:10		
θεοσέβεια	2:10			Δαλματία	4:10		

Figures of Speech in the Letters of Paul

CHART 44

FIGURE OF SPEECH	DEFINITION	EXAMPLES IN PAUL'S LETTERS
Allegory	Presentation of an abstract or spiritual concept with the help of concrete images and events	1 Cor. 9:9; 10:3–4; 2 Cor. 3:12–16; Gal. 4:21–5:1 (see ἀλληγορούμενα in 4:24)
Alliteration	Two or more words having the same initial letter	Rom. 1:31; 8:19; 11:33; 2 Cor. 6:3; Col. 1:22; 1 Tim. 1:17
Anacoluthon	A breaking of the sequence of thought	Rom. 8:3; 1 Cor. 2:9; Gal. 2:4, 6–9; Phil. 3:19; Col. 1:26
Anadiplosis	Repetition of the same word or words at the end of one sentence and at the beginning of another	Rom. 8:17; 10:17; 11:30; 2 Cor. 5:17–18; 9:6; Gal. 4:31–5:1; Phil. 2:8
Anaphora	Repetition of the same word at the beginning of successive sentences	Rom. 8:33–35; 2 Cor. 11:19, 23–28; 1 Tim. 3:16; 2 Tim. 2:11–13
Antithesis	A setting of one word, phrase, or thought in contrast with another	Rom. 1:17–18; 3:4; 5:18; 6:7–8; 8:5, 13; 12:9; 15:12; 1 Cor. 1:18; 2:13–14; 2 Cor. 4:17–18; 5:6–8; 6:8–10; Phil. 2:12; 3:7
Anthropo-morphism	Ascribing human characteristics to non-human objects	Rom. 8:19–23; 2 Cor. 11:31
Assonance	Repetition of a vowel	Rom. 9:4; Eph. 5:14; Phil. 1:21; 1 Tim. 3:16
Asyndeton	Without conjunction	Rom. 9:1; 10:1; 11:1; 1 Cor. 4:8; 2 Cor. 7:2; 11:19–20, 23–28; Eph. 1:3; 3:1; Phil. 3:5; 1 Thess. 5:14
Chain-link transitions	Structural device that interlocks two textual units	Rom. 7:25; 10:16–17; 12:14–16; 13:13–14; 1 Cor. 8:7–8
Chiasm(us)	Inverted parallelism	Rom. 2:7–10; 3:27–31; 9:6–26; 1 Cor. 6:13–20; 12:31–14:1; 2 Cor. 1:12–7:15; Gal. 3:5–14; Eph. 4:1–16; Phil. 2:6–11; 1 Tim. 2:11–12; 2 Tim. 1:6–14; Titus 3:3–7
Climax (sorites)	Sequence of thought in which each phrase picks up the last word of the previous one	Rom. 5:3–5; 8:29–30; 10:13–15
Diatribe	Dialogue with imaginary interlocutor	Rom. 2:1–5, 17–24; 1 Cor. 6:12–20; Gal. 3:1–9, 19–22
Digression	An excursus on another subject (which sometimes amplifies the main point)	1 Cor. 2:6–16; 6:1–11; 7:17–24; 9:1–10:22; 13:1–13; 2 Cor. 6:14–7:1; 2 Thess. 1:5–10
Ellipsis	Omission of a word or words	1 Cor. 3:2; 7:21; 8:6; 12:30; 2 Cor. 11:18–20, 22–28; Eph. 1:18; 4:4; 5:17, 24; Phil. 4:5; 2 Thess. 3:2
Euphemism	Change of what is unpleasant for what is pleasant	Rom. 16:10–11; 1 Cor. 7:1–2; Gal. 6:10; 1 Thess. 4:13
Hendiadys	Two words used, but one thing meant	Rom. 3:8; Eph. 6:10
Hyperbaton	Unusual placing of a word in a sentence	Rom. 1:3; 5:8; 8:18; 11:13; 12:19; 14:1; 1 Cor. 3:9; 13:1; Eph. 6:8; 1 Tim. 1:15; 3:16; 6:5, 12
Hyperbole	Exaggeration, rhetorical overstatement	Rom. 9:3; 10:18; 1 Cor. 4:15; 13:1–3; 2 Cor. 12:7; Gal. 1:8

FIGURE OF SPEECH	DEFINITION	EXAMPLES IN PAUL'S LETTERS
Inclusio	Similar phrases or words at beginning and end of a shorter or larger literary unit	Rom. 1:5; 16:25; Phil. 1:3–11; 4:10–20
Irony	Expression of thought in a form that conveys its opposite	1 Cor. 4:8, 10; 2 Cor. 11:16–17, 19–21, 29; 12:5, 11, 13
Litotes	Affirming an idea by denying its opposite	Acts 21:39; Rom. 1:13, 16, 28; 1 Cor. 11:22
Meiosis	A belittling of one thing to magnify another	2 Cor. 11:16; 12:11
Merism	Extremes of one category describe its totality	Rom. 2:6–8; Gal. 5:19–21; 5:22–23
Metaphor	Comparison by representation	Rom. 6:3–4; 1 Cor. 3:6–17; 5:6-8; 6:19; 7:23; 13:12; 2 Cor. 2:14; 3:3; 5:1, 4; 6:7, 14-16; 11:2, 18–31; 12:2, 5, 7–11, 13; Gal. 2:4; 3:23–25; Eph. 2:19–22; 4:13–14, 22–24; 5:2, 22–32; 6:10–20; Phil. 1:22, 27; 2:17; 3:13–14, 20; 4:18; Col. 2:1, 14; 3:1, 8–11; 1 Thess. 2:7–8, 11; 2 Tim. 4:7
Metonymy	A word is substituted for the thing it is intended to suggest	1 Cor. 12:27–28; Eph. 2:11; Phil. 2:30; Col. 1:16; 1 Thess. 2:8; 2 Tim. 1:6
Oxymoron	A contradiction	1 Cor. 1:23; 2:2; Gal. 3:1; 2 Cor. 6:9; 8:2; 12:10 (see 1 Cor. 1:25)
Paradox	A statement that includes contradiction	Rom. 7:7; 9:30–31; 2 Cor. 4:7, 10–11; 6:9-10; 12:10; Gal. 5:13
Parallelism	Repetition of the same or opposite subject in successive lines	Rom. 4:25; 5:12, 15, 19; 11:12, 15; 1 Cor. 3:16; 8:6; 2 Cor. 5:6–8; 11:17–18, 22-23, 29–30; 12:1–2, 5; 2 Tim. 2:11–13
Paranomasia	Repetition of words close but not identical in sound	Rom. 1:23, 25, 29; 3:3; 1 Cor. 2:13; 13:8; 2 Cor. 1:13; 3:2; 10:12; Gal. 5:7; Eph. 3:6; Phil. 1:4; 2 Thess. 3:2–3
Personification	Concepts, things or animals are spoken of as persons	Rom. 5:12–14, 21; 6:9, 12–23; 8:18–25; 9:20; 10:6-8; 1 Cor. 12:15–16; 13:4–7; 15:54; 2 Cor. 11:18; 12:7
Pleonasm	When more words are used than the grammar requires	1 Cor. 14:5; 2 Cor. 7:13; 11:16, 18, 21, 23–28; 1 Tim. 5:19
Polysyndeton	Superfluous repetition of a conjunction (→ asyndeton)	Rom. 8:38–39; 9:4; 2 Cor. 12:13
Simile	Comparison by resemblance	Rom. 9:27; 1 Cor. 3:10; 9:26; Phil. 2:17, 22; 1 Thess. 2:7; 5:2, 4; 2 Tim. 2:3; 4:6
Synecdoche	The exchange of one idea for another associated idea	whole → part: Rom. 8:22 (creature = humanity) See also Rom 12:1; 2 Cor 11:18, 32-33
Typology	Events of the past are a pattern of future events	1 Corinthians 10 & Exodus 13–17, Numbers 20 (see τύποι in 10:6); 2 Cor 3:4–18 & Exodus 34

Paul's OT Quotations and Allusions — Survey

CHART 45

PAUL'S LETTER	OT QUOTATIONS	OT ALLUSIONS
Romans	79	123
1 Corinthians	18	118
2 Corinthians	14	42
Galatians	14	22
Ephesians	7	37
Philippians	—	17
Colossians	—	8
1 Thessalonians	—	18
2 Thessalonians	—	24
1 Timothy	2	21
2 Timothy	2	13
Titus	—	10
Philemon	—	—
TOTAL	**136**	**453**

Paul's OT Quotations and Allusions in OT Order — Survey

CHART 46

OT BOOKS	Quotations in Paul	Allusions in Paul	TOTAL
Exodus	8	28	36
Leviticus	5	14	19
Numbers	1	20	21
Deuteronomy	17	38	55
Joshua	—	—	—
Judges	—	1	1
Ruth	—	—	—
1 Samuel	1	3	4
2 Samuel	2	—	2
1 Kings	3	3	6
2 Kings	—	2	2
1 Chronicles	—	2	2
2 Chronicles	—	2	2
Ezra	—	—	—
Nehemiah	—	—	—
Esther	—	—	—
Job	2	18	20
Psalms	26	87	113
Proverbs	5	26	31
Ecclesiastes	1	1	2
Song of Songs	—	—	—
Isaiah	30	79	109
Jeremiah	3	28	31
Lamentations	—	1	1
Ezekiel	3	12	15
Daniel	—	14	14
Hosea	4	4	8
Joel	1	2	3
Amos	—	5	5
Obadiah	—	—	—
Jonah	—	1	1
Micah	—	3	3
Nahum	1	1	2
Habbakuk	2	1	3
Zephaniah	—	1	1
Haggai	—	—	—
Zechariah	1	6	7
Malachi	1	6	7
TOTAL	136	453	589

Paul's OT Quotations — Details

CHART 47

TEXT	QUOTATIONS	TEXT	QUOTATIONS
Rom. 1:17	Hab. 2:4	Rom. 11:8	Deut. 29:3; Is 29:10
Rom. 2:6	Prov. 24:12; Ps. 62:12	Rom. 11:9–10	LXX Ps. 68:23–24 (69:22–23)
Rom. 2:24	Isa. 52:5	Rom. 11:26–27a	Isa. 59:20–21
Rom. 3:4a	LXX Ps. 115:2 (116:11)	Rom. 11:27b	Isa. 27:9
Rom. 3:4b	LXX Ps. 50:6 (51:4)	Rom. 11:34	LXX Isa. 40:13
Rom. 3:10–12	Eccl. 7:20; Ps. 14:1–3 (cf. Ps. 53:1–3)	Rom. 11:35	LXX Job 41:3
Rom. 3:13a	LXX Ps. 5:10 (5:9)	Rom. 12:16–17	Prov. 3:7
Rom. 3:13b	LXX Ps. 139:4 (140:3)	Rom. 12:19	Deut. 32:35
Rom. 3:14	Ps. 10:7	Rom. 12:20	LXX Prov. 25:21–22
Rom. 3:15–17	Isa. 59:7-8; Prov. 1:16	Rom. 13:9a	LXX Deut. 5:17–21; LXX Ex. 20:13–17
Rom. 3:18	LXX Ps. 35:2 (36:1)	Rom. 13:9b	Lev. 19:18
Rom. 4:3 (9, 22)	Gen. 15:6	Rom. 14:11	Isa. 49:18; Jer. 22:24; LXX Isa. 45:23
Rom. 4:7–8	LXX Ps. 31:1–2 (32:1–2)	Rom. 15:3	LXX Ps. 68:10 (69:9)
Rom. 4:9	Gen. 15:6	Rom. 15:9	LXX Ps. 17:50 (18:49); 2 Sam. 22:50
Rom. 4:17	LXX Gen. 17:5	Rom. 15:10	LXX Deut. 32:43
Rom. 4:18	LXX Gen. 15:5	Rom. 15:11	Ps. 117:1
Rom. 4:22	Gen. 15:6	Rom. 15:12	LXX Isa. 11:10
Rom. 7:7	Ex. 20:17; LXX Deut. 5:21	Rom. 15:21	LXX Isa. 52:15
Rom. 8:36	LXX Ps. 43:23 (44:22)	1 Cor. 1:19	Isa. 29:14
Rom. 9:7	LXX Gen. 21:12	1 Cor. 1:31	Jer. 9:23–24
Rom. 9:9	Gen. 18:10, 14	1 Cor. 2:16	LXX Isa. 40:13
Rom. 9:12	LXX Gen. 25:23	1 Cor. 3:19	Job 5:13
Rom. 9:13	LXX Mal. 1:2–3	1 Cor. 3:20	LXX Ps. 93:11 (94:11)
Rom. 9:15	LXX Ex. 33:19	1 Cor. 5:13	LXX Deut. 17:7
Rom. 9:17	Ex. 9:16	1 Cor. 6:16	LXX Gen. 2:24
Rom. 9:20	LXX Isa. 29:16	1 Cor. 9:9	Deut. 25:4
Rom. 9:25	Hos. 2:25	1 Cor. 10:7	LXX Ex. 32:6
Rom. 9:26	LXX Hos. 2:1	1 Cor. 10:26	Ps. 24:1
Rom. 9:27–28	Isa. 10:22–23; LXX Hos. 2:1	1 Cor. 14:21	Isa. 28:11–12
Rom. 9:29	LXX Isa. 1:9	1 Cor. 14:25	Isa. 45:14
Rom. 9:33	Isa. 8:14; 28:16	1 Cor. 15:25	Ps. 110:1
Rom. 10:5	Lev. 18:5	1 Cor. 15:27	Ps. 8:7
Rom. 10:6	Deut. 9:4; 30:12–14	1 Cor. 15:32	LXX Isa. 22:13
Rom. 10:7	Ps. 107:26	1 Cor. 15:45	LXX Gen. 2:7
Rom. 10:8	Deut. 30:14	1 Cor. 15:54	Isa. 25:8
Rom. 10:11	Isa. 28:16	1 Cor. 15:55	Hos. 13:14
Rom. 10:13	LXX Joel 3:5 (2:32)	2 Cor. 3:16	Ex. 34:34
Rom. 10:15	Isa. 52:7; Nah. 2:1	2 Cor. 4:13	LXX Ps. 115:1 (116:10)
Rom. 10:16	LXX Isa. 53:1	2 Cor. 6:2	LXX Isa. 49:8
Rom. 10:18	LXX Ps. 18:5 (19:4)	2 Cor. 6:16	Lev. 26:11; Ezek. 37:27
Rom. 10:19	LXX Deut. 32:21	2 Cor. 6:17	Isa. 52:11; Ezek. 20:34
Rom. 10:20–21	LXX Isa. 65:1–2	2 Cor. 6:18	2 Sam. 7:14
Rom. 11:2	1 Sam. 12:22; Ps. 94:14	2 Cor. 8:15	Ex. 16:18
Rom. 11:3	1 Kings. 19:10, 14	2 Cor. 9:7	LXX Prov. 22:8
Rom. 11:4	1 Kings 19:18	2 Cor. 9:9	LXX Ps. 111:9 (112:9)

TEXT	QUOTATIONS	TEXT	QUOTATIONS
2 Cor. 9:10	Isa. 55:10	Gal. 5:14	Lev. 19:18
2 Cor. 10:17	Jer. 9:22–23	Eph. 1:22	Ps. 8:7
2 Cor. 13:1	Deut. 19:15	Eph. 4:8	Ps. 68:19
Gal. 3:6	LXX Gen. 15:6	Eph. 4:25	Zech. 8:16
Gal. 3:8	Gen. 12:3; 18:18	Eph. 4:26	LXX Ps. 4:5
Gal. 3:10	Deut. 27:26	Eph. 5:31	LXX Gen. 2:24
Gal. 3:11	Hab. 2:4	Eph. 6:2-3	LXX Ex. 20:12; LXX Deut. 5:16
Gal. 3:12	Lev. 18:5	1 Tim. 5:18a	Deut. 25:4
Gal. 3:13	Deut. 21:23; 27:26	1 Tim. 5:19	Deut. 19:15
Gal. 3:16	Gen. 13:15; 17:8; 24:7	2 Tim. 2:19a	Num. 16:5
Gal. 4:27	LXX Isa. 54:1	2 Tim. 2:19b	Isa. 26:13
Gal. 4:30	LXX Gen. 21:10		

Paul's OT Quotations — OT Order

CHART 48

TEXT	QUOTATIONS	TEXT	QUOTATIONS
Gen. 2:7	1 Cor. 15:45	2 KINGS	—
Gen. 2:24	1 Cor. 6:16; Eph. 5:31	1 CHRONICLES	—
Gen. 12:3	Gal. 3:8	2 CHRONICLES	—
Gen. 13:15	Gal. 3:16	EZRA	—
Gen. 15:5 LXX	Rom. 4:18	NEHEMIAH	—
Gen. 15:6	Rom. 4:3, 9, 22; Gal. 3:6 (LXX)	ESTHER	—
Gen. 17:5 LXX	Rom. 4:17	Job 5:13	1 Cor. 3:19
Gen. 17:8	Gal. 3:16	Job 41:3 LXX	Rom. 11:35
Gen. 18:10, 14	Rom. 9:9	Ps. 4:5 LXX	Eph. 4:26
Gen. 18:18	Gal. 3:8	Ps. 5:10 LXX (5:9)	Rom. 3:13a
Gen. 21:10	Gal. 4:30	Ps. 8:7	1 Cor. 15:27; Eph. 1:22
Gen. 21:12 LXX	Rom. 9:7	Ps. 10:7	Rom. 3:14
Gen. 24:7	Gal. 3:16	Ps. 14:1–3	Rom. 3:10–12
Gen. 25:23	Rom. 9:12	Ps. 17:50 LXX (18:49)	Rom. 15:9
Ex. 9:16	Rom. 9:17	Ps. 18:5 LXX (19:4)	Rom. 10:18
Ex. 16:18	2 Cor. 8:15	Ps. 24:1	1 Cor. 10:26
Ex. 20:12 LXX	Eph. 6:2-3	Ps. 31:1–2 LXX (32:1–2)	Rom. 4:7–8
Ex. 20:13–17 LXX	Rom. 13:9a	Ps. 35:2 LXX (36:1)	Rom. 3:18
Ex. 20:17	Rom. 7:7	Ps. 43:23 LXX (44:22)	Rom. 8:36
Ex. 32:6 LXX	1 Cor. 10:7	Ps. 50:6 LXX (51:4)	Rom. 3:4b
Ex. 33:19 LXX	Rom. 9:15	Ps. 62:12	Rom. 2:6
Ex. 34:34	2 Cor. 3:16	Ps. 68:10 LXX (69:9)	Rom. 15:3
Lev. 18:5	Rom. 10:5; Gal. 3:12	Ps. 68:19	Eph. 4:8
Lev. 19:18	Rom. 13:9b; Gal. 5:14	Ps. 68:23-24 LXX (69:22–23)	Rom. 11:9–10
Lev. 26:11	2 Cor. 6:16	Ps. 93:11 LXX (94:11)	1 Cor. 3:20
Num. 16:5	2 Tim. 2:19a	Ps. 94:14	Rom. 11:2
Deut. 5:16 LXX	Eph. 6:2-3	Ps. 107:26	Rom. 10:7
Deut. 5:21 LXX	Rom. 7:7; 13:9a	Ps. 110:1	1 Cor. 15:25
Deut. 9:4	Rom. 10:6	Ps. 111:9 LXX (112:9)	2 Cor. 9:9
Deut. 17:7 LXX	1 Cor. 5:13	Ps. 115:1 LXX (116:10)	2 Cor. 4:13
Deut. 19:15	2 Cor. 13:1; 1 Tim. 5:19	Ps. 115:2 LXX (116:11)	Rom. 3:4a
Deut. 21:23	Gal. 3:13	Ps. 117:1	Rom. 15:11
Deut. 25:4	1 Cor. 9:9; 1 Tim. 5:18a	Ps. 139:4 LXX (140:3)	Rom. 3:13b
Deut. 27:26	Gal. 3:10, 13	Prov. 1:16	Rom. 3:15–17
Deut. 29:3	Rom. 11:8	Prov. 3:7	Rom. 12:16–17
Deut. 30:12–14	Rom. 10:6, 8	Prov. 22:8 LXX	2 Cor. 9:7
Deut. 32:21	Rom. 10:19	Prov. 24:12	Rom. 2:6
Deut. 32:43	Rom. 15:10	Prov. 25:21–22 LXX	Rom. 12:20
Deut. 32:35	Rom. 12:19	Eccl. 7:20	Rom. 3:10–12
JOSHUA	—	SONG OF SONGS	—
JUDGES	—	Isa. 1:9	Rom. 9:29
1 Sam. 12:22	Rom. 11:2	Isa. 8:14	Rom. 9:33
2 Sam. 7:14	2 Cor. 6:18	Isa. 10:22–23	Rom. 9:27–28
2 Sam. 22:50	Rom. 15:9	Isa. 11:10 LXX	Rom. 15:12
1 Kings 19:10 ff.	Rom. 11:3–4	Isa. 22:13 LXX	1 Cor. 15:32

TEXT	QUOTATIONS	TEXT	QUOTATIONS
Isa. 25:8	1 Cor. 15:54	Isa. 65:1–2 LXX	Rom. 10:20–21
Isa. 26:13	2 Tim. 2:19b	Jer. 9:22–23	1 Cor. 1:31; 2 Cor. 10:17
Isa. 27:9	Rom. 11:27b	Jer. 22:24	Rom. 14:11
Isa. 28:11–12	1 Cor. 14:21	LAMENTATIONS	—
Isa. 28:16	Rom. 9:33; 10:11	Ezek. 5:11	Rom. 14:11
Isa. 29:10	Rom. 11:8	Ezek. 20:34	2 Cor. 6:17
Isa. 29:14	1 Cor. 1:19	Ezek. 37:27	2 Cor. 6:16
Isa. 29:16 LXX	Rom. 9:20	DANIEL	—
Isa. 40:13 LXX	Rom. 11:34; 1 Cor. 2:16	Hos. 2:1 LXX	Rom. 9:26–28
Isa. 45:14	1 Cor. 14:25	Hos. 2:25	Rom. 9:25
Isa. 45:23 LXX	Rom. 14:11	Hos. 13:14	1 Cor. 15:55
Isa. 49:8 LXX	2 Cor. 6:2	Joel 3:5 LXX (2:32)	Rom. 10:13
Isa. 49:18	Rom. 14:11	AMOS	—
Isa. 52:5	Rom. 2:24	OBADIAH	—
Isa. 52:7	Rom. 10:15	JONAH	—
Isa. 52:11	2 Cor. 6:17	MICAH	—
Isa. 52:15 LXX	Rom. 15:21	Nah. 2:1	Rom. 10:15
Isa. 53:1 LXX	Rom. 10:16	Hab. 2:4	Rom. 1:17; Gal. 3:11
Isa. 54:1 LXX	Gal. 4:27	ZEPHANIAH	—
Isa. 55:10	2 Cor. 9:10	HAGGAI	—
Isa. 59:7–8	Rom. 3:15–17	Zech. 8:16	Eph. 4:25
Isa. 59:20–21	Rom. 11:26–27a	Mal. 1:2–3 LXX	Rom. 9:13

Paul's OT Allusions — Details

CHART 49

PAUL	OT ALLUSION	PAUL	OT ALLUSION
Rom. 1:1	Ps. 78:70	Rom. 8:31	Ps. 118:6
Rom. 1:1	Ps. 105:26	Rom. 8:32	Gen. 22:16
Rom. 1:9	Deut. 11:13; 1 Sam. 12:3	Rom. 8:33	Isa. 50:8
Rom. 1:10	Job 12:7-9	Rom. 8:34	Job 34:29; Ps. 110:1
Rom. 1:16	Ps. 119:46	Rom. 8:36	Zech. 11:4
Rom. 1:17	Ps. 98:2; Isa. 51:5–6, 8	Rom. 9:3	Ex. 32:32
Rom. 1:18	Ps. 73:1; Prov. 11:5	Rom. 9:4	Ex. 4:22; 16:10; Deut. 14:1; Hos. 11:1
Rom. 1:20	Ps. 19:2; Isa. 40:26, 28	Rom. 9:5	Ex. 13:5; Ps. 41:14
Rom. 1:21	2 Kings 17:15; Ps. 76:6; 94:11; Jer. 2:5	Rom. 9:14	Deut. 32:4
Rom. 1:22	Jer. 10:14	Rom. 9:16	Isa. 49:10
Rom. 1:23	Deut. 4:15-18; Ps. 106:20; Jer. 2:11	Rom. 9:18	Ex. 4:21; 7:3
Rom. 1:27	Lev. 18:22; 20:13	Rom. 9:20	Job 9:12; Isa. 45:9
Rom. 2:5	Deut. 9:27; Ps. 110:5; Zeph. 1:14–15	Rom. 9:21	Jer. 18:6
Rom. 2:11	2 Chron. 19:7	Rom. 9:22	Isa. 13:5; 54:16
Rom. 2:15	Isa. 51:7; Jer. 31:33	Rom. 9:28	Isa. 28:22; Dan. 5:28
Rom. 2:17	Micah 3:11	Rom. 9:31	Prov. 15:9; Isa. 51:1
Rom. 2:21	Ps. 50:16–21	Rom. 10:6, 7	Prov. 30:4
Rom. 2:24	Ezek. 36:20	Rom. 10:7	Deut. 30:13; Ps. 71:20
Rom. 2:26	Deut. 30:16	Rom. 11:2	Jer. 31:37
Rom. 2:29	Deut. 30:6; Jer. 4:4; 9:25f.	Rom. 11:8	Isa. 6:9
Rom. 3:1	Ps. 103:7; 147:19	Rom. 11:9	Ps. 35:8
Rom. 3:1–2	Deut. 4:7–8	Rom. 11:16	Num. 15:17–21
Rom. 3:4	Ps. 116:11	Rom. 11:17	Judg. 9:9
Rom. 3:15	Prov. 1:16	Rom. 11:26	Ps. 14:7
Rom. 3:20	Gen. 6:12; Ps. 143:2	Rom. 11:27	Jer. 31:33f.
Rom. 3:21	Ps. 71:2, 24; Isa. 51:5–6, 8; Dan. 9:16	Rom. 11:29	Ps. 110:4
Rom. 3:25	Lev. 16:13–15	Rom. 11:33	Job 5:9; 9:10
Rom. 4:10	Gen. 17:10–11	Rom. 11:34	Job 15:18; Jer. 23:18
Rom. 4:13	Gen. 22:17–18	Rom. 12:1	Dan. 2:18
Rom. 4:17	Isa. 48:13	Rom. 12:9	Ps. 97:10; Amos 5:15
Rom. 4:19	Gen. 17:17	Rom. 12:16	Prov. 3:7; Isa. 5:21
Rom. 4:24	Isa. 53:5, 12	Rom. 12:17	Prov. 3:4
Rom. 4:25	Isa. 53:5	Rom. 12:20	2 Kings 6:22
Rom. 5:1	Isa. 32:17; 53:5	Rom. 13:1	Prov. 8:15
Rom. 5:5	Ps. 22:6; 25:20	Rom. 15:8	Ps. 89:3; Micah 7:20
Rom. 5:12	Gen. 2:17	Rom. 15:16	Isa. 66:20
Rom. 5:15	Isa. 53:11f.	1 Cor. 1:2	Ps. 99:6; Joel 3:5
Rom. 5:19	Isa. 53:11	1 Cor. 1:10	Isa. 33:18
Rom. 7:10	Gen. 2:17	1 Cor. 1:19	Ps. 33:10
Rom. 7:11	Gen. 3:13	1 Cor. 1:20	Job 12:17; Isa. 19:11
Rom. 7:14	Ps. 51:7	1 Cor. 1:24	Job 12:13
Rom. 8:3	Lev. 16	1 Cor. 1:30	Jer. 23:5–6
Rom. 8:14	Deut. 14:1	1 Cor. 2:9	Isa. 52:15; 64:3; 65:16; Jer. 3:16
Rom. 8:20	Gen. 3:17–19	1 Cor. 2:10	Job 11:7; Prov. 20:27; Dan. 2:22
Rom. 8:26	Isa. 28:11	1 Cor. 2:11	Zech. 12:1
Rom. 8:27	Ps. 139:1	1 Cor. 2:16	Jer. 23:18
Rom. 8:29	Gen. 1:27	1 Cor. 3:10	Isa. 3:3

PAUL	OT ALLUSION	PAUL	OT ALLUSION
1 Cor. 3:13	Mal. 3:19	1 Cor. 14:34	Gen. 3:16; Dan. 2:47
1 Cor. 3:15	Amos 4:11	1 Cor. 15:3	Isa. 53:5–6, 8–9, 12
1 Cor. 3:17	Ps. 66:5; 79:1	1 Cor. 15:4	Hos. 6:2; Jonah 2:1
1 Cor. 4:4	Job 28:22	1 Cor. 15:21	Gen. 3:17
1 Cor. 4:10	Prov. 3:7	1 Cor. 15:24	Dan. 2:44
1 Cor. 4:12	Ps. 109:28	1 Cor. 15:38	Gen. 1:11–12
1 Cor. 4:13	Prov. 21:18	1 Cor. 15:39	Gen. 1:20, 24; 8:17
1 Cor. 5:1	Lev. 18:6	1 Cor. 15:49	Gen. 5:3
1 Cor. 5:7	Ex. 12:19, 21; 13:7	1 Cor. 15:58	Isa. 65:23
1 Cor. 6:2	Dan. 7:22	1 Cor. 16:13	Ps. 31:25
1 Cor. 6:17	Deut. 10:20; Ps. 73:28	2 Cor. 3:3	Ex. 31:18; 32:15; Deut. 9:10–11; Prov. 7:3; Ezek. 11:19; 36:26
1 Cor. 8:4	Deut. 6:4	2 Cor. 3:7	Ex. 34:30
1 Cor. 8:5	Ps. 136:2	2 Cor. 3:9	Deut. 27:26
1 Cor. 8:6	Mal. 2:10	2 Cor. 3:10	Ex. 34:29–30, 35
1 Cor. 9:7	Deut. 20:6	2 Cor. 3:13	Ex. 34:33, 35
1 Cor. 9:13	Num. 18:8, 31; Deut. 18:1-3	2 Cor. 3:18	Ex. 16:7, 10; 24:17
1 Cor. 9:16	Jer. 20:9	2 Cor. 4:6	Gen. 1:3; Ps. 112:4; Isa. 9:1
1 Cor. 10:1	Ex. 13:21; 14:22	2 Cor. 4:7	Lam. 4:2
1 Cor. 10:3	Ex. 16:4, 35; Deut. 8:3; Ps. 78:24	2 Cor. 5:10	Eccl. 12:14
1 Cor. 10:4	Ex. 17:6; Num. 20:7-11; Ps. 78:15, 35	2 Cor. 5:12	1 Sam. 16:7
1 Cor. 10:5	Num. 14:16; Ps. 78:31	2 Cor. 5:17	Isa. 43:18f.
1 Cor. 10:6	Num. 11:4, 34; Ps. 106:14	2 Cor. 6:9	Ps. 118:17
1 Cor. 10:8	Num. 25:1, 9; 26:62	2 Cor. 6:14	Deut. 32:10
1 Cor. 10:9	Num. 21:5; Ps. 78:18	2 Cor. 6:15	1 Kings 18:21
1 Cor. 10:10	Ex. 16:2–3; Num. 14:2, 36; 16:11–35	2 Cor. 6:17	Ezek. 20:41
1 Cor. 10:13	Ps. 145:13	2 Cor. 6:18	Isa. 43:6; Jer. 31:9; Amos 3:13
1 Cor. 10:18	Lev. 7:6, 15	2 Cor. 7:6	Isa. 49:13
1 Cor. 10:20	Lev. 17:7; Deut. 32:17; Ps. 106:37	2 Cor. 7:15	Ps. 1:11
1 Cor. 10:21	Isa. 65:11; Mal. 1:7, 12	2 Cor. 8:21	Prov. 3:4
1 Cor. 10:22	Deut. 32:21	2 Cor. 9:6	Prov. 11:24
1 Cor. 10:26	Ps. 50:12; 89:12	2 Cor. 9:7	Deut. 15:10
1 Cor. 11:3	Gen. 3:16	2 Cor. 9:10	Hos. 10:12
1 Cor. 11:7	Gen. 1:27	2 Cor. 10:4	Prov. 21:22
1 Cor. 11:8	Gen. 2:2–23	2 Cor. 10:8	Jer 24:6
1 Cor. 11:9	Gen. 2:18	2 Cor. 11:3	Gen. 3:13
1 Cor. 11:10	Gen. 6:2; 24:65; Ps. 138:1	2 Cor. 11:20	Ps. 53:5
1 Cor. 11:24	Lev. 24:7; Ps. 38:1; 70:1	2 Cor. 11:24	Deut. 25:3
1 Cor. 11:25	Jer. 31:31; 32:40; Zech. 9:11	2 Cor. 12:7	Num. 33:55, Ezek. 28:34
1 Cor. 12:2	Ps. 115:5; Hab. 2:18–19	Gal. 1:15	Isa. 49:1
1 Cor. 12:3	Num. 21:3	Gal. 2:6	Deut. 10:17
1 Cor. 13:1	Ps. 150:5	Gal. 2:16	Gen. 6:12; Ps. 143:2
1 Cor. 13:3	Dan. 3:19–20	Gal. 3:10	Deut. 28:58; 30:10
1 Cor. 13:5	Zech. 8:17	Gal. 3:17	Ex. 12:40
1 Cor. 13:12	Gen. 32:31; Num. 12:8	Gal. 3:19	Lev. 26:46; Deut. 5:4-5
1 Cor. 14:5	Num. 11:29	Gal. 4:8	2 Chron. 13:9; Isa. 37:19; Jer. 2:11
1 Cor. 14:16	1 Chron. 16:36	Gal. 4:22	Gen. 16:15; 21:2,9
1 Cor. 14:20	Jer. 4:22	Gal. 4:23	Gen. 17:16

PAUL	OT ALLUSION	PAUL	OT ALLUSION
1 Cor. 14:25	1 Kings 18:39; Zech. 8:23	Gal. 4:26	Ps. 87:5
Gal. 4:29	Gen. 21:9	1 Thess. 4:5	Ps. 79:6; Jer. 10:25
Gal. 5:12	Deut. 23:2	1 Thess. 4:6	Ps 94:2
Gal. 6:7	Job 4:8; Prov. 22:8	1 Thess. 4:8	Ezek. 36:27; 37:14
Gal. 6:16	Ps. 125:5; 128:6	1 Thess. 5:3	Jer. 6:14; Isa. 13:8
Eph. 1:6	Deut. 32:15; 33:5, 26; Isa. 44:2; Dan. 3:35 LXX	1 Thess. 5:8	Job 2:9; Isa. 59:17
Eph. 1:14	Mal. 3:17	1 Thess. 5:14	Prov. 14:29; Isa. 57:15
Eph. 1:17	Isa. 11:2	1 Thess. 5:15	Prov. 20:22
Eph. 1:19	Isa. 40:26; Dan. 4:27	1 Thess. 5:19	Num. 11:26-29
Eph. 1:20	Ps. 110:1	1 Thess. 5:22	Job 1:1, 8
Eph. 1:23	Jer. 23:24	2 Thess. 1:8	Isa. 66:4, 15; Jer. 10:25
Eph. 2:14	Isa. 9:5; Micah 5:4	2 Thess. 1:9	Isa. 2:10, 21
Eph. 2:17	Isa. 52:7; 57:19	2 Thess. 1:10	Ps. 68:36; 89:8; Isa. 2:10, 17
Eph. 2:20	Isa. 28:16	2 Thess. 1:12	Isa. 66:5; Mal. 1:11
Eph. 3:15	Ps. 147:4	2 Thess. 2:3	Ps. 89:23; Isa. 57:3–4
Eph. 4:9	Ps. 63:10	2 Thess. 2:4	Ezek. 28:2; Dan. 11:36
Eph. 4:14	Isa. 57:20	2 Thess. 2:8	Ezek. 21:24f.
Eph. 4:24	Gen. 1:26–27	2 Thess. 2:8	Job 4:9; Ps. 33:6; Isa. 11:4
Eph. 4:26	Deut. 24:15	2 Thess. 3:1	Ps. 147:15
Eph. 5:2	Ps. 40:7	2 Thess. 3:2	Isa. 25:4
Eph. 5:16	Amos 5:13	2 Thess. 3:5	1 Chron. 29:18
Eph. 5:18	Prov. 23:31	2 Thess. 3:8	Jer. 20:18
Eph. 5:26	Ezek. 16:9	1 Tim. 1:1	Ps. 24:5
Eph. 6:4	Prov. 2:2; 3:11	1 Tim. 2:2	Jer. 29:7
Eph. 6:7	2 Chron. 19:6	1 Tim. 2:6	Ps. 49:8
Eph. 6:9	Lev. 25:43	1 Tim. 2:8	Ps. 141:2
Eph. 6:10	Isa. 40:26	1 Tim. 2:12	Gen. 3:16
Eph. 6:14	Isa. 11:5; 59:17	1 Tim. 2:13	Gen. 1:27; 2:7, 22
Eph. 6:15	Isa. 52:7; Nah. 2:1	1 Tim. 2:14	Gen. 3:6, 13
Eph. 6:17	Isa. 49:2; 59:17; Hos. 6:5	1 Tim. 4:1	Isa. 19:14
Phil. 1:11	Prov. 3:9; 11:30; Amos 6:13	1 Tim. 4:3	Gen. 9:3
Phil. 1:19	Job 13:16	1 Tim. 4:4	Gen. 1:31
Phil. 1:22	Ps. 104:13	1 Tim. 5:5	Jer. 49:11
Phil. 2:7	Isa. 53:3, 11	1 Tim. 5:18	Num. 18:31
Phil. 2:10–11	Isa. 45:23	1 Tim. 6:1	Isa. 52:5
Phil. 2:15	Deut. 32:5; Dan. 12:3	1 Tim. 6:7	Job 1:21
Phil. 2:16	Isa. 49:4; 65:23	1 Tim. 6:11	1 Sam. 2:27; 1 Kings 13:1
Phil. 4:3	Ps. 69:29	1 Tim. 6:16	Ex. 33:20
Phil. 4:5	Ps. 145:18	1 Tim. 6:17	Ps. 62:11
Phil. 4:18	Gen. 8:21; Isa. 56:7; Ezek. 20:41	2 Tim. 2:7	Prov. 2:6
Col. 1:17	Prov. 8:23f.	2 Tim. 2:19	Lev. 24:16; Job 36:10; Isa. 28:16
Col. 2:3	Prov. 2:3; Isa. 45:3	2 Tim. 3:8	Ex. 7:11
Col. 2:22	Isa. 29:13	2 Tim. 3:11	Ps. 34:20
Col. 3:1	Ps. 110:1	2 Tim. 3:15	Ps. 119:98
Col. 3:10	Gen. 1:26-27	2 Tim. 4:15	Ps. 28:4; 62:13; Prov. 24:12
Col. 4:1	Lev. 25:43, 53	2 Tim. 4:17	Ps. 22:22; Dan. 6:21, 28
1 Thess. 2:4	Jer. 11:20	Titus 1:16	Ps. 14:1
1 Thess. 2:16	Gen. 15:16	Titus 2:11	Gen. 35:7

PAUL	OT ALLUSION	PAUL	OT ALLUSION
1 Thess. 3:13	Zech. 14:5	Titus 2:14	Ex. 19:5; Deut. 7:6; 14:2; Ps. 130:8; Ezek. 37:23
Titus 3:4	Ps. 31:20	Titus 3:6	Joel 3:1
Titus 3:5	Deut. 9:5		

Paul's OT Allusions in OT Order

CHART 50

OT TEXT	ALLUDED IN	OT TEXT	ALLUDED IN	OT TEXT	ALLUDED IN
Gen. 1:3	2 Cor. 4:6	Ex. 7:11	2 Tim. 3:8	Num. 11:4	1 Cor. 10:6
Gen. 1:11–12	1 Cor. 15:38	Ex. 12:19	1 Cor. 5:7	Num. 11:26–29	1 Thess. 5:19
Gen. 1:20, 24	1 Cor. 15:39	Ex. 12:21	1 Cor. 5:7	Num. 11:29	1 Cor. 14:5
Gen. 1:26–27	Eph. 4:24; Col. 3:10	Ex. 12:40	Gal. 3:17	Num. 11:34	1 Cor. 10:6
Gen. 1:27	Rom. 8:29; 1 Cor. 11:7; 1 Tim. 2:13	Ex. 13:5	Rom. 9:5	Num. 12:8	1 Cor. 13:12
Gen. 1:31	1 Tim. 4:4	Ex. 13:7	1 Cor. 5:7	Num. 14:2	1 Cor. 10:10
Gen. 2:7	1 Tim. 2:13	Ex. 13:21	1 Cor. 10:1	Num. 14:16	1 Cor. 10:5
Gen. 2:17	Rom. 5:12; 7:10	Ex. 14:22	1 Cor. 10:1	Num. 14:36	1 Cor. 10:10
Gen. 2:18	1 Cor. 11:9	Ex. 16:2–3	1 Cor. 10:10	Num. 15:17–21	Rom. 11:16
Gen. 2:22	1 Tim. 2:13	Ex. 16:4	1 Cor. 10:3	Num. 16:11–35	1 Cor. 10:10
Gen. 2:22–23	1 Cor. 11:8	Ex. 16:7	2 Cor. 3:18	Num. 18:8	1 Cor. 9:13
Gen. 3:6	1 Tim. 2:14	Ex. 16:10	Rom. 9:4; 2 Cor. 3:18	Num. 18:31	1 Cor. 9:13; 1 Tim. 5:18
Gen. 3:13	Rom. 7:11; 2 Cor. 11:3; 1 Tim. 2:14	Ex. 16:35	1 Cor. 10:3	Num. 20:7–11	1 Cor. 10:4
Gen. 3:16	1 Cor. 11:3; 14:34; 1 Tim. 2:12	Ex. 17:6	1 Cor. 10:4	Num. 21:3	1 Cor. 12:3
Gen. 3:17	1 Cor. 15:21	Ex. 19:5	Titus 2:14	Num. 21:5	1 Cor. 10:9
Gen. 3:17–19	Rom. 8:20	Ex. 24:17	2 Cor. 3:18	Num. 25:1	1 Cor. 10:8
Gen. 5:3	1 Cor. 15:49	Ex. 31:18	2 Cor. 3:3	Num. 25:9	1 Cor. 10:8
Gen. 6:2	1 Cor. 11:10	Ex. 32:15	2 Cor. 3:3	Num. 26:62	1 Cor. 10:8
Gen. 6:12	Rom. 3:20; Gal. 2:16	Ex. 32:32	Rom. 9:3	Num. 33:55	2 Cor. 12:7
Gen. 8:17	1 Cor. 15:39	Ex. 33:20	1 Tim. 6:16	Deut. 4:7-8	Rom. 3:1–2
Gen. 8:21	Phil. 4:18	Ex. 34:29–30	2 Cor. 3:10	Deut. 4:15–18	Rom. 1:23
Gen. 9:3	1 Tim. 4:3	Ex. 34:30	2 Cor. 3:7	Deut. 5:4-5	Gal. 3:19
Gen. 15:16	1 Thess. 2:16	Ex. 34:33	2 Cor. 3:13	Deut. 6:4	1 Cor. 8:4
Gen. 16:15	Gal. 4:22	Ex. 34:35	2 Cor. 3:10, 13	Deut. 7:6	Titus 2:14
Gen. 17:10–11	Rom. 4:10	Lev. 7:6	1 Cor. 10:18	Deut. 7:9	1 Cor. 10:13; 2 Cor. 1:18
Gen. 17:16	Gal. 4:23	Lev. 7:15	1 Cor. 10:18	Deut. 8:3	1 Cor. 10:3
Gen. 17:17	Rom. 4:19	Lev. 16	Rom. 8:3	Deut. 9:5	Titus 3:5
Gen. 21:2	Gal. 4:22	Lev. 16:13–15	Rom. 3:25	Deut. 9:10-11	2 Cor. 3:3
Gen. 21:9	Gal. 4:22, 29	Lev. 17:7	1 Cor. 10:20	Deut. 9:27	Rom. 2:5
Gen. 22:16	Rom. 8:32	Lev. 18:6	1 Cor. 5:1	Deut. 10:17	Gal. 2:6
Gen. 22:17–18	Rom. 4:13	Lev. 18:22	Rom. 1:27	Deut. 10:20	1 Cor. 6:17
Gen. 24:65	1 Cor. 11:10	Lev. 20:13	Rom. 1:27	Deut. 11:13	Rom. 1:9
Gen. 32:31	1 Cor. 13:12	Lev. 24:7	1 Cor. 11:24	Deut. 14:1	Rom. 8:14; 9:4
Gen. 35:7	Titus 2:11	Lev. 24:16	2 Tim. 2:19	Deut. 14:2	Titus 2:14
Ex. 4:21	Rom. 9:18	Lev. 25:43	Eph. 6:9; Col. 4:1	Deut. 15:10	2 Cor. 9:7
Ex. 4:22	Rom. 9:4	Lev. 25:53	Col. 4:1	Deut. 18:1-3	1 Cor. 9:13
Ex. 7:3	Rom. 9:18	Lev. 26:46	Gal. 3:19	Deut. 20:6	1 Cor. 9:7
Deut. 23:2	Gal. 5:12	Job 9:12	Rom. 9:20	Ps. 78:24	1 Cor. 10:3
Deut. 24:15	Eph. 4:26	Job 11:7	1 Cor. 2:10	Ps. 78:31	1 Cor. 10:5

OT TEXT	ALLUDED IN	OT TEXT	ALLUDED IN	OT TEXT	ALLUDED IN
Deut. 25:3	2 Cor. 11:24	Job 12:7–9	Rom. 1:10	Ps. 78:70	Rom. 1:1
Deut. 27:26	2 Cor. 3:9	Job 12:13	1 Cor. 1:24	Ps. 79:1	1 Cor. 3:17
Deut. 28:53	Rom. 2:9	Job 12:17	1 Cor. 1:20	Ps. 79:6	1 Thess. 4:5
Deut. 28:58	Gal. 3:10	Job 13:16	Phil. 1:19	Ps. 87:5	Gal. 4:26
Deut. 30:6	Rom. 2:29	Job 15:18	Rom. 11:34	Ps. 89:3	Rom. 15:8
Deut. 30:10	Gal. 3:10	Job 28:22	1 Cor. 4:4	Ps. 89:8	2 Thess. 1:10
Deut. 30:13	Rom. 10:7	Job 34:29	Rom. 8:34	Ps. 89:12	1 Cor. 10:26
Deut. 30:16	Rom. 2:26	Job 36:10	2 Tim. 2:19	Ps. 89:23	2 Thess. 2:3
Deut. 32:4	Rom. 9:14	Ps. 1:11	2 Cor. 7:15	Ps. 94:2	1 Thess. 4:6
Deut. 32:5	Phil. 2:15	Ps. 14:1	Titus 1:16	Ps. 94:11	Rom. 1:21
Deut. 32:10	2 Cor. 6:14	Ps. 14:7	Rom. 11:26	Ps. 97:10	Rom. 12:9
Deut. 32:15	Eph. 1:6	Ps. 19:2	Rom. 1:20	Ps. 98:2	Rom. 1:17
Deut. 32:17	1 Cor. 10:20	Ps. 22:6	Rom. 5:5	Ps. 99:6	1 Cor. 1:2
Deut. 32:21	1 Cor. 10:22	Ps. 22:22	2 Tim. 4:17	Ps. 103:7	Rom. 3:1
Deut. 33:5	Eph. 1:6	Ps. 24:5	1 Tim. 1:1	Ps. 104:13	Phil. 1:22
Deut. 33:26	Eph. 1:6	Ps. 25:20	Rom. 5:5	Ps. 105:26	Rom. 1:1
JOSHUA	/	Ps. 28:4	2 Tim. 4:15	Ps. 106:14	1 Cor. 10:6
Judg. 9:9	Rom. 11:17	Ps. 31:20	Titus 3:4	Ps. 106:20	Rom. 1:23
RUTH	/	Ps. 31:25	1 Cor. 16:13	Ps. 106:37	1 Cor. 10:20
1 Sam. 2:27	1 Tim. 6:11	Ps. 33:6	2 Thess. 2:8	Ps. 109:28	1 Cor. 4:12
1 Sam. 12:3	Rom. 1:9	Ps. 33:10	1 Cor. 1:19	Ps. 110:1	Rom. 8:34; Eph. 1:20; Col. 3:1
1 Sam. 16:7	2 Cor. 5:12	Ps. 34:20	2 Tim. 3:11	Ps. 110:4	Rom. 11:29
2 SAMUEL	/	Ps. 35:8	Rom. 11:9	Ps. 110:5	Rom. 2:5
1 Kings 13:1	1 Tim. 6:11	Ps. 38:1	1 Cor. 11:24	Ps. 112:4	2 Cor. 4:6
1 Kings 18:21	2 Cor. 6:15	Ps. 40:7	Eph. 5:2	Ps. 115:5	1 Cor. 12:2
1 Kings 18:39	1 Cor. 14:25	Ps. 41:14	Rom. 9:5	Ps. 116:11	Rom. 3:4
2 Kings 6:22	Rom. 12:20	Ps. 49:8	1 Tim. 2:6	Ps. 118:6	Rom. 8:31
2 Kings 17:15	Rom. 1:21	Ps. 50:12	1 Cor. 10:26	Ps. 118:17	2 Cor. 6:9
1 Chron. 16:36	1 Cor. 14:16	Ps. 50:16–21	Rom. 2:21	Ps. 119:46	Rom. 1:16
1 Chron. 29:18	2 Thess. 3:5	Ps. 51:7	Rom. 7:14	Ps. 119:98	2 Tim. 3:15
2 Chron. 13:9	Gal. 4:8	Ps. 53:5	2 Cor. 11:20	Ps. 125:5	Gal. 6:16
2 Chron. 19:6	Eph. 6:7	Ps. 62:11	1 Tim. 6:17	Ps. 128:6	Gal. 6:16
2 Chron. 19:7	Rom. 2:11	Ps. 62:13	2 Tim. 4:15		
EZRA	/	Ps. 63:10	Eph. 4:9	Ps. 130:8	Titus 2:14
NEHEMIAH	/	Ps. 66:5	1 Cor. 3:17	Ps. 136:2	1 Cor. 8:5
ESTHER	/	Ps. 68:36	2 Thess. 1:10	Ps. 138:1	1 Cor. 11:10
Job 1:1	1 Thess. 5:22	Ps. 69:29	Phil. 4:3	Ps. 139:1	Rom. 8:27
Job 1:8	1 Thess. 5:22	Ps. 70:1	1 Cor. 11:24	Ps. 141:2	1 Tim. 2:8
Job 1:21	1 Tim. 6:7	Ps. 71:2	Rom. 3:21	Ps. 143:2	Rom. 3:20; Gal. 2:16
Job 2:9	1 Thess. 5:8	Ps. 71:20	Rom. 10:7	Ps. 145:13	1 Cor. 10:13
Job 4:8	Gal. 6:7	Ps. 71:24	Rom. 3:21	Ps. 145:18	Phil. 4:5
Job 4:9	2 Thess. 2:8	Ps. 73:1	Rom. 1:18	Ps. 147:4	Eph. 3:15
Job 5:9	Rom. 11:33	Ps. 73:28	1 Cor. 6:17	Ps. 147:15	2 Thess. 3:1
Job 9:10	Rom. 11:33	Ps. 78:18	1 Cor. 10:9	Ps. 147:19	Rom. 3:1
Ps. 150:5	1 Cor. 13:1	Isa. 25:4	2 Thess. 3:2	Isa. 57:19	Eph. 2:17
Prov. 1:16	Rom. 3:15	Isa. 28:11	Rom. 8:26	Isa. 57:20	Eph. 4:14

OT TEXT	ALLUDED IN	OT TEXT	ALLUDED IN	OT TEXT	ALLUDED IN
Prov. 2:2	Eph. 6:4	Isa. 28:16	Eph. 2:20; 2 Tim. 2:19	Isa. 59:17	Eph. 6:14, 17; 1 Thess. 5:8
Prov. 2:3	Col. 2:3	Isa. 28:22	Rom. 2:9; 9:28	Isa. 64:3	1 Cor. 2:9
Prov. 2:6	2 Tim. 2:7	Isa. 29:13	Col. 2:22	Isa. 65:11	1 Cor. 10:21
Prov. 3:4	Rom. 12:17; 2 Cor. 8:21	Isa. 32:17	Rom. 5:1	Isa. 65:16	1 Cor. 2:9
Prov. 3:7	Rom. 12:16; 1 Cor. 4:10	Isa. 33:18	1 Cor. 1:10	Isa. 65:23	1 Cor. 15:58; Phil. 2:16
Prov. 3:9	Phil. 1:11	Isa. 37:19	Gal. 4:8	Isa. 66:4	2 Thess. 1:8
Prov. 3:11	Eph. 6:4	Isa. 40:26	Rom. 1:20; Eph. 1:19; 6:10	Isa. 66:5	2 Thess. 1:12
Prov. 7:3	2 Cor. 3:3	Isa. 40:28	Rom. 1:20	Isa. 66:15	2 Thess. 1:8
Prov. 8:15	Rom. 13:1	Isa. 43:6	2 Cor. 6:18	Isa. 66:20	Rom. 15:16
Prov. 8:23f.	Col. 1:17	Isa. 43:18f.	2 Cor. 5:17	Jer. 2:5	Rom. 1:21
Prov. 11:5	Rom. 1:18	Isa. 44:2	Eph. 1:6	Jer. 2:11	Rom. 1:23; Gal. 4:8
Prov. 11:24	2 Cor. 9:6	Isa. 45:3	Col. 2:3	Jer. 3:16	1 Cor. 2:9
Prov. 11:30	Phil. 1:11	Isa. 45:9	Rom. 9:20	Jer. 4:4	Rom. 2:29
Prov. 14:29	1 Thess. 5:14	Isa. 45:23	Phil. 2:10–11	Jer. 4:22	1 Cor. 14:20
Prov. 15:9	Rom. 9:31	Isa. 48:13	Rom. 4:17	Jer. 6:14	1 Thess. 5:3
Prov. 20:22	1 Thess. 5:15	Isa. 49:1	Gal. 1:15	Jer. 9:25f.	Rom. 2:29
Prov. 20:27	1 Cor. 2:10	Isa. 49:2	Eph. 6:17	Jer. 10:14	Rom. 1:22
Prov. 21:18	1 Cor. 4:13	Isa. 49:4	Phil. 2:16	Jer. 10:25	1 Thess. 4:5; 2 Thess. 1:8
Prov. 21:22	2 Cor. 10:4	Isa. 49:10	Rom. 9:16	Jer. 11:20	1 Thess. 2:4
Prov. 22:8	Gal. 6:7	Isa. 49:13	2 Cor. 7:6	Jer. 18:6	Rom. 9:21
Prov. 23:31	Eph. 5:18	Isa. 50:8	Rom. 8:33	Jer. 20:9	1 Cor. 9:16
Prov. 24:12	2 Tim. 4:15	Isa. 51:1	Rom. 9:31	Jer. 20:18	2 Thess. 3:8
Prov. 30:4	Rom. 10:6, 7	Isa. 51:5–6	Rom. 1:17; 3:21	Jer. 23:5–6	1 Cor. 1:30
Eccl. 12:14	2 Cor. 5:10	Isa. 51:7	Rom. 2:15	Jer. 23:18	Rom. 11:34; 1 Cor 2:16
SONG OF SONGS	/	Isa. 51:8	Rom. 1:17; 3:21	Jer. 23:24	Eph. 1:23
Isa. 2:10, 21	2 Thess. 1:9	Isa. 52:5	1 Tim. 6:1	Jer. 24:6	2 Cor. 10:8
Isa. 2:10, 17	2 Thess. 1:10	Isa. 52:7	Eph. 2:17; 6:15	Jer. 29:7	1 Tim. 2:2
Isa. 3:3	1 Cor. 3:10	Isa. 52:15	1 Cor. 2:9	Jer. 31:9	2 Cor. 6:18
Isa. 5:21	Rom. 12:16	Isa. 53:3	Phil. 2:7	Jer. 31:31	1 Cor. 11:25
Isa. 6:9	Rom. 11:8	Isa. 53:5	Rom. 4:25; 5:1	Jer. 31:33	Rom. 2:15
Isa. 9:1	2 Cor. 4:6	Isa. 53:5–6	1 Cor. 15:3	Jer. 31:33f.	Rom. 11:27
Isa. 9:5	Eph. 2:14	Isa. 53:8–9	1 Cor. 15:3	Jer. 31:37	Rom. 11:2
Isa. 11:2	Eph. 1:17	Isa. 53:11	Rom. 5:19; Phil. 2:7	Jer. 32:40	1 Cor. 11:25
Isa. 11:4	2 Thess. 2:8	Isa. 53:11f.	Rom. 5:15	Jer. 49:11	1 Tim. 5:5
Isa. 11:5	Eph. 6:14	Isa. 53:12	Rom. 4:24; 1 Cor. 15:3	Lam. 4:2	2 Cor. 4:7
Isa. 13:5	Rom. 9:22	Isa. 54:16	Rom. 9:22	Ezek. 11:19	2 Cor. 3:3
Isa. 13:8	1 Thess. 5:3	Isa. 56:7	Phil. 4:18	Ezek. 16:9	Eph. 5:26
Isa. 19:11	1 Cor. 1:20	Isa. 57:3–4	2 Thess. 2:3	Ezek. 20:41	2 Cor. 6:17; Phil. 4:18
Isa. 19:14	1 Tim. 4:1	Isa. 57:15	1 Thess. 5:14	Ezek. 21:24f.	2 Thess. 2:8
Ezek. 28:2	2 Thess. 2:4	Dan. 9:16	Rom. 3:21	Micah 7:20	Rom. 15:8
Ezek. 28:34	2 Cor. 12:7	Dan. 11:36	2 Thess. 2:4	Nah. 2:1	Eph. 6:15
Ezek. 36:20	Rom. 2:24	Dan. 12:3	Phil. 2:15	Hab. 2:18–19	1 Cor. 12:2
Ezek. 36:26	2 Cor. 3:3	Hos. 6:2	1 Cor. 15:4	Zeph. 1:14–15	Rom. 2:5
Ezek. 36:27	1 Thess. 4:8	Hos. 6:5	Eph. 6:17	HAGGAI	/

OT TEXT	ALLUDED IN	OT TEXT	ALLUDED IN	OT TEXT	ALLUDED IN
Ezek. 37:14	1 Thess. 4:8	Hos. 10:12	2 Cor. 9:10	Zech. 8:17	1 Cor. 13:5
Ezek. 37:23	Titus 2:14	Hos. 11:1	Rom. 9:4	Zech. 8:23	1 Cor. 14:25
Dan. 2:18	Rom. 12:1	Joel 3:1	Titus 3:6	Zech. 9:11	1 Cor. 11:25
Dan. 2:22	1 Cor. 2:10	Joel 3:5	1 Cor. 1:2	Zech. 11:4	Rom. 8:36
Dan. 2:44	1 Cor. 15:24	Amos 3:13	2 Cor. 6:18	Zech. 12:1	1 Cor. 2:11
Dan. 2:47	1 Cor. 14:25	Amos 4:11	1 Cor. 3:15	Zech. 14:5	1 Thess. 3:13
Dan. 3:19–20	1 Cor. 13:3	Amos 5:13	Eph. 5:16	Mal. 1:7	1 Cor. 10:21
Dan. 3:35LXX	Eph. 1:6	Amos 5:15	Rom. 12:9	Mal. 1:11	2 Thess. 1:12
Dan. 4:27	Eph. 1:19	Amos 6:13	Phil. 1:11	Mal. 1:12	1 Cor. 10:21
Dan. 5:28	Rom. 9:28	OBADIAH	/	Mal. 2:10	1 Cor. 8:6
Dan. 6:21	2 Tim. 4:17	Jonah 2:1	1 Cor. 15:4	Mal. 3:17	Eph. 1:14
Dan. 6:28	2 Tim. 4:17	Micah 3:11	Rom. 2:17	Mal. 3:19	1 Cor. 3:13
Dan. 7:22	1 Cor. 6:2	Micah 5:4	Eph. 2:14		

Paul's Intertestamental Allusions (NT Order)

CHART 51

PAUL	INTERTEST.	PAUL	INTERTEST.	PAUL	INTERTEST.
Rom. 1:4	T. Levi. 18:7	Rom. 9:4	Sir. 44:12	1 Cor. 11:7	Sir. 17:3
Rom. 1:18	1 En. 91:7	Rom. 9:4	Sir. 44:18	1 Cor. 11:7	Wis. 2:23
Rom. 1:19–32	Wis. 13–15	Rom. 9:19	Wis. 12:12	1 Cor. 11:24	Wis. 16:6
Rom. 1:19	2 Bar. 54:17f.	Rom. 9:21	Wis. 15:7	1 Cor. 12:2	3 Macc. 4:16
Rom. 1:21	Wis. 13:1	Rom. 9:22	2 Bar. 59:6	1 Cor. 13:13	3 Ezra 4:38
Rom. 1:21	1 En. 99:8	Rom. 9:24	Jubil. 2:19	1 Cor. 15:19	2 Bar. 21:13
Rom. 1:23	Wis. 12:24	Rom. 9:31	Sir. 27:8	1 Cor. 15:29	2 Macc. 12:43f.
Rom. 1:23	Wis. 11:15	Rom. 9:31	Wis. 2:11	1 Cor. 15:32	Wis. 2:5f.
Rom. 1:25	As. Mos. 5:4	Rom. 10:6	4 Ezra 4:8	1 Cor. 15:34	Wis. 13:1
Rom. 1:26	T. Jos. 7:8	Rom. 10:6	Bar. 3:29	2 Cor. 5:14	Wis. 9:15
Rom. 2:3	Pss. Sol. 15:8	Rom. 10:7	Wis. 16:13	2 Cor. 11:14	L. A. E.
Rom. 2:4	Wis. 11:23	Rom. 11:4	2 Macc. 2:4	2 Cor. 12:2	T. Levi 2
Rom. 2:5	Pss. Sol. 9:5	Rom. 11:15	Sir. 10:20f.	2 Cor. 12:12	Wis. 10:16
Rom. 2:5	T. Levi 3:2	Rom. 11:25	4 Ezra 4:35f.	Gal. 1:5	4 Macc. 18:24
Rom. 2:11	Sir. 35:12f.	Rom. 11:25	T. Zeb. 9	Gal. 2:6	Sir. 35:13
Rom. 2:15	Wis. 17:11	Rom. 11:33	Wis. 17:1	Gal. 4:10	1 En. 72–82
Rom. 2:15	2 Bar. 57:2	Rom. 11:33	2 Bar. 14:8ff.	Gal. 6:1	Wis. 17:17
Rom. 2:15	T. Reu. 4:3	Rom. 12:1	T. Levi 3:6	Gal. 6:17	3 Macc. 2:29
Rom. 2:17	2 Bar. 48:22	Rom. 12:15	Sir. 7:34	Eph. 1:6	Sir. 45:1
Rom. 2:17	Pss. Sol. 17:1	Rom. 12:21	T. Benj. 4:3f.	Eph. 1:6	Sir. 46:13
Rom. 2:22	T. Levi 14:4	Rom. 13:1	Sir. 4:27	Eph. 1:17	Wis. 7:7
Rom. 2:29	Jubil. 1:23	Rom. 13:1	Wis. 6:3f.	Eph. 3:9	3 Macc. 2:3
Rom. 3:3	Pss. Sol. 8:28	Rom. 13:9	4 Macc. 2:6	Eph. 4:14	Sir. 5:9
Rom. 4:13	Jubil. 19:21	Rom. 13:10	Wis. 6:18	Eph. 4:24	Wis. 9:3
Rom. 4:13	2 Bar. 51:3	Rom. 15:4	1 Macc. 12:9	Eph. 6:13	Wis. 5:17
Rom. 4:13	Sir. 44:21	Rom. 15:8	Sir. 36:20	Eph. 6:14	Wis. 5:18
Rom. 4:13	2 Bar. 14:13	Rom. 15:16	4 Macc. 7:8	Eph. 6:16	Wis. 5:19, 21
Rom. 4:17	2 Bar. 48:8	Rom. 15:23	T. Dan 5:2	Eph. 6:24	Pss. Sol. 4:25
Rom. 4:17	Sir. 44:19	Rom. 16:27	4 Macc. 18:24	Phil. 4:5	Wis. 2:19
Rom. 5:3	T. Jos. 10:1	1 Cor. 1:24	Wis. 7:24f.	Phil. 4:13	Wis. 7:23
Rom. 5:5	Sir. 18:11	1 Cor. 2:9	Sir. 1:10	Phil. 4:18	Sir. 35:6
Rom. 5:12	4 Ezra 3:21f.,26	1 Cor. 2:9	Apoc. El.	Col. 1:22	1 En. 102:5
Rom. 5:12	2 Bar. 54:15	1 Cor. 2:16	Wis. 9:13	Col. 2:3	Sir. 1:24f.
Rom. 5:12	2 Bar. 23:4	1 Cor. 4:13	Tobit 5:19	Col. 2:3	1 En. 46:3
Rom. 5:12	Wis. 2:24	1 Cor. 4:14	Wis. 11:10	1 Thess. 1:3	4 Macc. 17:4
Rom. 5:16	4 Ezra 7:118f.	1 Cor. 4:17	1 En. 104:13	1 Thess. 3:11	Judith 12:8
Rom. 7:7	4 Macc. 2:5f.	1 Cor. 6:2	Wis. 3:8	1 Thess. 4:6	Sir. 5:3
Rom. 7:10	Pss. Sol. 14:1	1 Cor. 6:12	Sir. 37:28	1 Thess. 4:13	Wis. 3:18
Rom. 7:12	4 Ezra 9:37	1 Cor. 6:13	Sir. 36:18	1 Thess. 5:1	Wis. 8:8
Rom. 7:23	4 Ezra 7:72	1 Cor. 6:18	Sir. 23:17	1 Thess. 5:2	Wis. 18:14f.
Rom. 8:18	2 Bar. 15:8	1 Cor. 6:18	T. Reu. 5:5	1 Thess. 5:3	Wis. 17:14
Rom. 8:18	2 Bar. 32:6	1 Cor. 7:19	Sir. 32:23	1 Thess. 5:3	1 En. 62:4
Rom. 8:19	4 Ezra 7:11	1 Cor. 9:10	Sir. 6:19	1 Thess. 5:8	Wis. 5:18
Rom. 8:19	4 Ezra 7:75	1 Cor. 9:25	Wis. 4:2	2 Thess. 2:1	2 Macc. 2:7
Rom. 8:22	4 Ezra 10:9	1 Cor. 10:1	Wis. 19:7	1 Tim. 1:17	Tobit 13:7, 11
Rom. 8:28	Pss. Sol. 4:25	1 Cor. 10:20	Bar. 4:7	1 Tim. 1:17	Tobit 14:5
Rom. 9:4	2 Macc. 6:23	1 Cor. 10:23	Sir. 37:28	1 Tim. 2:2	2 Macc. 3:11

PAUL	INTERTEST.	PAUL	INTERTEST.	PAUL	INTERTEST.
1 Tim. 2:2	Bar. 1:11f.	2 Tim. 2:19	Sir. 17:26	2 Tim. 4:17	1 Macc. 2:60
1 Tim. 3:16	4 Macc. 6:31	2 Tim. 2:19	Sir. 23:10	Titus 2:11	2 Macc. 3:30
1 Tim. 6:15	2 Macc. 12:15	2 Tim. 2:19	Sir. 35:3	Titus 2:11	3 Macc. 6:9
1 Tim. 6:15	2 Macc. 13:4	2 Tim. 3:11	Pss. Sol. 4:23	Titus 3:4	Wis. 1:6
1 Tim. 6:15	3 Macc. 5:35	2 Tim. 3:16	4 Macc. 7:16	PHILEMON	
1 Tim. 6:15	Sir. 46:5	2 Tim. 4:8	Wis. 5:16		

Paul's Intertestamental Allusions (Extra-biblical order)

CHART 52

INTERTEST.		PAUL	INTERTEST.		PAUL
1 Esdras	4:38	1 Cor. 13:13	Baruch	1:11	1 Tim. 2:2
4 Esdras	3:21	Rom. 5:12		3:29	Rom. 10:6
	4:35	Rom. 11:25		4:7	1 Cor. 10:20
	7:11	Rom. 8:19	Sirach	1:10	1 Cor. 2:9
	7:72	Rom. 7:23		1:24	Col. 2:3
	7:75	Rom. 8:19		4:27	Rom. 13:1
	7:118	Rom. 5:16		5:3	1 Thess. 4:6
	8:60	Rom. 1:21		5:9	Eph. 4:14
	9:37	Rom. 7:12		6:19	1 Cor. 9:10
	10:9	Rom. 8:22		7:34	Rom. 12:15
1 Maccabees	2:60	2 Tim. 4:17		10:20	Rom. 11:15
	12:9	Rom. 15:4		17:3	1 Cor. 11:7
2 Maccabees	2:4	Rom. 11:4		17:26	2 Tim. 2:19
	2:7	2 Thess. 2:1		18:11	Rom. 5:5
	3:11	1 Tim. 2:2		23:10	2 Tim. 2:19
2 Maccabees	3:30	Titus 2:11		23:17	1 Cor. 6:18
	6:4	Rom. 1:28		27:8	Rom. 9:31
	6:23	Rom. 9:4		32:23	1 Cor. 7:19
	12:15	1 Tim. 6:15		35:3	2 Tim. 2:19
	12:43	1 Cor. 15:29		35:6	Phil. 4:18
	13:4	1 Tim. 6:15		35:12	Rom. 2:11
3 Maccabees	2:3	Eph. 3:9		35:15	Gal. 2:6
	2:29	Gal. 6:17		36:18	1 Cor. 6:13
	4:16	Rom. 1:28; 1 Cor. 12:2		36:20	Rom. 15:8
	5:35	1 Tim. 6:15		37:28	1 Cor. 6:12; 10:23
	6:9	Titus 2:11		44:12	Rom. 9:4
4 Maccabees	1:26	Rom. 1:29–31		44:18	Rom. 9:4
	2:5	Rom. 7:7		44:19	Rom. 4:17
	2:15	Rom. 1:29–31		44:21	Rom. 4:13
	6:31	1 Tim. 3:16		45:1	Eph. 1:6
	7:8	Rom. 15:16		46:5	1 Tim. 6:15
	7:16	1 Tim. 3:16		46:13	Eph. 1:6
	17:4	1 Thess. 1:3	Wisdom of Sol.	1:6	Titus 3:4
	18:24	Rom. 16:27; Gal. 1:5		2:5	1 Cor. 15:32
Tobit	5:19	1 Cor. 4:13		2:11	Rom. 9:31
	13:7, 11	1 Tim. 1:17		2:19	Phil. 4:5
	14:5	Gal. 4:4		2:23	1 Cor. 11:7
Judith	12:8	1 Thess. 3:11		2:24	Rom. 5:12
				3:8	1 Cor. 6:2

INTERTEST.		PAUL	INTERTEST.		PAUL
Wisdom of Sol.	3:18	1 Thess. 4:13		17:1	Rom. 2:17
	4:2	1 Cor. 9:25	Enoch	46:3	Col. 2:3
	5:16	2 Tim. 4:8		62:4	1 Thess. 5:3
	5:17	Eph. 6:13		72–82	Gal. 4:10
	5:18	Eph. 6:14; 1 Thess. 5:8		91:7	Rom. 1:18
	5:19, 21	Eph. 6:16		99:8	Rom. 1:21
	6:3	Rom. 13:1		102:5	Col. 1:22
	6:18	Rom. 13:10		104:13	1 Cor. 4:17
	7:7	Eph. 1:17	Ass. Mos.	5:4	Rom. 1:25
	7:23	Phil. 4:13	Apoc. Bar.	14:8	Rom. 11:33
	7:24	1 Cor. 1:24		14:13	Rom. 4:13
	8:8	1 Thess. 5:1		15:8	Rom. 8:18
	9:3	Eph. 4:24		21:13	1 Cor. 15:19
	9:13	1 Cor. 2:16		23:4	Rom. 5:12
	9:15	2 Cor. 5:1, 4		32:6	Rom. 8:18
	10:16	2 Cor. 12:12		48:8	Rom. 4:17
	11:10	1 Cor. 4:14		48:22	Rom. 2:17
	11:15	Rom. 1:23		51:3	Rom. 4:13
	11:23	Rom. 2:4		54:15	Rom. 5:12
	12:12	Rom. 9:19		54:17	Rom. 1:17
	12:24	Rom. 1:23		57:2	Rom. 2:15
	13–15	Rom. 1:19–32		59:6	Rom. 9:22
	13:1	Rom. 1:21; 1 Cor. 15:34	Apoc. Elijah		1 Cor. 2:9
	15:7	Rom. 9:21	Test. Reuben	4:3	Rom. 2:15
	16:6	1 Cor. 11:24		5:5	1 Cor. 6:18
	16:13	Rom. 10:7	Test. Levi	2	2 Cor. 12:2
	17:1	Rom. 11:33		3:2	Rom. 2:5
	17:11	Rom. 2:15		3:6	Rom. 12:1
	17:14	1 Thess. 5:3		14:4	Rom. 2:22
	17:17	Gal. 6:1		18:7	Rom. 1:4
	18:14	1 Thess. 5:2	Test. Zebulon	9	Rom. 11:25
	19:7	1 Cor. 10:1	Test. Dan	5:2	Rom. 15:33
Jubilees	1:23	Rom. 2:29	Test. Joseph	7:8	Rom. 1:26
	2:19	Rom. 9:24		10:1	Rom. 5:3
	19:21	Rom. 4:13	Test. Benj.	4:3	Rom. 12:21
Psalms of Sol.	4:23	2 Tim. 3:11	Life of Adam	9	2 Cor. 11:14
	4:25	Rom. 8:28; Eph. 6:24			
	8:28	Rom. 3:3			
	9:5	Rom. 2:5			
	14:1	Rom. 7:10			
	15:8	Rom. 2:3			

ROMANS: A Snapshot

CHART 53

Place of Writing	Paul is about to leave Greece (see 15:25–26). He was probably in Corinth; see his reference to Phoebe from Cenchrae (16:1), one of Corinth's two ports. Gaius, Paul's host, is mentioned (16:23), and was a Christian from Corinth who was baptized by Paul (1 Cor. 1:14)
Audience	Mostly Gentiles (1:5–6, 8–15; 6:19; 11:13; 15:14–24) but also Jews (2:17–29; 14:1–15:6; 16:7, 11)
Occasion	Paul did not found the church in Rome and had not been able to visit the congregations (1:13). His letter makes contact with the believers, introduces himself, announces plans for a visit (1:15; 15:22–29). In addition, there is division among the Roman congregations (16:17), probably along ethnic lines of Jews and Gentiles (1:16; 2:11; 3:9, 22; 10:12). Jews boast over Gentiles (2:17; 3:29), and Gentiles boast over Jews (11:17–18; 14:1). The expulsion of Jews from Rome under emperor Claudius in AD 49 (see Acts 18:1–2) and their return under Nero in AD 54 is often considered a geopolitical background for the congregations' ethnic problems.
Structure	Salutation (1:1–17) 　A　No divine favoritism for Jews regarding sin and against Gentiles 　　　regarding salvation (since it is apart from the Law) (1:18–5:21) 　　　　B　Apart from the Law? So what about lawful living (6–8; see 3:8)? 　　　　　C　No favoritism? So what about Israel's election (9–11; see 3:3)? 　　　　B'　Lawful living in an ungodly world (12–13) 　A'　No favoritism between Jewish and Gentile believers (14:1–16:23) Doxology (16:24–26)
Special Features	• The phrase "obedience of faith" envelops the letter (1:5; 16:26) • The phrase "righteousness of God" occurs nine times in Paul's letters, eight of which here in Romans: Rom. 1:17; 3:5, 21–22, 25–26; 10:3 (2x); 2 Cor. 5:21 • Paul says "by no means" (μὴ γένοιτο) fourteen times in his letters, ten times in Romans: Rom. 3:4, 6, 31; 6:2, 15; 7:7, 13; 9:14; 11:1, 11; 1 Cor. 6:15; Gal. 2:17; 3:21; 6:14 • "Diatribe style" (dialogue, Q&A): 2:1–5, 17–24; 9:19–21; 11:17–24; 14:4, 10 • There were at least seven house churches in Rome (16:3–5, 10–11, 14–15) • Thirty-five names mentioned in 16:1–24
Purpose(s)	1. *Apologetics*: To defend the gospel and dispel doubts about his mission in light of various accusations and misunderstandings especially from Jews (see the four questions in 3:1–8; dress-rehearsal for his defense in Jerusalem?). 　2. *Pastoral*: To unite a church threatened by division (14:1; 15:7; 16:17) caused by a form of early Christian anti-Semitism (see 11:18). Paul's gospel of no divine favoritism for Jews finds direct application for Gentiles who are not to disregard the "weak" (see "judge" language in chs. 2 and 14). 　3. *Mission*: To prepare the Roman congregation as a base for future mission work in Spain (15:24, 28).

Key Words in Romans

CHART 54

		JEWS AND GENTILES
circumcision	περιτομή	31xPaul: Rom. 2:25 (2x), 26, 27, 28, 29; 3:1, 30; 4:9, 10 (2x), 11, 12 (2x); 15:8; also 1 Cor. 7:19; Gal 2:7, 8, 9, 12; 5:6, 11; 6:15; Eph. 2:11; Phil. 3:3, 5; Col. 2:11; 3:11; 4:11; Titus 1:10
to circumcise	περιτέμνω	9xPaul: 1 Cor. 7:18; Gal. 2:3; 5:2, 3; 6:12, 13; Col. 2:11
uncircumcision	ἀκροβυστία	20xNT: Acts 11:3; Rom. 2:25, 26 (2x), 27; 3:30; 4:9, 10 (2x), 11 (2x), 12; also 1 Cor. 7:18, 19; Gal. 2:7; 5:6; 6:15; Eph. 2:11; Col. 2:13; 3:11
Greek	Ἕλλην	6xRom.; singular: 1:16; 2:9, 20; 10:12; plural: 1:14; 3:9 (13xPaul)
non-Greek	βάρβαρος	6xNT: Acts 28:2, 4; Rom. 1:14; 1 Cor. 14:11; Col. 3:11
Israel	Ἰσραήλ	17xPaul: Rom. 9:6, 27, 31; 10:19, 21; 11:2, 7, 25, 26; 1 Cor. 10:18; 2 Cor. 3:7, 13; Gal. 6:16; Eph. 2:12; Phil. 3:5
Israelite	Ἰσραηλίτης	3xPaul: Rom. 9:4; 11:1; 2 Cor. 11:22
Jew(s)	Ἰουδαῖος	26xPaul; singular: Rom. 1:16; 2:9, 10, 17, 28, 29; 3:1; 10:12; Gal. 2:14; 3:28; Col 3:11; plural: Rom. 3:9, 29; 9:24; 1 Cor. 1:22, 23, 24; 9:20; 10:32; 12:13; 2 Cor. 11:24; Gal. 2:13, 15; 1 Thess. 2:14
Jew(s) and Greek(s)		Rom. 1:16; 2:9, 10; 3:9, 29; 9:24; 10:12; 1 Cor. 1:22, 24; 10:32; 12:13; Gal. 3:28; Col. 3:11
kinsman	συγγενής	4xPaul: Rom. 9:3; 16:7, 11, 21
law	νόμος	74xRom.: 2:12 (2x), 13 (2x), 14 (4x), 15, 17, 18, 20, 23 (2x), 25 (2x), 26, 27 (2x); 3:19 (2x), 20 (2x), 21 (2x), 27 (2x), 28, 31 (2x); 4:13, 14, 15 (2x), 16; 5:13 (2x), 20; 6:14, 15; 7:1 (2x), 2 (2x), 3, 4, 5, 6, 7 (3x), 8, 9, 12, 14, 16, 21, 22, 23 (3x), 25 (2x); 8:2 (2x), 3, 4, 7; 9:31 (2x); 10:4, 5; 13:8, 10 (121xPaul)
under the law	ὑπὸ νόμον	Rom. 6:14-15; 1 Cor. 9:20; Gal. 3:23; 4:4, 5, 21; 5:18
giving of the law	νομοθεσία	1xNT: Rom. 9:4 (see also 2 Macc. 6:23; 4 Macc. 5:35; *Jos. A.J.* 6.93)
commandment	ἐντολή	14xPaul: Rom. 7:8, 9, 10, 11, 12, 13; 13:9; 1 Cor. 7:19; 14:37; Eph. 2:15; 6:2; Col. 4:10; 1 Tim. 6:14; Titus 1:14; see verb in Acts 13:47
order	ἐπιταγή	7xNT: Rom. 16:26; 1 Cor. 7:6, 25; 2 Cor. 8:8; 1 Tim. 1:1; Titus 1:3; 2:15
work	ἔργον	15xRom.: 2:6, 7 (ἔργου ἀγαθοῦ), 15; 3:20, 27, 28; 4:2, 6; 9:12, 32; 11:6; 13:3, 12; 14:20; 15:18 (68xPaul)
work(s) of the law	ἔργα νόμου	9xNT: Rom. 3:20, 28; Gal. 2:16 (3x); 3:2, 5, 10; singular in Rom. 2:15
nations / Gentiles	ἔθνος	29xRom.: 1:5, 13; 2:14, 24; 3:29 (2x); 4:17, 18; 9:24, 30; 10:19 (2x); 11:11, 12, 13, 25; 15:9 (2x), 10, 11, 12 (2x), 16 (2x), 18, 27; 16:4, 26 [all plural except 10:19] (54xPaul)
non-Greek	βάρβαρος	6xNT: Acts 28:2,4; Rom. 1:14; 1 Cor. 14:11; Col. 3:11
		SIN PROBLEM / JUDGMENT
boast (verb)	καυχάομαι	37xNT: Rom. 2:17, 23; 5:2, 3, 11; 1 Cor. 1:29, 31 (2x); 3:21; 4:7; 13:3; 2 Cor. 5:12; 7:14; 9:2; 10:8, 13, 15, 16, 17 (2x); 11:12, 16, 18 (2x), 30 (2x); 12:1, 5 (2x), 6, 9; Gal. 6:13, 14; Eph. 2:9; Phil. 3:3; James 1:9; 4:16; verb: κατακαυχάομαι = 4xNT: Rom. 11:18 (2x): James 2:13; 3:14
boast (noun)	καύχημα	11xNT: Rom. 4:2; 1 Cor. 5:6; 9:15, 16; 2 Cor. 1:14; 5:12; 9:3; Gal. 6:4; Phil. 1:26; 2:16; Heb. 3:6

condemn (verb)	κατακρίνω	5xPaul: Rom. 2:1; 8:3, 34; 14:23; 1 Cor. 11:32
death	θάνατος	22xRom.: 1:32; 5:10, 12 (2x), 14, 17, 21; 6:3, 4, 5, 9, 16, 21, 23; 7:5, 10, 13 (2x), 24; 8:2, 6, 38 (47xPaul)
despise (verb)	ἐξουθενέω	2xRom.: 14:3, 10 (8xPaul)
die (verb)	ἀποθνήσκω	3xRom.: 5:6, 7 (2x), 8, 15; 6:2, 7, 8, 9, 10 (2x); 7:2, 3, 6, 10; 8:13, 34; 14:7, 8 (3x), 9, 15 (42xPaul)
disobey	ἀπειθέω	5xPaul: Rom. 2:8; 10:21; 11:30, 31; 15:31
division	διχοστασία	2xPaul: Rom. 16:17; Gal. 5:20
favoritism	προσωπολημψία	3xPaul: Rom. 2:11; Eph. 6:9; Col. 3:25
difference	διαστολή	3xPaul: Rom. 3:22; 10:12; 1 Cor. 14:7
flesh	σάρξ	26xRom.: 1:3; 2:28; 3:20; 4:1; 6:19; 7:5, 18, 25; 8:3 (3x), 4, 5 (2x), 6, 7, 8, 9, 12 (2x), 13; 9:3, 5, 8; 11:14; 13:14 (91xPaul)
judge (verb)	κρίνω	18x Rom. 2:1 (3x), 3, 12, 16, 27; 3:4, 6, 7; 14:3, 4, 5 (2x), 10, 13 (2x), 22 (41xPaul)
judgment	κρίμα	6x Rom.: 2:2, 3; 3:8; 5:16; 11:33; 13:2 (12xPaul)
sin (noun)	ἁμαρτία	48xRom.: 3:9, 20; 4:7,8; 5:12 (2x), 13 (2x), 20, 21; 6:1,2, 6 (2x), 7, 10, 11, 12, 13, 14, 16, 17, 20, 22, 23; 7:5, 7 (2x), 8 (2x), 9, 11, 13 (3x), 14, 17, 20, 23, 25; 8:2, 3 (3x), 10; 11:27; 14:23 (64xPaul)
sin (verb)	ἁμαρτάνω	7x Rom.: 2:12 (2x); 3:23; 5:12, 14, 16; 6:15 (17xPaul)
slavery	δουλεία	4xPaul: Rom. 8:15, 21; Gal. 4:24; 5:1
be a slave to	δουλεύω	7xRom.: 6:6; 7:6, 25; 9:12; 12:11; 14:18; 16:18 (17xPaul)
transgressor	παραβάτης	2xRom.: 2:25, 27; transgression/παράβασις=2xRom.: 2:23; 4:15; 5:14
unrighteousness	ἀδικία	7xRom.: 1:18 (2x), 29; 2:8; 3:5; 6:13; 9:14; adj.: ἄδικος = 1xRom.: 3:5
unbelief	ἀπιστία	4xRom.: 3:3; 4:20; 11:20, 23; verb: ἀπιστέω = 1xRom.: 3:3
SALVATION / SOLUTION		
Abraham	Ἀβραάμ	19xPaul: Rom. 4:1, 2, 3, 9, 12, 13, 16; 9:7; 11:1; 2 Cor. 11:22; Gal. 3:6, 7, 8, 9, 14, 16, 18, 29; 4:22
baptism	βάπτισμα	2xPaul: Rom. 6:4; Eph. 4:5
	βαπτισμός	4xNT: Mark 7:4; Col. 2:12; Heb. 6:2; 9:10
to baptize	βαπτίζω	13xPaul: Rom. 6:3 (2x); 1 Cor. 1:13, 14, 15, 16 (2x), 17; 10:2; 12:13; 15:29; Gal. 3:27
adoption	υἱοθεσία	5xNT: Rom. 8:15, 23; 9:4; Gal. 4:5; Eph. 1:5
call / be called (verb)	καλέω	8xRom.: 4:17; 8:30 [2x]; 9:7, 12, 24, 25, 26 (33xPaul)
calling (noun)	κλῆσις	9xPaul: Rom. 11:29; 1 Cor. 1:26; 7:20; Eph. 1:18; 4:1, 4; Phil. 3:14; 2 Thess. 1:11; 2 Tim. 1:9; adjective: κλητός = 4xRom.: 1:1, 6, 7; 8:28
covenant	διαθήκη	9xPaul: Rom. 9:4; 11:27; 1 Cor. 11:25; 2 Cor. 3:6, 14; Gal. 3:15, 17; 4:24; Eph. 2:12
election (noun)	ἐκλογή	5xPaul: Rom. 9:11; 11:5, 7, 28; 1 Thess. 1:4
elected (adjective)	ἐκλεκτός	6xPaul: Rom. 8:33; 16:13; Col. 3:12; 1 Tim. 5:21; 2 Tim. 2:10; Titus 1:1
faith (noun)	πίστις	40xRom.: 1:5, 8, 12, 17 (3x); 3:3, 22, 25, 26, 27, 28, 30 (2x); 4:5, 9, 11, 12, 13, 14, 16 (2x), 19, 20; 5:1, 2; 9:30, 32; 10:6, 8, 17; 11:20; 12:3, 6; 14:1, 22, 23 (2x); 16:26 (142xPaul)
faith, to have (verb)	πιστεύω	21xRom.: 1:16; 3:2, 22; 4:3, 5, 11, 17, 18, 24; 6:8; 9:33; 10:4, 9, 10, 11, 14 (2x), 16; 13:11; 14:2; 15:13 (54xPaul)

faith of Christ	πίστις ['Iης.] Χριστοῦ	6xNT: Rom. 3:22, 26; Gal. 2:16; 3:22; Eph. 3:12; Phil. 3:9
foreknow (verb)	προγινώσκω	2xPaul: Rom. 8:29; 11:2
freedom (noun)	ἐλευθερία	7xPaul: Rom. 8:21; 1 Cor. 10:29; 2 Cor. 3:17; Gal. 2:4; 5:1, 13
to free (verb)	ἐλευθερόω	5xPaul: Rom. 6:18, 22; 8:2, 21; Gal. 5:1
Gospel	εὐαγγέλιον	60xPaul: Rom. 1:1, 9, 16; 2:16; 10:16; 11:28; 15:16, 19; 16:25; 1 Cor. 4:15; 9:12, 14 (2x), 18 (2x), 23; 15:1; 2 Cor. 2:12; 4:3, 4; 8:18; 9:13; 10:14; 11:4, 7; Gal. 1:6, 17, 11; 2:2, 5, 7, 14; Eph. 1:13; 3:6; 6:15, 19; Phil. 1:5, 7, 12, 16, 27 (2x); 2:22; 4:3, 15; Col. 1:5, 23; 1 Thess. 1:5; 2:2, 4, 8f; 3:2; 2 Thess. 1:8; 2:14; 1 Tim. 1:11; 2 Tim. 1:8, 10; 2:8; Philem. 1:13
grace (noun)	χάρις	24xRom.: 1:5, 7; 3:24; 4:4, 16; 5:2, 15 (2x), 17, 20, 21; 6:1, 14, 15, 17; 7:25; 11:5, 6 (3x); 12:3, 6; 15:15; 16:20 (100xPaul; 155xNT)
give freely (verb)	χαρίζομαι	1xRom.: 8:32 (16xPaul)
gift (noun)	χάρισμα	16xNT: Rom. 1:11; 5:15, 16; 6:23; 11:29; 12:6; 1 Cor. 1:7; 7:7; 12:4, 9, 28, 30f; 2 Cor. 1:11; 1 Tim. 4:14; 2 Tim. 1:6; 1 Peter 4:10
heir	κληρονόμος	8xPaul: Rom. 4:13, 14; 8:17; Gal. 3:29; 4:1, 7; Titus 3:7
justify, to make right (verb)	δικαιόω	24xPaul: Rom. 2:13; 3:4, 20, 24, 26, 28, 30; 4:2, 5; 5:1, 9; 6:7; 8:30 ... [see below: "to make right, justify"]
justification	δικαίωσις	2xPaul: Rom. 4:25; 5:18 [see below: "be put right"]
kingdom of God	ἡ βασιλεία τοῦ θεοῦ	4xPaul: Rom. 14:17; 1 Cor. 4:20; Col. 4:11; 2 Thess. 1:5; see Acts 14:22; 19:8; 20:25; 28:23, 31
love (God's)	ἀγάπη	5:5, 8; 8:39; "love of Christ": Rom. 8:35; "love of the Spirit": 15:30
mercy	ἔλεος	3xRom.: 9:23; 11:31; 15:9 (10xPaul)
have mercy (verb)	ἐλεέω	7x Rom.: 9:15, 18; 11:30, 31, 32; 12:8 (12xPaul)
obedience (noun)	ὑπακοή	7xRom.: 1:5; 5:19; 6:16; 15:18; 16:19, 26 (11xPaul)
obedience of faith	ὑπακοή πίστεως	2xRom.: 1:5; 16:26
obey (verb)	ὑπακούω	4xRom.: 6:12, 16, 17; 10:16 (11xPaul)
predestine (verb)	προορίζω	5xPaul: Rom. 8:29, 30; 1 Cor. 2:7; Eph. 1:5, 11
promise, to promise	ἐπαγγελία, ἐπαγγέλλομαι	31xPaul: Rom. 4:13, 14, 16, 20, 21; 9:4, 8, 9; 15:8; 2 Cor. 1:20; 7:1; Gal. 3:14, 16, 17, 18 (2x), 19, 21, 22, 29; 4:23, 28; Eph. 1:13; 2:12; 3:6; 6:2; 1 Tim. 2:10; 4:8; 2 Tim. 1:1; Titus 1:2
reconciliation (noun)	καταλλαγή	4xNT: Rom. 5:11; 11:15; 2 Cor. 5:18, 19
reconcile (verb)	καταλλάσσω	6xNT: Rom. 5:10; 1 Cor. 7:11; 2 Cor. 5:18, 19, 20
remnant	λεῖμμα	1xNT: Rom. 11:5; noun: ὑπόλειμμα = 1xNT: Rom. 9:27 (Isa 10:22)
to make right, justify (verb)	δικαιόω	24xPaul: Rom. 2:13; 3:4, 20, 24, 26, 28, 30; 4:2, 5; 5:1, 9; 6:7; 8:30 (2x), 33; 1 Cor. 4:4; 6:11; Gal. 2:16 (3x), 17; 3:8, 11, 24; 5:4; 1 Tim. 3:16; Titus 3:7
be put right, justification	δικαίωσις	2xPaul: Rom. 4:25; 5:18
righteous (adjective)	δίκαιος	7xRom.: 1:17; 2:13; 3:10, 26; 5:7, 19; 7:12 (17xPaul)
righteousness (noun)	δικαιοσύνη	34xRom.: 1:17; 3:5, 21, 22, 25, 26; 4:3, 5, 6, 9, 11 (2x), 13, 22; 5:17, 21; 6:13, 16, 18, 19, 20; 8:10; 9:30 (3x); 31; 10:3 (3x), 4, 5, 6, 10; 14:17 (58xPaul)
righteousness of God	δικαιοσύνη θεοῦ	9xPaul: Rom. 1:17; 3:5, 21, 22, 25, 26; 10:3 (2x); 2 Cor. 5:21
righteous deed	δικαίωμα	5xPaul: Rom. 1:32; 2:26; 5:16, 18; 8:4 (δικαίωσις = Rom. 4:25; 5:18)

save (verb)	σῴζω	8xRom.: 5:9, 10; 8:24; 9:27; 10:9, 13; 11:14, 26 (29xPaul)
salvation (noun)	σωτηρία	5xRom.: 1:16; 10:1, 10; 11:11; 13:11 (18xPaul)
Spirit	πνεῦμα	34xRom.: 1:4, 9; 2:29; 5:5; 7:6; 8:2, 4, 5 (2x), 6, 9 (3x), 10, 11 (2x), 13, 14, 15 (2x), 16 (2x), 23, 26 (2x), 27; 9:1; 11:8; 12:11; 14:17; 15:13, 16, 19, 30 (146xPaul)
WORDS NOT FOUND IN ROMANS (sample)		
(2nd) coming	παρουσία	14xPaul: 1 Cor. 15:23; 16:17; 2 Cor. 7:6, 7; 10:10; Phil. 1:26; 2:12; 1 Thess. 2:19; 3:13; 4:15; 5:23; 2 Thess. 2:1, 8, 9
cross	σταυρός	10xPaul: 1 Cor. 1:17, 18; Gal. 5:11; 6:12, 14; Eph. 2:16; Phil. 2:8; 3:18; Col. 1:20; 2:14 (but see συσταυρόω in Rom. 6:6; Gal. 2:19)
to crucify	σταυρόω	8xPaul: 1 Cor. 1:13, 23; 2:2, 8; 2 Cor. 13:4; Gal. 3:1; 5:24; 6:14
demons	δαιμόνια	5xPaul: 1 Cor. 10:20, 21; 1 Tim. 4:1
devil	διάβολος	8xPaul: Eph. 4:27; 6:11; 1 Tim. 3:6, 7, 11; 2 Tim. 2:26; 3:3; Titus 2:3
down payment	ἀρραβών	3xPaul: 2 Cor. 1:21-22; 5:5; Eph. 1:14
fornication, fornicate	πορνεία, πορνεύω	6x Paul: 1 Cor. 5:9, 10, 11; 6:9, 18; 10:8; Eph. 5:5; 1 Tim. 1:10
head of the church	(Jesus)	Eph. 1:22; 4:15; 5:23; Col. 1:18; 2:10, 19; see 1 Cor. 11:3
savior	σωτήρ	Eph. 5:23; Phil. 3:20; 1 Tim. 1:1; 2:3; 4:10; 2 Tim. 1:10; Titus 1:3; etc.
temple	ναός	8xPaul: 1 Cor. 3:16, 17; 6:19; 2 Cor. 6:16; Eph. 2:21; 2 Thess. 2:4

1 CORINTHIANS: A Snapshot

CHART 55

Audience	Former pagans in Corinth (and beyond, 1:2b) who practiced idolatry (12:2)
Occasion	Paul planted the church at the end of his second mission journey (Acts 18:1–17) and stayed eighteen months (18:11). After he left, Paul received two oral reports about problems in the church (1 Cor. 1:11; 16:17) and responded to them in the first six chapters. But the Corinthians also wrote a letter to Paul which is lost to us, and in which they addressed various issues that Paul dealt with in chapters 7–16. Timothy brought Paul's letter to the Corinthians (4:17; 16:10) and, while there, helped the church work through the problems.

Structure	Salutation (1:1–9)
	    A. The **cross**, true and false wisdom and divisions in Corinth (1:10–4:17)
	    B. True and false **sexuality** (4:18–7:40)
	    C. True and false **worship** (8:1–14:40)
	    D. The **resurrection** and consummation (15:1–58)
	    E. The **collection** and other final matters (16:1–18)
	Subscription (16:19–24)

Special Features	• A previous letter of Paul to the Corinthians is mentioned (5:9) • Corinthian slogans (1:12; 6:12, 13; 7:1; 8:1, 4, 5-6, 8; 11:2), e.g., 1:12 "I follow Paul … "; 6:12 "Everything is permissible for me" (NIV 1984) • Phrase 'Now concerning' (Περὶ δὲ; 7:1, 25; 8:1; 12:1; 16:1, 12) indicates issues mentioned by the Corinthians in their letter to Paul • Paul asks eleven times: "Do you not know …?" (Οὐκ οἴδατε ὅτι; 3:16; 5:6; 6:2–3, 9, 15–16, 19; 9:13, 24; 12:2; elsewhere only in Rom 6:16), implying that despite their pride in knowledge, they lack significant understanding. • Pervasive use of A-B-A structure, e.g., A Fornication (5) – B Lawsuits (6:1–8) – A Fornication (6:9–20); also 1:10–3:4; 3:5–4:17; 7:1–40; 8:1–11:1; 12:4–31; 13:1–13; 14:1–40; 15:1–58 • See extensive parallels with 1 Timothy in chart 68
Purpose(s)	1. *Apologetics*: Especially at the beginning of the letter (chs. 1-4) Paul defends his authority. Some in the church oppose Paul in favor of Peter and Apollos as if these leaders would disagree with each other (1:12). Paul reminds them that he is the "father" of the church (4:15) who has the right to direct them in their affairs (4:3, 9–13; 7:40; 9:1; 12:28; 14:37). This defense of his authority provides the basis for all other appeals in the following chapters of the letter. 2. *Pastoral*: There is not only division between Paul and the church but also schisms among the members themselves (σχίσματα in 1:10; 11:18; 12:25). Paul aims to unite the church by transforming her pagan values in light of the crucified and risen Lord (*kurios* [κύριος] occurs 66x in 1 Cor.; 274x in Paul's letters).

Key Words in 1-2 Corinthians

CHART 56

CROSS / KNOWLEDGE / WISDOM — IGNORANCE / FOOLISHNESS		
boast (verb)	καυχάομαι	6x 1Cor.: 1:29, 31; 3:21; 4:7; [13:3 (but here it means: to burn!)] (35xPaul)
puff/blow up	φυσιόω	7xNT: 1 Cor. 4:6, 18, 19; 5:2; 8:1; 13:4; Col. 2:18
cross	σταυρός	10xPaul: 1 Cor. 1:17, 18; Gal. 5:11; 6:12, 14; Eph. 2:16; Phil. 2:8; 3:18; Col. 1:20; 2:14
crucify / be cruc.	σταυρόω	8xPaul: 1 Cor. 1:13, 23; 2:2, 8; 2 Cor. 13:4; Gal. 3:1; 5:24; 6:14
debater	συζητητής	1xNT: 1 Cor. 1:20
scribe	γραμματεύς	5x Acts/Paul: Acts 4:5; 6:12; 19:35; 23:9; 1 Cor. 1:20
foolish	μωρός	6xPaul: 1 Cor. 1:25, 27; 3:18; 4:10; 2 Tim. 2:23; Titus 3:9
foolish	ἄφρων	8xPaul: Rom. 2:20; 1 Cor. 15:36; 2 Cor. 11:16, 19; 12:6, 11; Eph. 5:17
foolishness	μωρία	5x NT: 1 Cor. 1:18, 21, 23; 2:14; 3:19
show to be f.	μωραίνω	4xNT: Matt. 5:13; Luke 14:34; Rom. 1:22; 1 Cor. 1:20
wisdom	σοφία	17x1 Cor.: 1:17, 19, 20, 21 [2x], 24, 30; 2:1, 4, 5, 6, 7, 13; 3:19; 12:8; 1x 2 Cor.: 1:12 (28xPaul)
wise	σοφός	11x1 Cor.: 1:19, 20, 25, 26, 27; 3:10, 18 (2x), 19, 20; 6:5 (20xNT, 16xPaul)
knowledge	γνῶσις	16x1–2 Cor.: 1 Cor. 1:5; 8:1 [2x], 7, 10, 11; 12:8; 13:2, 8; 14:6; 2 Cor. 2:14; 4:6; 6:6; 8:7; 10:5; 11:6 (29xNT, 23xPaul)
to know	γινώσκω	16x 1 Cor.: 1:21; 2:8, 11, 14, 16; 3:20; 4:19; 8:2, 3; 13:9, 12; 14:7, 9 (30xPaul)
to know	ἐπιγινώσκω	9x1–2 Cor.: 1 Cor. 13:12 [2x]; 14:37; 16:18; 2 Cor. 1:13 [2x], 14; 6:9; 13:5
to know	οἶδα	25x1 Cor.: 1:16; 2:2, 11, 12; 3:16; 5:6; 6:2, 3, 9, 15, 16, 19; 7:16 [2x]; 8:1, 4; 9:13, 24; 11:3; 12:2; 13:2; 14:11, 16; 15:58; 16:15 (103xPaul)
"do you not k."	οὐκ οἴδατε ὅτι	12xNT: Rom. 6:16; (11:2); 1 Cor. 3:16; 5:6; 6:2,3,9, 15, 16, 19; 9:24; James 4:4
be ignorant	ἀγνοέω	16xPaul: Rom. 1:13; 2:4; 6:3; 7:1; 10:3; 11:25; 1 Cor. 10:1; 12:1; 14:38; 2 Cor. 1:8; 2:11; 6:9; Gal. 1:22; 1 Thess. 4:13; 1 Tim. 1:13
ignorance	ἀγνωσία	2xNT: 1 Cor. 15:34; 1 Peter 2:15
mind	νοῦς	7x1 Cor.: 1:10; 2:16; 14:14, 15, 19 (21xPaul)
opinion	γνώμη	9xNT: Acts 20:3; 1 Cor. 1:10; 7:25, 40; 2 Cor. 8:10; Philem. 1:14; Rev. 17:13, 17
spiritual (things)	πνευματικός	15x1 Cor.: 2:13[2x], 15; 3:1; 9:11; 10:3, 4[2x]; 12:1; 14:1, 37; 15:44[2x], 46 [2x]
weak	ἀσθενής	11x1 Cor.: 1:25, 27; 4:10; 8:7, 9, 10; 9:22; 11:30; 12:22 (15xPaul)
weakness	avsqe,neia	8x1–2 Cor.: 1 Cor. 2:3; 15:43; 2 Cor. 11:30; 12:5, 9, 10; 13:4 (12xPaul)
to be weak	ἀσθενέω	9x1–2 Cor.: 1 Cor. 8:11, 12; 2 Cor. 11:21, 29 (2x); 12:10; 13:3, 4, 9 (16xPaul)
power	δύναμις	15x1 Cor.: 1:18, 24; 2:4, 5; 4:19, 20; 5:4; 6:14; 12:10, 28, 29; 14:11; 15:24, 43, 56 (49xPaul)
strong	ἰσχυρός	5xPaul: 1 Cor. 1:25, 27; 4:10; 10:22; 2 Cor. 10:10

MARRIAGE — SEXUAL IMMORALITY / TO JUDGE — LAWSUIT		
body	σῶμα	46x1 Cor.: 1 Cor. 5:3; 6:13 [2x], 15, 16, 18 [2x], 19, 20; 7:4 [2x], … (91xPaul)
to marry	γαμέω	12xPaul: 1 Cor. 7:9 [2x], 10, 28 [2x], 33, 34, 36, 39; 1 Tim. 4:3; 5:11, 14
virgin	παρθένος	7xPaul: 1 Cor. 7:25, 28, 34, 36, 37, 38; 2 Cor. 11:2
freedom / right	ἐξουσία	10x 1 Cor.: 7:37; 8:9; 9:4, 5, 6, 12, 18; 11:10; 15:24 (27xPaul)
shame	ἐντροπή	2xNT: 1 Cor. 6:5; 15:34 (see also noun: ἀτιμία in 11:14; 15:43)
to be ashamed	καταισχύνω	10xPaul: Rom. 5:5; 9:33; 10:11; 1 Cor. 1:27; 11:4, 5, 22; 2 Cor. 7:14; 9:4
fornication	πορνεία	10xPaul: 1 Cor. 5:1; 6:13, 18; 7:2; 2 Cor. 12:21; Gal. 5:19; Eph. 5:3; Col. 3:5; 1 Thess. 4:3
fornicator	πόρνος	6x Paul: 1 Cor. 5:9, 10, 11; 6:9; Eph 5:5; 1 Tim. 1:10
to fornicate	πορνεύω	3xPaul: 1 Cor. 6:18; 10:8 [2x]; prostitute (πόρνη) = 2xPaul: 1 Cor. 6:15, 16
adulterer	μοιχός	3xNT: Luke 18:11; 1 Cor. 6:9; Heb. 13:4
commit adultery	μοιχεύω	3xPaul: Rom. 2:22; 13:9
effeminate (adj.)	μαλακός	4xNT: Matt 11:8; Luke 7:25; 1 Cor. 6:9
sodomite	ἀρσενοκοίτης	2xNT: 1 Cor. 6:9; 1 Tim. 1:10
to judge	κρίνω	17x1 Cor.: 2:2; 4:5; 5:3, 12 [2x], 13; 6:1, 2[2x], 3, 6; 7:37; 10:15, 29; 11:13, 31, 32 (41xPaul)
to examine	ἀνακρίνω	10xPaul: 1 Cor. 2:14, 15; 4:3, 4; 9:3; 10:25, 27; 14:24
to differentiate	διακρίνομαι	7xPaul: Rom. 4:20; 14:23; 1 Cor. 4:7; 6:5; 11:29, 31; 14:29
differentiation	διάκρισις	2xPaul: Rom. 14:1; 1 Cor. 12:10
lawsuit, judgment	κρίμα	12xPaul: Rom. 2:2, 3; 3:8; 5:16; 11:33; 13:2; 1 Cor. 6:7; 11:29, 34; Gal. 5:10; 1 Tim. 3:6; 5:12; lawsuit, judgment (κριτήριον) = 2xPaul : 1 Cor. 6:2,4
master, lord	κύριος	66x1 Cor.: 1:2, 3, 7, 8, 9, 10, 31; 2:8, 16; 3:5, 20; 4:4, 5, 17, 19; … (274xPaul)
IDOL, IDOL FOOD		
love (noun)	ἀγάπη	10x1 Cor.: 4:21; 8:1; 13:1, 2, 3, 4 [3x], 8, 13; 14:1; 16:14, 24 (75xPaul)
beloved	ἀγαπητός	6x1–2 Cor.: 1 Cor. 4:14, 17; 10:14; 15:58; 2 Cor. 7:1; 12:19 (27xPaul)
to love (verb 1)	ἀγαπάω	6x 1–2 Cor.: 1 Cor. 2:9; 8:3; 2 Cor. 9:7; 11:11; 12:15 (2x) (34xPaul)
to love (verb 2)	φιλέω	2xPaul: 1 Cor. 16:22; Titus 3:15
to edify	οἰκοδομέω	9xPaul: Rom. 15:20; 1 Cor. 8:1,10; 10:23; 14:4[2x], 17; Gal. 2:18; 1 Thess. 5:11
edification	οἰκοδομή	9x1–2 Cor.: 1 Cor. 3:9; 14:3, 5, 12, 26; 2 Cor. 5:1; 10:8; 12:19; 13:10 (15xPaul)
idolatry	εἰδωλολατρία	4xNT: 1 Cor. 10:14; Gal. 5:20; Col. 3:5; 1 Peter 4:3
idol's temple	εἰδωλεῖον	1xNT: 1 Cor. 8:10
idolator	εἰδωλολάτρης	7xNT: 1 Cor. 5:10, 11; 6:9; 10:7; Eph. 5:5; Rev. 21:8; 22:15
idol	εἴδωλον	11xNT: Acts 7:41; 15:20; Rom. 2:22; 1 Cor. 8:4, 7; 10:19; 12:2; 2 Cor. 6:16; 1 Thess. 1:9; 1 John 5:21; Rev. 9:20
food for idols	εἰδωλόθυτος	9xNT: Acts 15:29; 21:25; 1 Cor. 8:1, 4, 7, 10; 10:19; Rev. 2:14, 20
meat for idols	ἱερόθυτος	1xNT: 1 Cor. 10:28
sacrifice	θυσία	5xPaul: Rom. 12:1; 1 Cor. 10:18; Eph. 5:2; Phil. 2:17; 4:18
altar	θυσιαστήριον	4xPaul: Rom. 11:3; 1 Cor. 9:13; 10:18
demon	δαιμόνιον	5xPaul: 1 Cor. 10:20 [2x], 21 [2x]; 1 Tim. 4:1

PROPHECY — SPEAKING IN TONGUES		
gift / ministry	χάρισμα	16xPaul; singular: Rom. 1:11; 5:15, 16; 6:23; 1 Cor. 1:7; 7:7; 2 Cor. 1:11; 1 Tim. 4:14; 2 Tim. 1:6; plural: Rom. 11:29; 12:6; 12:4, 9, 28, 30, 31
varieties	διαιρέσεις	3xPaul: 1 Cor. 12:4, 5, 6
prophecy	προφητεία	9xPaul: Rom. 12:6; 1 Cor. 12:10; 13:2,8; 14:6,22; 1 Thess. 5:20; 1 Tim. 1:18; 4:14
to prophecy	προφητεύω	11xPaul: 1 Cor. 11:4, 5; 13:9; 14:1, 3, 4, 5 [2x], 24, 31, 39
prophet	προφήτης	14xPaul: Rom. 1:2; 3:21; 11:3; 1 Cor. 12:28, 29; 14:29, 32 [2x], 37; Eph. 2:20; 3:5; 4:11; 1 Thess. 2:15; Titus 1:12
tongue	γλῶσσα	30xActs/Paul: Acts 2:3, 4, 11, 26; 10:46; 19:6; Rom. 3:13; 14:11; 1 Cor. 12:10 [2x], 28, 30; 13:1, 8; 14:2, 4, 5[2x], 6, 9, 13, 14, 18, 19, 22, 23, 26, 27, 39; Phil. 2:11
to speak in tongues	λαλέω γλῶσσαι	17xNT: Mark 16:17; Acts 2:4, 11; 10:46; 19:6; 1 Cor. 12:30; 13:1; 14:2, 4, 5 [2x], 6, 13, 18, 23, 27, 39
kinds of tongues	γένη γλῶσσαι	2xNT: 1 Cor. 12:10, 28 (new tongues [καῖναι γλῶσσαι] = 1xNT: Mark 16:17)
other tongues	ἕτεραι γλῶσσαι	1xNT: Acts 2:4; "various kinds of tongues" (see ἑτέρῳ γένη γλωσσῶν in 1 Cor. 12:10)
DEATH — RESURRECTION		
sleep, fall asleep	κοιμάω	9xPaul: 1 Cor. 7:39; 11:30; 15:6, 18, 20, 51; 1 Thess. 4:13, 14, 15
death	θάνατος	8x1 Cor.: 3:22; 11:26; 15:21, 26, 54, 55 [2x], 56 (47xPaul)
to die	ἀποθνήσκω	7x1 Cor.: 8:11; 9:15; 15:3, 22, 31, 32, 36 (42xPaul)
resurrection	ἀνάστασις	8xPaul: Rom. 1:4; 6:5; 1 Cor. 15:12, 13, 21, 42; Phil. 3:10; 2 Tim. 2:18
to raise	ἐγείρω	20x1 Cor.: 6:14; 15:4, 12, 13, 14, 15, 16, 17, 20, 29, 32, etc. (41xPaul)
to make alive	ζωοποιέω	7xPaul: Rom. 4:17; 8:11; 1 Cor. 15:22, 36, 45; 2 Cor. 3:6; Gal. 3:21
to baptize	βαπτίζω	10x1 Cor.: 1:13, 14, 15, 16 (2x), 17; 10:2; 12:13; 15:29 [2x] (13xPaul)
incorruptibility	ἀφθαρσία	7xPaul: Rom. 2:7; 1 Cor. 15:42, 50, 53, 54; Eph. 6:24; 2 Tim. 1:10
corruption	φθορά	9xNT: Rom. 8:21; 1 Cor. 15:42, 50; Gal. 6:8; Col. 2:22; 2 Pet. 1:4; 2:12 [2x], 19

Believers from Corinth Mentioned in the New Testament

CHART 57

	Name	Text	Further Information
1.	Aquila	Acts 18:2	Jew
2.	Priscilla	Acts 18:2	Jew
3.	Titius Justus	Acts 18:7	God-fearing Gentile
4.	Crispus	1 Cor. 1:14	Jew, synagogue leader
5.	Gaius	1 Cor. 1:14; Rom. 16:23	Paul's host
6.	Stephanas	1 Cor. 1:16; 16:15, 17	
7.	Fortunatus	1 Cor. 16:17	
8.	Achaicus	1 Cor. 16:17	
9.	Lucius	Rom. 16:21	Jew
10.	Jason	Rom. 16:21	Jew
11.	Sosipater	Rom. 16:21	Jew
12.	Tertius	Rom. 16:22	Paul's secretary
13.	Erastus	Rom. 16:23	City treasurer
14.	Quartus	Rom. 16:23	

2 CORINTHIANS: A Snapshot

CHART 58

Occasion	When Paul wrote the letter he was ready for a third visit (12:14; 13:1) in which he still feared to find at least some unrepentant sinners (12:20-21). He looked back already to two visits (Acts 18; 2 Cor. 2:1) and three previous letters written to the Corinthians. Their relationship was strained by rebellion against his authority, leading to a painful visit (2:1) followed by a tearful letter (2:4). Yet Titus brought back to Paul good news of "godly sorrow" (7:11) which led to the repentance of many (7:9), making Paul proud of them (1:14; 3:1-3; 7:8–16).

Structure	Salutation (1:1–11)
	    A. Paul's explanation of his conduct and apostolic ministry (1–7)
	    B. Paul's summons to complete the collection (8–9)
	    C. Paul's defense of his apostolic authority (10–13)
	Subscription (13:11–13)

Special features	• composite character with abrupt transitions (e.g., between chs. 7/8 & 9/10) • mention of a previous severe letter by Paul to Corinthians (2:3–4, 9; 7:12) • lists of apostolic suffering (1:3–11; 4:7–12; 6:4–10; 11:23–29; 12:7–10) • comparison in 3:7–18 between Paul and Moses, the new and old covenant • a (Merkabah) mystic experience in 12:1–4 (by Paul?) • Paul frequently mentions his sufferings (4:7–12; 6:4–10; 11:23–29; 12:10)
Purpose(s)	1. *Apologetics*: Some in the Corinthian church still questioned Paul's authority (1:15–22; 6:11–13; 7:2), fostered by the propaganda of "false apostles" (11:13). Their issue had to do with how divine power manifests itself in the life of an apostle. The false apostles were "peddling" the word of God (2:17), using deception and distorting the word of God (4:2), commending themselves (10:12), and searching to impress with "letters of commendation" (3:1, from Jerusalem?) and Jewish lineage (11:21–23). Paul, on the other hand, explains that his many sufferings (1 Cor 4:9–13; 2 Cor 4:7–12; 6:4–10; 11:23–29; 12:7–10) do not cast doubts on his calling but show that suffering is a prominent part of apostolic ministry in which divine "power is perfected in [human] weakness" (12:9). 2. *Pastoral*: (a) The Corinthians are encouraged to restore (a) the repentant sinner (2:5–11), their loyalty (b) to Paul (6:11–13; 7:2–3) and (c) to the one who sent him ("be reconciled to God," 5:20) and, resulting from these renewed relationships, (d) the commitment of participating in the collection for the saints in Jerusalem (chs. 8–9).

Charts *on the* Life, Letters, *and* Theology *of* Paul

119

Paul's Corinthian Correspondence

CHART 59

(1)	Paul's first visit: He planted a church in Corinth on his second missionary journey (Acts 18).
(2)	**First Letter**: Paul wrote a letter to Corinth that is lost to us (1 Cor. 5:9–11).
(3)	The Corinthians responded with a letter (see 1 Cor. 7:1 "Now concerning the things about which you wrote"; see further "now concerning" [Περὶ δὲ] in 8:1; 12:1; 16:1, 12).
(4)	Apollos visited Corinth, helped believers through his teaching (Acts 18:27–19:1).
(5)	**Second Letter**: Paul wrote 1 Corinthians to counter divisions in the church that took sides especially with him or Apollos (1:12), and to respond to reports about issues (1:11; 5:1) and questions (e.g., 7:1) from Corinthians' letter.
(6)	Timothy brought the letter to the Corinthians (1 Cor. 16:10–11).
(7)	Paul's second visit: In this painful visit (2 Cor. 2:1) Paul had to realize that his second letter (1 Corinthians) was not well received.
(8)	**Third Letter**: Paul followed his painful visit with a tearful letter (2:4; also 7:8–12), also lost to us, in which he confronted the church's internal problems.
(9)	Titus delivered this letter to the church and brought back to Paul good news of repentance and affection for Paul (2 Cor. 7:6–7, 13–16).
(10)	**Fourth Letter**: Paul responded to Titus' report (7:6–7) with another letter (2 Corinthians) in which he expressed his joy about the Corinthians' repentance.
(11)	Titus and "the brother" came to prepare the Corinthians' contribution for the poor in Jerusalem (2 Cor. 8:6, 17–18; 12:17–18).
(12)	Paul announced his "third visit" (2 Cor 12:14) to resolve remaining tension between him and the church (see 2 Cor. 10–13).

GALATIANS: A Snapshot

CHART 60

Audience	Former pagans (and Gentile proselytes? 3:26–28) who recently converted (1:6) from practicing idolatry (4:8)
City	"Galatia" (1:2) could refer to North Galatia (see Acts 16:6, leading to a later date for the letter) or to South Galatia (see Acts 14:1, 8, 20, allowing for a date before the council in Jerusalem in Acts 15)

Structure	Salutation (1:1–5)
	    A. Rebuke (1:6–4:11)
	        Autobiography (1:13–2:21)
	        Argument from Scripture: Abraham (3:1–4:11)
	    B. Request (Gal 4:12–6:10)
	        Autobiography (Gal 4:12–20)
	        Allegory from Scripture: Abraham (Gal 4:21–31)
	        Ethical instruction (Gal 5:1–6:10)
	Subscription (Gal 6:11–18)

Special Features	• four self-contained narrative units (1:12–2:21; 3:4–29; 4:1–7; 4:21–31)
	• Gal. 1–2 as autobiographical insight into Paul's life before and after conversion
	• Sarah – Hagar allegory (4:21–31)
	• male body language is prevalent: "foreskin" (ἀκροβυστία), "circumcision" (περιτομή), "sperm" (σπέρμα, 3:16), "castrate" (ἀποκόπτω, 5:12 NRS)
	• Key Words:
	  "gospel" (1:6, 7, 11; 2:2, 5, 7, 14)
	  "faith / to believe" (1:23; 2:7, 16 [3x], 20; 3:2, 5, 6, 7, 8, 9 [2x], 11, 12,
	    14, 22 [2x], 23 [2x], 24, 25, 26; 4:9; 5:5, 6, 22; 6:10)
	  "circumcise / circumcision" (2:3, 7, 8, 9, 12; 5:2, 3, 6, 11; 6:12, 13, 15)
	  "law" (2:16 [3x], 19 [2x], 21; 3:2, 5, 10 [2x], 11, 12, 13, 17, 18, 19, 21
	    [3x], 23, 24; 4:4, 5, 21 [2x]; 5:3, 4, 14, 18, 23; 6:2, 13)

Occasion	False teachers (1:7; 3:1; 4:17; 5:7–10; 6:12–13) mislead Christians in Galatia to turn away from Paul's gospel (1:6; 4:9; 5:4) and accept Judaism ("circumcision" 5:2, 6; 6:15; life "under law" 4:21; 5:18), at least partially as a pragmatic escape from persecution by Jews (4:29; 6:12; 5:11–12). In this confusion, Paul, the missionary to the Gentiles, is the enemy (4:16); and Jewish insistence on separation from Gentiles (see 2:12) is splitting the church (5:15, 26) along social and racial lines (3:26–29).
Purpose(s)	1. *Apologetics*: Paul defends his mission to the Gentiles with a circumcision-free gospel against opposition from rival Jewish Christian missionaries in Galatia. 2. *Pastoral*: Paul shames (1:6; 3:1–4) and warns (5:1–4) the Galatians for their attention to a "different gospel" (1:6). He identifies with their existential and theological challenge (2:1–14; 5:11) in order to establish resistance against the intruders and to overcome communal infighting (5:15, 26) by walking "by the Spirit" (5:16).

EPHESIANS: A Snapshot

CHART 61

Ephesus in Acts	• Paul was first hindered by the Spirit to speak in Asia / Ephesus (16:6) • He first visited Ephesus briefly at the end of his second journey (18:18–22) • In Ephesus, Paul met Apollos from Alexandria (18:24–28) and twelve men (19:1–7) who only knew the baptism of John. • Paul went to the synagogue, where Jews and Greeks heard him (19:8–10) • Paul visited Ephesus for two and a half years on the third journey (19:1–41). God did extraordinary miracles (19:11); but Paul also had a confrontation with Demetrius, who made silvers shrines for the goddess Artemis (19:23–41).
Other Info about Ephesus	• Paul fought "wild beasts" in Ephesus (1 Cor. 15:32; are these maybe human opponents? See 1 Cor. 16:9) • Other Christian ministers in Ephesus: Priscilla and Aquila (Acts 18:24–28); Tychicus (Eph. 6:21; 2 Tim. 4:12); Timothy (1 Tim. 1:3); Onesiphorus (2 Tim. 1:8)
Audience	"[A]t Ephesus" in 1:1 is missing in early and important manuscripts (P46, ℵ*, B*). The address "at Ephesus" could have been added later because (just as in Rev. 2:1?) Ephesus was the capitol of the region and thus the first and foremost among the churches addressed by this circular letter. The Laodiceans might have belonged to the recipients as well (see Col. 4:16).
Structure	Salutation (1:1–2) 　I. Knowing your calling (see 1:18): The mystery of Christ 　　A Eulogy (1:3–14) 　　　B Thanksgiving and petition (1:15–23) 　　　　C The mystery of Christ (2:1–3:13) 　　　B' Petition (3:14–19) 　　A' Doxology (3:20–21) 　II. Living your calling (see 4:1): The manner worthy of Christ 　　A Unity (4:1-6) and diversity in the body of Christ (4:7–16) 　　　B Lay off the old self—put on the new self (4:17–5:21) 　　　　C Household code (5:22-6:9) 　　　　　D The armor of God (6:10–17) 　　　　　　E Petition (6:18–20) and announcement of Tychicus (6:21–22) Subscription (6:23–24)
Special Features	• many verbal and conceptual similarities between Ephesians and Colossians • impersonal address (1:15; 3:1; 6:23; no personal greetings at the end) • "church" (ἐκκλησία) is exclusively used for the universal church (1:22; etc.) • Eph. 1:3–14 is the longest sentence in the New Testament • cosmic Christology (1:3–4, 9–10, 20-23; 2:6; 4:8–10), realized eschatology (1:3, 20–22; 2:2–8; 6:17), developed ecclesiology (1:23; 2:19–22; 4:16; 5:23)
Purpose(s)	The letter does not address any specific problem. The theme of the universal church, uniting Jews and Gentiles (2:11–22; 4:3–7), is expected to shape Christian identity and enable spiritual growth. It could also hint at a problem of anti-Semitism clashing with Jewish pride (2:11), leading to ethnic disunity in the local church (see also Romans).

Parallels between Ephesians and Colossians

CHART 62

EPHESIANS	COLOSSIANS
1:1 **Paul, an apostle of Christ Jesus by the will of God,** **to the saints** who are at Ephesus, and who are **faithful in Christ Jesus:** ² **Grace to you and peace from God our Father** and …	1:1 **Paul, an apostle of Jesus Christ by the will of God,** and Timothy our brother, ² **to the saints and faithful** brethren **in Christ** who are at Colossae: **Grace to you and peace from God our Father.**
1:3 Blessed be the **God** and **Father of our Lord Jesus Christ,**	1:3 We give thanks to **God, the Father of our Lord Jesus Christ,**
1:4 … that we would be **holy and blameless before Him.**	1:22 in order to present you **before Him holy and blameless** and beyond reproach—
1:13 In Him, you also, after **listening to the message of truth, the gospel** of your salvation—	1:5 …, of which you previously **heard in the word of truth, the gospel,** …
1:15 **For this reason** I too, having **heard** of the faith in the Lord Jesus which exists among you and your love for all the saints, ¹⁶ do **not cease** giving thanks for you, while making mention of you in my **prayers;**	1:9 **For this reason also,** since the day we **heard** of it, we have **not ceased** to **pray** for you and to ask …
1:21 far above all **rule** and **authority** and power and **dominion,** and every name that is named, not only in this age but also in the one to come. ²² And He put all things in subjection under His feet, and gave Him as head over all things to **the church,** ²³ which is His **body,** the fulness of Him who fills all in all.	1:16 For by Him all things were created, both in the heavens and on earth, visible and invisible, whether thrones or **dominions** or **rulers** or **authorities**— all things have been created by Him and for Him. ¹⁷ He is before all things, and in Him all things hold together. ¹⁸ He is also **head** of the **body, the church;**
2:1 And **you were dead in your trespasses** and sins, …	2:13 When **you were dead in your transgressions** …
2:11 Therefore remember that formerly you, the Gentiles in the **flesh,** who are called "Uncircumcision " by the so-called "**Circumcision,**" which is performed in the flesh by human **hands**—	2:11 and in Him you were also circumcised with a **circumcision** made without **hands,** in the removal of the body of the **flesh** by the circumcision of Christ;
NIV (1984) 2:15 by abolishing in his flesh the law with its commandments and **regulations.** …	2:14 having canceled out the certificate of debt consisting of **decrees** against us, …
NET 2:15 … He did this to **create** in himself one **new man** out of two, …	NET 3:9 Do not lie to one another since you have put off the old **man** with its practices ¹⁰ and have been clothed with the **new man** that is being **renewed** in knowledge according to the image of the one who **created** it.
3:4 … you can understand my insight into the **mystery of Christ,** ⁵ which in **other generations was not made known** to the sons of men, as it has **now been revealed to His** holy apostles and prophets in the Spirit;	1:26 that is, the **mystery which has been hidden from the past ages and generations; but has now been manifested to His** saints, … 4:3 … that we may speak forth the **mystery of Christ** …
NET 4:2 with all **humility** and **gentleness,** with **patience, bearing with one another** in **love,** ³ making every effort to keep the unity of the Spirit in the **bond** of **peace.** ⁴ There is one body and one Spirit, just as you too were **called** to the **one** hope …	NET 3:12 … kindness, **humility, gentleness,** and **patience,** ¹³ **bearing with one another** and forgiving one another, … ¹⁴ And to all these virtues add **love,** which is the perfect **bond.** ¹⁵ Let the **peace** of Christ be in control in your heart (for you were in fact **called** as **one** body …
NIV 4:16 From him **the whole body,** joined and **held together** by every **supporting ligament, grows** and builds itself up in love, as each part does its work.	NIV 2:19 … from whom **the whole body, supported** and **held together** by its **ligaments** and sinews, **grows** as God causes it to grow.

EPHESIANS	COLOSSIANS
4:25 Therefore, **laying aside falsehood**, ... [29] Let no unwholesome word proceed **from your mouth**, ... [31] Let all **bitterness** and **wrath** and **anger** and clamor and **slander** be put away from you, along with all **malice**.	3:8 But now you also, **put** them all **aside: anger, wrath, malice, slander,** and abusive speech **from your mouth**. [9] Do not **lie** to one another, ... [19] Husbands, love your wives, and do not be **embittered** against them.
5:3 But **immorality** or any **impurity** or greed must not even be named among you, as is proper among saints; ... [6] Let no one deceive you with empty words, for because of these things the **wrath of God comes upon the sons of disobedience.** [7] Therefore do not be partakers with them; [8] for you were **formerly** darkness, **but now** you are Light in the Lord; ...	3:5 Therefore consider the members of your earthly body as dead to **immorality, impurity,** passion, evil desire, and **greed,** which amounts to idolatry. [6] For it is because of these things that **the wrath of God will come upon the sons of disobedience,** [7] and in them you also **once** walked, when you were living in them. [8] **But now** you also, put them all aside: anger, wrath, malice, slander, ...
5:19 ... speaking to one another in **psalms and hymns and spiritual songs, singing** and making melody **with your heart to the Lord;** [20] always **giving thanks** for **all** things **in the name of our Lord Jesus** Christ **to God,** even **the Father;**	3:16 ... admonishing one another with **psalms and hymns and spiritual songs, singing** with thankfulness **in your hearts to God.** [17] And whatever you do in word or deed, do **all in the name of the Lord Jesus, giving thanks** through Him **to God the Father.**
5:22 **Wives, *be subject* to your** own **husbands, as to the Lord.** ... [25] **Husbands, love your wives,** just as Christ also loved the church ... 6:1 **Children, obey your parents in the Lord,** for this is right. ... [4] **Fathers, do not** provoke **your children** to anger; but bring them up in the discipline ... NIV [5] **Slaves, obey your earthly masters** with respect and fear, and **with sincerity of heart,** just as you would obey Christ. [6] Obey them not only **to win their favor when their eye is on you,** but like slaves of Christ, doing the will of God from your heart. [7] Serve wholeheartedly, as if you were serving **the Lord, not people,** [8] **because you know** that **the Lord** will reward each one for whatever good they do, whether they are slave or free. [9] And **masters,** treat **your slaves** in the same way. Do not threaten them, **since you know that** he who is both their **Master** and yours is in **heaven,** and there is no favoritism with him.	3:18 **Wives, be subject to your husbands, as** is fitting in **the Lord.** [19] **Husbands, love your wives,** and do not be embittered against them. [20] **Children, be obedient to your parents** in all things, for this is well-pleasing to the **Lord.** [21] **Fathers, do not** exasperate **your children,** so that they will not lose heart. NIV [22] **Slaves, obey your earthly masters** in everything; and do it, not only **when their eye is on you and to curry their favor,** but **with sincerity of heart** and reverence for the **Lord.** [23] Whatever you do, work at it with all **your heart, as** working for **the Lord, not** for **human masters,** [24] **since you know** that you will receive an inheritance from **the Lord** as a reward. It is the Lord Christ you are serving. ... and **there is no favoritism.** 4:1 **Masters,** provide **your slaves** with what is right and fair, **because you know that** you also have a **Master in heaven.**
6:18 With all **prayer** and petition pray at all times ..., [19] and pray on my behalf, that utterance may be given to me in the opening of my mouth, to make known with boldness the **mystery** of the gospel, [20] for which I am an ambassador in chains; that in proclaiming it I may speak boldly, **as I ought to speak.**	4:2 Devote yourselves to **prayer,** ... [3] praying at the same time **for us** as well, that God may open up to us a door for the word, so that we may speak forth the **mystery** of Christ, for which I have also been imprisoned; [4] that I may make it clear in **the way I ought to speak.**
NKJ 6:21 But that you also may know my affairs and how I am doing, **Tychicus, a beloved brother and faithful minister in the Lord, will make all things known to you;** ESV 6:22 **I have sent him to you for this very purpose, that you may know how we are, and that he may encourage your hearts.** ... NKJ 6:24 **Grace be with** all those who love our Lord Jesus Christ in sincerity. **Amen.**	NKJ 4:7 **Tychicus, a beloved brother, faithful minister,** and fellow servant in the Lord, will tell you all the news about me. ESV 4:8 **I have sent him to you for this very purpose, that you may know how we are and that he may encourage your hearts,** [9] and with him Onesimus, our faithful and beloved brother, who is one of you. They **will tell you of everything** that has taken place here. NKJ 4:18 ... **Grace be with** you. **Amen.**

PHILIPPIANS: A Snapshot

CHART 63

Audience	The Philippian believers were the first European Christians (Acts 16:11–40)
Philippi in Acts	Led to the city by divine intervention (Acts 16:6–10), Paul founded the church on his second missionary journey. Lydia, a proselyte or God-fearer (16:13–15), and the Philippian jailor (Acts 16:25–34) are among the first converts. After exorcizing a slave girl, Paul and Silas are imprisoned on charges of anti-Roman activities, but later released. Luke emphasizes the city's Roman character: • Only here in Acts is Paul charged with anti-Roman behavior (Acts 16:21) • Luke calls only Philippi a "colony" (Acts 16:12) • Only for Philippi did Luke mention titles of city officials such as the "chief magistrates" (Acts 16:20, στρατηγοί) and the "policemen" (16:35, ῥαβδοῦχοι)
Opposition mentioned	Paul's imprisonment (1:13, 17); Christian opponents of Paul (1:15–17); suffering of Philippians (1:29–30); Judaizers (3:2–3); see also 1:28; 3:18–29
Occasion	The Philippians suffer persecution (1:28-30); they are discouraged by Paul's imprisonment (1:12–26) and by Epaphroditus' illness (2:25–30); they hear of Judaizers (3:2–3) and experience internal division (4:3–4; 1:27; 2:2–4)

Structure	Salutation (1:1–3)
	    A. Thanksgiving and petition (1:4–11)
	    B. Pattern: Paul's positive outlook on his suffering (1:12–26)
	    C. Plea and patterns for humble unity in humiliating suffering (1:27–2:30)
	    D. Warning, plea, and pattern for redefining honor and shame (3:1–21)
	    E. Plea for unity and purity (4:1–9)
	    F. Praise for donation and pattern for contentment (4:10–20)
	Subscription (4:21–23)

Special Features	• So-called "Christ hymn" (2:6–11; Latin *Carmen Christi*); only in this letter does Paul call Jesus a "slave" (2:7, NRS μορφὴν δούλου) • Only in Philippians and Romans does Paul call himself a "slave" in the prescript (1:1, HCSB; Rom. 1:1, HCSB) • Paul's many self-references (1:12–26; 2:16–19, 23, 3:4–14; 4:12–13) • Only in Philippians and 1–2 Thessalonians does Paul *not* call himself an "apostle" • Only in Philippians does Paul address "overseers and deacons" (1:1) • Only in Philippians does Paul list his social honors as a Pharisaic Jew (3:5–6) • Paul uses the Roman term "conduct yourselves" (πολιτεύομαι 1:27; cf. 3:20) for his more common term "to walk" (περιπατέω, e.g., Gal. 5:16) when describing Christian behavior. • Women play an instrumental part in the church (Acts 16; Phil. 4:2–3)
Purpose(s)	1. *Apologetics*: to defend (shameful) suffering as a pattern of Christian life. 2. *Pastoral*: to strengthen faith and fellowship of believers who disagree in their definition of honor and, because of that, are discouraged because of suffering and sickness.

COLOSSIANS: A Snapshot

CHART 64

Audience	The church was founded by Paul's co-worker Epaphras (1:7–8; 4:12–13), probably during Paul's Ephesian ministry (see Acts 19:10, 26). The apostle had not met the believers in Colossae and in Laodicea (2:1).
City	Colossae, not mentioned in Acts, was situated in the Lycus valley close to Laodicea (eleven miles; see Col. 2:1; 4:16) along a major trade route from the Aegean sea to Asia Minor. The textile industry supported the local economy, as much so as its strategic location. An earthquake some time between AD 60–64 destroyed the city. The church was founded by coworkers of Paul (Col. 2:1).
Population	Estimates are difficult because of the earthquake. A Jewish minority of maybe two thousand people can be deduced from a statement by Cicero about the temple tax.
Occasion	A certain "philosophy" (2:8) threatened the faith of believers since it promoted certain views on diet and Sabbath (2:16), worship of angels (2:18), and ascetic behavior (2:21 "Do not handle, do not taste, do not touch!"), resulting in "severe treatment of the body" (2:23).
Structure	Salutation (1:1–2) and extended thanksgiving (1:3–23) 　A. Christian principles: knowing God's mystery without deception (2:1–23) 　B. Christian practice (3:1–4:6) Subscription (4:7–18)
Special features	• Colossians has many parallels with Ephesians and Philemon (charts 62, 75) • The letter is also addressed to the church in Laodicea (4:16) • Parallels between Colossians and Galatians show the essentially Jewish nature of the Colossian heresy:

SUBJECT	GALATIANS	COLOSSIANS
Circumcision	2:1–10, 12; 5:1–12; 6:15	2:8–15
Sabbath, special days	4:10	2:16
Food laws	2:11–18	2:16, 21–22
Elements of the world [τὰ στοιχεῖα τοῦ κόσμου] and angels	4:3, 9; 3:19	2:8, 18, 20
Denial of social and ethnic distinctions	3:28	3:11

Purpose(s)	1. *Pastoral*: Paul's goal was to find the believers "complete in Christ" (1:28). He had only good things to say about their past (1:21–22) and current (1:1–4) walk of faith. The exhortations largely contend with general statements, apart from the household code (3:18–4:1). But the need to persevere (1:23) and to withstand possible deception through alternative beliefs (2:4–23) motivate this letter. 2. *Apologetics*: Paul did not say that the Colossian believers have already a problem with the deceptive "philosophy" (2:8), but the danger was real and it was a "struggle" (2:1) for the apostle to protect those from error that have not met him face to face. The heresy reduced the divinity of Christ (1:13–22; 2:9–15) and elevated the importance of certain practices (2:16–23).

1 THESSALONIANS: A Snapshot

CHART 65

Audience	Former pagans who worshiped idols (1:9)
Acts and Thessalonica	On his second missionary journey, Paul enters Thessalonica and preaches in the synagogue (17:1–9). While some Jews and many God-fearing Greeks respond well, others become "jealous" and accuse him of anti-imperial intentions (17:5–6). Their ensuing plot urges Paul and Silas to leave for Berea. Aristarchus, a believer from Thessalonica, who later travelled with Paul on his third journey (20:4; also Secundus), was dragged into the Ephesian theater (19:29), later sailed with Paul to Rome (27:2) and became thus Paul's "fellow prisoner" (Col. 4:10; Philem. 1:24). As Proverbs 17:17 says, "A friend loves at all times, [a]nd a brother is born for adversity."
Structure	Salutation (1:1–2) and thanksgiving (1:4–10) 　A. Paul interprets his suffering and absence (2:1–3:13) 　B. Paul instructs about specific issues (4:1–5:24) Subscription (5:25–28)
Special Features	• Only here does Paul use in his address the name of the people ("Thessalonians" 1:1) instead of the city (e.g., 1 Cor. 1:2; Phil. 1:1 etc.) • The letter mentions three authors (1:1) and maintains a "we" throughout the letter (e.g., 2:7–8; 3:1), with the exception of the "I" in 2:18; 3:5; 5:27. • The Thessalonian believers were known all over Greece and beyond (1:7–8) • The theme of "wait[ing] for His Son from heaven" in 1:10 is repeated at the end of every chapter (see 2:19; 3:13; 4:13–18; 5:23) • The phrase "as you know" or similar as superfluous rehearsals in 1:5; 2:1–2, 5, 9–11; 3:3b–4; 4:1–2, 6, 10–11; 5:1; except in 4:13! • Paul compares himself to a father (2:10–12), a mother (2:7), a little child (2:7 NET), and an orphan (2:17, NIV) and uses other kinship terms such as "brother" (4:6–8) and "love of the brethren" (φιλαδελφία, 4:9; also only in Rom. 12:10)
Occasion	Some Thessalonian believers rejected prophecy (5:19–22), were idle (4:10–12), and had problems with sexual ethics (4:3–8). These issues may have stemmed from influence of local pagan cults (see commentaries to 4:4 and 5:7) and deep uncertainty about the future of fellow believers who had died prior to the parousia (4:13–18), possibly due to "persecution" (so NRS for θλῖψις in 1:6; 3:3, 7). Their suffering (1:6; 2:15) and death (4:13–18) and Paul's suffering (2:2; 3:3–4, 7) and absence (2:17–20) were misunderstood as signs of the apostle's desertion and of divine wrath (1:10; 5:9).
Purpose(s)	*Pastoral:* Paul seeks to restore the believers' confidence in God by strengthening their trust in him as the caring father and mother of their faith (chs. 2–3). He explains that God's wrath is not upon the persecuted (1:10; 5:9) but upon the persecutor (2:16). His absence is not his personal choice but Satan's work (2:18). Only after Paul dispelled doubts about his care for the Thessalonians and calling as an apostle does he advance to specific "commandments" (4:2) about individual issues in the church.

2 THESSALONIANS: A Snapshot

CHART 66

Structure	Salutation (1:1-2) and thanksgiving (1:3–12)
	    A. Paul corrects misunderstanding (2:1–12)
	      B. Paul comforts with divine assurance (2:13–3:5)
	    A' Paul corrects misbehavior (3:6–15)
	Subscription (3:16–18)

Special Features	• This letter shares more details about "when the Lord Jesus will be revealed (ἀποκάλυψις) from heaven" (1:7) than any of his other letters. • Only in 2 Thessalonians does Paul ever mention a reason for the delay of Christ's second coming (see the "restrainer," ὁ κατέχων in 2:6–7) • Five signs will precede the second coming: the apostasy (2:3), the "man of lawlessness" (2:3), the removal of "he who now restrains" (2:6–7), the destruction of the lawless one (2:8), the "deluding influence" (2:11–12)
Occasion	Maybe as a misunderstanding of Paul's repeated emphasis on the coming of the Lord in the first letter to the Thessalonians (1:10; 2:19; etc.), some in the church claimed that the day of the Lord "has come" (ἐνέστηκεν in 2:2; not KJV's "is at hand") and (as a consequence?) stopped working (3:6–12). In addition, this letter is preceded by Paul's second visit to Macedonia (see 2:5; 2 Cor. 2:13; 7:5; 9:2, 4; Acts 20:1–2), which most likely also included a stop in Thessalonica, Macedonia's capitol. During this visit, Paul taught that a "man of lawlessness" and "son of destruction" (2:3) would come, maybe a reference to the emperor Claudius (AD 41–53) who was feared to continue his predecessor Caligula's plan of erecting his picture in Jerusalem's temple (*Ann.* 12.54; see 2 Thess. 2:4). But after Claudius' death, Nero (AD 54–68) took the throne and he had initially a *positive* influence on politics. The question is at hand: Did this "man of lawlessness" not appear, did Paul make a mistake, or worse—was he even a false prophet?
Purpose(s)	1. *Apologetics*: Paul corrects a false teaching promoted in his name (2:2) about the second coming of the Lord and about the "man of lawlessness." The delay of both is explained with reference to "he who now restrains" (2:6–7). 2. *Pastoral*: Having talked about God's "judgment" (1:5; 2:2), "affliction" (1:6), and "eternal destruction" (1:9; 2:8), Paul assures the believers in Thessalonica of divine favor and salvation (2:13–14) and exhorts to withdraw support for troublemakers (ἀπὸ παντὸς ἀδελφοῦ ἀτάκτως, 3:6) whose millenarian excitement ignored apostolic traditions of working for one's own bread.

Similarities between 1 and 2 Thessalonians

CHART 67

STRUCTURAL SIMILARITIES	
Prescript	
1 Thess. 1:1	2 Thess. 1:1–2
First Thanksgiving	
1 Thess. 1:2f.	2 Thess. 1:3
1 Thess. 1:6f.	2 Thess. 1:4
1 Thess. 1:2–3	2 Thess. 1:11
Second Thanksgiving	
1 Thess. 2:13	2 Thess. 2:13
Transition to Application	
1 Thess. 3:11, 13	2 Thess. 2:16–17
Petition and Warning	
1 Thess. 4:1	2 Thess. 3:1
1 Thess. 4:1	2 Thess. 3:6
1 Thess. 4:10–12	2 Thess. 3:10–12
Church in Disorder	
1 Thess. 5:14	2 Thess. 3:6–7, 11
Subscription	
1 Thess. 5:23	2 Thess. 3:16
1 Thess. 5:28	2 Thess. 3:18

VERBAL SIMILARITIES	
Prescript	
1 Thess. 1:1 Paul and Silvanus and Timothy, To the church of the Thessalonians in God the Father and the Lord Jesus Christ: Grace to you and peace.	2 Thess. 1:1–2 Paul and Silvanus and Timothy, To the church of the Thessalonians in God our Father and the Lord Jesus Christ: Grace to you and peace from God the Father and the Lord Jesus Christ.
Other Similarities	
1 Thess. 2:9 For you recall, brethren, our labor and hardship, how working night and day so as not to be a burden to any of you, we proclaimed to you the gospel of God.	2 Thess. 3:8 nor did we eat anyone's bread without paying for it, but with labor and hardship we kept working night and day so that we might not be a burden to any of you;
Transition	
1 Thess. 3:11 Now may our God and Father Himself and Jesus our Lord …	2 Thess. 2:16 Now may our Lord Jesus Christ Himself and God our Father, …
Subscription	
1 Thess. 5:23 Now may the God of peace Himself …	2 Thess. 3:16 Now may the Lord of peace Himself …
1 Thess. 5:28 The grace of our Lord Jesus Christ be with you. [last sentence of the letter]	2 Thess. 3:18 The grace of our Lord Jesus Christ be with you all. [last sentence of the letter]

1 TIMOTHY: A Snapshot

CHART 68

Timothy	Timothy lived in Lystra, his mother was Jewish and his father Greek (Acts 16:1). Paul met him on his second journey, circumcised him and took him along for ministry. Timothy, a "man of God" (1 Tim. 6:11), had a good reputation (Acts 16:2) and knew the Old Testament from his childhood (2 Tim. 3:14–15). He was deeply committed to serving the new churches (Phil. 2:19–20), although his natural timidity needed occasional encouragement (2 Tim. 1:6–7; 1 Tim. 4:12–16). Paul forged a close friendship with Timothy and called him "my true child in the faith" (1 Tim. 1:2; 2 Tim. 1:2). Timothy was listed in six letters as a cowriter beside Paul (2 Cor., Phil., Col., 1 Thess., 2 Thess., Philem.); and, while often traveling with Paul (e.g., Acts 16–18; Rom. 16:21), was also sent as Paul's representative to local churches (Acts 18:5; 19:22; 1 Thess. 3:2, 6; 1 Cor. 4:17; 16:10–11; Phil. 2:19–24; 1 Tim. 1:3).
City	Ephesus (1:3)

Structure	Salutation (1:1–2)
	  A On Timothy and the opponents: law (1:3–20)
	    B On specific church groups: men, women, overseers, deacons (2:1–3:13)
	  A' On Timothy and the opponents: asceticism (3:14–4:16)
	    B' On specific church groups: widows, elders, slaves (5:1–6:2)
	  A" On Timothy and the opponents: greed (6:3–21a)
	Subscription (6:21b)

Special Features	• frequent use of "to instruct" and "instructions" (e.g., 1:3, 5, 18; 4:11; 5:7)
	• many similarities between the churches in Ephesus and Corinth:
	  - Timothy represents Paul in both churches (1 Cor. 4:17; 1 Tim. 1:3)
	  - Paul "hands someone over to Satan" (1 Cor. 5:1–5; 1 Tim. 1:20)
	  - wealthy members cause problems (1 Cor. 11:17–22; 1 Tim. 2:9–10; 6:17–19)
	  - heads of households recommended as leaders (1 Cor. 16:15–18; 1 Tim. 3:4)
	  - metaphor "household of God" is applied to the church (1 Cor. 3:9; 1 Tim. 3:15)
	  - those who claim superior wisdom / knowledge (1 Cor. 1:17; 1 Tim. 6:20–21)
	  - women should marry; it is not a sin (1 Cor. 7:2, 36; 1 Tim. 5:14; 4:3)
	  - place of widows (1 Cor. 7; 1 Tim. 5) and roles of women (1 Cor. 11; 1 Tim. 2) are uncertain
	  - women's wardrobe (1 Cor. 11:2–16; 1 Tim. 2:8-10) and speech (1 Cor. 14:33–36; 1 Tim. 2:11–15)
	  - dispute over food (1 Cor. 8–10; 1 Tim. 4:3) and financial support of ministers (1 Cor. 9; 1 Tim. 5)

Occasion	Paul opens with a reminder that he left Timothy in Ephesus to counter false teaching (ἑτεροδιδασκαλεῖν, 1:3). The letter itself is not very specific about the erroneous doctrines, but glimpses are evident in the following: • myths, endless genealogies (1:4); teachers of the law (1:7) • forbid marriage, abstain from food (4:3); worldly fables (4:7) • controversial questions and disputes about words (6:4) • "worldly... chatter," what is falsely called "knowledge" (γνῶσις, 6:20)
Purpose(s)	More than simply offering a "manual for church order", Paul wrote 1 Timothy in order to combat a proto-Gnostic (6:20) distortion of "godliness" (εὐσέβεια, 6:5) which separates faith and practice for the sake of personal gain.

2 TIMOTHY: A Snapshot

CHART 69

Structure	Salutation (1:1–2)
	  A Paul and Timothy – "Hold fast" (1:3–2:13)
	    B Timothy and opponents – "Avoid them" (2:14–3:9)
	  A' Paul and Timothy – "Do the ministry" (3:10–4:18)
	Subscription (4:19–22)

Special Features	• use of the same metaphors in 2 Timothy and Philippians:

PHILIPPIANS	2 TIMOTHY
2:17 But even if I am being poured out as a drink offering upon the sacrifice and service of your faith, I rejoice and share my joy with you all.	4:6 For I am already being poured out as a drink offering, and the time of my departure has come.
1:27 … with one mind striving together (συναθλοῦντες) for the faith of the gospel … ³⁰ experiencing the same conflict (ἀγῶνα) which you saw in me, and now hear to be in me.	2:5 Also if anyone competes as an athlete (ἀθλῇ), … unless he competes according to the rules (ἀθλήσῃ). 4:7 I have fought the good fight (τὸν καλὸν ἀγῶνα), I have finished the course, I have kept the faith;
4:13 I can do all things through Him who strengthens me (ἐνδυναμοῦντί με).	4:17 But the Lord stood with me and strengthened me (ἐνεδυνάμωσέν με), …

• apart from 2:2 and 4:22 (TNIV "Grace be with you all [ὑμῶν].") , the letter is focused solely on Timothy
• explicit attention to specific opponents: Phygelus and Hermogenes (1:15), Hymenaeus and Philetus (2:17), Demas and Alexander (4:9, 14)
• metaphors of medicine: vice as sickness (2:17), the teacher as a physician (1:13; 2:15)
• interpersonal character of faith: God has entrusted Paul (1:12), Paul entrusts Timothy (1:14), and Timothy is to entrust others (2:2)
• analogy between Moses/Joshua & Paul/Timothy: 1:6; 2:1, 19, 24; 3:8, 17; …

Occasion	Paul is in prison (1:8; 2:9), possibly in Rome (1:17), and he expects to suffer martyrdom soon (4:6). Many Christians in Asia (1:15) and Rome (4:16) left Paul and some opposed him (2:18; 4:14–15). False teaching about the resurrection (2:18) gained a large following and fake religious behavior (3:5) abounds, attracting especially some women (3:6).
Purpose(s)	1. *Pastoral*: As an old imprisoned leader on death-row (4:6), Paul encourages Timothy, a younger successor and key leader, to endure (2:13; 3:14; 4:15) by following Paul's model of ministry and of suffering in the face of opposition. 2. *Practical*: Paul asks for Timothy's soon arrival (4:9) "before winter" (4:21) and requests the delivery of clothes and books (4:13). 3. *Organizational*: If the greeting to a group in 4:22 indicates that the letter was also expected to be read by other believers, then Paul probably wanted to prepare them for accepting Timothy as Paul's successor.

Charts *on the* Life, Letters, and Theology *of* Paul

131

TITUS: A Snapshot

CHART 70

Audience	Paul calls Titus, who is never mentioned in the Book of Acts, "my brother" (2 Cor. 2:13) and even "my true child" (Titus 1:4). As a Greek (Gal. 2:3) "partner and fellow worker" (2 Cor. 8:23) beside the Jewish apostle, Titus served at least the churches in Corinth (2 Cor. 2:6–7, 13; 8:6, 16; 12:18), Dalmatia (2 Tim. 4:10; a province of Illyricum [modern-day Albania], see Rom 15:19) and the island Crete (Titus 1:5). As an uncircumcised Gentile, Titus embodies Paul's gospel of circumcision-free salvation and becomes thus a test case for the Jewish believers in Jerusalem (Gal. 2:1–3) and their acceptance of Gentile converts.
City	Crete (1:5) is an island in the Aegean Sea, 156 miles from East to West and thirty-five miles from north to south
Acts and Crete	According to the book of Acts, Cretans experienced the Pentecostal outpouring of the Spirit in Jerusalem (2:11) and Paul stopped on the island while travelling to Rome as a prisoner (27:7, 12, 13, 21).

Structure	Salutation (1:1–4) and introduction (1:5–9)
	     A The problem of opponents (1:10–16)
	          B' Sound doctrine that includes lifestyle (2:1–3:8)
	     A' The problem of opponents (3:9–11)
	Subscription and closing (3:12–15)

Special Features	• Paul cites the "true" testimony (1:13) of a *Cretan* poet Epimenides (6th cent. BC) according to whom "*Cretans* are always liars, evil beasts, lazy gluttons" (1:12)—except Epimenides! • parallels in content between 1 Cor 6:9–11 & Titus 3:3–7: vices, then/now, washed, justified, Spirit, heirs
Occasion	There are many rebellious men, especially those of the circumcision (1:10), who promote Jewish myths and commandments of men (1:14); profess to know God but deny Him by their deeds (1:16); and instigate foolish controversies about genealogies and strife and disputes about the Law (3:9)
Purpose(s)	Paul left Titus in Crete to "set in order what remains and appoint elders in every city" (1:5). The repeated discussion of opponents highlights the need for leadership that is, as Paul repeats here twice, "above reproach" (1:6, 7)

Similarities between the Pastoral Epistles

CHART 71

	1 TIMOTHY, 2 TIMOTHY, TITUS	
1.	appearance (ἐπιφάνεια)	6xNT: used of Jesus' first coming (2 Tim. 1:10) and his second coming (2 Thess. 2:8; 1 Tim. 6:14; 2 Tim. 4:1, 8; Titus 2:13)
2.	to appear (ἐπιφαίνω)	4xNT: Luke 1:79; Acts 27:20; Titus 2:11; 3:4; adj. Acts 2:20
3.	controversies (ζήτησις)	7xNT: John 3:25; Acts 15:2, 7; 25:20; 1 Tim. 6:4; 2 Tim. 2:23; Titus 3:9; "speculation" (ἐκζήτησις), 1xNT: 1 Tim. 1:4
4.	godliness (εὐσέβεια)	15xNT: Acts 3:12; 1 Tim. 2:2; 3:16; 4:7, 8; 6:3, 5, 6, 11; 2 Tim. 3:5; Titus 1:1; 2 Peter 1:3, 6, 7; 3:11
5.	godly (εὐσεβῶς)	2xNT: 2 Tim. 3:12; Titus 2:12 (θεοσέβεια = 1xNT: 1 Tim. 2:10)
6.	impiety / impious (ἀσέβεια, ἀσεβής)	7xPaul: Rom. 1:18; … ; 1 Tim. 1:9; 2 Tim. 2:16; Titus 2:12
7.	holy (ὅσιος)	2xPaul: 1 Tim. 2:8; Titus 1:8
8.	unholy (ἀνόσιος)	2xNT: 1 Tim. 1:9; 2 Tim. 3:2
9.	knowledge of truth (ἐπίγνωσις ἀληθείας)	5xNT: 1 Tim. 2:4 (4:3); 2 Tim. 2:25; 3:7; Titus 1:1; Heb. 10:26
10.	lawfully, correctly (νομίμως)	2xNT: 1 Tim. 1:8; 2 Tim. 2:5
11.	teachers of the law (νομοδιδάσκαλος)	3xNT: Luke 5:17; Acts 5:34; 1 Tim. 1:7
12.	about the law (νομικός)	9xNT: Matt. 22:35; Luke 7:30; 10:25; 11:45,46,52; 14:3; Titus 3:9, 13
13.	malicious gossips (plural: διάβολοι)	3xNT: 1 Tim. 3:11: 2 Tim. 3:3; Titus 2:3
14.	moderation (σωφροσύνη)	3xNT: Acts 26:25; 1 Tim. 2:9, 15
15.	moderate (σώφρων)	4xNT: 1 Tim. 3:2; Titus 1:8; 2:2, 5
16.	moderately (σωφρόνως)	1xNT: Titus 2:12
17.	moderation (σωφρονισμός)	1xNT: 2 Tim. 1:7
18.	myths (μῦθος)	5xNT: 1 Tim. 1:4; 4:7; 2 Tim. 4:4; Titus 1:14; 2 Peter 1:16
19.	owner, master (δεσπότης)	4xPaul: for God (2 Tim. 2:21) and for a human master (1 Tim. 6:1, 2 [see οἰκοδεσποτεῖν in 5:14]; Titus 2:9)
20.	present age (ὁ νῦν αἰών)	3xNT: 1 Tim. 6:17; 2 Tim. 4:10; Titus 2:12
21.	reject! (present singl. imperative παραιτοῦ)	4xNT: 1 Tim. 4:7; 5:11; 2 Tim. 2:23; Titus 3:10
22.	sound teaching (ὑγιαινούσα διδασκαλία)	4xNT: 1 Tim. 1:10; 2 Tim. 4:3; Titus 1:9; 2:1
23.	sound words (ὑγιαίνοι λόγοι)	2xNT: 1 Tim. 6:3; 2 Tim. 1:13
24.	sound in faith (ὑγιαίνοι ἐν τῇ πίστει)	2xNT: Titus 1:13; 2:2
25.	teaching (διδασκαλία)	21xNT: (a) act of teaching (Rom. 12:7; 15:4); (b) passive sense: that which is taught, instruction, doctrines (Matt. 15:9; Mark 7:7; Eph. 4:14; Col. 2:22; 1 Tim. 1:10; 4:1, 6, 13, 16; 5:17; 6:1,3; 2 Tim. 3:10, 16; 4:3; Titus 1:9; 2:1,7, 10)
26.	teacher (διδάσκαλος)	Used in NT for Paul only in 1 Tim. 2:7; 2 Tim. 1:11; 3:10
27.	able to teach (διδακτικός)	2xNT: 1 Tim. 3:2 (overseer); 2 Tim. 2:24 (slave of the Lord)
28.	teaching what is good (καλοδιδάσκαλος)	1xNT: Titus 2:3
29.	teachers of the law (νομοδιδάσκαλος)	3xNT: Luke 5:17; Acts 5:34; 1 Tim. 1:7
30.	different teaching (ἑτεροδιδασκαλέω)	2xNT: 1 Tim. 1:3; 6:3
31.	this is a trustworthy statement (πιστὸς ὁ λόγος)	5xNT: 1 Tim. 1:15; 3:1; 4:9; 2 Tim. 2:11; Titus 3:8

32.	quarrel (μάχη)	3xPaul: 2 Cor. 7:5; 2 Tim. 2:23; Titus 3:9
33.	uncontentious (ἄμαχος)	2xPaul: 1 Tim. 3:3; Titus 3:2
34.	to be quarrelsome (μάχομαι)	1xPaul: 2 Tim. 2:24
35.	battle over words (λογομαχία, λογομαχέω)	2xNT: 1 Tim 6:4; 2 Tim 2:14
	1 TIMOTHY AND 2 TIMOTHY	
36.	abandon the truth (ἀστοχέω)	3xNT: 1 Tim. 1:6; 6:21; 2 Tim. 2:18
37.	clear conscience (καθαρά συνείδησις)	2xNT: 1 Tim. 3:9; 2 Tim. 1:3
38.	conceited (τυφόω)	3xNT: 1 Tim. 3:6; 6:4; 2 Tim. 3:4
39.	deposit (παραθήκη)	3xNT: 1 Tim. 6:20; 2 Tim. 1:12, 14; verb 1 Tim. 1:18; 2 Tim. 2:2
40.	empty chatter (κενοφωνία)	2xNT: 1 Tim. 6:20; 2 Tim. 2:16
41.	flee … pursue righteousness (…), faith, love	2xNT: 1 Tim. 6:11; 2 Tim. 2:22
42.	Grace, mercy *and* peace from God the Father and Christ Jesus our Lord	2xNT: 1 Tim. 1:2; 2 Tim. 1:2 (χάρις ἔλεος εἰρήνη ἀπὸ θεοῦ πατρὸς καὶ Χριστοῦ Ἰησοῦ τοῦ κυρίου ἡμῶν)
	faith and love, that (is found) in Christ Jesus (πίστις καὶ ἀγάπη ἡ ἐν Χριστῷ Ἰησοῦ)	2xNT: 1 Tim. 1:14; 2 Tim. 1:13
43.	Hymenaeus (Ὑμέναιος)	2xNT: 1 Tim. 1:20; 2 Tim. 2:17
44.	I solemnly charge you in the presence of God and of Christ Jesus	2xNT: 1 Tim. 5:21; 2 Tim. 4:1 (Διαμαρτύρομαι ἐνώπιον τοῦ θεοῦ καὶ Χριστοῦ Ἰησοῦ)
45.	laying hands (ἐπίθεσις τῶν χειρῶν) on Timothy	2xNT: 1 Tim. 4:14 (by the presbytery); 2 Tim. 1:6 (by Paul)
46.	love/rs of money (φιλαργυρία, φιλάργυρος)	3xNT: Luke 16:14; 1 Tim. 6:10; 2 Tim. 3:2
47.	not loving money (ἀφιλάργυρος)	2xNT: 1 Tim. 3:3; Heb. 13:5
48.	man of God (ἄνθρωπος θεοῦ)	2xNT: 1 Tim. 6:11; 2 Tim. 3:17
49.	preacher and apostle (Paul)	2xNT: 1 Tim. 2:7; 2 Tim. 1:11 (εἰς ὃ ἐτέθην ἐγὼ κῆρυξ καὶ ἀπόστολος)
50.	profane (βέβηλος)	5xNT: 1 Tim. 1:9; 4:7; 6:20; 2 Tim. 2:16; Heb. 12:16
51.	good fight (καλός ἀγών)	2xNT: 1 Tim. 6:12 (1:18 καλὴ στρατεία); 2 Tim. 4:7
52.	Timothy … child (Τιμοθέῳ … τέκνῳ)	2xNT: 1 Tim. 1:2; 2 Tim. 1:2
53.	turn aside (ἐκτρέπω)	5xNT: 1 Tim. 1:6; 5:15; 6:20; 2 Tim. 4:4; Heb. 12:13
	1 TIMOTHY AND TITUS	
54.	accusation (κατηγορία)	3xNT: John 18:29; 1 Tim. 5:19; Titus 1:6
55.	elder (πρεσβύτερος)	5xPaul: 1 Tim. 5:1, 2, 17, 19; Titus 1:5
56.	The overseer must be …	2xNT: 1 Tim. 3:2; Titus 1:7 (δεῖ … τὸν ἐπίσκοπον … εἶναι)
57.	empty talk/ers (ματαιολογία, ματαιολόγος)	1 Tim. 1:6; Titus 1:10
58.	fond of dishonest gain (αἰσχροκερδής)	2xNT: 1 Tim. 3:8; Titus 1:7; see 1:11 (αἰσχροῦ κέρδους)
59.	genealogy (γενεαλογία)	2xNT: 1 Tim. 1:4; Titus 3:9
60.	God my/our savior (θεός σωτήρ)	10xNT: Luke 1:47; 1 Tim. 1:1; 2:3; 4:10; Titus 1:3; 2:10, 13; 3:4; 2 Peter 1:1; Jude 1:25
61.	good work(s) (καλόν ἔργον)	8xPaul: 1 Tim. 3:1; 5:10, 25; 6:18; Titus 2:7, 14; 3:8, 14
62.	husband of one wife … keeping children …	1 Tim. 3:2, 4; Titus 1:6 (μιᾶς γυναικὸς ἀνήρ … τέκνα ἔχων)
63.	Let no one look down on / disregard you	1 Tim. 4:12 (καταφρονείτω); Titus 2:15 (περιφρονείτω)

64.	proper time (καιροῖς ἰδίοις)	3xNT: 1 Tim. 2:6; 6:15; Titus 1:3
65.	rebellious (ἀνυπότακτος)	4xNT: 1 Tim. 1:9; Titus 1:6, 10; Heb. 2:8
66.	redeem (λυτρόω)	3xNT: Luke 24:21; Titus 2:14; 1 Peter 1:18; see 1 Tim. 2:6
67.	temperate in the use of alcohol (νηφάλιος)	3xNT: 1 Tim. 3:2, 11; Titus 2:2
68.	true child (γνήσιον τέκνον)	2xNT: 1 Tim. 1:2; Titus 1:4
69.	turn aside to (ἐκτρέπω)	5xNT: 1 Tim. 1:6; 5:15; 6:20; 2 Tim. 4:4; Heb. 12:13
70.	uncontentious, gentle (ἄμαχος, ἐπιεικής)	2xNT: 1 Tim. 3:3; Titus 3:2
2 TIMOTHY AND TITUS		
71.	avoid! (pres. mid. imperative περιΐστασο)	2xNT: 2 Tim. 2:16; Titus 3:9
72.	for this reason (δι᾽ ἣν αἰτίαν)	3xPaul: 2 Tim. 1:6, 12; Titus 1:13
73.	from all eternity (πρὸ χρόνων αἰωνίων)	2xNT: 2 Tim. 1:9; Titus 1:2
74.	pleasure / lovers of pl. (ἡδοναί, φιλήδονοι)	2xPaul: 2 Tim. 3:4; Titus 3:3
75.	various pleasures (ἐπιθυμίαις ποικίλαις)	2xNT: 2 Tim. 3:6; Titus 3:3 (… and lusts [καὶ ἡδοναῖς])
76.	overturn, upset (ἀνατρέπω)	3xNT: literal: John 2:15; figurative: 2 Tim. 2:18; Titus 1:11
77.	remind (ὑπομιμνήσκω)	2xPaul: 2 Tim. 2:14; Titus 3:1
78.	turn away (ἀποστρέφω) from the truth	2xNT: 2 Tim. 4:4; Titus 1:14

Authorship of the Pastoral Epistles

CHART 72

ARGUMENTS	AGAINST PAULINE AUTHORSHIP	FOR PAULINE AUTHORSHIP
(1) VOCABULARY & STYLE	• Different vocabulary: 175 NT hapax legomena; 131 additional words occur in the PE that are not found in other Pauline letters. • Different words used for the same idea. • Different style: "more uniform, less animated, more typical of Hellenistic Greek, less of the jolting breaks in thought (anacolutha) characteristic of Paul's other epistles" (Polhill a:399).	• For particular topics (e.g., leadership), Paul drew from contemporary Hellenistic sources. • Statistics are misleading because the samples are too small. • The influence of a secretary could explain differences in style. • The undisputed letters are themselves not uniform in vocabulary and style.
(2) HERESY	• The problems addressed in the PE relate more to Gnostic speculations of the early second century (e.g., 1 Tim. 6:20). • The author of the PE rarely offers arguments (e.g., 1 Tim. 2:13–15; 4:3–5) but merely rejects and warns which is untypical of Paul.	Features of the heresies do not go beyond what is known from the other letters of Paul (e.g., denial of resurrection [1 Cor. 15:12; 2 Tim. 2:18], dietary regulations [Col. 2:16; 1 Tim. 4:3]) and fit within a first-century Jewish context.
(3) THEOLOGY	• Theology: expressions such as "God's righteousness," "freedom," "cross," "Son of God," and "body of Christ" are missing. • Eschatology: realized, focus on life in this world, no imminent parousia. • Ecclesiology: church structure is hierarchical (1 Tim. 3:1–7; Titus 1:5–9). • Soteriology: strong emphasis on works (e.g., 1 Tim. 2:10; 6:18; 2 Tim. 2:21; Titus 2:7); "faith" as a virtue (e.g., 1 Tim. 1:14) and as a body of belief (e.g., 1 Tim. 4:1).	• Since the undisputed letters never offer any systematic and complete theology of Paul, the presence or absence of certain themes in other letters does not argue against Pauline authorship. • Eschatology: future judgment and parousia are not absent (1 Tim. 4:1–4; 2 Tim. 3:2–4; 4:1). • Ecclesiology: leadership in the church is mentioned by Paul also in Acts 20:17, 28; Rom. 12:8; Eph. 4:11; Phil. 1:1; 1 Thess. 5:12. • Soteriology: see "good work(s)" also in 2 Cor. 9:8; Eph. 2:10; Col. 1:10; "faith" as virtue also in 1 Cor. 13:13; etc. and as a body of belief in Phil. 1:27.
(4) ETHICS	Ethics of the PE reflects a "bourgeois" ethic, a middle-class adaptation to the world. See prayer for authorities (1 Tim. 2:1–2), traditional role for women (2:9–15); household orders.	Conservative behavior is also reflected in Paul's call to avoid courts (1 Cor. 6:1–6), pay taxes (Rom. 13:1–5), subordination of women (1 Cor. 11:3) and his general sense of adaptation (1 Cor. 9:22).
(5) CHRONOLOGICAL DETAILS	• Paul left Trophimus in Miletus (2 Tim. 4:20) whereas on his third journey he took Trophimus with him (Acts 20:4, 15) and arrived with him in Jerusalem (21:29). • Neither Paul's letters nor Acts mention a mission in Crete (Tit 1:5).	• 1 Tim. 1:3 easily harmonizes with Acts 20:1–3. • Both Acts and Paul's letters are incomplete in their chronology of Paul's life and ministry. Plausible reconstructions that harmonize many of the PE's biographical details with the chronologies of Acts and Paul's letters have been suggested.
(6) 2ND-CENTURY SOURCES	• Marcion does not mention the PE in his list. • The early papyri P⁴⁶ (maybe AD 200) contains all of Paul's letters except the PE and Philemon.	• Since "the opposing arguments (ἀντιθέσεις) of what is false called 'knowledge' (γνῶσις)" are rejected in 1 Tim. 6:20, Marcion, a Gnostic who wrote a book called Antithesis ("opposing argument"), would not have accepted 1 Timothy in his list. • The reference to the PE's absence in P46 is a weak argument from silence since the papyrus misses some leaves.

Charts *on the* Life, Letters, and Theology *of* Paul

Locating the Pastoral Epistles within Paul's Ministry

CHART 73

	WITHIN ACTS				AFTER THE END OF ACTS	AFTER PAUL'S DEATH	
	Ponsot (1997)	Robinson (1976)	Van Bruggen (1981)	Bartlet (1913)	Ellis, Fee, Polhill	Quinn/Wacker	Pervo
1. Journey (Acts 13:1–14:28)							
2. Journey (Acts 15:36–18:22)	1 Timothy Titus						
Prison: Philippi (Acts 16)		1 Timothy Titus	1 Timothy Titus				
3. Journey (Acts 18:23–21:16)							
4. Journey (Acts 21:17–28:16)							
Prison: Jerusalem (Acts 21–23)							
Prison: Caesarea (Acts 24–26)		2 Timothy					
Prison: Rom.e (Acts 28)	2 Timothy?		2 Timothy	1–2 Timothy, Titus			
Release from Rome					1 Timothy, Titus		
5. Journey					2 Timothy		
Prison and death in Rome							
Between AD 70–100						1–2 Tim., Titus	
Between AD 100–130							1–2 Tim., Titus

137

PHILEMON: A Snapshot

CHART 74

Recipients	Philemon (1:1), Apphia and Archippus (1:2); only the latter is known from elsewhere, see Col. 4:17
City	Philemon lived in Colossae; see parallel use of names in Colossians and Philemon (chart 75): Onesimus in Col. 4:9 and Philem. 1:10 Epaphras in Col. 1:7; 4:12 and Philem. 1:23 Archippus in Col 4:17; Philem. 1:2

Structure	A. Imprisonment and partnership under grace (1:1–3) [5 names]
	  B. Philemon "refreshed" the saints by helping them (1:4–7)
	    C. Appeal to Philemon for Onesimus (1:8–10) ["Paul"]
	      D. Paul wanted to keep Onesimus, his "heart" (1:11–13)
	        E. Paul wants Philemon to accept Onesimus voluntarily (1:14)
	      D'. Philemon should receive Onesimus as a "beloved brother" (1:15–17) ["Paul"]
	    C'. Charge me for any debt of Onesimus (1:18–19)
	  B'. Philemon should "refresh" again by serving Paul (1:20–22) [5 names]
	A'. Imprisonment and partnership under grace (1:23v25)

Special features	• Because of its short size and personal content, this letter corresponds more to the typical ancient letter than any of Paul's other "letters." • As an ancient letter, Philemon is wholly devoted to a personal matter and largely devoid of theological key themes such as justification by faith, the law, etc. • Philemon mentions a lot of names: besides Paul and Jesus; see Timothy (1:1), Philemon (1:1), Apphia (1:2), Archippus (1:2), Onesimus (1:10), Epaphras (1:23), Mark (1:24), Aristarchus (1:24), Demas (1:24), Luke (1:24). The letter is thus personal, but not private.
Occasion	Onesimus is Philemon's slave (1:16) who possibly ran away from his owner (1:12), maybe after having stolen (1:18). He met Paul who converted him (1:10) and used him in his ministry (1:12, 13; Col. 4:7–9)
Purpose(s)	Paul sends Onesimus back to Philemon (1:12) with the plea to receive the slave as a "brother" (1:16; Col. 4:9) and maybe to return him to Paul for ministry (1:13).

Parallels between Colossians and Philemon

CHART 75

	Term / Concept	Colossians	Philemon
1.	Paul is a prisoner	4:3, 10, 18	1:1, 9, 10, 13, 23
2.	Faith in Jesus, love for saints	1:4 since we heard of your faith in Christ Jesus and the love which you have for all the saints;	1:5 because I hear of your love, and of the faith which you have toward the Lord Jesus, and toward all the saints;
3.	Epaphras	1:7; 4:12	1:23
4.	"certificate of debt"	2:14 (χειρόγραφον)	1:19 (ἐγὼ Παῦλος ἔγραψα τῇ ἐμῇ χειρί)
5.	Slave who does wrong (ἀδικέω)	3:25 For he [slave] who does wrong (ὁ γὰρ ἀδικῶν) will receive the consequences of the wrong which he has done, and that without partiality.	1:18 But if he [Onesimus, the slave] has wronged you (εἰ δέ τι ἠδίκησέν σε) in any way or owes you anything, charge that to my account;
6.	Onesimus	4:9	1:10
7.	Mark	4:10	1:24
8.	Aristarchus	4:10	1:24
9.	Luke	4:14	1:24
10.	Demas	4:14	1:24
11.	Archippus, a recipient	4:17	1:2

Philemon and Elements of Forgiveness

CHART 76

	STEPS	TEXTS
1.	OFFENSE	11 who formerly was useless to you 18 But if he has wronged you in any way or owes you anything
2.	COMPASSION	10 my child, Onesimus, whom I have begotten in my imprisonment
3.	INTERCESSION	9 for love's sake I rather appeal to you 10 I appeal to you for my child, Onesimus.
4.	SUBSTITUTION	18 charge that to my account 19 I will repay it
5.	RESTORATION TO FAVOR	15 For perhaps he was for this reason separated from you for a while, that you would have him back forever
6.	NEW RELATIONSHIP	16 no longer as a slave, but more than a slave, a beloved brother, especially to me, but how much more to you, both in the flesh and in the Lord. 17 If then you regard me a partner, accept him as you would me.

Romans 1:17 For in it the righteousness of God is revealed from faith to faith; as it is written, "But the righteous man shall live by faith" (Hab. 2:4). ["Righteousness of God" 8x Rom.: 1:17; 3:5, 21, 22, 25, 26; 10:3 [2x]; then only 2 Cor. 5:21]

   a) the righteousness is God's own
      (1) possessive genitive: God's justice or faithfulness (*attribute*)
      (2) subjective genitive: God's righteous-making, saving power (*activity*)
   b) righteousness as a status or quality attributed to humans
      (3) objective genitive: a human righteousness (maybe by faith) which counts before God
      (4) genitive of origin: righteousness as a human status which results from God's grace

Romans 11:26...and so all Israel will be saved (καὶ οὕτως πᾶς Ἰσραὴλ σωθήσεται)

   a)   Eschatological Miracle:
        Ethnic Israel will be saved through faith in Christ through his direct revelation at his parousia.
   b)   Ecclesiological View:
        "All Israel" refers to the church, consisting of Jews and Gentiles. They are saved through the new covenant that has already been inaugurated by virtue of Christ's resurrection.
   c)   Roman Mission View:
        "All Israel" refers to believing and hardened Jews in Rome.
   d)   Two-Covenant View ("Sonderweg" hypothesis):
        "All Israel" refers to ethnic Israel that is saved regardless of faith in Christ.
   e)   Total National Elect View:
        "All Israel" refers to all of the elect from ethnic Israel.

1 Corinthians 7:15 Yet if the unbelieving one leaves, let him leave; … not under bondage

   a)   Paul grants the privilege of remarriage in case of desertion
   b)   Paul allows for a separation that does not permit remarriage

1 Corinthians 7:21 [B]ut if you are able also to become free, rather do that.

   a)   "freedom" is the object (KJV, NAS, NIV): Paul discourages slavery
   b)   "slavery" is the object (NAB, NJB, NRS): Paul resists freedom from slavery
   c)   "calling" is the object: Paul does not commend or oppose slavery

2 Corinthians 3:6...who also made us adequate as servants of a new covenant, not of the letter, but of the Spirit; for the letter kills, but the Spirit gives life.

   a)   The New Covenant excludes the Old Testament Law: the letter that kills refers to the Mosaic covenant which is now obsolete
   b)   The New Covenant includes the Old Testament law
      (1)   The Law, now internally on the heart, is kept through the Spirit
      (2)   "Letter" refers not to the Old Testament but to a defective understanding of the law, as being merely written
      (3)   The contrast relates to two different interpretations of the law: 'letter' refers to an incorrect, legalistic interpretation, "Spirit" refers to the correct one

2 Corinthians 5:21 He made Him who knew no sin to be sin (ἁμαρτίαν ἐποίησεν) on our behalf, so that we might become the righteousness of God in Him.

   a)   Sin: "to be sin" (NAS); "God made him share our sin" (GNT); see Matt 27:46; Gal. 3:13
   b)   Sin-Offering: "to be the offering for our sin" (NLT); see Lev. 4:21, 24; 5:12; Isa. 53:10

Galatians 2:16 [A] man is not justified by the works of the Law but (ἐὰν μὴ) through faith in Christ Jesus

   a)   adversative: "*but* through faith": law and faith are antithetical
   b)   exceptive: "*except* through faith": law and faith can meet together
   c)   exceptive, yet exception only applies to "a man is not justified"

Galatians 3:19 The Law "was added because of transgressions ...."

   a)   because of *identifying* transgressions (cognitive function)

   b)   because of *provoking* transgressions (causative function)

Ephesians 2:14 ... and broke down the barrier of the dividing wall [15] by abolishing in His flesh the enmity, which is the Law of commandments contained in ordinances (τὸν νόμον τῶν ἐντολῶν ἐν δόγμασιν), so that in Himself He might make the two into one new man...

   a)   Paul is making a negative statement about the whole Mosaic law

   b)   Paul negates the ceremonial law (see Col. 2:14 [δόγμα], 20–21 [... Do not taste, ...])

Ephesians 5:21...and be subject to one another in the fear of Christ.

   a)   The text is connected grammatically to the *preceding* text (5:18–21, NAS, ESV, HCSB)

   b)   The text teaches mutual submission; women should submit to husbands and vice versa.

   c)   This verse summarizes the subject of submission explained next: "[21] And further, submit to one another out of reverence for Christ. [22] For wives, this means submit to your husbands as to the Lord" (NLT).

Philippians 2:5 Have this attitude (ἐν ὑμῖν) in yourselves which was also in Christ Jesus [ὃ καὶ ἐν Χριστῷ Ἰησοῦ]

   a)   Christ is an ethical example for the individual

        KJV "Let this mind be in you, which was also in Christ Jesus"

   b)   Christ is an ethical example for the Christian community

        TNIV "In your relationships with one another, have the same attitude of mind Christ Jesus had"

   c)   Paul appeals not to Christ's ethics but to the believers' union in Christ:

        RSV "Have this mind among yourselves, which is yours in Christ Jesus" (ESV)

        Silva "[Adopt] [then] this frame of mind in your community—which indeed [is proper for those who are] in Christ Jesus."

Philippians 2:6...who, although He [Christ] existed in the form of God, did not regard equality with God a thing to be grasped, [7] but emptied Himself, taking the form of a bond-servant, and being made in the likeness of men.

   a)   Verse 6 contrasts the *earthly* Jesus with Adam: "form of God" alludes to "image of God" in Genesis 1:27 and "equality with God" echoes "like God" in Genesis 3:5.

   b)   Verse 6 reflects Paul's belief in Christ's preexistence.

Colossians 2:18 Let no one keep defrauding you of your prize by delighting in self-abasement and <u>the worship of the angels</u> (θρησκείᾳ τῶν ἀγγέλων), ...

   a)   Objective genitive: humans worship angels (see ἐθελοθρησκία in 2:23)

   b)   Subjective genitive: humans worship together with the angels

Colossians 2:18 Let no one keep defrauding you of your prize by delighting in self-abasement and the worship of the angels, <u>taking his stand on visions</u> (ἃ ἑόρακεν ἐμβατεύων), ...

   a)   "investigate" visions seen in ecstatic experiences

   b)   "enter" into heaven to possess salvation

   c)   "entering," meaning initiation into the mystery cult

1 Thessalonians 4:3 For this is the will of God, your sanctification; that is, that you abstain from sexual immorality; [4] that each of you know how to possess <u>his own vessel</u> (τὸ ἑαυτοῦ σκεῦος) in sanctification and honor, [5] not in lustful passion, like the Gentiles who do not know God; ...

   a)   RSV: "... know how to take a wife for himself in holiness and honor"; see 1 Peter 3:7

   b)   NRS: "... know how to control your own body in holiness and honor"

   c)   "vessel" refers to the genital part of the male body; see 1 Sam. 21:5 (LXX 21:6)

1 Thessalonians 4:17 Then we who are alive and remain <u>will be caught up</u> (ἀρπαγησόμεθα) together with them in the clouds to meet the Lord in the air, ...

    a) The "rapture" refers to the church's sudden disappearance before the second coming
    b) The "rapture" is a symbolic motif of consolation against death

2 Thessalonians 2:3 Let no one in any way deceive you, for it will not come unless the apostasy comes first, and <u>the man of lawlessness</u> (ὁ ἄνθρωπος τῆς ἀνομίας) is revealed, the <u>son of destruction</u> (ὁ υἱὸς τῆς ἀπωλείας), who opposes and exalts himself above every so-called god or object of worship, so that he takes his seat in <u>the temple of God</u>, displaying himself as being God.

    a) Paul speaks metaphorically
        (1) about opposition against the ecclesial temple, i.e., the church (1 Cor. 3:16)
        (2) about opposition against the heavenly temple, i.e., God himself
        (3) about opposition against the temple in Jerusalem, thus symbolizing "the gravest act of defiance imaginable"
    b) Paul speaks prophetically
        (4) about the opposition against the second temple. Paul was wrong: The temple is destroyed and the end has not yet come
        (5) about a future opposition against a future temple

2 Thessalonians 2:6 And you know <u>what restrains</u> (τὸ κατέχον) him now, so that in his time he will be revealed. [7] For the mystery of lawlessness is already at work; only <u>he who now restrains</u> (ὁ κατέχων) will do so until he is taken out of the way.

    a) Roman empire   d) God   g) A supernatural being
    b) The church   e) The Holy Spirit   h) An imaginary figure
    c) Paul   f) The church

1 Timothy 2:11 A woman must quietly receive instruction with entire submissiveness. [12] But I do not allow a woman to teach or exercise authority over a man, but to remain quiet. [13] For it was Adam who was first created, and then Eve. [14] And it was not Adam who was deceived, but the woman being deceived, fell into transgression. [15] But women will be preserved through the bearing of children if they continue in faith and love and sanctity with self-restraint.

    a) The text is irrelevant today because it is deutero-Pauline (as is 1 Cor. 14:34-35)
    b) The text is irrelevant today because Paul's command is culturally conditioned
    c) The text is relevant because women have always been more gullible than men
    d) The text is relevant because Paul grounds the command in the order of creation

1 Timothy 3:1 [I]f any man aspires to the <u>office of overseer</u> (ἐπισκοπή), it is a fine work he desires to do. [2] An overseer (ἐπίσκοπος), then, must be above reproach, ...

    a) "office / position of a bishop" / "bishop" (KJV, NKJV)
    b) "office of an overseer" / "overseer" (NAS, NIV, TNIV, ESV)
    c) "elder" (NLT)

2 Timothy 1:18 the Lord grant to him [Onesiphorus] to find mercy from the Lord on that day—and you know very well what services he rendered at Ephesus.

    a) Onesiphorus is / may be dead
        (1) Paul prays for him
        (2) Paul merely expresses a wish, not a prayer
    b) Onesiphorus is not dead, and Paul prays for him

2 Timothy 3:16 πᾶσα γραφὴ θεόπνευστος καὶ ὠφέλιμος πρὸς διδασκαλίαν, ...
(Should we place the missing copula "is" *between* both adjectives or *before* them?)

    a) ASV "Every scripture INSPIRED of God <u>is</u> also PROFITABLE for teaching ..."
        (the first adjective is attributive, the second is predicate)
    b) NAS "All Scripture <u>is</u> INSPIRED by God and PROFITABLE for teaching ..."
        (both adjectives, which agree in case, number, and gender, are predicate)

Titus 1:5 … appoint elders … ⁶ [who have] children <u>who believe</u> (τέκνα ἔχων πιστά)

    a)   Term describes *believing*: "children who believe" (NAS, NIV, TNIV, ESV, NLT)

    b)   Term describes *behaving*: "faithful children" (KJV, NKJV, NET; HCSB); see the same adjective in 1 Tim. 3:11; 2 Tim. 2:2, 13; Titus 1:9; see parallel in 1 Tim. 3:4

Titus 3:5 …by the washing of regeneration and renewing by the Holy Spirit (διὰ λουτροῦ παλιγγενεσίας καὶ ἀνακαινώσεως πνεύματος ἁγίου) ⁶ whom He poured out upon us richly…

    a)   Through a washing of rebirth and of renewal which is associated with the Holy Spirit.

    b)   Through a washing of rebirth and of renewal which are associated with the Holy Spirit.

    c)   Through a washing associated with the Holy Spirit which brings rebirth and renewal.

    d)   Through a washing of rebirth and through a renewal associated with the Holy Spirit.

Philemon 1:18 But if (εἰ) he has wronged (ἠδίκησέν) you in any way or owes (ὀφείλει) you anything, charge that to my account (τοῦτο ἐμοὶ ἐλλόγα)"

    a)   Paul hints at Onesimus' crime (standard reading)

    b)   Paul does not hint at a crime since he simply asserts something for the sake of argument (first-class conditional)

Philemon 1:19 I, Paul, am writing this with my own hand, <u>I will repay it</u> (not to mention to you that you owe to me even your own self as well).

    a)   Paul offers to pay what Onesimus owes.

    b)   Paul offers compensation for the loss of Onesimus if Philemon should send the slave back to the apostle.

Part D

PAUL'S THEOLOGICAL CONCEPTS

Sources for Paul's Theology

CHART 78

	SOURCE	EXAMPLE
(1)	Old Testament	Rom. 4:3 For what does the <u>Scripture</u> say? "Abraham believed God, and it was credited to him as righteousness." (Gen. 15:6)
(2)	Targumim	Eph. 4:8 Therefore it says, "When He ascended on high, He led captive a host of captives, And He *gave* [instead of 'received'] gifts to men." (Ps. 68:18)
(3)	(Intertestamental) Jewish Traditions	Gal. 3:19 Why the Law then? It was added because of transgressions, having been <u>ordained through angels</u> by the agency of a mediator, until the seed should come to whom the promise had been made. (See *Jubilees* 1:25-27; *A.J.* 15.136)
(4)	General revelation	1 Cor. 11:14 Does not even <u>nature itself teach</u> you that if a man has long hair, it is a dishonor to him, [15] but if a woman has long hair, it is a glory to her? For her hair is given to her for a covering.
(5)	Greco-Roman culture	1 Cor. 15:33 Do not be deceived: "Bad company corrupts good morals." (proverb from Menander [ca. 344-292 BC], a Greek comic poet)
(6)	Direct revelations	Gal. 1:12 For I neither received it [gospel] from man, nor was I taught it, but I received it through a <u>revelation</u> of Jesus Christ.
(7)	Agrapha of Jesus (non-canonical sayings)	Acts 20:35 In everything I showed you that by working hard in this manner you must help the weak and remember the words of the <u>Lord Jesus, that He Himself said</u>, "It is more blessed to give than to receive."
(8)	Synoptic Traditions	1 Cor. 11:25 In the same way *He took* the cup also, after supper, saying, "<u>This cup is the new covenant in My blood</u>; do this, as often as you drink *it*, in remembrance of Me." (See Luke 22:20)
(9)	Early Christian traditions	1 Cor. 15:3 For I delivered to you as of first importance <u>what I also received</u>, that Christ died for our sins according to the Scriptures, [4] and that He was buried, and that He was raised on the third day according to the Scriptures, [5] and that He appeared to Cephas, then to the twelve. [6] After that He appeared to more than five hundred brethren at one time, most of whom remain until now, but some have fallen asleep; [7] then He appeared to James, then to all the apostles; …

Diversity in Paul's Thoughts

CHART 79

1.	Paul received the Gospel by revelation	Paul received the Gospel by tradition
	Galatians 1:12 For I neither received it [the gospel] from man, nor was I taught it, but I received it through a revelation of Jesus Christ.	1 Corinthians 15:3 For I delivered to you as of first importance what I also received, that Christ died for our sins according to the Scriptures, …
2.	Paul has a positive view of the law	Paul has a negative view of the law
	Romans 3:31 Do we then nullify the Law through faith? May it never be! On the contrary, we establish the Law. (See also 7:12, 14; 8:2; 1 Cor 7:19; 9:21; Gal. 3:21; 5:14; 6:2)	Romans 3:20 because by the works of the Law no flesh will be justified in His sight; for through the Law comes the knowledge of sin. (see also 4:15; 5:20; 6:14; 7:9; 10:4; Gal. 3:10–13)
3.	Judgment of the believer	Justification of the believer
	Romans 14:10 But you, why do you judge your brother? Or you again, why do you regard your brother with contempt? For we shall all stand before the judgment seat of God.	Romans 5:1 Therefore having been justified by faith, we have peace with God through our Lord Jesus Christ, …
4.	Romans	Galatians
	• "to the Jew first and also to the Greek" (1:16) • Abraham's "seed" are believers (4:13, 16, 18) • "Israel" is historical Israel (3:1; 9–11; 15:8) • loving one another (13:8) is illustrated with the Decalogue (13:9–10) • observance of circumcision (2:28; 3:1–2) and dietary laws (14:1–6) and is permitted.	• "neither Jew nor Greek" (3:28) • Abraham's "seed" is Christ (3:16) • "Israel of God" (6:16) refers to Christians • "love your neighbor" (5:14) is illustrated with a catalogue of vices and virtues (5:18–23) • observance of circumcision (5:1–12; 6:12–15) and dietary laws (2:11–14) is confronted.
5.	God is committed to ethnic Israel	The church is the spiritual transethnic Israel
	Romans 11:26 and so all Israel will be saved; just as it is written, "The Deliverer will come from Zion, He will remove ungodliness from Jacob."	Romans 4:11 [Abraham is] "the father of all who believe without being circumcised." (also 4:16; Gal. 3:7, 19; 6:16; see Hos. 2:1, 25 applied to Gentiles in Rom. 9:25-26)
6.	Paul expects Christ's coming before his death	Paul expects to die before Christ's coming
	1 Thessalonians 4:15 For this we say to you by the word of the Lord, that we who are alive and remain until the coming of the Lord, will not precede those who have fallen asleep. (but see also 5:1–3)	Philippians 1:20 … that with all boldness, Christ shall even now, as always, be exalted in my body, whether by life or by death. (also 2 Thess. 2:3; Phil. 3:11; but see Phil. 4:5)
7.	Men and women are equal (new creation)	Man is the head of the woman (old creation)
	Galatians 3:28 There is neither Jew nor Greek, there is neither slave nor free man, there is neither male nor female; for you are all one in Christ Jesus. (also 1 Cor 11:5)	1 Corinthians 11:3 But I want you to understand that Christ is the head of every man, and the man is the head of a woman, and God is the head of Christ. (also 1 Cor 14:34)
8.	Paul abolishes a slave's status	Paul maintains a slave's status
	Colossians 3:11 … there is no distinction between Greek and Jew, circumcised and uncircumcised, barbarian, Scythian, slave and freeman, but Christ is all, and in all.	Colossians 3:22 Slaves, in all things obey those who are your masters on earth, not with external service, as those who merely please men, but with sincerity of heart, fearing the Lord.
9.	Widows should not remarry	Widows should remarry
	1 Corinthians 7:39 A wife is bound as long as her husband lives; but if her husband is dead, she is free to be married to whom she wishes, only in the Lord. 40 But in my opinion she is happier if she remains as she is; and I think that I also have the Spirit of God.	1 Timothy 5:14 Therefore, I want younger widows to get married, bear children, keep house, and give the enemy no occasion for reproach; 15 for some have already turned aside to follow Satan.

Theological Concepts

CHART 80

NAMES OF GOD	
almighty (παντοκράτωρ)	2 Cor. 6:18
Father (πατήρ)	Rom. 1:7; 6:4; 1 Cor. 1:3; 8:6; 15:24; 2 Cor. 1:2; Gal. 1:1; Eph. 1:2–3, 17; Phil. 1:2; Col. 1:2; 1 Thess. 1:1, 3; 2 Thess. 1:1; 1 Tim. 1:2; 2 Tim. 1:2; Titus 1:4; Philem. 1:3; etc.
Abba! Father! (αββα ὁ πατήρ)	Rom. 8:15; Gal. 4:6 (in the NT elsewhere only Mark 14:36)
… of all	Eph. 4:6 (see 1 Cor. 8:6)
… of believers	Rom. 1:7; 8:15; 1 Cor. 1:3; 2 Cor. 1:2; Gal. 1:3; …
… of glory (τῆς δόξης)	Eph. 1:17
… of Jesus Christ	Rom. 8:3; 2 Cor. 1:3; 11:31; Gal. 4:4; Eph. 1:3
… of mercies (τῶν οἰκτιρμῶν)	2 Cor. 1:3
God the father (θεός πατήρ)	Gal. 1:1; Eph. 6:23; Phil. 2:11; 1 Tim. 1:2; 2 Tim. 1:2
Our God and Father	Gal. 1:4; Col. 1:2
Jesus Christ and God the Father	Gal. 1:1
God the Father and the Lord Jesus Christ	Eph. 6:23; 2 Thess. 1:2
God our Father and the Lord Jesus Christ	Rom. 1:7; 1 Cor. 1:3; 2 Cor. 1:2; Gal. 1:3; Eph. 1:2; etc.
God and Father of our Lord Jesus Christ	2 Cor 1:3; 11:31; Eph 1:3
God the Father and Christ Jesus our Lord	1 Tim. 1:2; 2 Tim. 1:2; Titus 1:4
God of	
… all comfort (πάσης παρακλήσεως)	2 Cor. 1:3; Rom. 15:5 (perseverance and c.)
… hope (τῆς ἐλπίδος)	Rom. 15:13
… love and peace (τῆς ἀγάπης καὶ εἰρήνης)	2 Cor. 13:11
… peace (τῆς εἰρήνης)	Rom. 15:33; 16:20; 1 Cor. 14:33; 2 Cor. 13:11 (love and p.); etc.
God our Savior (θεός σωτήρ ἡμῶν)	1 Tim. 1:1; 2:3; 4:10; Titus 1:3; 2:10, 13; 3:4
king (βασιλεύς)	1 Tim. 1:17; 6:15 ("king of kings"); see 2:2
Lord (κύριος)	Rom. 4:8 (Ps. 32:1–2); 9:28–29 (Isa. 28:22; 1:9); 10:16 (Isa. 53:1); 11:34 (Isa. 40:13); 15:11 (Ps. 117:1); 1 Cor. 3:20 (Ps. 94:11); 2 Cor. 6:17-18 (Isa. 52:11; 2 Sam. 7:14)
Lord of Lords (κύριος τῶν κυριευόντων)	1 Tim. 6:15 (see κύριος κυρίων in Rev. 17:14; 19:16)
Sovereign (δυνάστης)	1 Tim. 6:15
ATTRIBUTES OF GOD	
divine (θειότης)	Rom. 1:20
eternal (αἰώνιος) God	Rom. 16:26 (God); 1 Tim. 1:17 (king; see 6:15)
faithfulness of God (πίστις τοῦ θεοῦ)	Rom. 3:3
God is faithful (πιστός)	1 Cor. 1:9; 10:13; 2 Cor. 1:18; 1 Thess. 5:24; …
glory (δόξα) of God	Rom. 1:23; 3:7, 23; 5:2; 15:7; 1 Cor. 10:31; …
the riches of His glory	Rom. 9:23; Eph. 3:16

To Him be the glory forever and ever. Amen.	Gal. 1:5; Phil. 4:20; 1 Tim. 1:17; 2 Tim. 4:18
God dwells in unapproachable light	1 Tim. 6:16 (φῶς ... ἀπρόσιτον)
grace (χάρις) **of God**	Rom. 3:24; 5:15; 1 Cor. 3:10; 15:10 (2x); 2 Cor. 6:1; 8:1; ...
immortality (ἀθανασία)	1 Tim. 6:16
impartiality (προσωπολημψία)	Rom. 2:11 (see 3:29); 10:12
no distinction (διαστολή)	Rom. 3:22; 10:12
Jews and Gentiles (Ἰουδαῖοι καὶ ἔθνη)	Rom. 3:29; 9:24; 1 Cor. 1:23
Jews and Greeks (Ἰουδαῖος καὶ Ἕλλην)	Rom. 1:16; 2:9, 10; 3:9, 29; 9:24; 10:12; Gal. 3:28
incorruptible (ἄφθαρτος)	Rom. 1:23; 1 Tim. 1:17
invisible (ἀόρατος)	Rom. 1:20; Col. 1:15; 1 Tim. 1:17; see 6:16
kind (χρηστότης)	Rom. 2:4; 11:22 (2x); Eph. 2:7; Titus 3:4
living God (θεός ζῶν)	Rom. 9:26; 2 Cor. 3:3; 6:16; 1 Thess. 1:9; ...
one God (εἷς θεὸς)	Rom. 3:30; 1 Cor. 8:4, 6; Gal. 3:20; Eph. 4:6; 1 Tim. 2:5
only God (μόνος θεὸς)	Rom. 16:27 ("only wise God"); 1 Tim. 1:17; see 1 Thess. 1:9
omnipotent	Rom. 8:28; Eph. 1:11; Col. 1:17
power (δύναμις) **of God**	Rom. 1:16, 20; 15:19; 1 Cor. 1:18, 24; 2:5; etc.
riches	Rom. 2:4 (of his kindness); 9:23 (of glory; Eph. 1:18; 3:16; Phil. 4:19; Col. 1:27); 11:33 (of wisdom and knowledge); Eph. 1:7 (of grace; 2:7); 2:4 (of mercy)
righteousness (δικαιοσύνη) **of God**	Rom. 1:17; 3:5, 21–22, 25–26; 10:3 [2x]; 2 Cor. 5:21
severity (ἀποτομία)	Rom. 11:22 (2x)
Sovereign	Rom. 9:15–16, 18; Eph. 1:11; 4:6; 1 Tim. 6:15
wrath of God (ὀργὴ θεοῦ)	Rom. 1:18; 2:5; Eph. 5:6; Col. 3:6; 1 Thess. 2:16
ACTIVITIES OF GOD	
chooses (ἐκλεκτός, ἐκλέγομαι)	Rom. 8:33; 16:13; 1 Cor. 1:27–28; see Gal. 1:15
Creator	Rom. 11:36; 1 Cor. 8:6; 11:9; Eph. 3:9; 1 Tim. 4:3
crushes Satan "under your feet"	Rom. 16:20
eternal	
... power (κράτος αἰώνιον)	1 Tim. 6:16
... purpose (πρόθεσιν τῶν αἰώνων)	Eph. 3:11
forgives (ἀφίημι, ἄφεσις, χαρίζομαι)	Rom. 4:7; Eph. 1:7; 4:32; Col. 1:14; 2:13 (Acts 13:38; 26:18)
hates (μισέω)	Rom. 9:13 (Mal. 1:2–3)
judges (κρίνω)	Rom. 2:2–3, 12, 16; 3:6–7; 1 Cor. 5:13; 11:31–32; 2 Thess. 1:5
righteous judgment (δικαιοκρισία) of God	Rom. 2:5; see 2 Thess. 1:5 (δικαία κρίσις)
judgment seat of God	Rom. 14:10 (βῆμα τοῦ θεοῦ)
gives sinners over to impurity	Rom. 1:24, 26, 28
love of God (ἡ ἀγάπη τοῦ θεοῦ)	Rom. 5:5, 8; 8:39; 2 Cor. 13:14; Eph. 2:4; (6:23); 2 Thess. 3:5
beloved [of God] (ἀγαπητοί [θεοῦ])	Rom. 1:7; 11:28; see 9:25; 1 Thess. 1:4
God loves (ἀγαπάω)	Rom. 9:13; 2 Cor. 9:7; Eph. 1:6; 2:4; 2 Thess. 2:16
God has given us a Spirit of love	2 Tim. 1:7

love for mankind (φιλανθρωπία)	Titus 3:4
justifies (δικαιόω)	Rom. 3:24, 26, 30; 4:5; 8:33; 1 Cor. 6:11; Gal. 3:8; Titus 3:7
peace from God (εἰρήνη ἀπὸ θεοῦ)	Rom. 1:7; 1 Cor. 1:3; 2 Cor. 1:2; Gal. 1:3; Eph. 1:2; etc.
resurrects: gives life to the dead	Rom. 4:17; 2 Cor. 1:9
raised Jesus from the dead	Rom. 4:24; 6:4; 8:11; 10:9; 1 Cor. 6:14; 15:15; 2 Cor. 4:14; Gal. 1:1; Eph. 1:20; Col. 2:12; 1 Thess. 1:10; Acts 13:30
will make us / made us alive with /in Christ	Rom. 8:11; 1 Cor. 15:22; Eph. 2:5–6; Col. 2:12–13; 3:1
reveals	Rom. 1:17–18; 1 Cor. 2:10; Gal. 1:16; Phil. 3:15; etc.
through creation (κτίσις)	Rom. 1:18–20; 8:19–22; Col. 1:15, 23
through the word of God (ὁ λόγος τοῦ θεοῦ)	Rom. 9:6; 1 Cor. 14:36; 2 Cor. 2:17; …
saves (σῴζω)	Rom. 5:9, 10; 8:24; 9:27; Titus 3:5
ENEMIES OF GOD	
demons (δαιμόνια)	1 Cor. 10:20 (2x), 21(2x); 1 Tim. 4:1
devil (διάβολος)	Eph. 4:27; 6:11; 1 Tim. 3:6, 7, 11; 2 Tim. 2:26; 3:3; Titus 2:3
Satan (ὁ Σατανᾶς)	Rom. 16:20; 1 Cor. 5:5; 7:5; 2 Cor. 2:11; 11:14; 12:7; etc.
evil one, the (ὁ πονηρός)	Eph. 6:16 (see "the lawless one" [ὁ ἄνομος] in 2 Thess. 2:8)
idols (τὰ εἴδωλα)	Rom. 2:22; 1 Cor. 8:4, 7; 10:19; 12:2; 2 Cor. 6:16; 1 Thess. 1:9
sinners	Rom. 5:10; 8:7; 1 Cor. 15:25; Phil. 3:18; Col. 1:21; 1 Tim. 5:14
world forces (κοσμοκρατώροι) **of this darkness**	Eph. 6:12 (also spiritual *forces* of wickedness …)

Christological Concepts

CHART 81

CHRIST'S HUMANITY	
Adam, the last	1 Cor. 15:45; see Rom. 5:12–20 (Luke 3:38)
Born of a woman	Gal. 4:4
Seed of Abraham	Gal. 3:16 (Matt. 1:1)
Seed of David	Rom. 1:3; 15:12 ("Jesse," Isa. 11:10); 2 Tim. 2:8; Acts 13:22–23, 34–37 (Matt. 9:27)
with a body of flesh	Col. 1:22 (σῶμα τῆς σαρκὸς); see Rom. 1:3; 9:5; 1 Tim. 3:16
Christ was a Jew	Rom. 9:5; 15:8; Gal. 4:4 (Luke 2:21; John 4:9)
Brothers of the Lord	1 Cor. 9:5; Gal. 1:19 (James) (Mark 3:31)
Christ was obedient	Rom. 5:18-19; Phil. 2:8 ("faithfulness of Christ" [NET] in chart 89) (Matt. 26:42)
Christ testified before Pilate	1 Tim. 6:13 (Matt 27:11–14)
Christ suffered & was killed	2 Cor. 1:5; Phil. 3:10; 1 Thess. 2:15 (Matt. 16:21; 27:33–50)
Christ was buried	1 Cor. 15:4 (and he went to the dead: Rom. 10:7; Eph. 4:6)
Jesus of Nazareth	Acts 26:9 (Matt. 2:23; 21:11)
Jesus as a man (ἄνθρωπος)	Rom. 5:15; 1 Cor. 15:21, 47; Phil. 2:7; 1 Tim. 2:5; but see also Gal. 1:1, 11–12; Col. 3:23
Incarnation (implied)	2 Cor. 8:9; Col. 1:19–22; 1 Tim. 1:15; 3:16
Jesus was sent "in the likeness of sinful flesh"	Rom. 8:3 (ἐν ὁμοιώματι σαρκὸς ἁμαρτίας)
Jesus was a slave	Phil. 2:6 (μορφὴ δούλου)
EXPLICIT CHRISTOLOGY	
Christ Jesus (Χριστός Ἰησοῦς)	Rom. 1:1; 2:16; 3:24; 6:3, 11, 23; 8:1–2, 34, 39; 15:5, 16–17; 16:3; 1 Cor. 1:1–2, 4, 30; 4:15, 17; 15:31; 16:24; 2 Cor. 1:1; 13:5; Gal. 2:4, 16; 3:14, 26, 28; 4:14; 5:6, 24; Eph. 1:1 (2x); 2:6–7, 10, 13, 20; 3:1, 6, 11, 21; Phil. 1:1 (2x), 6, 8, 26; 2:5; 3:3, 8, 12, 14; 4:7, 19, 21; Col. 1:1, 4; 2:6; 4:12; 1 Thess. 2:14; 5:18; 1 Tim. 1:1 (2x), 2, 12, 14–16; 2:5; 3:13; 4:6; 5:21; 6:13; 2 Tim. 1:1 (2x), 2, 9–10, 13; 2:1, 3, 10; 3:12, 15; 4:1; Titus 1:4; Philem. 1:1, 9, 23
Jesus Christ (Ἰησοῦς Χριστός)	Rom. 1:4, 6–8; 2:16; 3:22; 5:1, 11, 15, 17, 21; 7:25; 13:14; 15:6, 30; 1:25, 27; 1 Cor. 1:2–3, 7–10; 2:2; 3:11; 6:11; 8:6; 15:57; 2 Cor. 1:2–3, 19; 4:5–6; 8:9; 13:5, 13; Gal. 1:1, 3, 12; 2:16; 3:1, 22; 6:14, 18; Eph. 1:2–3, 5, 17; 5:20; 6:23, 24; Phil. 1:2, 11, 19; 2:11, 21; 3:20; 4:23; Col. 1:3; 1 Thess. 1:1, 3; 5:9, 23, 28; 2 Thess. 1:1–2, 12; 2:1, 14, 16; 3:6, 12, 18; 1 Tim. 6:3, 14; 2 Tim. 2:8; Titus 1:1; 2:13; 3:6; Philem. 1:3, 25
exaltation	
resurrected	Rom. 1:4; 4:24, 25; 6:4–5, 9; 7:4; 8:11, 34; 10:9; 1 Cor. 6:14; Phil. 3:10; etc.
ascended	Eph. 4:8-10; 1 Tim. 3:16 ("taken up in glory")
seated at the right hand	of God ("enthronement"): Rom. 8:34; Eph. 1:20; 2:6; Col. 3:1 (1 Peter 3:18; see Ps. 110:1)
second coming	1 Cor. 15:23; 1 Thess. 2:19; 3:13; 4:15–17; 5:23; 2 Thess. 2:1, 8
firstborn (πρωτότοκος)	Rom. 8:29; Col. 1:15, 18
firstfruit (ἀπαρχή)	1 Cor. 15:20, 23
from heaven (ἐξ οὐρανοῦ)	1 Cor. 15:47
God (Christ is)	Rom. 9:5; Titus 2:10–13 (see also Acts 20:28; Phil. 2:6-8)

head of the church	Eph. 1:22; 4:15; 5:23; Col. 1:18; 2:10, 19; see 1 Cor. 11:3
image (εἰκών) **of God**	2 Cor. 4:4, 6 (see 3:18); Col. 1:15
judge	Rom. 2:16; 1 Cor. 4:4–5; 2 Cor. 5:10; 2 Thess. 1:7-10; 2 Tim. 4:1, 8 (ὁ δίκαιος κριτής)
Jesus rules as **king** (βασιλεύειν)	1 Cor. 15:25; see 2 Tim. 2:12 (συμβασιλεύσομεν); see "seated at the right hand"
kingdom of Christ	Eph. 5:5 (and Rev. 11:15); see Col. 1:13; 1 Cor. 15:24
Lord (κύριος)	• Rom. 10:12; 14:4 (2x), 6 (3x), 8 (3x); 16:2, 8, 11–13; 1 Cor. 3:5; 4:4–5; 11:23; etc. • used also for his incarnation: 1 Cor. 2:8; 7:10; 9:14; 1 Thess. 4:15 • Jesus as "Lord" of Septuagint Yahweh Texts: Rom. 10:13; 14:11; 1 Cor. 1:31; 2:16; 8:6; 10:26; 2 Cor. 10:17; Phil. 2:10–11; 1 Thess. 3:13; 2 Tim. 2:19
Lord Christ	Rom. 16:18; Col. 3:24 (and Luke 2:11; 1 Peter 3:15)
Lord Jesus	Rom. 10:9; 14:14; 1 Cor. 11:23; 12:3; 16:23; 2 Cor. 4:14; 11:31; Eph. 1:15; Phil. 2:19; Col. 3:17; 1 Thess. 4:1–2; 2 Thess. 1:7; 2:8; Philem. 1:5
Lord Jesus Christ / Jesus Christ our Lord	Rom. 1:4, 7; 5:1, 11, 21; 1 Cor. 1:2–3, 7–10; Eph. 1:2–3, 17; 5:20; 6:23–24; Phil. 1:2; 2:11; 3:20; 4:23; Col. 1:3; 2:6; 1 Thess. 1:1, 3; 5:9, 23, 28; 2 Thess. 1:1–2, 12; 2:1, 14, 16; 3:6, 12, 18; 1 Tim. 6:3, 14; Philem. 1:3, 25; etc.
Lord of glory	1 Cor. 2:8 (see 2 Cor. 4:4; 8:19, 23; Eph. 1:12; Phil. 3:21; 1 Thess. 1:9)
Lord of Lords	1 Tim. 6:15 [also: "Lord both of the dead and living" in Rom. 14:9]
mediator (μεσίτης)	1 Tim. 2:5
Passover (τὸ πάσχα)	1 Cor. 5:7
place of atonement	Rom. 3:25 (ἱλαστήριον)
power and wisdom of God	1 Cor. 1:24
rock (ἡ πέτρα)	1 Cor. 10:4 (that followed Israel in the wilderness)
Savior (σωτήρ)	Eph. 5:23; Phil. 3:20; 2 Tim. 1:10; Titus 1:4; 2:13; 3:6 (see use for God in 1:3; 2:10; 3:4)
sinless	2 Cor. 5:21 (see Rom. 8:3)
Son of God (υἱός θεοῦ)	Rom. 1:4; 2 Cor. 1:19; Gal. 2:20; Eph. 4:13; God as Christ's "father": 2 Cor. 1:3; 11:31; Eph. 1:3
Son, the	1 Cor. 15:28
His son	Rom. 1:3, 9; 5:10; 8:3, 29, 32; 1 Cor. 1:9; Gal. 1:16; 4:4, 7; 1 Thess. 1:10
Son of His love	Col. 1:13; see Eph. 1:6
subordinate to God	1 Cor. 3:23; 11:3; 15:28; Phil. 2:6–8
IMPLICIT CHRISTOLOGY	
co-creator	1 Cor. 8:6; Col. 1:15–16; see Eph. 2:10
divine	Col. 1:19; 2:9
exercises final judgment	1 Cor. 4:4–5; 15:23; 2 Cor. 5:10; 1 Thess. 1:10; 2 Tim. 4:1, 8
eternally existent	1 Cor. 8:6; 10:4, 9; 2 Cor. 8:9; Gal. 4:4; Phil. 2:6–7; Col. 1:15–18; maybe 1 Tim. 1:15
equal to the Spirit	• righteous in Christ (Phil. 3:8, 9) and in the Spirit (Rom. 14:17) • life in Christ (Col. 3:4) and in the Spirit (Rom. 8:11) • hope for eternal life in Christ (1 Cor. 15:19) and the Spirit (Gal. 6:8) • joy in the Lord (Phil. 4:4) and in the Spirit (Rom. 14:17) • truth in Christ (Rom. 9:1) and in the Spirit (1 Cor. 12:3-6) • fellowship in Christ (1 Cor. 1:9) and of the Spirit (2 Cor. 13:13) • sanctified in Christ (1 Cor. 1:9) and in the Spirit (Rom. 15:16) • sealed in Christ (Eph. 1:13) and in the Spirit (Eph. 4:30) • Christ (Rom. 8:34) and the Spirit (Rom. 8:26) intercede for us • God sent (ἐξαποστέλλω) his Son (Gal. 4:4) and the Spirit of his Son (Gal 4:6)

forgives sins	Col. 3:13
object of worship	1 Cor. 16:11 ("*maranatha*"); Phil. 2:10–11; 1 Tim. 1:12
omnipotent	Phil. 3:21; Col. 1:17
owner of …	the kingdom (Eph. 5:5), the churches (Rom. 16:16), the Spirit (Rom. 8:9; Phil. 1:19)
receives praise	Eph. 5:19; 1 Tim. 1:12; 2 Tim. 4:18
receives prayer	Rom. 10:9, 12–13; 1 Cor. 1:2; 16:22 (*Maranatha*); 2 Cor. 12:8; 1 Thess. 3:11–13; 5:28; 2 Thess. 2:16–17; 3:5, 16; 2 Tim. 1:16, 18
revealer	Col. 1:15
source of blessing	1 Cor. 1:3; 2 Cor. 1:2; Gal. 1:3; 1 Thess. 3:11; 2 Thess. 2:16
sustainer	1 Cor. 8:6; Col. 1:17
ENEMIES OF CHRIST	
rule, authority, power	1 Cor. 15:24, Eph. 1:21; Col. 2:15
death	1 Cor. 15:25
enemies of the cross of Christ	Phil. 3:18

Pneumatological Concepts

CHART 82

NAMES AND ATTRIBUTES OF THE SPIRIT	
Holy Spirit (πνεῦμα ἅγιον)	Rom. 5:5; 9:1; 14:17; 15:13, 16; 1 Cor. 6:19; 12:3; 2 Cor. 6:6; 13:13; Eph. 1:13; 4:30; 1 Thess. 1:5–6; 4:8; 2 Tim. 1:14; Titus 3:5 (see also Acts 19:2; 20:23, 28; 21:11; 28:25)
Spirit of God (πνεῦμα θεοῦ)	Rom. 8:9, 14 (see v.11); 15:19; 1 Cor. 2:11, 14; 3:16; 6:11; 7:40; 12:3; 2 Cor. 3:3; Eph. 4:30; Phil. 3:3 (see 1 Thess. 4:8)
Spirit of Christ (πνεῦμα Χριστοῦ)	Rom. 8:9; Gal. 4:6; Phil. 1:19 (see also Acts 16:7)
Spirit of the Lord (πνεῦμα κυρίου)	2 Cor. 3:17–18; other "Spirit" and "Lord" / "Jesus Christ" texts: Rom. 8:9; 1 Cor. 15:45; Gal. 4:6; Phil. 1:19
Spirit … Lord/Christ … God	1 Cor. 12:4-6; 2 Cor. 13:14
Spirit of holiness (πνεῦμα ἁγιωσύνης)	Rom. 1:4
Metaphors for the Spirit	
down payment (ἀρραβών)	2 Cor. 1:21–22; 5:5; Eph. 1:14
first fruits (ἀπαρχή)	Rom. 8:23; 1 Cor. 15:20, 23
seal (σφραγίζω)	2 Cor. 1:21–22; Eph. 1:13; 4:30
the mind (φρόνημα) **of the Spirit**	Rom. 8:27
the law (νόμος) **of the Spirit of life**	Rom. 8:2
the love (ἀγάπη) **of the Spirit**	Rom. 15:30
Spirit … flesh (σάρξ)	Rom. 8:4, 5 (2x), 6, 9 (3x), 13; 1 Cor. 5:5; 2 Cor. 7:1; Gal. 3:3; 4:29; 5:16, 17 (2x); 6:8 (2x); Phil. 3:3; Col. 2:5; 1 Tim. 3:16
Spirit … body (σῶμα)	Rom. 8:10, 11 (2x), 13, 23; 1 Cor. 5:3; 6:19; 7:34; 12:13 (2x); Eph. 4:4; 1 Thess. 5:23
Spirit … letter (γράμμα)	Rom. 2:29 (see 7:6); 2 Cor. 3:6
Spirit … natural (ψυχικός)	1 Cor. 2:13–16; 15:44, 46
God's Spirit … our spirit	Rom. 1:4, 9; 8:16
THE RECEPTION OF THE SPIRIT	
God gives the Spirit	Rom. 5:5; Gal. 3:5; 2 Cor. 5:5
… into our hearts	Gal. 4:6; 2 Cor. 1:22
to receive the Spirit by hearing the word	Gal. 3:2
God reveals his wisdom through the Spirit	1 Cor. 2:10
temple (ναός) **of the Holy Spirit**	1 Cor. 6:19
THE MINISTRY OF THE SPIRIT	
the promise (ἐπαγγελία) **of the Spirit**	Gal. 3:14; see Eph. 1:13
the demonstration (ἀπόδειξις) **of the Spirit**	1 Cor. 2:4
the gifts (χαρίσματα) **of the Spirit**	1 Cor. 12:4–11
the fellowship (κοινωνία) **of the Spirit**	2 Cor. 13:13; Phil. 2:1
the fruit (καρπός) **of the Spirit**	Gal. 5:22

the manifestation (φανέρωσις) of the Spirit	1 Cor. 12:7
the ministry (διακονία) of the Spirit	2 Cor. 3:8
the newness (καινότης) of the Spirit	Rom 7:6
the power (δύναμις) of the Spirit of God	Rom. 15:13, 19 (see 1 Cor. 2:4; Gal. 3:5)
the unity (ἑνότης) of the Spirit	Eph. 4:3
walk according to the Spirit	Rom. 8:4; Gal. 5:16
the Spirit …	
… hinders and forbids	Acts 16:6–7
… dwells (οἰκέω) in the believer	Rom. 8:9–11; 1 Cor. 3:16; 2 Cor. 6:16; Eph. 2:22; 1 Thess. 4:8; 1 Cor. 6:19; Eph. 5:18; 2 Cor. 1:22; Gal. 4:6; Rom. 5:5
… leads (ἄγω) believers	Rom. 8:14; Gal. 5:18
… helps (συναντιλαμβάνομαι) us	Rom. 8:26
… intercedes (ἐντυγχάνω) for the saints	Rom. 8:27
… enables believers to abound in hope	Rom. 15:13
… searches the depths of God	1 Cor. 2:10
… distributes spiritual gifts	1 Cor. 12:11
… gives life	Rom. 8:2, 6, 10–11, 13; 1 Cor. 15:45; 2 Cor. 3:6; Gal. 6:8
… lusts (ἐπιθυμέω) against the flesh (lit.)	Gal. 5:17
… reveals the mystery of Christ	Eph. 3:5; see 1 Cor. 2:10
… grieves (λυπέω)	Eph. 4:30 (see LXX Isa. 63:10)
help (ἐπιχορηγία) of the Spirit of Jesus	Phil. 1:19
… is quenched (σβέννυμι)	1 Thess. 5:19
… in/by the Spirit (ἐν [τῷ] πνεύματι)	
circumcision by the Spirit	Rom. 2:29
peace and joy in the Holy Spirit	Rom. 14:17
sanctified in the Holy Spirit	Rom. 15:16
justified in the Spirit	1 Cor. 6:11
speaking in the Spirit	1 Cor. 12:3
baptized in one Spirit	1 Cor. 12:13
praise in the Spirit	1 Cor. 14:16
commending ourselves… in the Holy Spirit	2 Cor. 6:4–6
access in one Spirit to the Father	Eph. 2:18
built together into a dwelling of God in the Spirit	Eph. 2:22
mystery of Christ was made known in the Spirit	Eph. 3:4–5
be filled in the Spirit	Eph. 5:18
praying the Spirit	Eph. 6:18
our love in the Spirit	Col. 1:8
Gospel came in power and in the Holy Spirit	1 Thess. 1:5
Christ was vindicated in the Spirit	1 Tim. 3:16

Sin, Death, and Judgment

CHART 83

TERM		REFERENCE
Adam	Ἀδάμ	Rom. 5:14; 1 Cor. 15:22, 45; 1 Tim. 2:13–14
corruption	φθορά	Rom. 8:21; 1 Cor. 15:42, 50; Gal. 6:8; Col. 2:22
curse	κατάρα	Gal. 3:10, 13 (2x); Heb. 6:8; James 3:10; 2 Peter 2:14
	ἀνάθεμα	Rom. 9:3; 1 Cor. 12:3; 16:22; Gal. 1:8, 9
cursed	ἐπικατάρατος	Gal. 3:10, 13
death	θάνατος	Of humans: Rom. 1:32; 5:12 (2x), 14, 17, 21; 6:16, 21, 23; 7:10, 13 (2x), 24; 8:2, 6, 38; 1 Cor. 3:22; 15:21, 26, 54, 55 (2x), 56; 2 Cor. 1:9, 10; 2:16 (2x); 3:7; 4:11–12; 7:10; 11:23; Phil. 1:20; 2:27, 30; 2 Tim. 1:10
to die	ἀποθνῄσκω	Humans die: Rom. 5:15; 7:2–3, 10; 8:13; 14:7, 8 (3x); 1 Cor. 9:15; 15:22, 31–32, 36; 2 Cor. 6:9; Phil. 1:21
dead	νεκρός	• to be dead in sin: Eph. 2:1, 5; Col. 2:13 • death of the body: Rom. 8:10 (v.11 "mortal") • the dead: Rom. 14:9; 1 Cor. 15:29; 1 Thess. 4:16; 2 Tim. 4:1
destruction	ἀπώλεια	Rom. 9:22; Phil. 1:28; 3:19; 1 Tim. 6:9
	ὄλεθρος	1 Cor. 5:5; 1 Thess. 5:1; 2 Thess. 1:9 ("eternal"); 1 Tim. 6:9
destroy, perish	ἀπόλλυμαι	Rom. 2:12; 14:15; 1 Cor. 1:18–19; 8:11; 10:9f; 15:18; 2 Cor. 2:15; 4:3; 2 Thess. 2:10
destroyer	ὀλοθρευτής	1 Cor. 10:10
enmity	ἔχθρα	Rom. 8:7; Gal. 5:20; Eph. 2:14, 16
enemy	ἐχθρός	Rom. 5:10; 11:28; 12:20; 1 Cor. 15:25, 26 (death); Phil. 3:18; Col. 1:21
flesh, according to the	κατὰ σάρκα	Rom. 1:3; 4:1; 8:4, 5, 12–13; 9:3, 5; 1 Cor. 1:26; 10:18; 2 Cor. 1:17; 5:16 (2x); 10:2–3; 11:18; Gal. 4:23, 29; Eph. 6:5; Col. 3:22
in the flesh	ἐν (τῇ) σαρκί	Rom. 2:28; 8:8–9; 2 Cor. 10:3; Gal. 2:20; 6:12; Eph. 2:11 (2x); Phil. 1:22; 3:3, 4 (2x); Col. 2:1; 1 Tim. 3:16; Philem. 1:16
futility, purposelessness	ματαιότης	Rom. 8:20; Eph. 4:17; the verb [ματαιόω] in Rom. 1:21
futile, purposeless	μάταιος	1 Cor. 3:20; 15:17; Titus 3:9
harden	σκληρύνω	Rom. 9:18; see also πωρόω: Rom. 11:7; 2 Cor. 3:14
hardening	πώρωσις	Rom. 11:25; Eph. 4:18
hate	μισέω	Rom. 7:15; 9:13 (God hates Esau); Titus 3:3 (one another)
impurity	ἀκαθαρσία	Rom. 1:24; 6:19; 2 Cor. 12:21; Gal. 5:19; Eph. 4:19; 5:3; Col. 3:5; 1 Thess. 2:3; 4:7
impure / unclean	ἀκάθαρτος	1 Cor. 7:14; 2 Cor. 6:17; Eph. 5:5
immorality (sexual)	πορνεία	1 Cor. 5:1 (2x); 6:13, 18; 7:2; 2 Cor. 12:21; Gal. 5:19; Eph. 5:3; Col. 3:5; 1 Thess. 4:3
immoral (sexual)	πόρνος	1 Cor. 5:9–11; 6:9; Eph. 5:5; 1 Tim. 1:10

TERM		REFERENCE
to be sexually immoral	πορνεύω	1 Cor. 6:18; 10:8 (2x)
judgment (God's)	κρίμα	Rom. 2:2–3; 3:8; 5:16; 11:33; 13:2; 1 Cor. 11:29, 34; 1 Tim. 3:6; 5:12
God will judge	κρίνω	Rom. 2:12, 16; 3:6–7; 1 Cor. 5:13; 11:31, 32; 2 Thess. 2:12; 2 Tim. 4:1
… by the law	διὰ νόμου	Rom. 2:12
… the secrets of man		Rom. 2:16 (τὰ κρυπτὰ τῶν ἀνθρώπων); see 1 Cor. 4:5
… the world	τὸν κόσμον	Rom. 3:6
… believers		1 Cor. 11:32 (in order to be "disciplined" [παιδευόμεθα])
righteous judgment of God	δικαία κρίσις	2 Thess. 1:5; see Rom. 2:5 (δικαιοκρισία)
judgment seat of God	βῆμα τοῦ θεοῦ	Rom. 14:10
saints will judge the world		1 Cor. 6:2–3; see Rom. 2:27
Christ Jesus will judge		2 Tim. 4:1 (the living and the dead); see 2 Cor. 5:10
condemnation	κατάκριμα	Rom. 5:16, 18; 8:1
condemned	κατακρίνω	Rom. 2:1; 8:3, 34; 14:23; 1 Cor. 11:32
justified by works of the law	ἔργων νόμου	Rom. 2:15 (singular); 3:20 (28); Gal. 2:16 (3x); 3:2, 5, 10
by works	ἐξ ἔργων	Rom. 3:20; 4:2; 9:12, 32; 11:6; Gal. 2:16 (3x); 3:2, 5, 10; Eph. 2:9; Titus 3:5 (see James 2:21, 24–25)
justified "in law"	ἐν νόμῳ	Gal. 3:11; 5:4
righteousness of my own		Phil. 3:9 (ἐμὴν δικαιοσύνην τ. ἐκ νόμου); see Rom. 10:3; Titus 3:5
natural man	ψυχικὸς ἄνθρωπος	1 Cor. 2:14
old self/man	παλαιὸς ἄνθρωπος	Rom. 6:6; Eph. 4:22; Col. 3:9
penalty	δίκη	2 Thess. 1:9 ("pay the penalty of eternal destruction")
Satan	Σατανᾶς	Rom. 16:20; 1 Cor. 5:5; 7:5; 2 Cor. 2:11; 11:14; 12:7; 1 Thess. 2:18; 2 Thess. 2:9; 1 Tim. 1:20; 5:15
devil	διάβολος	Eph. 4:27; 6:11; 1 Tim. 3:6; 2 Tim. 2:26
demons	δαιμόνια	1 Cor. 10:20 (2x), 21 (2x); 1 Tim. 4:1
sensuality	ἀσέλγεια	Rom. 13:13; 2 Cor. 12:21; Gal. 5:19; Eph. 4:19
sin	ἁμαρτία	Rom. 3:9, 20; 4:7–8; 5:12 (2x), 13 (2x), 20, 21; 6:1, 2, 6 (2x), 7, 10–14, 16–18, 20, 22–23; 7:5, 7 (2x), 8 (2x), 11, 13 (3x), 14, 17, 20, 23, 25; 8:2, 3 (3x), 10; 11:27; 14:23; 1 Cor. 15:3, 17, 56 (2x); 2 Cor. 5:21 (2x); 11:7; Gal. 1:4; 2:17; 3:22; Eph. 2:1; Col. 1:14; 1 Thess. 2:16; 1 Tim. 5:22, 24; 2 Tim. 3:6
to sin	ἁμαρτάνω	Rom. 2:12; 3:23; 5:12, 14, 16; 6:15; 1 Cor. 6:18; 7:28 (2x), 36; 8:12 (2x); 15:34; Eph. 4:26; 1 Tim. 5:20; Titus 3:11
sin, wrongdoing	ἁμάρτημα	Mark 3:28–29; Rom. 3:25; 1 Cor. 6:18
sinner	ἁμαρτωλός	Rom. 3:7; 5:8, 19; 7:13; Gal. 2:15, 17; 1 Tim. 1:9, 15
disobedience	παρακοή	Rom. 5:19 (Adam); 2 Cor. 10:6
disobey	avpeiqe,w	Rom. 2:8; 10:21 (Israel); 11:30 (Gentiles), 31 (Israel); 15:31

TERM		REFERENCE
disobedient	ἀπειθής	Rom. 1:30 (to parents); 2 Tim. 3:2 (to parents); Titus 1:16; 3:3
lawlessness	ἀνομία	Rom. 4:7; 6:19; 2 Cor. 6:14; 2 Thess. 2:3, 7; Titus 2:14
offense, wrongdoing	παράπτωμα	Rom. 4:25; 5:15 (2x), 16–20; 11:11–12; 2 Cor. 5:19; Gal. 6:1; Eph. 1:7; 2:1, 5; Col. 2:13 (2x)
transgress.,transgressor	παράβασις, -βάτης	Rom. 2:23, 25, 27; 4:15; 5:14; Gal. 2:18; 3:19; 1 Tim. 2:14
slavery (negative)	δουλεία	Rom. 8:15, 21 ("of corruption"); Gal. 4:24; 5:1
be a slave (negative)	δουλεύω	Rom. 6:6 ("to sin"); 9:12; 16:18; Gal. 4:8–9, 25; Titus 3:3
unbelief	ἀπιστία	Rom. 3:3; 4:20; 11:20, 23; 1 Tim. 1:13
unbeliever	ἄπιστος	1 Cor. 6:6; 7:12–13, 14 (2x); 10:27; 14:22 (2x), 23–24; 2 Cor. 4:4; 6:14–15; 1 Tim. 5:8; Titus 1:15
not believe	ἀπιστέω	Rom. 3:3; 2 Tim. 2:13
ungodly	ἀσεβής	Rom. 4:5; 5:6; 1 Tim. 1:9
ungodliness	ἀσέβεια	Rom. 1:18; 11:26; 2 Tim. 2:16; Titus 2:12
unrighteousness	ἀδικία	Rom. 1:18 (2x), 29; 2:8; 3:5; 6:13; 9:14; 1 Cor. 13:6; 2 Cor. 12:13; 2 Thess. 2:10, 12; 2 Tim. 2:19
unrighteous	ἄδικος	1 Cor. 6:1, 9
righteousness of / through the Law		Rom. 9:31; 10:3–5; Gal. 2:21; Phil. 3:6, 9a
wrath	ὀργή	Rom. 1:18; 2:5, 8; 3:5; 4:15; 5:9; 9:22; 12:19; Eph. 5:6; Col. 3:6
	θυμός	Rom. 2:8; 2 Cor. 12:20; Gal. 5:20; Eph. 4:31; Col. 3:8
	ἐκδίκησις	Rom. 12:19 (Deut. 32:35); 2 Thess. 1:8

Soteriology: Objective Basis of Salvation

CHART 84

TERM		REFERENCES
Abraham	Ἀβραάμ	Rom. 4:1–3, 9, 12–13, 16; 9:7; 11:1; 2 Cor. 11:22; Gal. 3:6–9, 14, 16, 18, 29; 4:22
adoption	υἱοθεσία	Rom. 8:15, 23; 9:4; Gal. 4:5; Eph. 1:5
Sons of God	υἱοὶ θεοῦ	Rom. 8:14, 19; 9:26; Gal. 3:26
children	τέκνα	"children of God" (Rom. 8:16, 21; Phil. 2:15), "children of the promise" (Rom. 9:8; Gal. 4:28); "beloved children" (Eph. 5:1; see also 1 Cor. 4:14, 17; 2 Tim. 1:2); "children of Light" (Eph. 5:8)
calling	κλῆσις	Rom. 11:29; 1 Cor. 1:26; 7:20; Eph. 1:18; 4:1, 4; Phil. 3:14; 2 Thess. 1:11; 2 Tim. 1:9; Heb. 3:1; 2 Pet. 1:10
Called	καλέω	Rom. 4:17; 8:30; 9:7, 12, 24–26; 1 Cor. 1:9; 7:15, 17–18, 20–22, 24; Gal. 1:6, 15; 5:8, 13; Eph. 4:1, 4; Col. 3:15; 1 Thess. 2:12; 4:7; 5:24; 2 Thess. 2:14; 1 Tim. 6:12; 2 Tim. 1:9
those called	κλητοί	Rom. 1:6–7; 8:28; 1 Cor. 1:2, 24
covenant, new	διαθήκη	plural: Rom. 9:4; Gal. 4:24; Eph. 2:12 singular: Rom. 11:27; 1 Cor. 11:25 (new); 2 Cor. 3:6 (new), 14; Gal. 3:15, 17
cross	σταυρός	1 Cor. 1:17–18; Gal. 5:11; 6:12, 14; Eph. 2:16; Phil. 2:8; 3:18; Col. 1:20; 2:14
crucified	σταυρόω	Jesus: 1 Cor. 1:13, 23; 2:2, 8; 2 Cor. 13:4; Gal. 3:1; 5:24; 6:14
Jesus' blood	αἷμα	Rom. 3:25; 5:9; 1 Cor. 10:16; 11:25, 27; Eph. 1:7; 2:13; Col. 1:20
Jesus' death	θάνατος	Rom. 5:10; 6:3–5, 9, 21, 23; 7:5, 10, 13 (2x), 24; 8:2, 6, 38; 1 Cor. 3:22; 11:26; Phil. 2:8 (2x); 3:10; Col. 1:22
Jesus died	ἀποθνῄσκω	Rom. 5:6, 8; 6:7–10; 8:34; 14:9, 15; 1 Cor. 8:11; 15:3; 2 Cor. 5:14–15; Gal. 2:21; 1 Thess. 4:14; 5:10
Jesus died "for us"	ὑπὲρ ἡμῶν	Rom. 5:6–8; 8:32 (4:25); 1 Cor. 15:3; 2 Cor. 5:14–15, 21; Gal. 1:4; 2:20 ("for me"); 3:13; Eph. 5:2; 1 Thess. 5:9–10; Titus 2:14
Jesus died for the ungodly		Rom. 5:6 (ὑπὲρ ἀσεβῶν), 8 (while we were still sinners), 10 (while we were enemies); see 4:5
Jesus delivered himself up		Gal. 2:20 (παραδόντος ἑαυτὸν); Eph. 5:2; Titus 2:14 (ἔδωκεν ἑαυτὸν)
God delivered him up		Rom. 8:32 (παρέδωκεν αὐτόν); see 4:25
Sacrifice	θύω(θυσία	1 Cor. 5:7 (τὸ πάσχα); Eph. 5:2 (προσφορὰ καὶ θυσία)
delivered	ῥύομαι	Rom. 7:24; 11:26; 2 Cor. 1:10; Col. 1:13; 1 Thess. 1:10
	ἐξαιρέω	Gal. 1:4
election	ἐκλογή	Acts 9:15; Rom. 9:11; 11:5, 7, 28; 1 Thess. 1:4; 2 Peter 1:10
to elect	ἐκλέγομαι	1 Cor. 1:27 (2x), 28; Eph. 1:4
elect (adj.)	ἐκλεκτός	Rom. 8:33; 16:13; Col. 3:12; 1 Tim. 5:21; 2 Tim. 2:10; Titus 1:1
to choose	αἱρέομαι	2 Thess. 2:13 ("God has chosen you from the beginning for salvation")
eternal life	ζωή αἰώνιος	Rom. 2:7; 5:21; 6:22–23; Gal. 6:8; 1 Tim. 1;16; 6:12; Titus 1:2; 3:7
foreknowledge	προοράω	Gal. 3:8 (see 4:9; 1 Cor. 8:3)
	προγινώσκω	Rom. 8:29; 11:2
forgiveness	ἄφεσις	Eph. 1:7; Col. 1:14; for verbal expressions see Rom. 4:7; Col. 2:13

TERM		REFERENCES
freedom	ἐλευθερία	Rom. 8:21; 1 Cor. 10:29; 2 Cor. 3:17; Gal. 2:4; 5:1, 13 (2x)
be set free	ἐλευθερόω	John 8:32, 36; Rom. 6:18, 22; 8:2, 21; Gal. 5:1
gift	δωρεά	Rom. 5:15, 17 (of righteousness), Eph. 3:7 (of God's grace)
glory	δόξα	Rom. 2:7, 10; 8:18, 21; 9:23; 1 Cor. 2:7; 15:43; 2 Cor. 3:8–10, 11 (2x), 18; 4:17; Eph. 1:18; 3:13; Phil. 3:21; Col. 3:4; 1 Thess. 2:11, 20; 2 Thess. 2:14; 2 Tim. 2:10; see "glorified" (δοξάζω) in Rom. 8:30
	συνδοξάζω	Rom. 8:17 (see ἐνδοξάζομαι in 2 Thess. 1:10, 12)
grace/favor	χάρις	Rom. 1:5, 7; 3:24; 4:4, 16; 5:2, 15 (2x), 17, 20–21; 6:1, 14, 15; 11:5, 6 (3x); 12:3, 6; 15:15; 16:20; 1 Cor. 1:3–4; 3:10; 15:10 (3x); 16:23; 2 Cor. 1:2, 12; 4:15; 6:1; 8:1, 9; 9:8, 14; 12:9; 13:13; Gal. 1:3, 6, 15; 2:9, 21; 5:4; 6:18; Eph. 1:2, 6–7; 2:5, 7–8; 3:2, 7–8; 4:7; 6:24; Phil. 1:2, 7; 4:23; Col. 1:2, 6; 4:18; 1 Thess. 1:1; 5:28; 2 Thess. 1:2, 12; 2:16; 3:18; 1 Tim. 1:2, 14; 6:21; 2 Tim. 1:2, 9; 2:1; 4:22; Titus 1:4; 2:11; 3:7, 15; Philem. 1:3, 25
receive favor	χαρίζομαι	Rom. 8:32; 1 Cor. 2:12; Gal. 3:18; Col. 2:13; 3:13
heaven	οὐρανός	2 Cor. 5:1–2; 12:2 ("third heaven"); Phil. 3:20 ("citizenship" in heaven); Col. 1:5
hope	ἐλπίς	Rom. 4:18; 5:2, 4–5; 8:20, 24 (3x); 12:12; 15:4, 13 (2x); 1 Cor. 9:10 (2x); 13:13; 2 Cor. 1:7; 3:12; 10:15; Gal. 5:5; Eph. 1:18; 2:12; 4:4; Phil. 1:20; Col 1:5, 23, 27; 1 Thess. 1:3; 2:19; 4:13; 5:8; 2 Thess. 2:16; 1 Tim. 1:1; Titus 1:2; 2:13; 3:7
to hope	ἐλπίζω	Rom. 8:24–25; 15:12, 24; 1 Cor. 13:7; 15:19; 16:7; 2 Cor. 1:10, 13; 5:11; 8:5; 13:6; Phil. 2:19, 23; 1 Tim. 3:14; 4:10; 5:5; 6:17; Philem. 1:22
inheritance	κληρονομία	Gal. 3:18; Eph. 1:14, 18; 5:5; Col. 3:24
inherit	κληρονομέω	1 Cor. 6:9, 10; 15:50 (2x); Gal. 4:30; 5:21
heir	κληρονόμος	Rom. 4:13–14; 8:17; Gal. 3:29; 4:1, 7; Titus 3:7
kingdom	βασιλεία	1 Cor. 15:24 • "kingdom of God" in Rom. 14:17; 1 Cor. 4:20; 6:9, 10; 15:50; Gal 5:21; Col 4:11; 1 Thess. 2:11; 2 Thess. 1:5 • "kingdom of Christ and of God" in Eph. 5:5 • "kingdom of his beloved Son" in Col. 1:13; see 2 Tim. 4:1, 18
love	ἀγάπη	• God's love: Rom. 5:5, 8; 8:39; 2 Cor. 13:11, 14; Eph. 2:4; Col. 1:13 • Christ's love: Rom. 8:35; 2 Cor. 5:14; Eph. 3:19; 1 Tim. 1:14 • Spirit's love: Rom. 15:30
love (verb)	ἀγαπάω	• God loves: Rom. 8:37; 9:13, 25; 2 Cor. 9:7; Eph. 2:4; 1 Thess. 1:4; 2 Thess. 2:13, 16 • Christ loves: Gal 2:20; Eph 5:2, 25
mercy	ἔλεος	Rom. 9:23; 11:31; 15:9; Gal. 6:16; Eph. 2:4; 1 Tim. 1:2; 2 Tim. 1:2, 16, 18; Titus 3:5
have mercy	ἐλεέω	Rom. 9:15, 18; 11:30–32; 1 Cor. 7:25; 2 Cor. 4:1; Phil. 2:27; 1 Tim. 1:13,16
predestined	προορίζω	Acts 4:28; Rom. 8:29–30; 1 Cor. 2:7; Eph. 1:5, 11
promise	ἐπαγγελία	Rom. 4:13–14, 16, 20; 9:4, 8–9; 15:8; 2 Cor. 1:20; 7:1; Gal. 3:14, 16–17, 18 (2x), 21–22, 29; 4:23, 28; Eph. 1:13; 2:12; 3:6; 6:2; 1 Tim. 4:8; 2 Tim. 1:1
reconciliation	καταλλαγή	Rom. 5:11; 11:15; 2 Cor. 5:18–19
reconcile	καταλλάσσω	Rom. 5:10; 1 Cor. 7:11; 2 Cor. 5:18–20
	ἀποκαταλ.	Eph. 2:16; Col. 1:20, 22
redemption	ἀπολύτρωσις	Rom. 3:24; 8:23; 1 Cor. 1:30; Eph. 1:7, 14; 4:30; Col. 1:14
redeem	λυτρόω	Titus 2:14 (also Luke 24:21; 1 Peter 1:18)
	ἐξαγοράζω	Gal. 3:13; 4:5

TERM		REFERENCES
regeneration		Titus 3:5 (παλιγγενεσία)
resurrection, Jesus'		Rom. 1:4; 4:17; 6:4–5, 9; 7:4; 8:11; 10:7, 9; 1 Cor. 15:12, 20; Gal. 1:1; Eph. 1:20; Phil. 3:10; Col. 1:18; 2:12; 1 Thess. 1:10; 2 Tim. 2:8
salvation	σωτηρία	Rom. 1:16; 10:1, 10; 11:11; 13:11; 2 Cor. 1:6; 6:2 (2x); 7:10; Eph. 1:13; Phil. 1:19, 28; 2:12; 1 Thess. 5:8–9; 2 Thess. 2:13; 2 Tim. 2:10; 3:15; see Titus 2:11
saved	σώζω	Rom. 5:9, 10; 8:24; 9:27; 10:9, 13; 11:14, 26; 1 Cor. 1:18, 21; 3:15; 5:5; 7:16 (2x); 9:22; 10:33; 15:2; 2 Cor. 2:15; Eph. 2:5, 8; 1 Thess. 2:16; 2 Thess. 2:10; 1 Tim. 1:15; 2:4, 15; 4:16; 2 Tim. 1:9; 4:18; Titus 3:5;
universalism	[concept]	Rom. 5:18; 15:7–12; 1 Cor. 15:28; Phil. 2:9–11; 1 Tim. 2:4; 4:10; Titus 2:11

Soteriology: Subjective Means of Salvation

CHART 85

TERM		REFERENCES
assurance	πληροφορία	Col. 2:2; 1 Thess. 1:5; see Rom. 8:28–30, 38–39
fully assured	πληροφορέω	Rom. 4:21; 14:5; Col. 4:12
baptism	βάπτισμα	Rom. 6:4; Eph. 4:5; see βαπτισμός in Col. 2:12
baptize/baptized	βαπτίζω	Rom. 6:3; 1 Cor. 1:13–17; 10:2; 12:13; 15:29; Gal. 3:27 (see also Acts 16:14–15, 33; 19:1–7)
Christ "in you"	Χριστὸς ἐν ὑμῖν	Rom. 8:10; 2 Cor. 13:5; Gal. 2:20 ("in me"); see also Gal. 4:19; Eph. 3:14
to die	ἀποθνήσκω	Christians died - to sin: Rom. 6:2, 7–8; 7:6; 2 Cor. 5:14; Gal. 2:19 - to the law: Gal. 2:19 - to the elements of the world: Col. 2:12
faith	πίστις	Rom. 1:5, 8, 12; 1 Cor. 2:5; 2 Cor. 1:24 (2x); Gal. 1:23; Eph. 1:15; Phil. 1:25; Col. 1:4; 1 Thess. 1:3; 2 Thess. 1:3; 1 Tim. 1:2; 2 Tim. 1:5; Titus 1:1; Philem. 1:5–6; etc.
to believe	πιστεύω	Rom. 1:16; 1 Cor. 1:21; 2 Cor. 4:13 (2x); Gal. 2:16; Eph. 1:13, 19; Phil. 1:29; 1 Thess. 1:7; 2 Thess. 1:10 (2x); 2:12; 1 Tim. 1:16; 3:16; 2 Tim. 1:12; Titus 3:8; etc.
	ὅτι	that we shall also live with Him (Rom. 6:8)
	ὅτι	that God raised Him from the dead (Rom. 10:9)
	ὅτι	that Jesus died and rose again (1 Thess. 4:14)
believe in Christ	εἰς Χριστὸν	Gal. 2:16 (Phil. 1:29 [π. εἰς αὐτόν])
	π. ἐπ' αὐτῷ	Rom. 9:33 (Isa. 28:16); 10:11; 1 Tim. 1:16 (3:16)
faith in Jesus Christ	π. εἰς Χρ.	Col. 2:5; εἰς Ἰησοῦν: Acts 20:21; 24:24; see 26:18
	π. evn VIhsou/j	Gal. 3:26 (?; compare NAS with NET); Eph. 1:15; Col. 1:4; 1 Tim. 1:14; 3:13; 2 Tim. 1:13; 3:15
	π. πρὸς τ. κύρ.	Philem. 1:5
faith of (Jesus) Christ	πίστις Ἰησ. Χρ.	Rom. 3:22, 26; Gal. 2:16; (see 2:20 ἐν πίστει … τοῦ υἱοῦ τοῦ θεοῦ τοῦ); 3:22; Phil. 3:9; Eph. 3:12 (αὐτοῦ)
believe God	π. τῷ θεῷ	Rom. 4:3, 17; Gal. 3:6; Titus 3:8 (2 Tim. 1:12)
believe in God	π. ἐπὶ τὸν …	Rom. 4:5 (δικαιοῦντα τὸν ἀσεβῆ), 24 (ἐγείραντα Ἰησοῦν)
faith toward God	π. πρὸς τ. θεὸν	1 Thess. 1:8; see Rom. 4:5 (1 Cor. 2:5 [ἐν δυνάμει θεοῦ])
faith from God	π. ἀπὸ θεοῦ	Eph. 6:23
faith(fulness) of God	π. τοῦ θεοῦ	Rom. 3:3 (Rom. 4:12, 16 faith of Abraham [π. Ἀβραάμ])
justified by faith	δικαι. πίστει	Rom. 3:28
	ἐκ/διὰ πίστεως	Rom. 3:26, 30 (2x); 5:1; Gal. 2:16 (2x); 3:8, 24
	π. εἰς δικαιος.	Rom. 4:9; 10:10
righteousness by faith	δικ. ἐκ πίστ.	Rom. 9:30; 10:6; Phil. 3:9 (διὰ π.)
righteousness of faith	δικ. τῆς πίστ.	Rom. 4:11, 13

TERM		REFERENCES
obedience of faith	ὑπακοὴν πίστ.	Rom. 1:5; 16:26
law of faith	νόμος πίστεως	Rom. 3:27
work of faith	ἔργον τῆς π.	1 Thess. 1:3
good fight (of faith)	ἀγὼν τῆς π.	1 Tim. 6:12 (1:18 καλή στρατεία); 2 Tim. 4:7
joy of faith	χαρὰ τῆς π.	Phil. 1:25
confession	ὁμολογία	2 Cor. 9:13; 1 Tim. 6:12–13
confess	ὁμολογέω	Rom. 10:9–10; 1 Tim. 6:12
"in Christ"	ἐν Χριστῷ	Rom. 3:24; 6:11, 23; 8:1, 2, 39; 9:1; 12:5; 15:17; 16:3, 7, 9–10; 1 Cor. 1:2, 4, 30; 3:1; 4:10, 15 (2x), 17; 15:18–19, 22, 31; 16:24; 2 Cor. 2:14, 17; 3:14; 5:17, 19; 12:2, 19; Gal. 1:22; 2:4, 17; 3:14, 26, 28; 5:6; Eph. 1:1, 3, 10, 12, 20; 2:6, 7, 10, 13; 3:6, 11, 21; 4:32; Phil. 1:1, 13, 26; 2:1, 5; 3:3, 14; 4:7, 19, 21; Col. 1:2, 4, 28; 1 Thess. 2:14; 4:16; 5:18; 1 Tim. 1:14; 3:13; 2 Tim. 1:1, 9, 13; 2:1, 10; 3:12, 15; Philem. 1:8, 20, 23
	ἐν κυρίῳ	Rom. 14:14; 16:2, 8, 11, 12 (2x), 13, 22; 1 Cor. 1:31; 4:17; 7:22, 39; 9:1–2; 11:11; 15:58; 16:19; 2 Cor. 2:12; 10:17; Gal. 5:10; Eph. 2:21; 4:1, 17; 5:8; 6:1, 10, 21; Phil. 1:14; 2:19, 24, 29; 3:1; 4:1–2, 4, 10; Col. 3:18, 20; 4:7, 17; 1 Thess. 3:8; 4:1; 5:12; 2 Thess. 3:4, 12; Philem. 1:16, 20
	εἰς Χριστὸν	Rom. 6:3; 16:5; 2 Cor. 1:21; Gal. 3:24, 27; Philem. 1:6
judgment by works		Rom. 2:5–8; 14:10–12; 1 Cor. 3:8, 13–15; 2 Cor. 5:10; (9:6; 11:15); Gal. 6:7–8; Eph. 6:7–8; Col. 3:23–25; 1 Tim. 5:24–25; 2 Tim. 4:7–8, 14
justification	δικαίωσις	Rom. 4:25; 5:18
just	δίκαιος	Rom. 1:17; 2:13; 3:10, 26; 5:7, 19; 7:12; Gal. 3:11; Phil. 4:8; 2 Thess. 1:5–6; 1 Tim. 1:9; 2 Tim. 4:8
justify, justified	δικαιόω	Rom. 2:13; 3:24, 26, 28, 30; 4:2, 5; 5:1, 9; 6:7; 8:30 (2x), 33; 1 Cor. 4:4; 6:11; Gal. 2:16 (3x), 17; 3:8, 11, 24; 5:4; Titus 3:7
righteousness	δικαιοσύνη	• Rom. 4:3, 1 Cor. 1:30; 2 Cor. 3:9; 2 Cor. 5:21; 6:7, 14; 9:10; 11:15; Gal. 3:6, 21; 5:5; Eph. 4:24; 5:9; 6:14; Phil. 1:11; 3:9b; 1 Tim. 6:11; 2 Tim. 2:22; 3:16; 4:8; Titus 3:5; etc. • "Righteousness of God": Rom. 1:17; 3:5, 21–22, 25, 26; 10:3 (2x); then only in 2 Cor. 5:21; see also 2 Cor. 9:9
love, to	ἀγαπάω	• love for God: Rom. 8:28; 1 Cor. 2:9; 8:3 • love for Christ: Eph. 6:24; 2 Tim. 4:8
new creation	καινὴ κτίσις	2 Cor. 5:17; Gal. 6:15
new man	καινὸς ἄνθρ)	Eph. 2:15; 4:23–24; Col. 3:9–10
obedience	ὑπακοή	Rom. 1:5 (of faith); 6:16; 15:18; 16:19, 26; 2 Cor. 7:15; 9:13; 10:5, 6 (of Christ); Philem. 1:21
obey	ὑπακούω	Rom. 6:16, 17; 10:16; Phil. 2:12; see πείθω in Gal. 5:7
perseverance	ὑπομονή	Rom. 2:7; 5:3; Col. 1:11; 1 Thess. 1:3; 2 Thess. 1:4; 3:5; 1 Tim. 6:11; 2 Tim. 3:10; see also 1 Cor. 15:2; Col. 1:22–23; 2 Tim. 4:7; etc.
persevere	ἐπιμένω	Rom. 11:22; Col. 1:23; 1 Tim. 4:16
apostasy		Rom. 8:12–13; 11:20–22; Gal. 1:6; 4:9; 5:4; 1 Tim. 1:6; 5:15; etc.
not inherit the kingdom of God		1 Cor. 6:9–11; Gal. 5:19–21; Eph. 5:5

TERM		REFERENCES
in vain		labored (Gal. 4:9-11; 1 Thess. 3:5); believed (1 Cor. 15:2); received God's grace (2 Cor. 6:1); run (Phil. 2:16)
examples of apostates		Phygelus and Hermogenes (2 Tim. 1:15); Hymenaeus (1 Tim. 1:20; 2 Tim. 2:17), Philetus (2 Tim. 2:17); Demas (2 Tim. 4:10); Alexander (1 Tim. 1:20; 2 Tim. 4:14)
preservation	[concept]	Rom. 14:4; 1 Cor. 1:8; 10:13; Phil. 1:6; 1 Thess. 5:23–24; 2 Thess. 3:3
repentance	μετάνοια	Rom. 2:4; 2 Cor. 7:9–10; 2 Tim. 2:25
repent	μετανοέω	2 Cor. 12:21
sanctification	ἁγιασμός	Rom. 6:19, 22; 1 Cor. 1:30; 6:11; 1 Thess. 4:3–4, 7; 2 Thess. 2:13; 1 Tim. 2:15
sanctified	ἁγιάζω	Rom. 15:16; 1 Cor. 1:2; 6:11; 7:14; Eph. 5:26; 1 Thess. 5:23; 2 Tim. 2:21
saints	ἅγιοι	Rom. 1:7; 8:27; 12:13; 15:25–26, 31; 16:2, 15; 1 Cor. 1:2; 6:1, 2; 14:33; 16:1, 15; 2 Cor. 1:1; 8:4; 9:1, 12; 13:12; Eph. 1:1, 15, 18; 2:19; 3:8, 18; 4:12; 5:3; 6:18; Phil. 1:1; 4:21–22; Col. 1:2, 4, 12, 26; 1 Thess. 3:13; 2 Thess. 1:10; 1 Tim. 5:10; Philem. 1:5, 7

Metaphors of Salvation

CHART 86

METAPHOR	MEANING	REFERENCE
Customs of Paul's Time		
justification	court of law: acquittal	e.g., Rom. 3:21–26
redemption	buying back a slave or a prisoner of war	e.g., Rom. 3:24
liberation and freedom	manumission: the freedom from slavery	e.g., Gal. 5:1, 13
reconciliation	exchange of hostility for friendship	2 Cor. 5:18–20
new citizenship	Roman citizenship was visibly displayed	Phil. 3:20
Metaphors from everyday life		
salvation	wholeness of health, rescue, preservation	e.g., Rom. 1:16
inheritance	a valuable possession that has been given	Rom. 4:13–14; 8:17
waking up	waking up from sleep	Rom. 13:11
putting off/on clothes	a boy growing to manhood changed the toga	e.g., Rom. 13:12, 14
receiving an invitation	chosen for receipt of a special benefit	Rom. 8:30; Gal. 1:6
writing a letter		2 Cor. 3:3
Metaphors from agriculture		
sowing and watering		1 Cor. 3:6–8
irrigation		1 Cor. 12:13c
water poured out		Rom. 5:5
grafting		Rom. 11:17–24
harvest		Rom. 8:23
Metaphors from commerce		
seal	stamp of visible ownership	2 Cor. 1:22
first installment	partial payment that secures legal claim	2 Cor. 1:22; 5:5
"into the name"	formula for transfer of ownership	1 Cor. 1:13–15
"confirm"	legal ratification	1 Cor. 1:6
"tested and approved"	from process of refining	Rom. 14:18
Building		1 Cor. 3:10–12
Metaphors from major events of life		
abortion	a child born dead (but made alive by grace)	1 Cor. 15:8
birth		1 Cor. 4:15; Gal. 4:19
adoption		Rom. 8:15, 23
engagement		2 Cor. 11:2
marriage		1 Cor. 6:17
death, crucifixion		Rom. 6:3–6; Gal. 6:14
Cultic metaphors		
Passover		1 Cor. 5:7
propitiation		Rom. 3:25

Participation with Christ

CHART 87

	TERM		REFERENCES
1.	suffer with Christ	συμπάσχω	Rom. 8:17; see Phil. 3:10; Col. 1:24
2.	crucified with Christ	συσταυρόω	Rom. 6:6; Gal. 2:20; see 5:24; 6:14
3.	died with Christ	• ἀπεθάνομεν σὺν Χριστῷ	Rom. 6:8; Col. 2:20; see 2 Cor. 4:10a; Phil. 3:10
		• συναποθνῄσκω	2 Tim. 2:11 (see Mark 14:31)
4.	conformed to his death	• σύμφυτος	Rom. 6:5a
		• συμμορφίζομαι	Phil. 3:10 (see 3:21; Rom. 8:21)
5.	buried with him	συνετάφημεν αὐτῷ	Rom. 6:4; Col. 2:12
6.	raised with Christ	• σύμφυτος	Rom. 6:5b; see 6:4
		• συνεγείρω	Eph. 2:6; Col. 2:12; 3:1
		• σὺν Ἰησοῦ ἐγερεῖ	2 Cor. 4:14
7.	made alive with Christ	συνεζωοποίησεν τῷ Χριστῷ	Eph. 2:5; Col. 2:13; see 2 Cor. 4:10b
8.	live with him	• ζήσομεν σὺν αὐτῷ	2 Cor. 13:4
		• συζήσομεν αὐτῷ	Rom. 6:8; 2 Tim. 2:11
9.	heirs with Christ	συγκληρονόμοι Χριστοῦ	Rom. 8:17
10.	glorified with him	συνδοξασθῶμεν	Rom. 8:17; see Phil. 3:21
11.	seated with him	συνεκάθισεν	Eph. 2:6
12.	reign with him	συμβασιλεύσομεν	2 Tim. 2:12

God's Sovereignty and Human Responsibility

CHART 88

SUBJECT	GOD'S SOVEREIGNTY	HUMAN RESPONSIBILITY
Salvation	Philippians 2:13 for it is God who is at work in you, both to will and to work for His good pleasure. (also 1 Cor. 1:30; Eph. 2:5, 8)	Philippians 2:12 So then, my beloved, just as you have always obeyed, nnot as in my presence only, but now much more in my absence, work out your salvation with fear and trembling; ... (also 1 Cor. 9:20–21; 15:2; 1 Tim. 4:10)
Faith	Romans 10:17 So faith comes from hearing, and hearing by the word of Christ. (also 1 Cor. 2:4–5; Gal. 5:22; Phil. 1:6)	1 Thessalonians 3:10 ...as we night and day keep praying most earnestly that we may see your face, and may complete what is lacking in your faith? (also Phil. 1:25–26; 1 Tim. 1:18–19; 6:11; 2 Tim. 2:22)
Sanctification	1 Thessalonians 5:23 Now may the God of peace Himself sanctify you entirely; and may your spirit and soul and body be preserved complete, without blame at the coming of our Lord Jesus Christ. (also Rom. 15:5; 2 Cor. 13:7)	1 Thessalonians 4:2 For you know what commandments we gave you by the authority of the Lord Jesus. 3 For this is the will of God, your sanctification; that is, that you abstain from sexual immorality;... (also 1 Tim. 6:12; 1 Cor. 12:31; Phil. 3:12–14)
Mission	1 Corinthians 1:21 ... God was well-pleased through the foolishness of the message preached to save (σῶσαι) those who believe.	1 Corinthians 9:22 To the weak I became weak, that I might win the weak; I have become all things to all men, that I may by all means save (σώσω) some. (also Rom. 11:14; 1 Cor. 7:16; 10:33)
Strength	2 Thessalonians 2:16 Now may our Lord Jesus Christ Himself and God our Father, who has loved us and given us eternal comfort and good hope by grace, 17 comfort (παρακαλέσαι) and strengthen (στηρίξαι) your hearts in every good work and word. (also 3:2)	1 Thessalonians 3:2 ...and we sent Timothy, our brother and God's fellow worker in the gospel of Christ, to strengthen (στηρίξαι) and encourage (παρακαλέσαι) you as to your faith, ... (also 2 Cor. 7:6)
Money	2 Corinthians 9:8 And God is able to make all grace abound to you, that always having all sufficiency in everything, you may have an abundance for every good deed;	1 Corinthians 4:12 ...and we toil, working with our own hands;... (also Acts 20:34; Eph. 4:28; 1 Thess. 4:9–12; 2 Thess. 3:6–15)

"Faith of Jesus Christ": What Does It Mean?

CHART 89

REFERENCE	NAS: OBJECTIVE GENTIVE	NET: SUBJECTIVE GENITIVE
Romans 3:3	If some did not believe, their unbelief will not nullify **the faithfulness of God** (τὴν πίστιν τοῦ θεοῦ), will it? [subj. gen.]	What then? If some did not believe, does their unbelief nullify the **faithfulness of God**? [subj. gen.]
Romans 3:22	even the righteousness of God **through faith in Jesus Christ** (διὰ πίστεως Ἰησοῦ Χριστοῦ) for all those who believe; for there is no distinction;	namely, the righteousness of God **through the faithfulness of Jesus Christ** for all who believe. For there is no distinction,
Romans 3:25–26	[25] whom God displayed publicly as a propitiation in His blood through faith. This was to demonstrate His righteousness, because in the forbearance of God He passed over the sins previously committed; [26] for the demonstration, I say, of His righteousness at the present time, that He might be just and the justifier of the one **who has faith in Jesus** (δικαιοῦντα τὸν ἐκ πίστεως Ἰησοῦ).	[25] God publicly displayed him at his death as the mercy seat accessible through faith. This was to demonstrate his righteousness, because God in his forbearance had passed over the sins previously committed. [26] This was also to demonstrate his righteousness in the present time, so that he would be just and the justifier of the one **who lives because of Jesus' faithfulness**.
Romans 4:16	… not only to those who are of the Law, but also to those who are of the **faith of Abraham** (ἐκ πίστεως Ἀβραάμ), who is the father of us all, [subj. gen.]	… not only to those who are under the law, but also to those who have the **faith of Abraham**, who is the father of us all [subj. gen.]
Galatians 2:16 (2x)	nevertheless knowing that a man is not justified by the works of the Law but **through faith in Christ Jesus** (διὰ πίστεως Ἰησοῦ Χριστοῦ), even we have believed in Christ Jesus (εἰς Χριστὸν Ἰησοῦν ἐπιστεύσαμεν), that we may be justified by **faith in Christ** (ἐκ πίστεως Χριστοῦ), and not by the works of the Law; …	yet we know that no one is justified by the works of the law but **by the faithfulness of Jesus Christ**. And we have come to believe in Christ Jesus, so that we may be justified **by the faithfulness of Christ** and not by the works of the law, because by the works of the law no one will be justified.
Galatians 2:20	I have been crucified with Christ; and it is no longer I who live, but Christ lives in me; and the *life* which I now live in the flesh I live by **faith in the Son of God** (ἐν πίστει … τοῦ υἱοῦ τοῦ θεοῦ), who loved me and gave Himself up for me.	I have been crucified with Christ, and it is no longer I who live, but Christ lives in me. So the life I now live in the body, I live because of the faithfulness of the Son of God, who loved me and gave himself for me.
Galatians 3:22	But the Scripture has shut up all men under sin, that the promise by **faith in Jesus Christ** (ἐκ πίστεως Ἰησοῦ Χριστοῦ) might be given to those who believe.	But the scripture imprisoned everything and everyone under sin so that the promise could be given—because of the **faithfulness of Jesus Christ**—to those who believe.
Ephesians 3:12	in whom we have boldness and confident access **through faith in Him** (διὰ τῆς πίστεως αὐτοῦ).	in whom we have boldness and confident access to God **because of Christ's faithfulness**.
Philippians 3:8–9	[8] More than that, I count all things to be loss in view of the surpassing value of **knowing Christ Jesus** (τῆς γνώσεως Χριστοῦ Ἰησοῦ) [obj. gen.]… [9] …not having a righteousness of my own derived from the Law, but that which is **through faith in Christ** (διὰ πίστεως Χριστοῦ), the righteousness which comes from God on the basis of faith,	[8] More than that, I now regard all things as liabilities compared to the far greater value of **knowing Christ Jesus** [obj. gen.]… [9] …not because I have my own righteousness derived from the law, but because I have the righteousness that comes **by way of Christ's faithfulness**—a righteousness from God that is in fact based on Christ's faithfulness.

Eschatological Concepts

CHART 90

TERM	REFERENCES
age (αἰών)	
this age (αἰών οὗτος)	Rom. 12:2; 1 Cor. 1:20; 2:6, 8; 3:18; 2 Cor. 4:4; Eph. 1:21 (see 2:2)
the present age (ὁ νῦν αἰών)	1 Tim. 6:17; 2 Tim. 4:10; Titus 2:12
the present evil age	Gal. 1:4 (ὁ αἰών ὁ ἐνέστως πονηρός)
the present time (ὁ νῦν καιρός)	Rom. 3:26; 8:18; 11:5; 2 Cor. 6:2; 8:14
the age to come (ὁ αἰών ὁ μελλῶν)	Eph. 1:21
the ages to come	Eph. 2:7 (οἱ αἰῶνα οἱ ἐπερχόμενοι)
the ends of the ages	1 Cor. 10:11 (τὰ τέλη τῶν αἰώνων)
apostasy, the (ἡ ἀποστασία)	2 Thess. 2:3 (see 1 Tim. 4:1 ἀποστήσονταί)
day, the (eschatological)	Rom. 2:16; 13:12; 2 Tim. 1:12, 18; 4:8
… of wrath (ἡμέρα ὀργῆς)	Rom. 2:5
… of revelation	Rom. 2:5 (of the righteous judgment of God)
… of (our/the Lord) Christ Jesus	1 Cor. 1:8; 5:5; 2 Cor. 1:14; Phil. 1:6, 10; 2:16; 2 Thess. 2:2
… each man's work will be revealed	1 Cor. 3:13
… of redemption	Eph. 4:30
… will come like a thief in the night	1 Thess. 5:2, 4 (see Matt. 24:43; 2 Peter 3:10; Rev. 3:3; 16:15)
… he comes to be glorified	2 Thess. 1:10 (in his saints)
the last days (ἐν ἐσχάταις ἡμέραις)	2 Tim. 3:1
destruction ὄλεθρος ἀπώλεια	1 Cor. 5:5; 1 Thess. 5:3; 2 Thess. 1:9 (eternal); 1 Tim. 6:9 Rom. 9:22; Phil. 1:28; 3:19; 2 Thess. 2:3 (son of destruction); 1 Tim. 6:9
end, the (τὸ τέλος)	Rom. 6:21–22; 1 Cor. 1:8; 10:11 ("the ends of the ages have come"); 15:24; 2 Cor. 1:13; Phil. 3:19
fullness of time (πλήρωμα τοῦ χρόνου)	Gal. 4:4; Eph. 1:10 (πλήρωμα τῶν καιρῶν)
mystery formerly hidden, now revealed	Rom. 16:25–26; 1 Cor. 2:7; Col. 1:26; Eph. 1:9-10; 2 Tim. 1:9–10
eternal life (ζωή αἰώνιος)	Rom. 2:7; 5:21; 6:22–23; Gal. 6:8; 1 Tim. 1:16; 6:12; Titus 1:2; 3:7 (hope of) (see 2 Cor. 4:16–5:4)
imperishable (ἀφθαρσία, ἄφθαρτος)	Rom. 2:7; 1 Cor. 9:25; 15:42, 50, 52–54; 2 Tim. 1:10
immortality (ἀθανασία)	1 Cor. 15:53–54; 1 Tim. 6:16
death is swallowed up in victory	1 Cor. 15:54 (Isa. 25:8)
glory, be glorified	Rom. 2:7, 10; 8:17–18, 21; 1 Cor. 15:43; 2 Cor. 4:17; Eph. 1:18; Col. 1:27; 3:4; 1 Thess. 2:12; 2 Thess. 2:14; 2 Tim. 2:10 (eternal)
hope (ἐλπίς, ἐλπίζω)	Rom. 4:18; 5:2 (of the glory of God), 4–5; 8:20, 24 (3x), 25; 12:12; 15:4, 12, 13 (2x); 1 Cor. 9:10 (2x); 13:7, 13; 15:19; 2 Cor. 1:7, 10; 3:12; Gal. 5:5 (of righteousness); Eph 1:18 (of his calling); 4:4; Col 1:5 (laid up in heaven), 23 (of the gospel), 27 (of glory); 1 Thess. 1:3 (in our Lord Jesus Christ); 2:19; 5:8 (of salvation); 2 Thess. 2:16; 1 Tim. 1:1; 4:10; 5:5; 6:17; Titus 1:2 (of eternal life; 3:7); 2:13 (blessed); no hope (Eph. 2:12; 1 Thess. 4:13)
awaiting eagerly (ἀπεκδέχομαι)	Rom. 8:19, 23, 25; 1 Cor. 1:7; Gal. 5:5; Phil. 3:20

TERM	REFERENCES
inheritance (κληρονομία)	Gal. 3:18; Eph. 1:14, 18; 5:5; Col. 3:24
heir (κληρονόμος)	Rom. 4:13–14; 8:17; Gal. 3:29; 4:1, 7; Titus 3:7
to inherit (κληρονομέω)	1 Cor. 6:9–10; 15:50; Gal. 4:30; 5:21
inherit the kingdom of God	1 Cor. 6:9–10; 15:50; Gal. 5:21; Eph. 5:5
Israel	Rom. 9:6, 27, 31; 10:19, 21; 11:2, 7, 25–26; 1 Cor. 10:18; 2 Cor. 3:7, 13; Gal. 6:16; Eph. 2:12; Phil. 3:5
judgment (κρίμα) (God's)	Rom. 2:2–3; 3:8; 5:16; 11:33; 13:2; 1 Cor. 11:29, 34; 1 Tim. 3:6; 5:12
God will judge (κρίνω)	Rom. 2:12, 16; 3:6–7; 1 Cor. 5:13; 11:31–32; 2 Thess. 2:12; 2 Tim. 4:1
… by the law (διὰ νόμου)	Rom. 2:12
… the secrets of man	Rom. 2:16 (τὰ κρυπτὰ τῶν ἀνθρώπων); see 1 Cor. 4:5
… the world (τὸν κόσμον)	Rom. 3:6
… believers	1 Cor. 11:32 (in order to be "disciplined" [παιδευόμεθα])
judgment seat (βῆμα) of God	Rom. 14:10
saints will judge the world	1 Cor. 6:2–3; see Rom. 2:27
Christ Jesus will judge	2 Tim. 4:1 (the living and the dead); see 2 Cor. 5:10
condemnation (κατάκριμα)	Rom. 5:16, 18; 8:1
condemned (κατακρίνω)	Rom. 2:1; 8:3, 34; 14:23; 1 Cor. 11:32
kingdom of God	Rom. 14:17; 1 Cor. 4:20; Eph. 5:5; Col. 4:11; 1 Thess. 2:12; 2 Thess. 1:5; 2 Tim. 4:1
lawless one, the (ὁ ἄνομος)	2 Thess. 2:8-9
resurrection ἀνάστασις	• Jesus: Rom. 1:4; 6:5; Phil. 3:10 • Believers: 1 Cor. 15:12–13, 21, 42; 2 Tim. 2:18
ἐξανάστασις	• Phil. 3:10
raised ἐγείρω	• Jesus: Rom. 4:24–25; 6:4, 9; 7:4; 8:11 (2x), 34; 10:9; 1 Cor. 6:14; 15:4, 12–14, 15 (3x), 16 (2x), 17, 20, 29, 32, 35, 42, 43 [2x], 44, 52; 2 Cor. 5:15; Gal. 1:1; Eph. 1:20; Col. 2:12; 1 Thess. 1:10; 2 Tim. 2:8 • Believers: 1 Cor. 6:14; 15:32; 2 Cor. 1:9; 4:14 • Connection between both: 1 Cor. 6:14; 15:20; 2 Cor. 4:14; Col. 2:12
ἐξεγείρω	1 Cor. 6:14 (of Jesus)
ἀνίστημι	• Jesus: Rom. 15:12; 1 Thess. 4:14 • Christians: Eph. 5:14; 1 Thess. 4:16
revelation (ἀποκάλυψις, ἀποκαλύπτω)	
… of the righteous judgment	Rom. 2:5
… of glory	Rom. 8:18
… of the Sons of God	Rom. 8:19
… of our Lord Jesus Christ	1 Cor. 1:7; see 2 Thess. 1:7–8
… of works (with fire)	1 Cor. 3:13
… of the man of lawlessness	2 Thess. 2:3, 6, 8
reward ἀνταπόδοσις, ἀνταποδίδωμι ἀντιμισθία, μισθός	Rom. 12:19; Col. 3:24; 2 Thess. 1:6 Rom. 1:27; 1 Cor. 3:8, 14
second coming (παρουσία) (Christ's)	1 Cor. 15:23; 1 Thess. 2:19; 3:13 (with all his saints; see 4:14); 4:15–17; 5:23; 2 Thess. 2:1, 8 (see 1:7–8)

TERM	REFERENCES
appearing (ἐπιφάνεια)	2 Thess. 2:8; 1 Tim. 6:14; 2 Tim. 4:1, 8; Titus 2:13
the second coming is near	Rom. 13:11–12; 1 Cor. 2:6; 7:29; 16:22 (*Maranatha!*); Phil. 4:5; 1 Thess. 4:15, 17; 2 Tim. 3:1
restrainer, the τὸ κατέχον, ὁ κατέχων	2 Thess. 2:6–7 (he delays the parousia)
Spirit	2 Cor. 3:7–8; Gal. 3:14; 5:18; Rom. 8:4 (see Ezek. 36:27)
wrath (ὀργή)	Rom. 1:18; 2:5; Eph. 5:6; Col. 3:6; 1 Thess. 2:16
God will abolish	1 Cor. 15:24 (all rule, authority, power), 25 (all enemies)
death is the last enemy	1 Cor. 15:26
penalty (δίκη)	2 Thess. 1:9
retribution (ἐκδίκησις, ἐκδικέω)	Rom. 12:19; 2 Thess. 1:8

The "Already" and "Not Yet"

CHART 91

TERM/CONCEPT	ALREADY	NOT YET
Redemption	Ephesians 1:7 In Him we have redemption (ἔχομεν τὴν ἀπολύτρωσιν) through His blood, the forgiveness of our trespasses, …	Ephesians 4:30 Do not grieve the Holy Spirit of God, by whom you were sealed for the day of redemption (εἰς ἡμέραν ἀπολυτρώσεως).
Adoption	Romans 8:15 For you have not received a spirit of slavery leading to fear again, but you have received a spirit of adoption (ἐλάβετε πνεῦμα υἱοθεσίας) as sons by which we cry out, "Abba! Father!"	Romans 8:23 And not only this, but also we ourselves, having the first fruits of the Spirit, even we ourselves groan within ourselves, waiting eagerly for our adoption as sons (υἱοθεσίαν ἀπεκδεχόμενοι), the redemption of our body.
Justification/Gift of Righteousness	Romans 5:1 Therefore having been justified (δικαιωθέντες) by faith, we have peace with God through our Lord Jesus Christ, …	Galatians 5:5 For we through the Spirit, by faith, are waiting for the hope of righteousness (ἐλπίδα δικαιοσύνης ἀπεκδεχόμεθα). (also Rom. 2:13)
Salvation	Ephesians 2:8 For by grace you have been saved (ἐστε σεσῳσμένοι) through faith; and that not of yourselves, *it is* the gift of God; … (also 2 Cor. 6:2)	Romans 5:9 Much more then, having now been justified by His blood, we shall be saved (σωθησόμεθα) from the wrath *of God* through Him. (see Rom. 13:11)
Glory	2 Corinthians 3:18 But we all, with unveiled face beholding as in a mirror the glory of the Lord, are being transformed into the same image from glory to glory, just as from the Lord, the Spirit.	1 Corinthians 15:42 So also is the resurrection of the dead. It is sown a perishable body, it is raised an imperishable body; [43] it is sown in dishonor, it is raised in glory; it is sown in weakness, it is raised in power;
New Creation	2 Corinthians 5:17 Therefore if anyone is in Christ, *he is* a new creature (καινὴ κτίσις); the old things passed away (παρῆλθεν); behold, new things have come (ἰδοὺ γέγονεν καινά).	2 Corinthians 5:2 For indeed in this *house* we groan, longing to be clothed with our dwelling from heaven, (see 5:4)
Sanctification	1 Corinthians 1:2 To the church of God which is at Corinth, to those who have been sanctified (ἡγιασμένοις) in Christ Jesus, saints by calling, … (See 6:11)	1 Thessalonians 5:23 Now may the God of peace Himself sanctify you entirely (ἁγιάσαι ὑμᾶς ὁλοτελεῖς); …
Dead to Sin	Romans 6:2 … How shall we who died (ἀπεθάνομεν) to sin still live in it? (Also 6:6-8)	Romans 8:13 … but if by the Spirit you are putting to death (θανατοῦτε) the deeds of the body, you will live. (Col. 3:5, NIV "Put to death …" / KJV "Mortify" [Νεκρώσατε] …)

Ecclesiological Concepts

CHART 92

NAMES OF THE CHURCH	REFERENCES
believers (πιστοί,)	Rom. 4:24; 1 Cor. 1:21; 6:6; 7:12–15; 14:22; 2 Cor. 6:15; Gal. 3:22; 1 Thess. 1:7; 2:10; 1 Tim. 4:3, 10; 6:2
beloved (ἀγαπητοί,)	Rom. 1:7; 12:19; 16:12; 2 Cor. 7:1; 12:19; Eph. 5:1; 6:21; Phil. 2:12; Col. 4:7, 9, 14; 1 Tim. 6:2; 2 Tim. 1:2; Philem. 1:16
my/our beloved	Rom. 16:5, 8–9; 1 Cor. 4:14, 17; 10:14; 15:58; Phil. 4:1; Col. 1:7; 1 Thess. 2:8; Philem. 1:1
body (σῶμα)	1 Cor. 12:12–31; Rom. 12:4–8; Eph. 1:23 (his); 4:4–13; Col. 1:18, 24; 2:19
body of Christ	1 Cor. 12:27; Rom. 12:5; Eph. 1:23; 4:4–13; Col. 1:18
one body (ἕν σῶμα)	Rom. 12:4-5; 1 Cor. 10:17; 12:12 [2x], 13, 20; Eph. 2:16; 4:4; Col. 3:15
head (κεφαλή)	1 Cor. 11:3; Eph. 1:22; 4:15; 5:23; Col. 1:18; 2:10, 19
bride/virgin	2 Cor. 11:2; Eph. 5:25–32
called (κλήτοι)	Rom. 1:6–7; 8:28; 1 Cor. 1:2, 24
chosen/elected/predestined (ἐκλογή, αἱρέομ., προορίζω, ..)	Rom. 8:29–30, 33; 16:13; 1 Cor. 1:27–28; Eph. 1:4–5, 11; Col. 3:12; 1 Thess. 1:4; 2 Thess. 2:13; 2 Tim. 2:10; Titus 1:1
church (ἐκκλησία)	Rom. 16:1, 4–5, 16, 23; 1 Cor. 1:2; 4:17; 6:4; 7:17; 10:32; 11:16, 18, 22; 12:28; 14:4, 5, 12, 19, 23, 28, 33ff; 15:9; 16:1, 19; etc.
church of God (ἐκκλησία [τοῦ] θεοῦ)	Acts 20:28; 1 Cor. 1:2; 10:32; 11:16, 22; 15:9; 2 Cor. 1:1; Gal. 1:13; 1 Thess. 2:14; 2 Thess. 1:4; 1 Tim. 3:5, 15
all the churches of Christ	Rom. 16:16 (αἱ ἐκκλησίαι πᾶσαι τοῦ Χριστοῦ)
citizens	Eph. 2:12 (πολιτεία), 19 (συμπολῖται); see Phil. 1:27 (πολιτεύομαι); 3:20 (πολίτευμα)
family	
brothers and sisters (ἀδελφοί)	Rom. 1:13; 7:1, 4; 8:12; 10:1; 11:25; 12:1; 15:14, 30; 16:17; 1 Cor. 1:10–11, 26; 2:1; 3:1; 4:6; 6:6; 7:24, 29; 10:1; 11:33; 12:1; 14:6, etc.
brotherly love (φιλαδελφία)	Rom. 12:10; Gal. 4:26; 1 Thess. 4:9
children	Rom. 8:16–17; 1 Cor. 4:14–21; also 1 Tim. 1:2; 2 Tim. 1:2; Titus 1:4
beloved child[ren]	Eph. 5:1 (τέκνα ἀγαπητὰ); 2 Tim. 1:2; Titus 1:4
child[ren] of God (τέκνα θεοῦ)	Rom. 8:16, 21; 9:8; Phil. 2:15
children of promise	Rom. 9:8 (τέκνα τῆς ἐπαγγελίας); Gal. 4:28
my (beloved) children	1 Cor. 4:14, 17; Gal. 4:19; see also 2 Cor. 6:13; 12:14; Phil. 2:22; 1 Thess. 2:7, 11; 1 Tim. 1:2, 18; 2 Tim. 2:1; Philem. 1:10
children of light (τέκνα φωτὸς)	Eph. 5:8
daughters (θυγατέραι)	2 Cor. 6:18
father	• Abraham: Rom. 4:11, 12, 16–18 • Paul: 1 Cor. 4:15; Phil. 2:22; 1 Thess. 2:11 • older believers: 1 Tim. 5:1
kiss (φίλημα)	Rom. 16:16; 1 Cor. 16:20; 2 Cor. 13:12; 1 Thess. 5:26
mother (μήτηρ)	Rom. 16:13; 1 Tim. 5:2
sister (ἀδελφή)	Rom. 16:1, 15; 1 Cor. 7:15; 9:5; 1 Tim. 5:2; Philem. 1:2

sons (υἱοί)	Gal. 4:5–7
sons of God (υἱοὶ θεοῦ)	Rom. 8:14, 19; 9:26; Gal. 3:26
adoption (υἱοθεσία)	Rom. 8:15, 23; Gal. 4:5; Eph. 1:5
fellowship of faith	Philem. 1:6 (ἡ κοινωνία τῆς πίστεώς)
field (γεώργιον)	1 Cor. 3:9 (God's)
household (οἰκεῖοι)	Gal. 6:10 (of faith); Eph. 2:19 (of God)
insiders	1 Cor. 5:12; 1 Thess. 4:12; 1 Tim. 3:7
Israel of God	Gal. 6:16
my work in the Lord	1 Cor. 9:1
people (λαός) **(of God)**	Rom. 9:26; 2 Cor. 6:16–18; Titus 2:14
saints (ἅγιοι)	Rom. 1:7; 8:27; 1 Cor. 1:2; 3:17; 2 Cor. 1:1; 8:4; Eph. 1:1, 15, 18; 2:19; 3:8, 18; 4:12; 5:3; 6:18; Phil. 1:1; 4:21–22; Col. 1:2, 4, 12, 22, 26; 3:12; 1 Thess. 3:13; 5:26; 2 Thess. 1:10; 1 Tim. 5:10; Philem. 1:5, 7; etc.
seal of my apostleship in the Lord	1 Cor. 9:2
temple (ναός)	1 Cor. 3:16–17; 2 Cor. 6:16; Eph. 2:21
house (οἶκος)	1 Tim. 3:15 (of God); 2 Tim. 2:20–21 (οἰκία)
building (οἰκοδομή)	1 Cor. 3:9; Eph. 2:21
dwelling (κατοικητήριον)	Eph. 2:22; see 3:17 (κατοικέω)
vessels of mercy (σκεύη ἐλέους)	Rom. 9:23
ACTIVITIES OF THE CHURCH	
baptism (βάπτισμα)	Eph. 4:5; "buried with Him through baptism" in Rom. 6:4 and Col. 2:12
to baptize, baptized (βαπτίζω)	Rom. 6:3; 1 Cor. 1:13–17; 10:2; 12:13; 15:29; Gal. 3:27 (see also Acts 16:14–15, 33; 19:1–7)
church discipline	
… by God	1 Cor. 11:30–32
… by the church	1 Cor. 5:11; 6:1–6; 2 Cor. 2:5–8; Gal. 6:1; 2 Thess. 3:6, 14–15
… by the servant of the Lord	1 Cor. 6:5; 15:34; 2 Cor. 7:8; 1 Tim. 1:18–20; 5:20; 2 Tim. 2:24–26; 3:5; Titus 1:9, 13; 2:15; 3:10–11
… by Paul	1 Cor. 5:5; 1 Tim. 1:20
come together (συνέρχομαι)	1 Cor. 11:17–18, 20, 33–34; 14:23, 26
eat together	Rom. 14:1–23; 1 Cor. 8–10; 11:17–34; Gal. 2:11–14; Col. 2:16
edification (οἰκοδομή, οἰκοδομέω)	Rom. 14:19; 15:2; 1 Cor. 8:1; 10:23; 14:3, 4–5, 12, 17, 26; 2 Cor. 10:8; 12:19; 13:10; Eph. 4:12, 16, 29; 1 Thess. 5:11
fellowship (κοινωνία)	Rom. 15:26; 2 Cor. 6:14; 8:4; 9:13; Gal. 2:9; Phil. 1:5; Philem. 1:6
giving to the poor	Rom. 15:25–27; 1 Cor. 16:1–4; 2 Cor. 8–9; Gal. 2:10; Titus 3:14; see Acts 24:17
leaders	1 Cor. 16:15–16; Gal. 6:6
deacons (διάκονοι)	1 Tim. 3:8–10, 12–13
elders (πρεσβύτερος)	Acts 14:23; 15:2, 4, 6, 22–23; 16:4; 20:17; 21:18; 1 Tim. 5:17, 19; Titus 1:5
leaders (προϊστάμενοι)	Rom. 12:8; 1 Thess. 5:12; see 1 Tim. 5:17 (elders who "lead")
leadership (κυβέρνησις)	1 Cor. 12:28
overseer (ἐπίσκοπος)	Acts 20:28; Phil. 1:1; 1 Tim. 3:2; Titus 1:7 (also 1 Peter 2:25)

presbytery (πρεσβυτέριον)	1 Tim. 4:14
Lord's Supper (κυριακὸν δεῖπνον)	1 Cor. 11:20–26
prayer	Eph. 6:18; Phil. 4:6; Col. 4:2; 1 Tim. 2:1
prayer (προσευχή, προσεύχομαι)	Rom. 8:26; 12:12; 15:30; 1 Cor. 7:5; 11:4–5, 13; 14:13, 15; Eph. 6:18; Phil. 4:6; Col. 4:2–3; 1 Thess. 5:17, 25; 2 Thess. 3:1; 1 Tim. 2:1, 8; 5:5; Philem. 1:22
petition (δέησις)	2 Cor. 1:11; 9:14; Eph. 6:18; Phil. 1:19; 4:6; 1 Tim. 2:1; 5:5
thanksgiving (εὐχαριστία, εὐχαριστέω)	Rom. 1:21; 14:6; 16:4; 1 Cor. 14:16–18; 2 Cor. 1:11; 4:15; 9:11–12; Eph. 5:4, 20; Phil. 4:6; Col. 1:12; 2:7; 3:17; 4:2; 1 Thess. 3:9; 5:18; 1 Tim. 2:1; 4:3–4
service, ministry (διακονία, διακονέω)	• ministry of Moses: 2 Cor. 3:7, 9a • ministry of Paul and his coworkers: Rom. 11:13; 15:31; 1 Cor. 16:15; 2 Cor. 3:8, 9b; 4:1; 5:18; 6:3; Col. 4:17; 1 Tim. 1:12; 2 Tim. 4:5 • other ministries: Rom. 12:7; 1 Cor. 1:5; 16:15; 2 Cor. 8:4; 9:1, 12–13; Eph. 4:12; 1 Tim. 3:10, 13; 2 Tim. 1:18; Philem. 1:13
singing to the Lord	Eph. 5:19; Col. 3:16 (with psalms, hymns, and spiritual songs)
worship (λατρεία, λατρεύω)	Rom. 1:25; 12:2; Phil. 3:3

Gifts of the Spirit

CHART 93

	1 Cor. 12:8–10		1 Cor. 12:28–30		Rom. 12:6–8		Eph. 4:11	
1.	λόγος σοφίας	word of wisdom	(first) apostles	ἀπόστολοι	προφητείαν	prophecy	ἀπόστολοι	apostles
2.	λόγος γνώσεως	word of knowledge	(second) prophets	προφῆται	διακονία	service	προφῆται	prophets
3.	πίστις	faith	(then) teachers	διδάσκαλοι	ὁ διδάσκων	teaching	εὐαγγελίσται	evangelists
4.	χαρίσματα ἰαμάτων	gifts of healing	(then) miracles	δυνάμεις	ὁ παρακαλῶν	exhortation	ποιμένα	pastors (and teachers)
5.	ἐνεργήματα δυνάμεων	effecting of miracles	gifts of healings	χαρίσματα ἰαμάτων	ὁ μεταδιδοὺς	giving	διδάσκαλοι	teachers
6.	προφητεία	prophecy	helps	ἀντιλήμψεις	ὁ προϊστάμενος	leading		
7.	διακρίσεις πνευμάτων	distinguishing of spirits	administrations	κυβερνήσεις	ὁ ἐλεῶν	showing mercy		
8.	γένη γλωσσῶν	various kinds of tongues	various kinds of tongues	γένη γλωσσῶν				
9.	ἑρμηνεία γλωσσῶν	interpretation of tongues	interpretation	διερμηνεύουσιν				

Greek term and English translation

House Churches and Homes in Paul's Ministry

CHART 94

CITY	HOUSE CHURCHES IN PAUL'S MINISTRY	REFERENCE
Cenchrae	• Church in the house of Phoebe	Rom. 16:1–2
Colossae	• Church in the house of Philemon	Philem. 1–2, 21–22
Corinth	• (House of Aquila and Priscilla) • Church in the house of Gaius • Church in the house of Chloe	(Acts 18:2–3, 11) Rom. 16:23 1 Cor. 1:11
Ephesus	• Church in the house of Aquila and Prisca	1 Cor. 16:19
Laodicea	• Church in the house of Nympha	Col. 4:15
Rome	• Church in the house of Prisca and Aquila • (Church in the house of Aristobulus) • (Church in the house of Narcissus) • (Church in the house of "Asyncritus, Phlegon, Hermes, Patrobas, Hermas and the brothers with them") • ("Philologus, Julia, Nereus and his sister, and Olympas and all the saints with them")	Rom. 16:3–5 Rom. 16:10 Rom. 16:11 Rom. 16:14 Rom. 16:15
Troas	• Church in the house of an unknown host	Acts 20:7–12
HOUSES/HOUSEHOLDS OF BELIEVERS IN PAUL'S MINISTRY		
Caesarea	• House of Philip the evangelist	Acts 21:8
Corinth	• House of Titus Justus • House of Crispus, the leader of the synagogue • House of Stephanas	Acts 18:7 Acts 18:8 1 Cor. 16:15; 1:16
Damascus	• House of Judas	Acts 9:11
Ephesus	• House of Onesiphorus	2 Tim. 1:16; 4:19
Philippi	• House of Lydia • House of the jailer	Acts 16:14–15 Acts 16:31, 34
Thessalonica	• House of Jason	Acts 17:5, 7

Criteria for the Selection of Elders

CHART 95

	1 Timothy 3:1-7			Titus 1:5-8
1.	ἀνεπίλημπτον	above reproach	above reproach	ἀνέγκλητος
2.	μιᾶς γυναικὸς ἄνδρα	husband of one wife	husband of one wife	μιᾶς γυναικὸς ἀνήρ
3.	νηφάλιον	sober-minded	children are believers and not open to charge of debauchery or insubordination	τέκνα ἔχων πιστά, μὴ ἐν κατηγορίᾳ ἀσωτίας ἢ ἀνυπότακτα
4.	σώφρονα	self-controlled	above reproach	ἀνέγκλητον
5.	κόσμιον	respectable	not arrogant	μὴ αὐθάδη
6.	φιλόξενον	hospitable	not quick-tempered	μὴ ὀργίλον
7.	διδακτικόν	able to teach	not a drunkard	μὴ πάροινον
8.	μὴ πάροινον	not a drunkard	not violent	μὴ πλήκτην
9.	μὴ πλήκτην, ἀλλὰ ἐπιεικῆ	not violent but gentle	not greedy for gain	μὴ αἰσχροκερδῆ
10.	ἄμαχον	not quarrelsome	hospitable	ἀλλὰ φιλόξενον
11.	ἀφιλάργυρον	not a lover of money	lover of good	φιλάγαθον
12.	τοῦ ἰδίου οἴκου καλῶς προϊστάμενον	manage his own house well	self-controlled	σώφρονα
13.	τέκνα ἔχοντα ἐν ὑποταγῇ μετὰ πάσης σεμνότητος	with all dignity keeping his children submissive	upright	δίκαιον
14.	μὴ νεόφυτον	not a recent convert	holy	ὅσιον
15.	μαρτυρίαν καλὴν ἔχειν ἀπὸ τῶν ἔξωθεν	well-thought-of by outsiders	disciplined	ἐγκρατῆ
16.			hold firm to the trustworthy word so that he may be able both to exhort in sound doctrine and to refute those who contradict.	ἀντεχόμενον τοῦ κατὰ τὴν διδαχὴν πιστοῦ λόγου, ἵνα δυνατὸς ᾖ καὶ παρακαλεῖν ἐν τῇ διδασκαλίᾳ τῇ ὑγιαινούσῃ καὶ τοὺς ἀντιλέγοντας ἐλέγχειν

Ethics

CHART 96

PRINCIPLES	
adiaphora ("non-essentials")	Rom. 14:5–6; 1 Cor. 7:39; 8:8
free choices	1 Cor. 7:39; 8:8; Rom. 14:5–6
no neutral ethical realm	1 Cor. 10:31; Col. 3:17; creation is always good (1 Tim. 4:4–5)
not cause someone to stumble	Rom. 14:13, 20; 1 Cor. 8:9; walk in love (Rom. 14:15)
search the "excellent"	Phil. 1:9–11 (τὰ διαφέροντα)
danger: legalism	Rom. 14:3; 1 Cor. 7:1 (if a slogan); 10:25; Col. 2:16–23; 1 Tim. 4:3
Christ in you	Gal. 2:20; 4:19; Rom. 8:10; 2 Cor. 13:5; Col. 1:17; see Eph. 3:17
Christ-likeness	Rom. 8:29; 13:13–14; 1 Cor. 11:1; 2 Cor. 3:18; 4:10–11; Gal. 4:19; Phil. 2:5–11; etc.
compromise (when others hinder the doing of God's will)	
necessity of social contacts	1 Cor. 5:9–10; 10:27
nature of God: patience	Rom. 2:4
danger: lawlessness	2 Cor. 6:14; Gal. 5:13
conscience (συνείδησις)	Rom. 2:15; 9:1; 13:5; (see also 14:1–15:6); 1 Cor. 8:8, 10, 12–13; 10:25, 27; etc.
fight (στρατεύομαι)	2 Cor. 10:3–4; 1 Tim. 1:18–19 (τὴν καλὴν στρατείαν)
fight (ἀγωνίζομαι(ἀγών)	1 Tim. 6:12 (fight of faith); 2 Tim. 4:7 (τὸν καλὸν ἀγῶνα)
armor (ὅπλον, πανοπλία)	Rom. 13:12 (τὰ ὅπλα τοῦ φωτός); 2 Cor. 6:7; 10:4; Eph. 6:11–13; see 1 Thess. 5:8
struggle (πάλη)	Eph. 6:12
flesh (σάρξ) (negative)	Rom. 7:25; 8:3–9, 12–13; 2 Cor. 1:17; Eph. 2:3; Phil. 3:4
flesh – spirit antithesis (πνεῦμα[τικός], σάρξ[-κινος])	Rom. 7:5–6, 14; 8:4, 5 (2x), 6, 9 (3x), 12–13; 1 Cor. 3:1; 5:5; 2 Cor. 7:1; Gal. 3:3; 4:29; 5:16–26; 6:8 (2x); Phil. 3:3; Col. 2:5
fruit (καρπός)	Rom. 1:13; 15:28; Gal. 5:22–23; Eph. 5:9; Phil. 1:11, 22; 4:17
bearing fruit (καρποφορέω)	Rom. 7:4, 5; Col. 1:6, 10
growing, growth (αὐξάνω, - ησις)	1 Cor. 3:6–7; 2 Cor. 9:10; 10:15; Eph. 2:21; 4:15–16; Col. 1:6, 10; 2:19
grow wonderfully	2 Thess. 1:3 (ὑπεραυξάνω)
abound (περισσεύω)	Rom. 15:13; 2 Cor. 4:15; 8:7; Phil. 1:9; 1 Thess. 4:10
progress (προκοπή)	Phil. 1:12, 25; 1 Tim. 4:15
baby (νήπιος)	Rom. 2:20; 1 Cor. 3:1; Eph. 4:14 (see 1 Cor. 14:20)
child (παιδίον)	1 Cor. 14:20
mature (τέλειος)	Rom. 12:2; 1 Cor. 2:6; 14:20; Eph. 4:13; Phil. 3:15; Col. 1:28; 4:12
new creation (καινὴ κτίσις)	2 Cor. 5:17; Gal. 6:15
new man (καινός ἄνθρωπος)	Eph. 2:15; 4:24; see Col. 3:10 (ὁ νέος)
old man (παλαιός ἄνθρωπος)	Rom. 6:6; Eph. 4:22; Col. 3:9
lay off (ἀποτίθημι)	Rom. 13:12, 14; Eph. 4:22–24; Col. 2:11; 3:8–12
put on (ἐνδύω)	Rom. 13:12; Gal. 3:27; Eph. 4:24; 6:11, 14; Col. 3:10, 12; 1 Thess. 5:8
to please God (ἀρέσκω)	1 Thess. 4:2; also 2:4, 15; Rom. 8:8; 1 Cor. 7:32; Gal. 1:10; see 2 Tim. 2:4
sanctification (ἁγιασμός)	Rom. 6:19, 22; 1 Cor. 1:30; 1 Thess. 4:3–4, 7; 2 Thess. 2:13; 1 Tim. 2:15

sanctify (ἁγιάζω)	Rom. 15:16; 1 Cor. 1:2; 6:11; 7:14; Eph. 5:26; 1 Thess. 5:23; 2 Tim. 2:21
holiness (ἁγιωσύνη)	2 Cor. 7:1; 1 Thess. 3:13
sin (in the life of a believer)	Rom. 6:12–14; 14:23; 1 Cor. 5:1; 6:18; 8:12; 15:34; Eph. 4:26; 1 Tim. 5:20, 22; etc.
transformation (μεταμορφόω)	Rom. 12:2; 2 Cor. 3:18
formation (μορφόω)	Gal. 4:19 ("until Christ is formed in you")
renewal (ἀνακαινόω, - νωσις)	Rom. 12:2; 2 Cor. 4:16; Col. 3:10; Titus 3:5; see Eph. 4:23 (ἀνανεόω)
vices	Rom. 1:29–31; 13:9, 13; 1 Cor. 5:9–11; 6:9–10; 2 Cor. 12:20; Gal. 5:19–21; Eph. 4:25–32; 5:3–5; Phil. 4:8–9; Col. 3:5; 1 Tim. 1:9–10; 6:4–5; 2 Tim. 3:2–5; Titus 2:3; 3:3
virtues	Gal. 5:22–23; 1 Tim. 3:2–7, 8–13; 6:11; 2 Tim. 2:22–25; 3:10; Titus 1:6–8; 2:4–10; 3:1f
PRACTICES	
coveting (ἐπιθυμία)	Rom. 7:7 (2x), 8; 13:9; 1 Cor. 5:10–11; 6:10; 10:6; 2 Cor. 9:5; Eph. 5:5
drunkenness (μέθη, κῶμος)	Rom. 13:13; 1 Cor. 5:11; 6:10; 11:21; Gal. 5:21; Eph. 5:18; 1 Thess. 5:7
government	Rom. 13:1–7 (see 3:8); 1 Tim. 2:1–2; Titus 3:1 (see Matt. 22:21; 1 Peter 2:13–14)
household codes	Eph. 5:22–33; Col. 3:18–4:1; 1 Tim. 2:1–15; 5:1–2; 6:1–2, 17–19; Titus 2:1–3:8
marriage	Rom. 7:2–3; 1 Cor. 7; Eph. 5:21-33
married woman	Rom. 7:2 (ὕπανδρος γυνὴ), 3 ("joined to another man," γένηται ἀνδρὶ)
to marry (γαμέω)	1 Cor. 7:9 (2x), 10, 28 (2x), 33–34, 36, 39; 1 Tim. 4:3; 5:11, 14
to give in marriage	1 Cor. 7:38 (2x) (γαμίζω)
divorce	1 Cor. 7:10–16, 39
one wife (μία γυνή)	1 Tim. 3:2, 12; Titus 1:6
celibacy	1 Cor. 7:1 (Corinthian slogan?), 7–8; reasons: 1 Cor. 7:26, 28–29, 32–35
sexuality	
adultery (μοιχεύω)	Rom. 2:22; 7:3; 13:9; 1 Cor. 6:9
homosexuality	Rom. 1:26–27; 1 Cor. 6:9–10 (μαλακοί, ἀρσενοκοῖται); 1 Tim. 1:9–11
impurity (ἀκαθαρσία)	(when beside πορνεία): 2 Cor. 12:21; Gal. 5:19; Eph. 5:3–5; Col. 3:5; see Rom. 1:24; "impure" (ἀκάθαρτος): 1 Cor. 7:14; 2 Cor. 6:17; Eph. 5:5
sexual immorality (πορνεία)	1 Cor. 5:1–11; 6:9–18; 7:2; 2 Cor. 12:21; Gal. 5:19; Eph. 5:3, 5; Col. 3:5; 1 Thess. 4:3; 1 Tim. 1:10; "act immorally" (πορνεύω): 1 Cor. 6:18; 10:8 (2x); "immoral people" (πόρνος): 1 Cor. 5:9–11; 6:9; Eph. 5:5; 1 Thess. 1:10
virgin (παρθένος)	1 Cor. 7:25, 28, 34, 36–38
widow (χήρα)	1 Cor. 7:8; 1 Tim. 5:3 (2x), 4–5, 9, 11, 16 (2x)
money	2 Corinthians 8–9
giving (μεταδίδωμι)	Rom. 12:8; Eph. 4:28; see Acts 20:35
giving to believers	Rom. 12:13; 15:14-32; 1 Cor. 16:1–4; 2 Cor. 8:1-9:15; Gal. 6:10b
giving to unbelievers	Rom. 12:14, 20; Gal. 6:10a
greed (πλεονεξία)	Rom. 1:29; 2 Cor. 9:5; Eph. 4:19; 5:3; Col. 3:5; 1 Thess. 2:5
greedy person (πλεονέκτης)	1 Cor. 5:10–11; 6:10; Eph. 5:5
leaders should be paid	1 Cor. 9:1–14; Gal. 6:6; 1 Thess. 5:12; 1 Tim. 5:17

Paul's financial support	from Philippians (Phil. 4:15–18), but not from Corinthians (1 Cor. 9:12, 15–19)
liberality (ἁπλότης)	Rom. 12:8; 2 Cor. 8:2; 9:11, 13
love(rs) of money	1 Tim. 6:10 (φιλαργυρία); 2 Tim. 3:2 (φιλάργυρος); see 1 Tim. 3:3 (ἀφιλάργυρος)
poverty (πτωχεία, πτωχός)	Rom. 15:26; 2 Cor. 6:10; 8:2, 8, 9 (2x); Gal. 2:10; 4:9; "become poor": 2 Cor. 8:9
rich (πλοῦτος)	• metaphorical: Rom. 2:4; 9:23; 11:12, 33; Eph. 1:7, 18; 2:7; 3:8, 16; Col. 1:27; 2:2 • material: 2 Cor. 8:2; Phil. 4:19; 1 Tim. 6:17
be / make rich (πλουτίζω, πλουτέω)	• metaphorical: Rom. 10:12; 1 Cor. 1:5; 4:8; 2 Cor. 6:10; 9:11; 1 Tim. 6:18 • material: 2 Cor. 8:9; 1 Tim. 6:9
sufficiency (αὐτάρκεια)	2 Cor. 9:8; 1 Tim. 6:6
suffice (ἀρκέω)	2 Cor. 12:9; 1 Tim. 6:8
content (αὐτάρκης)	Phil. 4:11
taxes (φόρος)	Rom. 13:6–7
slaves	• equal to the master in Christ: 1 Cor. 12:13; Gal. 3:28; Col. 3:11 • subordinate to the master: Eph. 6:5; Col 3:22–4:1; 1 Tim. 6:1; Titus 2:9 • debated text: 1 Cor. 7:21–23
women	• equal to men: 1 Cor. 7:3–5; 11:11–12; Gal. 3:28; see 2 Cor. 5:16–17 • subordinate to men: Rom. 7:2 (ὕπανδ.); 1 Cor. 11:3, 7–9; 14:34–35; 1 Tim. 2:9–15
work	• Paul worked: 1 Cor. 4:12; 1 Thess. 2:9; 2 Thess. 3:8–9; see Acts 20:34–35 • general instructions: 1 Cor. 10:31; Eph. 4:28; 6:6; Col. 3:17, 22; 1 Thess. 4:11; 2 Thess. 3:10–13

The Imperative in Paul's Letters

CHART 97

	ROMANS
6:11–13	[11] Even so **consider** yourselves to be dead to sin, but alive to God in Christ Jesus. [12] Therefore **do not let sin reign** in your mortal body so that you obey its lusts, [13] and **do not go on presenting the members of your body to sin** as instruments of unrighteousness; but **present yourselves to God** as those alive from the dead, and your members as instruments of righteousness to God.
6:19	so now **present your members as slaves to righteousness**, resulting in sanctification.
11:18	**do not be arrogant** toward the branches;
11:20	Quite right, they were broken off for their unbelief, but you stand by your faith. **Do not be conceited, but fear**;
12:1–3	[1] Therefore I urge you, brethren, by the mercies of God, to **present your bodies a living and holy sacrifice**, acceptable to God, which is your spiritual service of worship. [2] And **do not be conformed** to this world, but **be transformed** by the renewing of your mind, so that you may prove what the will of God is, that which is good and acceptable and perfect. [3] For through the grace given to me I say to everyone among you **not to think more highly of himself than he ought to think**; but to think so as to have sound judgment, as God has allotted to each a measure of faith.
12:14–17, 21	[14] **Bless** those who persecute you; **bless** and **do not curse**. [15] **Rejoice** with those who rejoice, and **weep** with those who weep. [16] Be of the same mind toward one another; do not be haughty in mind, but associate with the lowly. **Do not be wise in your own estimation**. [17] **Never pay back evil for evil** to anyone. … [21] **Do not be overcome by evil, but overcome evil with good**.
13:1	Every person is to **be in subjection to the governing authorities**. For there is no authority except from God, and those which exist are established by God.
14:1	**Now accept** the one who is weak in faith,
	1 CORINTHIANS
1:10	Now I exhort you, brethren, by the name of our Lord Jesus Christ, that you all **agree** and that there **be no divisions** among you, but that you **be made complete** in the same mind and in the same judgment.
3:10	But each man must be **careful** how he builds on it.
4:16	Therefore I exhort you, **be** imitators of me.
5:7	**Clean** out the old leaven so that you may be a new lump, just as you are in fact unleavened.
5:9	I wrote you in my letter **not to associate with immoral people**; (also 5:11)
5:13	"**Remove** the wicked man from among yourselves" (Deut. 13:5; 17:7, 12; 21:21: 22:21)
6:18	**Flee immorality.**
7:3	The husband **must fulfill his duty to his wife**, and likewise also the wife to her husband.
7:10	But to the married I give instructions, not I, but the Lord, that **the wife should not leave her husband**
9:9	"You shall **not muzzle the ox** while he is threshing" (Deut. 25:4)
10:7	**Do not be idolaters**, as some of them were;
11:6	For if a woman does not cover her head, **let her also have her hair cut off**; but if it is disgraceful for a woman to have her hair cut off or her head shaved, **let her cover her head**.
12:31	But earnestly **desire the greater gifts.**
14:1	**Pursue love, yet desire earnestly spiritual gifts**, but especially that you may prophesy.
14:34	The **women are to keep silent in the churches**;
15:34	**Become sober-minded** as you ought, and **stop sinning**; for some have no knowledge of God.
16:20	**Greet** one another with a holy kiss.
	2 CORINTHIANS
5:20	… we beg you on behalf of Christ, **be reconciled to God**.
6:14	**Do not be bound together with unbelievers**;
6:17	Therefore, "'**Come out** from their midst and **be separate**,' says the Lord. 'And **do not touch what is unclean**" (Isa. 52:11)
13:5	**Test yourselves** to see if you are in the faith; **examine yourselves!**

GALATIANS	
5:13	… through love **serve one another**.
5:16	But I say, **walk by the Spirit**, and you will not carry out the desire of the flesh.
6:1	… if anyone is caught in any trespass, you who are spiritual, **restore such a one** in a spirit of gentleness;
6:2	**Bear one another's burdens**, and thereby fulfill the law of Christ.
6:4	But **each one must examine his own work**, …
6:6	The one who is taught the word is to **share all good things** with the one who teaches him.
6:17	From now on **let no one cause trouble for me**, for I bear on my body the brand-marks of Jesus.
EPHESIANS	
4:25–31	25 Therefore, laying aside falsehood, "**Speak truth each one**" (Zech 8:16) … 26 "Be angry, and yet do not sin" (Ps 4:4); **do not let the sun go down on your anger**, 27 and **do not give the devil an opportunity**. 28 He who steals **must steal no longer**; but rather he must **labor**, … 29 **Let no unwholesome word proceed** from your mouth, but only such a word as is good for edification, 30 **Do not grieve the Holy Spirit** … 31 **Let all bitterness and wrath and anger and clamor and slander be put away from you**, along with all malice.
5:1–3, 5–11	1 Therefore **be imitators of God**, as beloved children; 2 and **walk in love**, just as Christ also loved you and gave Himself up for us, an offering and a sacrifice to God as a fragrant aroma. 3 But **immorality or any impurity or greed must not even be named** among you, as is proper among saints; … 5 For this **you know with certainty**, that no immoral or impure person or covetous man, who is an idolater, has an inheritance in the kingdom of Christ and God. 6 **Let no one deceive you** with empty words, for because of these things the wrath of God comes upon the sons of disobedience. 7 Therefore **do not be partakers** with them; 8 for you were formerly darkness, but now you are Light in the Lord; **walk as children of Light** 9 (for the fruit of the Light consists in all goodness and righteousness and truth), 10 trying to learn what is pleasing to the Lord. 11 **Do not participate** in the unfruitful deeds of darkness, …
5:25	**Husbands, love your wives**, just as Christ also loved the church and gave Himself up for her,
6:1–2	1 **Children, obey your parents** in the Lord, for this is right. 2 Honor your father and mother (Ex 20:12)
6:4	**Fathers, do not provoke your children to anger**, but bring them up in the discipline and instruction of the Lord.
6:5	**Slaves, be obedient to those who are your masters** …
6:9	And **masters, do the same things** to them, and give up threatening, …
PHILIPPIANS	
1:27	Only **conduct yourselves** in a manner worthy of the gospel of Christ, …
2:5	**Have this attitude in yourselves** which was also in Christ Jesus, …
2:12–13	12 … **work out your salvation** with fear and trembling; 13 for it is God who is at work in you, both to will and to work for His good pleasure.
3:17	Brethren, **join in following my example**, …
COLOSSIANS	
2:6	Therefore as you have received Christ Jesus the Lord, **so walk in Him**, …
3:5	Therefore **consider the members of your earthly body as dead** to immorality, impurity, passion, evil desire, and greed, which amounts to idolatry.
3:8	But now you also, **put them all aside**: anger, wrath, malice, slander, and abusive speech from your mouth.
1 THESSALONIANS	
4:2–3	2 For you know what commandments we gave you by the authority of the Lord Jesus. 3 For this is the will of God, your sanctification; that is, that you **abstain from sexual immorality;**
5:14–15	14 We urge you, brethren, **admonish the unruly, encourage the fainthearted, help the weak, be patient with everyone.** 15 See that **no one repays another with evil for evil, but always seek after that which is good for one another and for all people.**
5:19–22	19 **Do not quench the Spirit;** 20 do not despise prophetic utterances. 21 But examine everything carefully; hold fast to that which is good; 22 abstain from every form of evil.
2 THESSALONIANS	
3:10	… if anyone is not willing to work, then **he is not to eat**, either.
3:14–15	14 If anyone does not obey our instruction in this letter, take special note of that person and **do not associate with him**, so that he will be put to shame. 15 Yet **do not regard him as an enemy**, …

Vices in Paul's Letters

CHART 98

	VICE		REFERENCE
1.	evil	κακός	28xPaul: Rom. 1:30; 2:9; 3:8; 7:19, 21; 12:17 (2x); 13:3, 4 (2x), 10; 14:20; 16:19; 1 Cor. 10:6; 13:5; 15:33; 2 Cor. 13:7; Phil. 3:2; Col. 3:5; 1 Thess. 5:15 (2x); 1 Tim. 5:8; 6:10; 2 Tim. 3:13; 4:14; Titus 1:12
2.	evil, depravity	κακία	6xPaul: Rom. 1:29; 1 Cor. 5:8; 14:20; Eph. 4:31; Col. 3:8; Titus 3:3
3.	unrighteousness	ἀδικία	12xPaul: Rom. 1:18 (2x), 29; 2:8; 3:5; 6:13; 9:14; 1 Cor. 13:6; 2 Cor. 12:13; 2 Thess. 2:10, 12; 2 Tim. 2:19
4.	to do wrong	ἀδικέω	9xPaul: 1 Cor. 6:7, 8; 2 Cor. 7:2, 12 (2x); Gal. 4:12; Col. 3:25 (2x); Philem. 1:18
5.	unrighteous	ἄδικος	3xPaul: Rom. 3:5; 1 Cor. 6:1, 9
6.	lust(s)	ἐπιθυμία	17xPaul: Rom. 1:24; 6:12; 7:7, 8; 13:14; Gal. 5:16, 24; Eph. 2:3; 4:22; Col. 3:5; 1 Thess. 4:5; 1 Tim. 6:9; 2 Tim. 2:22; 3:6; 4:3; Titus 2:12; 3:3
7.	to desire, covet	ἐπιθυμέω	4xPaul: Rom. 7:7; 13:9; 1 Cor. 10:6; Gal. 5:17
8.	to lie	ψεύδομαι	5xPaul: Rom. 9:1; 2 Cor. 11:31; Gal. 1:20; Col. 3:9; 1 Tim. 2:7
9.	lie	ψεῦδος	4xPaul: Rom. 1:25; Eph. 4:25; 2 Thess. 2:9, 11
10.	liar	ψεύστης	3xPaul: Rom. 3:4; 1 Tim. 1:10; Titus 1:12
11.	false brother	ψευδάδελφος	2xPaul: 2 Cor. 11:26; Gal. 2:4
12.	lie	ψεῦσμα	1xPaul: Rom. 3:7
13.	false witness	ψευδόμαρτυς	1xPau: 1 Cor. 15:15
14.	falsely called	ψευδώνυμος	1xPaul: 1 Tim. 6:20
15.	speaking falsely	ψευδολόγος	1xPaul: 1 Tim. 4:2
16.	false apostle	ψευδαπόστολος	1xPaul: 2 Cor. 11:13
17.	sexual Immorality	πορνεία	10xPaul: 1 Cor. 5:1; 6:13, 18; 7:2; 2 Cor. 12:21; Gal. 5:19; Eph. 5:3; Col. 3:5; 1 Thess. 4:3
18.	immoral people	πόρνος	6xPaul: 1 Cor. 5:9, 10, 11; 6:9; Eph. 5:5; 1 Tim. 1:10
19.	prostitute	πόρνη	2xPaul: 1 Cor. 6:15, 16
20.	wicked	πονηρός	13xPaul: Rom. 12:9; 1 Cor. 5:13; Gal. 1:4; Eph. 5:16; 6:13, 16; Col. 1:21; 1 Thess. 5:22; 2 Thess. 3:2, 3; 1 Tim. 6:4; 2 Tim. 3:13; 4:18
21.	wickedness	πονηρία	3xPaul: Rom. 1:29; 1 Cor. 5:8; Eph. 6:12
22.	greediness	πλεονεξία	6xPaul: Rom. 1:29; 1 Cor. 5:8; Eph. 6:12
23.	covetous	πλεονέκτης	4xPaul: 1 Cor. 5:10, 11; 6:10; Eph. 5:5
24.	to take advantage	πλεονεκτέω	5xPaul: 2 Cor. 2:11; 7:2; 12:17, 18; 1 Thess. 4:6

	VICE		REFERENCE
25.	idolater	εἰδωλολάτρης	5xPaul: 1 Cor. 5:10, 11; 6:9; 10:7; Eph. 5:5
26.	idolatry	εἰδωλολατρία	3xPaul: 1 Cor. 10:14; Gal. 5:20; Col. 3:5; also Rom. 1:19–25
27.	idol	εἰδωλόθυτος	5xPaul: 1 Cor. 8:1, 4, 7, 10; 10:19
28.	to slander	βλασφημέω	8xPaul: Rom. 2:24; 3:8; 14:16; 1 Cor. 10:30; 1 Tim. 1:20; 6:1; Titus 2:5; 3:2
29.	blasphemer	βλάσφημος	2xPaul: 1 Tim. 1:13; 2 Tim. 3:2
30.	slander	βλασφημία	3xPaul: Eph. 4:31; Col. 3:8; 1 Tim. 6:4
31.	impurity	ἀκαθαρσία	9xPaul: Rom. 1:24; 6:19; 2 Cor. 12:21; Gal. 5:19; Eph. 4:19; 5:3; Col. 3:5; 1 Thess. 2:3; 4:7
32.	unclean	ἀκάθαρτος	3xPaul: 1 Cor. 7:14; 2 Cor. 6:17; Eph 5:5
33.	strife	ἔρις	9xPaul: Rom. 1:29; 13:13; 1 Cor. 1:11; 3:3; 2 Cor. 12:20; Gal. 5:20; Phil. 1:15; 1 Tim. 6:4; Titus 3:9
34.	to steal	κλέπτω	5xPaul: Rom. 2:21 (2x); 13:9; Eph. 4:28 (2x)
35.	thief	κλέπτης	3xPaul: 1 Cor. 6:10; 1 Thess. 5:2, 4
36.	arrogance	φυσίωσις	1xPaul: 2 Cor. 12:20
37.	be arrogant	φυσιόω, -ομαι	7xPaul: 1 Cor. 4:6, 18, 19; 5:2; 8:1; 13:4; Col. 2:18
38.	wrath	ὀργή	5xPaul: Rom. 2:8; Eph. 2:3; 4:31; Col. 3:8; 1 Tim. 2:8
39.	be angry	ὀργίζω	1xPaul: Eph. 4:26
40.	anger	παροργισμός	1xPaul: Eph. 4:26
41.	angry	ὀργίλος	1xPaul: Titus 1:7
42.	jealousy	ζῆλος	5xPaul: Rom. 10:2; 13:13; 1 Cor. 3:3; 2 Cor. 12:20; Gal. 5:20
43.	to be jealous	ζηλόω	2xPaul: 1 Cor. 13:4; Gal. 4:17
44.	ungodliness	ἀσέβεια	4xPaul: Rom. 1:18; 11:26; 2 Tim. 2:16; Titus 2:12
45.	ungodly	ἀσεβής	3xPaul: Rom. 4:5; 5:6; 1 Tim. 1:9
46.	quarrel	μάχη	3xPaul: 2 Cor. 7:5; 2 Tim. 2:23; Titus 3:9 (see the opposite, ἄμαχος, in 1 Tim. 3:3; Titus 3:2)
47.	be quarrelsome	μάχομαι	1xPaul: 2 Tim. 2:24
48.	quarrel about words	λογομαχία	1xPaul: 1 Tim. 6:4
49.	dispute about words	λογομαχέω	1xPaul: 2 Tim. 2:14
50.	to do adultery	μοιχεύω	3xPaul: Rom. 2:22 (2x); 13:9
51.	adulteress	μοιχαλίς	2xPaul: Rom. 7:3 (2x)
52.	adulterer	μοιχός	1xPaul: 1 Cor. 6:9

	VICE		REFERENCE
53.	envy	φθόνος	5xPaul: Rom. 1:29; Gal. 5:21; Phil. 1:15; 1 Tim. 6:4; Titus 3:3
54.	to envy	φθονέω	1xPaul: Gal. 5:26
55.	drunkenness	μέθη	2xPaul: Rom. 13:13; Gal. 5:21
56.	drunk	μέθυσος	2xPaul: 1 Cor. 5:11; 6:10
57.	to get drunk	μεθύσκω	2xPaul: 1 Cor. 11:21; 1 Thess. 5:7
58.	disputes	ἐριθεία	5xPaul: Rom. 2:8; 2 Cor. 12:20; Gal. 5:20; Phil. 1:17; 2:3
59.	disputes	ζήτησις	3xPaul: 1 Tim. 6:4; 2 Tim. 2:23; Titus 3:9 (see Acts 15:2, 7)
60.	useless speculat.	ἐκζήτησις	1xPaul: 1 Tim. 1:4
61.	disputant	συζητητής	1xPaul: 1 Cor. 1:20
62.	passion	πάθος	3xPaul: Rom. 1:26; Col. 3:5; 1 Thess. 4:5
63.	passion	πάθημα	2xPaul: Rom. 7:5; Gal. 5:24
64.	murder	φόνος	1xPaul: Rom. 1:29
65.	to murder	φονεύω	1xPaul: Rom. 13:9
66.	killer of father	πατρολῴας	1xPaul: 1 Tim. 1:9
67.	killer of mother	μητρολῴας	1xPaul: 1 Tim. 1:9
68.	killer of men	ἀνδροφόνος	1xPaul: 1 Tim. 1:9
69.	anger	Θυμός	4xPaul: 2 Cor. 12:20; Gal. 5:20; Eph. 4:31; Col. 3:8
70.	sensuality	ἀσέλγεια	4xPaul: Rom. 13:13; 2 Cor. 12:21; Gal. 5:19; Eph. 4:19
71.	strife	ἔχθρα	4xPaul: Rom. 8:7; Gal. 5:20; Eph. 2:14, 16
72.	reviler	λοίδορος	2xPaul: 1 Cor. 5:11; 6:10
73.	to revile, insult	λοιδορέω	1xPaul: 1 Cor. 4:12
74.	reproach	λοιδορία	1xPaul: 1 Tim. 5:14
75.	deceit	δόλος	3xPaul: Rom. 1:29; 2 Cor. 12:16; 1 Thess. 2:3
76.	to deceive	δολιόω	1xPaul: Rom. 3:13
77.	act shamefully	ἀσχημονέω	2xPaul: 1 Cor. 7:36; 13:5
78.	shameful	ἀσχήμων	1xPaul: 1 Cor. 12:23
79.	shameless deed	ἀσχημοσύνη	1xPaul: Rom. 1:27
80.	profane	βέβηλος	4xNT: 1 Tim. 1:9; 4:7; 6:20; 2 Tim. 2:16

	VICE		REFERENCE
81.	conceited	τυφόω	3xPaul: 1 Tim. 3:6; 6:4; 2 Tim. 3:4
82.	disturbance	ἀκαταστασία	3xPaul: 1 Cor. 14:33; 2 Cor. 6:5; 12:20
83.	malicious gossip	διάβολοι	3xPaul: 1 Tim. 3:11; 2 Tim. 3:3; Titus 2:3
84.	no understanding	ἀσύνετος	3xPaul: Rom. 1:21, 31; 10:19
85.	robber, swindler	ἅρπαξ	3xPaul: 1 Cor. 5:10, 11; 6:10
86.	insolent	ὑβριστής	2xPaul: Rom. 1:30; 1 Tim. 1:13
87.	to insult	ὑβρίζω	1xPaul: 1 Thess. 2:2
88.	bitterness	πικρία	2xPaul: Rom. 3:14; Eph. 4:31
89.	to be bitter	πικραίνω	1xPaul: Col. 3:19
90.	homosexuality	ἀρσενοκοίτης	2xPaul: 1 Cor. 6:9; 1 Tim. 1:10; see Rom. 1:27
91.	effeminate	μαλακός	1xPaul: 1 Cor. 6:9
92.	lovers of self	φίλαυτος	1xPaul: 2 Tim. 3:2
93.	lovers of money	φιλάργυρος	1xPaul: 2 Tim. 3:2
94.	lovers of pleasure	φιλήδονος	1xPaul: 2 Tim. 3:4
95.	addicted to wine	πάρουνος	2xPaul: 1 Tim. 3:3; Titus 1:7; see 1 Tim. 3:8; Titus 2:3
96.	arrogant	ὑπερήφανος	2xPaul: Rom. 1:30; 2 Tim. 3:2; see 2 Cor. 12:20
97.	boastful	ἀλαζών	2xPaul: Rom. 1:30; 2 Tim. 3:2
98.	bully	πλήκτης	2xPaul: 1 Tim. 3:3; Titus 1:7
99.	disob. to parents	γονεῦσιν ἀπειθεῖς	2xPaul: Rom. 1:30; 2 Tim. 3:2; see 1 Tim. 1:9
100.	dissension	διχοστασία	2xPaul: Rom. 16:17; Gal. 5:20
101.	empty talk	ματαιολογία	1xPaul: 1 Tim. 1:6
102.	empty talkers	ματαιολόγος	1xPaul: Titus 1:10
103.	excessive feasting	κῶμος	2xPaul: Rom. 13:13; Gal. 5:21
104.	factions	αἵρεσις	2xPaul: 1 Cor. 11:19; Gal. 5:20
105.	greedy	αἰσχροκερδής	2xPaul: 1 Tim. 3:8; Titus 1:7 (see 1 Peter 5:2)
106.	spreading rumors	ψιθυριστής	1xPaul: Rom. 1:29
107.	gossip	ψιθυρισμός	1xPaul: 2 Cor. 12:20

	VICE		REFERENCE
108.	irritate, be irrit.	παροξύνω	1xPaul: 1 Cor. 13:4 (also Acts 17:16); noun παροξυσμός also in Acts 15:39)
109.	slander	καταλαλιά	1xPaul: 2 Cor. 12:20
110.	slanderers	κατάλαλος	1xPaul: Rom. 1:30
111.	unholy	ἀνόσιος	2xPaul: 1 Tim. 1:9; 2 Tim. 3:2
112.	unloving	ἀστόργους	2xPaul: Rom. 1:31; 2 Tim. 3:3
113.	arrogant	αὐθάδης	1xPaul: Titus 1:7
114.	brag, boast	περπερεύομαι	1xPaul: 1 Cor. 13:4
115.	brutal	ἀνήμερος	1xPaul: 2 Tim. 3:3
116.	clamor	κραυγή	1xPaul: Eph. 4:31
117.	coarse jesting	εὐτραπελία	1xPaul: Eph. 5:4
118.	corrupting talk	λόγος σαπρός	1xPaul: Eph. 4:29
119.	double-tongued	δίλογος	1xPaul: 1 Tim. 3:8
120.	filthiness	αἰσχρότης	1xPaul: Eph. 5:4
121.	haters of good	ἀφιλάγαθος	1xPaul: 2 Tim. 3:3
122.	haters of God	θεοστυγής	1xPaul: Rom. 1:30 (see 2 Tim 3:4)
123.	irreconcilable	ἄσπονδος	1xPaul: 2 Tim. 3:3 (see also variant to Rom. 1:31)
124.	kidnapper	ἀνδραποδιστής	1xPaul: 1 Tim. 1:10
125.	malice	κακοήθεια	1xPaul: Rom. 1:29
126.	no self-control	ἀκρατής	1xPaul: 2 Tim. 3:3
127.	reckless	προπετής	1xPaul: 2 Tim. 3:4
128.	silly talk	μωρολογία	1xPaul: Eph. 5:4
129.	sorcery	φαρμακεία	1xPaul: Gal. 5:20
130.	treacherous	προδότης	1xPaul: 2 Tim. 3:4
131.	ungrateful	ἀχάριστος	1xPaul: 2 Tim. 3:2
132.	untrustworthy	ἀσύνθετος	1xPaul: Rom. 1:31
133.	unmerciful	ἀνελεήμονας	1xPaul: Rom. 1:31

Vices: Various Lists

CHART 99

	Romans	1 Corinthians	2 Corinthians	Galatians	Ephesians
	1:29–31	6:9–11	12:20	5:19–21	4:31
(1)	unrighteousness (3)	fornicators (18)	strive (33)	immorality (17)	bitterness (88)
(2)	wickedness (21)	idolaters (25)	jealousy (42)	impurity (31)	wrath (69)
(3)	greed (22)	adulterers (52)	angry tempers (69)	sensuality (70)	anger (38)
(4)	evil (2)	effeminate (91)	disputes (58)	idolatry (26)	clamor (116)
(5)	envy (53)	homosexuals (90)	slanders (109)	sorcery (129)	slander (30)
(6)	murder (64)	thieves (35)	gossip (107)	enmities (71)	all malice (2)
(7)	strife (33)	covetous (23)	arrogance (36)	strife (33)	
(8)	deceit (75)	drunkards (56)	disturbances (82)	jealousy (42)	
(9)	malice (124)	revilers (72)		outbursts of anger (69)	
(10)	gossips (106)	swindlers (85)		disputes (58)	
(11)	slanderers (110)			dissensions (100)	
(12)	haters of God (121)			factions (104)	
(13)	insolent (86)			envying (53)	
(14)	arrogant (96)			drunkenness (55)	
(15)	boastful (97)			carousing (103)	
(16)	inventors of evil (1)			and things like these	
(17)	disobedient to parents (99)				
(18)	without understanding (84)				
(19)	untrustworthy (132)				
(20)	unloving (112)				
(21)	unmerciful (133)				

Virtues in Paul's Letters

CHART 100

	VIRTUES		GOD	PAUL	CHRISTIANS
1.	beyond reproach	ἀνέγκλητος			1 Cor. 1:8; Col. 1:22; 1 Tim. 3:10; Titus 1:6–7
2.	blameless	ἄμωμος			Eph. 1:4; 5:27; Phil. 2:15; Col 1:22
3.	blameless	ἄμεμπτος		Phil. 3:6	1 Thess. 3:13
4.	children, bearing	τεκνογονία			1 Tim. 2:15
5.	children, bear/beget	τεκνογονέω			1 Tim. 5:14
6.	children, bring up	τεκνοτροφέω			1 Tim. 5:10
7.	children, to love them	φιλότεκνος			Titus 2:4
8.	compassion / mercy	οἰκτιρμός	Rom. 12:1; 1 Cor. 1:3		Phil. 2:1; Col. 3:12
9.	dignified, honorable	σεμνός			Phil. 4:8; 1 Tim. 3:8, 11; Titus 2:2
10.	dignity, reverence	σεμνότης			1 Tim. 2:2; 3:4; Titus 2:7
11.	faithfulness	πίστις	Rom. 3:3, 22 (of Jesus Christ)		2 Cor. 8:7; Gal. 5:22; Eph. 6:23; 1 Thess. 3:6; 5:8; 2 Thess. 1:4; 1 Tim. 1:14; 4:12; 6:11; 2 Tim. 1:13; 2:22; 3:10; Titus 2:2; Philem. 5
12.	faithful	πιστός	1 Cor. 1:9; 10:13; 2 Cor. 1:8; 1 Thess. 5:24; 2 Tim. 2:13	1 Cor. 7:25; 1 Tim. 1:12	1 Cor. 4:2; Eph. 6:21; Col. 1:7; 4:7; 1 Tim. 3:11; 2 Tim. 2:2; Titus 1:6
13.	gentleness	πραΰτης	(see Matt. 11:29)	1 Cor. 4:21; 2 Cor. 10:1	Gal. 5:23; 6:1; Eph. 4:2; Col. 3:12; 2 Tim. 2:25; Titus 3:2
14.	gentle	ἐπιεικής			Phil. 4:5; 1 Tim. 3:3; Titus 3:2
15.	gentleness	ἐπιείκεια	2 Cor. 10:1 (of Christ)		
16.	gentleness	πραϋπαθία			1 Tim. 6:11
17.	godliness	εὐσέβεια			1 Tim. 2:2; 3:16; 4:7, 8; 6:3.5–6, 11; 2 Tim. 3:5; Titus 1:1
18.	practice godliness	εὐσεβέω			1 Tim. 5:4
19.	godly	εὐσεβῶς			2 Tim. 3:12; Titus 2:12
20.	goodness	ἀγαθωσύνη			Rom. 15:14; Gal. 5:22; Eph. 5:9; 2 Thess. 1:11
21.	good	ἀγαθός	Rom. 7:12 (the law), 13 (2x); 8:28; 10:15; Phil. 1:6; 2 Thess. 2:16 (hope)		Rom. 2:7, 10; 3:8; 5:7; 7:18–19; 9:11; 12:2, 9, 21; 13:3–4; 14:16; 15:2; 16:19; 1 Cor. 7:9, 38; 11:17; 2 Cor. 5:10; 9:8; Gal. 6:6, 10; Eph. 2:10; 4:28, 29; Eph. 6:8; Col. 1:10; 1 Thess. 3:6; 2 Thess. 2:17; 1 Tim. 1:5, 19; 2:10; 5:10; 2 Tim. 2:21; 3:17; Titus 1:16; 2:5, 10; 3:1; Philem. 1:6, 14
22.	repay evil with good				Rom. 12:17; 1 Thess. 5:15
23.	good work(s)	ἔργον ἀγαθὸν			Rom. 2:7; 13:3; 2 Cor. 9:8; Eph. 2:10; Phil. 1:6; Col. 1:10; 1 Tim. 2:10; 5:10; 2 Tim. 2:21; 3:17; Titus 1:16; 3:1
24.	to do good	ἀγαθοεργέω			1 Tim. 6:18 (noun in Rom. 13:3?)

Charts *on the* Life, Letters, and Theology *of* Paul

	VIRTUES		GOD	PAUL	CHRISTIANS
25.	good reputation	εὔφημος			Phil. 4:8
26.	good reputation	μαρτυρία καλή			1 Tim. 3:7; 5:10
27.	humility	ταπεινοφροσύνη			Eph. 4:2; Phil. 2:3; Col. 3:12
28.	humble	ταπεινός			Rom. 12:16; 2 Cor. 10:1
29.	to be humble	ταπεινόω			2 Cor. 11:7; 12:21; Phil. 2:8; 4:12
30.	innocent	ἀκέραιος			Rom. 16:19; Phil. 2:15
31.	joy	χαρά	Rom. 15:13; 1 Thess. 1:6 (of the Holy Spirit)	Rom. 15:32; 2 Cor. 2:3; 7:4; Phil. 1:4; 2:2; 4:1; 1 Thess. 2:19, 20; 3:9; 2 Tim. 1:14; Philem. 1:7	Rom. 14:17; 2 Cor. 1:24; 7:13; 8:2; Gal. 5:22; Phil. 1:25; 2:29; Col. 1:11; 1 Thess. 1:6
32.	rejoice	χαίρω		Rom. 16:19; 1 Cor. 16:17; 2 Cor. 2:3; 6:10; 7:7, 9, 13, 16 13:9; Phil. 1:18 (2x); 2:17; 4:10; Col. 1:24; 2:5; 1 Thess 3:9	Rom. 12:12, 15 (2x); 1 Cor. 7:30; 13:6; 2 Cor. 13:11; Phil. 2:18, 28; 3:1; 4:4 (2x); 1 Thess. 5:16
33.	rejoice with	συγχαίρω		Phil. 2:17	1 Cor. 12:26; 13:6; Phil. 2:18
34.	kindness	χρηστότης	Rom. 2:4; 11:22 (3x); Eph. 2:7; Titus 3:4	2 Cor. 6:6	Rom. 3:12; Gal. 5:22; Col. 3:12
35.	to be kind	χρηστεύομαι			1 Cor. 13:4
36.	kind	χρηστός	Rom. 2:4		1 Cor. 15:33; Eph. 4:32
37.	love (noun)	ἀγάπη	Rom. 5:5, 8; 8:35 (Christ), 39; 15:30 (Spirit); 2 Cor. 5:14 (Christ); 13:11, 14; Eph. 1:4; 2:4; 3:17, 19 (Christ); 6:23; Col. 1:13; 2 Thess. 3:5; 1 Tim. 1:14; 2 Tim. 1:13	1 Cor. 16:24; 2 Cor. 2:4; 6:6; 8:7	Rom. 12:9; 13:10 (2x); 14:15; 1 Cor. 4:21; 8:1; 13:1–3, 4 (3x), 8, 13 (2x); 14:1; 16:14; 2 Cor. 2:8; 5:14; 8:8, 24; Gal. 5:6, 13, 22; Eph. 1:15; 4:2, 15–16; 5:2; Phil. 1:9, 16; 2:1, 2; Col. 1:4, 8; 2:2; 3:14; 1 Thess. 1:3; 3:6, 12; 5:8, 13; 2 Thess. 1:3; 2:10; 3:5; 1 Tim. 1:5; 2:15; 4:12; 6:11; 2 Tim. 1:7; 2:22; 3:10; Titus 2:2; Philem. 1:5, 7, 9
38.	to love	ἀγαπάω	Rom. 8:37; 9:13, 25 (2x); Eph. 5:2; 2 Cor. 9:7; Gal. 2:20 (Son of God); Eph. 1:6; 2:4; 5:2 (Christ); 25 (Christ); Col. 3:12; 1 Thess. 1:4; 2 Thess. 1:13; 2:16	2 Cor. 11:11; 12:15	Rom. 8:28 (God); 13:8 (2x), 9; 1 Cor. 2:9 (God); 8:3 (God); 2 Cor. 12:15; Gal. 5:14; Eph. 1:6; 5:25, 28 (3x), 33; 6:24 (our Lord Jesus Christ); Col. 3:19; 1 Thess. 4:9; 2 Tim. 4:8 (His appearing)
39.	to love	φιλέω			1 Cor 16:22 (the Lord); Titus 3:15
40.	love for mankind	φιλανθρωπία	Titus 3:4		

	VIRTUES		GOD	PAUL	CHRISTIANS
41.	brotherly love	φιλαδελφία			Rom. 12:10; 1 Thess. 4:9
42.	love to God	φιλόθεος			2 Tim. 3:4 (see Rom. 8:28; 1 Cor. 2:9)
43.	to love	φιλόστοργος			Rom. 12:10
44.	to love one's husband	φίλανδρος			Titus 2:4
45.	to love one's children	φιλότεκνος			Titus 2:4
46.	love of strangers / hospitality	φιλοξενία			Rom. 12:13; Heb. 13:2
47.	loving strangers / hospitable	φιλόξενος			1 Tim. 3:2; Titus 1:8; 1 Peter 4:9
48.	to show hospitality	ξενοδοχέω			1 Tim. 5:10
49.	loving good	φιλάγαθος			Titus 1:8
50.	kiss	φίλημα			Rom. 16:16; 1 Cor. 16:20; 2 Cor. 13:12; 1 Thess. 5:26
51.	lovely, pleasing	προσφιλής			Phil. 4:8
52.	not loving money	ἀφιλάργυρος			1 Tim. 3:3
53.	patience	μακροθυμία	Rom. 2:4; 9:22; 1 Tim. 1:16 (Christ Jesus)	2 Cor. 6:6; 2 Tim. 3:10	Gal. 5:22; Eph. 4:2; Col. 1:11; 3:12; 2 Tim. 4:2
54.	to be patient	μακροθυμέω			1 Cor. 13:4; 1 Thess. 5:14
55.	enduring difficulties w/out becoming angry	ἀνοχή	Rom. 2:4; 3:26		
56.	be patient, enduring	ἀνέχομαι		1 Cor. 4:12	2 Cor. 11:1 (4, 19–20); Eph. 4:2; Col. 3:13; 2 Thess. 1:4; 2 Tim. 4:3
57.	patient, tolerant	ἀνεξίκακος			2 Tim. 2:24
58.	peace	εἰρήνη	Rom. 1:7; 5:1; 15:13, 33; 16:20; 1 Cor. 1:3; 14:33; 2 Cor. 1:2; 13:11; Gal. 1:3; Eph. 1:2; 2:14–15, 17 (2x); 6:15, 23; Phil. 1:2; 4:7, 9; Col. 1:2; 3:15 (of Christ); 1 Thess. 1:1; 5:23; 1 Thess. 1:2; 3:16 (2x); 1 Tim. 1:2; 2 Tim. 1:2; Titus 1:4; Philem. 1:3		Rom. 3:17; 8:6; 14:17, 19; 1 Cor. 7:15; 16:11; Gal. 5:22; 6:16; Eph. 4:3; 2 Tim. 2:22
59.	to make peace	εἰρηνεύω	(see in Eph. 2:14–15; Col. 1:20 [εἰρηνοποιέω])		Rom. 12:18; 2 Cor. 13:11; 1 Thess. 5:13

193

	VIRTUES		GOD	PAUL	CHRISTIANS
60.	perseverance	ὑπομονή		2 Cor. 6:4; 12:12; 2 Tim. 3:10	Rom. 2:7; 5:3–4; 8:25; 15:4, 5; 2 Cor. 1:6; Col. 1:11; 1 Thess. 1:3; 2 Thess. 1:4; 3:5; 1 Tim. 6:11; Titus 2:2
61.	to persevere	ὑπομένω		2 Tim. 2:10	Rom. 12:12; 1 Cor. 13:7; 2 Tim. 2:12
62.	to endure	ὑποφέρω:		2 Tim. 3:11	1 Cor. 10:13
63.	endure hardships	κακοπαθέω		2 Tim. 2:9	2 Tim. 2:3; 4:5
64.	pure	ἀγνός			2 Cor. 7:11; 11:2; Phil. 4:8; 1 Tim. 5:22; Titus 2:5
65.	purity	ἀγνεία			1 Tim. 4:12; 5:2
66.	purity	ἀγνότης		2 Cor. 6:6	2 Cor. 11:3
67.	righteousness	δικαιοσύνη	Rom. 1:17; 3:5, 21, 22, 25, 26; 4:3, 5–6, 9, 11 (2x), 13, 22; 5:17 (gift of r.), 21; 9:30 (3x); 10:3 (2x), 6, 10; 1 Cor. 1:30 (Christ); 2 Cor. 3:9 (ministry of r.); 5:21; 9:9; Gal. 2:21; 3:6, 21; Phil. 1:11; 3:9	2 Tim. 4:8	Rom. 6:13, 16, 18–20; 8:10; 14:17; 1 Cor. 1:30; 2 Cor. 6:7, 14; 2 Cor. 9:10; 11:15; Gal. 5:5; Eph. 4:24; 5:9; 6:14; 1 Tim. 6:11; 2 Tim. 2:22; 3:16; 4:8
68.	right, righteous	δίκαιος	Rom. 7:12 (the Law); 2 Thess. 1:5 (God's judgment), 6; 2 Tim. 4:8	Phil. 1:7	Rom. 1:17; 2:13; 3:10, 26; 5:7, 19; Gal. 3:11; Eph. 6:1; Phil. 4:8; Col. 4:1; 1 Tim. 1:9; Titus 1:8
69.	self-control	ἐγκράτεια			Gal. 5:23
60.	to exercise self-control	ἐγκρατεύομαι			1 Cor. 7:9; 9:25
71.	self-controlled	ἐγκρατής			Titus 1:8
72.	sensible	σώφρων			1 Tim. 3:2; Titus 1:8; 2:2, 5
73.	sound judgment	σωφρονέω		2 Cor. 5:13	Rom. 12:3; Titus 2:6
74.	sensibility / moderation	σωφροσύνη			1 Tim. 2:9, 15
75.	sensibility / moderation	σωφρονισμός			2 Tim. 1:7
76.	sensible, moderate	σωφρόνως			Titus 2:12
77.	to share	μεταδίδωμι		Rom. 1:1; 1 Thess. 2:8	Rom. 12:8; Eph. 4:28; 1 Thess. 2:8
78.	to share generously	εὐμετάδοτος			1 Tim. 6:18
79.	sober, restraint	νήφω			1 Thess. 5:6, 8; 2 Tim. 4:5
80.	sober-minded	ἐκνήφω			1 Cor. 15:34
81.	temperate	νηφάλιος			1 Tim. 3:2, 11; Titus 2:2
82.	tenderhearted	εὔσπλαγχνος			Eph. 4:32
83.	uncontentious	ἄμαχος			1 Tim. 3:3; Titus 3:2
84.	virtue	ἀρετή			Phil. 4:8
85.	wash feet	πόδας ἔνιψεν			1 Tim. 5:10

Virtues: Various Lists

CHART 101

	1 Corinthians	Galatians	Ephesians	Colossians	Titus
	13:4–8	5:22–23	4:25–32	3:12–14	3:1–2
(1)	love is patient (53)	love (36)	put away falsehood (9)	compassion (8)	be submissive to rulers and authorities
(2)	… kind (34)	joy (30)	speak the truth	kindness (34)	obedient
(3)	… does not envy (43)	peace (57)	be angry and do not sin (39, 40)	humility (27)	ready for every good work (23)
(4)	… does not boast (112)	patience (52)	don't steal but work (34)	meekness (13)	speak evil of no one (28)
(5)	… is not proud (37)	kindness (33)	share with anyone in need (77)	patience (53)	avoid quarreling (46)
(6)	… is not rude (103)	goodness (20)	no corrupting talk (130)	bearing with one another (56)	be gentle (14)
(7)	… is not self-seeking	faithfulness (11)	good talk for building up (21)	forgiving each other as the Lord has …	show perfect courtesy toward all people (13)
(8)	… is not easily angered (106)	gentleness (13)	be kind (36)	put on love (37)	
(9)	… keeps no record of wrong (1)	self-control (68)	tenderhearted (82)		
(10)	… does not delight in evil (3)		forgiving one another as God in Christ forgave you		
(11)	… rejoices with the truth				
(12)	… always protects				
(13)	… always trusts				
(14)	… always hopes				
(15)	… always perseveres				
(16)	… never fails				

Household Codes

CHART 102

Ephesians 5:22–6:9	Colossians 3:18–4:1
5:22 **Wives**, be subject to your own husbands, as to the Lord. 23 For the husband is the head of the wife, as Christ also is the head of the church, He Himself being the Savior of the body. 24 But as the church is subject to Christ, so also the wives ought to be to their husbands in everything.	3:18 **Wives**, be subject to your husbands, as is fitting in the Lord.
25 **Husbands**, love your wives, just as Christ also loved the church and gave Himself up for her, 26 so that He might sanctify her, having cleansed her by the washing of water with the word, 27 that He might present to Himself the church in all her glory, having no spot or wrinkle or any such thing; but that she would be holy and blameless. 28 So husbands ought also to love their own wives as their own bodies. He who loves his own wife loves himself; 29 for no one ever hated his own flesh, but nourishes and cherishes it, just as Christ also does the church, 30 because we are members of His body. 31 For this reason a man shall leave his father and mother and shall be joined to his wife, and the two shall become one flesh (Gen. 2:24; Matt. 19:5). 32 This mystery is great; but I am speaking with reference to Christ and the church. 33 Nevertheless, each individual among you also is to love his own wife even as himself, and the wife must see to it that she respects her husband.	19 **Husbands**, love your wives and do not be embittered against them.
6:1 **Children**, obey your parents in the Lord, for this is right. 2 Honor your father and mother (which is the first commandment with a promise), 3 so that it may be well with you, and that you may live long on the earth (Ex. 20:12; Deut. 5:16).	20 **Children**, be obedient to your parents in all things, for this is well-pleasing to the Lord.
4 **Fathers**, do not provoke your children to anger, but bring them up in the discipline and instruction of the Lord.	21 **Fathers**, do not exasperate your children, so that they will not lose heart.
5 **Slaves**, be obedient to those who are your masters according to the flesh, with fear and trembling, in the sincerity of your heart, as to Christ; 6 not by way of eyeservice, as men-pleasers, but as slaves of Christ, doing the will of God from the heart. 7 With good will render service, as to the Lord, and not to men, 8 knowing that whatever good thing each one does, this he will receive back from the Lord, whether slave or free.	22 **Slaves**, in all things obey those who are your masters on earth, not with external service, as those who merely please men, but with sincerity of heart, fearing the Lord. 23 Whatever you do, do your work heartily, as for the Lord rather than for men, 24 knowing that from the Lord you will receive the reward of the inheritance. It is the Lord Christ whom you serve. 25 For he who does wrong will receive the consequences of the wrong which he has done, and that without partiality (προσωπολημψία).
9 And **masters**, do the same things to them, and give up threatening, knowing that both their Master and yours is in heaven, and there is no partiality (προσωπολημψία) with Him.	4:1 **Masters**, grant your slaves justice (δίκαιον) and fairness (ἰσότητα), knowing that you too have a Master in heaven.

1 Timothy 2, 5, 6	Titus 2:1–3:2
2:8 Therefore I want the **men** in every place to pray, lifting up holy hands, without wrath and dissension.	2:2 **Older men** are to be temperate, dignified, sensible, sound in faith, in love, in perseverance.
2:9 Likewise, I want **women** to adorn themselves with proper clothing, modestly and discreetly, not with braided hair and gold or pearls or costly garments, 10 but rather by means of good works, as is proper for women making a claim to godliness. 11 A woman must quietly receive instruction with entire submissiveness. 12 But I do not allow a woman to teach or exercise authority over a man, but to remain quiet. 13 For it was Adam who was first created, and then Eve. 14 And it was not Adam who was deceived, but the woman being deceived, fell into transgression. 15 But women will be preserved through the bearing of children if they continue in faith and love and sanctity with self-restraint.	3 **Older women** likewise are to be reverent in their behavior, not malicious gossips nor enslaved to much wine, teaching what is good, 4 so that they may encourage the **young women** to love their husbands, to love their children, 5 to be sensible, pure, workers at home, kind, being subject to their own husbands, so that the word of God will not be dishonored.
5:1 Do not sharply rebuke an **older man**, but rather appeal to him as a father, to the younger men as brothers,	6 Likewise urge the **young men** to be sensible; 7 in all things show yourself to be an example of good deeds, with purity in doctrine, dignified, 8 sound in speech which is beyond reproach, so that the opponent will be put to shame, having nothing bad to say about us.
5:2 the **older women** as mothers, and the **younger women** as sisters, in all purity.	
5:3 Honor **widows** who are widows indeed; … (5:3–16)	
6:1 All who are under the yoke as **slaves** are to regard their own masters as worthy of all honor so that the name of God and our doctrine will not be spoken against. 2 Those who have believers as their masters must not be disrespectful to them because they are brethren, but must serve them all the more, because those who partake of the benefit are believers and beloved. Teach and preach these principles.	9 Urge **bondslaves** to be subject to their own masters in everything, to be well-pleasing, not argumentative, 10 not pilfering, but showing all good faith so that they will adorn the doctrine of God our Savior in every respect. 11 For the grace of God has appeared, bringing salvation to all men, 12 instructing us to deny ungodliness and worldly desires and to live sensibly, righteously and godly in the present age, 13 looking for the blessed hope and the appearing of the glory of our great God and Savior, Christ Jesus, 14 who gave Himself for us to redeem us from every lawless deed, and to purify for Himself a people for His own possession, zealous for good deeds.
6:17 Instruct those who are **rich** in this present world not to be conceited or to fix their hope on the uncertainty of riches, but on God, who richly supplies us with all things to enjoy. 18 Instruct them to do good, to be rich in good works, to be generous and ready to share, 19 storing up for themselves the treasure of a good foundation for the future, so that they may take hold of that which is life indeed.	3:1 Remind **them** to be subject to rulers, to authorities, to be obedient, to be ready for every good deed, 2 to malign no one, to be peaceable, gentle, showing every consideration for all men.

Authority and Submission in Paul's Cosmology

CHART 103

	Authority	Subject	Reference
(1)	God	Christ	1 Cor. 11:3; 15:27–28
(2)	(Law / Righteousness of) God	All things & everyone	Rom. 8:7, 20; 9:21; 10:3
(3)	Christ	All things & everyone	1 Cor. 15:23–28; Eph. 1:20–22 (Ps. 110:1 and 8:7); Phil. 3:21; Col. 2:10
(4)	Government	Citizens	Rom. 13:1–7; 1 Tim. 2:2; Titus 3:1
(5)	Christ	Church	Eph. 1:22; 4:15; 5:23–24; Col. 1:18; 2:19; 2 Thess. 3:14
(6)	Leaders in the church	Church	1 Cor. 16:16; 2 Cor. 10:8; 1 Thess. 5:12–13; Titus 2:15
(7)	Christ	Every man	1 Cor. 11:3
(8)	Husbands	Wives	Rom. 7:2 (ὕπανδρος γυνή); 1 Cor. 11:3, 7; 1 Cor. 7:4 (her body); Eph. 5:22–24; Col. 3:18; 1 Tim. 2:11–15; Titus 2:5
(9)	Wives	Husband	1 Cor. 7:4 (his body)
(10)	Masters	Slaves	Eph. 6:5; Col. 3:22; Titus 2:9
(11)	Parents	Children	Eph. 6:1–2; Col. 3:20
(12)	Individual	Will	1 Cor. 7:37

Women: Equal and Subordinate to Men

CHART 104

EQUAL	SUBORDINATE
NLT Romans 16:1 I commend to you our sister **Phoebe**, who is a deacon in the church in Cenchrea. ² … for she has been helpful to many, and especially to me. ³ Give my greetings to **Priscilla** and Aquila, my co-workers in the ministry of Christ Jesus. ⁴ In fact, they once risked their lives for me. I am thankful to them, and so are all the Gentile churches. …⁶ Give my greetings to **Mary**, who has worked so hard for your benefit. ⁷ Greet Andronicus and **Junia**, my fellow Jews, who were in prison with me. They are highly respected among the apostles and became followers of Christ before I did. … ¹² Give my greetings to **Tryphena** and **Tryphosa**, the Lord's workers, and to dear **Persis**, who has worked so hard for the Lord. ¹³ Greet Rufus, whom the Lord picked out to be his very own; and also **his dear mother**, who has been a mother to me. ¹⁴ Give my greetings to Asyncritus, Phlegon, Hermes, Patrobas, Hermas, and the brothers and **sisters** who meet with them. ¹⁵ Give my greetings to Philologus, **Julia**, Nereus and **his sister**, and to Olympas and all the believers who meet with them.	Romans 7:2 For the married woman (lit.: "the woman under a man" [ἡ γὰρ ὕπανδρος γυνὴ]) is bound by law to her husband while he is living; but if her husband dies, she is released from the law concerning the husband.
1 Corinthians 7:4 The wife does not have authority over her own body, but the husband does; and likewise also the husband does not have authority over his own body, but the wife does. … ¹⁰ … the wife should not leave her husband ¹¹ … and that the husband should not divorce his wife. (This mutuality is also expressed in also 7:12–16, 28, 32–34.]	1 Corinthians 11:3 But I want you to understand that Christ is the head of every man, and the man is the head of a woman, and God is the head of Christ. … ⁷ For a man ought not to have his head covered, since he is the image and glory of God; but the woman is the glory of man.
1 Corinthians 11:11 However, in the Lord, neither is woman independent of man, nor is man independent of woman. ¹² For as the woman originates from the man, so also the man has his birth through the woman; and all things originate from God.	1 Corinthians 14:34 The women are to keep silent in the churches; for they are not permitted to speak, but are to subject themselves [ὑποτασσέσθωσαν], just as the Law also says. ³⁵ And if they desire to learn anything, let them ask their own husbands at home; for it is improper for a woman to speak in church.
2 Corinthians 6:18 "And I will be a father to you, And you shall be sons and daughters to Me," Says the Lord Almighty. (Quote from 2 Sam. 7:14/1 Chron. 17:13; maybe expanded with parts of Isa. 43:6?)	Ephesians 5:22 Wives, be subject to your own husbands, as to the Lord. ²³ For the husband is the head of the wife, as Christ also is the head of the church, He Himself being the Savior of the body. ²⁴ But as the church is subject [ὑποτάσσεται] to Christ, so also the wives ought to be to their husbands in everything.
Galatians 3:28 There is neither Jew nor Greek, there is neither slave nor free man, there is neither male nor female; for you are all one in Christ Jesus.	Colossians 3:18 Wives, be subject [ὑποτάσσεσθε] to your husbands, as is fitting in the Lord. ¹⁹ Husbands, love your wives, and do not be embittered against them.
	1 Timothy 2:11 A woman must quietly receive instruction with entire submissiveness [ἐν πάσῃ ὑποταγῇ]. ¹² But I do not allow a woman to teach or exercise authority [αὐθεντεῖν] over a man, but to remain quiet. ¹³ For it was Adam who was first created, and then Eve. ¹⁴ And it was not Adam who was deceived, but the woman being quite deceived, fell into transgression. ¹⁵ But women will be preserved through the bearing of children if they continue in faith and love and sanctity with self-restraint.
	Titus 2:3 Older women likewise are to be reverent in their behavior, not malicious gossips nor enslaved to much wine, teaching what is good, ⁴ that they may encourage the young women to love their husbands, to love their children, ⁵ to be sensible, pure, workers at home, kind, being subject [ὑποτασσομένας] to their own husbands, that the word of God may not be dishonored.

Women in Ministry

CHART 105

DESCRIPTOR	WOMEN	MEN
Apostle (ἀπόστολος)	Junia? (Rom. 16:7)	Apollos (1 Cor. 4:9) Brethren (2 Cor. 8:23) Cephas (Gal. 1:17–18) James, brother of the Lord (Gal. 1:19) Epaphroditus (Phil. 2:25)
Host/hostess of a house church	Lydia (Acts 16:40) Chloe (1 Cor. 1:11) Nympha? (Col. 4:15)	Ananias (Acts 9:10-18; 22:12-13) Aquila and Priscilla (Acts 18:3)
Minister (TNT, DBY, NAB) / Servant (KJV, NAS, CSB, ESV) / Deacon/ess (RSV, NRS, NIV, NLT, NJB) (διάκονος)	Phoebe (Rom. 16:1)	Christ (Rom. 15:8; Gal. 2:17) Apollos (1 Cor. 3:5) Paul (2 Cor. 3:6; 6:4 Eph. 3:7; etc.) Tychicus (Eph. 6:21; Col. 4:7) Philippian church leaders (Phil. 1:1) Epaphras (Col. 1:7) Timothy (1 Tim. 4:6)
Patron/Caretaker (προστάτις)	Phoebe (Rom. 16:2)	See: 'to lead,' 'to take care of' (προΐστημι): Leaders who care for the church (1 Tim. 5:17; 1 Thess. 5:17) Leaders who care for their families (1 Tim. 3:4–5, 12) Helpers (Titus 3:8, 14)
Prophet/Prophetess (προφητεύω)	1 Cor. 11:5; see Acts 21:9	Judas and Silas (Acts 15:32) Agabus (Acts 21:10)
Teacher (καλοδιδάσκαλος)	Titus 2:3	Barnabas (Acts 13:1; 15:35) Paul (Acts 15:35; 28:31; 1 Cor. 4:17; Col. 1:28) Apollos (Acts 18:25) Timothy (1 Tim. 4:11, 13, 16; 6:2)
General descriptors		
Shared the struggle (συναθλέω) in the Gospel	Euodia (Phil. 4:2–3) Syntyche (Phil. 4:2–3)	Paul (Phil. 4:3; see Col. 1:29; 2:1) Epaphras (Col. 4:12; ἀγωνίζομαι) Church in Philippi (Phil. 1:27)
Fellow-prisoner (συναιχμαλώτοι)	Junia (Rom. 16:7)	Andronicus (Rom. 16:7) Aristarchus (Col. 4:10) Epaphras (Philem. 1:23)
Who has worked (κοπιάω) hard for you	Mary (Rom. 16:6) Tryphaena (Rom. 16:12) Tryphosa (Rom. 16:12) Persis (Rom. 16:12)	Stephanas (1 Cor. 16:16) Paul (Gal. 4:11; Phil. 2:16; Col. 1:29; etc.) Leaders (1 Thess. 5:12) Elders (1 Tim. 5:17)
Fellow-worker (συνεργός)	Prisca (Rom. 16:3–5)	Aquila (Rom. 16:3) Urbanus (Rom. 16:9) Timothy (Rom. 16:21; 1 Thess. 3:2) Apollos and Paul (1 Cor. 3:9) Titus (2 Cor. 8:23) Epaphroditus (Phil. 2:25) Mark and Justus (Col. 4:10–11) Philemon (Philem. 1:1) Mark, Aristarchus, Demas, Luke (Philem. 1:24)

Paul and Slavery as an Ancient Institution

CHART 106

	STATEMENTS THAT REGULATE SLAVE-MASTER RELATIONSHIPS
Eph. 6:5, 8–9	[5] Slaves, be obedient to those who are your masters according to the flesh, with fear and trembling, in the sincerity of your heart, as to Christ; ... [8] knowing that whatever good thing each one does, this he will receive back from the Lord, whether slave or free. [9] And masters, do the same things to them, and give up threatening, knowing that both their Master and yours is in heaven, and there is no partiality with Him.
Col. 3:22, 25; 4:1	[22] Slaves, in all things obey those who are your masters on earth, not with external service, as those who merely please men, but with sincerity of heart, fearing the Lord. ... [25] For he who does wrong will receive the consequences of the wrong which he has done, and that without partiality. 4:1 Masters, grant to your slaves justice and fairness, knowing that you too have a Master in heaven.
1 Tim. 6:1–2	[1] All who are under the yoke as slaves are to regard their own masters as worthy of all honor so that the name of God and our doctrine may not be spoken against. [2] Those who have believers as their masters must not be disrespectful to them because they are brethren, but must serve them all the more, because those who partake of the benefit are believers and beloved.
Titus 2:9–10	[9] Urge bondslaves to be subject to their own masters in everything, to be well-pleasing, not argumentative, [10] not pilfering, but showing all good faith that they may adorn the doctrine of God our Savior in every respect.
	STATEMENTS THAT RELATIVIZE OR NEGATE SOCIAL DISTINCTIONS
1 Cor. 12:13	For by one Spirit we were all baptized into one body, whether Jews or Greeks, whether slaves or free, and we were all made to drink of one Spirit.
Gal. 3:28	There is neither Jew nor Greek, there is neither slave nor free man, there is neither male nor female; for you are all one in Christ Jesus.
Col. 3:11	a renewal in which there is no distinction between Greek and Jew, circumcised and uncircumcised, barbarian, Scythian, slave and freeman, but Christ is all, and in all.
	SLAVE DEALING AS A VICE
1 Tim. 1:9–10 (NIV 1984)	[9] We also know that law is made not for the righteous but for lawbreakers and rebels, the ungodly and sinful, the unholy and irreligious; for those who kill their fathers or mothers, for murderers, [10] for adulterers and perverts, for slave traders (ἀνδραποδισταῖς) and liars and perjurers—and for whatever else is contrary to the sound doctrine ...
	AMBIGUOUS STATEMENT
1 Cor. 7:21–23	[21] Were you called while a slave? Do not worry about it; but if you are able also to become free, rather do that. [22] For he who was called in the Lord while a slave, is the Lord's freedman; likewise he who was called while free, is Christ's slave. [23] You were bought with a price; do not become slaves of men.

Paul's Metaphorical Use of Slavery

CHART 107

	NEGATIVE USE	POSITIVE USE
Slave (δοῦλος)	• "Slaves of sin" (Rom. 6:16–17, 20) • body was "slave to impurity" (Rom. 6:19) • "Slaves of men" (1 Cor. 7:23) • slave vs. son (Gal. 4:1, 7) • slave vs. beloved brother (Philem. 16)	• "Slaves of obedience" (Rom. 6:16) • "Slaves to righteousness" (Rom. 6:19) • Jesus "took the form of a slave" (Phil. 2:7) • Paul: "Slave of Christ Jesus" (Rom. 1:1; Gal. 1:10; Phil. 1:1); "Slave of God" (Titus 1:1) • Paul and Timothy: "your slaves" (2 Cor. 4:5) • Timothy: "Slave of Christ" (Phil. 1:1; see 2:22) • Epaphras: "Slave of Christ" (Col. 4:12) • Leader of the church: "the Lord's slave" (2 Tim. 2:24) • Believers as "slaves of Christ" (Eph. 6:6; see 1 Cor. 7:22)
Slavery (δουλεία)	• Spirit of slavery vs. spirit of adoption (Rom. 8:15) • Creation is in slavery of corruption (Rom. 8:21) • Hagar, covenant from Mt. Sinai, Ishmael, slave (Gal. 4:24) • Freedom in Christ vs. "yoke of slavery" (Gal. 5:1)	
To be a slave (1) (δουλεύω)	• "no longer be slaves to sin" (Rom. 6:6) • "a slave to the law of sin" (Rom. 7:25 NIV) • Esau "will serve the younger" (Rom. 9:12) • "slaves … of their own appetites" (Rom. 16:18) • "you were slaves to those which by nature are not God" (Gal. 4:8; also v.9) • Jerusalem is "in slavery" (Gal. 4:25) • "enslaved to various lusts" (Titus 3:3)	• "serve in the newness of the Spirit" (Rom. 7:6) • "I … in my mind am a slave to God's law" (Rom. 7:25 NIV) • "serving the Lord" (Rom. 12:11) • "whoever thus serves Christ" (Rom. 14:18) • "through love serve one another" (Gal. 5:13) • Timothy served the Gospel (Phil. 2:22) • "to serve a living and true God" (1 Thess. 1:9)
To be a slave (2) (δουλόω)	• "bondage" for one-sided marriage (1 Cor. 7:15) • "bondage under the elemental things of the world" (Gal. 4:3) • "enslaved to much wine" (Titus 2:3)	• "became slaves of righteousness" (Rom. 6:18) • "enslaved to God" (Rom. 6:22) • Paul is a "slave to all" (1 Cor. 9:19)

Paul and Jesus

CHART 108

	CANONICAL TRADITIONS	
(1)	Romans 2:6 … who will **render to each person according to his deeds** (Ps. 62:12; Prov. 24:12).	Matthew 16:27 "For the Son of Man is going to come in the glory of His Father with His angels, and **will then repay every man according to his deeds** (Prov 24:12)."
(2)	Romans 14:14 I know and am convinced in the Lord Jesus that **nothing is unclean in itself**; …	Mark 7:19 **Thus He declared all foods clean.**
(3)	Romans 15:12 And again Isaiah says (Isa. 11:10), "There shall come the root of Jesse, And He who arises to rule over the Gentiles, **In Him shall the Gentiles hope.**" (see Rom. 1:3)	Matthew 12:17 This was to fulfill what was spoken through Isaiah the prophet: "Behold, My Servant whom I have chosen (Isa. 42:1); … [21] **"And in His name the Gentiles will hope** (Isa. 11:10)."
(4)	1 Corinthians 7:10 But <u>to the married I give instructions, not I, but the Lord</u>, that **the wife should not leave her husband** [11] (but if she does leave, she must remain unmarried, or else be reconciled to her husband), and that **the husband should not divorce his wife**.	Mark 10:9 "What therefore God has joined together, let no man separate." … [11] And He said to them, **"Whoever divorces his wife and marries another woman commits adultery** against her; [12] and **if she herself divorces her husband and marries another man, she is committing adultery.**"
(5)	1 Corinthians 9:9 … written in the Law of Moses, "You shall not muzzle the ox while he is threshing" (Deut. 25:4) … [14] So also <u>the Lord directed</u> those who proclaim the gospel to get their living from the gospel.	Luke 10:7 Stay in that house, eating and drinking what they give you; for **the laborer is worthy of his wages**.
(6)	1 Corinthians 11:23 For I <u>received from the Lord</u> that which I also delivered to you, that the Lord Jesus in the night in which He was betrayed took bread; [24] and when He had given thanks, He broke it and said, "**This is My body, which is for you; do this in remembrance of Me.**" [25] In the same way He took the cup also after supper, saying, "**This cup is the new covenant in My blood; do this, as often as you drink it, in remembrance of Me.**	Luke 22:19 And when He had taken some bread and given thanks, He broke it and gave it to them, saying, "**This is My body which is given for you; do this in remembrance of Me.**" [20] And in the same way He took the cup after they had eaten, saying, "**This cup which is poured out for you is the new covenant in My blood.**"
(7)	1 Corinthians 13:2 If I have the gift of prophecy, and know all mysteries and all knowledge; and if I have all **faith, so as to remove mountains**, but do not have love, I am nothing. (see Matt. 17:20)	Matthew 17:20 "… for truly I say to you, if you have faith the size of a mustard seed, you will say to this **mountain**, 'Move from here to there,' and it will **move**; and nothing will be impossible to you."
(8)	1 Thessalonians 4:15 For this <u>we say to you by the word of the Lord</u>, that we who are alive and remain until the coming of the Lord, will not precede those who have fallen asleep. [16] For the Lord Himself will descend from heaven with a shout, with the voice of the archangel and with the **trumpet** of God, and the dead in Christ will rise first. [17] Then we who are alive and remain will be caught up together with them in the **clouds** to **meet** (Matt. 25:6) the Lord in the air, and so we shall always be with the Lord.	Matthew 24:30 "And then the sign of the Son of Man will appear in the sky, and then all the tribes of the earth will mourn, and they will see the Son of Man coming on the **clouds** of the sky (Dan. 7:13) with power and great glory. [31] "And He will send forth His angels with a great **trumpet** (Isa. 27:13) and they will gather together His elect from the four winds, from one end of the sky to the other."
(9)	1 Thessalonians 5:2 … the day of the Lord will come just **like a thief in the night**.	Matthew 24:43 "But be sure of this, that if the head of the house had known at what time of the **night** the **thief** was coming, …"

(10)	1 Timothy 5:18 For the Scripture says, "You shall not muzzle the ox while he is threshing" (Deut. 25:4), and "**The laborer is worthy of his wages.**"	Luke 10:7 "Stay in that house, eating and drinking what they give you; for **the laborer is worthy of his wages**. Do not keep moving from house to house."

NON-CANONICAL TRADITIONS (AGRAPHA)

(11)	Acts 20:35 "… and remember the words of the Lord Jesus, that He Himself said, '**It is more blessed to give than to receive.**'"
(12)	1 Corinthians 15:3 For I delivered to you as of first importance what I also received, that Christ died for our sins according to the Scriptures, ⁴ and that He was buried, and that He was raised on the third day according to the Scriptures, ⁵ and that He appeared to Cephas, then to the twelve. ⁶ **After that He appeared to more than five hundred brethren** at one time, most of whom remain until now, but some have fallen asleep; ⁷ **then He appeared to James, then to all the apostles;** ⁸ and **last of all, as to one untimely born, He appeared to me also.**
(13)	2 Corinthians 12:8 Concerning this I implored the Lord three times that it might leave me. ⁹ And He has said to me, "**My grace is sufficient for you, for power is perfected in weakness.**" Most gladly, therefore, I will rather boast about my weaknesses, so that the power of Christ may dwell in me.

THEOLOGICAL CONTINUITY

(14)	The "kingdom of God" is present (Matt. 12:28; Rom. 14:17) and future (Mark 14:25; 1 Cor. 6:9–10)
(15)	Expectation of the possibly imminent coming of the king/dom (Matt. 4:17; Rom. 16:20; 1 Cor. 16:22)
(16)	"Abba, Father" (ἀββα ὁ πατήρ; Mark 14:36; Rom. 8:15; Gal. 4:6)
(17)	Jesus came to save sinners from sin (Matt. 1:21; 9:2; Rom. 5:12–21; 1 Tim. 1:15)
(18)	Inclusion of Gentiles (Matt. 28:19–20; Mark 13:10; Luke 24:46–47; Rom. 1:16–17; 10:12–13; 1 Cor. 1:22–24)
(19)	Justification of the sinner (Luke 18:13–14; Rom. 3:23–24)
(20)	Salvation by faith (Luke 8:12; Mark 16:16; Rom. 1:16; 10:10; Eph. 2:8)
(21)	The law is summed up in loving one's neighbor (Matt. 22:39–40; Rom. 13:8–10; Gal. 5:14)
(22)	Jesus: "Love your enemies" (Matt. 5:44). Paul: "Never pay back evil for evil" (Rom. 12:17–21; 1 Thess. 5:15)
(23)	Pay taxes to the rulers! (Matt. 17:24–27; 22:16–22; Rom. 13:6–7)
(24)	Judgment by works (see Prov. 24:12 in Matt. 16:27 and Rom. 2:6; Mark 10:29-30; Rom. 14:10; 2 Cor. 5:10)
(25)	Second coming of Christ (Matt. 16:27–28; 24:36–51; 1 Cor. 15:23; 1 Thess. 2:19; 3:13)

Paul and James

CHART 109

	PAUL	JAMES
faith, works, justified	Romans 3:20 … by the <u>works of the Law</u> no flesh will be <u>justified</u> in His sight; for through the Law comes the knowledge of sin. ²¹ But now apart from the Law the righteousness of God has been manifested, being witnessed by the Law and the Prophets, ²² even the righteousness of God through **faith** in/of Jesus Christ for all those who **believe**; for there is no distinction; ²³ for all have sinned and fall short of the glory of God, ²⁴ being <u>justified</u> as a gift by His grace through the redemption which is in Christ Jesus; ²⁵ whom God displayed publicly as a propitiation in His blood through **faith**. This was to demonstrate His righteousness, because in the forbearance of God He passed over the sins previously committed; ²⁶ for the demonstration, I say, of His righteousness at the present time, so that He would be just and the <u>justifier</u> of the one who has **faith** in Jesus. ²⁷ Where then is boasting? It is excluded. By what kind of law? Of <u>works</u>? No, but by a law of **faith**. ²⁸ For we maintain that a man is <u>justified</u> by **faith** apart from <u>works of the Law</u>. (See Gal. 2:16)	2:14 What use is it, my brethren, if someone says he has **faith** but he has no <u>works</u>? Can that **faith** save him? ¹⁵ If a brother or sister is without clothing and in need of daily food, ¹⁶ and one of you says to them, "Go in peace, be warmed and be filled," and yet you do not give them what is necessary for their body, what use is that? ¹⁷ Even so **faith**, if it has no <u>works</u>, is dead, being by itself. ¹⁸ But someone may well say, "You have **faith** and I have <u>works</u>; show me your **faith** without the <u>works</u>, and I will show you my **faith** by my <u>works</u>." ¹⁹ You believe that God is one. You do well; the demons also believe, and shudder. ²⁰ But are you willing to recognize, you foolish fellow, that **faith** without <u>works</u> is useless?
Abraham, Gen. 15:6, justified	Romans 4:1 What then shall we say that Abraham, our forefather according to the flesh, has found? ² For if Abraham was <u>justified</u> by <u>works</u>, he has something to boast about, but not before God. ³ For what does the Scripture say? "Abraham believed God, and it was credited to him as righteousness" (Gen. 15:6). ⁴ Now to the one who <u>works</u>, his wage is not credited as a favor, but as what is due. ⁵ But to the one who does not <u>work</u>, but **believes** in Him who <u>justifies</u> the ungodly, his **faith** is credited as righteousness. (See Gen. 15:6 in Gal. 3:6.)	2:21 Was not Abraham our father <u>justified</u> by <u>works</u> when he offered up Isaac his son on the altar? ²² You see that **faith** was working with his <u>works</u>, and as a result of the <u>works</u>, **faith** was perfected; ²³ and the Scripture was fulfilled which says, "And Abraham believed God, and it was reckoned to him as righteousness" (Gen. 15:6), and he was called the friend of God. ²⁴ You see that a man is <u>justified</u> by <u>works</u> and not by **faith** alone. ²⁵ In the same way, was not Rahab the harlot also <u>justified</u> by <u>works</u> when she received the messengers and sent them out by another way? ²⁶ For just as the body without the spirit is dead, so also **faith** without <u>works</u> is dead.
Ex. 20 and Lev. 19:18	Romans 13:8 Owe nothing to anyone except to love one another; for he who loves his neighbor has fulfilled the law. ⁹ For this, "You shall not commit adultery, You shall not murder, You shall not steal, You shall not covet" (Ex. 20:13–15, 17), and if there is any other commandment, it is summed up in this saying, "You shall love your neighbor as yourself" (Lev. 19:18). ¹⁰ Love does no wrong to a neighbor; therefore love is the fulfillment of *the* law. (See Lev. 19:18 in Gal. 5:14.)	2:8 If, however, you are fulfilling the royal law according to the Scripture, "You shall love your neighbor as yourself" (Lev. 19:18) you are doing well. ⁹ But if you show partiality, you are committing sin and are convicted by the law as transgressors. ¹⁰ For whoever keeps the whole law and yet stumbles in one point, he has become guilty of all. ¹¹ For He who said, "Do not commit adultery," also said, "Do not commit murder" (Ex. 20:14, 13). Now if you do not commit adultery, but do commit murder, you have become a transgressor of the law.

Modern Jewish Views of Paul

CHART 110

1. OLDER VIEW OF JEWISH SCHOLARS: IN CONTRAST TO JESUS, PAUL ABROGATED THE LAW	
Joseph Salvador (1796-1873)	Paul severed Christians from synagogue and Torah
Samuel Hirsch (1815-1889)	Paul set grace in antithesis to the law
Heinrich Graetz (1817-1891)	Paul changed Christianity from "a Judaean sect to an independent religion"
Elia Benamozegh (1823-1900)	Paul's new principle is "faith opposed as such to . . . works."
Isaac M. Wise (1819-1900)	Paul's "mystical and anti-law tendencies" oppose rabbinic rationality & law
Kaufmann Kohler (1843-1926)	Paul was a disciple of hellenism (gnosis, mystery religions) not of Gamaliel
Moritz Friedländer (1844-1919)	Paul's view of the Law is an "unbridgeable gulf" between him and the Jews
→ Gottlieb Klein (1852-1914)	Paul's universalism is Jewish (see prophets and rabbis, including Gamaliel)
Claude G. Montefiore (1858-1938)	There is "much in Paul which . . . is inexplicable by Judaism."
Joseph G. Klausner (1874-1958)	Paul changed his Jewish faith into a "half-pagan sect of compromise"
Martin Buber (1878-1965)	Jewish *emuna* ("faithfulness") contradicts Paul's *pistis* (merely intellectual)
Leo Baeck (1873-1956): early	Paul went beyond Judaism by borrowing from mystery religions (sacraments)
2. NEWER VIEW OF JEWISH SCHOLARS: PAUL IS MORE JEWISH THAN PREVIOUSLY THOUGHT	
Leo Baeck (1873-1956): later	It is rabbinic to view the law as not binding after the arrival of the Messiah
Hans J. Schoeps (1909-1980)	All elements of Paul's thoughts are Jewish, though not their combination
Samuel Sandmel (1911-1979)	Paul's Christology "is the climactic and logical conclusion" of Jewish history
Schalom Ben-Chorin (1913-1999)	Paul's Gentile mission fulfills Jewish hopes
David Flusser (born 1917)	Paul's theology was part of an inner-Jewish reform movement (Essenes)
Pinchas Lapide (born 1922)	Paul meant his gospel only for Gentiles, for the Jews are still God's people
Richard Rubenstein (born 1924)	Paul is a "revolutionary Jewish mystic" who expresses unconscious conflicts
→ H. Maccoby (born 1924)	Paul deviates from Judaism by fusing Gnosticism and mystery religions
Lester Dean (born 1954)	Paul does not abolish obedience to the Torah but adds belief in Christ
Alan F. Segal (born 1945)	Paul converted "to a new, apocalyptic, mystical, . . . form of Judaism."
Daniel Boyarin (born 1946)	Paul melts his Pharisaic identity with universalism of diaspora Judaism (Philo)

The "New Perspectives" on Paul

CHART 111

	"OLD PERSPECTIVES"	"NEW PERSPECTIVES"
1. Judaism of the first century	A religion of works-righteousness and legalistic perfectionism	A religion of "covenantal nomism": you get in by grace and stay in by obedience (Sanders)
2a. "Justification by works"	Individual attempt to find favor with God through obedience to God's laws	Corporate attempt to keep Gentiles out of the covenant through boundary markers
2b. "Works of the Law"	Ritual *and moral* laws that need to be obeyed in their totality in order to please God and earn his favor (emphasis on *activity*)	While the phrase does refer to observance of the law in principle (activity), Paul's missionary context highlighted particular laws ("boundary markers") that kept Jews and Gentiles apart (*identity*), e.g., Sabbath, dietary laws, circumcision (Dunn)
3. "Justification by faith"	*Forensic* act in which the guilty sinner is declared innocent	*Forensic* act in which the sinner is declared innocent as *one* important part of God's plan to save the world through Israel (covenant) and her Messiah (Christology) (Wright)
4. Paul's use of Abraham	Focus on Abraham's *faith*	Focus on Abraham's *fatherhood*
5. Paul's focus	Soteriology: *How* to get saved	Ecclesiology: *Who* gets saved?
6. Paul's target	Jewish nomism **(individual performance)**	Jewish nationalism and racialism (corporate privilege)
7. Older predecessors	Augustine, Luther, Bultmann	W. Wrede; G. F. Moore; H.-J. Schoeps, K. Stendahl, J. Parkes, E. Jacob
8. Modern proponents	Cranfield, Schreiner, Das, Thielman, Seifrid	E. P. Sanders, J. D. G. Dunn, N. T. Wright, T. Donaldson, D. A. Campbell, R. B. Hays
9. Criticism of the other view	Paul targets not just ethnic privilege but ethical inability to perform according to God's will	Older view understands Paul mostly through Luther's experience of medieval Catholicism

Comments

Chart Comments

Part A: Paul's Background & Context

1. Roman Emperors before and during Paul's Life and Ministry

While Paul might not have seen any of the Roman emperors in person, the chart shows that their decisions and ideas impacted the apostle's ministry both positively and negatively. For more information see T. S. Johnson 968–974; Aune (c); Horsley (1997–2004); Porter d:1010–1018; D. L. Jones; Alvarez (1999); Bernett (2007), esp. 264–351; Miller.

2. Roman Political Order

From the beginning Paul was destined not just to travel widely but also to travel up to the social and political elite. Jesus commissioned him to witness before "kings" (Acts 9:15). That divine plan is, ironically, mostly fulfilled through human antagonists who drag Paul and his companions before the authorities (e.g., Acts 16:19). His first convert explicitly mentioned by Luke is none less than Sergius Paulus, the proconsul (ἀνθύπατος) of the senatorial province Cyprus (Acts 13:6–12). Another proconsul, Gallio of Corinth, dismissed Jewish charges against Paul. In Ephesus Paul called "Asiarchs" among his friends (Acts 19:31), which were some type of public official (Kearsley). Later in Caesarea Maritima, the capitol of the imperial province, the apostle appeared before the governors (ἡγεμών) Felix (Acts 24:1–23) and Porcius Festus (24:27–25:12) and before King Herod Agrippa II (Acts 26:1–32) who also exonerated him. On Malta, Paul was welcomed and entertained for days by Publius, a "leading man of the island" (Acts 28:8). Luke finished with Paul's arrival and stay in Rome where he expected to meet the emperor (Acts 25:11, 21, 25; 26:32; 28:19). With this trail of contacts to public officials throughout the years, Paul can say that nothing in his Christian life happened "in a corner" (Acts 26:26). For descriptions of the Roman political order see Reasoner, Gill b:995–999; Rapske 978–984; Hanson, Oakman 64–70.

3. Roman Social Order

Friesen (35–37) created this "income poverty scale," not as a "precise measurements of the first century situation" (39) but as an approximate estimate of Paul's ancient social context. The numbers reflect a wide experience of "poverty and systemic inequality" in the Roman empire (37) that falls below the standards of modern day Uganda in terms of annual income per capita, life expectancy, infant mortality, etc. (see fig. 4 on p. 38). Analyzing the income level of church members, Friesen concludes that, with the exception of Gaius (Rom. 16:23), Chloe (1 Cor. 1:11) and a few other individuals, "the vast majority in Paul's assemblies hovered around the level of subsistence, just above or just below" (41). The social order of the Roman empire was characterized by a rigid class system that divided people into the elite (emperor, six hundred senators, twenty thousand equestrians, 150,000 decurions) and the non-elite (free-born citizens; free-born non-citizens; freedmen; slaves) without a middle class that is so typical of modern Western societies (see Jeffers 180–196; Burge, Cohick, Green 86–92; Duling 15-19). Membership to a group was conditioned on birth, heritage and minimum property qualifications. Thus, senators had to own 1 mio, equestrians 400,000 and decurions 150,000–200,000 sesterces. These requirements imposed extreme limits to social upward mobility (Hellerman c:48, 60–61, 182 n.75). The elite did not only command control over the land, but constantly ingrained its superior status through highly visible markers such as attire, occupation, seating at public events and privileges in the legal system. Such hierarchical order was duplicated in the religious cults, civil groups and local municipalities of non-elites (Hellerman c:56–59). In such a status-conscious society, honor (ascribed or acquired) was a central cultural value and public commodity, achieved through affirmation "by the larger social group to which the individual belonged" (Hellerman c:35). The ensuing "struggle for reputation" became "a primary social energy" in the society, fueled by an "insatiable desire for public esteem" (Hellerman c:34). Many strata of the Roman social order came together in the local church, including members of the social elite (e.g., Acts 13:7, 12; Rom. 16:10–11, 23; 1 Cor. 1:14, 26; Phil. 4:22; 17:34; see Tidball 888–889; Theissen a:69–119; Meeks 51–73; Fiensy b:226–230). Therefore, understanding the social dynamics between them and the accompanying universal quest for honor has offered helpful insights into some struggles in Paul's churches (Barton). The problem between the weak and the strong in 1 Corinthians 8 might have had as much to do with socioeconomic factors as with theological arguments (Theissen b:121–143). Paul's rejection of support from the Corinthians (1 Corinthians 9) is at least partially intended "to avoid dependency on some patron who might manipulate the situation to exercise power" (Thiselton a:127). The Christology in Philippians 2:6–11 receives social relevance on the background of Philippi's pronounced Roman character (Hellerman).

4. Roman Military Structure

The chart simplifies the structural complexity of the imperial Roman military which, depending on the emperor and the region, involved either more or less subordinate units and related forms of leadership. For a brief review see G. L. Thompson's article, for more thorough discussions see Broughton, Webster (esp. 97–166) and Southern (esp. 87–140). The numbers about the strength of a unit are "paper figures" since no one knows their exact size. Thus, the total number of men within a single legion was "somewhere between 5,000 and 6,000" (Southern 99). While Roman citizenship was typically a *prerequisite* for enlisting in the Roman army (see Acts 22:28), it was a *reward* in the auxiliary troops and in the Navy given at retirement for honorable service (Webster 142–145, 166). All of the Roman military encountered in the book of Acts probably belonged to the auxiliary branch of the army. Cornelius in Acts 10 was a "centurion" of the "Italian cohort" (Acts 10:1), meaning he was "presumably one of six" leaders in the cohort (Barrett c:1.499). In Jerusalem, Paul was protected from the Jewish mob by a Roman commander and his centurions (Acts 21:31), showing that the military strength at that time consisted of at least one cohort stationed at the fortress Antonia (Rapske 980). And later again, Luke mentions the impressive military protection that guarded Paul from the Jewish mob on the way to his trial in Caesarea. The commander "called to him two of the centurions and said, 'Get two hundred soldiers ready by the third hour of the night to proceed to Caesarea, with seventy horsemen and two hundred spearmen'" (Acts 23:23).

5. Greco-Roman Religions, Cults, and Philosophies

Klauck (2003) offers a book-long study of early Christianity's religious context mentioned in this chart. For a shorter overview see also Grant (19–42), Jeffers (89-109), and Esler (1–79).

If Paul would never have traveled outside of Palestine, he still would have encountered plenty of pagan religions. Yet, because of his itinerant ministry, he inevitably came face to face with a wide range of local and universal expressions of ancient paganism, polytheism and philosophy (see Kauppi). Paul makes polemic references to these varied forms of paganism (see Woyke; Grant 46–49), ranging from idols (2 Cor. 6:16; 1 Thess. 1:9-10) and "mute idols" (1 Cor. 12:2) to "many gods and many lords" (1 Cor. 8:4–6; see Gal. 4:8), from the practice of eating meat "sacrificed to idols" (1 Cor. 8:1) to the worship of images "in the form of corruptible man and of birds and four-footed animals and crawling creatures" (Rom. 1:23).

The gods and goddesses listed here mention first the twelve gods and goddesses of the "Olympian pantheon," followed by minor deities, and finally heroes (see Aune c:787). Some were worshiped widely, others only locally. Many more gods were worshiped than the ones listed here. In the Gentile context of Corinth, where there are "many gods and many lords," Paul insists that there is "one God" and "one Lord Jesus Christ by whom are all things, and we exist through Him" (1 Cor. 8:5–6). In Ephesus citizens worshiped a multitude of gods and goddesses, "including Aphrodite, Apollos, Asclepius, Athena, Cabiri, Demeter, Dionysus, Egyptian Cults, Ge, God Most High, Hecate, Hephaestus, Hercules, Hestia, the Mother goddess, Pluton, Poseidon, Zeus and other minor deities" (Trebilco b:19 n. 47; Arnold c:250). Above all stood Artemis as the most powerful deity of the city.

In ancient as well as modern times, people with special skills or positions (e.g., Acts 10:25; 14:8–20; 16:25–34; 28:1–6), including rulers (Acts 12:20–23), were often considered with divine honors or even viewed as the incarnation of a god (see Kezbere). The emperor Augustus received, according to Philo, "honors equal to those of the Olympian gods" (*Legat.* 1:149). These honors developed into an institution of emperor worship that grew in expressions and demand throughout the first century (Jones). There were emperor temples with temple taxes, high priests, processions, feasts, sacrifices, games, hymns, and confessions. Herod's building projects in honor of Caesar are just one expression of emperor worship in Judea (Caesarea Maritima, etc.; see Bernett). Since the 1990s, there has been a growing interest among Pauline scholars to interpret Paul's letters on the background of the emperor worship (Aune c:234–235, Jones, Strelan 94–113; Alvarez; Crossan/Reed; Horsley 1997–2004; Harrison 2002; Wright 2002; Finney; Oakes 2005; Saunders; Elliott 2008; Hardin; Kahl).

The "mystery cults" were secret cults that used rituals for initiation and redemption, understood as unity with the gods that leads to everlasting life (see Aune d:792–793; Meyer; Donfried 1985; Ulansey; Court; Speyer; Patella; Hengel c:91–97; g:455 n. 16). Pauline scholars continue to find occasional reliance on individual terms and concepts of mystery religions in the letters of the apostle (e.g., Hengel j:8; Rogers; House; Donfried 1985; Aune d:794). See BDAG for γνῶσις (1 Cor. 13:2), ἐμβατεύω (Col. 2:18), μυέω (Phil. 4:12), μυστήριον (Col. 2:2), and τελειόω (Phil. 3:12). The second-century Christian apologist Justin Martyr explained that "wicked demons have imitated in the mysteries of Mithra" the Lord's Supper by using bread and a cup of water together with words spoken over them (*1 Apol.* 66; see also Origen, Cels. 6.22–23). Yet, the differences are no less apparent. "Attis, Adonis, Osiris die, are mourned for, and return to life. Yet it is nowhere said that *soteria* [salvation] comes by their death" (Nock 83; also Hengel c:92, 133–136; e:199; Perrin).

Besides the gods and goddesses of the Greco-Roman pantheon, a variety of healers and miracle workers were known in the first century (see Cotter; F. Martin 155–198), including rulers (e.g., Caesar, Augustus, Vespasian), itinerant philosophers (e.g., Apollonius of Tyana), apostles (see Peter and Paul) or ordinary Christians (1 Cor. 12:10, 28). Paul has his own experience with ancient fortune-telling when he exorcises a "spirit of divination" (πνεῦμα πύθωνα) from a slave girl in Philippi (Acts 16:16; see Kauppi, 27–28). Paul also has no shortage of meeting magicians such as Bar-Jesus in Paphos on Cyprus (Acts 13:6–7) or the magicians in Ephesus who burned their expensive books after becoming Christians (Acts 19:19; see also φαρμακεία as a vice [Gal. 5:20] and "sorcerers" [original meaning of γόητες] who will deceive [2 Tim 3:13]). For studies on Paul and magic see Arnold b:580–583; Klauck 2003; Heininger; Twelvetree. Allusions to ancient astrology could be found in the reference to "principalities and powers" (Col. 1:16) and to the "elemental spirits of the world" (Gal. 4:3, 9; Col 2:8, 20) (Arnold b:582).

Ancient philosophers were the only providers of "pastoral care or therapists" available in the classical period (Klauck a:334). They studied theology together with physics, logic, and other subjects. More specifically, recent clarifications about philosophy "in the first century of the Mediterranean world" as "'a way of life' with an emphasis on 'spiritual exercises'" led "biblical scholars during the past decade" to identify Paul "with Epicureans (Clarence Glad), Cynics (F. Gerald Downing), Stoics (Troels Engberg-Pedersen), and moral philosophers in general (Abraham Malherbe)" (Keay 153). Paul did meet Epicurean and Stoic philosophers in Athens (Acts 17:18). The latter's influence is often traced in some of Paul's letters (Betz; DeWitt; Downing; DeSilva; Engberg-Pedersen; Thorsteinsson; M. Lee; Huttunen).

6. Paul's Greco-Roman Background

For Paul's Greco-Roman background see Engberg-Pedersen, Charles, Sampley (a-b), Lampe (a), Hock, Vegge, Craig Evans (b). For a discussion of both his Jewish and Greco-Roman background see P. Williams, Fleming,

Köster (b), Pitts, Fisk (301–310), Porter (2008). Craig Evans lists "some 600 potential parallels" (Evans b:117 n. 3) between Paul and pagan and Jewish literature and inscriptions (in Evans a:376–95). Paul's use of a variety of figures of speech throughout his letters (see comments below) suggests Hellenistic education beyond the primary level, although further verification is hard to come by. The most striking observation is what Fleming calls (with a West African missiologist) the "translatability of the Gospel" (Fleming 128). Paul does not feel obligated to limit himself to Christological expressions of previous early Christian traditions (although he does that, see 1 Cor. 15:1–3). Instead, he contextualizes his message by translating the good news into concepts and expressions familiar to the local culture of his particular audience. Such efforts destigmatize the culture and the gospel by using the familiar to communicate what is foreign. Be it the Cabirus cult in Thessalonica (Donfried a:28–31) or the cult of Asklepios in Corinth (Thiselton a:993–994), they all supplied Paul with terms and concepts that he employed in the service of his ministry. While Luke's mention of Paul's Roman citizenship does fit the author's pro-Roman depiction of early Christianity, there is no reason to deny the historicity of this legal property (see Riesner 147-156; Omerzu a:17–52).

7-8. First-Century Judaisms: Different Groups and Common Characteristics

First-century Judaism is not easily summarized without gross distortion. This chart offers only a sample of Jewish groups and merely indicates the variety of beliefs (see Grabbe for more details). Against F. C. Baur's view of a polarized early church, Russel (2008) argued that this Jewish heterodoxy forms the background for early Christian diversity. Maher (2003) traces the recent shifts in understanding ancient Judaism. Until the 1950s, second temple Judaism was perceived more or less as one normative orthodox movement. The discovery of the Dead Sea Scrolls diversified such a monolithic perception and the pendulum shifted to the opposite extreme: there was no single "Judaism" but only various "Judaisms," a plurality of groups with no common ground (Morton Smith; Neusner). The position in the middle suggests a "complex Judaism" (Hengel, Deines) which had a united front before outsiders while differing on the inside. John J. Collins also speaks of a "common ethic" among diaspora Jews according to which Jews used the Torah particularly to maintain their distinctive in the midst of a pagan society (Elliott/Reasoner 191): monotheism, election, circumcision, separation from Gentiles. Not all of them are equally important as normative concepts throughout the different Jewish groups. With reference to the Dead Sea Scrolls and various pseudepigrapha, Mark A. Elliot (*The Survivors of Israel*, 2000) recently observed a notion of Israel's apostasy and of remnant theology that questioned an unqualified notion of national election. Nanos argues with reference to Josephus (*A.J.* 20.17–96) that even circumcision was not a universal Jewish requirement for Gentile participation in Israel's blessings (Nanos b:133–134). Yet, the anecdotal evidence adduced renders this view as hardly representative for second temple Judaism. Stemberger (2001) uses Tacitus' description (*Histories* 5.5.2–5) as an elementary expression of commonalities: Jews have no community with Romans in the religious sphere, they do not dine with them, and Jews do not marry outsiders.

9. Paul's Jewish Background

For Paul's Jewish background see Nägeli (59–68), Boyarin, Chilton, Sanders, Witherington (b), Stegner, Aune (a), Polhill (27–35) Capes/Reeves/Richards (66–68), and Elliott/Reasoner. Horbury (166–173) reviews the struggles of the early twentieth-century religion-historical school about pinpointing the most dominant influence on Paul's thought. The matter cannot be easily decided by answering the question of whether Tarsus or Jerusalem was the place of Paul's education. For one thing, the relevant text (Acts 22:3, Paul was "brought up" [ἀνατεθραμμένος] in Jerusalem) poses interpretive challenges (compare NRSV with NIV; see Hock a:218 n.2; Marshall, Travis, Paul 36–37) and does not rule out the possibility that Paul spent his adolescent years in Tarsus (Deissmann b:92–93; Pitts 27–33). Yet, Chilton's certainty that Paul went to Jerusalem at age 21 (Chilton, xii, 25) is purely speculative as well. More important than the meaning of this single text is the understanding that the old divide between a purely Jewish Palestine and a hellenized diaspora in the first century is outdated (see especially Hengel 2003). Inscriptional evidence shows that Greek invaded Aramaic-speaking Israel already in the third century BC (M. O. Wise 439) and by the first century AD "a significant presence of elementary Greek education in Jerusalem" can be demonstrated (Pitts 41, see 33–43). Thus, even if Paul grew up early on in Jerusalem, he would have been exposed to Greek thoughts and terms as reflected in his letters.

Paul says of himself that he was "as to the Law, a Pharisee, as to zeal, a persecutor of the church, as to the righteousness which is in the Law, found blameless" (Phil. 3:5–6; Acts 23:6). More specifically, H. Hübner (1973) saw Paul as a follower of the conservative Shammai while J. Jeremias (1969) identified Pauline beliefs with the school of Hillel. Donfried (2004), on the other hand, showed many parallels between Paul and the Essenes, a Jewish group that opposed Pharisees as compromisers. Besides parallels between Ephesians 5:3–14 and Dead Sea Scrolls, 2 Corinthians 6:13-7:1 appears to Dahl nearly as a "christianized fragment of essene provenance" (Dahl b:335). Yet, while discussions today usually ask *what kind* of Judaism influenced Paul's life and theology, not all of the apostle's thoughts and actions can be explained based on a Jewish background. Jürgen Becker's view of a *consistent* discontinuity between Paul and ancient Judaisms is hard to maintain. Yet, Martin Hengel argued that unless further discoveries of relevant ancient texts tell us otherwise (e.g., d:174), the understanding of a crucified Messiah who died once (Rom. 6:10) "for our sins" (1 Cor. 15:3) to reconcile the whole world remains a unique Christian message that can historically be explained only as a result of Jesus' resurrection as the "church-forming ur-event" itself (Hengel, d:178). Similarly, Paul's prevalent emphasis on the "new covenant" (Gal. 4:21-31?; 1 Cor. 11:25; 2 Cor. 3:6, 14; Rom. 7:6; 11:27), while not absent from the Old Testament (Jeremiah 31), is not found in second temple Judaism. And where we do find it—as in the Dead Sea Scrolls—its understanding differs from Paul, since the "sectaries of Qumran saw the new covenant as a return to the original intentions of the Mosaic Torah" (Talbert e:19).

Part B: Paul's Life & Ministry

10. CHRONOLOGY OF PAUL'S LIFE

The chronology displayed here was taken from Schnelle (a:56). Riesner's survey of scholarship on the question of Paul's chronology (pages 3–28) shows the controversial nature of any suggestion in this regard. The absolute reference points are the expulsion of Jews from Rome by Claudius in AD 49 (see Acts 18:2) and Gallio's proconsulship in Achaia in AD 51–52 (Acts 18:12–16). Because of these historical reference points, "Paul's arrival in Corinth at the beginning of the year 50 provides a firm point from which the relative chronology of Paul's activity can be calculated both forwards and backwards." (Schnelle a:49). The following are important references for this relative chronology:

Gal. 1:18 "Then **three years later** [after conversion] I went up to Jerusalem."

Gal. 2:1 "Then after an interval of **fourteen years** [after conversion or after 1st visit?] I went up again to Jerusalem…"

Acts 18:11 Paul stayed for **one and a half years** in Corinth.

Acts 19:9–10 Paul stayed for ca. **two and a half years** in Ephesus.

Acts 20:3 Paul stayed in Greece for **three months**.

11. PARALLELS BETWEEN ACTS AND THE PAULINE CORPUS

See Porter (2001, esp. 117), Aejmelaeus, Porter (2001:117); Witherington (1998a:610–618); Walton (157–198), Marguerat (b:324–325). For additional parallels of people and places, see charts 12–14. The parallels caution against an exaggerated antithesis between the "Paul of Acts" and the "Paul of the letters" that dominated the older German research (so Schröter 58). As Paul's travel companion, it should not surprise that Luke's selective sketch of the apostle overlaps quite often with what we know from the letters themselves. It also makes good sense that the only speech of Paul in Acts addressed to *Christians* (Acts 20:18–35) shows the closest parallels to the letters, which were also written to believers. The differences between Acts and Paul's letters (see next chart) should be evaluated in light of their many commonalities (Brown 424). Based on the parallels, some scholars have concluded that the author of Acts knew the Pauline doctrine of justification by faith. And, although they are never mentioned or cited, he might have also been familiar with some of Paul's letters (e.g., Lindemann 1979, Aejmelaeus, Witherington, Pichler; for an introduction to the latter point see Walton 14–17). For others, the parallels are insufficient to suggest literary dependence and/or biographical connection between both sets of texts and their authors (e.g., Mount 107).

12. Differences between Acts and the Pauline Corpus

The list is suggestive and by far not complete. Consider, for examples the many names in chart 23 that appear in Acts but not in the letters and vice versa, or the collection for believers in Jerusalem mentioned in the letters (Rom. 15:25–27; 1 Cor. 16:1–4; 2 Cor. 8–9; Gal. 2:10) but not in Acts (except maybe 24:17 [Wenham/Walton 281]; see also the comparison in Pervo 150). In general, the Paul of Acts appears much more Jewish than the Paul we meet in his own letters. When evaluating these differences we need to consider (a) the many parallels between Acts and the Pauline corpus (see previous chart) and (b) the authors' different "aims, perspectives, knowledge of events and principles of selection" (DeSilva 494). Luke is interested, among other things, in Paul the missionary and church planter who speaks to (God-fearing?) unbelievers, whereas the letters express the apostle's written pastoral concerns for *established* churches with predominantly *Gentile* believers. Furthermore, Luke's portrait of Paul is driven by an imitation of the Jewish life of Christ (see chart 13), whereas Paul's letters imitate Greco-Roman styles of letter-writing and respond to situations at hand (see Marshall a:485). In addition, neither the letters nor Acts seek to tell us everything there is to know about Paul. If the earliest of Paul's letters date ca. AD 50 then we are left with seventeen years of his Christian life since his conversion in AD 33 that remain in the "dark," not to speak of his pre-Christian past (Schnelle a:41; Hengel / Schwemer 2–3; Witherington c:213–227). And even Luke's lengthy narrative about Paul's life as a Christian missionary (Acts 13–28) skips over "eight of the twelve years between 50 and 62" (Johnson a:61; also Polhill c:340, 379; see Acts 18:11; 19:10; 24:27; 28:30; see also the speed with which Luke reports Paul's traveling of over four hundred kilometers from Phrygia and Galatia to Asia and Troas in Acts 16:6–8; Jewett c:3). It is thus evident that, even when taken together, the book of Acts as well as the *Corpus Paulinum* offer only a collection of snapshots and depend therefore *necessarily* on each other *as equals* for the fullest possible portrait of Paul (Kümmel 254, Witherington 1998a:307–308, 430–438). Any arguments from silence run into this problem of the sources' brevity and situational selectivity (see Hengel g:453–454). When looking at the theological discrepancies between Acts and the letters we need to bear in mind that the letters alone already display a diversity that is not always easily harmonized (see chart 79). It is then no surprise to find that the problem is compounded when someone else's view on Paul (Luke's) is added to the apostle's own biographical snippets. These differences require methodologically that both sets of texts deserve "independent inquiry" as well as an "intentional separation of Paul's life and thought" (Phillips 47). Only then are we able to respect each portrait of Paul and endeavor a "disciplined comparison" (again Phillips 47) without blurring their distinctions and flattening their plurality. Considering all this and without being an optimist, some of the discrepancies can indeed be resolved (e.g., no. 20 and Wenham a:226–243; DeSilva 494–496). Maybe we can say that Luke has simplified Paul but not falsified him (Nolland xxxvi) or that "that which lies in the shadow in Paul's letters Luke has placed in the sun in Acts" (Jervell, 199). While Paul does not mention visits in the "synagogue," his contacts with this Jewish house of prayer and worship are implied in the punishments of lashes from the Jews (2 Cor. 11:24). And while Paul criticizes circumcision as a requirement for Gentiles, the circumcision of Timothy for the purpose of ministry (Acts 16:3) illustrates well the apostle's principle to become a Jew to the Jews (1 Cor. 9:20; so already Wikenhauser 15). The bottom line is that the "Paul we see in Acts is not un-Pauline, much less anti-Pauline, but in some cases a Paul we do not hear about in the epistles, and in some cases a familiar Paul, though from a different and fresh perspective. It is a Paul interpreted through the eyes of admiration and respect" (Witherington 1998a:438; also Bruce c:46–59).

13. Parallels between Jesus in Luke, and Paul in Acts

Mattill (1975) and Crossan/Reed (a:29) were the major sources for this chart (see also Talbert, d:218–220; Pervo 154). For the few important studies of these parallels see Evans (1884), Rackham (1901), Goulder (1964), Talbert (1974), Radl (1975), Muhlack (1979), Neirynck (1979), Heusler (2000), Omerzu (2003; c:154). Walton (34–40) helpfully summarizes the contributions of Rackham, Goulder, and Talbert. While not the focus of this chart, the Gospel of Luke and Acts also show many important *structural* parallels and patterns (Liefeld 39; Porter c:108–109; Lindemann b:225–237; Talbert c:xxiii–xxv). The chart does not include parallels in Luke–Acts between Paul and people other than Jesus, such as Peter (see next chart), Stephen (see 6:13 and 21:28), Elijah and Elisha. Nor should we overlook that people other than Paul are paralleled with Jesus (see Acts 7:60 and Luke 23:34 [Stephen]). Not all of Mattill's parallels are persuasive, but it is probably no exaggeration when he observes that Jesus-Paul parallels "are found in every chapter of Luke and in every chapter of Acts ix–xxviii, except the Petrine chapters x and xii" and that "we must avoid the common error of overlooking it altogether" (1975:36). To be sure, the depictions of Jesus and Paul are not identical (Schröter 44–45) and Acts is not a copycat of the Gospel (Marguerat a:44-45). For example, Jesus was not a Roman citizen and consequently did not appeal to Caesar during his trial (see Omerzu a:chs. 2–3). Furthermore, other gospels reveal parallels to Paul that Luke did not include (Mattill 1975:36; e.g., Matt. 23:27 and Acts 23:3). These differences show that Luke's literary and theological creativity was constrained intentionally (by historical interests) and unintentionally (lack of sources). The parallels do demonstrate the literary unity of "Luke–Acts" (so first called by Cadbury in 1927 [Marguerat a:43]; see Tannehill; Verheyden 1999). But more than that, these parallels point to the function of Luke's two-volume work as (among others) "an irresistible apology for Paul" (Mattill 1975:37) whose life is presented as an *imitatio* [of Luke's] *Christi*, a pedigree higher than any of the apostle's other social distinctions (see also Puskas/Crump 113; De Boer 376–377; so already Sahlin 1945). "Jesus goes before his disciples as archēgos (Acts 3:15; 5:31; Heb. 2:10; 12:2), that is, pioneer or leader," followed in astonishing biographical detail by his main successor (Talbert d:119). With regard to their pre-canonical unity and function, Mattill even explains (*pace* Maddox 11), in the words of H. Evans, that "the Acts are not the appendix to Luke, but St. Luke is the introduction to the Acts" (in Mattill 1975:17; see also Radl 1999; Barrett [1992] disagrees). Whether or not such an estimate is adequate, these parallels offer evidence for the heuristic value of reading the Gospel and Acts against the "canonical disunity" (Parsons/Pervo 8) as one book (see also the *inclusio* "salvation of God" in Luke 3:8 [with Isaiah 40:5] and Acts 28:28 [after Isaiah 6:9-10]; Marguerat a:48). And these parallels offer in particular an important corrective to those studies that continue to limit Luke's portrait of Paul to the book of Acts alone (e.g., Lenz 1993, Lang 2008). Beyond Luke-Acts, Murphy-O'Connor (2007) has compared the lives of Jesus and Paul and collected astonishing parallels between biographical details of both.

14. Parallels in Acts between Peter and Paul

Besides my own observations, some sources for these parallels and their discussion are Ehrman (121), Mattill (b:110–111), Talbert (c:xxvii–xxix) and especially Walton (35–36), reproducing Rackham's insights. In contrast to some early Christian perception of contrast between Peter and Paul (1 Cor. 1:12), Luke seeks to demonstrate their partnership in ministry. More specifically, the question of purpose regarding these parallels should not be answered in isolation from those between Jesus and Paul (see previous chart and comments). If the latter served to defend Paul and his mission to the Gentiles, then Luke's portrait of Peter "in the image of Paul" and that of Paul "in the image of Peter" most likely has the same purpose: "One can easily argue that the author included Peter primarily to demonstrate the legitimacy of Paul's apostolate to the Gentiles. The election of Matthias to replace Judas is an acknowledgement of the fact that Paul is not one of 'the twelve.' Yet the dramatic acts and experiences of the chief apostle, Peter, are matched one for one from the life of Paul and demonstrate that Paul is in no sense inferior. Nor is the mission to the Gentiles an innovation by Paul, since the first breakthrough was accomplished by Peter in response to divine revelation" (Madvig 147). In the story of Acts, "Cornelius is the first gentile to become a convert to Christianity (Acts 10:1–11:18, cf. 15:6–11)" (Gaventa b:1154). Significantly, it is the respected and Jewish pillar of early Christianity who converts the first Gentile, not the disputed Paul.

Furthermore, *Peter's* citation of Joel 2:28–32, finishing on the note that "everyone who calls on the name of the Lord will be saved" (Acts 2:21), subverts "criticism of Paul's Gentile mission" (Wall 550). The mission to the Gentiles is, therefore, not Paul's post-Easter aberration of Christianity's Jewish origins but finds support from the prime apostle, eyewitness of Jesus, and Jewish leader of the church in Jerusalem (see Clark 2001).

15. Autobiographical Information

This chart was inspired by Eve-Marie Becker's essay (82–83) and adds observations to her collection of Paul's autobiographical notes. Some of the information here can be debated. The Greek term for "kinsmen" (συγγενεῖς) in Romans 16 could be a metaphor for fictive kinship and would then not refer to Paul's blood relatives (Das 90–103). Tatum (126–130) offers a reconstruction of Paul's career based on the undisputed letters.

16. Comparison of Three Accounts of Paul's Conversion in Acts

All three accounts share basic components of Paul's experience: Paul was a zealous Pharisee, eagerly persecuting Christians, when on a road to Damascus he saw a "light" and "heard a voice" from Jesus who commissioned him to be his witness to Jews and Gentiles. The major difference between the three accounts is the location of the commission within the narrative. While in Acts 26, the shortest version, it appears immediately in Jesus' first and only address to Paul, it is mediated through Ananias in Acts 9 and 22. The comparison makes it obvious that none of the versions tell the full story. The first version omits Paul's question and Jesus' answer (points 10 and 11) and Ananias does not repeat Jesus' mission for Paul which naturally must have happened. In Acts 22, Jesus' vision to Ananias is radically shortened and the dialogue between Ananias and Paul now includes the mission "to all men" (22:15). And the version in Acts 26 does not mention Ananias at all and condenses all important components of the different dialogues to one speech of Jesus. For more discussion on the three accounts see Polhill (a:44–54); Kremer; Czachesz (60–91). For questions regarding the year of Paul's conversion see Riesner (64–74). The threefold repetition of Paul's conversion in the book of Acts highlights its importance in the eyes of Luke.

17. Saul – Paul: Did the Apostle change his name?

See the essays by Compton and Nobbs for a discussion of various views on Acts 13:9. Among Pauline scholars it is common to understand "Paul" as the apostle's chosen Latin sound-equivalent to his Jewish name, both of which he had from the very beginning (see Bruce b:38, Schnelle a:61–62, Murphy-O'Connor a:41–43, Bauckham c:210). Yet should it be accidental, as Nobbs (288) sees it, that the same context in which the apostle's names are mentioned (Acts 13:9) also contains the only references in the New Testament to individuals with the same name, namely a Gentile "*Paulus Sergius*" (13:7) and the Jewish "Saul son of Kish" (13:21)? On the other hand, a frequent popular understanding is that Saul changed his name to Paul right after his conversion to symbolize the radical change in his life. Yet both names are not mentioned in Acts 9, at his conversion, but in Acts 13, at the beginning of his mission. A mediating view could be taken that grants the existence of both names early on in Paul's life yet allows for Luke's attempted symbolism in the sense of views no. 2 and 4 (see Riesner 143–146).

18. Paul's Missionary Journeys

The traditional concept of "three missionary journeys" is "driven more by tradition than by inherent structural markers" (DeSilva 358). With this in mind, I included Paul's travel to Rome as a prisoner among the "missionary journeys" since mission in Rome is the stated purpose of Paul's last journey (Acts 23:11) and Luke finishes his book on that note (28:30–31). In addition, Paul witnessed to Felix (Acts 24:24:27), showing incessant missionary zeal even while being in chains. The definition of a "journey" is somewhat stretched by the way we typically conceive of Paul's itinerary. For example, extending the third missionary "journey" all the way to Paul's return in Jerusalem (Acts 21:16) overlooks that Paul was not continuously travelling but stayed in Ephesus for three years (Acts 19:10; 20:31). Wenham and Walton (276–280), therefore, finish the report of the "third journey" with Paul's ministry in Ephesus (Acts 19:41). The change in the prominent coworkers throughout Paul's journeys from Barnabas (last mentioned in 15:39) to Silas (last mentioned in 18:5), Timothy (last mentioned in 20:4) and, finally, Luke might reflect a historical and theological development of the early church as well as of Paul from a predominantly Jewish group of believers to the universal church (though Titus, who remained uncircumcised [Gal. 2:3], is not mentioned in Acts). That the accounts of the journeys are selective is not only evident from the many gaps in the reports, but also from the few lengthy speeches, with one speech each for the major groups of ministry across the first three journeys (Jews, Gentiles, Christians). The dates for these journeys are not absolute and vary from one chronological reconstruction to another (see, for example, Mowery, 227–228).

19. PAUL'S COWORKERS

See Zuck (137) for Paul's hosts and Peerbolte (a:228–230) and Ellis (c) for an alphabetical list of all coworkers, although Ellis does not mention five of Paul's seven travel companions found in Acts 20:4. Paul mentions thirty male and eleven female coworkers (see also chart 80). Most of them were Gentiles and only a handful of those were Jews (see Col. 4:11; also Paul's συγγενεῖς in Rom. 16:7, 11, 21). The chart shows that Paul was not an individualist but worked with a team (see Murray) within which Timothy stands out as the one closest to Paul (see also Phillips 157–189). A difference (of genre?) between Paul's letters and the Dead Sea Scrolls is obvious: While every one of the apostle's letters contains personal names, there is only one of the 870 separate scrolls "that records actual names of members of the Yahad" (Wise, Abegg, Cook 406). And while "the question of whether women lived at Qumran depends largely on the interpretation of the literary sources" (Magness 89), no such uncertainty exists about Paul's team and his churches.

20. ALL CITIES VISITED BY PAUL

For literature see Ramsay (1907), Köster (2004), Meeks (40–50) and Part 4, "Paul's Cities" (pages 153–222), in Wallace and Williams, *The Three Worlds of Paul of Tarsus* (1998). It is not quite clear why Wallace and Williams mention Joppa and Lydda (p.178–179) among "Paul's Cities" since Acts only reports *Peter's* visit to these places (Acts 9–11). Some unusual spelling of cities (e.g., Perge, Attaleia, Ephesos, Kos, Rhodos, Beroea) have also been harmonized with common English translations (e.g., Perga, Attalia, Ephesus, Cos, Rhodes, Berea). Paul visited more cities than those specifically mentioned in Acts and the *Corpus Paulinum*. The book of Acts refers to Paul's ministry in the regions of Phrygia and Galatia without offering names of specific cities (Acts 16:6; 18:23). Also, Paul's letter to Titus presupposes ministry on the island of Crete (Titus 1:5), about which Luke reports nothing. According to Schnabel's calculations (122), Paul traveled more than fifteen thousand miles, and that without modern amenities (vehicles, bridges, highways) and with full exposure to the weather, robbers, animals, lack of food and shelter, etc. (see Richards b:189–200)! There is "no underlying plan" explicitly offered in Acts that explains the details of Paul's itinerary (Peerbolte a:238). He is merely commissioned to be a witness to Gentiles, kings, and Israel (9:15; 22:21). We don't hear of his own desire to go to Rome until the third journey (19:21). There are at least four identifiable factors that influenced the apostle's itinerary:

(A) Persecution occasionally pushed Paul to escape from a city and move on (Acts 14:6; 17:10; also 20:3).

(B) At times, his disciples decided where Paul should go: in Damascus they simply "took Paul" (Acts 9:25, 27) by night to keep him from danger and sent him to Tarsus (9:30); at another occasion they brought him to Antioch (11:26; 15:22). Perhaps Paul visited Cyprus early on during his first journey (13:4) because Barnabas, maybe the leader on this first journey, came from here (4:36) and urged to evangelize his home country (McRay a:113–114).

(C) Paul himself initiates the second and third journey because he wanted to look after his churches (Acts 15:37; 18:23). Various indicators of human strategy are also perceptible.

It is evident that when he had a choice Paul was a Jewish missionary who sought out cities (1) that hosted synagogues (Acts 9:20; 13:5, 13; 14:1; 17:1, 10, 17; 18:4, 19; 19:8) or other Jewish places for assembly and prayer (Acts 16:13, 16) and (2) that were major (provincial) capitals (Ephesus, Athens, Rome) and urban trade centers located along major roads, including Roman colonies (Pisidia Antioch, Iconium, Philippi [πρώτη[ς] μερίδος τῆς Μακεδονίας, Acts 16:12] and Corinth), probably anticipating that converted businessmen and travelers would carry his gospel from there into other parts of the world (Peerbolte a:233–237). Yet Paul did not preach in every large city he passed through (see Acts 17:1, Amphipolis and Apollonia on the *Via Egnatia*; Gill 413–414; there were no synagogues in these cities [McRay b:1232]) nor did he visit every important city there was (e.g., Pergamum, Smyrna, Sardis in Asia and Kassandreia, Dion, and Pella in Macedonia [Gill 405]). Some of these "omissions" can be explained with reference to his coworkers who extended his ministry to cities he never visited (e.g., Colossae and Laodicea [see Col. 2:1; 4:16]; Rome [Rom. 1:10–15]). His avoidance of Asia and Bithynia on the second journey (Acts 16:6–7), the preference of travelling by ship on the third journey, and the bypassing of Ephesus on the way back (Acts 20:16) could be due to heightened concerns about trouble with Roman officials (French 57; Johnson a:143). Having said all this, we still do not know why Paul travelled from the beginning into the west of the empire instead of moving South (Egypt; Ethiopia [Acts 8:27]) or East (Mesopotamia, Parthia [Acts 2:9], India, China), places that did not lack either synagogues or large cities. Scholars have offered different possible explanations (see Wander 181–187 for a review of some views), ranging from (a) the table of the nations (Genesis 10) and its ancient reappropriations (e.g., *A.J.* 1.6) about migration patterns of the Japhethites (Bechard, esp. 385–387; Scott with reference to Rom. 15:19b [Ezek. 5:5], 24, 28), to (b) the ideological map in Isaiah 66:18-21 (Riesner), (c) Hadrian's *Panhellenion* (Nasrallah), or (d) Paul's biographical identity as a "*Greek* speaker … and *Roman* citizen" (Barnett 268). Given his principle of preaching "not where Christ was [already] named" (Rom 15:20), the question might remain open until we consider the other apostles' places of ministry (e.g., Eusebius, *E.H.* 3.1; also Bruce b:315). And maybe Paul learned early on to see himself as a major instrument in fulfilling Jesus' plan for a witness "to the remotest part of the earth" (Acts 1:8). If that phrase refers to Spain (Ellis b), it would not only explain Paul's move to the West from the very beginning of his missionary activity but also help to understand his expressed desire to preach there (Rom. 15:24, 28).

(D) After all these human and rational reasons have been considered, we must notice also what Stange (pp. 56–74) called the "irrational" element in Paul's itinerary: (1) he repeatedly has plans to visit churches but conditions them by saying "if the Lord permits" (Acts 18:21; Rom. 1:10; 15:32; 1 Cor. 4:19; 16:7; Phil. 2:24), thus indicating his expectation of divine guidance and prevention; (2) Paul's travel plans are prevented at times by the Holy Spirit (Acts 16:6, 7) and at other times by Satan (1 Thess. 2:18); (3) they are more often initiated by a revelation (Gal. 2:2), a vision (Acts 16:9–10), a christophany (Acts 23:11) or by the Holy Spirit (Acts 13:2, 4; 19:21–22 [Wenham/Walton 281]; see also the textual additions in Codex D in Acts 19:1 and 20:3). The motives for Paul's movements are thus of varied kinds and the total picture of the apostle is less that of a strategist but more that of a man of principles and pragmatics who operates under the sovereign leadership of God.

21. Major Cities in Paul's Ministry

For most of the information on these cities see the literature referred to in the comments to the previous chart in addition to relevant articles in standard dictionaries. Collins (b:24) and Winter (b:220) both offer this number for the population of ancient Corinth at the time of Paul's visit (yet see Murphy-O'Connor b:31). Trebilco (a:307) assumes an even higher estimate for the population of Ephesus: "between 200,000-250,000." Oakes (a:44–46) offers the total population of Philippi based mostly on the size of the theatre (ca. eight thousand seats). For the city's Roman culture and background see Hellerman's articles. Riesner (199) offers these numbers for the population of ancient Rome in the first century. The estimate about the size of the population in Thessalonica depends on the assumed size of the city (130–200 ha, 500 per ha) and the inclusion or exclusion of surrounding villages (Brocke 72).

22. ALL WOMEN MENTIONED BY AND AROUND PAUL

There is text-critical debate about the gender of the names "Junia" (see the discussion mentioned in the comments to chart 105) and "Nympha" (see Gehring 120). Even apart from the uncertainties surrounding these two names, the glimpses offered in this chart permit us to say that Paul is comfortable around women, be they at the bottom of society (Acts 16:15–18) or rich (Acts 16:14) and prominent (Acts 17:4, 12). He ministers to them, calls them to ministry and recommends them for that purpose (see charts 19, 105). Beyond being a matter of his personality, it is Paul's conviction that God does not favor men over women but invites both into his kingdom (Gal. 3:28).

23. ALL MEN MENTIONED BY AND AROUND PAUL

The list is not absolute because we don't always know with certainty whether the same name in two texts ("Jason") or different yet similar names in two texts (e.g., "Sosipater"/"Sopater," "Lucius"/"Luke") refer to the same person (Ellis c:186). If "Derbe" in Acts 20:4 belongs grammatically to Gaius, then we have three people with the same name in Paul's life. If it belongs to the following person (Timothy), then this could be the same Gaius as the one from Macedonia in Acts 19:29 (see Gillman).

24. SPEECHES OF PAUL IN ACTS

The list of speeches is taken from Soards (1993) and I added Paul and Silas' response to the jailer in 16:31. See also Porter (esp. 126–171) and Lang for a discussion. The word count is based on the Greek text in Nestle-Aland, 27th edition. The total of Paul's words in Acts is 2,741, including 186 words from scattered utterances such as "Who are You, Lord" in 9:5 and "yes" in 22:27 (see 9:5; 13:10–11; 16:18, 28, 37; 18:21; 19:2–4, 21; 20:10; 21:37, 29; 22:25, 27, 29; 23:17).

25. CONTEXTUALIZATION IN PAUL'S MISSIONARY SPEECHES

Fleming (86–88) offers a detailed chart that compares all three speeches while Bechard (ch. 6) describes in fascinating detail the similarities and "contrasting cultural settings" (415) of Paul's speeches in Lystra and Athens, the only two speeches in Acts that are addressed to Gentiles, besides Paul's defenses before Festus and Felix.

26. PAUL'S MIRACLES

For secondary sources on the subject see Alkier, Heininger, Peerbolte (b), and Derickson. For the *Acts of Paul* see Schneemelcher II:213–270. Miracles were part of Paul's life from the very beginning of his ministry to the reported end in Rome. The list of miracles in Acts is not complete: Luke refers to miracles by Paul in Iconium and Malta but does not specify them (Acts 14:3; 15:12; 28:9). He also does not report any miracles in Corinth whereas Paul refers to them in his letters (1 Cor. 2:4; 2 Cor. 12:12). It is telling that while Luke makes every effort to mention Paul's miracles in detail (as equal to Peter), the apostle himself offers only general references to them and hardly bothers to point them out. On the contrary, Paul mentions the sickness of Epaphroditus (Phil. 2:25–27), Timothy (1 Tim. 5:23) and Trophimus (2 Tim. 4:20) which he did not heal (Derickson 308–311). The silence of miracles in the letters has been interpreted both in favor and against a cessationist view (Derickson, esp. 304–305). For one thing, the Christians addressed in most of the letters would have known about Paul's miracles and did not need additional report. Paul also wanted to prevent a superficial attention to outward signs of authority (πρόσωπον, 2 Cor. 10:7) with which false apostles diverted attention from the gospel (2 Cor. 12:11–12; also 2 Thess. 2:9).

27. PAUL'S PRAYERS

"Pray without ceasing" (1 Thess. 5:17)! Paul did not merely commend faithful prayer (also Rom. 12:12, 14; Eph. 6:18; Phil. 4:6–7; Col. 4:2; 1 Tim. 2:1–2; 5:5) but, as the chart demonstrates, lived what he preached. Luke confirms that the apostle was a man of prayer (see Acts 9:11; 13:2–3; 14:23; 16:25; 20:36; 22:17; 28:8). Letters are not liturgies and, consequently, what we read here are not the prayers themselves but "reports about prayers addressed to the letters' readers" (Longenecker 206). As such, they give only indirect insight into Paul's actual and spontaneous communication with God and are loaded with epistolary function (e.g., *inclusio* in 1 Cor. 1:3; 16:23), rhetorical purpose (thanksgivings at the beginning indicate purpose and content of the letter), and reflected theological content. As Paul intercedes for the readers, so he asks for the same (1 Thess. 5:25), specifically that he may be rescued from wicked men (Rom. 15:30–32; 2 Thess. 3:2) and given the chance to visit the church (Philem. 1:22), for his deliverance (2 Cor. 1:10–11; Phil. 1:19), that he may have an opportunity to preach (Col. 4:3–4), and then "with boldness" (Eph. 6:19–20) and success (2 Thess. 3:1). This invitation for reciprocity between the apostle and the readers shows that "Paul continually lived within the flexible exchange of prayer and providence" (Crump 228). Paul also prayed to Jesus, the clearest example of which is found in 2 Corinthians 12:8–9 (see Ostmeyer 81–97). The list mostly stems from Coggan who offers short comments to each prayer. For further studies on the subject see Wiles, Gebauer, R. N. Longenecker, Crump (197–251), Ostmeyer (40–160).

28. NAMES, TITLES, AND METAPHORS FOR PAUL AND HIS MINISTRY

The titles Paul uses for himself speak of his self-perception (see Zuck 24–41 for a general survey). They are dispersed widely throughout his letters, and sometimes various terms appear together, such as "preacher, apostle, and teacher" in 1 Timothy 2:7 and 2 Timothy 1:11. While Paul refers to the gifts of an evangelist (Eph. 4:11; 2 Tim. 4:5), a pastor (Eph. 4:11) and a prophet (e.g., 1 Cor. 12:28; see Gal. 1:15–16; Keay 152–153), he never calls himself one (yet see the verb "to announce good news" [εὐαγγελίζω] applied to Paul's ministry in Acts 14:7, 21; 16:10; 17:18; Rom. 1:15; 15:20; 1 Cor. 1:17; 9:16, 18; 15:1, 2; 2 Cor. 10:16; 11:7; Gal. 1:8–9, 16, 23; 4:13; Eph. 3:8; see also καταγγέλλω in Acts 13:5, 38; 1 Cor. 9:14; Col. 1:28; etc.). Although he uses "Lord" (κύριος) sometimes for God (e.g., Rom. 14:11), human slave-masters (e.g., Eph. 6:5, 9) and mostly for Jesus (e.g., Rom. 1:4), Paul never addresses himself this way (see 1 Cor. 7:10, 12, 25; also 2 Cor. 1:24). Winter observed with regard to Romans 12–15 that Paul also avoids terms such as "member," "friend," and "patron" / "client" and with it their ancient Roman associations of inequality (Winter a:94–95; also Lampe a:493). On the contrary, Paul frequently employs terms such as "brother" (e.g., 1 Cor. 1:1), "fellow-worker" (e.g., Rom. 16:9), and "fellow soldier" (e.g., Phil. 2:25) which is evidence of "non-hierarchical language, within a framework that accommodates leaders and led" (Clarke b:95; also Peerbolte a:230; A. Long). Thus, the titles used, as well as those absent, nurture an *imitatio Christi* in which, contrary to cultural norms, the strong have obligations towards the weak. Yet, at times he has to insist on apostolic authority above that of prophets (e.g., 1 Cor. 12:28; 14:37) and sometimes Paul calls himself a "father" who threatens to come with a "stick" (1 Cor. 4:15, 21) and to whom the Philippians owe service (Phil. 2:30; see 2:22; Capes 45). Considering the democratic and the authoritarian ends of a spectrum, Paul's leadership style is found mostly around the middle (Best 11–34; Lampe a:500–501; Bartchy 170–178). For comprehensive discussions of Paul's metaphors see David Williams (1999) and Gerber (2005). See M. Mitchell (chs. 4–5) for the metaphor "abortion" in 1 Cor 15:8.

29. TRACKING PAUL'S OPPONENTS

The first obvious observation from this chart is that every one of Paul's canonical letters mentions opposition either to Paul, or to the church, or to both. Even more "theological" letters such as Romans and Ephesians were written under the pressure of a hostile environment (Rom. 15:31; Eph. 3:13; 4:1). Unfortunately, it is seldom clear who exactly the enemies were and what they were upset about (see the next chart plus comments). Easy solutions such as finding one opponent that fits the references in all letters, be they Jewish Christians (F. B.

Baur) or Gnostics (Schmithals), have not found much support (Sumney c:7–12; W. S. Campbell 515). Sumney's research offers helpful access to the debates about the opponents' identity.

30. Accusations against, and Misunderstandings of, Paul

For a discussion of the accusations mentioned in the book of Acts see Reimer (214–220), Tajra, and Omerzu (a:111–501). Although there must have been many more accusations and misunderstandings than those listed here, it is difficult to clearly identify them in the apostle's own letters. Attempts of mirror-reading the texts in order to find the readers' or opponents' arguments and accusations reflected in Paul's words are loaded with difficulties. Does the question in Romans 6:1 reflect a libertine attitude of believers in Rome? Does Paul's use of Abraham against circumcision in Galatians 3–4, for example, indicate that his Galatian opponents themselves supported circumcision with reference to the patriarch (see Wilson 58–59)? Paul never addresses the opponents directly and we know of their accusations only through Paul's *polemical* response (see Barclay 1987).

31. Paul's Sufferings

For literature see Bloomquist, Cunningham, Fitzgerald, Fredrickson, Hafemann (1990, 1993), Pobee. Paul mentions his sufferings especially often in the Corinthian correspondence (1 Cor. 4:10–13; 2 Cor. 4:7–12; 6:4–10; 11:23–29; 12:10). Scholars debate whether Paul makes positive use of a Greco-Roman "philosophic convention of hardship lists" (Fredrickson 179; Fitzgerald) according to which the "wise sage" demonstrates virtue and divine approval through perseverance in adversity, or whether Paul's sufferings prove to be part of the gospel's scandal which subverts values of his day (Shi 15–17, 188–265; see 2 Cor. 11:23). Beyond the question of rhetorical purpose, this list of suffering speaks about a man who was "in danger every hour" (1 Cor. 15:30) of his Christian life and who faced the daily possibility of violent death. More than half of the sufferings mentioned in this chart were inflicted on him by other people. And without exception, all of Paul's canonical letters mention human enmity against the apostle in one way or another (see chart 29). From the slanderous report in Romans 3:8 to the imprisonment in Philemon (see verses 1, 10, 13, 23), Paul wrote every word under the fire of heated opposition. Thus, quite contrary to the apostle's growing reputation in following centuries, he experienced in his own lifetime that "God has exhibited us apostles as last of all, as men condemned to death" (1 Cor. 4:9). According to Luke, such a burden was God's plan for the apostle from the beginning (Acts 9:16). While the chart focuses mostly on physical hardships, Paul also suffered emotionally. He "despaired of life" due to afflictions in Asia (2 Cor. 1:8). He grieved (2 Cor. 2:1), had "anguish of heart" and "many tears" (2 Cor. 2:4) following a painful visit to the Corinthian church (see 2 Cor. 2:1–11; 7:12). There was "great sorrow" and "unceasing grief" concerning persistent Jewish opposition to his gospel (Rom. 9:2). The rhetorical purpose of opening his heart to the churches (see 2 Cor. 6:11) lies, at least partially, in the affirmation of their common bond. The sharing of suffering and the related emotions "is the necessary condition for true friendship" (Fredrickson 182). The bold expressions of affection offer proof of unity between the apostle and the Christian communities.

32. Why Did Luke Finish Acts without Reporting about Paul's End?

For a brief review of the various explanations see Omerzu c:128–144, who herself concludes that the abrupt ending of Acts reflects Luke's lack of traditions about Paul's death (c:152–156). The three categories of explanations are not airtight divisions but overlap in meaning.

Luke finishes Luke-Acts and his portrait of Paul with the apostle imprisoned in Rome, waiting for his trial. While the last verses don't offer a closing of Paul's life, they do present a climax for Luke-Acts: The long quotation of Isaiah 6:9–10 in response to Jewish rejection (Acts 28:26–27) and the positive note on Gentile reception of the Gospel (Acts 28:28) culminate Luke's efforts in explaining the historical shift from a very Jewish Jesus (Luke 2:21–52) to a mostly Gentile church. And the finishing reference to Paul "preaching the kingdom of God and teaching concerning the Lord Jesus Christ with all openness, unhindered" (Acts 28:31) fulfills the repeated expression of divine necessity that Paul "must witness at Rome also" (Acts 23:11; also 19:21; 27:24). Luke has prepared the reader for a negative outcome of Paul's trial, given the hints that indicate inevitable suffering (Acts 14:22), if not martyrdom (Acts 20:23-24, 38) in the likeness of Jesus (Acts 21:11; Luke 18:32; see chart 13). Such clear indicators make it unlikely that Luke intentionally omitted Paul's death because it would have compromised his pro-Roman apologetic (so Holloway; see Omerzu c:135 in response to such a view).

33. TRADITIONS OF PAUL'S MISSIONARY JOURNEY TO SPAIN

See Meinardus for a brief discussion of these traditions, including local folklore from Spain of the eighth and tenth century. Paul himself merely describes plans for traveling to Spain. We have no certain information from himself or any other source of the first century that he actually made this journey. Clement's vague reference to the "extreme limit of the west" is often understood as a reference to Spain, but not unanimously so. The certainty of such a visit increases with the distance of time to the apostle's life.

34. TRADITIONS OF PAUL'S MARTYRDOM

For I Clement see Holmes 51–53; for "The Acts of Paul" see Schneemelcher II:262–263; for Clement of Alexandria see *The Anti-Nicene Fathers*, VII:486; for Tertullian see Eusebius, trans. K. Lake, I:181 and Jurgens, *Faith of the Early Fathers*, 152; for Lactantius, see *The Anti-Nicene Fathers*, VII:120 and 301-302; for Eusebius see trans. K. Lake, I:181–182 and 191. These traditions from the late second century about Paul's martyrdom under Nero in Rome are sometimes contested. Relying on traditions about Paul's journey to Spain (e.g., Rom 15:28; *1 Clem.* 5.7; Muratorian Canon 38–39), Barnes argues that "Paul was tried and executed by a provincial governor in Spain." Later, Catholic Christians transferred his place of martyrdom to Rome in order to support "the concept of apostolic succession" (35). See Horn for a discussion about historical, theological and literary aspects of Paul's death.

Part C: Paul's Letters

35. MANUSCRIPTS (PAPYRI AND UNCIALS) OF PAUL'S LETTERS

See Aland's *Kurzgefaßte Liste* for the papyri (3–16, only until P 99) and the majuscules (pages 19–44). The *Institut für neutestamentliche Textforschung* in Münster, Germany, provides supplementary updates for the papyri at http://www.uni-muenster.de/NTTextforschung/. A list of the papyri of Paul's letters in the *canonical* order is offered in Comfort, Barrett 8–9.

36. SECRETARIES, COWRITERS, AND CARRIERS

The only explicit reference to a named secretary is found in Rom 16:22 (Tertius). Yet, the statement found at the end of four letters that Paul wrote the greeting with his "own hand" could indicate that someone else wrote the rest of the letter, although the phrase could also legally function as a guarantee (Arzt-Grabner 240–243; Dunn f:339–340). Paul did not use a secretary because of illiteracy but because it was the custom (Richards b:61). The influence of the secretary in ancient letter writing varies from that of a (1) "transcriber" to whom the letter is simply dictated to a (2) "contributor" who can make "minor editorial changes" or even offer "significant contributions" (Richards b:74) and finally the (3) "composer" who used a "set form, vocabulary and style" to write stereotyped letters based on guidelines (Richards b:75). Paul's use of such help may fall somewhere in between the transcriber and the composer (Richards b:92–93).

Whether the cowriters were actually involved in composing and writing the letters is difficult to determine. In 1 Corinthians, for example, Paul uses "the singular Greek pronoun for 'I' eighty six times in the letter" (Terry 3), thus highlighting his own thoughts as a single individual writer. Yet, Murphy O'Connor (e:1–10) seeks to show that the sudden shift from "I" to "we" in 1 Cor. 1:18–31 and 2:6–16 demonstrates Sosthenes' perceptible contribution to the writing of the letter. Paul might mention cowriters also to enhance their reputation and thereby improve their opportunities for ministry. Yet, at times they may also have served as secretaries (so Godet 76). In this case, their absence in 1–2 Timothy and Titus could have contributed to "certain linguistic and lexical peculiarities" (Towner b:87) in comparison with the other letters of Paul. Although Timothy is present when Paul writes Romans (Rom. 16:21), he is not mentioned as a co-author, maybe because he was not known to the Roman congregations (Klauck c:301). Manuscripts of later centuries (minuscules) often added the name of the supposed carrier or secretary, some of which found their way (through the Textus Receptus) into the King James Version (see Comfort 480–81, 529, 555, 601, 618, 639, 649, 656–57, 691–92).

With the exception of Galatians and 1–2 Thessalonians, Paul chose carriers from his own team. This practice saved money and guaranteed additional help in understanding the letter if needed. For more information on their role and their task of traveling long distances see Richards' discussion (b:188–209).

37. GROUPING PAUL'S LETTERS

The Book of Acts mentions four of Paul's imprisonments (Philippi ch. 16, Jerusalem ch. 21, Caesarea ch. 23, and Rome ch. 28), some of which are possible provenances for the so-called "prison letters." Not all scholars distinguish between disputed and pseudepigraphical letters (see Beker 3, note).

38. HOW MANY LETTERS DID PAUL WRITE?

Even when one credits all thirteen letters from Romans to Philemon as authentically Pauline, an answer to this question remains impossible. Paul mentions a now lost letter to the Laodiceans (Col. 4:16), and although some suppose that it is either the same as our Ephesians (Marcion; Harnack) or that it was merged with Colossians (Boismard), most consider the letter simply lost. Other lost letters by Paul are mentioned in 1 Corinthians 5:9 and 2 Corinthians 2:4 and 7:8. As can be seen from chart 41, some early collections of the New Testament writings considered the letter to the Hebrews to be written by Paul (including Eusebius, *Church History* III.3; see also Harding 134–135). Furthermore, partition theories of 1 Corinthians, 2 Corinthians, Philippians, and 1–2 Thessalonians would, if found to be true, add substantially to the number of writings by the apostle (see Jervis 57–68; Weima/Porter 64–68). While some rejected the authenticity of at least some of the thirteen canonical letters as Pauline already in the second century (Marcion rejected 1–2 Timothy and Titus), the church usually held all canonical letters as authentically Pauline until the nineteenth century. Schleiermacher is generally credited with having been the first to question Pauline authorship of the Pastoral Epistles in 1807 (see Polhill a:398). Ferdinand C. Baur wrote in 1845 that it is "the result of *recent* criticism" to question the authenticity of some letters (245; italics added). The radical Dutch position was held by Allard Pierson, S. A. Naber, Abraham D. Loman, W. C. Van Manen, and G. A. Van Den Bergh Van Eysinga (see also Völter whose conclusions are only slightly less radical). According to Detering's extensive review (1992), Allard Pierson's *Bergrede* from 1878 began this total rejection of Pauline authorship and it basically ceased with the death of Van Eysinga in 1957. The majority of Pauline scholars today affirms Pauline authorship only for seven letters: Ephesians, Colossians, 2 Thessalonians, 1–2 Timothy and Titus are often called "deutero-Pauline" (see Krodel 1993). The strength of the consensus about these letters' inauthenticity diminishes from the Pastorals (very strong; so already Marcion, see Tertullian, *Marc.* 5.21) to Ephesians (strong), Colossians (less strong) to 2 Thessalonians (weak) (see Crossan/Reed a:106; Aune b:344). The five criteria for evaluating authenticity are the following: "internal data, format, style, vocabulary, and thought/theology" (Brown 588).

This denial of Pauline authorship for the so-called "disputed" letters remains in my eyes speculative, despite the majority support it receives. Knowing that the subject deserves deeper and longer discussion, I suggest, in all brevity, seven observations for this position: (1) The criteria for measuring authenticity are not used consistently. Hoehner took the five criteria, applied them to Galatians and concluded that Paul could not have written this letter. Yet, Galatians is unanimously understood as genuinely Pauline while Ephesians, a letter with a similar word count and vocabulary, is understood to be pseudepigraphic by the same standards. Hoehner finds that the consensus position has accepted a "double standard" (Hoehner b:168) which simply exempts the "undisputed" letters from the same rigorous application of criteria for authenticity that render the "disputed" letters inauthentic. (2) *Stylistic* differences between disputed and undisputed letters do not outweigh "significant stylistic differences" (Johnson a:60, 64) between undisputed letters such as 1 and 2 Corinthians (Wright d:18-19; Stuckenbruck 118; see also Turner's [80] division of Paul's letters into four groups of differing style [excluding the Pastorals]). The problem is here one of insufficient data for making a decision about authorship based on vocabulary or style. Using the higher number of hapax legomena in the Pastoral Epistles as evidence for pseudepigraphy (Harrison 1921), for example, "fails to give adequate attention to the smallness of the sample and the wide variations in the undisputed Pauline corpus" (Johnson a:69; also Guthrie b:7-8; O'Donnell 85-101, 387-394). Leaning on Yule, a statistician, Hoehner explains that we need samples of at least "10,000 words similar in length and content" for "proper comparison" (Hoehner b:169 n.37; also Radday 13). Yet Romans, the longest letter of Paul, only counts 7114 words. Establishing objective criteria of style for differentiating between disputed and undisputed letters are thus hard to come by (also Metzger b:91-94; Mounce cxii-cxvii; Herzer a:1280; Ebner/Schreiber 459-460). (3) Similarly, *theological* differences between disputed and undisputed letters do not outweigh significant diversity between undisputed letters or significant diversity within one undisputed letter such as Romans (see chart 79; Johnson a:82). The answer to the question: 'when does diversity between two thoughts constitute inherent *complexity*, natural *development* within Paul's theology or even post-Pauline *departure* from him?' depends quite often on the scholar's personal imagination. What is coherent for the majority of Pauline scholars is still inconsistent for E. P. Sanders and Heikki Räisänen. And what is a departure from Paul for the majority still makes sense as Pauline theology for Ridderbos and Schreiner. The consensus answer also requires the ability to say that we have *all* puzzle pieces of Paul's theology contained in the seven undisputed letters, which strikes me as overconfident. Here as before, truly *objective* criteria are hard to come by. (4) Frequent speculations about "interpolations" in undisputed letters show that theological differences between disputed and undisputed letters can only be maintained by purging the latter from anything that disturbs the presupposed portrait of Paul who is often conceived of as a charismatic, pro-Jewish, egalitarian and social radical (Elliott [25-28] proposes these interpolations in the undisputed letters: 1 Thess 2:14-16; 1 Cor 14:34-35 [also Epp a:15-20; Pervo 47]; Rom 13:1-7; also Crossan/Reed xiii, see Fisk 295-296). Pauline scholarship today is in this regard dangerously close to Schweitzer's dictum of 19th century Jesus research which had the tendency to find what it was looking for (see Johnson a:56, 58). (5) The overemphasis on differences often leads to oversight of similarities between Pauline and "deutero-Pauline" letters such as those between Colossians and Galatians (chart 64), Colossians and Philemon (chart 75), 1 Timothy and 1 Corinthians (chart 68), and 2 Timothy and Philippians (chart 69). In his commentary on Philemon (2000), which he affirms as authentically Pauline, Markus Barth writes, for example, that "just as Ephesians and Colossians are twins, so also Colossians and PHM [Philemon] bear signs of stemming from the same author, the same place and situation, at about the same time" (126; see also Knox 1938). Yet, while Colossians is considered deutero-Pauline, Philemon is never classified as such. Fee expresses a justified surprise in this regard: "It remains one of the singular mysteries in NT scholarship that so many scholars reject Pauline authorship of Colossians yet affirm the authenticity of Philemon" (b:289 n. 2). (6) Until we can limit the use of secretaries with *reasonable certainty* to the function of mere transcribers, large stylistic variances can be explained with reference to their demonstrable influence on Paul's letters (see chart 36; Richards b:154–155), including Ephesians (Turner 84), Colossians (Moo b:31) and the Pastoral Epistles (Bruce b:443–444, Ellis e:661, Towner b:86–87). (7) The common perception among modern scholars that pseudepigraphy was an acceptable, maybe even respectable, way of honoring a deceased figure of authority not only trivializes the act of deception but lacks historical warrants and runs into a *non-sequitur*: just because pseudepigraphy was widespread in antiquity, it does not follow that it was an acceptable literary convention (see 2 Thess. 2:2; *Bapt.* 17.5; see Frenschkowski; Guthrie a:1011–1027; Wilder; Herzer; Marshall reviews recent scholarship on this point [c:288–292]).

Considering these and other weaknesses in the consensus position, variables in our understanding, and open questions, it should not surprise that plausible arguments for Pauline authorship for all "disputed" letters by respectable scholars continue to appear even in prominent places of scholarship. The Anchor Bible Commentary series, for example, offers volumes on Ephesians (Barth 1974, a:36–61, 170, 224, 244, 250, 335, 382), Colossians (Barth 1995, b:114-125), 1-2 Thessalonians (Malherbe 2000), and 1–2 Timothy (Johnson 2001) that, if not argue for Pauline authorship, raise serious objections against considering the "disputed" letters inauthentic.

39. Other Literature Ascribed to Paul

See Meeks and Fitzgerald (2007) for a commented collection of these writings in English translation and Harding (138-144) for a brief introduction to some of them. The most discussed and most important of these works are the *Acts of Paul* (see Howe, Bauckham 1993, Bovon) which have been linked to the canonical Paul in various ways (Büllesbach reviews seven different proposals). 2 Thessalonians 2:2 testifies that opponents of Paul wrote letters in his name even during his lifetime. That problem continued into the second century, as the Muratorian Canon testifies: "There is current also (an epistle) to the Laodiceans, another to the Alexandrians, forged in Paul's name for the sect of Marcion, and several others, which cannot be received in the catholic Church; for it will not do to mix gall with honey" (Schneemelcher I:36).

40. Paul's Letters: Total Numbers of Words and Vocabulary

For the numbers of words see Klauck (c:331 n. 24), for the stichoi see Aune (b:345), for the vocabulary see Morgenthaler (164) and for the pages see Roller (38). The (rounded up) numbers about the pages per letter are an estimated *minimum* since they consider a rather high average of 450 words per page. "Stichoi" is the Greek word for "lines" which was "a unit of measure by which the length of manuscripts was calculated, by which copyists were paid for their work … and by which the commercial value of a manuscript was determined" (Aune b:449). All of Paul's letters make up a little less than twenty-five percent of the New Testament (total 137,332 words). A strict division into letters to churches and to individuals is somewhat blurred by the fact that each of the "private" letters "concludes with blessings in the plural" (Harding 133 n.12; see the plural "you" [ὑμῶν] in 1 Tim. 6:21; 2 Tim. 4:22; Titus 3:15; Philem. 1:25). The canonical arrangement is clearly organized in descending order of length, with the exception of the shorter Galatians preceding the longer Ephesians. Most Greek letters in antiquity average between 130 and 200 words (Roller 34–35), with very few exceeding beyond 1,000 words (one letter allegedly from Plato counts even 8,896 words; Roller 35). Cicero's Latin letters are usually longer and average 294 words, the largest one counting 4,530 words (Roller 360–361). According to Seneca, a letter should not be longer than one page ("ought not fill the reader's left hand" *Ep.* 45.13, cited in Klauck c:51). It is evident that by any means of comparison with ancient standards of writing, Paul's letters exceed the norm, including his shortest letter (Roller 37). His letter to the Romans is "one of the longest real letters from antiquity" (Klauck c:301). Beyond the length, A. T. Robertson characterized Paul's letters as "the most personal and the most powerful writing of antiquity. … He is abrupt, paradoxical, bold, antithetical, now like a torrent, now like a summer brook" and "in Ro. 8 and 1 Cor. 13 he reaches the elevation and dignity of Plato" (Robertson 129).

41. Various Arrangements of Paul's Letters

See Capes 286; Keck and Furnish 53, Parker 249–256. Romans is given in bold print to highlight the shifting position of Paul's largest letters from one list to another. Hebrews is shaded to make its presence and absence among the lists quickly visible. The Sahidic Canon is represented by Codex Chester-Beatty A from around AD 600. With the exception of the Corinthian letters, Galatians and Romans, the Muratorian Canon follows the order of P[46]. Dahl (a:154) argues that the author of Muratori followed an early canonical list and repositioned the three letters to improve the list's chronology. Much of the early Egyptian church considered Hebrews to be Pauline (see also Clement in Eusebius, *H.E.* 6.14; for modern proponents see Farrar 1891 and Reymond 2003). The oldest extant manuscripts (01, A, B., D) place Hebrews in the middle of the Pauline letters. If the symbolism of the number 7 (14 letters as 2x7) was the decisive reason is less clear (so Beker 27, Schmithals 255, Klauck c:331). Eusebius also mentions that the Roman church never accepted Pauline authorship of Hebrews (*H.E.* 3.3), a position supported with good reasons (Anderson 436–437). Tertullian (ca. 150–220 AD) ascribed Hebrews even to Barnabas (Tertullian, *Modesty*, 20.2). Our modern arrangement goes back to late Byzantine manuscripts via Erasmus (Trobisch 24–25) and "reflects the ambiguity regarding the relationship of Hebrews to the Pauline tradition" (J. W. Thompson 198).

42. Formal Structural Components of Paul's Letters

For discussions of these formal components see Roetzel 51–66, O'Brien 550–553, Polhill a:122–126, and especially Jervis 69–157 with more detailed charts on individual parts. *Superscriptio*, *Adscriptio* and *Salutatio* are formal rhetorical terms frequently used by scholars today. The presence of a salutation and a subscription are the most consistent formal components in each of Paul's letters (Jervis 40). While Jervis discusses the "apostolic parousia" in a chapter separate from the "conclusion," it appears at the *end* of the letter often enough to justify its inclusion in this *last* component (exceptions are indicated with parentheses). A "prescript" contains the "formal features that introduce ancient letters" (Aune b:372) while the "preface" (or "proem" from Greek *prooimion*) refers to the "introduction, preamble, preface, beginning" of a letter (Aune b:367). Aune offers a helpful chart that compares the prescripts of letters from the New Testament and Ignatius (Aune b:373–376).

A comparison of these formal structural components yields rich results for the understanding of the individual letter, especially when Paul deviates from his norm. It is a telling silence, for example, that of all letters to churches, only 2 Corinthians and Galatians do not include a word of thanks, prayer or praise in their opening section. Furthermore, while all letters to churches address the believers as "saints," such a descriptor is missing in Galatians. The prescript of Romans, on the other hand, stands out because of various unique features (Jervis 72–83) such as its extraordinary length, thereby "seeking to establish credibility" with an audience that has not met him in person (Jervis 78). The thanksgiving in 1 Corinthians 1:4–9 is remarkable because "Paul singles out the Corinthians' gift of speech and knowledge and that they do not fall short in any grace-gift (*charisma*), but he omits any mention of their love (contrast Phil. 1:9; Col. 1:4; 1 Thess. 1:3; 2 Thess. 1:3; Philem. 1:5) or work (contrast Phil. 1:6; Col. 1:10; 1 Thess. 1:3; 2 Thess. 1:11). Both appear to be wanting in the Corinthian church" (Garland 31). The opening of Philippians is highly anomalous since only here does Paul greet the leaders of the church with their formal title "overseers and deacons" (Phil. 1:1). On the other hand, Paul calls himself and Timothy "slaves" without adding the title "apostle," thus modeling from the outset what he will ask later, that "with humility of mind let each of you regard one another as more important than yourselves" (Phil. 2:3; see Hellerman d:783).

43. *Hapax Legomena* in Paul's Letters

The numbers are taken from Aune (b:345; Words), Aland (449–460; Hapax) and Morgenthaler (164; Vocabulary). Their presence in *each* of Paul's letters demonstrates the individual character of their content shaped by the specific situation of author and audience. Every letter of Paul is unique and differs from all the others in vocabulary, style, and means of expression. Paul "was not a static but a creative thinker" (Hoehner a:52). Using the frequency of *hapax legomena* for conclusions about authorship fails due to insufficient statistical data (see O'Donnell 85–101, 387–394).

44. Figures of Speech in the Letters of Paul

The figures of speech, definitions as well as references, were selected from a variety of sources such as Bullinger, Bühlmann/Scherer, Aune (b), Longenecker's monograph or commentaries by Fee, Garland, the *Dictionary of Paul and His Letters*, etc. See also Tolmie's impressive list of "Rhetorical Techniques" found just in the letter to the Galatians alone (249–256) and Dodson's discussion of personification in Romans. The examples for each figure of speech are not exhaustive. And some figures of speech such as paranomasia can only be identified in the original Greek language. The likelihood that Paul reached the upper levels of formal education is estimated by some as very low (Forbes 151) and by others as very "clear" (Hock a:209; Witherington b:94-98, d:2 ["in the upper one to two percent of the population in education"]). One could read Paul's self-deprecation of being "unskilled in speech" (ἰδιώτης τῷ λόγῳ, 2 Cor. 11:6) and his profession as a tent-maker (Acts 18:3) as an indication of the former. Yet his enemies assess his letters as "weighty and strong" (βαρεῖαι καὶ ἰσχυραί, 2 Cor. 10:10), which indicates skills of speech beyond the elementary level. This long list of figures of speech certainly adds support to this assumption. His manual labor could indicate a loss of status after his conversion (Hock a:218 n. 1, b:14-18), or simply a freely chosen pragmatic source of income for an itinerant preacher that enables Paul to reject financial support (2 Cor. 11:7-11; 12:13-14; 1 Thess. 2:9) in order to avoid awkward obligations towards patrons (see Omerzu a:47). Furthermore, Paul dares to take on his own defense when being accused by a skilled orator (ῥήτωρ) before the governor Felix (Acts 24:1-21). When explicitly referring to his own education (Gal. 1:14), he mentions that he excelled above his contemporaries (see Thiselton a:23-29 for a fuller discussion of Paul's socioeconomic status).

45-50. Paul's OT Quotations and Allusions

Apart from a few additions, the data for the lists of OT quotations and allusions was taken from Appendix IV in *Novum Testamentum Graece*, 27th edition. Paul relies repeatedly on the Septuagint, the Greek translation of the Hebrew Old Testament (Roetzel 11-12, Waaler 51). There are no quotations from fifteen OT books, and no allusions from nine OT books. The sources of some citations are unclear (1 Cor. 2:9; 9:10; 1 Tim. 5:18). Some of the allusions listed are questionable, such as the one to Isaac (Genesis 22) in Romans 8:32 (see Schwartz 263-265). The Paul of Acts is making ample use of the Old Testament as well, using Scripture for Christology (Ps. 2:7; Isa. 55:3; Ps. 16:10; Hab. 1:5 in 13:32-42), for describing the character of his ministry (Isa. 49:6 in Acts 13:46-47), for confronting pagan apotheosis in Lystra and Derbe (Ex. 20:11 and Ps. 146:6 in 14:14-15)—thus showing an orthodox spirit of Torah obedience (Ex. 22:27 in 23:4-5) and accusing the disbelief of his contemporaries (Isa. 6:9 in 28:25-27). Paul himself sometimes introduces his quotation with a formula, such as "it is written" (i.e., Rom. 1:17). But often enough his mind (maybe unconsciously) makes use from a (memorized) treasure of Scripture without pause for explicit introduction (i.e., Rom. 2:6 quotes Prov. 24:12; Ps. 62:13; Rom. 11:34-35 quotes Isa. 40:13; Job 41:3). Beside these more obvious quotations and allusions of the Old Testament, the reader of Paul's letters needs to be prepared for additional formative influence of the Jewish Scriptures on major lines of thinking. Rosner (1999, 177-180; also Ciampa/Rosner 695-752, esp. 709) and Waaler (54-71), for example, have demonstrated the many links between 1 Corinthians 5-10 and the book of Deuteronomy (see, for example, the *Shema* in Deut. 6:1-4 and 1 Cor. 8:1-6)—a connection that is not obvious when looking at the biblical text, at this chart, or other lists of Paul's OT quotations and allusions. Although Philippians, Colossians, 1 Thessalonians, 2 Thessalonians, Titus, and Philemon contain no quotation from (or even an allusion to) the Old Testament, subtle allusions to the Hebrew Bible in each of them except Philemon merit these letters' inclusion in the *Commentary on the New Testament Use of the Old Testament* (2007; see Silva 635, Beetham).

For Paul, the Old Testament has direct bearing on the present time (1 Cor. 10:11; Rom. 4:23-24; 15:4). He says explicitly that it was written "for us" (1 Cor. 9:9-10; 10:6, 11) and introduces citations repeatedly with "the Lord says" (1 Cor. 14:21; Rom. 12:19; see 2 Tim. 3:16-17) (Stuhlmacher 252). Paul makes creative use of typological (see τύπος in Rom. 5:14; 1 Cor. 10:6; also 9:8-10) and allegorical (see ἀλληγορέω in Gal. 4:24) interpretations of the Old Testament. Yet, the biggest surprise in studying the apostle's use of the Old Testament is the "puzzling shift" of meaning (Hays b:1). In Romans 10:1-8, Paul pitches Leviticus 18:5 against Deuteronomy 30:11-14, saying that the former speaks about a righteousness based on the law while the latter supports a righteousness based on faith (see Evans a:335-336; Bekken 2007). First Corinthians 10:4 identifies the rock in the wilderness with Christ and in Galatians 3-4 Paul uses the story of Abraham (esp. Gen. 15:6 in Gal. 3:6; also Rom. 4:3) to argue against circumcision, although Abraham himself was given circumcision as a sign of God's covenant with him (Gen. 17; see now Schliesser 2007). In addition, Paul repeatedly reverses roles: The Old Testament text speaks of Yahweh, but Paul applies it to Christ (Joel 2:23 [3:5 LXX] in Rom. 10:13). Or the OT speaks of

Gentiles, and the apostle refers it to Israel (Isa. 52:5 in Rom. 2:24) and vice versa (Hos. 2:25 in Rom. 9:25–26; Hays [b:67] calls this example one of "scandalous inversion"). In a "shocking reversal," Paul "associates the Hagar-Ishmael-slavery symbolic complex not with the Gentiles but with Sinai and the Law" (Hays b:114). Some of these theological reversals have precedents in the Old Testament itself (see Grech 225 with reference to Isa. 19:19–25 and Ex. 3:7–9; 8:16–24). Interest in studying Paul's use of Scripture has increased since the 1980s, using theological, historical, literary, rhetorical, and social scientific angles on the subject (Stanley 4–7). Since 2005, "The Paul and Scripture Seminar" of the Society of Biblical Literature offers a platform for bringing the various approaches into a dialogue (see Porter, Stanley 2008). Additional challenges arise when one compares the use of an OT text in Paul with that of another writer of the New Testament. Genesis 15:6 is cited by Paul in the service of justification by faith as opposed to justification by works of the law (Rom. 4:3) whereas James uses the same text in order to argue for justification by works (James 2:23–24; see chart 109). Habakkuk 2:4 is used in Romans 1:17 and Galatians 3:11 as a proof text for Paul's gospel of justification by faith, whereas it is used in Hebrews 10:38–39 to encourage perseverance and warn of apostasy.

51-52. PAUL'S INTERTESTAMENTAL ALLUSIONS

The data was taken from Appendix IV in *Novum Testamentum Graece*, 27th edition. See also Evans (a:378–395). Maybe the most frequently observed parallels between Paul and intertestamental literature are the frequent echoes of Wisdom of Solomon in Romans 1, culminating in the conclusion that the sin of idolatry is "the source and cause and end of every evil" (Wis. 14:27 and Rom. 1:24, 26, 28; see Schreiner d:523; Witherington h:63; Dodson 2008).

53. ROMANS: A SNAPSHOT

For a detailed defense of Romans 16 as an "integral part of the letter" see Das 10–23 (for another view see Comfort 477–480). For the counting of house churches in Romans 16 see Lampe (b:146–147). For the diatribe style see Watson (1993). Paul wrote this letter late in the 50s on his last missionary journey (see the reference to collection for Jerusalem in Rom. 15:25–27 and Acts 24:17). The structure is my proposal and suggests that the first five chapters are driven by Paul's emphasis on God's ethnic impartiality regarding sin and salvation. The Jews are as much sinners as the Gentiles and, since justification happens "apart from the Law" (3:21), the Gentiles are as much objects of God's salvation as the Jews: "For there is no partiality with God" (2:11), "there is no distinction" (3:22), they "are all under sin" (3:9). There is a difference of order (Jews first, then Greeks; 1:16; 2:9–10), but not of outcome (judgment) or opportunity (grace). The follow-up questions by a Jewish interlocutor, as expressed in Romans 3:1–8, determine the development of Romans 6–11 (so also Penna 60–89): First, if Jews are as liable for their sins in God's judgment just as Gentiles are (so Romans 2), do they have no advantage over Gentiles whatsoever (Rom 3:1–2)? And if that is so, does that "not nullify the faithfulness of God" (3:3)? The short answers in 3:2 and 3:4 are elaborated in Romans 9–11. Second, if the Law is irrelevant for justification, does obedience to it matter at all, or is anarchy the logical conclusion (Rom 3:5–8)? Paul's answers in 3:6 and 3:8 are expanded in Romans 6–8. The parenetic section in Romans 12–16 picks up the concerns of anarchy and impartiality in an inverted order. The principles of lawful living in Romans 6–8 are translated into specific Christian conduct (Romans 12–13). And *God's* impartiality between Jews and Gentiles (Romans 1–5) is translated into *Christian* impartiality between the weak and the strong (Romans 14–15:13) and demonstrated (1) by Paul himself, a Jewish missionary for Gentile believers (15:14–24), (2) by a collection of Gentile Christians for Jewish believers in Jerusalem (15:25–31), and (3) by a long list of greetings whose thirty-five names include Jews and Greeks, slave and free, male and female (Clarke 2002). The three purposes given for Romans feed into each other (Fisk 319–321). This particular defense of the Gospel aids in solving the house churches' disunity and lays the groundwork for future cooperation with Paul's mission in Spain.

54. Key Words in Romans

Instead of simply listing all terms alphabetically, the three groupings of the key words are offered as a guide for further study. The terms "cross" and "crucifixion" are strikingly absent (except συσταυρόω in 6:6). While Paul's theology in 1 Corinthians and Galatians depends on Jesus' death as a crucified one (e.g., 1 Cor. 1:23; Gal. 3:10, 13), Paul emphasizes in Romans the physical (death) and soteriological benefits of the crucifixion.

55. 1 Corinthians: A Snapshot

Hurd (67–68) charts various proposals about identifying Corinthian slogans in the letter, some of which find more support (6:12; 8:1, 4) than others (7:1; 8:5–6, 8). The structure was proposed (with few modifications) by Ciampa/Rosner. It shows that the apparently disconnected discussion of many issues in the letter (so Kümmel 199) does develop along the lines of four topics: cross / wisdom (1–4), fornication / sexuality (5–7), idolatry / worship (8–14) and resurrection (15), the first three of which receive first a negative and then a positive treatment. While the focus on the cross (1:13, 17, 18, 23; 2:2, 8) and the resurrection (ch. 15) form a theological *inclusio* of the letter, the attacks on sexual immorality and idolatry reflect common Jewish criticism of pagan vices (e.g., Sib. Or. 3; Ciampa / Rosner, 207). Furthermore, Terry has pointed out that all of the many issues addressed share two things: They are rooted in Greek culture, and "[a]lmost every argument appeals to Christ in some way" (Terry 10; e.g., 1:23; 5:7; 6:13; 7:17; 10:21; 11:3, 23; 12:27; 15:17; 16:7, 22). The pervasive A-B-A structures in 1 Corinthians as a "basic form of argumentation" (Fee c:16) with a *digressio* in the center are frequently noticed (K. Bailey 156; Collins b:14; Terry 6; Garland 150, 298, etc.; Chiu). For the Corinthian correspondence see Fisk (321–323).

56. Key Words in 1–2 Corinthians

The categories offered for organizing the key words follow somewhat the structure of the letter: cross / wisdom / foolishness (chs. 1–4), sexuality (chs. 5–7), worship (chs. 8–14), resurrection (ch. 15). Paul never uses "salvation" (σωτηρία) in this letter, and other central soteriological terms occur only rarely: "to save / be saved" (σώζω, 29x Paul, 8x 1 Cor), "faith" (πίστις, 142x Paul, 7x 1 Cor), "to believe" (πιστεύω, 54x Paul, 9x 1 Cor). While he employs "sin" (ἁμαρτία) forty-eight times in Romans, it appears only four times in 1 Corinthians (15:3, 17, 56 [2x]).

57. Believers in Corinth Mentioned in the New Testament

See Murphy-O'Connor (b:182) for these names and further thoughts on the size of the Corinthian community.

58. 2 Corinthians: A Snapshot

The most important feature to come to grips with for interpreting 2 Corinthians is the "composite character" of the letter (Aune b:115). Various abrupt transitions have suggested to scholars that the letter consists of fragments from previous letters with different purposes. For example, 8:1 begins to speak about a collection for the saints in Jerusalem without any recognizable transition in chapters 1–7. Also, a fairly positive view of the Corinthian believers' faith and obedience in chapters 1–9 finishes in 9:15 with this praise, "Thanks be to God for His indescribable gift!" Yet 10:1 begins with a negative accusation against Paul by the Corinthians (he is bold in his letters but weak when face-to-face) that leads to the apostle's defense in chapters 10–13 (compare also 12:20 "I am afraid" with 7:16 "I rejoice"). In addition to these abrupt transitions, chapters 10–13 reveal various verbal parallels to chapters 1–9 such as "Did I exploit (ἐπλεονέκτησα) you …?" in 12:17 and "We have exploited (ἐπλεονεκτήσαμεν) no one" (both NIV) in 7:2 (also 10:2 and 8:22; 10:6 and 2:9; 12:16 and 4:2; 13:2 and 1:23; 13:10 and 2:3; see Barrett a:13). Harris reviews and evaluates different issues of integrity for more than forty pages (b:8–50) and belongs to the few who maintain the literary unity of the letter (also Matera; Long; Belleville b:84-103). The structure presented here leans on his proposal (b:ix-xi).

59. PAUL'S CORINTHIAN CORRESPONDENCE

For further discussion see Hafemann, Fisk 321–325, Bruce b:264–279.

60. GALATIANS: A SNAPSHOT

Discussion about the location of Galatia "is presently at an impasse" (Nanos xiv), and the interest in the subject for the interpretation of the letter seems to decrease in scholarship (for a review see Fisk 299–300; Wenham a:226–243). The structure is borrowed from Hansen. In the section on "rebuke" (1:6–4:11), Paul uses both his own story (vs. egocentrism) and that of Abraham (vs. ethnocentrism) to demonstrate how the "new life in Christ . . . unites Jewish and Gentile Christians" (Hansen b:147). This then becomes the preparation and paradigm for the request beginning with 4:12, "become as I am." The advantage of this epistolary (vs. rhetorical) structure, as I see it, is the ability to understand the autobiographical narrative in 4:12–20 not as a digression but as an integral part of Paul's argument. The 2002 volume *The Galatians Debate* (edited by Nanos) offers over twenty essays by as many different scholars that represent important discussions and points of view regarding this letter.

61. EPHESIANS: A SNAPSHOT

Numerous inscriptions found in Ephesus permit a fairly thorough understanding of its culture during Paul's ministry (Köster; Trebilco; Witetschek 7–139). It is possible that Ephesians is the letter "from Laodicea" (Col. 4:16), written as a circular letter to be read in several Asian churches (Harnack; Lincoln 3-4). Insights from Dahl's study (c:349–350) were helpful for parts of my own analysis of Ephesians' structure. For some of the special theological features see Fisk 285–286. There are striking similarities between Ephesians and Romans: (1) At the heart of both letters' concern stands the unity between Gentiles and Jews in the church of Christ (Eph. 2-3; Rom. 1–5). (2) The logic between theology and parenesis in both letters is the same: as God included you Gentiles into the people of God, so you are to include Jewish believers into the church (Eph. 4:3; Rom. 14:1–15:13). (3) Only in Romans and Ephesians does "mystery" refer to the inclusion of Gentiles into the people of God (Eph. 3:6; Rom. 11:25). (4) The decalogue in Paul's letters is explicitly mentioned only in Romans (see 13:9 [Ex. 20:13–17]; 7:7 [Deut. 5:21]) and Ephesians (6:2–3). They are the only letters among Paul's correspondence that address clearly mixed congregations. All other letters are written to what seems to be exclusively Gentile churches. Consequently Paul has no problems in emphasizing the Mosaic law / the decalogue when Jewish believers are addressed (see Holtz 237).

62. PARALLELS BETWEEN EPHESIANS AND COLOSSIANS

For a detailed Greek synopsis, see Van Kooten 239–289. There are more parallels than those offered in this chart. An accurate synopsis of all parallels needs to work with the Greek text, since English translations do not always render the same term in both letters with the same English word or phrase (the NAS, for example, translates δόγματα in Eph. 2:15 with "ordinances" and in Col. 2:14 with "decrees"). In these cases I have tried to use a translation that expresses the Greek parallels better than the NAS. It is easier to observe the parallels than to explain them (see Polhill 1973 for various proposals). Witherington's remarks offer a minimalist conclusion of most Pauline scholars: "Even the most conservative commentators on these documents have to admit that Col. 4.7-9 and Eph. 6.21-22 seem to indicate some sort of literary relationship between these two documents. Few would dispute that these two documents are more similar than any other two documents in the Pauline corpus, and perhaps in the NT" (Witherington e:103). On the other hand, the "order of the similar material" agrees "only about half the time" (Talbert b:5). And there are, of course, many differences between both letters, too. The situational problem of the "philosophy" (Col. 2:8) and the "Christ hymn" (Col. 1:15–20) are unique to Colossians. The Spirit is mentioned only once in Colossians (1:8), but frequently in Ephesians (1:13–14, 17; 2:18; etc.; see Talbert b:5 for more examples). The differences led Talbert to postulate the literary independence between both letters (Talbert b:3–6). An identification of the letter from the "church of the Laodiceans" (Col. 4:16) with Ephesians (see Lincoln lxxiii) would nicely explain the high verbal identity between their references to Tychicus as their common carrier (Col. 4:7–9; Eph. 6:21–22). Their similarity in content helps at times in interpreting the letters. Thus, the parallel with Ephesians 5:18–20 suggests that the "psalms and hymns and spiritual songs" in Colossians 3:16 go together with the preceding two participles "teaching and admonishing" (NAS) and should not be separated from them by a comma (so NIV and the interpunction in NA[27]; see Hengel e:186).

63. Philippians: A Snapshot

Only thirty to forty percent of the citizens in Philippi are estimated to have been Roman citizens. That explains why Paul did not often rely upon his Roman citizenship (Acts 16:37) since most of his converts would not have had this defense available in light of similar sufferings (Hellerman c:112–114). Apart from Philippi in Acts 16:12, Luke "never formally describes the technical status of any other city" (Sherwin-White 95)! This special attention to Philippi's Romanness (colony and offices) suggests "Luke's awareness of the heightened sensitivity to social status and public honor which characterized the colony" (Hellerman b:422). That is also reflected in Paul's letter to the Philippians since only here does he a) specifically address "overseers and deacons" (Phil 1:1), b) "delineate his own social honors and achievements as a Pharisaic Jew (3:5–6)" and c) "substitute the term πολιτεύομαι (1:27; cf. 3:20) for his more common περιπατέω" when describing Christian conduct (Hellerman b:423). The warning in 2:3 about "selfishness or empty conceit" (κενοδοξία, a *hapax*, literally "empty honor") and following depiction of Christ who descended from equality with God to the status of a slave on the cross (2:6–11) has special meaning in such a context. The structure is my attempt and takes its cue from 3:17, "Brethren, join in following my example, and observe those who walk according to the pattern you have in us." Paul confronts the Roman definition of honor and shame with patterns of Christian conduct (see the references to himself, to Christ [2:6–11], to Timothy and Epaphroditus [2:19–30]) that plea for unity and perseverance in suffering for Christ.

64. Colossians: A Snapshot

The nature of the "philosophy" (2:8) that threatens the church in Colossae is the bone of contention. Proposals about the exact nature of the false teaching range from Jewish mysticism (Dunn 1996) to pagan magic (Arnold), with syncretistic Judaism as a position in the middle (Schweizer). While scholars frequently mention some similarities with Galatians, Allan Bevere observed and discussed in depth five parallels (a:55–121) which together strengthen "the *Jewish* character of the Colossian philosophy with the synagogue as its target" (Bevere a:121; italics added).

65. 1 Thessalonians: A Snapshot

Thessalonica was the capitol of Macedonia, positioned at the Via Egnatia. Donfried's article from 1985 urged a reading of the letter against the broader Greco-Roman background and was instrumental in "breaking with the dominant translation of 1 Thess. 4:4" (Donfried b:xx) in which σκεῦος refers not to one's wife (so RSV) but to genital organs (see NRSV). The translation of θλῖψις in 1:6; 3:3, 7 as either (mental) "affliction" (RSV) or (physical) "persecution" (NRSV, see Still 208–217) has a lot of bearing on the reconstruction of the church's problems (see Donfried b:xxi–xxiii). The structure is mine and tries to capture the dynamic that is expressed somewhat in the proverb, "People don't care what you know until they know that you care." Paul could have jumped right into addressing the visible vices of the church (sexual sin, idleness, etc.). Yet he realized that he needed to earn the believers' trust first and respond to a deeper need for certainty. He showed empathy with their underlying loss of confidence in him, in themselves, and in God and sought to restore a personal connection that served as a foundation for believing and living. Both main sections B (2:1–3:13) and C (4:1–5:24) end with prayers (3:11–13; 5:23–24) that contain the word "blameless" and the phrase "at the coming of our Lord Jesus" (Aune b:460). Apart from the significant exception in 4:13 (Οὐ θέλομεν δὲ ὑμᾶς ἀγνοεῖν), Paul frequently appeals to familiar knowledge throughout the letter (e.g., "as you know" in 1:5), a habit which Dahl called "superfluous rehearsals and reminders" (see Donfried b:40). For Paul's use of the four kinship metaphors in 1 Thessalonians 2 see Burke 130–162; Gaventa 2007 (for the reading of either νήπιοι ["infant," NLT, NET] or ἤπιοι ["gentle," usual translation] in 1 Thess. 2:7 see Gaventa a:18–20; also Metzger a:230–233).

66. 2 Thessalonians: A Snapshot

Although Pauline authorship for 2 Thessalonians was already rejected by Schmidt in 1801 and by Wrede in 1903, Goulder (b:96 n. 2) observed that "until 1980 almost all commentators held to Pauline authenticity" (see also Fisk 284 n. 3, Röcker 223–230). While that might be a minority position today, it still finds ample and studious support (Jervis 56 n. 1, Still 46–60, Jewett, Malherbe, Nicholls 182–221). A lot depends in this regard on the understanding of the relationship between First and Second Thessalonians. The text in 2:1–12 is an "interpretive jungle" (Burge, Cohick, Green) and Augustine spoke for many: "I frankly confess I do not know what he means" (*Civ.* 20.19). I followed Roh's reconstruction (2007, esp. 32–66) according to which the "man of lawlessness" refers to Claudius and "he who now restrains " to Nero. Thus, the letter does not correct 1 Thessalonians but actualizes Paul's previous eschatology in the context of the current situation (Roh 128).

67. Similarities between 1 and 2 Thessalonians

For the data see Schnelle b:371–372 who concludes a literary dependence of 2 Thessalonians on 1 Thessalonians. Frame (46) observes with regard to the formal epistolary outline of 1 and 2 Thessalonians that "no other two extant letters of Paul agree so closely in this respect."

68. 1 Timothy: A Snapshot

The rather simple structure offered here is taken from Van Neste's insightful study (2004, esp. ch. 3) which observes the alternation between sections devoted to Timothy and the opponents and instructions about specific groups in the church (see also Johnson a:138). While the discussion of opponents link together 1:3–20 (law), 3:14–4:16 (asceticism) and 6:3–21a (greed), the units on the church groups show a "common ethical or value system" (143) as can be seen, for example, in parallel terms and phrases such as "acceptable before God" (2:1–2; 5:4), "prayer (δέησις) and petition (προσευχή)" (2:1; 5:5), and a concern to be "above criticism" (ἀνεπίλημπτος, 3:2; 5:7). Johnson (a:144) observes the many fascinating parallels between the churches in Ephesus and Corinth (also Fuchs 5–14), to which I would add that both letters support salaried ministers with a quote from Deuteronomy 25:4, followed by a reference/quotation of a dominical tradition (1 Cor. 9:9, 14; 1 Tim. 5:18). Johnson suggests that 1) the matters addressed in 1 Timothy fit firmly into Paul's lifespan (against non-Pauline authorship), 2) 1 Timothy should be compared to 1 Corinthians as 2 Timothy to Philippians, and 3) instead of counting 1 Timothy always to the "Pastorals" (see still Marshall/ Towner 1–2), we should disregard this artificial grouping and read each of the three documents as individual "letters" (Johnson a:145; see also Wieland 15–16, 248–249).

69. 2 Timothy: A Snapshot

Timothy is most likely still in Ephesus (compare 1:16–18 and 4:19; 4:12 and Acts 20:4; 4:19 and Acts 18:24–26). Being in a Roman prison, maybe already for years (see Acts 28:30), Paul is somewhat emotionally drained. "All in Asia have turned away from me" (1:15), yet Tychicus and Trophimus, believers from Asia (see Acts 20:4), are still involved in his ministry (4:12, 20). "Only Luke is with me" (4:11), yet Paul is surrounded by believers who send their greetings to Timothy (4:21). On the other hand, Paul is still actively involved. The prison conditions are not too bad, for he still can write a letter, send out delegates (4:12), plan his ministry (4:11) and expect to receive books and clothes (4:13). Keeping the faith (4:7) and being strengthened by the Lord (4:17) are as real for Paul as the bars in front of his window.

For the parallels between Philippians and 2 Timothy see Aageson (73–78) and Harrison (b:92–99), who believes that Philippians was "written towards the end of Paul's one and only Roman imprisonment" and the parallel authentic Pauline fragments of 2 Timothy "at the end of that imprisonment, on the eve, or perhaps on the very day of his martyrdom" (93; also Johnson a:319). I made only a few modifications to Van Neste's proposal for the structure of the letter (2004, ch. 5). Both A-sections 1:3–2:13 and 3:10–4:8 share (a) the "use of the first person singular referents," (b) the focus on Timothy and Paul while 2:14–3:9 focuses on Timothy and the opponents, (c) the explicit theme of suffering (1:6–2:13; 3:10–12), (d) reference to Timothy's spiritual beginnings (1:5; 3:10–17) (Van Neste 231). While Van Neste views 3:10–17 as a hinge between what precedes and what follows, all of the previous parallels are included in 3:10–17 and justify in viewing the hinge as part of A'. If we extend A' to include 4:9–19, then (e) general desertion (1:15a; 4:16), (f) named deserters (1:15b; 4:10), and (g) named supporters (Onesiphorus in 1:16–18; Luke, Mark, Tychicus in 4:11–12) could be added as parallels. For the special features of medical language and the interpersonal character of faith see Johnson a:325–326, 393–394. For the study of the analogy between Moses/Joshua and Paul/Timothy see Seán Charles Martin.

70. Titus: A Snapshot

Mayer-Haas (13) points out Titus' representative character as an uncircumcised Gentile, which could explain his absence in Luke's second volume with its focus on a torah-observant Paul (22–24). For the information on Crete see Pattengale. For the structure see Van Neste (ch. 7) who also proposed to view the middle section 2:1–3:8 as two chiastic cycles that each include a part on lifestyle (2:1–10; 3:1–2), a doctrinal basis (2:11–14; 3:3–7), and a summary exhortation (3:15; 3:8). For the parallels between 1 Corinthians 6:9–11 and Titus 3:3–7 see Weidemann (43).

71. Similarities between the Pastoral Epistles

In this chart cognates are kept together even though individual terms might fall into different categories (e.g., "godly" [εὐσεβῶς] is found only in 2 Timothy 3:12 and Titus 2:12, but was grouped in the first category since related terms occur in all three letters). Besides my own studies with aids such as Bibleworks 7.0 and the concordance by Kohlenberger III, Goodrick and Swanson, other sources used were Harrison a:137-178, Murphy-O'Connor's article (1991), W. A. Richards (2002) and Fuchs (2003). The largest number of similarities between the Pastoral letters have to do with the false teachings and with descriptions of salvation. These similarities have led to a consensus over the past two hundred years to regard the three letters as one body of "Pastoral Epistles" that mutually interpret each other (e.g., Ebner/Schreiber 456–458). Yet, a growing number of studies have highlighted on the one hand each of the three letters' unique parallels with other letters of Paul (see charts 68 and 69) and, on the other hand, their differences from each other (see Murphy O'Connor 1991, Fuchs, Wieland; for more studies see Fuchs 3 n. 7). Three examples suffice to illustrate the point: (1) Only in 1 Timothy among Paul's letters is God called "king" (βασιλεύς in 1 Tim. 1:17; 6:15; see 2:2; compare with Titus 3:1), a suitable title for God in an address to Christians that live in the Asian capitol of emperor worship. (2) The Old Testament is never quoted in the letter to the Greek Titus but in both letters addressed to circumcised Timothy (1 Tim. 5:18–19; 2 Tim. 2:19). (3) "Lord" (κύριος) as a title for Christ appears in every book of the New

Testament except in Titus and 1-3 John (Fuchs 95–98). These and other observations warrant the respect of each letter's individuality. Yet, William A. Richards goes to the opposite extreme when he ignores the similarities between these three letters and considers them as "independent projects by three different authors over what may have been a lengthy period of time (50–150 CE)" (Marshall c:284). Towner accounts for their differences and similarities, the latter of which "justify recognizing that the three letters form a second important contextual horizon" (Towner b:29, italics added; also Polhill a:398).

72. Authorship of the Pastoral Epistles

The chart surveys only some of the arguments typically used against Pauline authorship of 1–2 Timothy and Titus, together with their rebuttals. For a defense of non-Pauline authorship see Schnelle b:379–383; Pokorny/ Heckel 654–669; Häfner in Ebner/Schreiber 459–463; for rebuttals see Martin c:300–306; Polhill a:398–406; L. T. Johnson a:55–90; Fuchs 175–220. Different authors give different weight to these criteria. For Häfner (in Schreibner/Ebner 459–460), considerations of vocabulary, style, and chronology are inconclusive. Yet, the Pastoral Epistles' discussion of heresy, ecclesiology, and theological themes make the distinctions to the undisputed letters evident. Johnson, on the other hand, reduces these "historical-critical" arguments to egalitarian desires and social pressures of a modern academic majority (a:56, 58). Due to their similarities (see the previous chart), scholars will usually either reject all three letters as non-Pauline or accept all three as Pauline. An exception is Murphy-O'Connor who accepts 2 Timothy as Paul's letter (a:356–359; d:403–418). See also my comments to chart 38.

73. Locating the Pastoral Epistles within Paul's Ministry

See Guthrie (a:651) for a brief review of four proposals for the dating of the Pastoral Epistles. Dating the Pastorals during the apostle's ministry reported in Acts was common in the early church and continued until the nineteenth century. This view was later rejected not because it was unconvincing but because the Pastorals' assumed inauthenticity did not require any date during Paul's life (Van Bruggen a:21). While locating the Pastoral Epistles historically after the end of Acts may be the "simplest solution" (so Polhill 405), it does have its challenges. For example, the locations of ministry mentioned in the Pastoral Epistles presuppose much work in the East (Ephesus [1 Tim 3:14]; Troas [2 Tim 4:13]; Miletus [2 Tim 4:20]), an area that Paul had left after the third journey and did not expect to see again (see Acts 20:25). Also, harmonizing the data of the Pastoral Epistle with the chronology of Acts and Paul's letters is at least as plausible of a solution for their historical location (see DeSilva 734–735). Van Bruggen (followed, for example, by Fuchs [5–30] and Towner [b:10–15, c:14–20]) has offered a reconstruction according to which Paul interrupted his three-year ministry in Ephesus on the third missionary journey (Acts 19; see 20:31) for an "interim journey" (b:93) to Macedonia (see 1 Tim. 1:3) and Crete (Titus 1:5) which led to the writing of 1 Timothy and Titus shortly thereafter. The basic arguments, other than those above, are that (1) Paul talks about a young Timothy (1 Tim. 4:12) which points to an earlier date (Van Bruggen a:15–16; 32–34; 49–50; b:91–96); (2) while Paul expresses hope to return to Ephesus in 1 Tim 3:14–15 and while further visits in Asia are presupposed (2 Tim. 4:13 [Troas] and 4:20 [Milet]), the apostle does not expect any further visits to Asia *after* the third missionary journey (Acts 20:22–25); (3) the content of 1 Timothy with its detailed instructions about the basic structure and services of a church "points to a time of building, when not everything has taken shape and been formalized yet" (Van Bruggen b:92).

74. Philemon: A Snapshot

With twenty-five verses and 335 Greek words, Philemon is the shortest of Paul's letters, but that does not diminish its significance. The letter often serves a test-case for Paul's ethics (Kreitzer b:14–15), in which the rules of Colossians 3:22–4:1 for slaves and masters find specific application in the relationship between

Onesimus the slave and Philemon the master. Philemon is also a wonderful illustration of Paul's word in Colossians 4:6, "Let your speech always be with grace, as though seasoned with salt . . ." (Radford 332). While the names of Colossian Christians in this letter suggest Colossae as the city of Philemon's home, other cities in the Lycus Valley were also proposed (Laodicea, so Goodspeed and Lightfoot; see Barth/Blanke c:127). A minimalist proposal for a structure of Philemon observes the typical epistolary progression from the salutation (1:1–3) to thanksgiving (1:4–7), the body of the letter (1:8–22) and the greetings and subscription (1:23–25). Yet a closer look at the syntax, key words as well as the progression of thought reveals an inverted order with central focus on Paul's plea to Philemon for his voluntary acceptance of Onesimus (Heil 2001; I changed some of Heil's headings to make the repetitions more explicit; for other suggested chiasms see Harvey 278–282). The traditional understanding of the letter's occasion is that Onesimus was a slave owned by Philemon who ran away and maybe also stole from his owner (since at least John Chrysostom, c. AD 347–407). Yet the letter does not say that Onesimus ran away but that he "was separated" (ἐχωρίσθη), maybe implying providential circumstances (*passivum divinum*? See Kreitzer b:63). We also do not read that Onesimus stole from his owner but that he "wronged" Philemon and "owes" him something (v.18, which, being mentioned in a first class conditional statement, could have been uttered simply for the sake of argument [Pearson 269–270]). Both assumptions, that Onesimus is a fugitive and a criminal, have come under severe suspicion at least since the 1930s. According to John Knox (1935), Onesimus is *Archippus'* slave and Philemon an influential church leader. Using a letter to Philemon as leverage, Paul asks Archippus to give up Onesimus (see Col. 4:17) for Christian service (see Philem. 1:10; "send back" in v. 12 understood as "send up" [for legal decision by Philemon], Kreitzer b:57; "repay" in v.19 as "compensation for the loss of his slave," Pearson 278). Other hypothetical reconstructions of the letter's occasion picture Onesimus either as an asylum-seeker, a slave sent from the church in Colossae (Winter 1984) or even as Philemon's physical brother (Callahan 1993) (see Kreitzer b:61–69). What these alternative scenarios do reveal is the amount of questions about the historical background that remain unanswered by this short letter (see the ten questions in Capes 237 and the seven textual and grammatical issues discussed by Pearson). Despite these new interpretive efforts, the traditional understanding finds ongoing scholarly support (see Barclay 1991, Nordling), maybe affirmed by the regulations in Colossians 3:25 about the slave "who does wrong."

75. PARALLELS BETWEEN COLOSSIANS AND PHILEMON

Knox (a:13–14) suggested the parallel between Colossians 2:14 and Philemon 1:19 (also Kreitzer a:92–93) while Bevere argued for a parallel of the *cheirograph* with Ephesians 2:15 (Bevere 2009). Regardless of the question if the metaphor in Colossians 2:14 is borrowed from the world of commerce or reminds of the emperor's remission of debts after the earthquake in the Lycus Valley in AD 60 (so Kreitzer), the parallel in Philemon 1:19 invokes the memory of the metaphor or event in Paul's petition to Philemon. The parallels between both letters demonstrate the likelihood that Philemon lived in Colossae (see comments to previous chart) and explain why commentaries usually discuss both of these letters together. Both letters' mentioning of the wrongdoing of a slave explains why the household code in Colossians differs at this point from Ephesians when slaves, not the master (as in Eph. 6:9), are warned of God's impartiality. We should at least mention the parallels between Philemon and Philippians (see Thurston/Ryan 177–178).

76. PHILEMON AND ELEMENTS OF FORGIVENESS

Based on a traditional reading of the letter (Onesimus wronged Philemon), Tenney (317) outlined these "elements of forgiveness" and I added verse 17 to the last element. Knox rightly cautions against reading the letter as an attempt to remove a personal offense in order to restore a personal relationship since there is "not one word about any repentance on the part of the slave and there is no explicit appeal for forgiveness or pity on the part of the master" (a:3). The commercial (verses 17–18 κοινωνός, προσλαμβάνω, ὀφείλω, ἐλλογέω; Arzt-Grabner 227–240) and juridical (verse 19 ἐγὼ Παῦλος ἔγραψα τῇ ἐμῇ χειρί; Arzt-Grabner 240–244) language shows that Paul seeks Philemon's "forgiveness" by settling financial debt in a contractual way. But here (v.19) and elsewhere (Col. 2:14) the apostle himself uses such financial language of business partners as metaphors for spiritual forgiveness. It is indeed Philemon's own *spiritual* forgiveness that Paul subtly appeals to when requesting *financial* "forgiveness" for Onesimus (see Matt. 6:12 "And forgive us our debts, as we also have forgiven our debtors.").

77. KEY TEXTS AND THEIR INTERPRETATIONS

For literature on these key texts and their interpretations see the following suggestions:

Romans 1:17 — Wright f:200–201; Moo 70–72; Stott 61–64
Romans 11:26 — Merkle 2000; Scott 1993
1 Corinthians 7:15 — Fee c:303–304
1 Corinthians 7:21 — Thiselton 553–559
2 Corinthians 3:6 — Grindheim
2 Corinthians 5:21 — Harris 449–456
Galatians 2:16a — Owen
Galatians 3:19 — Wallace 1990
Ephesians 2:14 — Balla 187–192c
Ephesians 5:21 — Talbert b:130–132
Philippians 2:5 — Silva 2005:95–96
Philippians 2:6–7 — Hellerman b:421–433
Colossians 2:18a — Arnold a:90–95
Colossians 2:18b — Arnold 104–157
1 Thessalonians 4:3 — Yarborough; Konradt (2001)
1 Thessalonians 4:17 — Luckensmeyer 254–260
2 Thessalonians 2:3 — Wanamaker 247–248
2 Thessalonians 2:6–7 — Röcker 422–458; Paul Metzger 15–47
1 Timothy 2:11-15 — Schreiner
1 Timothy 3:1–2 — Merkle 2003, esp. 148–157
2 Timothy 1:18 — Weiser 140–146
2 Timothy 3:16 — Mounce 565–570; Marshall/Towner 790–794
Titus 1:5 — Grubbs
Titus 3:5 — Marshall/Towner 317-318
Philemon 18 — Pearson 268–271
Philemon 19 — Pearson 277–278

Part D: Paul's Theological Concepts

78. SOURCES FOR PAUL'S THEOLOGY

The influences on Paul's theology were as varied as the apostle's education and life experience in various ancient Mediterranean cultures. More texts could be added to illustrate the use of each source. For Paul's use of the (1) Old Testament see charts 45–50. For his use of the (2) targumim and (3) intertestamental traditions see charts 9 and 51–52. (4) References to general revelation are also found in Romans 1:26-27 and Acts 14:17–18. A glimpse of the influence of the (5) Greco-Roman culture can be found in chart 6. (6) Special revelation is claimed elsewhere in Paul's letters (e.g., Eph. 3:13). Luke reports multiple direct revelations of Jesus to Paul (Acts 9:4–6; 18:9–10; 22:17–21; 23:11). The one revelation of supreme importance for all of Paul's theology is his encounter with the risen Christ on the road to Damascus (Acts 9). (7) Other agrapha (2 Cor. 12:9; 1 Thess. 4:15–17) and (8) various explicit parallels (e.g., Luke 10:7 in 1 Tim. 5:18; Luke 22:20 in 1 Cor. 11:25) and echoes to Jesus' teaching can be detected (Fisk 310–314, Kim 474–492; Carter). The continuities and contrasts between Jesus and Paul have been the subject of intensive studies and debates (see Wedderburn, Wenham, Holzbrecher, Still). Finally, (9) pre-Pauline Christian traditions are also often argued for in Romans 1:3–4, Philippians 2:6–11, and Galatians 4:4–5 (see Häußer; Ralph P. Martin c:248–275).

79. Diversity in Paul's Thoughts

These (and more) opposite concepts must have been *one* reason why Peter found some things difficult to understand in Paul's letters (2 Peter 3:15–16). This diversity indicates how little Paul wrote as a systematic theologian and how much of his thoughts are tied to particular historical settings and pastoral needs. Scholars offer, of course, manifold reasons for this diversity. The differences in eschatology between the Thessalonian epistles are at times the main reasons for regarding 2 Thessalonians as non-Pauline (J. Bailey). Similarly, Kreitzer finds Colossians' support of the status quo to be "the product of a later disciple" (b:17) while seeing in Philemon the authentic Pauline abolitionist position on slavery. Yet, besides overlooking Paul's positive metaphorical use of slavery (see chart 107), Barth reminds that "Paul sends Onesimus back to his master (Philem. 12)" and acts thus "in full accordance with the substance of HT [Haustafeln] admonitions to slaves: to subordinate themselves to their masters" (Barth c:229; see Col. 3:22–25). Elsewhere, tension between two letters is explained with development of thought (so already Origen; see Markschies 168; Jürgen Becker 3–5). With regard to the differences between Romans and Galatians, Jervell thinks that new circumstances force Paul to "reconsider his earlier views" (60) so that Romans corrects earlier polemical exaggerations in Galatians. Daniel B. Wallace, on the other hand, suggests that Paul has merely *refined* his views" and that what develops is Paul's "*articulation*" of his theology of Israel (237–238, italics his). Considering the varying audiences in both letters is at least part of the solution. Paul addresses Gentile Christians in Galatians and Jewish Christians in Romans, a difference which implicates dissimilar questions and pressures (Holtz 211–212, 232–237; see also Gielen 95–103; Sänger). Regarding Paul's diverse views on the remarriage of widows, Polhill notices that "it is interesting how time and circumstances can alter one's opinion" (Polhill a:242). Yet Schreiner finds it in general "not really convincing" that Paul's theology underwent any development (Schreiner d:38 n. 5; e:138–140) and concludes with regard to this difference that "[d]espite the emphasis in 1 Corinthians 7, Paul likely viewed marriage and children as the calling for the majority of believers" (Schreiner d:416). When tensions are found within a single letter, as is the case with Paul's view of the law and of Israel's salvation in Romans, the impression of inconsistency (Räisänen c:288; d:151) is at least understandable (but see also Van Spanje's critique and Gadenz's exegesis, here 117). Paul also does not seem to believe that God's commitment to ethnic Israel and to the church as the spiritual transethnic Israel (see Ladd a:23–24) are incompatible. Yet he "never explains how these two understandings . . . fit together" (Thielman 710). Theological diversity accompanies the letters of Paul whether one looks at all thirteen letters or only at the "undisputed" ones, and whether one compares two different letters or two texts of the same letter. That renders theological differences as a criterion for inauthenticity meaningless. Efforts at describing Paul's theology need to (a) constantly keep in mind the partial truth contained in single texts, (b) avoid atomistic exegesis and (c) balance any given text with relevant parallels. Such caution and care enables F. F. Bruce (c:86) to offer a commendable solution to the tension between Galatians 1:11–12 and 1 Corinthians 15:3–4 when saying that the "*core* of the gospel, then, came to Paul by unmediated revelation [Gal. 1]. But many of the *details* of the gospel story were such that he could know of them only from those who had witnessed them [1 Cor. 15]" (italics added; see Price for a radically different answer). For a brief discussion on the debate about theological diversity in Paul's letters see Klein, Blomberg, Hubbard (439–440), Fisk (292–295), Marshall (b:43–61), and Dunn (g:118–123 "Was Paul a Consistent Thinker?")

80. Theological Concepts

"[Y]et for us there is but one God, the Father, from whom are all things, and we exist for Him" (1 Cor 8:6a). Paul's confession of God as "one" ($\epsilon \hat{\iota}_S$) reflects at the heart a monotheistic heritage from Judaism (see the *Shema* in Deut. 6:4–9). The use of "Abba" for God, on the other hand, belongs to the distinctives of Christian prayer and is without parallel in contemporary Jewish sources (Hengel h:498). The poetic force of Paul's theology is sometimes lost in the English translation, such as, for example, the alliteration with the sixfold alpha [α] in 1 Timothy 1:17. The chart seeks to offer a rich *sample* of Paul's theology and is therefore not exhaustive either in the left or the right column. The list of "enemies" could be expanded, from "Belial" in 2 Corinthians 6:15 (a Jewish name for Satan, e.g., *Jubil.* 1:20), to "the tempter" (1 Thess. 3:5, ὁ πειράζων) and the "many gods" (1 Cor. 8:5 θεοὶ πολλοί; see Woyke for a study of gods and idols mentioned in Pauline literature).

81. Christological Concepts

"... and one Lord, Jesus Christ, by whom are all things, and we exist through Him" (1 Cor. 8:6b). "For I determined to know nothing among you except Jesus Christ, and Him crucified" (1 Cor. 2:2). Paul is not just an apostle, but, as this window into his priorities reveals, first and foremost "an apostle of Jesus Christ" (1 Cor. 1:1). The references to the Gospels indicate Paul's familiarity with the Gospel traditions (oral or written). Referring to Jesus as "Christ" is a habit among Christians which they largely owe to Paul (seventy-two percent of references to "Christ" in the NT is found in Paul's letters; see Morris a:39). Paul regarded Jesus so much the Messiah of the Old Testament promises (see 2 Cor. 1:20) that he made "Christ" even part of Jesus' personal name. On the other hand, Paul never refers to Jesus with the Synoptic titles "Son of Man" or "Son of David," never calls him Jesus "of Nazareth" (except in Acts 26:9), the concepts of priesthood (e.g., Heb. 2:17) are applied to Paul (Rom. 15:16), not to Jesus, and the apostle "says nothing about a virgin birth as the means of incarnation" (Gundry 6, also 13; see further Witherington f:114). Thus, Christ's preexistent deity (see Rom. 9:5; Phil. 2:6) and his humanity are taught without offering a historical bridge from the former to the latter. The titles and terms listed here are not intended to be a complete reference to Paul's understanding of Christ's humanity and divinity. Many more traces of the historical Jesus can be found (see Barnett 18–20). Howell astutely observes the "overlapping of roles, functions, attributes and prerogatives assigned to both God and Christ in the Pauline literature" (Howell 468). And the expression "in Christ," for example, is alternatively also reflected in phrases such as "'in him' (Eph. 1:4, 9, 10), 'in the beloved' (Eph. 1:6) and 'in whom' (Eph. 1:7, 11, 13)" (Schreiner d:156). Though not without heavy challenges to their meaning (see Fuller's discussion), the richest Christological expressions in Paul's letters are found in the so-called "hymns" such as Phil. 2:6–11 (see now Park); Col. 1:15–20 and 1 Tim. 3:16 (Martin a:422) and "creedal" statements such as Rom. 1:3–4; 3:24–26; and 2 Cor 5:18–21 (Martin b:191). "Jesus is Lord" (Rom. 10:9; 1 Cor. 12:3; Phil. 2:11) is the most basic confession of Pauline Christianity that stands beside the apostle's equally explicit monotheism (see 1 Cor. 8:6a). There are many attempts to delineate Paul's Christology from first century Judaism, such as the Hebrew concept of "corporate personality" (Capes), Jewish throne mysticism (Eskola 2001) or divine agency (Hurtado). For a review of these and other proposals, see Eskola (a:6–13) and Lee (2–19). What should not be forgotten in these efforts is "the importance of early Christian contributions in the development of early christological thinking (e.g., the impact made by Jesus on his followers through his teaching and deeds, his resurrection/exaltation, their own exegesis of OT scriptures, etc.)" (Lee 21; see Hengel c:74–145).

Gordon Fee (2007) has served us with a most in-depth exegetical study of Paul's Christology (also Schnelle/Söding 2000; Boers 2006; Schreiner d:151–188; f:305–338; Schnelle a:410–477; Dunn d:163–315). For the implicit Christology see, among others, Harris (a:315–317) and for the Septuagint citations/allusions where κύριος refers to Christ or to God in Pauline letters see Capes (1993), Fee (b:631–638), and Bauckham (b:186–191). For most of the parallels between Christ and the Spirit see Witherington (f:108). Like maybe no other scholar in the twentieth century, Martin Hengel has argued that "important basic features of Christology and soteriology ... must have existed already" three years after Jesus death and resurrection since otherwise Paul's conversion remains inexplicable (h:510–511; i:27–51, esp. 29).

82. Pneumatological Concepts

Paul mentions the (Holy) Spirit (πνεῦμα) in every one of his letters except Philemon. He might only be referred to once, as in Colossians (1:8; see also "spiritual" in 1:9; 3:16 and "power" in 1:11, 29; Fee a:637) and Titus (3:5), or twice as in 2 Thessalonians (2:2, 13; see also "power" in 1:11). But that says nothing about the Spirit's importance in letters that are driven by the occasion at hand. More important than the quantity is the Spirit's significance. Fee's voluminous study (1994) offers eight hundred pages of analysis and one hundred pages of synthesis regarding the Holy Spirit in the letters of Paul. He explains that Paul's "'changed eschatological perspective' derives from two experienced realities" (805) which are the resurrection of Christ and the gift of the Spirit who was both "the *certain evidence* that the future had dawned, and the *absolute guarantee* of its final consummation" (806). The three metaphors in particular (down payment, first fruit, and seal) make clear that the coming of the Spirit marks, together with Christ's resurrection, the watershed between the old and new age. The Holy Spirit, in Paul's mind, is not simply a power but a personality with cognition (Rom. 8:27) and emotion (Eph. 4:30). As a personality, believers can have "fellowship" with the Spirit (2 Cor. 13:13). As power, the Spirit enables everything in the Christian walk from justification (1 Cor. 6:11) to sanctification (Rom. 8:4; 15:16). Paul is also a realist: "the coming of the Spirit means not that divine perfection has set in, but 'divine infection'" (Fee a:817). For further studies see Horn 59–75, Dunn d:413–441.

83. Sin, Death, and Judgment

While the notion of "sin" stands at the center of Paul's understanding regarding the human predicament, its origin is not tied to Satan (a connection may be found in 1 Tim. 5:15, 19), but to Adam, whose transgression established the universal reign of physical (Rom. 5:12) and spiritual (Eph. 2:1) death. Paul usually grasps the individual as part of a corporate drama of judgment and salvation (Son 2001). "Works of the flesh" are defined comprehensively, including 1) sexual sins, 2) religious sins, 3) relational sins, and 4) sins concerning food and liquor (Gal. 5:19–21). The condition of the unbeliever is pictured in radically pessimistic terms (Rom. 1:18–3:20). Although Paul does not speak anywhere of "hell," the sinner's inevitable experience of God's wrath (Rom. 1:18) and "eternal destruction" (2 Thess. 1:9) communicate the same disastrous outcome. For further discussion see Konradt (2003), Schreiner f:522–539.

84. Soteriology: Objective Basis of Salvation

This chart focuses on Paul's manifold expressions of God's saving activity in Christ, not on categories known from systematic theology, although I am aware that the division into objective basis and subjective means of salvation (borrowed from Schreiner/Caneday, chs. 2–3, see p. 89; see also the distinction of part 2 from part 3 in their *New Testament Theology* [2008]) introduces a doctrinal distinction that may be foreign to Paul's dense theological discourse. When looking up the references, be prepared that English translations might render the Greek terms differently. The references are limited to their *soteriological* use. That means that at times a concordance will list more uses of a term in Paul's letters (e.g., χάρις occurs one hundred times) than those listed in this chart. The list is merely an indiscriminate start for studying Paul's soteriology. It does not define the terms (see Fitzmyer a:59–71), does not relate them to each other (see, for example, Rom. 3:24 "being justified as a gift by His grace through the redemption which is in Christ Jesus" or Rom. 8:30 "predestined . . . called . . . justified . . . glorified" [also Rom. 5:1–11; Eph. 1:3–14]) or help to weigh the significance of each for Paul's overall understanding. Some soteriological ideas do not appear together in a letter, probably because Paul followed different rhetorical strategies. Thus, Paul never refers to "Abraham" and the "old covenant" / "new covenant" in the same letters. In Galatians 3–4, for example, where Paul uses the *antiquity* of God's covenant with Abraham as an indicator for its *priority* over the Mosaic covenant, it would compromise the logic to label the Mosaic covenant as "old" (as he does in 2 Cor. 3:14). There is considerable debate regarding the extent of *cultic* descriptions of Christ's death in Paul's letters. Are they only found in 1 Cor. 5:7 (Passover) and Rom. 3:25 (propitiation; Vahrenhorst 275–279 [he overlooks Gal. 4:4–5; see Schwartz 260–263]) or do they include also the "for" (ὑπέρ) formula as in 2 Cor. 5:21, Rom. 8:3, and other texts (Finlan; Stuhlmacher 195; Boers 196-198)? First Corinthians 15:3 expresses the basic and most important soteriological expression in Paul's theology: "Christ died for our sins according to the Scriptures." This interpretation of Jesus' death as the Messiah's vicarious suffering with universal atoning significance is the reason why Jesus was not forgotten as another victim of Roman brutality (see Hengel d:146–184)! And, this interpretation of Jesus' death challenged alternative institutions and traditions of atonement such as sacrifice in a temple, prayer (so among the Essenes, e.g., 1QS 9.3–6) and fasting (so among the Pharisees, *Pss. Sol.* 3.8; see Luke 18:12; see Lührmann 45–46), and thereby created Christian victims of Jewish and Roman persecution.

85. Soteriology: Subjective Means of Salvation

As for the previous chart, I used the concordance by Kohlenberger III et. al., as well as Bible Works 7.0. And again as before, the focus of this chart is on the Pauline expression of soteriology, not on categories known in systematic theology (e.g., "imputation" [see Bird a:71–85], "atonement"). A surprise might be the inclusion of "sanctification" in this chart, but the term's meaning in 1 Corinthians 1:30 and 6:11, as well as in 2 Thessalonians 2:13, refers "not to a second work of grace, nor does it refer primarily to something that takes place in the believer after conversion—although that, too, is surely expected. Rather, their conversion itself may be described in terms of 'sanctification,' both in its sense of their being now set apart for God's purposes and in its more ethical sense of their walking in God's ways, so as to reflect his character" (Fee a:79). Different studies have highlighted individual aspects of this subjective side of Paul's soteriology. Paul's notion of "justification" has received more discussion than any other aspect of the apostle's soteriology (see McGrath [1984]; N. T. Wright [2009]; D. A. Campbell [2009]). Barcley (1999) studied the phrase "Christ in you" and Yinger (1999) analyzed Paul's statements on the believers' judgment according to deeds. The thorniest issue would be the relationship between justification and judgment in Pauline thought. Ortlund (2009) reviewed in this regard no less than fourteen different proposals! The subtitle of the second volume of *Justification and Variegated Nomism* (eds. Carson, O'Brien, Seifrid) is telling: *The Paradoxes of Paul*.

86. Metaphors of Salvation

The chart basically follows the collection of metaphors offered by James Dunn (i:120) who uses these to show the diversity of soteriological expressions in Paul's letters. For the definitions see also David J. Williams, Danker, Finlan. Hengel explained repeatedly that Paul's thoughts in particular and ancient thinking in general were prone to a "multiplicity of approaches" and a variety of facets that escape a purely analytical approach which searches for schema and patterns (Hengel f: 315). The reader needs to be prepared for a multitude of images mixed together in a single statement. In Romans 3:24–25, for example, Paul uses metaphors "of the law court, and of the sacrifices, and of manumission" (Morris b:1003).

87. Participation with Christ

According to Paul, God's purpose for believers is to be "conformed (συμμόρφους) to the image of His Son" (Rom. 8:29). This chart demonstrates the comphrenensive nature of this vision. It does not shield the believer from suffering or even from sin. But it also does not keep the church from glory. Union with Christ is conceived thus not merely in spiritual terms but lived out in the physical body of the believer. For further discussion see Beasley-Murray; Schnelle a:479–481.

88. God's Sovereignty and Human Responsibility

It is striking how Paul's confidence in God's initiative and provision never excludes the demand for human will and action and vice versa. Paul prays to God for the salvation of the Jews which expresses his belief in divine sovereign control over human decisions (Rom. 10:1). Yet we also know of the apostle's restless efforts and creative strategies to persuade people (1 Cor. 9:20–23; 1 Tim. 4:10a; 2 Tim. 2:25a). With regard to moral behavior, we could highlight Paul's pessimistic statements about human abilities (e.g., Rom. 3:10, 19–20), his expectation of sanctification by God (1 Thess. 5:23) and the agency of the Spirit (Rom. 8:1–11) and of Christ (Gal. 2:20) in the obedience of the believer. Yet, all of these statements are balanced in their contexts with imperatives that require obedience (1 Thess. 4:2–3; Rom. 8:12–13) and perseverance (1 Cor. 15:2, 58; 16:13; Col. 1:22; see 2 Tim. 4:7) and that warn about the possibility of losing salvation (see Rom. 11:20–22; Gal. 1:6; 4:9; 5:4). This duality in Paul's thinking is underlined in the chart by showing how both aspects often appear within the same letter and are thus heard by the same ears. The complexity in Paul's thoughts is reflected in ongoing discussions about the apostle's understanding of divine sovereignty and human responsibility (Gundry-Volf 1991; Laato 1995; Eskola 1998; Yinger 1999; Oropeza 2000; Carson, O'Brien, Seifrid 2004; Barclay, Gathercole 2008).

89. "Faith of Jesus Christ": What Does It Mean?

The enigmatic Greek expression πίστις Ἰησοῦ Χριστοῦ literally translates as "faith of Jesus Christ" and occurs eight times in Paul's letters (cf. Gal. 2:16 [twice], 20; 3:22; Rom. 3:22, 26; Phil. 3:9; Eph. 3:12). In contrast to older translations (see the chart in McRay a:356), modern translations usually interpret and render with "faith *in* Jesus Christ" (italics added; the genitive "Jesus Christ" is the grammatical *object* of "faith"; see NAS, but also ASV, CSB, ESV, NAB, NIV, NKJ, NRS, RSV), although the Greek does not mention the preposition "in." The phrase is thus understood to speak of the *believer's* faith who is saved by believing in Jesus Christ. If it would not be for this phrase, so Dunn explains, the expression "belief in Christ" would be relatively absent from the undisputed letters (Dunn h:66–67; see Gal. 2:16; Phil. 1:29). Yet, a challenge to this interpretation is at least as old as the 1891 study by Johannes Haussleiter who regarded the expression as a reference to *Jesus'* own faith (Hays a:142; the genitive "Jesus Christ" is here grammatically the *subject* of "faith"; see NET). Many have followed suit since then, with a developing list of arguments (see Hays a:141–148; c:36 n.3; Johnson c:59–62). Among the theological implications are a decreased focus on "our own cognitive disposition or confessional orthodoxy" as the means of our salvation (Hays c:55; see Hultgren 218) as well as an increased emphasis on "the same sort of faith-obedience" and "costly self-sacrificial burden-bearing" that Christ revealed (Hays c:56). As the three indented texts in the chart show, there are formal parallels to both grammatical understandings in the immediate contexts of at least some occurrences: In Romans 3:3 ("the faithfulness of God" [with the article in the Greek]) and 4:16 ("the faith of Abraham" [in Greek without the article, as all occurrences of πίστις Ἰησοῦ Χριστοῦ, except Eph. 3:12]) the genitive is clearly understood as subjective and in Phil. 3:8 ("knowing Jesus Christ") it is clearly an objective genitive. Paul can use the same grammatical form for a variety of references. Therefore, reducing ambiguity among interpretive options requires the inclusion of other exegetical and theological arguments. For a review of both sides of the debate see Hays (1983 [2nd ed. 2002], 1997), Dunn (1997), Matlock, Tonstad, McRay a:352–359, Schreiner f:574–575, and especially the collection of essays in Bird and Sprinkle. Schliesser (257–267) discusses at least five different proposals for translating the expression and suggests, with Schlatter, a "genitivus relationis" in which the objective and the subjective understanding come together (262–263).

90. Eschatological Concepts

Many of Paul's soteriological concepts (charts 84–85) are also eschatological in nature, such as the fulfillment of Abraham's promise and with it the inclusion of the Gentiles (Gal. 3:14), the inauguration of the "new covenant" (1 Cor. 11:25; 2 Cor. 3:6), and so on. Paul did not only believe that the timeline of history has an end sometime in the future but that, in light of the Messiah's appearance (Gal. 4:4; see Kreitzer d:256) and the giving of the Holy Spirit, "the ends of the ages have [already] come" (1 Cor. 10:11) and that "the day is near" (Rom. 13:12). Though Paul considered it possible for Christ to return during his lifetime, he never regarded this as *necessary* (see Morris a:88–89), as the expectation of his death also indicates (Phil. 1:20–23; see 2 Cor. 1:9; 5:1–11; 2 Tim. 4:6–7). "He maintains both Christ's imminence and his own death in the Philippian letter (Phil. 1:6,20f; 3:20;

4:5). Paul may be simply borrowing from traditional and contemporary prophetic language which stressed the coming eschatological events were near even though those events might point to the distant future (Joel 2:1,15; Obad. 15; Ezek. 12:23–25; 4 Ezra 11:44; cf. Rev. 1:1–3)" (Oropeza 175). While the apostle teaches a simple order of few end-time events (1 Cor. 15:22–24, 51–52; 1 Thess. 4:15–17; 2 Thess. 2:1–12), he did not indulge in elaborate schemes or calculations about specific years that would elapse until their occurrence.

91. The "Already" and the "Not Yet"

The phrase "already and not yet" captures a rather complex concept of Pauline eschatology. For it conveys the seeming paradox that "the present evil age" (Gal. 1:4) and the "new creation" (2 Cor. 5:17) are not simply successive stages of redemptive history but exist simultaneously. Jesus' ministry, death and resurrection occurred at "the fullness of the time" (Gal. 4:4) and indicate the "ends of the ages" (1 Cor. 10:11). The giving of the Holy Spirit as the "first fruit" (Rom. 8:23), "down payment" (2 Cor. 1:21–22), and "seal" (Eph. 1:13) speaks of the initial participation in God's kingdom. Thus, we are not standing at a midpoint in God's history at which the old age has ceased and the new age has yet to come as if both succeed each other chronologically. The old age has neither ceased nor is the new age yet to come since both are here and overlap. When "the end... the day of our Lord Jesus Christ" (1 Cor 1:8) will come, the old age will completely disappear and all benefits of redemption will unfold (see also Matt. 13:24–30). This eschatological tension between the already and not yet underlies all of Paul's theology and goes a long way in explaining the opposing statements within this chart. This eschatological tension also renders the "attempt to force justification, sanctification and salvation into a neat past-present-future framework" as too simplistic (McGrath c:518). Special recognition for highlighting this concept of "already and not yet" is usually given to Geerhardus Vos and George E. Ladd. Despite different emphases (see Ladd b:66-67, 713; Witherington g:35) and few objections (see Karlberg), the "already and not yet" expression and idea is pervasive among Pauline scholars. For discussion see Dunn (d:466–472), Ellis (d:889), McGrath (b:195), Mott (273–274), Schreiner/Caneday (38–48), Thiselton (b:11–19).

92. Ecclesiological Concepts

Paul loves the church and showers titles of honor on her, such as "those who have been chosen of God, holy and beloved" (Col. 3:12). In every one of his letters to the churches he calls the believers "saints," with the telling exception of that to the Galatians. The activities of the church are by far not limited to the terms listed here. The next chart on the gifts of the Spirit offers deeper insight into the manifold ministries of the believers. For a study on fictive kinship in Paul's letters see Aasgaard (2004).

93. Gifts of the Spirit

Only "prophecy" is mentioned in all four lists and "teaching" in three of them. Gifts of healing, miracles and tongues are limited to the Corinthian lists. In total, Paul mentions twenty different gifts in all four lists, although some gifts might be similar or even identical despite their different names (e.g., "administration" in 1 Cor. 12:28 and "leading" in Rom. 12:8). Most importantly, all four texts mention the exercise of these gifts in the context of the church as "one body" (Rom. 12:4–5; 1 Cor. 12:20 [also 10:17]; Eph. 4:4, 16 [also 2:16; Col. 3:15]). This context highlights the purpose of the gifts as given "for the common good" (1 Cor. 12:7), for the "care for one another" (1 Cor. 12:25), the "edification" of the church (1 Cor. 14:5, 12, 26), and "for the equipping of the saints for the work of service, to the building up of the body of Christ, until we all attain to the unity of the faith" (Eph. 4:12–13). Furthermore, in his most elaborate explanation of spiritual gifts in 1 Corinthians 12, Paul *pluralized* them against the reduction to a single important gift (1 Cor. 12:4–6, 29-30), *democratized* them against the tendency to neglect the "less honorable" (1 Cor. 12:23) such as those of ethnic minorities or slaves (12:13, see 12:12–27), and *prioritized* them against the Corinthian overestimate of speaking in tongues (12:28). Paul uses various terms for spiritual gifts: "spiritual things" (πνευματικά [the Corinthians' term?], 1

Cor. 12:1; 14:1), "spirits" (πνεύματα, 1 Cor. 14:12), "manifestations of the Spirit" (φανέρωσις τοῦ πνεύματος, 1 Cor. 12:7), " "gift" (χάρις, Eph. 4:7), "gifts" (δόματα, Eph. 4:8), "gifts" or "services" (χαρίσματα, Rom. 12:6; 1 Cor. 12:4, 31), "ministries" (διακονίαι, 1 Cor. 12:5), "results" or "effects" (ἐνεργήματα, 1 Cor. 12:6) (Schreiner d:352). The last three terms appear in a synonymous parallelism in 1 Cor. 12:4–6 and mutually explain each other. This indicates that, contrary to the conventional understanding, Paul uses "gifts" not as a reference to special *abilities* but to *ministries* which God uses to build up His church (see Berding). Augustine reasonably argued that Paul possessed all of the nine gifts in 1 Cor. 12:28–30 himself (*De gest. Pel.* 14.32 [*NPNF* 5:197–198]).

94. House Churches and Homes in Paul's Ministry

Entries in parenthesis (…) and all of those under "Houses/Households of Believers" refer to texts that do not clearly say if the house was also used as a gathering for the church. Gehring is more confident when he says that Lydia's house, for example, became "a meeting place for worship" (Gehring 131). We might gather from Aquila and Prisca's house church in Ephesus (1 Cor. 16:19) and Rome (Rom. 16:3–5) that the reference in Acts 18:2–3 points a similar public use of their private home in Corinth (Gehring 135 n. 91). We hear Paul say to the Ephesian elders that he taught "publicly and from house to house" (Acts 20:20; see 20:7–8). The presence of house churches is clearly attested for Cenchrae, Colossae, Corinth, Ephesus, Laodicea, and Rome. Based on the names listed in Romans 16, Lampe finds "at least seven different Christian islands … in the capital of the Empire" (Lampe b:147). References to the "whole church" in 1 Corinthians 14:23 (11:20) and Romans 16:23 could then denote the assembly of various house churches in one place (Meeks 75). The house as the *physical* place for the believers' meetings influenced Paul's *theological* concept of the church as the "household of God" (1 Tim. 3:15). Evidence for structural changes of private homes specifically for the purpose of Christian worship is not found until the middle of the second century, followed by "larger buildings and halls" in the third century and the first basilica in the fourth century (Gehring 13). For a discussion of the social and theological significance of house churches as the space of the earliest Christian gatherings see Meeks 75–77, Barton 1131–1132, and Gehring ch. 4.

95. Criteria for the Selection of Elders

As far as we can gather from the NT writings, each local church has its own "elders" who led the church (Acts 14:23; Phil. 1:1; Titus 1:5 ["elders in every city"]). Paul's language of leadership is not limited to "elders" and employs a variety of terms, such as "those who … have charge over you" (προΐστημι, 1 Thess. 5:12; see also 1 Tim. 3:5; 5:17). Titus seems to regard the term "elders" (πρεσβύτεροι, plural) in 1:5 as synonymous with that of "overseer" (ἐπίσκοπος, singular) in 1:7 (see also cf. Acts 20:17, 27; 1 Tim. 3:1–7; Phil. 1:1; 1 Peter 5:1–2). The translation of the latter term with "bishop" (KJV, NKJV, RSV, NRSV) presents an anachronism for first-century ecclesiology. The order according to which bishops are separate from elders and rule over them is first found in letters from Ignatious from Antioch (110 AD; e.g., Ign. *Magn.* 2.1; see Bulley 2000). Paul lists these qualifications for elders in letters to his coworkers Timothy and Titus who are to select local leaders for the congregations. The following are a sample of the important matters of debate regarding these lists: (1) Does "not a drunkard" mean total avoidance of alcohol or merely the temperate use of it? (2) Does τέκνα … πιστά in Titus 1:6 refer to children who believe or who behave (see Grubbs and chart 77). (3) While "husband of one wife" certainly excludes polygamists from leadership, does it also apply to divorced men? Moral characteristics dominate both lists. The quality of the work depends on the character of the worker! For discussions see Campbell (1998); Grubbs; Merkle (2003).

96. Ethics

Maybe the most important question regarding Paul's *principles* of ethics is that of the Christian's possibility or impossibility to obey God's will. The apostle mentions the existence of sin in the life of his disciples simultaneously with his expectation of the believers' growth and transformation. A key text for consideration is Romans 7:14–25 (see Boers 36–46). Although Paul does not offer a casuistic manual for Christian behavior, "Virtue and vice lists . . . appear in every letter except Philemon and the Thessalonian correspondence" (Osborne a:393), showing the apostle's interest in specific Christian behavior. One could also consider the ten issues addressed in 1 Corinthians (Terry 3) not just as situational advice for local problems but as a *representative* samples of specific Pauline ethics, especially in light of the repeated reference: "as I teach everywhere in every church" (1 Cor. 4:17; 7:17; 11:16). Schlatter (16) said so pointedly that Paul does not know any other Christianity than the one whose only purpose is that of ethics, of goodness, of unity with the will of God. For a general introduction to Paul's ethics, see Furnish (2009), for specific attention to ethics in most of Paul's letters see Van der Watt (167–413). Miller (129–131) suggests that "impurity" (ἀκαθαρσία), when used beside "immorality" (πορνεία) could be an indirect reference to homosexual behavior (see also Rom 1:24) so as to avoid mentioning shameful action (see Eph 5:11–12). I offered some comments on Paul's view of women in the comments to charts 22, 104, and 105.

97. The Imperative in Paul's Letters

This representative (not exhaustive) sample of various imperatives in Paul's letters illustrates the "obedience of faith" among the Gentiles of which the apostle speaks in Romans 1:5 and 16:26 (see also Isa. 2:3; Jer. 31:33; John 15:10; Rom. 2:13 [par. Matt. 16:27]; 1 Cor. 7:19; Gal. 6:2). Related to this obedience within the New Covenant, Paul also speaks of the believer's judgment according to works (e.g., Rom. 14:10; 1 Cor. 3:8, 13–15; 2 Cor. 5:10; etc.). The believer's obedience and related judgment demonstrate that the faith/grace—law antithesis in Paul's letters (e.g., Rom. 6:14) does not abolish the categories of "command" and judgment from the Christian's new way of life. The imperative *follows* the indicative of salvation, as in Colossians 3:3, 5: "For you have died [indicative], … Therefore consider the members of your earthly body as dead … [imperative]." Harris (d:324) concludes, "This paradoxical dialectic is common in Paul (e.g. Rom. 6:2, 12; Gal. 5:25; Phil. 2:12–13)." For various attempts to harmonize the believer's justification and judgment see Ortlund (2009).

98–99. Vices in Paul's Letters

Lists of vices and virtues appear "in all the Pauline letters except 1 Thessalonians, 2 Thessalonians and Philemon" (Kruse 962). According to Kruse (962), they fulfill various functions, such as (1) to depict the depravity of unbelievers (e.g., Rom. 1:29–31; 1 Cor. 5:9–11); (2) to encourage believers to avoid the vices and practice the virtues (Rom. 13:13; 1 Cor. 6:9–10); (3) to expose/denounce the failure of the false teachers (1 Tim. 1:3–11); (4) to describe what is required of church leaders (1 Tim. 6:11; 2 Tim. 2:22–25); and (5) to advise a young pastor (2 Tim. 3:2–5).

The most important lists of vices are the following: Rom. 1:29–31; 1 Cor. 5:10–11; 6:9–11; 2 Cor. 12:20; Gal. 5:19–21; Eph. 4:31; 5:3–5; Col. 3:5, 8–9; 1 Tim. 1:9–10; 2 Tim. 2:22–25; 3:2–5. The vices in the first of the two charts are listed according to their frequency and don't claim to cover all vices in Paul's letters. The number in parenthesis after the vice in the lists (chart 99) refers to the term in the previous chart (chart 98). The Greek terms in chart 98 represent the lexical entry, with the exception of the plural διάβολοι ("malicious gossip") which differs in meaning from the singular. At times I chose the definition of the lexicon to make the meaning of the term more explicit (e.g., κῶμος: NAS "carousing," meaning "excessive feasting"; πορνεία: NAS "immorality" meaning "sexual immorality"; ἅρπαξ: NAS "swindler," meaning "robber"). Occasionally, the same term can describe a vice and a virtue even in the same letter: see "jealousy" (2 Cor. 12:20 and 7:7, 11; 9:2; 11:2), "wrath" (Rom. 2:8 and 1:18; Eph. 4:31 and 5:6; Col. 3:6 and 3:8; etc.), and "desire" (1 Thess. 2:17 and 4:5). The chart lists only those references that refer to the meaning of the term as a vice, not to the use of it as a virtue. The reader needs to be conscious of the word-idea fallacy. For example, Romans 1 does not mention the word "idolatry," but that is precisely the *idea* described in Romans 1:19–25. Paul does not follow any obvious pattern in his vice lists and they seem to focus on the individual congregation's need. Thus love in 1 Corinthians 13 is described as "not arrogant" because that is one of congregation's big problems (see φυσιόομαι in 1 Cor. 4:6, 18–19; 5:2; 8:1). Yet, as different as Paul's various lists are, there are occasional commonalities: 2 Corinthians 12:20 and Galatians 5:20 mention the same four vices in the same order: "strife, jealousy, outbursts of anger, disputes" (ἔρις, ζῆλος, θυμοί, ἐριθεῖαι). And the lists of vices in Romans 1 and in 2 Timothy 3 share four (five with a variant) expressions in common: "arrogant" (ὑπερήφανος), "boastful" (ἀλαζών), "disobedient to parents" (γονεῦσιν ἀπειθεῖς), "unloving" (ἀστόργους), maybe even "irreconcilable" (ἄσπονδος; See variant to Rom 1:31). Paul himself was growing towards practicing these virtues. He said that "love is not provoked" (παροξύνομαι, 1 Cor 13:5), and yet, that seems to be what happened between him and Barnabas (παροξυσμός, Acts 15:39).

100–101. VIRTUES IN PAUL'S LETTERS

Paul frequently lists virtues in his letters, e.g., 1 Cor. 4:12–13; 13:4–8; 2 Cor. 6:6; Gal. 5:22–23; Eph. 4:1–3; 5:25–32; Phil. 4:8; Col. 3:12–14; 1 Thess. 5:1–22; 2 Tim. 2:22; 3:10; Titus 3:1–2. The alphabetical list of virtues in chart 100 is not trying to be complete. Regarding chart 101: the number in [ ] after the virtue refers to the term with the same number in chart 100 and the number in ( ) refers to the term in the chart on vices (chart 98). In chart 100, Greek cognates (e.g., "joy" and "rejoice") and, at times, semantically related terms are kept together (e.g., various words for "love"). A virtue in one situation might be a vice in another. We should bear (ἀνέχομαι) with other Christians (Eph. 4:2), but not with false leaders (2 Cor. 11:4, 19, 20). Humility (ταπεινοφροσύνη) is a virtue (Col. 3:12), but self-abasement is not (Col. 2:18, 23). Virtues are, of course, not just expressed in the positive presence of these characteristics, but also in the absence of their opposites: Love "is not jealous, … does not brag, and is not arrogant, does not act unbecomingly; it does not seek its own, is not provoked, does not take into account a wrong suffered" (1 Cor. 13:4–5; also 1 Tim. 3:8). Love is not only the most frequently mentioned virtue (quantity), but it is also the most important one (1 Cor. 13:1–7; Col. 3:14; 1 Tim. 1:5) and frequently paired either with faith (1 Thess. 3:6; 5:8; 2 Thess. 1:3; 1 Tim. 1:5, 14; 2:15; 4:12; 6:11; 2 Tim. 3:10; Titus 2:2; Philem. 1:5) or with faith and hope (1 Cor. 13:13; Col. 1:4–5; 1 Thess. 1:3; 5:8). Close terminological similarity exists between Ephesians 5:5–11 and 1 Corinthians 5:9–11; 6:9–10 (Dahl b:337).

In Paul's theology, a virtuous Christian life is not an optional addition to justifying faith. Jesus died for our sins so that "He might rescue us out of this present evil age" (Gal. 1:4) and the appearance of salvation also means that believers "deny ungodliness and worldly desires" (Titus 2:12). The virtues in Paul's letters are thus a necessary explication of the apostle's soteriology. The columns for "God" (which includes also references to Jesus Christ and the Holy Spirit) and "Paul" were added to demonstrate that Paul does not ask for anything the believer has not already experienced and received. The expression "just as" makes this explicit, e.g., "accept one another, just *as* Christ also accepted us" (Rom. 15:7; Eph. 4:32; 5:2, 25, 29; Col. 3:13) or "Give no offense either to Jews or to Greeks or to the church of God; just as I also please all men in all things …" (1 Cor. 10:32–33; see also 11:1; Phil. 4:9). The goal, then, of virtuous living is not the achievement of abstract moral ideals but being conformed "to the image of His Son" (Rom. 8:29). God does not merely set this goal but enables growth towards it. For Paul frequently reveals that God is not just the model of virtues, but their mediator as well: "may the Lord cause you to increase and abound in love for one another, and for all people" (1 Thess. 3:12; also Rom. 15:5, 13; 2 Cor. 13:7; 2 Tim. 1:13; 3:10; Titus 2:2). It is significant in this regard that the virtues in Galatians 5:22–23 are described as the "gift of the Spirit" who empowers the believer to do what God desires (also Rom. 8:4; Gal. 5:16; Eph. 3:16–19). Such divine assistance does not exclude human efforts of "discipline … for the purpose of godliness" (1 Tim. 4:7; also 1 Cor. 9:27).

102. HOUSEHOLD CODES

For an introduction about the household codes see Towner (1993) and Balch (1992); for more substantive discussions see Bart/Blanke (c:151–170), Wagener, Gehring (229–287), and Hering. The small caps in this chart represent quotations from the Old Testament. Other household codes in early Christian literature can be found in 1 Peter 2:18–3:7 as well as later in *Did.* 4:9–11*; *Barn.* 19:5–7*; *1 Clem* 21:6–9;* Ign. *Pol.* 5:1–2; and Pol. *Phil.*

4:2–6:3. Colossians, Ephesians and those texts marked with an * contain instructions for fathers but none for mothers (Titus 2:4 is a short note on the side). Directives for masters are absent in 1 Timothy and Titus as well as in 1 Peter 2:18–3:7. While "household" as a reference to the nuclear family is not absent from the Pastoral Epistles (e.g., "his own household" [τοῦ ἰδίου οἴκου], 1 Tim. 3:4), their focus is on the church as the "household of God" (see 1 Tim 3:15). That explains why Paul does not speak here about children/fathers and wives/husbands but about men/women as related to teaching/instruction (1 Tim. 2:8–9) and why he includes the relationships between older/younger men and women, the widows, and the rich, as well as behavior towards rulers. This focus on the church leads some scholars to exclude 1 Timothy and Titus from a discussion about household codes.

Ephesians and Colossians mention three pairs of relationships found within the individual house of church members: wife/husband, children/fathers, slaves/masters. In each of these pairs the subordinate party is mentioned first. The instructions follow a pattern of a) address (e.g., "wives"), b) imperative (e.g., "submit to husbands"), c) amplification (e.g., "as to the Lord"), d) motivation ("husband is head of the wife as Christ is head of the church") (see Hoehner a:728; also Wagener 17).

The same three pairs of relationships are also mentioned, for example, by Aristotle (*Pol.* 1.2.1), Josephus (*C. Ap.* 2.200–201, 206, 215) and Philo (*Hypoth.* 7.14). Philo also talks in similar contexts about the younger men/older men (*Spec.* 2.226; see 1 Tim. 5:1) and about the relationship to rulers (*Spec.* 2.227; see Titus 3:1). For samples of parallels in non-biblical sources see Walter T. Wilson 310, 312, 360, 412. Various backgrounds to and influences on Paul's household codes have been postulated, ranging from the Old Testament to Aristotle (see Wagener 15–61; Hering 9–60). The answer to the question of background usually comes with a conclusion about the function of these instructions, fluctuating between the "humanizing" and "paganizing" ends of the spectrum.

Any discussion of background and function needs to first take full account of the content and qualifications of Paul's specific instructions. In the relevant texts of 1 Timothy and Titus, for example, "God" is referenced occasionally (1 Tim. 6:2, 17; Titus 2:5, 10–11, 13), but there is only one reference to "Christ" or "Jesus" (Titus 2:13). The instructions are motivated explicitly by an evangelistic interest that is oriented to outsiders' reception of the gospel: "so that the word of God will not be dishonored" (Titus 2:5, 9; see 1 Tim. 6:1). Yet, while a reference to "God" is strikingly absent in their household codes (except in Eph. 6:6), Colossians and Ephesians discuss human relationships frequently with mentioning of the "Lord" in the life of the individual believer (esp. Colossians) and with reference to the pattern of Christ's relationship to the church (esp. Ephesians; see "Lord" in Eph. 5:22 [not in 5:25–33!]; 6:1, 4, 7–9; Col. 3:18, 20, 22–24; "Christ" in Eph. 5:23–25, 29, 32; 6:5, 6; Col. 3:24; "Master" in Eph. 6:9; Col. 4:1). Thus, social relationships of all parties addressed are organized "within the framework of Christ's lordship" (Henderson 424). In addition, as Polaski has pointed out, while the subordinate member is only addressed once in each household codes, the male head of the household hears his orders from the Lord three times (as husband, father, and master). "Rhetorically the effect is to stress the differences between the similar moral codes with their typical directives to subordinates only and the mutuality of this Christian social order" (Polaski, 98–99). See also the comments to the next four charts.

103. Authority and Submission in Paul's Cosmology

The Pauline language reflected in this chart is that of "subordinate" and "submission" (ὑποτάσσομαι, ὑποταγή), "head" or "preeminence" (κεφαλή), and "authority" (ἐξουσία, ἐξουσιάζω). It is evident that creation is organized hierarchically in Paul's cosmology. The apostle is especially verbal about the organization of *human* relationships, probably because of (occasional?) early Christian trends subversive to such order. It is easy to misread single statements in this regard, whether the angle is "from above" or "from below." Three observations are offered for a proper perspective: (1) As the chart shows, God is the only one who does not have any superior over him. In Paul's worldview, everyone always has to obey someone and is accountable for the action done to those who submit. Thus no human "superior" authority is absolute since it has to subordinate to a variety of authorities itself, "knowing their Master and yours is in heaven, and there is no partiality with Him" (Eph. 6:9). A case in point is Philemon, the slave master who himself is called to "obedience" by Paul (Phlm 21; see Barth, Blanke 155). (2) The Lord's own submission to God demands the adoption of the same behavior by all followers, including those of superior social standing. Although the *term* "submission" does not occur in Phil. 2:6–8, the *concept* is nevertheless defined and sanctified by Christ's own "1) refusal to claim equality with God or forsaking rights; 2) servanthood (μορφὴν δούλου) and obedience; 3) humility; 4) humiliation and suffering; and 5) volition" (Parks 120). The preceding and following exhortations clearly portray Christ's voluntary submission to God as the paradigm for Christian conduct (Phil. 2:1–5, 12-18). Elsewhere, Paul uses Christ's sacrificial behavior not towards God but towards the church as an example for the husband's action towards his wife ("loved the church and gave Himself up for her" Eph. 5:25). Consequently, in his own role as an apostle, Paul's "authority" (ἐξουσία) is a function given "by the Lord" for "building you up (εἰς οἰκοδομὴν) and not for destroying you" (2 Cor. 10:8). The highest principle for Christian conduct applies to any of these hierarchical relationships: "love one another. ... Love does no wrong to a neighbor" (Rom. 13:8, 10). (3) Hierarchy and equality are not mutually exclusive concepts in Paul's cosmology. *Distinctions* within humanity are balanced by Paul's expressions of *unity* before God in sin (Rom. 3:9, 22–24) and salvation (Rom. 1:16; 10:12; Gal. 3:28; 1 Cor. 12:13; and Col. 3:11). As a result, submission in Paul's understanding is not in and of itself an oppressive concept but part of God's created order that is re-created in Christ.

104. WOMEN: EQUAL AND SUBORDINATE TO MEN

Paul's understanding regarding the roles of men and women in the church as well as in the family are understandably the ongoing subject of intense debate. Different views on this subject reflect the much larger erosion of consensus in modern Western societies concerning sex (hetero-, homo-, bi-, transsexual) and gender (e.g., controversies about statements by Lawrence Summer in 2005 and Eva Herman in 2006). Personal and cultural perceptions and projections of "male" and "female" and the related question of "nature" and "nurture" belong to every reader's pool of presuppositions. At the same time, the complexity of Paul's thought contributes to disagreements among interpreters who have to wrestle with a host of difficult questions such as (1) text-critical intricacies (1 Cor. 14:34–35; Rom. 16:7 [see next chart]), (2) philological challenges (the meaning of αὐθεντεῖν in 1 Tim. 2:12 [Belleville a:82–87; Wolters] and κεφαλή in 1 Corinthians 11:3 [Kroeger; Grudem; Lakey 6–36]), (3) the complexity of Paul's seemingly opposite statements in the same context which run "the risk of sabotaging his own argument" (Furnish b:77), (4) Paul's diverse ancient historical contexts (Brooten, Eisen, Fiensy a:46–48), (5) the hermeneutical question of the cultural and the transcultural in the Bible (Webb, Osborne, Knight III, Meadors), (6) basic biblical-theological concepts such as the Trinity (Bilezikian; Kovach/Schemm). The spectrum of views on the subject is large. For Schüssler Fiorenza, Galatians 3:28 asserts that "patriarchal marriage ... is no longer constitutive of the new community in Christ" (227–228) and that patriarchal texts such as Col. 3:18. are "late" (the last third of the first century) and belong to the "post-Pauline tradition" (237; also Walker b:101). Yet, statements of distinction between men and women are not limited to the disputed letters of Paul (see 1 Cor. 11:2–16), and the challenge remains to find a consistent point of view that is able to accommodate both emphases. Closer to a synthesis are attempts that reckon with both sets of texts in the undisputed letters, yet find the more authentic Pauline attitude in the egalitarian voice. Hogan thinks that Paul's comments in 1 Corinthians 11:2–16 were "dictated by the particular circumstances of the Corinthian church," while "Paul's own attitude toward the conventions may, however, be more clearly expressed in his more personal communication, specifically the letter to Philemon and the greetings to his Roman acquaintances" (44). Odell-Scott understands the patriarchal voice in 1 Corinthians 11:3–10 as "quoted material from the Corinthian letter to Paul" to which the apostle replies with 11:11–12, "where he contends that in the Lord, woman and man are codependent and co-originating (consistent, as I will argue, with his egalitarian discussion of husbands and wives in 1 Corinthians chapter 7)" (Odell-Scott a:213; similarly Padgett). Most complexity is credited to Paul by those that tribute both sets of texts with equal hermeneutical value. Hove argues that "oneness in Galatians 3:28 does not imply unqualified equality" (127). While not devoid of social implications (136–137), this text does "not primarily address the issue of sexual roles" (132) and therefore does not contradict the call to submit elsewhere (see Motyer [1989] and Hansen [2010] for other explanations). The complementarian and egalitarian positions on the subject are represented well in the two collections of essays edited by Piper/Grudem and Pierce/

Groothuis as well as in *Two Views on Women in Ministry* by Belleville, Blomberg, Keener, and Schreiner (2005). For six different interpretive strategies in dealing with Paul's texts on gender see Lakey 154–176. *One*-sided conclusions of Paul as either a "feminist" or a "chauvinist" and "misogynist" miss the "tension in Paul's thoughts on women and gender—that is, that he is neither a consistent egalitarian nor a consistent patriarchalist" (Gundry-Volf, b:186).

105. Women in Ministry

While fewer in numbers, this chart shows that Paul's female coworkers receive, with some exceptions (σύνδουλος, κοινωνός, [συς]στρατιώτης), at least one of the descriptors also used for male workers. The most debated designations are those found in Romans 16. Is "Junia"/"Junias" (Greek IOYNIAN, so the original writing in capital letters without accentuation) in Rom 16:7 the name of a female (Ἰουνίαν, with an acute) or male (Ἰουνιᾶν, with a circumflex), and does that individual belong to the apostles, or is he/she highly regarded by the apostles (is ἐπίσημοι exclusive or inclusive)? Epp has made a strong case for a female apostle, but not without criticism (see Das 97–100; Wolters 2008; Huttar 2009). The other frequently discussed question regarding women and leadership in Romans 16 surrounds the titles for Phoebe in Romans 16:1–2. She is first called a *diakonos* (διάκονος), which either could mean simply "servant" (most translations) or designate the office of a "minister" or "deacon/ess" (NRSV; see Hentschel 167–172). Second, she is also called *prostatis* (προστάτις), a *hapax legomenon* that is usually translated with "helper" but at times also with a leadership term such as "benefactor" (NRSV) or "patron" (ESV). Should the meaning of the related verb *proistēmi* (προΐστημι), used for leadership in the church in Romans 12:8, 1 Thessalonians 5:12, and 1 Timothy 5:17, be applied to Phoebe (so already Bengel [1687–1752], according to Gehring 143 n. 137; see also McCabe; differently Clarke 115–118)? See comments to chart 104 for related questions.

106–107. Paul and Slavery

Paul makes only a few references to the ancient institution of slavery, and one of them is notoriously difficult to interpret (see 1 Cor. 7:21–22 in chart 77). The negation of social distinctions in Christ and the disqualification of "slave dealers" (or "kidnappers") in 1 Timothy 1:10 stand side by side with christologically qualified regulations (not abolitions) of the master-slave relationship (see esp. Col. 3:11 and 3:22), demonstrating that a non-contextual reading of Paul's ethical instructions as "timeless truth" "fails to comprehend the complexity of either moral reasoning or biblical interpretation" (Harrill b:196). Paul makes abundant use of slavery as a metaphor, either in a positive or in a negative sense. That is sometimes obscured by the inconsistent translation of δουλεύω with "to serve" rather than with "to serve as a slave" or "be enslaved." It is particularly distorting when the NAS thus severs, for example, the statement in Romans 8:15 "you have not received a spirit of slavery" from the predicament of being enslaved just previously expressed in Romans 7:6, 25. Similarly, many translations do not permit to connect the later instructions in Romans 12:11 and 14:18 with 6:19 "present your members as slaves to righteousness" (see also Phil. 1:1; 2:22). The modern reader might be surprised to find any positive reference at all to slavery in Paul's letters. Typically, the background for such use is found either in the "Servant of God" tradition of the Old Testament (e.g., Isa. 40–55; yet the LXX uses δοῦλος / δοῦλοι τοῦ θεοῦ only in Ezra 5:11; Neh. 10:30; and Isa. 42:19; see also Rev. 15:3) or in the Greco-Roman institution of ancient slavery (Byron 72–76). Maybe the positive experience of "managerial slaves" of wealthy owners (Dale B. Martin 1990) or the benefits of the "imperial slaves" (Michael J. Brown 2001; see Phil. 4:22) who had opportunity for "upward mobility" served "as an inspiration of hope for the lower classes" (Byron 77; Meeks 20). These benign aspects of ancient slavery are the subject of debate in extensive research projects (McKeown 30–51). Paul's positive use of slavery as a metaphor indicates that not every master was abusive and violent. Such a background would also help us understand that the apostle's affirmative statements about slavery are not an unqualified support and timeless approval of the "totalizing ideology" of the human institution *per se* (so wrongly Harrill b:117; for a critical response to Harrill see Nicklas; for pertinent comments see Hoehner a:800–804; Harris 1999;

R. McL. Wilson 327–330; Blomberg 281–282). Moreover, Paul calls Jesus a "slave" once (Phil. 2:7) and "Lord" many times (see chart 81), which probably informed the apostle's ethics on this point more than any cultural experience. Byron offers a studious review about important texts, past and current debates related to Paul and slavery (see my review at bookreviews.org).

108. PAUL AND JESUS

The differences between Jesus and Paul are obvious to any reader of the New Testament. While both were Jewish contemporaries of each other with strong ties to Jerusalem, their paths never crossed and they thought and spoke in largely different terms and concepts. This is the more astonishing since Paul finds "Christ crucified" so much at the heart of his ministry (Fisk 310). And yet, this biographical gap stands in no relation to their theological commonalities. At times, Paul quotes canonical and non-canonical words of Jesus and does so very consciously (see the underlined words). But more often, core theological concepts of the apostle stand in direct continuity to his Lord. Thus, Paul's creative teaching remains connected to the content of Jesus' preaching. Paul's reference "according to the flesh" in 2 Cor. 5:16 does not devaluate knowledge of *Jesus'* earthly existence (so Bultmann) but qualifies the *believer's* new mode of understanding (see Nöh). For more data and discussion see chart 81; Fisk 311–312; Barclay 492–503; Barnett 11–22; Schlatter; Mohrlang; Wedderburn; Wenham (1995, 2002); Yeung; Holzbrecher; Still; Bird/Willits (2011).

109. PAUL AND JAMES

It is striking that both authors not only use the same terms (works, faith, justified) but also cluster them in a similar way. In addition, some of the same Old Testament texts were employed (Gen. 15:6; Ex. 20:13–15; Lev. 19:18), even though not in similar contexts. And yet, despite these parallels, James' statement that "a man is justified by works" (2:24) sounds like the opposite of Paul's teaching that "a man is justified by faith apart from works of the Law" (Rom. 3:28). While the references to the decalogue and to Lev. 19:18 appear within the immediate context of justification in James 2, Paul's positive reference to the commandments of the Torah stands disconnected from the immediate discourse on justification (the last occurrence of "to justify" [δικαιόω] in Romans appears in 8:33). A flat contradiction between both authors seems obvious (so Luther). Yet Paul's references to James in Galatians 1:19 and 2:9 are quite positive and don't show disagreement on the content of the gospel (Gal. 2:12 is ambiguous regarding James' attitude; see Davids a:457). According to Augustine, Paul speaks of works *before* justification, James of works *after* justification (see Augustine, trans. Lombardo, 4). But that ignores the significance of works as the instrument of justification in James 2:24. Another solution shows the different use of the same terms (Burchard 131) and contrasts James' ecclesiological-ethical discourse with Paul's soteriological context (Popkes 38). Thus, with the exception of 2:23, the faith James speaks of is that of demons (2:19) which is "dead" (2:17, 26) and "useless" (2:20), quite contrary to Paul's obedient faith (Rom. 1:5; 16:26). And the "works" in James are purely ethical while the phrase "works of the Law" in Romans also encompasses ritual prescriptions such as circumcision (Davids b:346). The term "justify" would also then have to carry different meanings: either the contrast is between "imputed righteousness" (Paul) and merely "showing to be righteous" (James; see Maxwell 376) or between "initial justification" (Paul) and "final justification" that is by works (James; see Moo c:41–43, 141). Finally, even the use of Abraham and Genesis 15:6 would have to be different (see Schliesser ch. 3; Flüchter ch. 6; Maxwell 376). Paul uses the patriarch and the proof text to reject circumcision (Gen. 17) as a requirement for justification (see Rom. 4:9–12), while James uses the same proof text in anticipation of Abraham's subsequent obedience (Gen. 22). For other proposals and further discussions see Davids a:457–458; Ladd 638–639; Stuhlmacher 348; Marshall a:692–693; Jenkins 63–64.

110. MODERN JEWISH VIEWS OF PAUL

See Hagner, and especially Meißner who, in chapter 2 of his book (p. 9–140), discusses each of the mentioned Jewish scholars' analyses of Paul and divides them into these two paradigms. The list of names is, of course, not complete. Thus, Pamela Eisenbaum (*Paul was not a Christian*, 2009) should be added to the second paradigm. Klein and Maccoby are not put in bold print because they deviate from their contemporary Jewish view of Paul. The short description after each scholar only indicates the individual scholar's point of view but does not capture the often more nuanced perspective. In general, it can be said that every negative position certainly also admits Jewish aspects in Paul's life and theology and every positive view of Paul's Jewishness is also aware of discontinuities between him and his Jewish contemporaries. Interestingly, the renewed modern Jewish interest in Paul *precedes* the beginnings of the Christian "New Perspective" on Paul since the 1970s with its quest for the Jew of Tarsus (E. P. Sanders).

111. THE "NEW PERSPECTIVES" ON PAUL

This last chart speaks about what is perhaps the loudest subject in Pauline scholarship today. The "new perspective" on Paul has pushed since the 1980s for nothing less but a paradigm shift for understanding the apostle's theology. It is not a single "school" of thought since proponents such as Ed P. Sanders, James D. G. Dunn and Nicholas T. Wright have, according to Wright, "at least as much disagreement between ourselves as we do with those outside this (very small, and hardly charmed) circle" (Wright, c:28; therefore "new *perspectives*" [plural!]). Nor does the "new" contribution of this perspective seek to overturn every "old" understanding of Paul. The united concern is a rejection of viewing the Judaism of Paul's day as a religion of works-righteousness that attempts to earn God's favor by obedience to the law. That traditional understanding, so it is argued, does not fit manifold ancient Jewish expressions of gratitude for God's grace and mercy "as the only ground of hope, of the assurance of sins forgiven" (Dunn g:4; e.g., 1QS 11.11–15). If the evidence requires a new understanding of ancient Judaism, then we also need a new answer to the question what Paul was opposing when he rejected the "works of the law" and what he was offering when he spoke of "justification by faith." The responses of the "new perspectives" highlight the multiethnic context of Paul's mission, at the heart of which stood the obstacle to overcome a deep-seated Jewish (and Gentile) nationalism (Gal 2:1–15; Acts 10–11). Proponents of the "new perspective" have often been criticized for having an anti-Lutheran bias and for compromising the traditional Protestant understanding of justification by faith. That charge is at least partially due to "confusions and misunderstandings" (see Dunn g:17–41) and because, as Dunn confesses, his "early formulations were not sufficiently refined" (Dunn g:18, 23, 28 n. 107). Considering the fog about who thinks what in this debate, it is imperative for a fair hearing to let the proponents speak for themselves. Dunn's "The New Perspective: whence, what and whither?" (chapter 1 in his *The New Perspective on Paul*) and Wright's *Justification* (2009), especially chapter 4, provide accessible summaries, including explicit affirmation of forensic justification (Wright) as well as of the reformational *sola gratia* and *sola fide* (Dunn). Westerholm's (b:1–38) concise review of thirty-two Pauline scholars, organized into five different views of ancient Judaism, offers a fair and helpful survey of the "new perspective's" proponents, opponents, and spin-offs. Various collections of essays discuss key exegetical and theological issues in critical interaction with the new perspectives (Carson, O'Brien and Seifrid 2004, Bachmann 2005).

Though insufficient to do justice to the subject, I offer the following as a brief observation. The "old perspective" of Reformation theology found Paul to be speaking about the inevitable predicament of evil *inside* of the *human* heart. The "new perspective" finds Paul addressing the *Jewish* insistence on *outside* boundary markers that keep Gentiles out. Both have put their finger on something evident in Paul's letters that I like to summarize with a paraphrase of 1 Samuel 16:7, "Jewish opponents look at the outside appearance but Paul looks at the heart." A text like Galatians 5:3 shows the connection between the main concern of both perspectives: The first part of 5:3 ("every man who receives circumcision") picks up the Jewish zeal for circumcision as a mark of distinction on the outside flesh of the human body. It reflects the ethnic interest to limit the privilege of divine favor to Israel and those Gentiles who are willing to bear the sign of Israel's covenant (Gal. 2:12). The second part of 5:3 ("he is under obligation to keep the whole Law") reflects Paul's prophetic reminder about the need for obedient behavior. *Being* part of God's people obligates them to *do* all of God's law. There would be no need for this reminder if the Jews and Judaizers would have been zealous to do the law in order to gain God's favor. But this proto-Pelagian attitude is not what Paul is confronted with. This is also confirmed by 6:13, "For those who are circumcised do not even keep the Law themselves, but they desire to have you circumcised so that they may boast in your flesh." A similar situation emerges from Romans 2. Here, Paul begins by saying that God will judge not just the Gentiles but also the Jews by what they do (2:1–16), for God "will render to each person according to his deeds" (2:6, quoting Ps. 62:12; Prov. 24:12; see Matt. 16:27), and that without partiality (2:11). This standard of judgment is a surprise for his Jewish contemporaries who boast on what they *have*, namely the name "Jew," the Law, the knowledge of God's will, etc. (2:17–20). Paul confronts this boasting about ethnic privilege with the reality of ethical failures of stealing, adultery, and idolatry (2:21–24). And, anticipating the argument that circumcision exempts Jews from God's judgment despite ethical failures, Paul goes on to deconstruct this foundational reliance on an outside feature of the flesh (2:25–29).

Bibliography

Aageson, James W. *Paul, the Pastoral Epistles, and the Early Church.* Library of Pauline Studies. Peabody, MA: Hendrickson, 2008.

Aasgaard, Reidar. *'My Beloved Brothers and Sisters!' Christian Siblingship in Paul.* JSNTSup 265. London: T&T Clark, 2004.

Aejmelaeus, Lars. *Die Rezeption der Paulusbriefe in der Miletrede* (Apg 20,18-35). AASF B/232. Helsinki: Suomalainen Tiedeakatemia, 1987.

Agosto, Efrain. "Paul and Commendation." In: *Paul in the Greco-Roman World: A Handbook*, ed. J. Sampley, 101-133. Harrisburg: Trinity Press International, 2003.

Aland, K., ed. *Vollständige Konkordanz zum Griechischen Neuen Testament. Band II: Spezialübersichten.* Berlin: Walter de Gruyter, 1978.

Aland, Kurt, Michael Welte, Beate Koster, Klaus Junack. *Kurzgefaßte Liste der Griechischen Handschriften des Neuen Testaments.* 2nd edition. Arbeiten zur Neutestamentlichen Textforschung. Berlin: de Gruyter, 1994.

Alkier, S. *Wunder und Wirklichkeit in den Briefen des Apostels Paulus. Ein Beitrag zu einem Wunderverständnis jenseits von Entmythologisierung und Rehistorisierung.* WUNT 134. Tübingen: Mohr Siebeck, 2001.

Alvarez Cineira, David. *Die Religionspolitik des Kaisers Claudius und die paulinische Mission.* Herder's Biblical Studies, Freiburg: Herder, 1999.

Anderson, Charles P. "The Epistle to the Hebrews and the Pauline Letter Collection." *HTR* 59 (1966): 429–438.

Arnold, Clinton E. *The Colossian Syncretism: The Interface between Christianity and Folk Belief at Colossae.* Grand Rapids, MI: Baker, 1996.

_____. "Magic." In: *Dictionary of Paul and His Letters*, eds. G. F. Hawthorne, R. P. Martin, D. G. Reid, 580–583. Downers Grove, IL: IVP, 1993.

_____. "Ephesus." In: *Dictionary of Paul and His Letters*, eds. G. F. Hawthorne, R. P. Martin, D. G. Reid, 249–253. Downers Grove, IL: IVP, 1993.

Arzt-Grabner, Peter. *Philemon.* Papyrologische Kommentare zum Neuen Testament, Band 1. Göttingen: V&R, 2003.

Augustine. *On Faith and Works* (*De fide et operibus*, ca. AD 412). Translated and annotated by Gregory J. Lombardo. New York: Newman Press, 1988.

Aune, David E. "Apocalypticism." In: *Dictionary of Paul and His Letters*, eds. G. F. Hawthorne, R. P. Martin, D. G. Reid, 25–35. Downers Grove, IL: IVP, 1993.

_____. *The Westminster Dictionary of New Testament and Early Christian Literature and Rhetoric.* Louisville, KY: Westminster, 2003.

_____. "Emperors, Roman." In: *Dictionary of Paul and His Letters*, eds. G. F. Hawthorne, R. P. Martin, D. G. Reid, 233-235. Downers Grove, IL: IVP, 1993.

_____. "Religions, Greco-Roman." In: *Dictionary of Paul and His Letters*, eds. G. F. Hawthorne, R. P. Martin, D. G. Reid, 786-796. Downers Grove, IL: IVP, 1993.

Bachmann, Michael, ed. *Lutherische und Neue Paulusperspektive. Beiträge zu einem Schlüsselproblem der gegenwärtigen exegetischen Diskussion.* WUNT 182. Tübingen: Mohr Siebeck, 2005.

Bailey, Daniel P. *Jesus as the Mercy Seat: The Semantics and Theology of Paul's Use of hilastērion in Romans 3:25.* Ph.D. Thesis, University of Cambridge, 1999. See abstracts in TynB 51.1 (2000): 155–158.

Bailey, John A. "Who Wrote II Thessalonians?" *NTS* 25 (1978–79): 131–45.

Bailey, Kenneth E. "The Structure of I Corinthians and Paul's Theological Method with Special Reference to 4:17." *Novum Testamentum* 25 (1983): 152–181.

Balch, David L. "Household Codes." In: *The Anchor Bible Dictionary*, ed. D. N. Freedman, 3:318–320. New York: Doubleday, 1992.

_____. "Paul, Families, and Households." In: *Paul in the Greco-Roman World: A Handbook*, ed. J. Sampley, 258–292. Harrisburg, PA: Trinity Press International, 2003.

Balla, Peter. *Challenges to New Testament Theology: An Attempt to Justify the Enterprise.* WUNT 2.95. Tübingen: Mohr Siebeck, 1997.

Barclay, John M. G. "Mirror-Reading a Polemical Letter: Galatians as a Test Case." *JSNT* 31 (1987): 73–93.

_____. "Paul, Philemon and the Dilemma of Christian Slave-Ownership." *NTS* 37 (1991): 161–186.

_____. "Jesus and Paul." In: *Dictionary of Paul and His Letters*, eds. G. F. Hawthorne, R. P. Martin, D. G. Reid, 492–503. Downers Grove, IL: IVP, 1993.

Barclay, John M. G. and Simon Gathercole, eds. *Divine and Human Agency in Paul and His Cultural Environment.* New York: T&T Clark, 2008.

Barcley, W. B. *"Christ in You": A Study in Paul's Theology and Ethics.* Lanham, MD: University Press of America, 1999.

Barnes, Timothy D. *Early Christian Hagiography and Roman History.* TrC 5. Tübingen: Mohr Siebeck, 2010.

Barnett, Paul. *Paul, Missionary of Jesus: After Jesus.* Volume 2. Grand Rapids, MI: Eerdmans, 2008.

Barrett, C. K. *A Commentary on the Second Epistle to the Corinthians.* Harper's New Testament Commentaries. Peabody, MA: Hendrickson, 1973.

_____. "The Third Gospel as a Preface to Acts? Some Reflections." In: *The Four Gospels 1992.* FS F. Neirynck, II. BETL 100. Leuven: Leuven University Press, 1992.

_____. *A Critical and Exegetical Commentary on the Acts of the Apostles.* The International Critical Commentary on the Holy Scriptures of the Old and New Testaments. Edinburgh: T&T Clark, 2004.

Bartchy, S. "Who Should Be Called 'Father'? Paul of Tarsus between the Jesus Tradition and Patria Potestas." In: *The Social World of the New Testament: Insights and Models*, ed. J. H. Neyrey and E. C. Stewart, 165–179. Peabody, MA: Hendrickson, 2008.

Barth, Markus. *Ephesians 1-3.* Anchor Bible 34. New York: Doubleday, 1974.

_____ & Helmut Blanke. *Colossians.* Anchor Bible 34B. New York: Doubleday, 1995.

_____ & Helmut Blanke. *The Letter to Philemon*. ECC. Grand Rapids, MI: Eerdmans, 2000.

Bartlet, J. V. "The Historic Setting of the Pastoral Epistles." *The Expositor* 8.5 (1913): 28–36, 161–167, 256–263, 325–347.

Barton, S. C. "Social Values and Structures." In: *Dictionary of New Testament Background*, eds. C. A. Evans, Stanley E. Porter, 1127–1134. Downers Grove, IL: IVP, 2000.

Bauckham, R. "The Acts of Paul as a Sequel to Acts." In: *The Book of Acts in its Ancient Literary Setting*, eds. B. W. Winter and A. D. Clarke, 105-152. Grand Rapids, MI: Eerdmans, 1993.

_____. *Jesus and the God of Israel: God Crucified and Other Studies on the New Testament's Christology of Divine Identity*. Grand Rapids, MI: Eerdmans, 2008.

_____. "Paul and Other Jews with Latin Names in the New Testament." In: *Paul, Luke and the Graeco-Roman World: Essays in Honour of Alexander J. M. Wedderburn*, ed. Stanley E. Porter, 202–220. JSNTSupp. 217. Sheffield: Sheffield Academic Press, 2002.

Baur, Ferdinand C. *Paul: The Apostle of Jesus Christ, His Life and Work, His Epistles and His Doctrine. A Contribution to a Critical History of Primitive Christianity*. 2nd ed. Trans. Ed. Zeller. Rev. A. Menzies. Vol. I. London: Williams and Norgate, 1876.

Beale, G. K. "Peace and Mercy Upon the Israel of God: The Old Testament Background of Galatians 6,16b." *Biblica* 80 (1999): 204–223.

Beasley-Murray, G. R. "Dying and Rising with Christ." In: *Dictionary of Paul and His Letters*, eds. G. F. Hawthorne, R. P. Martin, D. G. Reid, 218–222. Downers Grove, IL: IVP, 1993.

Bechard, Dean Philip. *Paul Outside the Walls: A Study of Luke's Socio-Geographical Universalism in Acts 14,8–20*. AnBib 143. Rome: Editrice Pontificio Istituto Biblico, 2000.

Becker, Eve-Marie and Peter Pilhofer, eds. *Biographie und Persönlichkeit des Paulus*. WUNT 187. Tübingen: Mohr Siebeck, 2005.

Becker, Eve-Marie. "Autobiographisches bei Paulus." In: *Biographie und Persönlichkeit des Paulus*, eds. E.-M. Becker and P. Pilhofer, 67–87. WUNT 187. Tübingen: Mohr Siebeck, 2005.

Becker, Jürgen. *Paulus: Der Apostel der Völker*. 3rd ed. UTB. Tübingen: Mohr Siebeck, 1998.

Beetham, Christopher. *Echoes of Scripture in the Letter of Paul to the Colossians*. Biblical Interpretation Series 96. Leiden: Brill, 2008.

Beker, Johan Christiaan. *Paul the Apostle: The Triumph of God in Life and Thought*. Minneapolis: Fortress Press, 1980.

Bekken, Per Jarle. *The Word Is Near You: A Study of Deuteronomy 30:12–14 in Paul's Letter to the Romans in a Jewish Context*. BZNW 144. Berlin: de Gruyter, 2007.

Bell, Richard H. "Rom. 5.18–19 and Universal Salvation." *NTS* 48 (2002): 417–432.

Belleville, Linda L., Craig L. Blomberg, Craig S. Keener, and Thomas R. Schreiner. *Two Views on Women in Ministry*. Revised Edition. Grand Rapids, MI: Zondervan, 2005.

Belleville, Linda. "Women in Ministry: An Egalitarian Perspective." In: *Two Views on Women in Ministry*, ed. L. Belleville, et al, 21–103. Revised Edition. Grand Rapids, MI: Zondervan, 2005.

_____. *Reflections of Glory: Paul's Polemical Use of the Moses-Doxa Tradition in 2 Corinthians 3.1–18*. JSNTSup. 52. Sheffield: JSOT Press, 1991.

Berding, Kenneth. *What Are Spiritual Gifts? Rethinking the Conventional View*. Grand Rapids, MI: Kregel, 2006.

Berger, Klaus. *Paulus*. München: Beck, 2002.

Bernett, Monika. *Der Kaiserkult in Judäa unter den Herodiern und Römern*. WUNT 203. Tübingen: Mohr Siebeck, 2007.

Best, Ernest. "Paul's Apostolic Authority—?" In: *The Pauline Writings*, eds. Stanley E. Porter and Craig A. Evans, 11-34. London: T&T Clark International, 2004.

Bevere, Allan R. *Sharing in the Inheritance: Identity and the Moral Life in Colossians*. JSNTSup 226. London: Sheffield Academic Press, 2003.

_____. "The *Cheirograph* in Colossians 2:14 and the Ephesian Connection." In: *Jesus and Paul: Global Perspectives in Honor of James D. G. Dunn for His Seventieth Birthday*, eds. B. J. Oropeza, C. K. Robertson, and D. C. Mohrman, 199–206. LNTS 414. New York: T&T Clark, 2009.

Bilezikian, Gilbert. "Hermeneutical Bungee-Jumping: Subordination in the Godhead." *JETS* 40 (1997): 57–68.

Bird, Michael F. *The Saving Righteousness of God: Studies on Paul, Justification, and the New Perspective*. Paternoster Biblical Monographs. Milton Keynes: Paternoster, 2007.

_____. "Mark: Interpreter of Peter and Disciple of Paul." In: *Paul and the Gospels: Christologies, Conflicts and Convergences*, ed. M. F. Bird and J. Willitts, 30–61. LNTS 411. London: T&T Clark International, 2011.

Bird, Michael F. and Preston M. Sprinkle, eds. *The Faith of Jesus Christ: Exegetical, Biblical, and Theological Studies*. Peabody, MA: Hendrickson, 2010.

Bird, M. F. and J. Willitts, eds. *Paul and the Gospels: Christologies, Conflicts and Convergences*. LNTS 411. London: T&T Clark International, 2011.

Blomberg, Craig L. *From Pentecost to Patmos: An Introduction to Acts Through Revelation*. Nashville: B&H Academic, 2006.

Bloomquist, L. Gregory. *The Function of Suffering in Philippians*. JSNT. Sheffield: JSOT Press, 1993.

Boers, Hendrikus. *Christ in the Letters of Paul: In Place of a Christology*. BZNW 140. Berlin: de Gruyter, 2006.

Boismard, M.-É. "Paul's Letter to the Laodiceans." In: *The Pauline Canon*, ed. Stanley E. Porter, 45–57. Leiden: Brill, 2004.

Bovon, Francois. "Canonical and Apocryphal Acts of Apostles." *Journal of Early Christian Studies* 11.2 (2003): 65–194.

Boyarin, Daniel. *A Radical Jew: Paul and the Politics of Identity*. Berkeley: University of California Press, 1994.

Brocke, Christoph vom. *Thessaloniki—Stadt des Kassander und Gemeinde des Paulus. Eine frühe christliche Gemeinde in ihrer heidnischen Umwelt*. WUNT 2.125. Tübingen: Mohr-Siebeck, 2000.

Brooten, Bernadette. *Women Leaders in the Ancient Synagogue: Inscriptional Evidence and Background Issues*. Brown Judaic Studies 36. Chico, CA: Scholars, 1982.

Broughton, T. R. S. "The Roman Army." In: *The Beginnings of Christianity. Part I: The Acts of the Apostles*, ed. F. J. Foakes Jackson and Kirsopp Lake, 427–445. London: MacMillan, 1933.

Brown, Raymond E. *An Introduction to the New Testament*. The Anchor Bible Reference Library. Doubleday: New York, 1997.

Bruce, F. F. "Is the Paul of Acts the Real Paul?" *BJRL* 58 (1976): 282–305.

_____. *Paul: Apostle of the Heart Set Free*. Grand Rapids, MI: Eerdmans, 1979.

_____. "'All things to All Men': Diversity in Unity and Other Pauline Tensions." In: *Unity and Diversity in New Testament Theology. Essays in Honor of George E. Ladd*, ed. Robert A.Guelich, 82-99. Grand Rapids, MI: Eerdmans, 1978.

_____. *The Acts of the Apostles: The Greek Text with Introduction and Commentary*. 3rd rev. ed. Grand Rapids,

MI: Eerdmans, 1990.

Büllesbach, Claudia. "Das Verhältnis der Acta Pauli zur Apostelgeschichte des Lukas. Darstellung und Kritik der Forschungsgeschichte." In: *Das Ende des Paulus: Historische, theologische und literaturgeschichtliche Aspekte*, ed. F. W. Horn, 215–237. BZNW 106. Berlin: de Gruyter, 2001.

Bulley, Colin. *The Priesthood of Some Believers. Developments from the General to the Special Priesthood in the Christian Literature of the First Three Centuries.* Paternoster Biblical and Theological Monographs. Carlisle: Paternoster Press, 2000.

Burge, Gary M., Lynn H. Cohick, and Gene L. Green. *New Testament in Antiquity: A Survey of the New Testament within Its Cultural Contexts.* Grand Rapids, MI: Zondervan, 2009.

Burke, Trevor J. *Family Matters: A Socio-Historical Study of Kinship Metaphors in 1 Thessalonians.* JSNTSup 247. London: T&T Clark International, 2003.

Byron, John. *Recent Research on Paul and Slavery.* Recent Research in Biblical Studies, vol. 3. Sheffield: Sheffield Phoenix Press, 2008.

_____. "The Epistle to Philemon: Paul's Strategy for Forging the Ties of Kinship." In: *Jesus and Paul: Global Perspectives in Honor of James D. G. Dunn for His Seventieth Birthday*, eds. B. J. Oropeza, C. K. Robertson, and D. C. Mohrman, 207–216. LNTS 414. New York: T&T Clark, 2009.

Callahan, Allen Dwight. "Paul's Epistle to Philemon: Toward an Alternative Argumentum." *Harvard Theological Review* 86 (1993): 357–376.

Campbell, D. A. *The Quest for Paul's Gospel: A Suggested Strategy.* JSNTS 274. London: T&T Clark, 2005.

_____. *The Deliverance of God: An Apocalyptic Rereading of Justification in Paul.* Grand Rapids, MI: Eerdmans, 2009.

Campbell, R.A. *The Elders: Seniority with Earliest Christianity.* Edinburgh: T. & T. Clark, 1998.

Campbell, W. S. "Judaizers." In: *Dictionary of Paul and His Letters*, eds. G. F. Hawthorne, R. P. Martin, D. G.Reid, 512-515. Downers Grove, IL: IVP, 1993.

Capes, David B. *Old Testament Yahweh Texts in Paul's Christology.* WUNT 2.47. Tübingen: Mohr Siebeck, 1993.

Capes, David B., Rodney Reeves, and E. Randolph Richards. *Rediscovering Paul: An Introduction to His World, Letters and Theology.* Downers Grove, IL: IVP, 2007.

Carson, D. A., Peter T. O'Brien, Mark A. Seifrid, eds. *Justification and Variegated Nomism. Volume 2: The Paradoxes of Paul.* Grand Rapids, MI: Baker, 2004.

Carter, Christopher L. *The Great Sermon Tradition as a Fiscal Framework in 1 Corinthians: Towards a Pauline Theology of Material Possessions.* LNTS 403. New York: T&T Clark, 2010.

Chang, Hae-Kyung. "The Christian Life in a Dialectical Tension? Romans 7:7–25 Reconsidered." *Novum Testamentum* 49.3 (2007): 257–280.

Charles, J. D. "Pagan Sources in the New Testament." In: *Dictionary of New Testament Background*, eds. S. E. Porter, C. A. Evans, 756–763. Downers Grove, IL: IVP, 2000.

Chilton, Bruce. *Rabbi Paul: An Intellectual Biography.* New York: Doubleday, 2004.

Chilton, Bruce and Craig Evans, eds. *The Missions of James, Peter, and Paul: Tensions in Early Christianity.* NovTSup. 115. Leiden: Brill, 2005.

Chiu, José Enrique Aguilar. *1 Cor 12–14: Literary Structure and Theology.* Analecta Biblica 166. Rome: Editrice Pontificio Istituto Biblico, 2007.

Ciampa, Roy E., Brian S. Rosner. "The Structure and Argument of 1 Corinthians: A Biblical/Jewish Approach." *NTS* 52 (2006): 205–218.

_____. "I Corinthians." In: *Commentary on the New Testament Use of the Old Testament*, eds. G. K. Beale and D. A. Carson, 695-752. Grand Rapids, MI: Baker, 2007.

Clark, Andrew C. *Parallel Lives: The Relation of Paul to the Apostles in the Lucan Perspective.* Carlisle: Paternoster Press, 2001.

Clarke, Andrew D. "Jew and Greek, Slave and Free, Male and Female: Paul's Theology of Ethnic, Social and Gender Inclusiveness in Romans 16." In: *Rome in the Bible and the Early Church*, ed. Peter Oakes, 103–125. Grand Rapids, MI: Baker, 2002.

_____. *Called to Serve: A Pauline Theology of Church Leadership.* LNTS 362. London: T & T Clark, 2008.

Coggan, Donald. *The Prayers of the New Testament.* Washington, DC: Corpus Books, 1967.

Collins, Raymond F. *Letters That Paul Did Not Write: The Epistle to the Hebrews and the Pauline Pseudepigrapha.* Good News Studies 28. Wilmington, DE: Glazier, 1994.

_____. *First Corinthians.* Sacra Pagina. Collegeville, MN: The Order of St. Benedict, 1999.

Comfort, Philip W. and David P. Barrett, eds. *The Text for the Earliest New Testament Greek Manuscripts.* Wheaton, IL: Tyndale House Publishers, 2001.

Comfort, Philip W. *New Testament Text and Translation Commentary.* Carol Stream, IL: Tyndale House Publishers, Inc. 2008.

Compton, Michael. "From Saul to Paul: Patristic Interpretation of the names of the apostle." In: *Dominico Eloquio: In Lordly Eloquence. Essays on Patristic Exegesis in Honor of Robert Louis Wilken*, eds. P. M. Blowers, A. R. Christman, D. G. Hunter, R. D. Young, 50–68. Grand Rapids, MI: Eerdmans, 2002.

Cotter, Wendy. *Miracles in Greco-Roman Antiquity. A Sourcebook.* New York, NY: Routledge, 1999.

Court, John M. "Mithraism among the mysteries." In: *Religious Diversity in the Graeco-Roman World: A Survey of Recent Scholarship*, ed. D. Cohn-Sherbock and J. M. Court, 182–195. Sheffield: Sheffield Academic Press, 2001.

Cranfield, C. E. B. "'The Works of the Law' in the Epistle to the Romans." *JSNT* 43 (1991): 89–101.

_____. *On Romans and Other New Testament Essays.* Edinburgh: T&T Clark, 1998.

Cranford, Michael. "Election and Ethnicity: Paul's View of Israel in Romans 9:1–13." *JSNT* 50 (1993): 27–41.

Crossan, J. D. and J. L. Reed. *Excavating Jesus: Beneath the Stones, Behind the Texts.* San Francisco: Harper Collins, 2001.

_____. *In Search of Paul: How Jesus' Apostle Opposed Rome's Empire with God's Kingdom.* San Francisco: Harper Collins, 2004.

Crump, David. *Knocking on Heaven's Door: A New Testament Theology of Petitionary Prayer.* Grand Rapids, MI: Baker Academic, 2006.

Cunningham, Scott. *"Through Many Tribulations": The Theology of Persecution in Luke–Acts.* Sheffield: Sheffield Academic Press, 1997.

Czachesz, István. *Commission Narratives. A Comparative Study of the Canonical and Apocryphal Acts.* Studies on Early Christian Apocrypha, Vol. 8. Leuven: Peeters, 2007.

Dahl, Nils Alstrup. "Welche Ordnung der Paulusbriefe wird vom Muratorischen Kanon vorausgesetzt?" In: *Studies In Ephesians*, 147–163. WUNT 131. Tübingen: Mohr Siebeck, 2000.

_____. "Der Epheserbrief und der verlorene, erste Brief des Paulus an die Korinther." In: *Studies in Ephesians*, 335-348. WUNT 131. Tübingen: Mohr Siebeck, 2000.

_____. "Das Geheimnis der Kirche nach Epheser 3,8-10." In: *Studies in Ephesians*, 349-363. WUNT 131. Tübingen: Mohr Siebeck, 2000.

Danker, Frederick William, rev. and ed. *A Greek-English Lexicon of the New Testament and Other Early Christian Literature*. 3rd ed. Chicago: University of Chicago Press, 2000.

Das, A. Andrew. *Solving the Romans Debate*. Minneapolis: Fortress, 2007.

Dessau, H. "Der Name des Apostels Paulus." *Hermes* 45 (1910): 347–368.

Davis, Casey W. *Oral Biblical Criticism: The Influence of the Principles of Orality on the Literary Structure of Paul's Epistle to the Philippians*. JSNTSup 172. Sheffield: Sheffield Academic Press, 1999.

Davids, P. H. "James and Paul." In: *Dictionary of Paul and His Letters*, eds. G. F. Hawthorne, R. P. Martin, D. G.Reid, 457–460. Downers Grove, IL: IVP, 1993.

_____. "James." In: *New Dictionary of Biblical Theology*, ed. T. Desmond Alexander and Brian S. Rosner, 342-346. Downers Grove, IL: IVP, 2001.

DeBoer, Martinus C. "Images of Paul in the Post-Apostolic Period." *CBQ* 42 (1980): 359–380.

Deissmann, Adolf. *Light from the Ancient Near East: The New Testament Illustrated by Recently Discovered Texts of the Graeco-Roman World*. 4th ed. New York: Harper & Brothers, 1922.

_____. *St. Paul: A Study in Social and Religious History*. Trans. L. R. M. Strachan. London: Hodder and Stoughton, 1912.

Derickson, Gary W. "The Cessation of Healing Miracles in Paul's Ministry." *BibSac* 155 (1998): 299–315.

DeSilva, David A. *An Introduction to the New Testament: Contexts, Methods & Ministry Formation*. Downers Grove, IL: IVP, 2004.

_____. "Paul and the Stoa: A Comparison." *JETS* 38.4 (1995): 549–564.

Detering, Hermann. *Paulusbriefe ohne Paulus? Die Paulusbriefe in der holländischen Radikalkritik*. Kontexte 10. Frankfurt a.M.: Peter Lang, 1992.

_____. "The Dutch Radical Approach to the Pauline Epistles." *Journal of Higher Criticism* 3.2 (1996): 163–193.

DeWitt, Norman Wentworth. *St. Paul and Epicurus*. Minneapolis: University of Minnesota Press, 1954.

Dodson, Joseph R. *The "Powers" of Personification: Rhetorical Purpose in the Book of Wisdom and the Letter to the Romans*. BZNW 161. Berlin: de Gruyter, 2008.

Donaldson, T. *Paul and the Gentiles: Remapping the Apostle's Convictional World*. Minneapolis: Fortress, 1997.

Donfried, Karl Paul. "The Cults of Thessalonica and the Thessalonian Correspondence." *NTS* 31 (1985): 336–356. Reprint in *Paul, Thessalonica and Early Christianity*, 21–48.

_____. *Paul, Thessalonica and Early Christianity*. Grand Rapids, MI: Eerdmans, 2002.

_____. "Paul the Jew – But of What Sort?" In: *Testimony and Interpretation: Early Christology in Its Judeo-Hellenistic Milieu: Studies in Honour of Petr Pokorný*, ed. Jiři Mrázek and Petr Pokorný, 11–27. JSNTSup 272. London: T&T Clark, 2004.

Downing, F. Gerald. *Cynics, Paul and the Pauline Churches: Cynics and Christian Origins II*. London: Routledge, 1998.

Duling, Dennis C. *The New Testament: History, Literature, and Social Context*. 4th edition. Belmont, CA: Wadsworth, 2003.

Dunn, J. D. G. "The New Perspective on Paul." *BJRL* 65 (1983): 95–122. (repr. *Jesus, Paul, and the Law*, 195–212)

_____. *Romans*. 2 vols. Word Biblical Commentary. Dallas, TX: Word Books, 1988.

_____. *Jesus, Paul, and the Law: Studies in Mark and Galatians*. Louisville, KY: Westminster, 1990.

_____. *The Theology of Paul the Apostle*. Grand Rapids, MI: Eerdmans, 1998.

_____. "The Incident at Antioch (Gal 2:11–18)." In: *The Galatians Debate*, ed. M. Nanos, 199–234. Peabody, MA: Hendrickson, 2002.

_____. *The Epistles to the Colossians and to Philemon*. NIGTC. Grand Rapids, MI: Eerdmans, 1996.

_____. *The New Perspective on Paul*. Revised Edition. Grand Rapids, MI: Eerdmans, 2008.

_____. "Once More: ΠΙΣΤΙΣ ΧΡΙΣΤΟΥ." In: *Pauline Theology. Vol. IV: Looking Back, Pressing On*, ed. E. E. Johnson and D. M. Hay, 60–81. Atlanta, GA: Scholars Press, 1997.

_____. "Diversity in Paul." In: *Religious Diversity in the Graeco-Roman World: A Survey of Recent Scholarship*, ed. D. Cohn-Sherbock and J. M. Court, 107–123. Sheffield: Sheffield Academic Press, 2001.

Dunn, James, ed. *Pauline Theology*. Atlanta, GA: Society of Biblical Literature, 2002.

Dunn, James, ed. *The Cambridge Companion to St. Paul*. Cambridge: Cambridge University Press, 2003.

Ehrman, Bart D. *The New Testament: A Historical Introduction to the Early Christian Writings*. Oxford: Oxford University Press, 1997.

Ebner, Martin and Stefan Schreiber, eds. *Einleitung in das Neue Testament*. UTB. Stuttgart: Kohlhammer, 2008.

Eisen, Ute E. *Women Officeholders in Early Christianity: Epigraphical and Literary Studies*. Collegeville, MN: Liturgical Press, 2000.

Eisenbaum, Pamela. *Paul was not a Christian: The Real Message of a Misunderstood Apostle*. New York: HarperCollins Publishers, 2009.

Ellis, E. Earle. *Pauline Theology: Ministry and Society*. Grand Rapids, MI: Eerdmans, 1989.

_____. " 'The End of the Earth' (Acts 1:8)." *Bulletin for Biblical Research* 1 (1991): 123–132.

_____. "Coworkers, Paul and His." In: *Dictionary of Paul and His Letters*, eds. G. F. Hawthorne, R. P. Martin, D. G.Reid, 183–189. Downers Grove, IL: IVP, 1993.

_____. "Paul." *New Bible Dictionary*, 3rd ed., eds. I. H. Marshall, J. I. Packer, D. J. Wiseman. Downers Grove IVP, 1996.

_____. "Pastoral Letters." In: *Dictionary of Paul and His Letters*, eds. G. F. Hawthorne, R. P. Martin, D. G.Reid, 658–666. Downers Grove, IL: IVP, 1993.

Elliot, Mark Adam. *The Survivors of Israel: A Reconsideration of the Theology of Pre-Christian Judaism*. Grand Rapids, MI: Eerdmans, 2000.

Elliott, Neil. *The Rhetoric of Romans: Argumentative Constraints and Strategy and Paul's Dialogue with Judaism*. JSNTSup 45. Sheffield: Sheffield Academic, 1990 (Minneapolis: Fortress Press, 2006).

_____. *The Arrogance of Nations: Reading Romans in the Shadow of Empire*. Paul in Critical Contexts Series. Minneapolis: Fortress, 2008.

Elliott, Neil and Mark Reasoner, eds. *Documents and Images for the Study of Paul*. Minneapolis: Fortress, 2010.

Engberg-Pedersen, Troels, ed. *Paul in Hellenistic Context*. Minneapolis: Fortress Press, 1995.

Engberg-Pedersen, Troels. "Paul's Stoicizing Politics in Romans 12–13: The Role of 13:1–10 in the Argument." *JSNT* 29.2 (2006): 163–172.

_____. *Paul and the Stoics*. Edinburgh : T & T Clark, 2000.

_____. *Cosmology and Self in the Apostle Paul: The Material Spirit*. Oxford: Oxford University Press, 2010.

Epp, Eldon Jay. *Junia: The First Woman Apostle*. Minneapolis: Fortress Press, 2005.

_____. "Minor Textual Variants in Romans 16:7." In: *Transmission and Reception: New Testament Text-Critical and Exegetical Issues*, ed. J. W. Childers and D. C. Parker, 123–141. Texts and Studies 3.4. Piscataway, NJ: Georgias Press, 2006.

Eskola, Timo. *Messiah and the Throne. Jewish Merkabah Mysticism and Early Christian Exaltation Discourse.* WUNT 2.142. Tübingen: Mohr Siebeck, 2001.

_____. *Theodicy and Predestination in Pauline Soteriology.* WUNT 2.100. Tübingen: Mohr Siebeck, 1998.

Esler, Philip F., ed. *The Early Christian World.* Volume I. London: Routledge, 2000.

Eusebius. *Ecclesiastical History.* Trans. K. Lake. Cambridge, MA: Harvard University Press, 2001.

Evans, Craig A. *Ancient Texts for New Testament Studies: A Guide to the Background Literature.* Peabody, MA: Hendrickson, 2005.

_____. "Paul and the Pagans." In: *Paul: Jew, Greek, and Roman*, ed. Stanley E. Porter, 115–139. Pauline Studies, vol. 5. Leiden: Brill, 2008.

Evans, Howard H. *St. Paul the Author of the Acts of the Apostles and of the Third Gospel.* London: Wyman & Sons, 1884–1886.

Farnell, F. David. "When Will the Gift of Prophecy Cease?" *BibSac* 150 (1993): 171–202.

Farrar, F. W. *The Epistle of Paul the Apostle to the Hebrews. With Notes and Introduction.* Cambridge: Cambridge University Press, 1891.

Fee, Gordon F. *God's Empowering Presence: The Holy Spirit in the Letters of Paul.* Peabody, MA: Hendrickson, 1994.

_____. *Pauline Christology: An Exegetical-Theological Study.* Peabody, MA: Hendrickson, 2007.

_____. *The First Epistle to the Corinthians.* NICNT. Grand Rapids, MI: Eerdmans, 1987.

Fiensy, David A. "The Roman Empire and Asia Minor." In: *The Face of New Testament Studies. A Survey of Recent Research*, eds. Scot McKnight, Grant R. Osborne, 36–56. Grand Rapids, MI: Baker, 2004.

_____. "The Composition of the Jerusalem Church." In: *The Book of Acts in Its First Century Setting. Volume 4: Palestinian Setting*, ed. Richard Bauckham, 213–236. Grand Rapids, MI: Eerdmans, 1995.

Finlan, Stephen. *The Background and Content of Paul's Cultic Atonement Metaphors.* Academia Biblica 19. Atlanta, Society of Biblical Literature, 2004.

Finney, Mark T. "Christ Crucified and the Inversion of Roman Imperial Ideology in 1 Corinthians." *Biblical Theology Bulletin* 35 (2005): 20–33.

Fisk, Bruce N. "Paul: Life and Letters." In: *The Face of New Testament Studies: A Survey of Recent Research*, eds. Scot McKnight and Grant R. Osborne, 283–325. Grand Rapids, MI: Baker, 2004.

Fitzgerald, John T. *Cracks in an Earthen Vessel: An Examination of the Catalogues of Hardships in the Corinthian Correspondence.* SBLDS 99. Atlanta, GA: Scholars Press, 1988.

Fitzmyer, Josef A. *Paul and His Theology: A Brief Sketch.* Edgewood Cliffs, NJ: Prentice Hall, 1987.

_____. *According to Paul: Studies in the Theology of the Apostle.* New York: Paulist Press, 1993.

Fleming, Dean. *Contextualization in the New Testament: Patterns for Theology and Mission.* Downers Grove, IL: IVP, 2005.

Flüchter, S. and Lars Schnor. "Die Anrechnung des Glaubens zur Gerechtigkeit. Ein rezeptionsgeschichtlicher Versuch zum Verständnis von Gen 15,6 MT." *Biblische Notizen* 109 (2001): 27–44.

Flüchter, Sascha. *Die Anrechnung des Glaubens zur Gerechtigkeit: Auf dem Weg zu einer sozialhistorisch orientierten Rezeptionsgeschichte von Gen 15,6 in der neutestamentlichen Literatur.* Tübingen: Francke, 2010.

Forbes, Christopher. *Prophecy and Inspired Speech in Early Christianity and its Hellenistic Environment*. WUNT 2.75. Tübingen: Mohr Siebeck, 1995.

Frame, James E. *A Critical and Exegetical Commentary on the Epistles of St. Paul to the Thessalonians*. ICC. Edinburgh: T&T Clark, 1912.

Fredrickson, David E. "Paul, Hardships, and Suffering." In: *Paul in the Greco-Roman World: A Handbook*, ed. J. Sampley, 172–197. Harrisburg: Trinity Press International, 2003.

French, David. "Acts and the Roman Roads of Asia Minor." In: *The Book of Acts in Its First Century Setting. Volume 2: Graeco-Roman Setting*, eds. D. W. J. Gill and C. Gempf, 49–58. Grand Rapids, MI: Eerdmans, 1994.

Frenschkowski, Marco. "Pseudepigraphie und Paulusschule: Gedanken zur Verfasserschaft der Deuteropaulinen, insbesondere der Pastoralbriefe." In: *Das Ende des Paulus: Historische, theologische und literaturgeschichtliche Aspekte*, ed. F. W. Horn, 239-272. BZNW 106. Berlin: de Gruyter, 2001.

Friesen, Steve J. "Paul and Economics: The Jerusalem Collection as an Alternative to Patronage." In: *Paul Unbound: Other Perspectives on the Apostle*, ed. Mark D. Given. Peabody, MA: Hendrickson, 2010.

Fuchs, Rüdiger. Unerwartete *Unterschiede: Müssen wir unsere Ansichten über die Pastoralbriefe revidieren?* TVG Bibelwissenschaftliche Monographie 12. Wuppertal: R. Brockhaus, 2003.

Fuller, Reginald H. "The Theology of Jesus or Christology? An Evaluation of the Recent Discussion." *Semeia* 30 (1984): 105–116.

Furnish, Victor Paul. *The Moral Teaching of Paul: Selected Issues*. 3rd rev. ed. Nashville, TN: Abingdon, 2009.

_____. *The Theology of the First Letter to the Corinthians*. New Testament Theology. Cambridge: Cambridge University Press, 1999.

Gadenz, Pablo T. *Called from the Jews & from the Gentiles: Pauline Ecclesiology in Romans 9–11*. WUNT 2.267. Tübingen: Mohr Siebeck, 2009.

Garland, David E. *1 Corinthians*. BECNT. Grand Rapids, MI: Baker, 2003.

Gaventa, Beverly R. *Our Mother Saint Paul*. Louisville, KY: Westminster, 2007.

_____. "Cornelius." In: *The Anchor Bible Dictionary*, ed. D. N. Freedman, 1:1154–1156. New York: Doubleday, 1992.

Gebauer, Roland. *Das Gebet bei Paulus: Forschungsgeschichtliche und exegetische Studien*. TVG. Giessen: Brunnen Verlag, 1989.

Gehring, Roger W. *House Church and Mission: The Importance of Household Structures in Early Christianity*. Peabody, MA: Hendrickson, 2004.

George, Timothy. *Galatians*. The New American Commentary 30. Nashville: Broadman and Holman, 1994.

Gerber, Christine. *Paulus und seine "Kinder": Studien zur Beziehungsmetaphorik der paulinischen Briefe*. BZNW 136. Berlin: de Gruyter, 2005.

Gielen, Marlis. "Paulus—Gefangener in Ephesus? Teil 1" *Biblische Notizen* 131 (2006): 79–103.

Gill, David W. J. "Macedonia." In: *The Book of Acts in Its First Century Setting. Volume 2: Graeco-Roman Setting*, eds. D. W. J. Gill and C. Gempf, 397–417. Grand Rapids, MI: Eerdmans, 1994.

_____. "Roman Political System." In: *Dictionary of New Testament Background*, eds. C. A. Evans, Stanley E. Porter, 995–999. Downers Grove, IL: IVP, 2000.

Gillman, John. "Gaius." In: *The Anchor Bible Dictionary*, ed. D. N. Freedman, 2:869. New York: Doubleday, 1992.

Godet, F. *Einleitung in das Neue Testament. Erster Band: Die Briefe des Apostels Paulus*. Trans. E. Reineck. Hannover: Verlag von Carl Meyer, 1894.

Gorman, Michael J. *A Theological Introduction to Paul and His Letters*. Grand Rapids, MI: Eerdmans, 2004.

Goulder, Michael D. *Type and History in Acts*. London: SPCK, 1964.

_____. "Silas in Thessalonica." *JSNT* 48 (1992): 87–106.

Grant, Robert M. *Gods and the One God*. Ed. Wayne A. Meeks. Philadelphia: The Westminster Press, 1986.

Grech, Prosper. "Inner-biblical Reinterpretation and Modern Hermeneutics." In: *Philosophical Hermeneutics and Biblical Exegesis*, eds. Petr Pokorný and Jan Roskovec, 221–237. WUNT 153. Tübingen: Mohr Siebeck, 2002.

Grindheim, Sigurd. "The Law kills but the Gospel gives Life: The Letter-Spirit Dualism in 2 Corinthians 3.5–18." *JSNT* 84 (2001): 97–115.

Grubbs, Norris C. "The Truth About Elders and Their Children: Believing or Behaving in Titus 1:6?" *Faith & Mission* 22.2 (2005): 3–15.

Grudem, Wayne. "Does *kephalē* ('Head') Mean 'Source' or 'Authority over' in Greek Literature? A Survey of 2,336 Examples." *Trinity Journal* 6 (1985): 38–59

_____. "The Meaning of *kephalē*: A Response to Recent Studies." *Trinity Journal* 11 (1990): 3–72.

_____. "The Meaning of κεφαλή ('head'): An Evaluation of New Evidence, Real and Alleged." *JETS* 44.1 (2001): 25–65. Reprint in: *Biblical Foundations for Manhood and Womanhood*, ed. Wayne A. Grudem, 144-202. Wheaton, IL: Crossway Books, 2002.

Gundry, Robert H. "1. Hermeneutic Liberty, Theological Diversity, and Historical Occasionalism in the Biblical Canon." In: *The Old is Better: New Testament Essays in Support of Traditional Interpretations*, 1–17. WUNT 178. Tübingen: Mohr Siebeck, 2005.

Gundry-Volf, Judith M. *Paul and Perseverance: Staying in and Falling away*. Louisville, KY: Westminster John Knox, 1991.

_____. "Paul on Women and Gender: A Comparison with Early Jewish Views." In: *The Road from Damascus: The Impact of Paul's Conversion on His Life, Thought, and Ministry*, ed. R. N. Longenecker, 184–212. McMaster New Testament Studies. Grand Rapids, MI: Eerdmans, 1997.

Guthrie, Donald. *New Testament Introduction*. 4th ed. Downers Grove, IL: IVP, 1990.

_____. *The Pastoral Epistles and the Mind of Paul*. The Tyndale New Testament Lecture, 1955. London: The Tyndale Press, 1956.

Hafemann, S. J. "Suffering." In: *Dictionary of Paul and His Letters*, eds. G. F. Hawthorne, R. P. Martin, and D. G. Reid, 919–921. Downers Grove, IL: IVP, 1993.

_____. *Suffering and Ministry in the Spirit: Paul's Defense of His Ministry in 2 Corinthians, 2:14–3:3*. Grand Rapids, MI: Eerdmans, 1990.

_____. "Corinthians, Letters to the." In: *Dictionary of Paul and His Letters*, eds. G. F. Hawthorne, R. P. Martin, and D. G. Reid, 164–179. Downers Grove, IL: IVP, 1993.

Hagner, Donald A. "Paul in Modern Jewish Thought." In: *Pauline Studies: Essays presented to Professor F. F. Bruce on his 70th Birthday*, eds. D. A. Hagner and M. J. Harris, 143–165. Grand Rapids, MI: Eerdmans, 1980.

Hansen, Bruce. *All of You Are One: The Social Vision of Galatians 3.28, 1 Corinthians 12.13 and Colossians 3.11*. Library of New Testament Studies 409. London: T&T Clark, 2010.

Hansen, G. Walter. "Galatians, Letter to the." In: *Dictionary of Paul and His Letters*, eds. G. F. Hawthorne, R. P. Martin, and D. G. Reid, 323–334. Downers Grove, IL: IVP, 1993.

_____. "A Paradigm of the Apocalypse: The Gospel in the Light of Epistolary Analysis." In: *The Galatians Debate*, ed. M. Nanos, 143–154. Peabody, MA: Hendrickson, 2002.

Hanson, K. C. and Douglas E. Oakman. *Palestine in the Time of Jesus: Social Structures and Social Conflicts*. Minneapolis: Fortress Press, 1998.

Hardin, Justin K. *Galatians and the Imperial Cult: A Critical Analysis of the First-Century Social Context of Paul's Letter*. WUNT 2.237. Tübingen: Mohr Siebeck, 2008.

Harding, Mark. "Disputed and Undisputed Letters of Paul." In: *The Pauline Canon*, ed. Stanley E. Porter, 129–168 Leiden: Brill, 2004.

Harnack, Adolf. *Apocrypha IV: Die Apokryphen Briefe des Paulus an die Laodicener und Korinther*. Kleine Texte für Vorlesungen und Übengen, 12. Berlin: Walter de Gruyter, 1931.

Harrer, G. A. "Saul Who Is Also Called Paul." *HTR* 33 (1940): 19–33.

Harrill, J. Albert. *The Manumission of Slaves in Early Christianity*. HUT 32. Tübingen: Mohr Siebeck, 1995.

_____. *Slaves in the New Testament: Literary, Social, and Moral Dimensions*. Minneapolis: Fortress Press, 2006.

Harris, Murray J. *Jesus as God: The New Testament Use of Theos in Reference to Jesus*. Grand Rapids, MI: Baker, 1992.

_____. *The Second Epistle to the Corinthians*. NIGTC. Grand Rapids, MI: Eerdmans, 2005.

_____. *Slave of Christ: A New Testament Metaphor for Total Devotion to Christ*. New Studies in Biblical Theology. Downers Grove, IL: IVP, 1999.

_____. "Colossians." In: *New Dictionary of Biblical Theology*, ed. T. D. Alexander, B. S. Rosner, 322–326. Downers Grove, IL: IVP, 2000.

Harrison, J. R. "Paul and the Imperial Gospel at Thessaloniki." *JSNT* 25 (2002): 71–96.

Harrison, P. N. *The Problem of the Pastoral Epistles*. London: Oxford University Press, 1921.

_____. *Paulines and Pastorals*. London: Villiers Publication, 1964.

Harvey, John D. *Listening to the Text: Oral Patterning in Paul's Letters*. ETS Studies 1. Grand Rapids, MI: Baker, 1998.

Häußer, Detlef. *Christusbekenntnis und Jesusüberlieferung bei Paulus*. WUNT 2.210. Tübingen: Mohr Siebeck, 2006.

Hawthorne, G. F., R. P. Martin, and D. G. Reid, eds. *Dictionary of Paul and His Letters*. Downers Grove, IL: IVP, 1993.

Hays, Richard B. *The Faith of Jesus Christ: The Narrative Substructure of Galatians 3:1–4:11*. 2nd ed. The Biblical Resource Series. Grand Rapids, MI: Eerdmans, 2002.

_____. *Echoes of Scripture in the Letters of Paul*. New Haven: Yale University Press, 1989.

_____. "ΠΙΣΤΙΣ and Pauline Christology." In: *Pauline Theology. Vol. IV: Looking Back, Pressing On*, ed. E. E. Johnson and D. M. Hay, 35–60. Atlanta, GA: Scholars Press, 1997.

Heil, J. P. "The Chiastic Structure and Meaning of Paul's Letter to Philemon." *Biblica* 82 (2001): 178–206.

Heininger, Bernhard. "Im Dunstkreis der Magie: Paulus als Wundertäter der Apostelgeschichte." In: *Biographie und Persönlichkeit des Paulus*, ed. Eve-Marie Becker and Peter Pilhofer, 271–291. WUNT 187. Tübingen: Mohr Siebeck, 2005.

Hellerman, Joseph H. "The Humiliation of Christ in the Social World of Roman Philippi, Part 1." *BibSac* 160 (2003): 321–336.

_____. "The Humiliation of Christ in the Social World of Roman Philippi, Part 2." *BibSac* 160 (2003): 421–433.

_____. *Reconstructing Honor in Philippi. Carmen Christi as Cursus Pudorum*. SNTSMS, vol. 132. Cambridge: Cambridge University Press, 2005.

_____. "ΜΟΡΦΗ ΘΕΟΥ as a Signifier of Social Status in Philippians 2:6." *JETS* 52.4 (2009): 779–797.

Henderson, Suzanne Watts. "Taking Liberties with the Text: The Colossians Household Code as Hermeneutical Paradigm." *Interpretation* 60.4 (2006): 420–432.

Hengel, Martin. *Judaism and Hellenism: Studies in Their Encounter in Palestine during the Early Hellenistic Period.* Eugene, OR: Wipf & Stock Publishers, 2003 (first published in 1974).

_____. The Pre-Christian Paul. Philadelphia: Trinity Press International, 1991.

_____. "Der Sohn Gottes." In: *Studien zur Christologie: Kleine Schriften IV*, 74–145. WUNT 201. Tübingen: Mohr Siebeck, 2006. (reprint from the 2nd edition from 1977 of the book with the same title)

_____. "Der stellvertretende Sühnetod Jesu: Ein Beitrag zur Entstehung des urchristlichen Kerygmas." In: *Studien zur Christologie: Kleine Schriften IV*, 146–185. WUNT 201. Tübingen: Mohr Siebeck, 2006. (reprint from *IKZ* 9 [1980]: 1–25.135–147)

_____. "Hymnus und Christologie." In: *Studien zur Christologie: Kleine Schriften IV*, 185–204. WUNT 201. Tübingen: Mohr Siebeck, 2006. (reprint from *Wort in der Zeit*, ed. W. Haubeck and M. Bachmann, 1980, pp. 1-23)

_____. "Setze dich zu meiner Rechten!« Die Inthronisation Christi zur Rechten Gottes und Psalm 110,1." In: *Studien zur Christologie: Kleine Schriften IV*, 281–367. WUNT 201. Tübingen: Mohr Siebeck, 2006. (reprint from *Le Trône de Dieu*, ed. M. Philonenko, 1993, pp. 108–194)

_____. "Das Mahl in der Nacht, »in der Jesus ausgeliefert wurde« (1 Kor 11,23)." In: *Studien zur Christologie: Kleine Schriften IV*, 451-495. WUNT 201. Tübingen: Mohr Siebeck, 2006 (reprint from *Le Repas de Dieu—Das Mahl Gottes,* ed. C. Grappe, 2004, pp. 115–160).

_____. "Abba, Maranatha, Hosanna und die Anfänge der Christologie." In: *Studien zur Christologie: Kleine Schriften IV*, 496–534. WUNT 201. Tübingen: Mohr Siebeck, 2006 (reprint from *Denkwürdiges Geheimnis*, ed. I. U. Dalferth, 2004, 145–183).

_____. "Christologie und neutestamentliche Chronologie: Zu einer Aporie in der Geschichte des Urchristentums." In: *Studien zur Christologie: Kleine Schriften IV*, 27–51. WUNT 201. Tübingen: Mohr Siebeck, 2006 (reprint from *Neues Testament und Geschichte*, ed. H. Baltensweiler, 1972, 43–67).

_____. "Der Kreuzestod Jesu Christi als Gottes souveräne Erlösungstat. Exegese über 2. Korinther 5,11–21." In: *Studien zur Christologie: Kleine Schriften IV*, 1–26. WUNT 201. Tübingen: Mohr Siebeck, 2006 (reprint from *Theologie und Kirche*, ed. Evangelische Landessynode in Württemberg, 1967, pp. 60–89).

_____. "The Geography of Palestine in Acts." In: *The Book of Acts in Its First Century Setting. Volume 4*: Palestinian Setting, ed. Richard Bauckham, 27–78. Grand Rapids, MI: Eerdmans, 1995.

Hengel, Martin and Anna M. Schwemer. *Paulus zwischen Damaskus und Antiochien: Die unbekannten Jahre des Apostles.* WUNT 108. Tübingen: Mohr Siebeck, 1998.

Hentschel, Anni. *Diakonia im Neuen Testament: Studien zur Semantik unterer besonderer Berücksichtigung der Rolle von Frauen.* WUNT 2.226. Tübingen: Mohr Siebeck, 2007.

Hering, James P. *The Colossian and Ephesian Haustafeln in Theological Context: An Analysis of Their Origins, Relationship, and Message.* New York: Peter Lang, 2007.

Herzer, Jens. "Abschied vom Konsens? Die Pseudepigraphie der Pastoralbriefe als Herausforderung an die neutestamentliche Wissenschaft." *Theologische Literaturzeitung* 129 (2004): 1268-1281.

_____. "Fiktion oder Täuschung? Zur Diskussion über die Pseudepigraphie der Pastoralbriefe." In: *Pseudepigraphie und Verfasserfiktion in frühchristlichen Briefen*, eds. Jörg Frey, Jens Herzer, Martina Janßen u. Clare K. Rothschild, 489-536. WUNT 246. Tübingen: Mohr Siebeck, 2009.

_____. *Constructing Pseudonymity: The Pastoral Epistles between Claim and Criticism* (forthcoming).

Heusler, Erika. *Kapitalprozesse im lukanischen Doppelwerk. Die Verfahren gegen Jesus und Paulus in exegetischer und rechtshistorischer Analyse.* NTA NF 38. Münster: Aschendorff, 2000.

Hock, Ronald F. "Paul and Greco-Roman Education." In: *Paul in the Greco-Roman World: A Handbook*, ed. J. Sampley, 198–227. Harrisburg, PA: Trinity Press International, 2003.

_____. "The Problem of Paul's Social Class: Further Reflections." In: *Paul's World*, ed. Stanley E. Porter, 7–18. Pauline Studies 14. Leiden: Brill, 2008.

Hoehner, Harold. *Ephesians: An Exegetical Commentary.* Grand Rapids, MI: Baker, 2002.

_____. "Did Paul Write Galatians?" In: *History and Exegesis: New Testament Essays in Honor of Dr. E. Earle Ellis*, ed. Sang-Won Son, 150–169. New York: T&T Clark International, 2006.

Hogan, Pauline N. *"No Longer Male and Female": Interpreting Galatians 3.28 in Early Christianity.* LNTS 380. London: T&T Clark, 2008.

Holmes, Michael W., ed. *The Apostolic Fathers: Greek Texts and English Translation.* 3rd ed. Grand Rapids, MI: Baker, 2007.

Holloway, Paul A. "Inconvenient Truths: Early Jewish and Christian History Writing and the Ending of Luke–Acts." In: *Die Apostelgeschichte im Kontext antiker und frühchristlicher Historiographie*, ed. Jörg Frey, Clare K. Rothschild, and Jens Schröter, 418–433. BZNW 162. Berlin: de Gruyter, 2009.

Holtz, Gudrun. *Damit Gott sei alles in allem: Studien zum paulinischen und frühjüdischen Universalismus.* BZNW 149. Berlin: de Gruyter, 2007.

Holzbrecher, Frank. *Paulus und der historische Jesus: Darstellung und Analyse der bisherigen Forschungsgeschichte.* Texte und Arbeiten zum neutestamentlichen Zeitalter 48. Tübingen: Francke, 2007.

Horbury, William. *Herodian Judaism and New Testament Study.* WUNT 193. Tübingen, 2006.

Horn, Friedrich W., ed. *Das Ende des Paulus: Historische, theologische und literaturgeschichtliche Aspekte.* BZNW 106. Berlin: de Gruyter, 2001.

Horn, Friedrich W. "Kurios und Pneuma bei Paulus." In: *Paulinische Christologie: Exegetische Beiträge. Hans Hübner zum 70. Geburtstag*, ed. Udo Schnelle and Thomas Söding, 59–75. Göttingen: V&R, 2000.

Horrell, David G. *An Introduction to the Study of Paul.* 2nd ed. London: T&T Clark, 2006.

Horsley, Richard A., ed. *Paul and Empire: Religion and Power in Roman Imperial Society.* Harrisburg, PA: Trinity Press International, 1997.

Horsley, Richard A., and Neil Asher Silberman. *The Message and the Kingdom: How Jesus and Paul Ignited a Revolution and Transformed the Ancient World.* New York: Grosset/Putnam, 1997.

Horsley, Richard A., ed. *Paul and Politics: Ekklesia, Israel, Imperium, Interpretation.* Harrisburg, PA: Trinity Press International, 2000.

Horsley, Richard A., ed. *Paul and the Imperial Roman Order.* Harrisburg, PA: Trinity Press International, 2004.

House, Wayne H. "Tongues and Mystery Religions of Corinth." *Bibliotheca Sacra* 140 (1983): 134–150.

Hove, Richard. "Does Galatians 3:28 Negate Gender-Specific Roles?" In: *Biblical Foundations for Manhood and Womanhood*, ed. Wayne A. Grudem, 104–143. Wheaton, IL: Crossway Books, 2002.

Howe, E. Margaret. "Interpretations of Paul in *The Acts of Paul and Thecla*." In: *Pauline Studies: Essays presented to Professor F. F. Bruce on his 70th Birthday*, ed. D. A. Hagner and M. J. Harris, 33–49. Grand Rapids, MI: Eerdmans, 1980.

Howell, Jr., Don H. "God-Christ Interchange in Paul: Impressive Testimony to the Deity of Jesus." *JETS* 36.4 (1993): 467-479.

Hultgren, Arland J. "Salvation: Its Forms and Dynamics in the New Testament." *Dialog* 45.3 (2006): 215–222.

Hurd, John Coolidge. *The Origin of I Corinthians*. Macon, GA: Mercer University Press, 1983.

Hurtado, L. W. *One God, One Lord: Early Christian Devotion and Ancient Jewish Monotheism*. Philadelphia: Fortress Press, 1988. British edition by SCM Press. Second edition, Edinburgh: T. & T. Clark, 1998.

_____. *At the Origins of Christian Worship: The Context and Character of Earliest Christian Devotion (the 1999 Didsbury Lectures)*. Carlisle: Paternoster Press, 1999; Grand Rapids, MI: Eerdmans, 2000.

_____. *Lord Jesus Christ: Devotion to Jesus in Earliest Christianity*. Grand Rapids, MI: Eerdmans, 2003.

Huttar, David. "Did Paul Call Andronicus an Apostle in Romans 16:7?" *JETS* 52.4 (2009): 747–778.

Huttunen, Niko. *Paul and Epictetus on Law: A Comparison*. LNTS 405. New York: T&T Clark, 2009.

Jeffers, James S. *The Greco-Roman World of the New Testament: Exploring the Background of Early Christianity*. Downers Grove, IL: IVP, 1999.

Jenkins, C. Ryan. "Faith and Works in Paul and James." *BibSac* 159 (2002): 62–78.

Jervell, Jacob. "Paul in the Acts of the Apostles." In: *The Unknown Paul*, 68–76. Minneapolis: Augsburg, 1984.

_____. "The Letter to Jerusalem." *StTh* 25 (1971): 61–73; reprinted in *The Romans Debate*, rev. ed., ed. K. P. Donfried, 53–64. Peabody, MA: Hendrickson, 1991.

Jervis, L. Ann. *The Purpose of Romans. A Comparative Letter Structure Investigation*. JSNTSupp. 55. Sheffield: JSOT Press, 1991.

Jewett, Robert. *The Thessalonian Correspondence: Pauline Rhetoric and Millennium Piety*. Philadelphia: Fortress, 1986.

_____. "A Matrix of Grace: The Theology of 2 Thessalonians as a Pauline Letter." In: *Pauline Theology. Volume 1: Thessalonians, Philippians, Galatians, Philemon*, ed. J. M. Bassler, 63–70. Minneapolis: Fortress Press, 1991.

_____. "Mapping the Route of Paul's 'Second Missionary Journey' From Dorylaeum to Troas." *TynB* 48.1 (1997): 1–22.

Johnson, L. T. *The First and Second Letters to Timothy: A New Translation with Introduction and Commentary*. AB. New York: Doubleday, 2001.

_____. *The Writings of the New Testament: An Interpretation*. Rev. Ed. Minneapolis: Fortress Press, 2002.

_____. *Reading Romans: A Literary and Theological Commentary*. Macon, GA: Smyth & Helwys Publishing, 2001.

Johnson, T. S. "Roman Emperors." In: *Dictionary of New Testament Background*, eds. C. A. Evans, Stanley E. Porter, 968–974. Downers Grove, IL: IVP, 2000.

Jones, Michael E. *The End of Roman Britain*. New York: Cornell University Press, 1998.

Jones, Donald L. "Roman Imperial Cult." In: *The Anchor Bible Dictionary*, ed. D. N. Freedman, 5:806–809. New York: Doubleday, 1992.

Jurgens, William A. *Faith of the Early Fathers*. Volume 1. Collegeville, MN: Liturgical Press, 1970.

Kahl, Brigitte. *Galatians Re-Imagined. Reading with the Eyes of the Vanquished*. Minneapolis, MN: Fortress Press, 2010.

Karlberg, Mark W. "(Review of) *The Holy Spirit*. By Sinclair B. Ferguson." *JETS* 42 (1999): 529–531.

Kauppi, Lynn Allan. *Foreign but Familiar Gods: Greco-Romans Read Religion in Acts*. LNTS 277. London: T&T Clark, 2006.

Kearsley, R. A. "The Asiarchs." In: *The Book of Acts in Its First Century Setting. Volume 2: Graeco-Roman Setting*, eds. D. W. J. Gill and C. Gempf, 363–376. Grand Rapids, MI: Eerdmans, 1994.

Keay, Robert D. "Paul the Spiritual Guide: A Social Identity Perspective on Paul's Apostolic Self-Identity." *TynB* 56.1 (2005): 151–155.

Keck, Leander E. and Victor P. Furnish. *The Pauline Letters. Interpreting Biblical Texts*. Nashville: Abingdon Press, 1984.

Kenny, Anthony J. P. *A Stylometric Study of the New Testament*. Oxford: Clarendon, 1986.

Kezbere, Ilze. *Umstrittener Monotheismus: Wahre und falsche Apotheose im lukanischen Doppelwerk*. NTOA 60. Göttingen: V&R, 2007.

Kim, S. "Jesus, Sayings of." In: *Dictionary of Paul and His Letters*, eds. G. F. Hawthorne, R. P. Martin, D. G. Reid, 474–492. Downers Grove: IVP, 1993.

Klauck, Hans Josef. *The Religious Context of Early Christianity: A Guide to Graeco-Roman Religions*. London: T&T Clark, 2003.

_____. *Magic and Paganism in Early Christianity: The World of the Acts of the Apostles*. Minneapolis: Fortress Press, 2003.

_____. *Ancient Letters and the New Testament: A Guide to Context and Exegesis*. Waco, TX: Baylor University Press, 2006.

Klein, William W. "Paul's Use of *Kalein*: A Proposal." *JETS* 27 (1984): 53–64.

Knight III, George W. "The Scriptures Were Written for Our Instruction." *JETS* 39 (1996): 3–13.

Knox, John. *Philemon among the Letters of Paul: A New View of its Place and Importance*. Chicago: The University of Chicago Press, 1935.

_____. "Philemon and the Authenticity of Colossians." *The Journal of Religion* 18.2 (April 1938): 144–160.

Kohlenberger III, John R., Edward W. Goodrick and James A. Swanson. *The Exhaustive Concordance to the Greek New Testament*. Grand Rapids, MI: Zondervan, 1995.

Konradt, Matthias. *Gericht und Gemeinde: Eine Studie zur Bedeutung und Funktion von Gerichtsaussagen im Rahmen der paulinischen Ekklesiologie und Ethik im 1 Thess und 1 Kor*. BZNW 117. Berlin: de Gruyter, 2003.

_____. "Zu Paulus´ sexualethischer Weisung in 1 Thess 4,4f." *ZNW* 92 (2001): 128–135.

Köstenberger, A. J., T. R. Schreiner, H. S. Baldwin, eds. *Women in the Church: A Fresh Analysis of 1 Timothy 2:9-15*. 2nd ed. Grand Rapids, MI: Baker, 2005.

Köster, Helmut, ed. *Ephesos: Metropolis of Asia*. HTS 41. Valley Forge, PA: Trinity International Press, 1995.

_____. *Paul and His World: Interpreting the New Testament in its Context*. Minneapolis: Fortress Press, 2007.

_____. *Cities of Paul, Images and Interpretations: from the Harvard New Testament and Archaeology Project*. Minneapolis: Fortress Press, 2004.

Kovach, Stephen D., Peter R. Schemm, Jr. "A Defense of the Doctrine of the Eternal Subordination of the Son." *JETS* 42 (1999): 461–476.

Kreitzer, Larry J. "Living in the Lycus Valley: Earthquake Imagery in Colossians, Philemon and Ephesians." In: *Testimony and Interpretation: Early Christology in Its Judeo-Hellenistic Milieu: Studies in Honour of Petr Pokorný*, ed. Jiři Mrázek and Petr Pokorný, 81–94. JSNTSup 272. London: T&T Clark, 2004.

_____. *Philemon*. Readings. Sheffield: Sheffield Phoenix Press, 2008.

_____. "Resurrection." In: *Dictionary of Paul and His Letters*, eds. G. F. Hawthorne, R. P. Martin, D. G. Reid, 805–812. Downers Grove: IVP, 1993.

_____. "Eschatology." In: *Dictionary of Paul and His Letters*, eds. G. F. Hawthorne, R. P. Martin, D. G. Reid,

253–269. Downers Grove: IVP, 1993.

Kremer, J. "Die dreifache Wiedergabe des Damaskuserlebnisses Pauli in der Apostelgeschichte. Eine Hilfe für das rechte Verständnis der lukanischen Osterevangelien." In: *The Unity of Luke-Acts*, ed. J. Verheyden, 329–355. Bibliotheca Ephemeridum Theologicarum Lovaniensium 142. Leuven: Leuven University Press, 1999.

Krodel, Gerhard, ed. *The Deutero-Pauline Letters: Ephesians, Colossians, 2 Thessalonians, 1-2 Timothy, Titus.* Proclamation Commentaries. Rev. Ed. Minneapolis: Fortress Press, 1993.

Kroeger, Catherine. "Head." In: *Dictionary of Paul and His Letters*, ed. G. F. Hawthorne, R. P. Martin, D. G. Reid, 375–377. Downers Grove: IVP, 1993.

Kruse, C. G. "Virtues and Vices." In: *Dictionary of Paul and His Letters*, eds. G. F. Hawthorne, R. P. Martin, D. G. Reid, 962–963. Downers Grove, IL: IVP, 1993.

Kümmel, W. G., P. Feine, and J. Behm. *Introduction to the New Testament.* 14th rev. ed. Trans. A. J. Mattill, Jr. Nashville: Abingdon, 1966.

Kuula, Kari. *The Law, the Covenant and God's Plan, Volume 1: Paul's Polemical Treatment of the Law in Galatians.* Helsinki: Finnish Exegetical Society; Göttingen: V&R, 1999.

Laato, Tim. *Paul and Judaism. An Anthropological Approach.* Atlanta, GA: Scholars Press, 1995.

Ladd, George Eldon. "Historic Premillennialism." In: *The Meaning of the Millennium: Four Views*, ed. G. E. Ladd, R. G. Clouse, 17–40. Downers Grove, IL: IVP, 1977.

_____. *A Theology of the New Testament.* Revised Edition. Grand Rapids, MI: Eerdmans, 1993.

Lakey, Michael. *Image and Glory of God: 1 Corinthians 11:2–16 as a Case Study in Bible, Gender and Hermeneutics.* LNTS 418. New York: T&T Clark, 2010.

Lamp, Jeffrey S. "Paul, the Law, Jews, and Gentiles: A Contextual and Exegetical Reading of Romans 2:12–16." *JETS* 42 (1999): 37–51.

Lampe, Peter. "Paul, Patrons, and Clients." In: *Paul in the Greco-Roman World: A Handbook*, ed. J. Sampley, 488–523. Harrisburg, PA: Trinity Press International, 2003.

_____. "Paths of early Christian mission into Rome: Judaeo-Christians in the households of pagan masters." In: *Celebrating Romans: Template for Pauline Theology. Essays in Honor of Robert Jewett*, ed. Sheila E. McGinn, 143–148. Grand Rapids, MI: Eerdmans, 2004.

Lang, Manfred. *Die Kunst des christlichen Lebens. Rezeptionsästhetische Studien zum lukanischen Paulusbild.* Arbeiten zur Bibel und ihre Geschichte 29. Leipzig: Evangelische Verlagsanstalt, 2008.

Lee, Aquila H. *From Messiah to Preexistent Son: Jesus' Self-Consciousness and Early Christian Exegesis of Messianic Psalms.* WUNT 2.192. Tübingen: Mohr Siebeck, 2005.

Lee, Michelle V. *Paul, The Stoics, and The Body of Christ.* SNTSM 137. New York: Cambridge University, 2006.

Lenz, Jr., John Clayton. *Luke's Portrait of Paul.* SNTSMS 77. Cambridge: Cambridge University Press, 1993.

Lichtenberger, Hermann. *Das Ich Adams und das Ich der Menschheit. Studien zum Menschenbild in Römer 7.* WUNT 164. Tübingen: Mohr Siebeck, 2004.

Liefeld, Walter L. *Interpreting the Book of Acts.* Guides to NT Exegesis. Grand Rapids, MI: Baker, 1995.

Lincoln, Andrew T. *Ephesians.* WBC 42. Dallas, TX: Thomas Nelson, 1990.

Lindemann, A. *Paulus im ältesten Christentum. Das Bild des Apostels und die Rezeption der paulinischen Theologie in der frühchristlichen Literatur bis Marcion.* BHTh 58. Tübingen: Mohr Siebeck, 1979.

_____. "Einheit und Vielfalt im lukanischen Doppelwerk. Beobachtungen zu Reden, Wundererzählungen und Mahlberichten." In: *The Unity of Luke–Acts*, ed. J. Verheyden, 225–254. BETL 142. Leuven: Leuven University Press, 1999.

Long, Adrian. *Paul and Human Rights: A Dialogue with the Father of the Corinthian Community*. Sheffield: Sheffield Phoenix, 2009.

Long, Fredrick J. Long. *Ancient Rhetoric and Paul's Apology: The Compositional Unity of 2 Corinthians*. SNTSMS 131. Cambridge: Cambridge University Press, 2004.

Longenecker, Bruce W. *Rhetoric at the Boundaries: The Art and Theology of New Testament Chain-Link Transitions*. Waco, TX: Baylor University Press, 2005.

Longenecker, Richard N. "Prayer in the Pauline Letters." In: *Into God's Presence: Prayer in the New Testament*, ed. R. N. Longenecker, 203–227. Grand Rapids, MI: Eerdmans, 2001.

Lowe, Chuck. "'There is No Condemnation' (Romans 8:1): But Why Not?" *JETS* 42 (1999): 231–250.

Luckensmeyer, David. *The Eschatology of First Thessalonians*. NTOA 71. Göttingen: V&R, 2009.

Lührmann, Dieter. "Paul and the Pharisaic Tradition." *JSNT* 36 (1989): 75–94; reprint in: *The Pauline Writings*, ed. S. E. Porter and C. A. Evans, 35–53. London: T&T Clark International, 2004.

Maddox, Robert. *The Purpose of Luke–Acts*. Edinburgh: T&T Clark, 1992.

Madvig, Donald H. "The Missionary Preaching of Paul: A Problem in New Testament Theology." *JETS* 20.2 (1977): 147–155.

Magness, Jodi. "Women at Qumran." In: *What Athens has to do with Jerusalem: Essays on Classical, Jewish, and early Christian Art and Archaeology in honor of Gideon Foerster*. Edited by by Leonard V. Rutgers, 89–123. Imprint Leuven: Peeters, 2002.

Maher, Michael. "Knowing the Tree by its Roots: Jewish Context of the Early Christian Movement." In: *Christian Origins. Worship, Belief and Society*, 1–28. JSNTSup 241. Sheffield: Sheffield Academic Press, 2003.

Malherbe, Abraham J. *The Letters to the Thessalonians: A New Translation with Introduction and Commentary*. AB 32B. New York: Doubleday, 2000.

_____. *Paul and the Popular Philosophers*. Minneapolis: Fortress Press, 2006.

Malina, Bruce J. and John J. Pilch. *Social-Science Commentary on the Letters of Paul*. Minneapolis: Fortress Press, 2006.

Marguerat, Daniel. *The First Christian Historian: Writing the "Acts of the Apostles."* SNTSMS 121. Cambridge: Cambridge University Press, 2002.

_____. "Paul après Paul: Une histoire de réception." *NTS* 54 (2008): 317–337.

Markschies, Christoph. "Paul, the Apostle." In: *The Westminster Handbook to Origen*, ed. J. A. McGuckin, 167–169. Louisville, KY: Westminster John Knox Press, 2004.

Marshall, I. H. *New Testament Theology: Many Witnesses, One Gospel*. Downers Grove, IL: IVP, 2004.

_____. "A New Understanding of the Present and the Future: Paul and Eschatology." In: *The Road from Damascus: The Impact of Paul's Conversion on His Life, Thought, and Ministry*, ed. Richard N. Longenecker, 43–61. Grand Rapids, MI: Eerdmans, 1997.

_____. "The Pastoral Epistles in Recent Study." In: *Entrusted with the Gospel: Paul's Theology in the Pastoral Epistles*, ed. A. J. Köstenberger and T. L. Wilder, 268–324. Nashville: B&H Academics, 2010.

Marshall, I. H. and Ph. H. Towner. *A Critical and Exegetical Commentary on the Pastoral Epistles*. ICC. London: T&T Clark, 1999.

Marshall, I. H., Stephen Travis, and Ian Paul. *Exploring the New Testament: A Guide to the Letters & Revelation*. Volume Two. Downers Grove, IL: IVP, 2002.

Martin, D. B. *Slavery as Salvation: The Metaphor of Slavery in Pauline Christianity*. New Haven, CT: Yale University Press, 1990.

Martin, Francis. *Narrative Parallels to the New Testament.* Atlanta, GA: Scholars Press, 1988.

Martin, Ralph P. "Hymns, Hymn Fragments, Songs, Spiritual Songs." In: *Dictionary of Paul and His Letters*, eds. G. F. Hawthorne, R. P. Martin, D. G. Reid, 419–423. Downers Grove, IL: IVP, 1993.

————. "Creed." In: *Dictionary of Paul and His Letters*, eds. G. F. Hawthorne, R. P. Martin, D. G. Reid, 190–192. Downers Grove, IL: IVP, 1993.

————. *New Testament Foundations: A Guide for Christian Students. Volume 2: The Acts, the Epistles, the Apocalypse.* Grand Rapids, MI: Eerdmans, 1978.

Martin, Seán Charles. *Pauli Testamentum: 2 Timothy and the Last Words of Moses.* Rome: Gregorian University Press, 1997.

Martyn, J. Louis. *Theological Issues in the Letters of Paul.* Nashville: Abingdon, 1997.

————. "Nomos plus genitive noun in Paul." In: *Early Christianity and Classical Culture. Comparative Studies in Honor of Abraham J. Malherbe*, ed. J. T. Fitzgerald, Th. H. Olbright, L. M. White, 575–587. Leiden: Brill, 2003.

Matera, Frank J. *II Corinthians: A Commentary.* The New Testament Library. Louisville, KY: Westminster John Knox Press, 2003.

Matlock, R. B. "'Even the Demons Believe': Paul and πίστις Χριστοῦ." *CBQ* 64 (2002): 300–318.

————. "The Rhetoric of πίστις in Paul: Galatians 2.16, 3.22, Romans 3.22, and Philippians 3.9." *JSNT* 30.2 (2007): 173–203.

Mattill, Andrew J. "The Purpose of Acts: Schneckenburger Reconsidered." In: *Apostolic History and the Gospel. Biblical and Historical Essays Presented to F.F. Bruce*, eds. W. Ward Gasque and Ralph P. Martin, 108–122. Exeter: The Paternoster Press, 1970.

————. "The Jesus-Paul Parallels and the Purpose of Luke–Acts: H. H. Evans Reconsidered." *NovT* 17.1 (1975): 15–46.

————. "The Date and Purpose of Luke–Acts: Rackham Reconsidered." *CBQ* 40.3 (1978): 335–350.

Maxwell, David R. "Justified by works and not by faith alone: Reconciling Paul and James." *Concordia Journal* 33.4 (2007): 375–378.

Mayer-Haas, Andrea. "Titus im Zeugnis des Neuen Testaments.: Eine Einführung." In: *Ein Meisterschüler: Titus und sein Brief. Michael Theobald zum 60. Geburtstag*, ed. H.-U. Weidemann and W. Eisele, 11–30. Stuttgarter Bibelstudien 214. Stuttgart: Verlag Katholisches Bibelwerk, 2008.

McCabe, Elizabeth A. "A Reevaluation of Phoebe in Romans 16:1–2 as a Diakonos and Prostatis: Exposing the Inaccuracies of English Translations." In: *Women in the Biblical World: A Survey of Old and New Testament Perspectives*, Vol. 1, ed. Elizabeth A. McCabe. Lanham, MD: University Press of America, 2009.

McDonough, S. M. "Small Change: from Saul to Paul Again." *JBL* 125 (2006): 390–391.

McGrath, Alister E. *Iustitia Dei: A History of the Christian Doctrine of Justification.* Cambridge: Cambridge University Press, 1982.

————. "Cross, Theology of." In: *Dictionary of Paul and His Letters*, eds. G. F. Hawthorne, R. P. Martin, D. G.Reid, 192–197. Downers Grove: IVP, 1993.

————. "Justification." In: *Dictionary of Paul and His Letters*, eds. G. F. Hawthorne, R. P. Martin, D. G. Reid, 517–523. Downers Grove: IVP, 1993.

McKeown, Niall. *The Invention of Ancient Slavery?* Duckworth Classical Essays. London: Gerald Duckworth & Co., 2007.

McRay, John. *Paul: His Life and Teaching.* Grand Rapids, MI: Baker, 2003.

_____. "Thessalonica." In: *Dictionary of New Testament Background*, eds. C. A. Evans, Stanley E. Porter, 1231-1233. Downers Grove, IL: IVP, 2000.

Meadors, Gary T., ed. *Four Views on Moving Beyond the Bible to Theology*. Grand Rapids, MI: Zondervan, 2009.

Mealand, D. L. "The Extent of the Pauline Corpus: A Multivariate Approach." *JSNT* 59 (1995): 61–92.

Meeks, Wayne A. *The First Urban Christians: The Social World of the Apostle Paul*. 2nd ed. New Haven, CT: Yale University Press, 2003.

Meeks, Wayne A. and John T. Fitzgerald, eds. *The Writings of St. Paul. A Norton Critical Edition*. New York: W. W. Norton & Company, 2007.

Meinardus, Otto F. A. "Paul's Missionary Journey to Spain: Tradition and Folklore." *BA* 41.2 (1978): 61–63.

Meißner, Stefan. *Die Heimholung des Ketzers. Studien zur jüdischen Auseinandersetzung mit Paulus*. WUNT 2.87. Tübingen: Mohr Siebeck, 1996.

Merkle, Ben L. "Romans 11 and the Future of Ethnic Israel." *JETS* 43 (2000): 709–721.

_____. *The Elder and Overseer: One Office in the Early Church*. Studies in Biblical Literature 57. New York: Lang, 2003.

Metzger, Bruce. *The Text of the New Testament: Its Transmission, Corruption and Restoration*. 3rd edition. New York: Oxford University Press, 1992.

_____. "A Reconsideration of Certain Arguments Against the Pauline Authorship of the Pastoral Epistles." *ExpT* 70 (1958–59): 91–94.

Metzger, Paul. *Katechon. II Thess 2,1–12 im Horizont apokalytpischen Denkens*. BZNW 135. Berlin: de Gruyter, 2005.

Meyer, Marvin W. "Mystery Religions." In: *The Anchor Bible Dictionary*, ed. D. N. Freedman, 4:941–945. New York: Doubleday, 1992.

Middendorf, Michael Paul. *The "I" in the Storm: A Study of Romans 7*. St. Louis: Concordia Academic Press, 1997.

Miller, Colin. "The Imperial Cult in the Pauline Cities of Asia Minor and Greece." *CBQ* 72 (2010): 314–332.

Miller, Ed. "More Pauline references to homosexuality?" *EQ* 77.2 (2005): 129–134.

Mills, Watson E. *An Index to Periodical Literature on the Apostle Paul*. Leiden: Brill, 1993.

Mitchell, Matthew W. *Abortion and the Apostolate: A Study in Pauline Conversion, Rhetoric, and Scholarship*. Gorgias Dissertations: Biblical Studies 42. Piscataway, NJ: Gorgias, 2009.

Mitchell, S. Anatolia. *Land, Men, and Gods in Asia Minor. Vol. 2: The Rise of the Church*. Oxford: Clarendon Press, 1993.

Mohrlang, Roger. *Matthew and Paul: A Comparison of Ethical Perspectives*. Cambridge: Cambridge University Press, 1985.

Moo, Douglas J. "'Law,' 'Works of the Law,' and Legalism in Paul." *WTJ* 45 (1983): 73–100.

_____. *The Letter to the Colossians and to Philemon*. Pillar New Testament Commentary. Grand Rapids, MI: Eerdmans, 2008.

_____. *The Letter of James*. Pillar NT Commentary. Grand Rapids, MI: Eerdmans, 2000.

Morgenthaler, R. *Statistik des neutestamentlichen Wortschatzes*. Zürich: Gotthelf-Verlag, 1958.

Morris, Leon. *New Testament Theology*. Grand Rapids, MI: Zondervan, 1986.

_____. "Redeemer, Redemption." In: D. R. W. Wood and I. Howard Marshall, *New Bible Dictionary*, 3rd ed., ed. D. R. W. Wood and I. H. Marshall, 1003–1004. Downers Grove, IL: InterVarsity Press, 1996.

Morton, A. Q. and J. McLeman. *Paul, the Man and the Myth*. New York: Harper & Row, 1966.

Mosse, Martin. *The Three Gospels: New Testament History Introduced by the Synoptic Problem*. PBM. Eugene, OR: Wipf & Stock, 2007.

Mott, S. C. "Ethics." In: *Dictionary of Paul and His Letters*, eds. G. F. Hawthorne, R. P. Martin, D. G. Reid, 269–275. Downers Grove, IL: IVP, 1993.

Motyer, Stephen. "The Relationship Between Paul's Gospel of 'All One in Christ Jesus' (Gal. 3:28) and the 'Household Codes'." *Vox Evangelica* 19 (1989): 33–48.

Mounce, Robert H. *Pastoral Epistles*. WBC 46. Nashville: Thomas Nelson, 2000.

Mount, Christopher. *Pauline Christianity: Luke–Acts and the Legacy of Paul*. NovTSupp 104. Leiden: Brill, 2002.

Mowery, Robert L. "Paul and Caristanius at Pisidian Antioch." *Biblica* 87.2 (2006): 223–242.

Muhlack, Gudrun, *Die Parallelen von Lukas-Evangelium und Apostelgeschichte*. Theologie und Wirklichkeit 8. Frankfurt: Peter Lang, 1979.

Murphy-O'Connor, Jerome (a). *Paul: A Critical Life*. New York: Oxford University Press, 1996.

————. *St. Paul's Corinth. Texts and Archaeology*. 3rd rev. ed. Collegeville, MN: Liturgical Press, 2002.

————. *Jesus and Paul: Parallel Lives*. Collegeville, MN: Liturgical Press, 2007.

————. "2 Timothy Contrasted with 1 Timothy and Titus." *Revue Biblique* 98 (1991): 403–418.

————. "Co-authorship in the Corinthian Correspondence." *Revue Biblique* 100 (1993): 562-70; republished in: *Keys to First Corinthians: Revisiting the Major Issues*. Oxford: Oxford University Press, 2009, 1–10.

Murray, George W. "Paul's Corporate Evangelism in the Book of Acts." *Bibliotheca Sacra* 155 (1998): 189-200.

Nägeli, Theodor. *Der Wortschatz des Apostels Paulus: Beitrag zur sprachgeschichtlichen Erforschung des Neuen Testaments*. Goettingen: Vandenhoeck & Ruprecht, 1905.

Nanos, Mark D. (a) "Introduction." In: *The Galatians Debate: Contemporary Issues in Rhetorical and Historical Interpretation*, ed. Mark D. Nanos, xi–xli. Peabody, MA: Hendrickson, 2002.

————— (b). "Paul and Judaism. Why not Paul's Judaism?" In: *Paul Unbound: Other Perspectives on the Apostle*, ed. Mark D. Given, 117 –-160. Peabody, MA: Hendrickson, 2010.

Nasrallah, Laura. "The Acts of the Apostles, Greek Cities, and Hadrian's Panhellenion." *JBL* 127.3 (2008): 533–566.

Neirynck, F. "The Miracle Stories in the Acts of the Apostles. An Introduction." In: *Actes des Apôtres. Traditions, rédaction, théologie*, ed. J. Kremer 169–213. BETL 48. Leuven: Peeters, 1979.

Neubrand, Maria. *Abraham. Vater von Juden und Nichtjuden. Eine exegetische Studie zu Römer 4*. Würzburg: Echter Verlag, 1997.

Neumann, Kenneth J. *The Authenticity of the Pauline Epistles in the Light of Stylostatistical Analysis*. SBLDS 120. Atlanta, GA: Scholars, 1990.

Neusner, Jacob. *The Babylonian Talmud: A Translation and Commentary*. Peabody, MA: Hendrickson Publishers, 2011.

————. *The Jerusalem Talmud: A Translation and Commentary*. Peabody, MA: Hendrickson Publishers, 2008.

Nicholl, Colin R. *From Hope to Despair in Thessalonica: Situating 1 and 2 Thessalonians*. SNTMS 126. Cambridge: Cambridge University Press, 2004.

Nicklas, Tobias. "The Letter to Philemon: A Discussion with J. Albert Harrill." In: *Paul's World*, ed. S. Porter, 201-220. Pauline Studies, vol. 4. Leiden: Brill, 2008.

Nobbs, Alanna. "Cyprus." In: *The Book of Acts in Its First Century Setting. Volume 2: Graeco-Roman Setting*, ed. D. W. J. Gill, C. Gempf, 279–289. Grand Rapids, MI: Eerdmans, 1994.

Nöh, Rüdiger. *Der irdische Christus: Eine Exegese von 2 Korinther 5,16.* Nürnberg: VTR, 1998.

Nolland, John. *Luke 1–9:20.* WBC 35A. Nashville: Thomas Nelson, 1989.

Nordling, John G. "Onesimus Fugitivus: A Defense of the Runaway Slave Hypothesis in Philemon." *JSNT* 41 (1991): 97–119.

Oakes, Peter. *Philippians: From People to Letter.* MSSNTS 110. Cambridge: Cambridge University Press, 2001.

————. "Re-mapping the Universe: Paul and the Emperor in 1 Thessalonians and Philippians." *JSNT* 27.3 (2005): 301–322.

O'Brien, P. T. "Letters, Letter Forms." In: *Dictionary of Paul and His Letters,* eds. G. F. Hawthorne, R. P. Martin, and D. G. Reid, 550–553. Downers Grove, IL: IVP, 1993.

O'Donnell, Matthew Brook. *Corpus Linguistics and the Greek of the New Testament.* New Testament Monographs 6. Sheffield: Sheffield Phoenix Press, 2005.

Odell-Scott, David W. "Patriarchy and Heterosexual Eroticism: The Question in Romans and Corinthians." In: *Gender, Tradition and Romans: Shared Ground, Uncertain Borders,* ed. Cristina Grenholm and Daniel Patte, 209–225. Romans Through History and Cultures Series. London: T&T Clark International, 2005.

————. "Let the Women Speak in Church: An Egalitarian Interpretation of 1 Cor 14:33b-36." *Biblical Theology Bulletin* 13 (1983): 90–93.

Omerzu, Heike. *Der Prozess des Paulus. Eine exegetische und rechtshistorische Untersuchung der Apostelge- schichte.* BZNW 115. Berlin: de Gruyter, 2002.

————. "Das traditionsgeschichtliche Verhältnis der Begegnungen von Jesus mit Herodes Antipas und Paulus mit Agrippa II." *StudNTUmwelt* 28 (2003): 121–145.

————. "Das Schweigen des Lukas: Überlegungen zum offenen Ende der Apostelgeschichte." In: *Das Ende des Paulus: Historische, theologische und literaturgeschichtliche Aspekte,* ed. F. W. Horn, 127–156. BZNW 106. Berlin: de Gruyter, 2001.

Oropeza, B. J. *Paul and Apostasy. Eschatology, Perseverance, and Falling Away in the Corinthian Congregation.* WUNT 115. Tübingen: Mohr Siebeck, 2000.

Ortlund, Dane. "Justified by Faith, Judged According to Works: Another Look at a Pauline Paradox." *JETS* 52 (2009): 323–339.

Osborne, G. "Hermeneutics/Interpreting Paul." In: *Dictionary of Paul and His Letters,* eds. G. F. Hawthorne, R. P. Martin, and D. G. Reid, 388–397. Downers Grove, IL: IVP, 1993.

————. "Hermeneutics and Women in the Church." *JETS* 20 (1977): 337–352.

Ostmeyer, Karl-Heinrich. *Kommunikation mit Gott und Christus: Sprache und Theologie des Gebetes im Neuen Testament.* WUNT 197. Tübingen: Mohr Siebeck, 2006.

Owen, Paul L. "The 'Works of the Law' in Romans and Galatians: A New Defense of the Subjective Genitive." *JBL* 126.3 (2007): 553–577.

Padgett, Alan. "Paul on Women in the Church: The Contradictions of Coiffure in 1 Corinthians 11:2–16." *JSNT* 20 (1984) : 69-86.

Park, M. Sydney. *Submission within the Godhead and the Church in the Epistle to the Philippians: An Exegetical and Theological Examination of the Concept of Submission in Philippians 2 and 3.* LNTS 361. New York: T&T Clark, 2007.

Parker, D. C. *An Introduction to the New Testament Manuscripts and Their Texts.* Cambridge: Cambridge

University Press, 2008.

Parks, M. Sydney. *Submission within the Godhead and the Church in the Epistle to the Philippians: An Exegetical and Theological Examination of the Concept of Submission in Philippians 2 and 3.* Library of the New Testament. London: T&T Clark International, 2007.

Parsons, Mikeal Carl, Richard I. Pervo. *Rethinking the Unity of Luke and Acts.* Minneapolis: Fortress, 1993.

Patella, Michael. *Lord of the Cosmos: Mithras, Paul, and the Gospel of Mark.* New York: T&T Clark, 2006.

Pattengale, Jerry A. "Crete." In: *The Anchor Bible Dictionary*, ed. D. N. Freedman, 1:1206. New York: Doubleday, 1992.

Pearson, Brook W. R. "Assumptions in the Criticism and Translation of Philemon." In: *Translating the Bible: Problems and Prospects*, ed. S. E. Porter and R. S. Hess, 253–280. JSNTSupp 173. Sheffield: Sheffield Academic Press, 1999.

_____. "Antioch (Pisidia)." In: *Dictionary of New Testament Background*, eds. C. A. Evans, Stanley E. Porter, 31–34. Downers Grove, IL: IVP, 2000.

Peerbolte, L. J. Lietaert. *Paul the Missionary.* Leuven: Peeters, 2003.

_____. "Paul the Miracle Worker: Development and Background of Pauline Miracle Stories." In: *Wonders Never Cease: The Purpose of Narrating Miracle Stories in the New Testament and Its Religious Environment*, ed. M. Labahn, B. J. L. Peerbolte, 180–199. The Library of New Testament Studies. London: T&T Clark, 2006.

Penna, Romano. *Paul the Apostle, Jew and Greek alike: A Theological and Exegetical Study. Volume 1. Trans.* Thomas P. Wahl. Collegeville, MN: The Liturgical Press, 1996.

Perrin, Nicholas. "On Raising Osiris in 1 Corinthians 15." *TynB* 58 (2007): 117–128.

Pervo, Richard I. *The Making of Paul: Constructions of the Apostle in Early Christianity.* Minneapolis: Fortress Press, 2010.

Phillips, Thomas E. *Paul, His Letters, and Acts.* Library of Pauline Studies. Peabody, MA: Hendrickson, 2009.

Pichler, Josef. *Paulusrezeption in der Apostelgeschichte. Untersuchungen zur Rede im pisidischen Antiochien.* IthS 50. Innsbruck/Wien: Tyrolia-Verlag, 1997.

_____. "Das theologische Anliegen der Paulusrezeption im lukanischen Werk." In: *The Unity of Luke–Acts*, ed. J. Verheyden, 731–743. BETL 142. Leuven: Leuven University Press, 1999.

Pierce, Ronald W., Rebecca M. Groothuis, eds. *Discovering Biblical Equality. Complementarity without Hierarchy.* 2nd ed. Downers Grove, IL: IVP, 2005.

Piper, John, Wayne Grudem, eds. *Recovering Biblical Manhood & Womanhood.* Rev. ed. Wheaton, IL: Crossway Books, 2006.

Pitts, Andrew W. "Hellenistic Schools in Jerusalem and Paul's Rhetorical Education." In: *Paul's World*, ed. Stanley E. Porter, 19–50. Pauline Studies 14. Leiden: Brill, 2008.

Price, Robert M. "Apocryphal Apparitions: 1 Corinthians 15:3–11 as a Post-Pauline Interpolation." *JHC* 2.2 (1995): 69–99.

Pobee, John S. *Persecution and Martyrdom in the Theology of Paul.* JSNTSupp 6. Sheffield: JSOT Press, 1985.

Polaski, Sandra Hack. *A Feminist Introduction to Paul.* St. Louis: Chalice Press, 2005.

Polhill, John B. *Paul and His Letters.* Nashville: Broadman & Holman, 1999.

_____. "The Relationship between Ephesians and Colossians." *Review & Expositor* 70.4 (1973): 439–450.

_____. *Acts.* NAC 26. Nashville: Broadman & Holman, 1992.

Pokorný, Petr and Ulrich Heckel. *Einleitung in das Neue Testament. Seine Literatur und Theologie im Überblick.* UTB. Tübingen: Mohr Siebeck, 2007.

Ponsot, H. "Les Pastorales, Seraient-elles les premières lettres de Paul?" *Lumière et Vie* 231 (1997): 83–93; 232 (1997): 79–90; 233 (1997): 83–89.

Popkes, Wiard. *Der Brief des Jakobus*. THNT 14. Leipzig: Evangelische Verlagsanstalt, 2001.

Porter, Stanley E., ed. *Paul and His Opponents*. Pauline Studies 2. Leiden: Brill, 2005.

Porter, Stanley E., ed. *Paul: Jew, Greek, and Roman*. Pauline Studies 5. Leiden: Brill, 2008.

Porter, Stanley E. "Peace, Reconciliation." In: *Dictionary of Paul and His Letters,* eds. G. F. Hawthorne, R. P. Martin, and D. G. Reid, 695–699. Downers Grove, IL: IVP, 1993.

_____. *The Paul of Acts: Essays in Literature, History and Theology*. Library of Pauline Studies. Peabody, MA: Hendrickson, 2001.

_____. "Scripture Justifies Mission: The Use of the Old Testament in Luke-Acts." In: *Hearing the Old Testament in the New Testament*, ed. Stanley E. Porter, 104–126. McMaster New Testament Studies. Grand Rapids, MI: Eerdmans, 2006.

_____. "Rome: Overview." In: *Dictionary of New Testament Background*, eds. C. A. Evans and Stanley E. Porter, 1010–1018. Downers Grove, IL: IVP, 2000.

Porter, Stanley E. and Christopher D. Stanley, eds. *As It Is Written: Studying Paul's Use of Scripture*. SBL Symposium. Atlanta, GA: Society of Biblical Literature, 2008.

Puskas, Charles and David Crump. *An Introduction to the Gospels and Acts*. Grand Rapids, MI: Eerdmans, 2008.

Quinn, Jerome D. and William C. Wacker. *The First and Second Letters to Timothy*. ECC. Vols. 1–2. Grand Rapids, MI: Eerdmans, 1995.

Rackham, Richard B. *The Acts of the Apostles*. 2nd ed. London: Methuen & Co., 1904.

Radday, Yehuda T. and Haim Shore. *Genesis: An Authorship Study*. Analecta biblica 103. Rome: Biblical Institute Press, 1985.

Radford, Lewis B. *The Epistle to the Colossians and the Epistle to Philemon*. Westminster Commentaries. London: Methuen & Co, 1931.

Radl, W. *Paulus und Jesus im lukanischen Doppelwerk: Untersuchungen zu Parallelmotiven im Lukasevangelium und in der Apostelgeschichte*. EHS 23/49. Frankfurt: Peter Lang, 1975.

_____. "Die Beziehungen der Vorgeschichte zur Apostelgeschichte, dargestellt an Lk 2,22–39." In: *The Unity of Luke–Acts*, ed. J. Verheyden, 297–312. Bibliotheca Ephemeridum Theologicarum Lovaniensium 142. Leuven: Leuven University Press, 1999.

Räisänen, Heikki. "Sprachliches zum Spiel des Paulus mit nomos." In: *Glaube und Gerechtigkeit: In Memoriam Rafael Gyllenberg*, ed. J. Kiilunen, 131–154. Helsinkii: Kirjapaino, 1983.

_____. "Galatians 2.16 and Paul's Break with Judaism." *NTS* 31 (1985): 543–553.

_____. *Paul and the Law*. WUNT 29. Tübingen: Mohr Siebeck, 1987.

_____. *The Rise of Christian Beliefs: The Thought World of Early Christianity*. Minneapolis: Fortress, 2010.

Rapske, B. M. "Roman Governors." In: *Dictionary of New Testament Background*, eds. C. A. Evans, Stanley E. Porter, 978–984. Downers Grove, IL: IVP, 2000.

Reasoner, Mark. *Romans in Full Circle: A History of Interpretation*. Louisville, KY: Westminster John Knox Press, 2005.

_____. "Political Systems." In: *Dictionary of Paul and His Letters*, eds. G. F. Hawthorne, R. P. Martin, and D. G. Reid, 718–723. Downers Grove, IL: IVP, 1993.

Reicke, B. "Chronologie der Pastoralbriefe." *ThLZ* 101 (1976): 81–94.

Reicke, Paul. *Re-examining Paul's Letters: The History of the Pauline Correspondence*. Harrisburg, PA: TPI, 2001.

Reimer, Andy M. *Miracle and Magic: A Study in the Acts of the Apostles and the Life of Apollonius of Tyana*. JSNTSup 235. Sheffield: Sheffield Academic Press, 2002.

Reinhardt, Wolfgang. "The Population Size of Jerusalem and the Numerical Growth of the Jerusalem Church." In: *The Book of Acts in Its First Century Setting. Volume 4: Palestinian Setting*, ed. Richard Bauckham, 237–265. Grand Rapids, MI: Eerdmans, 1995.

Reymond, Robert. *Paul, Missionary Theologian: A Survey of his Missionary Labours and Theology*. Fern, Scotland: Christian Focus Publications, 2003.

Richards, E. Randolph. *The Secretary in the Letters of Paul*. WUNT 2.42. Tübingen: Mohr Siebeck, 1991.

_____. *Paul and First-Century Letter Writing: Secretaries, Composition and Collection*. Downers Grove, IL: IVP, 2004.

Richards, William A. *Difference and Distance in Post-Pauline Christianity: An Epistolary Analysis of the Pastorals*. Studies in Biblical Literature 44. New York: Peter Lang, 2002.

Ridderbos, Herman. *Paul: An Outline of His Theology*. Grand Rapids, MI: Eerdmans, 1975.

Riesner, Rainer. *Paul's Early Period: Chronology, Mission Strategy, Theology*. Grand Rapids, MI: Eerdmans, 1998.

Roberts, A. and J. Donaldson, eds. *The Anti-Nicene Fathers*. Volume VII. Grand Rapids, MI: Eerdmans, 1970.

Robertson, A. T. *A Grammar of the Greek New Testament in the Light of Historical Research*. Nashville: Broadman Press, 1934.

Robinson, J. A. T. *Redating the New Testament*. Eugene, OR: Wipf & Stock, 2001.

Röcker, Fritz W. *Belial und Katechon: Eine Untersuchung zu 2 Thess 2,1–12 und 1 Thess 4,13–5,11*. WUNT 2.262. Tübingen: Mohr Siebeck, 2009.

Roetzel, Calvin J. *The Letters of Paul: Conversations in Context*. 4th ed. Louisville, KY: Westminster John Knox, 1998.

Rogers, Cleon L., Jr. "The Dionysian Background of Ephesians 5:18." *Bibliotheca Sacra* 136 (1979): 249–257.

Roh, Taeseong. *Der zweite Thessalonicherbrief als Erneuerung apokalyptischer Zeitdeutung*. NTOA 62. Göttingen: V&R, 2007.

Roller, Otto. *Das Formular der Paulinischen Briefe: Ein Beitrag zur Lehre vom Antiken Briefe*. BWANT. Stuttgart: Kohlhammer, 1933.

Rosner, Brian S. *Paul, Scripture, & Ethics: A Study of 1 Corinthians 5–7*. Biblical Studies Library. Grand Rapids, MI: Baker, 1999.

Russel, Peter J. *Heterodoxy within Second-Temple Judaism and Sectarian Diversity within the Early Church: A Correlative Study*. Lewiston, NY: Mellen, 2008.

Sahlin, H. *Der Messias und das Gottesvolk: Studien zur protolukanischen Theologie*. ASNU 12. Uppsala: lmqvist och Wiksells Boktrykeri, 1945.

Sampley, J. Paul, ed. *Paul in the Greco-Roman World: A Handbook*. Harrisburg, PA: Trinity Press International, 2003.

_____. "Introduction." *Paul in the Greco-Roman World: A Handbook*, ed. J. Paul Sampley, 1–15. Harrisburg, PA: Trinity Press International, 2003.

Sanders, Ed Parish. *Paul and Palestinian Judaism: A Comparison of Patterns of Religion*. Philadelphia: Fortress, 1977.

_____. *Paul: A Very Short Introduction.* Oxford: Oxford University Press, 1991.

Sänger, Dieter. "Die Adressaten des Galaterbriefs und das Problem einer Entwicklung in Paulus' theologischem Denken." In: *Beiträge zur urchristlichen Theologiegeschichte*, ed. W. Kraus, 247–275. BZNW 163. Berlin: de Gruyter, 2009.

Saunders, Ross. "Paul and the Imperial Cult." In *Paul and His Opponents*, ed. Stanley E. Porter, 227–238. Pauline Studies, vol. 2. Leiden: Brill, 2005.

Schlatter, Adolf. *Jesus und Paulus: Eine Vorlesung und Einige Aufsätze.* 3rd ed. Stuttgart: Calwer, 1961.

Schliesser, Benjamin. *Abraham's Faith in Romans 4: Paul's Concept of Faith in Light of the History of Reception of Genesis 15:6.* WUNT 2.224. Tübingen: Mohr Siebeck, 2007.

Schmithals, Walter. "Der Hebräerbrief als Paulusbrief: Beobachtungen zur Kanonbildung." *Die Weltlichkeit des Glaubens in der Alten Kirche. FS Ulrich Wickert*, ed. D. Wyrwa, 319–337. BZNW 85. Berlin: De Gryter, 1997. Reprint in *Paulus, die Evangelien und das Urchristentum: Beiträge von und zu Walter Schmithals zu seinem 80. Geburtstag*, ed. C. Breytenbach, 252–271. Arbeiten Zur Geschichte Des Antiken Judentums Und Des Urchristentums. Leiden: Brill, 2004.

Schnabel, Eckhard J. *Paul the Missionary: Realities, Strategies and Methods.* Downers Grove, IL: IVP, 2008.

Schneemelcher, Wilhelm. *New Testament Apocrypha.* Volumes 1–2. Rev. Ed. Trans. R. McL. Wilson. Louisville, KY: Westminster / John Knox Press, 1991–1992.

Schnelle, Udo. *Apostle Paul: His Life and Theology.* Trans. M. E. Boring. Grand Rapids, MI: Baker, 2005.

_____. *Einleitung in das Neue Testament.* 2nd ed. UTB. Göttingen: V&R, 1996.

Schnelle, Udo and Thomas Söding, eds. *Paulinische Christologie: Exegetische Beiträge. Hans Hübner zum 70. Geburtstag.* Göttingen: V&R, 2000.

Schreiner, Thomas R. "'Works of Law' in Paul" *Novum Testamentum* 33 (1991): 217–244.

_____. "Does Romans 9 Teach Individual Election Unto Salvation? Some Exegetical and Theological Reflections." *JETS* 36 (1993): 25–40.

_____. *The Law and its Fulfillment: A Pauline Theology of Law.* Grand Rapids, MI: Baker, 1993.

_____. *Paul: Apostle of God's Glory in Christ.* Downers Grove, IL: IVP, 2001.

_____. *Interpreting the Pauline Epistles.* Guides to New Testament Exegesis. Grand Rapids, MI: Baker, 1990.

_____. *New Testament Theology: Magnifying God in Christ.* Grand Rapids, MI: Baker, 2008.

Schreiner, Thomas and Ardel B. Caneday. *The Race Set Before Us: A Biblical Theology of Perseverance & Assurance.* Downers Grove, IL: IVP, 2001.

Schröter, Jens. "Actaforschung seit 1982: IV. Israel, die Juden und das Alte Testament. Paulusrezeption." *Theologische Rundschau* 73.1 (2008): 1–59.

Schüssler Fiorenza, Elisabeth. "The Praxis of Coequal Discipleship." In: *Paul and Empire: Religion and Power in Roman Imperial Society*, ed. R. A. Horsley, 224–241. Harrisburg, PA: Trinity Press International, 1997.

Schwartz, Daniel R. "Two Pauline allusions to the redemptive mechanism of the crucifixion." *JBL* 102.2 (1983): 259–268.

Scott, James M. "All Israel Will Be Saved." In: *Restoration: Old Testament, Jewish & Christian Perspectives*, ed. J. M. Scott, 489–526. Supplements to the Journal for the Study of Judaism 72. Leiden: Brill, 2001.

_____. "Restoration of Israel." In: *Dictionary of Paul and His Letters*, eds. G. F. Hawthorne, R. P. Martin, and D. G. Reid, 796–805. Downers Grove, IL: IVP, 1993.

_____. "Luke's Geographical Horizon." In: *The Book of Acts in Its Graeco-Roman Setting*, ed. D. W. J. Gill, C. Gempf, 483–544. Grand Rapids, MI: Eerdmans, 1994.

_____. "Paul's 'Imago Mundi' and Scripture." In: *Evangelium, Schriftauslegung, Kirche. FS für Peter*

Stuhlmacher zum 65. Geburtstag, ed. J. Ådna, S. J. Hafemann, O. Hofius, 366–381. Göttingen: V&R, 1997.

Seifrid, Mark A. "The Subject of Rom. 7:14–25." *Novum Testamentum* 34.4 (1992): 313–333.

_____. *Christ, Our Righteousness: Paul's Theology of Justification*. Downers Grove, IL: IVP, 2000.

Sherwin-White, A. N. *Roman Society and Roman Law in the New Testament*. Oxford: Clarendon Press, 1963.

Shi, Wenhua. *Paul's Message of the Cross as Body Language*. WUNT 2.254. Tübingen: Mohr Siebeck, 2008.

Silva, Moises. "Old Testament in Paul." In: *Dictionary of Paul and His Letters*, eds. G. F. Hawthorne, R. P. Martin, and D. G. Reid, 630–642. Downers Grove, IL: IVP, 1993.

_____. *Philippians*. 2nd ed. BECNT. Grand Rapids, MI: Baker Academic, 2005.

Soards, Marion L. *The Speeches in Acts: Their Content, Context, and Concerns*. Louisville, KY: Westminster John Knox, 1993.

Son, S. Aaron. *Corporate Elements in Pauline Anthropology*. Roma: Pontifical Biblical Institute Publications, 2001.

Southern, Pat. *The Roman Army: A Social and Institutional History*. Oxford: Oxford University Press, 2006.

Spencer, Aida Besancon. "The Wise fool (and the foolish Wise): A Study of Irony in Paul." *NovT* 23 (1981): 349–360.

Speyer, Wolfgang. "Zu den antiken Mysterienkulten." In: *Frühes Christentum im antiken Strahlungsfeld. Kleine Schriften III*, 103–119. WUNT 213. Tübingen: Mohr Siebeck, 2007.

Stange, Erich. *Paulinische Reisepläne*. Beiträge zur Förderung christlicher Theologie 22. Gütersloh: C. Bertelsmann, 1918.

Stanley, Christopher D. "Paul and Scripture: Charting the Course." In: *As It Is Written: Studying Paul's Use of Scripture*, eds. S. E. Porter, C. D. Stanley, 3–12. SBL Symposium. Atlanta, GA: Society of Biblical Literature, 2008.

Stegner, W. "Jew, Paul the." In: *Dictionary of Paul and His Letters*, eds. G. F. Hawthorne, R. P. Martin, and D. G. Reid, 503–511. Downers Grove, IL: IVP, 1993.

Stemberger, G. "Was There a 'Mainstream Judaism' in the Late Second Temple Period?" *Review of Rabbinic Judaism* 4 (2001): 189–208.

Still, Todd D., ed. *Jesus and Paul Reconnected: Fresh Pathways into an Old Debate*. Grand Rapids, MI: Eerdmans, 2007.

Still, Todd D. *Conflict at Thessalonica: A Pauline Church and its Neighbours*. JSNTSupp 183. Sheffield: Sheffield Academic Press, 1999.

Stott, John. *The Message of Romans: God's Good News for the World*. BST. Downers Grove, IL: InterVarsity, 1994.

Stowers, Stanley K. *A Rereading of Romans: Justice, Jews, and Gentiles*. New Haven, CT: Yale University Press, 1994.

Strelan, Rick. *Paul, Artemis, and the Jews in Ephesus*. BZNW 80. Berlin: de Gruyter, 1996.

Stuckenbruck, Loren T. "Colossians and Philemon." In: *The Cambridge Companion to St. Paul*, ed. J. D. G. Dunn, 116–132. Cambridge: Cambridge University Press, 2003.

Stuhlmacher, Peter. *Biblische Theologie des Neuen Testaments. Volume 1: Grundlegung. Von Jesus zu Paulus*. 2nd ed. Göttingen: V&R, 1997.

Sumney, Jeffrey. *Identifying Paul's Opponents. The Question of Method in 2 Corinthians*. JSNTSup. 40. Sheffield: JSOT Press, 1990.

_____. *"Servants of Satan," "False Brothers" and Other Opponents of Paul*. JSNTSup. 188. Sheffield: Sheffield Academic Press, 1999.

_____. "Studying Paul's Opponents: Advances and Challenges." In: *Paul and His Opponents*, ed. Stanley E. Porter, 7–58. Pauline Studies 2. Leiden: Brill, 2005.

_____. "Paul and His Opponents: The Search." In: *Paul Unbound: Other Perspectives on the Apostle*. Peabody, MA: Hendrcikson, 2010.

Tajra, Harry W. *The Trial of St. Paul: A Juridical Exegesis of The Second Half of the Acts of the Apostles*. WUNT 2.35. Tübingen: Mohr Siebeck, 1989.

Talbert, Charles H. *Literary Patterns, Theological Themes, and the Genre of Luke-Acts*. SBLMS 20. Missoula, MT: Scholars Press, 1974.

_____. *Ephesians and Colossians*. Paideia. Grand Rapids, MI: Baker, 2007.

_____. *Reading Acts : A Literary and Theological Commentary on the Acts of the Apostles*. Rev. ed. Macon, GA: Smyth & Helwys Publishing, 2005.

_____. *Reading Luke : A Literary and Theological Commentary on the Third Gospel*. Rev. ed. Macon, GA: Smyth & Helwys Publishing, 2002.

_____. "Paul, Judaism, and the Revisionists." *Catholic Biblical Quarterly* 63 (2001): 1–22.

Tannehill, Robert C. *Narrative Unity of Luke–Acts: A Literary Interpretation*. 2 vols. Minneapolis: Fortress Press, 1990.

Tatum, Gregory. *New Chapters in the Life of Paul: The Relative Chronology of His Career*. CBQMS 41. Washington, DC: The Catholic Biblical Association of America, 2006.

Tenney, Merrill C. *New Testament Survey*. Rev. ed. Grand Rapids, MI: Eerdmans, 1980.

Terry, Ralph Bruce. "Patterns of Discourse Structure in I Corinthians." *Journal of Translation and Textlinguistics* 7 (1996): 1–30.

Theissen, Gerd. "Social Stratification in the Corinthian Community: A Contribution to the Sociology of Early Hellenistic Christianity." In: *The Social Setting of Pauline Christianity: Essays on Corinth*, 69–119. Edinburgh: T&T Clark, 1982.

_____. "The Strong and the Weak in Corinth: A Sociological Analysis of a Theological Quarrel." In: *The Social Setting of Pauline Christianity: Essays on Corinth*, 21–143. Edinburgh: T&T Clark, 1982.

Thielman, Frank. *Theology of the New Testament. A Canonical and Synthetic Approach*. Grand Rapids, MI: Zondervan, 2005.

Thiselton, Anthony C. *The First Epistle to the Corinthians*. NIGTC. Grand Rapids, MI: Eerdmans, 2000.

_____. *The Living Paul: An Introduction to the Apostle's Life and Thought*. Downers Grove, IL: IVP, 2009.

Thomas, Robert L. "Tongues … Will Cease." *JETS* 17 (1974): 81–89.

Thompson, J. W. "The Epistle to the Hebrews and the Pauline Legacy." *Restoration Quarterly* 47.4 (2005): 197–206.

Thompson, G. L. "Roman Military." In: *Dictionary of New Testament Background*, eds. S. E. Porter, C. A. Evans, 991–995. Downers Grove, IL: IVP, 2000.

Thorsteinsson, Runar M. "Paul and Roman Stoicism: Romans 12 and Contemporary Stoic Ethics." *JSNT* 29.2 (2006): 139–161.

_____. *Roman Christianity and Roman Stoicism: A Comparative Study of Ancient Morality*. Oxford: Oxford University Press, 2010.

Thurston, Bonnie B. and Judith M. Ryan. *Philippians and Philemon*. Sacra Pagina. Collegeville, MN: Liturgical Press, 2009.

Tidball, D. J. "Social Setting of Mission Churches." In: *Dictionary of Paul and His Letters*, eds. G. F. Hawthorne, R. P. Martin, D. G. Reid, 883–891. Downers Grove, IL: IVP, 1993. DPL, 883–891.

Tolmie, D. François. *Persuading the Galatians: A Text-Centered Rhetorical Analysis of a Pauline Letter*. WUNT

2.190. Tübingen: Mohr Siebeck, 2005.

Tonstad, Sigve. "πίστις Χριστοῦ: Reading Paul in a New Paradigm." *AndUnivSemStud* 40 (2002): 37–59.

Towner, P. H. "Households and Household Codes." In: *Dictionary of Paul and His Letters*, ed. G. F. Hawthorne, R. P. Martin, D. G. Reid, 417–419. Downers Grove, IL: IVP, 1993.

_____. *The Letters to Timothy and Titus*. NICNT. Grand Rapids, MI: Eerdmans, 2006.

_____. *1–2 Timothy & Titus*. The IVP New Testament Commentary Series. Downers Grove, IL: IVP, 1994.

Trebilco, Paul. "Asia." In: *The Book of Acts in Its First Century Setting. Volume 2: Graeco-Roman Setting*, eds. D. W. J. Gill and C. Gempf, 291–362. Grand Rapids: Eerdmans, 1994.

_____. *The Early Christians in Ephesus from Paul to Ignatius*. WUNT 166. Tübingen: Mohr Siebeck, 2004.

Trobisch, David. *The First Edition of the New Testament*. Oxford: Oxford University Press, 2000.

Turner, Nigel. *A Grammar of New Testament Greek*. Vol. 4, Style. Edinburgh: T&T Clark, 1976.

Twelftree, Graham H. "Jesus and Magic in Luke–Acts." In: *Jesus and Paul: Global Perspectives in Honor of James D. G. Dunn for His Seventieth Birthday*, eds. B. J. Oropeza, C. K. Robertson, and D. C. Mohrman, 46–58. LNTS 414. New York: T&T Clark, 2010.

Ulansey, David. "Solving the Mithraic Mysteries." *BAR* 20.5 (1994): 40–53.

Ulrichs, Karl Friedrich. *Christusglaube. Studien zum Syntagma* πίστις Χριστοῦ *und zum paulinischen Verständnis von Glaube und Rechtfertigung*. WUNT 2.227. Tübingen: Mohr Siebeck, 2007.

Vahrenhorst, Martin. *Kultische Sprache in den Paulusbriefen*. WUNT 230. Tübingen: Mohr Siebeck, 2008.

Van Bruggen, Jakob. *Die geschichtliche Einordnung der Pastoralbriefe*. Wuppertal: Brockhaus, 1981.

_____. *Paul: Pioneer For Israel's Messiah*. Trans. Ed M. Van der Maas. Phillipsburg, NJ: P&R Publishing, 2005.

Van der Watt, Jan G., ed. *Identity, Ethics, and Ethos in the New Testament*. BZNW 141. Berlin: de Gruyter, 2006.

Van Kooten, George H. *Cosmic Christology in Paul and the Pauline School: Colossians and Ephesians in the Context of Graeco-Roman Cosmology with a New Synopsis of the Greek Texts*. WUNT 2.171. Tübingen: Mohr Siebeck, 2003.

Van Neste, Ray. *Structure in the Pastoral Epistles*. JSNTSupp 280. London: T&T Clark, 2004.

_____. "Cohesion and Structure in the Pastoral Epistles." In: *Entrusted with the Gospel: Paul's Theology in the Pastoral Epistles*, eds. A. J. Köstenberger, T. L. Wilder, 84–104. Grand Rapids, MI: Baker, 2010.

Van Spanje, T. E. *Inconsistency in Paul? A Critique of the Work of Heikki Räisänen*. WUNT 2.110. Tübingen: Mohr Siebeck, 1999.

Vegge, Tor. *Paulus und das antike Schulwesen. Schule und Bildung des Paulus*. BZNW 134. Berlin: de Gruyter, 2006.

Verheyden, J., ed. *The Unity of Luke–Acts*. BETL 142. Leuven: Leuven University Press, 1999.

Völter, Daniel. *Paulus und Seine Briefe. Kritische Untersuchungen zu einer neuen Grundlegung der Paulinischen Briefliteratur und ihrer Theologie*. Strassburg: J. H. Ed. Heitz (Heitz & Mündel), 1905.

Vos, Geerhardus. *The Pauline Eschatology*. Phillipsburg, NJ: Presbyterian and Reformed Publishing Co., 1986. (first 1930)

Waaler, Erik. *The Shema and The First Commandment in First Corinthians: An Intertextual Approach to Paul's*

Re-reading of Deuteronomy. WUNT 2.253. Tübingen: Mohr Siebeck, 2008.

Wagener, Ulrike. *Die Ordnung des 'Hauses Gottes.'* WUNT 2.65. Tübingen: Mohr Siebeck, 1994.

Walker, Jr., William O. "Translation and Interpretation of *ean me* in Galatians 2:16." *JBL* 116 (1997): 515–520.

_____. "The 'Theology of Woman's Place' and the 'Paulinist' Tradition." *Semeia* 28 (1983): 101–112.

Wall, R. W. "Intertextuality, Biblical." In: *Dictionary of New Testament Background*, eds. C. A. Evans, Stanley E. Porter, 541–551. Downers Grove, IL: IVP, 2000.

Wallace, Daniel B. "Galatians 3:19–20: A Crux Interpretum for Paul's View of the Law." *WTJ* 52 (1990): 225–245.

Wallace, Richard and Wynne Williams. *The Three Worlds of Paul of Tarsus.* London: Routledge, 1998.

Walters, James C. "Paul, Adoption, and Inheritance." In: *Paul in the Greco-Roman World: A Handbook*, ed. J. Sampley, 42–76. Harrisburg, PA: Trinity Press International, 2003.

Walton, Steve. *Leadership and Lifestyle. The Portrait of Paul in the Miletus Speech and 1 Thessalonians.* MSSNTS 108. Cambridge: Cambridge University Press, 2000.

Wanamaker, Charles A. *The Epistles to the Thessalonians.* NIGTC. Grand Rapids, MI: Eerdmans, 1990.

Wander, Bernd. "Warum wollte Paulus nach Spanien? Ein forschungs- und motifgeschichtlicher Überblick." In: *Das Ende des Paulus: Historische, theologische und literaturgeschichtliche Aspekte*, ed. F. W. Horn, 175–195. BZNW 106. Berlin: de Gruyter, 2001.

Watson, D. F. "Diatribe." In: *Dictionary of Paul and His Letters*, ed. G. F. Hawthorne, R. P. Martin, D. G. Reid, 213–214. Downers Grove, IL: IVP, 1993.

Watson, Francis. *Paul, Judaism and the Gentiles: A Sociological Approach.* SNTSMS 56. Cambridge: Cambridge University Press, 1986.

_____. *Paul and the Hermeneutics of Faith.* London: T&T Clark International, 2004.

Webb, William J. *Slaves, Women & Homosexuals. Exploring the Hermeneutics of Cultural Analysis.* Downers Grove, IL: IVP, 2001.

_____. "A Redemptive-Movement Hermeneutics: The Slavery Analogy." In *Discovering Biblical Equality: Complementarity Without Hierarchy*, ed. R. W. Pierce and R. M. Groothuis. 2nd ed. Downers Grove, IL: IVP, 2005.

Webster, Graham. *The Roman Imperial Army of the First and Second Centuries A.D.* 3rd ed. Norman, OK: Oklahoma University Press, 1998.

Wedderburn, A. J. M., ed. *Paul and Jesus: Collected Essays.* JSOTS. Sheffield: Sheffield Academic Press, 1989.

Weidemann, Hans-Ulrich. "Titus, der getaufte Heide—Überlegungen zu Tit 3,1–8." In: *Ein Meisterschüler: Titus und sein Brief. Michael Theobald zum 60. Geburtstag*, ed. H.-U. Weidemann and W. Eisele, 31-54. Stuttgarter Bibelstudien 214. Stuttgart: Verlag Katholisches Bibelwerk, 2008.

Weima, Jeffrey A. D. and Stanly E. Porter. *An Annotated Bibliography of 1 and 2 Thessalonians.* Leiden: Brill, 1998.

Weiser, Alfons. *Der Zweite Brief an Timotheus.* EKK 16.1. Düsseldorf: Benziger Verlag, 2003.

Wenham, David. "Acts and the Pauline Corpus II: The Evidence of Parallels." In: *The Book of Acts in Its First Century Setting. Volume 1: Ancient Literary Setting*, ed. Bruce W. Winter, Andrew D. Clarke, 215–258. Grand Rapids, MI: Eerdmans, 1993.

_____. *Paul: Follower of Jesus or Founder of Christianity?* Grand Rapids, MI: Eerdmans, 1995.

_____. *Paul and Jesus: The True Story.* London: SPCK, 2002.

Wenham, David and Steve Walton. *Exploring the New Testament: A Guide to the Gospels & Acts.* Downers Grove, IL: IVP, 2001.

Westerholm, Stephen. *Perspectives Old and New on Paul: The "Lutheran" Paul and His Critics.* Grand Rapids,

MI: Eerdmans, 2004.

_____. "The 'New Perspective' at Twenty-Five." In: *Justification and Variegated Nomism. Volume 2: The Paradoxes of Paul*, ed. D. A. Carson, Peter T. O'Brien, and Mark A. Seifrid, 1–38. Grand Rapids, MI: Baker, 2004.

Wieland, George M. *The Significance of Salvation: A Study of Salvation Language in the Pastoral Epistles*. Paternoster Biblical Monographs. Eugene, OR: Wipf and Stock Publishers, 2006.

Wikenhauser, Alfred. *Die Apostelgeschichte*. Das Regensburger Neue Testament. Regensburg: Friedrich Pustet, 1951.

Wilder, T. L. "New Testament Pseudonymity and Deception." *TynB* 50.1 (1999): 156–158.

_____. *Pseudonymyti, the New Testament and Deception: An Inquiry into Intention and Reception*. Lanham, MD: University Press of America, 2004.

Wiles, Gordon P. *Paul's Intercessory Prayers: the Significance of the Intercessory Prayer Passages in the Letters of Paul*. SNTSMS 24. Cambridge: Cambridge University Press, 1974.

Williams, David J. *Paul's Metaphors: Their Context and Character*. Peabody, MA: Hendrickson, 1999.

Williams, P. J., ed. *The New Testament in Its First Century Setting: Essays on Context and Background in Honour of B. W. Winter on his 65th birthday*, Grand Rapids: Eerdmans, 2004.

Willitts, Joel. "Paul and Matthew: A Descriptive Approach from a Post-New Perspective Interpretative Framework." In: *Paul and the Gospels: Christologies, Conflicts and Convergences*, ed. M. F. Bird and J. Willitts, 62–85. LNTS 411. London: T&T Clark International, 2011.

Wills, Garry. *What Paul Meant*. New York: Penguin, 2006.

Wilson, R. McL. *Colossians and Philemon: A Critical and Exegetical Commentary*. London: T&T Clark International, 2005.

Wilson, Todd A. *The Curse of the Law and the Crisis in Galatia: Reassessing the Purpose of Galatians*. WUNT 2.225. Tübingen: Mohr Siebeck, 2007.

Wilson, Walter T. *Pauline Parallels: A Comprehensive Guide*. Louisville, KY: Westminster John Knox Press, 2009.

Winter, Bruce. "Roman Law and Society in Romans 12-15." *Rome in the Bible and the Early Church*, ed. Peter Oakes, 67–102. Grand Rapids, MI: Baker, 2002.

_____. *After Paul Left Corinth: The Influence of Secular Ethics and Social Change*. Grand Rapids, MI: Eerdmans, 2001.

Winter, Sara B. C. "Methodological Observations on a New Interpretation of Paul's Letter to Philemon." *Union Seminary Quarterly Review* 39 (1984): 203–212.

Wise, Isaac M. *The Origin of Christianity and a Commentary to the Acts of the Apostles*. Cincinnati, OH: Block & Co., 1868.

Wise, M., M. Abegg, E. Cook. *The Dead Sea Scrolls: A New Translation*. San Francisco: Harper, 1996.

Wise, M. O. "Languages of Palestine." In: *Dictionary of Jesus and the Gospels*, ed. J. B. Green and Scot McKnight, 434–444. Downers Grove: IVP, 1992.

Witetschek, Stephan. *Ephesische Enthüllungen. Vol. 1: Frühe Christen in einer antiken Großstadt*. Biblical Tools and Studies 6. Leuven: Peeters, 2008.

Witherington III, Ben. *The Acts of the Apostles: A Socio-Rhetorical Commentary*. Grand Rapids, MI: Eerdmans, 1998.

_____. *The Paul Quest: The Renewed Search for the Jew of Tarsus*. Downers Grove, IL: IVP, 1998.

_____. *New Testament History: A Narrative Account*. Grand Rapids, MI: Baker, 2001.

_____. *Conflict and Community: A Socio-Rhetorical Commentary on 1 and 2 Corinthians*. Grand Rapids, MI: Eerdmans, 1995.

_____. *The Letters to Philemon, the Colossians, and the Ephesians. A Socio-Rhetorical Commentary on the Captivity Epistles*. Grand Rapids, MI: Eerdmans, 2007.

_____. "Christology." In: *Dictionary of Paul and His Letters*, eds. G. F. Hawthorne, R. P. Martin, and D. G. Reid, 100–115. Downers Grove, IL: IVP, 1993.

_____. *The Problem with Evangelical Theology: Testing the Exegetical Foundations of Calvinism, Dispensationalism, and Wesleyanism*. Waco, TX: Baylor University Press, 2005.

_____. *Paul's Letter to the Romans: A Socio-Rhetorical Commentary*. Grand Rapids, MI: Eerdmans, 2004.

_____. *The Indelible Image: The Theological and Ethical Thought World of the New Testament. Volume One: The Individual Witnesses*. Downers Grove, IL: IVP, 2009.

Wolters, A. "A Semantic Study of αὐθέντης and Its Cognates." *Journal of Greco-Roman Christianity and Judaism* 1 (2000): 145–175.

_____. "ΙΟΥΝΙΑΝ (Romans 16:7) and the Hebrew Name *Yĕhunni*." *JBL* 127 (2008): 397–408.

_____. "ΑΥΘΕΝΤΗΣ and Its Cognates in Biblical Greek." *JETS* 52.4 (2009): 719–729.

Woyke, Johannes. *Götter, "Götzen," Götterbilder: Aspekte einer paulinischen "Theologie der Religionen."* BZNW 132. Berlin: De Gruyter, 2005.

Wright, N. T. *The Climax of the Covenant: Christ and the Law in Pauline Theology*. Minneapolis: Fortress, 1992.

_____ . *What Saint Paul Really Said: Was Paul of Tarsus the Real Founder of Christianity?* Grand Rapids, MI: Eerdmans, 1997.

_____. *Justification: God's Plan & Paul's Vision*. Downers Grove, IL: IVP, 2009.

_____. *Paul in Fresh Perspective*. Minneapolis: Fortress Press, 2005.

_____. "Romans." In: *The New Interpreter's Bible*, Volume X. Nashville: Abingdon Press, 2002.

_____. "On Becoming the Righteousness of God. 2 Corinthians 5:21." In: *Pauline Theology, Volume II*, ed. D. M. Hay, 200–208. Minneapolis: Augsburg Fortress, 1993.

_____. "Paul and Caesar: A New Reading of Romans." In: *A Royal Priesthood: The Use of the Bible Ethically and Politically*, ed. Bartholemew, C., 173–193. Carlisle: Paternoster, 2002.

Yarborough, Robert W. "Sexual Gratification in 1 Thess 4:1–8." *TrinJ* 20.2 (1999): 215–232.

Yeung, Maureen W. *Faith in Jesus & Paul: A Comparison with Special Reference to 'Faith that can remove Mountains' and 'Your faith has healed / saved You*. WUNT 2.147. Tübingen: Mohr Siebeck, 2002.

Yinger, K. L. *Paul, Judaism, and Judgment According to Deeds*. Cambridge: Cambridge University Press, 1999.

Young, Richard A. "The Knowledge of God in Romans 1:18–23: Exegetical and Theological Reflections." *JETS* 43 (2000): 695–707.

Zoccali, Christopher. "'And so all Israel will be saved': Competing Interpretations of Romans 11:26 in Pauline Scholarship." *JSNT* 30 (2008): 289–318.

Zuck, Roy B. *Teaching as Paul Taught*. Grand Rapids, MI: Baker, 1998.